THE ENGLISH LANGUAGE ON TRIAL

Many lawsuits arise over disagreements about language and about the meanings of everyday words, phrases, and sentences. This book draws on over fifty cases involving disputed meanings in the American legal system where the author served as an expert witness or consultant, to explore the interaction between language and law. Stepping back from the legal specifics and their outcomes, it analyzes the disputes from the perspective of the language sciences, especially semantics and pragmatics, and language comprehension. It seeks to understand why, and in what areas of English grammar, lexis, and usage, they have arisen among speakers who do not normally miscommunicate and disagree like this. The cases involve contracts, patents, advertising, trademarks, libel, and defamation, and descriptive insights and methods from the language sciences are applied to each case to make explicit the meanings that speakers would normally assign to English.

JOHN A. HAWKINS is Distinguished Professor of Linguistics at the University of California, Davis and Emeritus Professor of English and Applied Linguistics at the University of Cambridge. His recent publications include *Cross-linguistic Variation and Efficiency* (Oxford University Press, 2014) and *Criterial Features in L2 English* (with Luna Filipović; Cambridge University Press, 2012).

STUDIES IN ENGLISH LANGUAGE

The aim of this series is to provide a framework for original studies of English, both present-day and past. All books are based securely on empirical research, and represent theoretical and descriptive contributions to our knowledge of national and international varieties of English, both written and spoken. The series covers a broad range of topics and approaches, including syntax, phonology, grammar, vocabulary, discourse, pragmatics and sociolinguistics, and is aimed at an international readership.

Already published in this series:

Haruko Momma: *From Philology to English Studies: Language and Culture in the Nineteenth Century*
Raymond Hickey (ed.): *Standards of English: Codified Varieties around the World*
Benedikt Szmrecsanyi: *Grammatical Variation in British English Dialects: A Study in Corpus-Based Dialectometry*
Daniel Schreier and Marianne Hundt (eds.): *English as a Contact Language*
Bas Aarts, Joanne Close, Geoffrey Leech and Sean Wallis (eds.): *The Verb Phrase in English: Investigating Recent Language Change with Corpora*
Martin Hilpert: *Constructional Change in English: Developments in Allomorphy, Word Formation, and Syntax*
Jakob R. E. Leimgruber: *Singapore English: Structure, Variation, and Usage*
Christoph Rühlemann: *Narrative in English Conversation: A Corpus Analysis of Storytelling*
Dagmar Deuber: *English in the Caribbean: Variation, Style and Standards in Jamaica and Trinidad*
Eva Berlage: *Noun Phrase Complexity in English*
Nicole Dehé: *Parentheticals in Spoken English: The Syntax-Prosody Relation*
Jock O. Wong: *The Culture of Singapore English*
Marianne Hundt (ed.): *Late Modern English Syntax*
Irma Taavitsainen, Merja Kytö, Claudia Claridge and Jeremy Smith (eds.): *Developments in English: Expanding Electronic Evidence*

Arne Lohmann: *English Coordinate Constructions: A Processing Perspective on Constituent Order*
Nuria Yáñez-Bouza: *Grammar, Rhetoric and Usage in English: Preposition Placement 1500–1900*
Anita Auer, Daniel Schreier and Richard J. Watts (eds.): *Letter Writing and Language Change*
John Flowerdew and Richard W. Forest: *Signalling Nouns in English: A Corpus-Based Discourse Approach*
Jeffrey P. Williams, Edgar W. Schneider, Peter Trudgill and Daniel Schreier (eds.): *Further Studies in the Lesser-Known Varieties of English*
Jack Grieve: *Regional Variation in Written American English*
Douglas Biber and Bethany Gray: *Grammatical Complexity in Academic English: Linguistics Change in Writing*
Gjertrud Flermoen Stenbrenden: *Long-Vowel Shifts in English, c. 1050–1700: Evidence from Spelling*
Zoya G. Proshina and Anna A. Eddy (eds.): *Russian English: History, Functions, and Features*
Raymond Hickey (ed.): *Listening to the Past: Audio Records of Accents of English*
Phillip Wallage: *Negation in Early English: Grammatical and Functional Change*
Marianne Hundt, Sandra Mollin and Simone E. Pfenninger (eds.): *The Changing English Language: Psycholinguistic Perspectives*
Joanna Kopaczyk and Hans Sauer (eds.): *Binomials in the History of English: Fixed and Flexible*
Alexander Haselow: *Spontaneous Spoken English: An Integrated Approach to the Emergent Grammar of Speech*
Christina Sanchez-Stockhammer: *English Compounds and Their Spelling*
David West Brown: *English and Empire: Language History, Dialect, and the Digital Archive*
Paula Rodríguez-Puente: *The English Phrasal Verb, 1650–Present: History, Stylistic Drifts, and Lexicalisation*
Erik. R. Thomas (ed.): *Mexican American English: Substrate Influence and the Birth of an Ethnolect*
Thomas Hoffmann: *English Comparative Correlatives: Diachronic and Synchronic Variation at the Lexicon-Syntax Interface*
Nuria Yáñez-Bouza, Emma Moore, Linda van Bergen and Willem B. Hollmann (eds.): *Categories, Constructions, and Change in English Syntax*
Raymond Hickey (ed.): *English in the German-Speaking World*
Axel Bohmann: *Variation in English World-wide: Registers and Global Varieties*
Raymond Hickey (ed.): *English in Multilingual South Africa: The Linguistics of Contact and Change*
Jeremy J. Smith: *Transforming Early English: The Reinvention of Early English and Older Scots*
Tobias Bernaisch: *Gender in World Englishes*

Lorena Pérez-Hernández: *Speech Acts in English: From Research to Instruction and Textbook Development*
Elisabeth Reber: *Quoting in Parliamentary Question Time: Exploring Recent Change*
Marco Condorelli: *Standardising English Spelling: The Role of Printing in Sixteenth and Seventeenth-Century Graphemic Developments*
Irma Taavitsainen (ed.): *Genre in English Medical Writing, 1500–1820: Sociocultural Contexts of Production and Use*
Elisa Mattiello: *Transitional Morphology: Combining Forms in Modern English*
Theresa Neumaier: *Conversation in World Englishes: Turn-Taking and Cultural Variation in Southeast Asian and Caribbean English*
Elnora ten Wolde: *The English Binominal Noun Phrase: A Cognitive-Functional Approach*
Małgorzata Kowalczyk: *Borrowings in Informal American English*
Daniela Landert: *Methods in Historical Corpus Pragmatics: Epistemic Stance in Early Modern English*
Claudia Claridge, Ewa Jonsson and Merja Kytö: *Intensifiers in Late Modern English: A Sociopragmatic Approach to Courtroom Discourse*
Leslie Arnovick: *Verbal Medicines: The Curative Power of Prayer and Invocation in Early English Charms*
Tony McEnery, Isobelle Clarke and Gavin Brookes: *Learner Language, Discourse and Interaction: A Corpus-Based Analysis of Spoken English*
Eva Berlage: *Composite Predicates in English: Processes of Specialization*
Sven Leuckert and Teresa Pham: *Non-canonical English Syntax: Concepts, Methods, and Approaches*
Mikko Laitinen and Paula Rautionaho (eds): *Data-Intensive Investigations of English*
John A. Hawkins: *The English Language on Trial: Witnessing Disputed Meanings in American Courts*

Earlier titles not listed are also available

THE ENGLISH LANGUAGE ON TRIAL

Witnessing Disputed Meanings in American Courts

JOHN A. HAWKINS
University of California, Davis
University of Cambridge

CAMBRIDGE
UNIVERSITY PRESS

CAMBRIDGE
UNIVERSITY PRESS

Shaftesbury Road, Cambridge CB2 8EA, United Kingdom

One Liberty Plaza, 20th Floor, New York, NY 10006, USA

477 Williamstown Road, Port Melbourne, VIC 3207, Australia

314–321, 3rd Floor, Plot 3, Splendor Forum, Jasola District Centre, New Delhi – 110025, India

103 Penang Road, #05–06/07, Visioncrest Commercial, Singapore 238467

Cambridge University Press is part of Cambridge University Press & Assessment, a department of the University of Cambridge.

We share the University's mission to contribute to society through the pursuit of education, learning and research at the highest international levels of excellence.

www.cambridge.org
Information on this title: www.cambridge.org/9781009682824

DOI: 10.1017/9781009682794

First published 2026
First paperback edition 2026

Cover image: Asimmetria nella Simmetria [Asymmetry in Symmetry] by Giovanni Venturini

A catalogue record for this publication is available from the British Library

ISBN 978-1-009-68278-7 Hardback
ISBN 978-1-009-68282-4 Paperback

To Luna
Moja Najveća Ljubav

Contents

Preface

Many lawsuits arise over disagreements about language and about the meanings of everyday words, phrases, and sentences. For example, your medical insurance coverage is written in English. What exactly does it cover? Your new invention has been developed after consulting the US Patent Office, to make sure it does not infringe anybody else's patent. These patents are written in English. What exactly do they describe, and are you safe to develop your product or not? You wish to identify your product with a trademark. Are you free to do so without risk of unfair competition by depriving others of the use of a common "generic" or "descriptive" term in English?

The present book draws on more than fifty cases in which language has played a central role in the American legal system and in which I was retained over a thirty-five-year period as an expert witness or consultant. The cases involved contract interpretations, patents, copyright infringements, advertising, trademarks, libel, and defamation, and in all of them certain words and phrases of English, and their uses in context, were critical. In effect, the English language itself was "on trial" in these cases. This book steps back from the legal specifics and their outcomes, and analyzes and classifies the disputed meanings from the perspective of the language sciences, especially semantics and pragmatics within linguistics and philosophy, and language comprehension within psycholinguistics. It seeks to understand why these lawsuits have arisen among English speakers who do not normally miscommunicate or disagree with one another over the meanings they assign to their words and phrases.

There have been a number of books and handbooks in recent years that explore the relevance of linguistics to the law and that describe lawsuits in detail in which linguists (often sociolinguists and applied linguists) have given testimony. The focus of the present book is different: It is the English language itself and the analyses of English given by the opposing parties. It raises some key linguistic questions that need to be asked about these disputes. How, and in what areas of English lexis and grammar and in the use of English, have they arisen? What aspects of English have given rise to these disputed meanings among lawyers and their clients?

For example, when a case centers around a certain key word of English, are we seeing a reflection in these courtroom disagreements of the kinds of challenges that lexicographers regularly face when they try to define the full set of senses that a word can convey, or the full extent of a single word sense? Are these general problems in lexicography and word meaning being played out in the courtroom? Or is it some elusive and "non-compositional" property of a word combination or construction that a nonlinguist might fail to capture that is responsible for the disagreement? Is it a syntactic ambiguity in phrasal attachments that underlies the dispute, with the opposing parties seizing on different preferred meanings from among those that are logically possible? More generally with respect to ambiguity, which is rampant in English and arises at all levels of linguistic analysis (words, word combinations, whole clauses) and can potentially lead to many alternative interpretations, has one of the parties failed to give sufficient attention to the "disambiguating" role of context? Is one logically possible meaning being seized upon because it confers a legal or financial benefit, even though it is dispreferred in the sentence and context in question, in which case why is it dispreferred? And when the parties disagree over whether a text does or does not "imply" something negative about a person, in a libel suit, what kind of implication or inference are they appealing to, and can a solid argument be made from well-established rules of pragmatic inference to show that the information in question is indeed present in the minds of readers?

These are the kinds of linguistic and analytical questions that this book addresses, arising from lawsuits that I have witnessed directly. There is a rich body of scientific work that can help us describe the disputed language in cases such as this, and this work is increasingly being applied by linguists to lawsuits in which they are asked to consult as they assist the triers of fact. But here I want to use language science in order to better understand why we are having a dispute over meaning in the first place and a resulting lawsuit, and I want to share with the language science community, and especially with the field of English linguistics, a set of conflicting interpretations and analyses of English words and phrases that have arisen in the American legal system. By gathering my personal experiences together in book form, my aim is to try and better understand where, how, and why these disputed meanings have arisen, and can be expected to arise in the future.

A related goal of this book is to increase awareness in the language science community of just how many lawsuits do crucially involve matters of language. Even in America where expert witness testimony by linguists is much more common than in Britain (where language consultants seem to be primarily phoneticians advising on speaker identification), I have been surprised by how unaware many linguists are about what has been happening in the courtroom. I hope my book will add to this awareness and interest in matters of language and law through its detailed focus on syntactic, semantic, and pragmatic properties of English, and the conflicting interpretations they have given rise to.

I hope also that this book will be read by legal scholars and by practicing lawyers and judges. The disputed meanings I have witnessed and my analyses of them have clear relevance, as one reviewer of the present book pointed out, for the more high-profile cases of language-based legal interpretation that we all hear about in the press involving constitutional amendments, firearms, abortion, voting rights, and marriage equality. Some of the insights and clarifications that I incorporate from the language sciences to the disputed meanings in this book could be usefully applied by legal scholars to their debates about originalism, textualism, canonical, and practical interpretations, and I would be delighted if the present book could serve as a conduit from language science to the law in this way. There is an attitude I have heard among some lawyers (even in America) of "We know our own language, so you aren't needed." But it is one thing to know and be able to speak a language; it is quite a different matter to step back and describe and analyze it correctly, and to explain why there is a disagreement, and I hope this book will help to make that distinction clear.

For a similar reason I would like this book to be read by other social scientists and by business and marketing people, and by anyone in the educated general public who is fascinated by our most human and vital attribute, our language, and by the problems that can arise in society when there are disagreements over something that works perfectly well most of the time but which can break down and lead to disputes in this very public and visible forum.

The English language is at the center of legal disputes like this for reasons that are actually rather interesting. First, the rules of English, and the precise meanings of many words and phrases, are quite complex, much more so than lay people realize (including many lawyers!). Second, the knowledge that native speakers possess of these rules and meanings is almost entirely unconscious. The job of the language scientist is to describe, and make conscious, these unconscious and complex processes that underlie everyday language use. Depending on the meanings that can be shown to be present in people's minds when they use English, a patent will or will not have been infringed, a contract will or will not cover a particular possession or service, a book will or will not have damaged someone's reputation, and a trademark will or will not be a legitimate label for a product. All of these cases reduce, in essence, to a question of language and linguistic usage: What exactly do writers and readers of English understand these words, phrases, and sentences to mean?

When there are such disputes, we have to unravel the unconscious processes that underlie the normal use of English, and make them conscious and explicit, so that we can clearly identify the source of the problem, explain why we actually have a lawsuit, and point to the correct solution for the triers of fact. This book is accordingly being written in a way that provides a background into the unconscious subtleties and complexities of the English language for non-linguistics readers, and at the same time it delves into many technical syntactic, semantic, and pragmatic details of the words and phrases in question for the benefit of specialists in linguistics. I have tried to write it in a way that will make it accessible to a broad readership.

My personal involvement with language in the law started by accident. I remember it was a sunny fall afternoon in Los Angeles, California, back in 1988, and I was sitting in my Linguistics Department office at USC (the University of Southern California), where I had a long window and a commanding view over the Athletic Field, then filled with the massive (and loud) Trojan Marching Band. They were practicing their routine for next Saturday's football game. In the distance was the gleaming white Hollywood sign on the Hollywood Hills. It was hard to concentrate with all this noise and the visual distractions, so I was quite pleased when a phone call came in, relayed to me by my secretary, asking to speak with the chair of the Linguistics Department. "That's me," I said. "What can I do for you?" It turned out it was an attorney from a nearby law firm in California who needed, urgently, an English language expert for a lawsuit in which his client was taking a medical insurance company to court for refusing to provide coverage on account of the language in the policy. At issue was the word DISEASE and what exactly this word meant in relation to conditions of the heart, on this occasion a heart attack.

I had had inquiries like this before, and I would normally refer them to a colleague of mine who held a joint appointment in Linguistics and the Law School. But on this occasion, something about the case intrigued me, as the lawyer explained the details (which I could just about hear over the Trojan Marching Band!), and I realized this was something that my own background and PhD in English linguistics equipped me to handle just as well as my colleague could, so I agreed to take it on.

I had no idea at the time that this would be the first step into a career in language and the law that would run parallel, albeit part-time, to my main career as a university researcher and teacher at USC, then Cambridge University in England, and now UC Davis. A similar inquiry came in some months after the first, from a large intellectual property law firm in Los Angeles with an equally urgent need for a language consultant, this time to protect a client's trademark, AIR DOOR, and again I signed on. And shortly after that I was contacted by one of the major media communications law firms in Beverly Hills needing a language consultant for a libel suit involving a Hollywood celebrity. And so began this parallel career that has now lasted thirty-five years, of roughly one to two cases per year, serving as a consultant and often as expert witness in trials and depositions. The law firms in question have been mainly in California, but also in New York, Chicago, Washington, Washington, DC, Texas, Oregon, and Montana, with a couple in London and Europe. In all of these cases, certain words and phrases of English, and their meanings in context, have been critical.

My primary career, as I mentioned, has been as a linguistics professor. My usefulness in litigation (I have been told by several lawyers) has been precisely that I am not primarily an expert witness, but an established academic and professor with an extensive publication record who has actually done some of the foundational work on English and language generally that I could apply to these legal disputes. And having now accumulated more than fifty consultancies, I have a large enough sample and database so that I can examine it all from an English linguistics perspective, step back from the legal specifics, and try to see some general patterns and reach some conclusions about how and why these legal disputes have arisen. In particular my aim, as I explained, is to analyze, classify, and better understand the disputed meanings in American courts from the perspective of the language sciences. To this end I draw especially on core branches of linguistics itself and on the neighboring fields of the philosophy of language and the psychology of language (so-called psycholinguistics).

My focus is on English, therefore. I will not be giving details of the law and legal outcomes in individual cases, except when these are directly relevant and needed for the linguistic analysis, for example when

I discuss the classification of terms in trademark law and the eligibility or not of particular words or word combinations for trademark status. Furthermore, I will not even mention the names of the celebrities who were involved in my libel and defamation cases. I don't want to add to the often damaging allegations made against them, and I don't want the paparazzi mining this book for salacious details, so I use pseudonyms throughout. Nor do I mention many specific companies. Some critical sentences have been converted to parallel ones so as not to reveal the participants in question. It is not important for our purposes who was actually using the English language on these occasions and who or what is being referred to. What is important is the language itself, the word, the construction, the ambiguity, and the analytical issues about meaning that are raised by these disputes over meaning. The main exception to this practice of anonymity is when discussing trademarks, where identification is unavoidable. Readers interested in pursuing more of the legal specifics of the cases I discuss can do so by consulting the Appendix, which gives the year and location of the case and the dates of my declarations, depositions, and trial appearances, plus the law firms that retained me and brief details of each case. This book is primarily a contribution to English and general linguistics, therefore, using a revealing and interesting set of data from American courts. Some background readings for readers who are new to linguistics and language science are recommended at the end of Chapter 1, as are further readings in language and the law following the conclusions in Chapter 8.

Acknowledgments

There are many people whose help and support were critical in making this book possible and that I would like to acknowledge.

Let me begin by mentioning some of the lawyers I worked with. For an academic like myself whose main job has been to write books and articles on linguistics and teach students in a university setting, it has certainly been an interesting experience to be asked to apply this expertise to the resolution of real-world issues in American courts. It was not always straightforward. There were numerous details of intellectual property law I needed to learn, along with the mind-set and practices of people engaged in a different discipline, the law. These plus the factual and legal details of the lawsuits in question had to be mastered rapidly. In particular, I had to develop a skill for identifying points in my discipline, linguistics, that could complement and add precision and relevance to the legal arguments being made. It was important for these reasons to be able to work with lawyers who were supportive, helpful, and understanding, and who recognized the potential contributions that my discipline could make to theirs. In this respect I would like to especially mention and thank Roy Anderson (Los Angeles), Marty Glick (San Francisco), John Slafsky (Palo Alto), David Perkins and Ben Clossick (London), Adam Rosenberg and Daniel Brown (Seattle), Tony Glassman and Alex Rufus-Isaacs (Beverly Hills), Vincent Cox (Century City), and John Cone (Dallas). I would also like to recognize the impressive and dedicated (late) trademark survey analyst, Gerald Ford (of Long Beach), with whom I collaborated on some cases.

It was not always pleasant doing this legal consulting and delivering my opinions. Depositions can be stressful, with often hostile questions in a video-recorded environment under oath and your subsequently transcribed answers then being repeated back at you in the following trial. Declarations must often be written under real time pressure. There was occasional pressure from one or two lawyers for me to make linguistic arguments I did not want to make, which I had to resist. On one occasion

I even had a menacing personal threat directed against me outside the courtroom by an opposing expert who was "mad as hell" about my testimony and vowed to do things I won't repeat here if I ever crossed his path again. (I took this as an indication that I must have made some very good linguistic points!) Despite all of this, it has been a privilege to be able to serve in this applied capacity in the pursuit of just outcomes for many lawsuits that ultimately involved the English language.

I would also like to acknowledge several fellow linguists who have helped me over the years and with whom I have discussed semantics and pragmatics: Ed Keenan (UCLA) and the late Pieter Seuren (Nijmegen), my UC Davis linguistics colleague Patrick Farrell (who also did legal consulting), and UC Davis psycholinguist Fernanda Ferreira, from whom I took the concept of "good enough parsing," which I apply in this book. I also learned a lot about the law and legal philosophy from my many conversations with former USC colleague and dean Marshall Cohen, who deserves special mention here. I am most grateful as well to two anonymous reviewers of the present book who gave me invaluable feedback, one of them on the relationship between linguistics and the law and the other on English linguistics.

My sincere thanks also to the incredibly efficient and most helpful editor of the Cambridge Studies in English Language series in which this book is privileged to appear, Merja Kytö (Uppsala University). No less efficient and helpful were Cambridge University Press & Assessment, who have handled the whole publication process with such professionalism and made it such a pleasant experience. This book was written during a full year's sabbatical leave from the University California, Davis from 2023 to 2024, for which I am most grateful, as I am for the University Library and other resources that I continue to use at Cambridge University in my capacity as the Emeritus Professor of English and Applied Linguistics there. I would also like to express my sincere gratitude to the artist Giovanni Venturini, who painted the striking and thematically perfect courtroom scene specifically for the cover of this book. It depicts the asymmetries between the opposing parties within the visual symmetries of the courtroom. Thank you, Giovanni!

Finally, and most significantly, this book owes its existence to my amazing wife, Luna Filipović, herself a forensic linguist and author of Cambridge University Press's *Bilingualism in Action: Theory and Practice* and a forthcoming Oxford University Press book on multilingualism in the justice system. She convinced me that I had something to tell that was worth telling, she insisted that I do it, she helped with its whole conception as a contribution to both English linguistics and the law, and it is primarily because of her that it is now seeing the light of day. She has been my mentor and muse in so many other projects as well, as a result of our unique and shared mind-set in matters of language and linguistics, and the special bond that has enabled us to triumph over many obstacles, of geographical distance and separation, age difference, and institutional policies and practices that have not always been helpful. This bond not only created a beautiful little girl, Aria, now nine, the fourth of the four lovely daughters we have between us (along with Kathryn, Kirsten, and Luzzi); it has been the foundation for so much more, both for what has already been and for what is yet to come. In the words of the incomparable John Lennon and Paul McCartney, born like me in Liverpool, England: "Though I know I'll never lose affection for people and things that went before. . . . There is no one compares with you." This book is for you, Lovely Luna: "Moja najveća ljubav."

Stylistic Conventions

The stylistic conventions of this book follow the practice that is widely used in legal writing of using capital letters for words of the object language under discussion, here English. Hence, SUBSTANTIALLY stands for the English word "substantially," ALTHOUGH stands for the English word "although," and so on. This is a practice that I have used myself as a consulting linguist in my declarations and reports to American courts, and it is one that I find both convenient and clarifying. There is a second stylistic convention that I use systematically in this book, namely that of reserving single quotes (i.e. ' . . . ') for describing and defining the meanings that are associated with words and phrases, for example when dictionaries define their proposed meanings using semantic paraphrases. These paraphrases are, of necessity, in the form of other words and phrases of English that are deemed to have an equivalent sense to the word or phrase being defined, and I find it helpful to distinguish the object language orthographically from its semantics in this way. So, the basic meaning of the English word SUBSTANTIALLY is defined in one major dictionary as 'to a considerable extent or in a way that has real substance and significance.' Apart from these two features I have followed normal stylistic practices for written English in this book, and the Cambridge stylesheet in particular.

Abbreviations

adj	adjective
adv	adverb
AHD	*The American Heritage Dictionary of the English Language*
app	application
BYU	Brigham Young University
COCA	Corpus of Contemporary American English
disting	distinguished (from)
ed.	editor
edn	edition (of a book)
eds.	editors
esp.	especially
et al.	and the other authors
F&W	*Funk & Wagnall's Standard Dictionary of the English Language*
FCPA	Foreign Corrupt Practices Act
HPBRM	Half Price Books, Records, Magazines, Inc.
iWeb	The iWeb Corpus
n	noun
NOW	News on the Web Corpus
NP	noun phrase
OED	*Oxford English Dictionary*
p.	page
P	preposition
pp.	pages
PP	prepositional phrase
RHD	*The Random House Dictionary of the English Language*
S	sentence or clause
TTAB	Trademark Trial and Appeal Board
UC Davis	University of California, Davis

US	United States of America
USC	University of Southern California
USPS	United States Postal Service
USPTO	United States Patent and Trademark Office
V	verb
V'	a phrasal combination with the verb and within VP
vb	verb
VP	verb phrase
v.	versus
vi	intransitive verb
vs.	versus
vt	transitive verb
WTNID	*Webster's Third New International Dictionary*

CHAPTER 1

Introduction

Creating Meanings in Everyday Language Use

When there are legal disputes in the American legal system involving the English language and the meanings of everyday words and phrases, language experts will often be called in and asked to write a report and perhaps give testimony in a legal deposition or trial. These experts may be professors of English, of linguistics, psycholinguistics, sociolinguistics, or the philosophy of language. In other words, they will be specialists in one or more branches of the "language sciences." Their job is to provide an analysis of the meaning and usage of the relevant words, phrases, and sentences, and to describe (in terms that a potential jury can understand) how an "average reader" will interpret the language in question.

The English language is often at the center of legal disputes like this for what are rather interesting reasons. First, the precise meanings of certain words and phrases are not always easy to pin down. Second, the rules of English, and indeed all languages, are very complex – much more than people realize who haven't studied grammar. We confront this complexity when we try to learn a foreign language as an adult and realize just how difficult it is. Moreover, the knowledge that we all possess and share as native speakers about these rules is almost entirely unconscious. We use our language effortlessly and effectively most of the time. We can generally answer certain questions about individual words and sentences when asked by foreigners anxious to improve their English. For example, we can tell the learner whether a particular sentence sounds OK and whether we would use it ourselves, or whether it sounds ungrammatical and we wouldn't use it. In other words, we can make what are called "native-speaker judgments" about our language. But we cannot, without linguistic training, turn this unconscious knowledge into a more conscious formulation for a rule of English using the technical grammatical terms that are found in grammars of English, for example in the *Comprehensive Grammar of the English Language* by Randolph Quirk, Sidney Greenbaum, Geoffrey Leech, and Jan Svartvik (Longman, London & Seminar Press, New York, 1985).

Professional linguists devote years of their lives to figuring out how these rules work in just one small area of language, and the results of these many contributions over many decades and even centuries are then compiled into a comprehensive and authoritative grammar of English like this one.

I personally devoted several years of study when I was writing my PhD to just two words of English: the definite article THE and the indefinite article A! Some of my key findings and examples of English usage were then incorporated into this Quirk et al. *Comprehensive Grammar of the English Language*. Admittedly the articles of English are among the most common words in the language, but still I have had to contend all my life with the amazement of my family, friends, and nonlinguist colleagues, exclaiming, "How can you possibly spend years of your life working on just two words of the English language like this?" My answer is always "Very easily, and there's still a lot more to be said!" Native speakers possess this rich unconscious knowledge of the rules governing the grammar and meanings of the words and phrases in their language, and most of the time communication proceeds smoothly. But when disagreements arise, as they do in certain lawsuits, the language sciences provide a body of scientific knowledge about meaning and usage that can be helpful to the trier of fact. Increasingly linguists are in fact contributing to legal judgements and applying their theories and methods to the law. Language science can also help us understand why we have a lawsuit in the first place, and this is one of the primary goals of the present book. I want to use language science in order to better understand why, where, and how these disputes arise.

In the chapters that follow I provide an analysis of many lawsuits in which language played a central role. They have been selected from more than fifty cases for which I was retained as a consultant involving contract interpretation, patents, copyright infringement, advertising, trademarks, libel, and defamation. In all these cases, certain words and phrases of English, and their uses in context, were critical. My sample of cases is now large enough that I can step back from it all and give a representative overview of the kinds of legal and linguistic disputes to whose resolution the language sciences can contribute. In particular, this book asks some fundamental questions about the language side of all this: What areas and properties of English give rise to these disputes, can we expect them in some areas and not in others (and if so which), and can we explain through our theories and analytical techniques and corpus searches why we are seeing these disagreements among language users who do not normally disagree in the meanings they assign in their unconscious use of language?

Are there aspects of word meaning that are hard to define that lexicographers have difficulties with as well, and are these inherent difficulties ultimately responsible for the disagreement? Are there subtle properties of meaning in word combinations and in whole sentences that a nonlinguist would fail to capture, and are these central to the dispute? When the parties disagree over whether a text does or does not "imply" something negative about a person, in a libel suit, what kind of implication are they appealing to, and can a solid argument be made from well-established theories of pragmatic inference to show that the information is indeed present in the minds of readers? Are some linguists who give testimony better informed about semantic and pragmatic theories than others, and better able to explain the unconscious thought processes going on in the minds of readers? And are legal and even financial considerations interfering with the proper analysis of ambiguity resolution in context? These questions take center stage in the present book, with its focus on the English language and the theories and analytical tools of the language sciences.

The financial consequences of these legal decisions that I was involved with were often considerable. Sometimes the survival of a whole company or firm was at stake – their viability and the jobs of their employees. Settlements could be in the millions, sometimes hundreds of millions of dollars. And the reputations of public figures could be ruined or salvaged, depending on the outcomes of these law cases.

Before I get into the disputed meanings at the heart of these lawsuits, I need to set out, if only briefly, how meanings are created in the normal case in everyday English, when things don't go wrong and communication proceeds smoothly and language is used effectively and cooperatively. We will then have a basic foundation on which to analyze and classify the problems that arise when there are disagreements involving language in the law, and I will be better able to describe and explain what is going on.

1.1 Individual Words

The meaning of a whole sentence results from many different components and processes of interpretation. At the most basic level we have individual words, like BACHELOR, PROFESSOR, CUP, GLASS, SING, WALK, FIGHT, HAPPY, and so on. Each of these has a basic sense or meaning, and typically more than one, and dictionaries will list these words alphabetically and give a description of the different senses they can convey, in effect by using paraphrases in terms of other words or phrases. So

PROFESSOR as a noun is defined by the *Webster's New Collegiate Dictionary* (9th edn, 1986) as

> '1 **:** one that professes, avows, or declares 2 **a :** a faculty member of the highest academic rank at an institution of higher education b : a teacher at a university, college, or sometimes secondary school c : one that teaches or professes special knowledge of an art, sport, or occupation requiring skill . . . .'

The intransitive verb SING in the same dictionary includes the following definitions:

> '1 **a :** to produce musical tones by means of the voice **b :** to utter words in musical tones and with musical inflections and modulations **c :** to deliver songs as a trained or professional singer 2 **:** to make a shrill whining or whistling sound 3 **a :** to relate or celebrate something in verse **b :** to compose poetry 4 **:** to produce musical or harmonious sounds . . . .'

And SING as a transitive verb is defined as

> '1 **:** to utter with musical inflections; *esp* : to interpret in musical tones produced by the voice 2 **:** to relate or celebrate in verse 3 **:** CHANT, INTONE 4 **:** to bring or accompany to a place or state by singing <*~s* the child to sleep>.'

Everyone is familiar with dictionaries and uses them not infrequently, to check things like the spellings of various words, or their precise meanings and usage. Dictionaries do differ significantly from one another, however, in sheer size, and in the details and manner of their coverage and presentation, for example whether they also include earlier uses and meanings of a word in the history of English, whether they cover the worldwide features of English in the UK, US, Australia, New Zealand, and elsewhere, or regional dialects. They differ in how they order the various senses of a word. Do they give the oldest recorded uses first or the most common uses in the modern language first?

The most obvious and visible difference between dictionaries of English concerns how large they are and how many words they contain and define. A small dictionary like the *Longman Dictionary of American English* (published in 2000) lists just 44,000 words, phrases, and idioms. A commonly used everyday dictionary by American students and professors is the *Merriam-Webster's Collegiate Dictionary*, whose eleventh edition (2003) sits on my office desk and has 165,000 entries. A slightly larger dictionary, often found on university campuses in libraries and student workspaces, is the *American Heritage Dictionary of the English Language*. The third edition of this (1992) has more than 200,000 entries; the fourth edition (2000) added nearly 10,000 new words and their definitions; and the fifth edition (2011) added yet another 10,000, largely in order to cover the rapid expansion that we have seen in English vocabulary as the language adapts to new technologies and worldwide developments, serving the linguistic needs of an ever-expanding set of global English users. Larger still in size and coverage is the second edition of *Random House Webster's Dictionary* (1997), with some 315,000 entries, and even larger (to the point of being almost impossible to lift and carry without doing serious damage to the book itself and its spine) is the *Webster's Third New International Dictionary of the English Language Unabridged* (1993), with more than 450,000 words.

All of these dictionaries with *Webster's* in the name go back ultimately to the great American lexicographer Noah Webster, who was at pains to record the distinctive features of American as opposed to British English and who compiled *A Compendious Dictionary of the English Language* in 1806 and *An American Dictionary of the English Language* in 1828. Meanwhile, back in England, work began in 1857 on what has now become the largest lexicographic resource on the English language worldwide: the *Oxford English Dictionary* (*OED*), with more than 600,000 words. The first edition of the *OED* was published in ten volumes in 1928, the second edition in 1989 had twenty volumes, and now the third edition has been adapted for online access and is still being updated on a regular basis.

It is often not realized that dictionary writing is very hard. Why? Well, selecting the right words and phrases to put in these paraphrases for the meanings of even basic words like PROFESSOR and SING takes a lot of careful thought and consideration. Have I captured exactly what these words mean? Do my formulations cover all the uses that are recorded in the database that I have available to me? Different publishing houses will each have a database that has been compiled over previous decades by earlier dictionary writers and that current lexicographers can now access. Am I missing something? Do I need to adjust my definition slightly, given certain uses and intended meanings that I see in the database or that have been brought to my attention by scholars or dictionary users?

In addition to this fundamental challenge for the dictionary writer, of actually getting the paraphrase right using other words and phrases of English, there are four further types of problems that lexicographers must contend with every time they set about defining the meaning of a word. And interestingly we are going to see in this book that in each of these cases where lexicographers have problems, lawyers and their clients have problems too!

First, there are "lexical ambiguities." Just about every word of English has more than one sense. Look at the very different meanings that can be conveyed by the noun BACHELOR (from the *Merriam-Webster's Collegiate Dictionary*, 11th edn), meanings as different as 'young knight,' 'someone who has received a certain type of degree,' 'unmarried man,' and 'male animal without a mate':

> '**1 :** a young knight who follows the banner of another **2 :** a person who has received what is usu. the lowest degree conferred by a four-year college, university, or professional school <~ of arts> **3 a** : an unmarried man **b** : a male animal (as a fur seal) without a mate during breeding time.'

Dictionaries have to capture and paraphrase all these different possibilities. The bigger ones will list more of them and make more fine-tuned distinctions between senses; the smaller ones will list fewer and make fewer distinctions.

A second challenge for dictionary writers is what we call "vagueness" as opposed to "ambiguity." We have ambiguity whenever there are clearly definable different senses of a word, as we have just seen with BACHELOR. Vagueness involves trying to establish the precise extent of each sense. What exactly is covered and compatible with a particular word sense, albeit not mentioned explicitly in its semantic definition, such that a word is "vague" with respect to these possibilities? So, for a verb like HIT in English, there has to be some physical contact or striking if it is the case that JOHN HIT BILL. But this sentence does not tell us whether John did it with his left hand or his right hand, so the sentence is vague in this respect. Both possibilities exist, but we don't have two different senses listed in the dictionary (one for hitting with the left hand, one for the right). Similarly the color adjective RED is vague with respect to all the many different shades of this color that you will find (often numbered) in a paint store, and for which there are sometimes more specific terms of English such as CRIMSON, SCARLET, FIRE-ENGINE RED, and so forth. So the challenge posed by vagueness involves finding and specifying the precise semantic properties that are inherent and essential in a word and establishing the extent of the word's coverage. And when there are words with closely related meanings, where exactly is the boundary between a CUP and a GLASS, or between a CHAIR and a STOOL, and so on?

Third, some of the different senses listed for a given word are nonliteral and extended uses of a more basic sense, such as metaphors. Consider the senses listed for the (transitive) verb FIGHT (in the *Merriam-Webster's*

Collegiate Dictionary, 11th edn). They range from the purely physical and violent to extended nonphysical opposition, surmounting an obstacle, overcoming something, and so on:

> '1 **a** (1) : to contend against in or as if in battle or physical combat; (2) : to box against in the ring **b** (1) to attempt to prevent the success or effectiveness of <the company *fought* the takeover attempt> (2) : to oppose the passage or development of <~ a bill in Congress> **2 a:** WAGE, CARRY ON <~ a battle> **b :** to take part in (as a boxing match) **3 :** to struggle or endure or surmount <~ a cold> **4 a :** to gain by struggle <~*s* his way through> **b :** to resolve by struggle <*fought* out their differences in court> **5 a :** to manage (a ship) in a battle or storm **b :** to cause to struggle or contend **c :** to manage in an unnecessarily rough or awkward manner.'

When a basic literal physical violence meaning is commonly extended like this, the extensions are listed in dictionaries. On other occasions we invent new metaphors spontaneously as part of the effective and everyday use of language, and these semantic possibilities assigned to words by native speakers are generally not listed. A major challenge for lexicographers is then to decide at what point a metaphorical extension should be listed in a dictionary entry, and when the entry should limit itself to the more basic conventional meanings from which numerous metaphorical extensions can be derived in actual usage?

A fourth and particularly subtle challenge for lexicographers comes from the fact that we need to distinguish knowledge of the English language and so-called linguistic meanings from knowledge of the world. But what happens when the world changes dramatically over successive generations? The things that CAR and MOVIE refer to today are radically different from what they were one hundred years ago, and the images we have in our minds when these words are used are now quite different. So, has the meaning of these English words changed as well over this period, or is it just the world that has changed and the actual language and its meanings have stayed the same? This is a profound philosophical question and one that is, or at least should be, of fundamental concern to lexicographers. Are they describing the English language when they define words like this, or rather the nature of the world that English language speakers currently inhabit, and how exactly do we distinguish the two? Putting this another way, where is the boundary between a dictionary of words and an encyclopedia of things that these words refer to? This may seem like idle philosophizing. Trust me – it is not, as we shall see.

In all these situations dictionary writers are challenged when they try to give adequate descriptions and paraphrases for individual words, precisely because the number and nature of the distinct meanings involved, their full extent, and whether or not these meanings have expanded or declined over time or whether only the world around us has changed, are all far from easy to determine. We will see in §2 that legal disputes have arisen in all of these situations in which lexicographers have difficulties.

For example, the word SUBSTANTIALLY is ambiguous between quite distinct senses, just like BACHELOR is ambiguous. One of its senses is exemplified in THE SUN IS SUBSTANTIALLY LARGER THAN THE EARTH (i.e., 'all of the sun is larger than all of the earth'). A second sense is seen in MY PAINTING IS SUBSTANTIALLY COMPLETE (i.e., 'most of it is, but not yet all'). Whether the patent in question was infringed depended on which of these two quite distinct meanings the readers (and their lawyers!) selected (see §2.1).

Is the word DISEASE broad enough in its semantic coverage, and is it vague enough so that it can refer to the medical condition in question, just like HITTING can subsume actions with both the left hand and the right hand? If so, the insurance company can avoid paying up and can exclude coverage for the costs related to this particular (disputed) instance of a DISEASE (see §2.2.1).

Is FIGHT used and intended literally in a given context (a promotional flyer for an event), in which case it refers to, and can even incite, violence? Or is it understood metaphorically, as it regularly is when we talk about verbal or political disagreements (see §2.3.1)?

And does a TANGIBLE item that is referred to in a movie contract from some decades ago, covering articles for sale derived from the movie, still cover derivative items that are no longer physical and touchable in today's computerized online movie business, but still visibly and perceptually similar to these (see §2.4)?

The disputed meanings for individual words in all these situations arose often precisely because there are deep linguistic and philosophical challenges for lexicographers. Remember Shakespeare's famous question (in *Romeo and Juliet*): "What's in a name?," specifically in the word ROSE. It's often not easy to define. There is then the further difficulty of establishing how the context interacts with, and selects from, the different senses defined by the dictionary and how an unbiased reader will understand a given word in the context in question (see §1.4). Many disputed meanings in American courts have arisen precisely when and because words are hard to define, or else the role of the context was not straightforward or was not considered sufficiently by one of the parties. There were also legal and financial incentives for exploiting these difficulties and ambiguities in the pursuit of a particular linguistic argument that was favorable to one of the parties in the case.

1.2 Word Combinations

When words combine together into phrases and different kinds of multiword units, their meanings also combine. These combinations can be what we call "compositional," which means that the meaning of the whole is straightforwardly and transparently derivable from the meanings of the individual parts. Or else the combination is "noncompositional" and not so easily derivable from its parts. For example, a COMPUTER STORE is a store that sells computers (compositional), while a CHAIN STORE does not sell chains (noncompositional). Rather, it has a distinctive meaning that is assigned to the whole combination, 'one of numerous usu. retail stores having the same ownership and selling the same line of goods' (*Merriam-Webster's Collegiate Dictionary*, 11th edn). This combination functions very much like a single word here; the parts do not enable us to derive the meaning of the whole, and so the dictionary lists it and defines its combinatorial meaning along with all the individual words that it lists and defines. In a phrase like CRIMINAL LAWYER there is an ambiguity along exactly this dimension. It can refer to someone who is a lawyer and who also happens to be criminal (compositional), or else it refers to a type of lawyer – namely 'a lawyer who specializes in criminal law' (noncompositional; *Merriam-Webster's Collegiate Dictionary*, 11th edn).

Traditionally semantic theories in linguistics and philosophy have focused more on compositional meanings since these are the easier to describe. But noncompositional meanings are also highly productive, and indeed ubiquitous in a language like English, and they are gaining increasing attention in models of grammar and meaning in linguistics, especially those that examine whole constructions (see e.g. Adele Goldberg's 2006 *Constructions at Work*, Oxford University Press, Oxford). So, consider the meaning of GIVE A KICK (to someone) versus just plain KICK. There is no literal 'giving' going on here, as in GIVE A PRESENT. Instead, MARY GAVE JOHN A KICK adds what we call an "aspectual" meaning to the effect that this was a single act of kicking, whereas MARY KICKED JOHN leaves this unspecified and vague. The kicking could have been repeated, or not. And compare WASH THE DISHES with the "phrasal verb" WASH UP THE DISHES. The UP in this combination has nothing to do with its literal directional meaning in UP THE HILL. It also adds an aspectual meaning, this time to the effect that the action of washing the dishes was completed, i.e. this is a non-compositional characteristic of the whole phrase or construction.

It is sometimes hard to pin down what exactly the added contribution is of certain words in these multiword constructions, or whether there is any additional contribution at all compared with corresponding single words. What is the difference between RENTING OUT YOUR APARTMENT and just plain RENTING IT? Very little, it seems. But when there is some perceptible difference, describing precisely what it is, and which sets of words it arises with, can be challenging.

Consider a word combination that we are going to discuss in detail in §3.1 involving the surface of a component within a dental implant as this was described in a patent. In normal transparent English the component could be referred to as a SURFACE THAT ENGAGES A WRENCH or ... THAT ENGAGES WITH A WRENCH. The phrase that was actually used in the patent was A WRENCH-ENGAGING SURFACE. Now, this construction has a rather intriguing and subtle noncompositional element of meaning, and this noncompositional meaning turned out to be crucial to determining whether or not the patent was infringing somebody else's patent. The basic point was that this surface was not just one that could engage with a wrench, or possibly with a hammer or a spanner or any such tool. Rather the surface was one that was designed specifically for this purpose, i.e. for the purpose of engaging with the wrench. In a similar manner, an OIL-BURNING HEATER is not just one that can burn oil among various fossil fuels; it is designed specifically so that it does burn oil, and this is how it produces heat. Thus the purpose is part of the overall meaning of these phrases.

The precise syntax of word combinations is also very important in a legal context (i.e. how exactly the words are put together grammatically and what kinds of syntactic units result), which then affects how the meanings of the parts combine together. One of the most common types of word combinations in English, which figures prominently in trademarks and trademark law, is that of "compound nouns" (also called "noun compounds" and "complex nominals") such as ROACH MOTEL (for an insect trap) or WORLD BOOK (for an encyclopedia). Trademarks are identifying names for companies and their products and brands. The examples just given have the same [Noun$_1$ Noun$_2$] structure as FLOWER POT. The righthand Noun$_2$ is what we call the syntactic "head" here, and the Noun$_1$ on the left is actually a grammatically reduced modifier of this head.

To see what I mean by "grammatically reduced," consider the fact that a FLOWER POT will typically have lots of flowers in it, but you can't actually call it a *FLOWERS POT, for reasons of English grammar (this "*" signals ungrammaticality). You can put a plural -s on the head $Noun_2$ when there are several of them, FLOWER POTS, but not on the modifier. Similarly, you cannot add a preposition or other grammatical material to the $Noun_1$ to make clear what its semantic relation is to the head $Noun_2$, i.e. to make explicit that it is a POT WITH FLOWERS or POT WITH FLOWERS IN (IT) unless you position these modifying phrases to the right of POT, as I just did. If you try to add these clarifying elements to the modifying $Noun_1$ on the left, the result is again ungrammatical: *A WITH FLOWER(S) POT. So the grammar of $Noun_1$ $Noun_2$ compounds in English is quite restrictive for these "prenominal modifiers" and different from word combinations like POTS WITH FLOWERS that have "post-nominal modification" in which all the component words retain their full grammatical integrity in the phrasal combination.

One important consequence of these grammatical restrictions in compounds is that the semantic relationship of the modifying word when it occurs on the left of the head word is much less explicit and less clear than it is when the order is reversed and additional prepositions are present on the right. And this turns out to be highly relevant for trademark law and for determining whether certain types of word combinations are eligible for trademark status.

Consider the following compound nouns with PAPER as the first element: PAPER FACTORY, PAPER PLATE, PAPER CLIP, PAPER MONEY, and PAPER TIGER. The manner in which PAPER as the modifying $Noun_1$ combines semantically with its head $Noun_2$ is different in each case. A PAPER FACTORY normally refers to a factory that makes paper, as in the more explicit A FACTORY FOR MAKING PAPER, or just A FACTORY FOR PAPER, though it could also refer in the context of an architect's plan to a miniature model and hence to a factory made of paper, i.e. a FACTORY OF PAPER. Similarly, a PAPER PLATE is a plate made of paper, but a PAPER CLIP is not typically a clip made of paper (though it could be!) but rather a (metal) clip for holding papers together. PAPER MONEY is money in the form of paper bank notes rather than coins, and a PAPER TIGER has an extended metaphorical sense referring to someone who is outwardly strong like a tiger but basically weak and lacking strength like paper.

The semantic possibilities here and the different ways of combining PAPER, or any $Noun_1$ with its head $Noun_2$ in [$Noun_1$ $Noun_2$] sequences, are vast, and crucially their interpretation depends not only on the meanings of these individual words, but on our knowledge of the world, about factories and plates and clips, and so on. And since these expressions are reduced, compared with FACTORY FOR (MAKING) PAPER, there is less explicit description going on and more enrichment of these reduced grammatical forms through real-world knowledge, imagination, and inferencing, in order to derive the appropriate and relevant meaning for different occasions of use. All of this is highly relevant for the distinction made in trademark law between terms that are "suggestive" versus those that are more "descriptive" and "generic" (see §3.3 and §5.5).

1.3 Whole Clauses

As we move beyond word combinations such as compound nouns and into whole clauses, there will be new elements of grammatical meaning that we have to describe, in addition to the meanings of the individual words and any compounds they contain. So a clause with an intransitive verb like THE BIRD CHIRPED describes a situation in which there is a single participant, the bird, and an action or state that is being "predicated" (as we say) of this entity. This is rather different from a clause with a transitive verb, like THE BOY BOUNCED THE BALL, in which there are two participants and an activity that brings them together and in which there are grammatical components of meaning added – namely that the boy is the semantic "agent" of this activity, the one who is doing it, while the ball is the thing (the "patient") that the agent is acting upon with respect to this bouncing action. These brief examples suffice to show, once again, that it is not enough to just add up the meanings of all the words in a sentence, as given in a dictionary, in order to describe what a sentence means. The construction and the clause in which these words appear add important elements of ("grammatical") meaning, like the agent and patient "thematic roles," as we call them, of a transitive clause.

As more words are added to a sentence and clauses become larger, so the possibilities for combining them together syntactically and semantically become greater, and as they do so, the sentence can express different meanings and may become ambiguous in its sentence structure and not just in the meanings of its words. One productive set of grammatical ambiguities involves so-called attachment ambiguities. Consider the sentence THE DETECTIVE SPOTTED THE GIRL WITH A TELESCOPE. There are two quite distinct interpretations for this and two quite distinct phrasal attachments. In one, the grammatical subject of the sentence, THE DETECTIVE, is the person who has the telescope and who is using it to perform the action in question, spotting the girl. In the other, the direct object

THE GIRL has the telescope and the detective has managed to spot her in a way that is not further specified. In the first "reading," as we say, the prepositional phrase WITH A TELESCOPE attaches to the verb SPOTTED and forms part of the verb phrase that is predicated of THE DETECTIVE and describes what he or she did (i.e. 'the detective spotted with a telescope this particular girl'). In the second, WITH A TELESCOPE attaches directly to GIRL within the object noun phrase, where it serves to identify which girl we are talking about, and it exerts no semantic influence or effect outside of this object noun phrase (i.e. 'the detective spotted this particular girl who had a telescope').

Talk of syntactic attachments and of attachment ambiguities like this may seem like the stuff of technical grammar and logic classes, with no real bearing on the real world and matters of corporate business. But nothing could be further from the truth. We are going to see examples of exactly this type (in §4.1) in legal disputes, with the two parties assigning different attachments to key phrases in the sentence.

When we have larger and more complex sentences, they will typically consist of more than one clause, a main clause plus one or more subordinate clauses, and precisely how these are put together, and depending on the grammatical words that are selected for different subordinate clauses (so-called subordinate conjunctions), there will be further elements of grammatical meaning added to a sentence, over and above the combined lexical meanings from all of its words. These grammatical meanings can again be quite subtle and almost hidden, yet very real in the unconscious understanding of everyday sentences within a text. "Conditional" sentences like IF YOU WORK HARD, YOU WILL PASS YOUR EXAM introduce a prior condition in the subordinate clause ('working hard') for the fulfillment of the event in the main clause ('passing your exam'). "Causal" clauses with a BECAUSE subordinating conjunction, BECAUSE YOU WORKED HARD, YOU PASSED YOUR EXAM, make explicit that what happened in the first clause was the cause of what happened in the second. Various "temporal" conjunctions like BEFORE and AFTER signal when the event in the subordinate clause happens in relation to the event in the main clause: YOU MUST WORK HARD BEFORE YOU TAKE YOUR EXAM, and AFTER YOU TAKE YOUR EXAM, YOU CAN RELAX.

Now consider sentences with a subordinate clause containing the subordinating conjunction ALTHOUGH, in combination with a main clause, e.g. ALTHOUGH JOHNNY WAS SHORT (subordinate clause) HE WAS A GREAT BASKETBALL PLAYER (main clause). Semantically this ALTHOUGH clause introduces what we call a "concessive" relation into the sentence. Here is how this works. Normally the best basketball players are tall, for obvious reasons: This puts them closer to the hoop that they throw the ball into, so if they're closer to the hoop, they are more accurate and score more points. On this occasion we have an exception to the normal rule: Johnny was short, and despite this he was a great basketball player. So concessive clauses like this introduce an exception to what is known to be a normal rule. I will return to clauses with ALTHOUGH in §4.3, where we will see that this concessive meaning played a crucial role in a libel suit.

1.4 Resolving Ambiguities and the Role of Context

We have just referred in the last section to attachment ambiguities within whole clauses, and in §1.1 we discussed ambiguities involving lexical items such as BACHELOR and SUBSTANTIALLY.

How do hearers and readers know, in all these cases of ambiguity, which particular meaning the speaker or writer intends? I have mentioned that numerous lawsuits arise precisely because words, phrases, and whole clauses can regularly be interpreted in more than one way. The different parties in a lawsuit can then select different meanings and claim that this is what the writer or speaker intended.

In everyday language use it is crucially the context that "disambiguates" between the different semantic possibilities that a word or word combination or whole sentence allows, i.e. it is the context that enables the hearer or reader to figure out the meaning that is intended. By "context" we mean a number of interrelated things: The other words and phrases within a given sentence and their meanings, or the other sentences in the larger text in which the sentence in question appears, or the physical environment and situation in which the sentence (if spoken) is actually uttered, and the "mutual knowledge" of the speaker or writer and hearer or reader, including their knowledge about the real world that they bring to their understanding of a given sentence. This whole issue of how exactly the context serves to delimit the everyday understanding of ambiguous words and phrases has been extensively researched and discussed in the language sciences. In a useful summary volume (*Discourse Analysis*, Cambridge University Press, Cambridge, 1983), Gillian Brown and George Yule show how the textual, situational, and real-world context in which words are uttered or written limits their interpretations and supports the intended one. They cite Dell Hymes (pp. 37–38): "The use of a linguistic form identifies a range of meanings. A context can support a range of meanings. When a form is used in a context . . . the context eliminates from consideration the meanings possible to the form other than those the context can support."

So, for example, a context can eliminate the basic literal meaning of FIGHT when there is no reference to any physical violence, and instead its metaphorical meaning is clearly intended, in a political debate or a sports context, as one of the many "metaphors we live by" (to cite the title of George Lakoff and Mark Johnson's book, University of Chicago Press, Chicago, 1980). Similarly the ambiguity of SUBSTANTIALLY (recall §1.1) can be resolved within the context of the dental patent in question by carefully reading the full patent and inspecting the visual drawings.

Normally the context performs this task of eliminating unintended meanings very successfully, effectively removing the other meaning possibilities completely from our conscious awareness, though subconsciously psychologists have found evidence, in controlled experiments conducted in psycholinguistic labs, that these alternative meaning possibilities are nonetheless briefly activated in language processing before being dispelled by the context (see e.g. David A. Swinney, 1979, "Lexical Access during Sentence Comprehension: (Re)consideration of Context Effects," *Journal of Verbal Learning and Verbal Behavior* 18: 645–660). Some less technical proof for how this works in everyday language use comes from a perhaps surprising source: linguistic humor.

Many jokes provide clear evidence for the reality of these ambiguities and for how they are normally resolved in context. What typically happens is that the speaker intends the contextually most natural and appropriate meaning, only to have the hearer then respond by invoking the contextually unintended and unexpected interpretation. The contrast between these different senses, and the surprising reversal in the meaning assigned from that which is most natural and obvious in context, creates the humor. Consider the exchange shown in (1) (from the movie *Mary Poppins*):

(1) Guilty-looking car driver to neighbor:
I'M TERRIBLY SORRY, BUT I RAN OVER YOUR CAT!
CAN I REPLACE IT FOR YOU?
Neighbor:
THAT'S ALL VERY WELL, BUT DO YOU CATCH MICE?

Here the ambiguity is based on the verb REPLACE and its "argument structure", i.e. the individuals and entities that figure in the event in question. The meaning that is most natural and intended by the guilty-looking car driver is 'Can I replace your cat with another cat for you?' But there is another meaning that is compatible with the semantics of REPLACE, but far less plausible given our knowledge of how the world works and of what the driver was offering, namely, 'Can I be the one who actually replaces your cat for you?,' and it is this second, clearly unintended interpretation that the neighbor picks up on by questioning whether the car driver can actually do the job that the cat was there to do – namely catch mice!

A second example, one of my favorite linguistic jokes in fact, is from comedian Benny Hill and is shown in (2):

(2) Benny Hill dressed up as an irate mother of schoolboy Johnny talking to his headmaster:
THERE ARE FORTY PUBS IN THIS TOWN AND MY JOHNNY HASN'T BEEN IN ONE OF THEM.
Headmaster:
OH YES, WHICH ONE'S THAT?

This is a joke based on what we call a "quantifier scope ambiguity." The sentence used by the irate mother (Benny Hill!) has two logically possible and logically quite distinct meanings. The first, and the one she/he intends, is 'Johnny has not been in any of the forty pubs in this town,' i.e. in 'not one.' But the headmaster chooses the other possible meaning: 'There is one of the forty pubs that Johnny has not been in' i.e. 'one not,' and he asks which one that is. In this second meaning it is implied that Johnny has been in the remaining pubs, possibly all of them, which goes completely counter to the irate mother's claim that Johnny has not been in any of the forty pubs. The brilliance of the joke lies in the linguistic fact that the two meaning possibilities are so contrary to one another, and that the context makes it so clear that the irate mother intends the one, while the headmaster cleverly invokes the other unintended meaning through his question and in the process completely contradicts the claim about Johnny's innocence with respect to pub crawling.

Again we have an initial meaning that the irate mother intends about her son Johnny, and a second clearly unintended interpretation that the headmaster then invokes in his response to her. It is the contrast between these two meanings, and both the unexpectedness and inappropriateness of the second meaning given the first, that creates the humor.

A final example, involving an argument structure ambiguity again as in (1), and again from comedian Benny Hill, is what underlies the humorous use of BOUNCE in the following sentence that evokes a TV commercial that was very well-known by Benny Hill's audience at the time:

(3) Well-known TV commercial:
TRILL MAKES YOUR BUDGIE BOUNCE WITH HEALTH
Benny Hill trying to make his budgie bounce like you bounce a ball:
I'VE FED MY BUDGIE THREE PACKETS OF TRILL AND HE STILL WON'T BOUNCE!

The verb BOUNCE has a basic intransitive sense exemplified by THE BALL BOUNCES, plus a nonliteral extension of this in YOUR BUDGIE BOUNCES WITH HEALTH, which is invoked by the TV commercial with the meaning that the bird is healthy and full of active movement like a bouncing ball. There is also a transitive use of BOUNCE, as in I BOUNCED THE BALL, meaning 'I performed an action that caused the ball to bounce.' The TV commercial about the packet of seeds for budgies clearly intended the intransitive and extended meaning of BOUNCE in BOUNCE WITH HEALTH, and this is what everyone watching would understand it to mean. Benny Hill walks on stage performing the transitive action of bouncing a (clearly toy) budgie, thus invoking instead the transitive sense of BOUNCE, like you bounce a ball, and then proclaims that his budgie did not bounce in this transitive sense after he fed it lots of Trill, implying that it should have done so since the commercial claimed that it would, at least in the intransitive sense of BOUNCE that holds for balls that have been made to bounce in the transitive sense.

What we have in this example, therefore, and what Benny Hill is exploiting in his humor, is actually three closely related meanings associated with the ambiguous verb BOUNCE: First, the transitive use (as in BOUNCE A BALL, here the budgie!); second, the literal intransitive (the BALL BOUNCES); and third the extended nonliteral intransitive (the budgie BOUNCES WITH HEALTH). The last of these is invoked in the TV commercial. The first is invoked by Benny Hill's actions trying to bounce the toy budgie like a ball. Benny Hill's use of the literal intransitive BOUNCE, the second meaning, then creates the humorous contrast between this second intransitive (literal) meaning of the budgie bouncing like a ball, which he invokes through his actions, and the third (nonliteral) intransitive meaning ('bouncing with health'), as in the TV commercial, which everyone knows about and which is the normal contextually appropriate use of BOUNCE in relation to budgies, but which Benny Hill's own actions prevent hearers from assigning.

For readers who are interested in these kinds of ambiguities, and their deliberate exploitation for humor and other purposes, I have to recommend a wonderful 2003 book by Lehigh University economics professor Robert J. Thornton: *The Lexicon of Intentionally Ambiguous Recommendations (LIAR)* (Sourcebooks, Naperville, Illinois). His book is full of "positive-sounding" reference letters, which disguise a meaning that is not actually positive at all (e.g. "YOU'LL BE LUCKY IF YOU CAN GET THIS PERSON TO WORK FOR YOU"!). The sheer extent of such ambiguities in English is displayed to great effect in this book, as is the mischief to which a letter writer can resort who is reluctant to say anything explicitly and unambiguously negative about a job candidate.

1.5 Inferential Processes

We move now from the role of speakers/writers and hearers/readers in selecting between the alternative meanings that can be assigned to words and sentences, to their role in going beyond these meanings and assigning additional meanings through reasoning and inference. In fact, much of the information that is conveyed in everyday speaking and writing is in the form of "implications." The relevant information is not literally said, and expressed directly by the meanings of the words, phrases, and clauses within a sentence, as these are described in dictionaries and grammars, but it is nonetheless just as real in the minds of hearers and readers as that which is explicitly said. A number of technical distinctions are made in linguistics and philosophy between different kinds of implications, and these will have important consequences for language in the law (as we shall see in Chapter 5).

One type, familiar to anyone who has studied logic, is called "logical implication" or "entailment" (the two terms are equivalent). The sentence HARRY WAS EATING AN APPLE logically implies, or entails, HARRY WAS EATING A FRUIT, since if the former is true, the latter must be true as well. This kind of implication holds whenever the truth of one sentence P guarantees the simultaneous truth of another sentence Q. If a text contains HARRY WAS EATING AN APPLE, therefore, the text does not literally say that Harry was eating a piece of fruit, but it does clearly imply it, logically. These implications follow directly from the meanings of individual words and phrases in a sentence, therefore, and they hold regardless of the different contexts in which the sentence can be used and regardless of which individual HARRY is referring to.

A second type of implication, which is rather more complex and sometimes elusive, but nonetheless just as real in the minds of everyday language users, is called "implicature" or "contextual inference". The term "implicature" goes back to Paul Grice's (1975) paper "Logic and Conversation" (in P. Cole and J. Morgan, eds., *Speech Acts*, Academic Press, New York, 41–58). This kind of implication depends both on sentence meaning and on the additional information that a context provides. Consider a short text consisting of sentences (4a) and (4b):

(4) (a) MY FRIEND HARRY LIKES TO VACATION IN PLACES WHERE HE DOESN'T KNOW ANYBODY.
(b) HARRY IS CURRENTLY VACATIONING IN NEW YORK.

Sentence (4b), following as it does after (4a), implies (more precisely "implicates") that Harry does not know anybody in the place where he is currently vacationing, i.e. it implicates (5):

(5) HARRY DOES NOT KNOW ANYBODY IN NEW YORK.

This inference follows from the information given in both (4a) and (4b). Sentence (4b) uttered or written in isolation would clearly imply nothing about whether Harry has acquaintances in New York, but when it follows (4a) like this, the implicature is clear and very real.

We saw in the last section that the information supplied in a text leads the reader to choose certain meanings for its words and phrases when these are ambiguous. We now see that it also leads the reader to enrich the meanings in what is said by drawing inferences like this. By altering the contextual information given, the precise choice of words, or the positioning of a sentence in a text, a writer can convey quite different implicatures. These implicatures are both psychologically real and important aspects of communication. They are particularly important in libel suits, as we shall see. There may be nothing damaging or libelous in the meaning that can be assigned to a single sentence per se, but when that sentence is interpreted in combination with the information given in the rest of the text, the resulting implicature can be very negative indeed.

There is an interesting test that semanticists use for distinguishing between the two types of implications that we have talked about: logical implications and contextual implications or implicatures. It is called "cancellability." With logical implications you cannot deny something that is entailed using what we call a "cancelling clause." That is, you cannot say,

HARRY WAS EATING AN APPLE, BUT HE WASN'T EATING A FRUIT! That is contradictory and makes no sense, precisely because HARRY WAS EATING AN APPLE entails HARRY WAS EATING A FRUIT. The truth of the former guarantees the truth of the latter, so you can't deny the latter when you assert the former. But with contextual implications, the inference in question is not inherent in the meaning of the relevant individual sentence. It depends instead crucially on the additional information supplied by the context. An implicature made by a sentence can then be cancelled by, in effect, changing and denying the previous context. To utter (4b') after (4a) is not inherently contradictory:

(4b') HARRY IS CURRENTLY VACATIONING IN NEW YORK, BUT IN FACT HE KNOWS SEVERAL PEOPLE THERE.

The cancelling clause BUT IN FACT HE KNOWS SEVERAL PEOPLE THERE denies the implicature derived from the earlier (4a). It does not contradict something that is inherent in the meaning of HARRY IS CURRENTLY VACATIONING IN NEW YORK, i.e. in (4b). There is no contradiction in (4b'), as there was in the contradictory APPLE and FRUIT sentence provided previously. The reader is simply being told not to draw the inference that was derived from the earlier text. In effect, the reader is being told that the information that led him or her to enhance the meaning of (4b) and to infer (5) from it is not altogether correct.

So cancellability distinguishes between our two types of implication, logical and contextual. It also does something else, of considerable use to us when we have a dispute over what exactly is implied contextually. It provides evidence for the reality of an implicature, and it helps us determine what that implicature is exactly. (4b') is completely appropriate when it follows (4a) and denies the implicature that is set up by this earlier information. But if (4b') were uttered in isolation, or in a context in which there were no (4a) preceding it, and hence if there were no implicature of (5) in the hearer's or reader's mind to begin with, then there would be nothing to cancel, and the cancelling clause in (4b') would sound weird and inappropriate. To the extent that a BUT clause or other cancellation is a possible cancellation and sounds appropriate in context, therefore, this gives us evidence that the inference in question has indeed been drawn in the hearer/reader's mind. It confirms for us that it is real, and depending on the content of the cancellation, it helps us identify what the inference is exactly that has been drawn by the reader.

The type of implicature we have exemplified so far has been based on additional information supplied by an earlier sentence in a text, here (4a) preceding (4b). We will see several examples of this type playing a key role in disputed meanings and lawsuits (in §§4.2–4.3 and §§5.1–5.3). But the additional information that is crucial for implicatures can also come from other sources and from other types of mutual knowledge.

A second type of inference and of implicature comes from the fact that if I utter something like GARY JUST GOT DIVORCED, then there is what philosophers call a "presumption of truth", i.e. there is an implicature to the effect that the speaker believes this to be the case, and has evidence for it. If this is not the case, then the English language gives us various means for removing the presumption of truth, such as "modal verbs" GARY MAY HAVE JUST GOTTEN DIVORCED, or "modal adjectives" IT'S POSSIBLE THAT GARY JUST GOT DIVORCED, or verbs of reporting MARY SAID THAT GARY JUST GOT DIVORCED. Unless one of these devices is used, then the hearer will understand the speaker to be implicating that he or she believes that what is said is true. If the speaker has evidence to the contrary and still asserts GARY JUST GOT DIVORCED, then, of course, the speaker is lying. In fact, lying is only possible precisely because there is a presumption of truth in the normal case. If the sentences we utter could be either true or false, and there were no regular commitment to truth, then the hearer would not automatically assume that the speaker did necessarily believe what was being said.

A third and especially common type of inference and of implicature derives from our knowledge of the real world. Interestingly, this type is regularly evoked in what are called "suggestive" terms in trademark law. Let us return to the trademark ROACH MOTEL, first mentioned in §1.2, which is classified as "suggestive" and can as a consequence serve as an appropriate proper name for the insect trap made by this particular manufacturer. This mark is suggestive, not "generic" or "descriptive" like INSECT TRAP would be (see §3.3 and also §5.5). ROACH MOTEL appeals to our linguistic knowledge of word meanings and word combinations, plus crucially our general knowledge of how the world works and of the entities and things that are in it. A MOTEL is defined in *Merriam-Webster's Collegiate Dictionary* (11th edn) as 'an establishment which provides lodging and parking and in which the rooms are usu. accessible from an outdoor parking area.' Clearly this is an establishment that exists for humans only, not for animals and certainly not for insects. So MOTEL does not apply to roaches, and it is not being used descriptively and literally here. In fact, the combination ROACH MOTEL is semantically incongruous. By inference, we try to make sense of this incongruity, using our knowledge of the world (on this occasion our general knowledge of insects and pests and pest removal), and we reason that the "establishment" in question is one that is compatible with roaches, and specifically one that does for roaches what we all want to do with them, namely get rid of them, on this occasion by trapping them and removing them. Thus a form of contextual inference, crucially involving knowledge of the world in combination with linguistic knowledge, enables us to apply the term ROACH MOTEL to something that it does not literally describe, namely an insect trap. The genius of suggestive terms like this lies precisely in the reasoning process that makes use of additional world knowledge to achieve a linguistic effect, namely referring to something that ROACH MOTEL does not literally describe. With (4b) we saw a similar reasoning process at work, resulting in whole sentences conveying additional information that was not inherent in their linguistic meanings and that was based crucially on other material in the text itself.

Context and mutual knowledge between speaker/writer and hearer/reader also have a profound role to play in literary effects, such as "irony" and "metaphor." They are vital in determining whether a sentence is to be understood as literally true, or as deliberately and recognizably false. This is what irony is all about, saying e.g. THAT WAS A TERRIBLE MEAL when everyone knows it was excellent. Metaphor involves saying something that is partly true, for example when Johnny, a young boy, is called an ELEPHANT, if he is large and clumsy and has some of the properties of an elephant without literally being one. "Hyperbole" involves saying something that is clearly exaggerated and recognized by the speech participants as being so (see §2.3 for further discussion of these nonliteral and extended meanings).

In summary we have three major types of implicatures that are used in everyday communication: (a) implicatures that arise from information given in the preceding text and which lead to an enrichment in the information conveyed, (b) inferences that arise from the presumption of truth, and (c) implicatures that arise from real-world knowledge in combination with linguistic knowledge. We shall see, especially in Chapter 5, that all three have been at the basis of lawsuits involving implications made in language use.

1.6 Reference and Identification

An important process in everyday language usage involves "reference" to people and things in the world. English, like other languages, has numerous grammatical devices for this purpose including nouns (PROFESSOR) and personal pronouns (HE and SHE) and proper names (JOHN SMITH and SUSIE JONES), plus other items with a semantics that enables speakers and hearers to refer in this way. How exactly such reference is achieved, however, and to whom and to what reference is made on different occasions of language use, is quite complex and subtle. Very often the context of utterance plays a key role in determining the reference. Use of THE PROFESSOR in (6) and (7) results in two quite different people being referred to: one associated with the mathematics class and the other with the linguistics class.

(6) (Talking of a mathematics class) THE PROFESSOR IS A NICE GUY.

(7) (Talking of a linguistics class) THE PROFESSOR IS A NICE GUY.

Similarly HE in (8) and (9) refers to two quite different individuals, depending on the previous utterance:

(8) (Talking of some student) HE'S A NICE GUY.

(9) (Talking of some professor) HE'S A NICE GUY.

The definite description THE PROFESSOR in (6) and (7) achieves its "unique" reference within the appropriate class, and the speaker thereby makes clear to the hearer which professor is being referred to. Similarly, in the immediate context of a reference to SOME STUDENT in (8), HE can achieve unambiguous and unique reference back to this individual. For detailed discussion of how the context serves to delimit definite references like these and make them unambiguous and unique within the relevant sets of entities in question, see my 2015 *Definiteness and Indefiniteness: A Study in Reference and Grammaticality Prediction* (Routledge, New York, a reissue of an earlier 1978 book of mine). With proper names it also has to be clear among the interlocutors which JOHN and SUSIE are being talked about.

Lawsuits can arise over who or what exactly such noun phrases refer to, which people or entities in the world they pick out and evoke in the minds of language users, and how they achieve this reference. A crucial aspect of a trademark, for example, and of trademark law, involves determining whether some word or phrase can achieve unique identification of the company that produces the product in question or whether it gives instead a more common and "generic" description that applies to, and can refer to, the products of lots of companies. So in §3.4 I shall summarize trademark litigation over whether a term like APP STORE refers uniquely to the product of one particular company or whether it refers to lots of similar products on the basis of its common descriptive and legally generic meaning. We shall see that it does not (any longer at least) make unique reference to the product of just one company, and so it is not a good trademark. A "suggestive" term like ROACH MOTEL, on the other hand, does make unique and source-identifying reference to the product of just one company. It achieves this uniqueness by using a word combination that appeals ultimately to inference and to an extension in the literal meaning of one of the component words in a way that other competitors have not thought of doing and do not need to do, and so this is a good trademark.

A key distinction is made in the language sciences between what is called "sense" and "reference." The sense of a term is its general meaning that makes it available to users so they can refer to people and entities that have the semantic properties associated with the dictionary definitions and grammar of these terms. Unique identification of one particular entity from among this set of possible referents then requires some additional grammatical devices, like the definite article THE in THE PROFESSOR, or alternatively proper name status as in JOHN and SUSIE, plus crucially the further disambiguating role of context, as illustrated previously.

Even when we have a definite article, and a clear context, there can still be an ambiguity in reference in certain cases. A lawsuit can arise over the precise reference that a definite noun phrase like THE POLICE has and over the way in which the speaker and hearer's "mutual knowledge" comes into play. A distinction is made between "referential" and "attributive" uses of such phrases: The former refers to individuals who are mutually known and identifiable to speaker and hearer; the latter refers to the police in general and whoever they might be. This makes a big difference in a lawsuit in which certain individuals are accused of a crime and suffer reputational damage. Is it the police force in general that people are talking about (the attributive use), or are certain individuals whose identities are known to the interlocutors being clearly identified when THE POLICE is uttered (the referential use) so that they as individuals stand accused of various crimes? This issue is discussed further (with linguistic references given) in §6.4.

With this short background on how meanings are created, and how reference is achieved in everyday language use, we can now give a more detailed discussion of the disputed meanings that have arisen in American court cases in which I have been involved. The disputes can be classified, and clarified I believe, on the basis of the different ways in which meanings are created in the normal case, when communication does not break down and there are no disagreements. The normal cases help us identify the source of the problem when there is one. The following chapters (Chapters 2–6) largely follow the sequence of section headings in this introductory chapter, with questions of resolving ambiguities and the role of context discussed throughout each, and with one further chapter added on certain disputes that involved spelling and punctuation (Chapter 7). I conclude in Chapter 8.

Before I begin, I recognize and I hope that there will be many readers of this book who are not specialists in the English language or in some branch of the language sciences and for whom a background reading list may be helpful for my analysis of the disputed meanings in the chapters that follow. I will accordingly make some suggestions for further readings in the next section (§1.7). I will be giving references to numerous general and specialist works in linguistics throughout the book, and to technical articles in journals and edited books, but the next section gives my own suggested sampler of a few good background readings in different branches of the language sciences. Some of these will be referred to again later in the chapters that follow where they are most relevant, but pulling them together now may be helpful. These are items that I would recommend for academic and practicing lawyers, for social scientists and for all keen observers of human behavior, and for anyone who is fascinated by English and by human language generally, and by the uses and sometimes misuses to which it can be put.

1.7 A Background Reading Sampler

There are a number of books that introduce the field of linguistics as a whole and contain chapters on its component areas of phonetics and phonology, morphology (i.e. word structure), syntax, and semantics, plus the various interdisciplinary connections with philosophy, psychology, sociology, anthropology, and computer science that make up the language sciences generally. One of my favorites is

O'Grady, William, John Archibald, Mark Aronoff, and Janie Rees-Miller (2017) *Contemporary Linguistics: An Introduction*, 7th edn, Bedford/St. Martin's, Boston.

Another generally good one is

Fromkin, Victoria, Robert Rodman, and Nina Hyams (2017) *An Introduction to Language*, 11th edn, Cengage Learning, Wadsworth.

For applications of general linguistics specifically to the description of English, I mentioned the following landmark work by Randolph Quirk at the outset of this chapter:

Quirk, Randolph, Sidney Greenbaum, Geoffrey Leech, and Jan Svartvik (1985) *A Comprehensive Grammar of the English Language*, Longman, London.

Another important general description of English with broad coverage is

Pullum, Geoffrey K., and Rodney Huddleston (2002) *The Cambridge Grammar of the English Language*, Cambridge University Press, Cambridge.

Because of rapidly evolving developments in the field of syntax in the last few decades, and because there are now many different models and partial theories out there, this part of linguistics is often most difficult for introductory textbooks to cover (the O'Grady et al. syntax chapter is a better introduction than that in Fromkin et al.). I accordingly recommend the following book in addition:

Tallerman, Maggie (1998) *Understanding Syntax*, Arnold, London.

For those readers who become really intrigued by the kinds of syntactic processes that I introduced in §1.3 on word combinations and in §1.4 on whole clauses (and to which I return in Chapters 3 and 4, respectively), I recommend the very sensible detailed model of syntax developed by Peter Culicover and Ray Jackendoff:

Culicover, Peter W., and Ray Jackendoff (2005) *Simpler Syntax*, Oxford University Press, Oxford.

What is especially important for the present book, with its emphasis on disputed meanings, is semantics, the study of meaning, and the related "pragmatics" that involves meaning in context (recall §1.4). The introductory texts cited here give some useful background on semantics and pragmatics. Also useful, and more detailed, is the following:

Cruse, Alan (2000) *Meaning in Language: An Introduction to Semantics and Pragmatics*, Oxford University Press, Oxford.

Even more detailed still, on the semantics side, is the authoritative two-volume work by John Lyons, to which I shall be referring for some important clarifications that need to be made in some of our cases:

Lyons, John (1977) *Semantics* (2 vols.), Cambridge University Press, Cambridge.

Much of our information about the meanings of individual words comes, of course, from dictionaries of English. I gave an overview in §1.1 of some of the different dictionaries of English, and how they try to define word meanings using their paraphrases. I will make extensive use of these throughout this book, especially of the larger and more detailed ones that have been compiled on the basis of large databases of words and phrases. I will also make extensive use of computerized corpora of different kinds in which I can observe the occurrence and frequencies of these words and phrases. For an introductory text on what we call the "mental lexicon," i.e. our knowledge of all these words and how they are stored and arranged in the mind, I suggest the very readable

Aitchison, Jean (1993) *Words in the Mind: An Introduction to the Mental Lexicon*, Blackwell, Oxford.

Many of our disputed meanings arise because one of the parties in the dispute has not looked sufficiently carefully at the wider context in which the words, phrases, or clauses in question were uttered or written. In other words, that party has not considered the pragmatics properly. In addition to the general textbooks above and Cruse's useful *Meaning in Language* (2000), there are two textbooks on pragmatics by Cambridge University Press from the early 1980s that I still consider among the best:

Levinson, Stephen C. (1983) *Pragmatics*, Cambridge University Press, Cambridge.

Brown, Gillian, and George Yule (1983) *Discourse Analysis*, Cambridge University Press, Cambridge.

A lot of the key insights involving context-dependent inference, or "implicature," go back to the Oxford and UC Berkeley philosopher of language Paul Grice and his much-cited paper from 1975:

Grice, H. Paul (1975) "Logic and Conversation," in P. Cole and J. Morgan (eds.), *Speech Acts*, Academic Press, New York.

The theory of "speech acts" was initiated by another Oxford philosopher, John Austin, and was further developed by his American student and UC Berkeley professor John Searle:

Austin, John L. (1962) *How to Do Things with Words*, Clarendon, Oxford.

Searle, John R. (1969) *Speech Acts*, Cambridge University Press, Cambridge.

These are eminently readable as introductions to these branches of pragmatics. So is the following classic on how we regularly use words to create metaphors by Lakoff and Johnson:

Lakoff, George, and Mark Johnson (1980) *Metaphors We Live By*, University of Chicago Press, Chicago and London.

Also helpful here, I find, is John Searle's chapter on metaphor:

Searle, John R. (1993) "Metaphor," in A. Ortony (ed.), *Metaphor and Thought*, 2nd edn, Cambridge University Press, Cambridge.

More advanced books on pragmatics and inferencing that I shall be referring to are

Sperber, Dan, and Deirdre Wilson (1995) *Relevance: Communication and Cognition*, 2nd edn, Basil Blackwell, Oxford.

Levinson, Stephen C. (2000) *Presumptive Meanings: The Theory of Generalized Conversational Implicature*, MIT Press, Cambridge, MA.

Finally, for a general psycholinguistic introduction to ambiguity resolution and the role of context (§1.4), inferential processes (§1.5), reference and identification (§1.6), and all the other topics and issues that psychologists of language address (as opposed to the authors we have cited hitherto, who are primarily linguists and philosophers), I would refer readers to these two classic texts:

Clark, Herbert H., and Eve V. Clark (1977) *Psychology and Language: An Introduction to Psycholinguistics*, Harcourt Brace Jovanovich, New York.

Garnham, Alan (1985) *Psycholinguistics: Central Topics*, Methuen, London.

And for an updated introduction I suggest the following excellent text by my UC Davis colleague Matt Traxler:

Traxler, Matthew J. (2023) *Introduction to Psycholinguistics: Understanding Language Science*, 2nd edn, Wiley Blackwell, Hoboken, NJ.

I will make reference to several of these items at different points in this book, and will also cite further books and papers when these may be helpful to nonlinguists and/or linguists alike.

CHAPTER 2

Disputes over Individual Words

We saw in §1.1 that individual words like PROFESSOR, BACHELOR, SING, and FIGHT each have some basic meaning, and typically more than one, that dictionaries try to describe. They do so using paraphrases, i.e. they use other words and phrases and even whole sentences to convey the relevant meaning of the word in question as accurately as possible. I pointed out, however, that it is not straightforward getting these paraphrases right, in a way that captures the essential meaning of a word and the full set of things and events and states of affairs that it can refer to, and I mentioned four major challenges for lexicography. We will now see that where lexicographers have a problem, lawyers and their clients can have a problem too, or they may be encouraged to create one for legal and/or financial reasons.

The first source of difficulty involves lexical ambiguity. Just about every word of English has more than one basic sense, and legal disputes center around which meaning is intended in a given case. This can seriously impact what is being described in a patent, for example, and whether there is an actual infringement by that patent of another product and its patent, as we will see in §2.1.

Second, we have the extent of a meaning (or "vagueness") problem. How many entities, actions, states of affairs can be covered by the sense in question? Disputes now center around whether something is subsumed under a particular word sense (in a medical insurance contract, for example); see §2.2.

A third problem involves metaphors and other nonliteral meanings and extensions of a basic sense. Is the word in question being used literally or metaphorically in a particular context? If readers understand the literal sense, then this could be libelous, or the writer may be accused of inciting violence, with certain classes of words. If it is clear that these words are understood in a nonliteral sense, then there may be no libel or incited violence; see §2.3.

Fourth we have the issue of word meanings in relation to a changing world, in particular a world of rapidly advancing technology. Computer screens can now blur the distinction between image and physical reality, with consequences for words of English that involve physical perception and touching and their applicability to the relevant items; see §2.4.

2.1 Lexical Ambiguity

In a patent infringement case involving a dental implant (Los Angeles, 1996), the court called for "extrinsic evidence" to help resolve a tricky case of lexical ambiguity. It involved the adverb SUBSTANTIALLY and how it should be interpreted, since the parties disagreed. I was asked (by the defense) to supply this extrinsic evidence. At issue was the precise positioning of one part of the implant, consisting of a "WRENCH-ENGAGING SURFACE" (recall §1.2 and see further §3.1), and another part, THE TOP SURFACE OF THE ANCHORING MEANS, i.e. the means by which the artificial tooth would be held in place within the jawbone. The first part was described in the patent of the defending party as being SUBSTANTIALLY ENTIRELY BELOW the second. The plaintiff claimed that this infringed their own dental implant patent, in which these two parts were level, and their lawyers argued that the meaning of SUBSTANTIALLY ENTIRELY BELOW was compatible with an interpretation in which they were level. The lawyers for the defense argued that this was not a possible interpretation for the language of their patent and that the first part needed to be, and was, entirely below the second. Hence there was no infringement of the prosecuting party's patent in this respect.

There are a number of linguistic issues that needed to be considered here: the precise meanings of key individual words first of all, primarily SUBSTANTIALLY and also ENTIRELY. Another issue was the grammar of these two adverbs in combination, and whether this sequence is even fully acceptable in English. Finally, we have the larger context of the whole patent and what it tells us and shows us in the visual drawings. The clause to be analyzed is given in (1):

(1) ... AN INTERNAL, WRENCH-ENGAGING SURFACE LYING ... SUBSTANTIALLY ENTIRELY BELOW THE TOP SURFACE OF THE ANCHORING MEANS.

This clause is stylistically awkward at best because of the sequence SUBSTANTIALLY ENTIRELY BELOW, and this awkwardness complicates its interpretation, though we shall see that there is a good reason for why the patent writer chose this particular formulation. There was also evidence in the patent itself for what the patent writer intended and for how this phrase should be, and would be, interpreted in context after a careful reading.

2.1.1 *The Lexical Semantics of SUBSTANTIALLY and ENTIRELY*

The adverb SUBSTANTIALLY is formed from the adjective SUBSTANTIAL, which in turn is derived from the noun SUBSTANCE. Major dictionaries of English define the meaning of SUBSTANTIAL in terms such as the following (from *The American Heritage Dictionary of the English Language*, 5th edn, Houghton Mifflin Company, 2011):

> 'Considerable in importance, value, degree, amount or extent; . . . Ample; . . . Of, relating to, or having substance; . . . True or real.'

Using these concepts, we can define the general meaning of the adverb SUBSTANTIALLY as

> 'to a considerable extent or in a way that has real substance and significance.'

This general meaning combines with the meanings of the other words and phrases with which SUBSTANTIALLY combines syntactically to yield different possible interpretations. It is helpful when discussing these to use the terminology of Quirk, Greenbaum, Leech, and Svartvik in their 1972 *A Grammar of Contemporary English* (Longman, London, and Seminar Press, New York), henceforth Quirk et al., who have analyzed the many types of adverb meanings in English in considerable detail.

The first possibility, corresponding to the notion of 'to a considerable extent' in the definition, is what Quirk et al. call a "booster." It can be seen in sentence (2):

(2) THE SUN IS SUBSTANTIALLY LARGER THAN THE EARTH.

This meaning can be paraphrased as 'the sun, in its entirety, is to a considerable extent larger than the earth.' Other boosters in English are MUCH (LARGER . . .), CONSIDERABLY (LARGER . . .), and FAR (LARGER . . .).

A second possibility, referred to as a "downtoner" in Quirk et al. is seen in (3):

(3) MY PAINTING IS SUBSTANTIALLY COMPLETE.

This meaning is 'in most respects my painting is complete, but some of it is not complete.' Clearly this is very different from the booster sense. Some other downtoners of English are MOSTLY (COMPLETE), MORE OR LESS (COMPLETE), and PARTLY (COMPLETE).

The selection of the intended interpretation for SUBSTANTIALLY depends on the accompanying adjective or adjective phrase. LARGER THAN in (2) selects the booster meaning; COMPLETE in (3) selects the downtoner. But some sentences are ambiguous within the sentence itself, and the selection of the intended interpretation must then be made by the larger context (the text itself or our general knowledge of the world). Consider the problem sentence of the patent (1) without the word ENTIRELY:

(4) THE WRENCH-ENGAGING SURFACE LIES SUBSTANTIALLY BELOW THE TOP SURFACE OF THE ANCHORING MEANS.

This sentence with SUBSTANTIALLY BELOW is ambiguous and could receive different interpretations in different contexts. The booster meaning is 'the wrench-engaging surface lies a considerable distance below the top surface of the anchoring means.' The downtoner meaning is 'most of the wrench-engaging surface lies below the top surface of the anchoring means, but some of it is not below.' In this latter case some of the wrench-engaging surface would be above the top of the anchoring means or conceivably just level with it.

Consider a parallel example of an ambiguous sentence with SUBSTANTIALLY from everyday experience that is perhaps easier to visualize. Imagine a New York high-rise building with a large square advertising billboard on one of its sides. If we say that "THE BILLBOARD IS SUBSTANTIALLY BELOW THE TOP OF THE BUILDING," where is it exactly? This is in fact ambiguous in the same way that (4) is. Either the billboard is far down the side of the building and at a considerable distance from the top (the booster meaning), or most of it is below (the downtoner) and some of it may be protruding above the top, or may be level with it.

ENTIRELY, meanwhile, has a meaning that stresses reference to all (or all parts of) the object in question. It is paraphrasable by 'in its entirety; all of it.' In Quirk et al.'s terminology ENTIRELY is a "maximizer," and maximizers like boosters are both referred to as "amplifiers" and they are contrasted with downtoners. Consider the problem sentence of (1) now without SUBSTANTIALLY and with ENTIRELY alone:

(5) THE WRENCH-ENGAGING SURFACE LIES ENTIRELY BELOW THE TOP SURFACE OF THE ANCHORING MEANS.

The meaning of (5) can be paraphrased as 'all of the wrench-engaging surface lies below the top.' This sentence is not compatible with part of the wrench-engaging surface not being below the top of the anchoring means. That is, it is not compatible with part of the wrench-engaging surface lying above the top of the anchoring means. Nor is it compatible with part of the wrench-engaging surface lying level with the top, since then not all of it would be below. Other maximizers in English are COMPLETELY (BELOW . . .), FULLY (BELOW . . .), TOTALLY (BELOW . . .), THOROUGHLY (BELOW . . .), and so on.

2.1.2 *Combining SUBSTANTIALLY with Other Adverbs*

SUBSTANTIALLY in its booster meaning is semantically compatible with the maximizer meaning of ENTIRELY. Both refer to the wrench-engaging surface 'in its entirety.' The downtoner meaning of SUBSTANTIALLY is not semantically compatible with ENTIRELY, however: The former refers to only part of the wrench-engaging surface (the part lying below the surface in question); the latter still tries to refer to all of it! This is the first piece of evidence for how readers will interpret the meaning of SUBSTANTIALLY ENTIRELY BELOW. They will select the booster meaning. But we have seen that this syntactic combination of adverbs is stylistically awkward, despite its semantic compatibility. This awkwardness is not limited to adverbs of just this type. There are numerous restrictions in the grammar of English on permitted combinations of adverbs (see Quirk et al. for full details).

Without going into these details, it is sufficient to note here that combinations of a booster (like CONSIDERABLY) with a maximizer (like FULLY and ENTIRELY) have quite generally a rather marginal status grammatically, despite the fact that they are semantically compatible with one another (cf. CONSIDERABLY FULLY, CONSIDERABLY ENTIRELY, etc.). Their meanings are quite coherent and compatible with each other, but their syntax and the resulting grammaticality or acceptability of combining them like this will vary, depending on the particular adverbs chosen.

In short, combining the booster sense of SUBSTANTIALLY with the meaning of ENTIRELY is semantically possible, though it is considered stylistically awkward by native speakers for reasons having to do with the grammar of English, not with the semantics. The downtoner sense of SUBSTANTIALLY, on the other hand, is not compatible with the meaning of ENTIRELY, and combinations of downtoners with words like ENTIRELY (maximizers) are either fully ungrammatical for both semantic and syntactic reasons, or they require rather forced and marginal interpretations that attempt to make the entirety of the WRENCH-ENGAGING SURFACE somehow compatible with only some of it.

Assuming, therefore, that the reader can see past the stylistic awkwardness of SUBSTANTIALLY ENTIRELY BELOW in (1) and assign a clear meaning to it, the meaning that he or she will most plausibly assign is the semantically coherent one: 'All of the internal wrench-engaging surface lies below the top surface of the anchoring means, to a considerable extent or in a way that has real substance or significance.'

There is an interesting further linguistic detail in this case that came to light during discovery and prior to my deposition. The original wording that the patent examiner had agreed to did not contain both SUBSTANTIALLY and ENTIRELY together, but just ENTIRELY on its own, i.e. THE WRENCH-ENGAGING SURFACE LIES ENTIRELY BELOW THE TOP SURFACE . . ., as in (5). The adverb SUBSTANTIALLY was added later prior to finalization of the patent, and this addition then led to the patent infringement claim that I have described, on account of the alleged overlap in meaning between the downtoner sense of SUBSTANTIALLY and the nature of the plaintiff's patent. The original formulation of the defendant's patent was unambiguously in favor of the booster and maximizer meanings for the disputed phrase, therefore, and quite possibly and plausibly the patent writer was unconsciously aware of the ambiguity of SUBSTANTIALLY when this word was added later and so kept ENTIRELY in the sequence with it, in order to clarify that it was the booster meaning that was intended (i.e. the entirety of the surface in question was to a considerable extent below the top surface of the anchoring means).

2.1.3 *The Disambiguation of SUBSTANTIALLY in Context*

A disambiguation of SUBSTANTIALLY in favor of the booster meaning was further supported by the wider context of the accused patent itself. Remember the useful quote from Dell Hymes given in §1.4: "The use of a linguistic form identifies a range of meanings. A context can support a range of meanings. When a form is used in a context . . . the context eliminates from consideration the meanings possible to the form other than those the context can support."

Here the contextual information in the patent's specification made clear the intended interpretation. Specifically, all the drawings of the dental implant that illustrated the location of the wrench-engaging surface relative to the top surface of the anchoring means (and there were several such drawings) showed quite unambiguously that the wrench-engaging surface was entirely below the top surface of the anchoring means. None of them showed any portion of the wrench-engaging surface above or even level with the top surface of the anchoring means.

The drawings therefore showed that the wrench-engaging surface was entirely below the top surface of the anchoring means, thus reinforcing the most natural interpretation resulting from the combination of SUBSTANTIALLY with ENTIRELY. Hence the wider context supported the booster meaning of SUBSTANTIALLY and ruled out the downtoner meaning. The plaintiff and the plaintiff's lawyer paid insufficient attention to the visual context of the defendant's patent and tried to make a linguistic argument in favor of one of the semantic possibilities (the downtoner meaning) of the ambiguous word SUBSTANTIALLY that was favorable to their case. But since the booster meaning was the one required by the context, and not the downtoner one, the plaintiff's linguistic argument collapsed and with it the legal argument for patent infringement (though see §3.1 for discussion of a second alleged infringement involving the phrase WRENCH-ENGAGING SURFACE itself).

2.2 The Extent of a Meaning (or Its Permitted "Vagueness")

In §1.1 we asked "What's in a name?," and we will now see some disputes that get to the heart of this question when what is at issue is the precise extent and coverage of a word's meaning, i.e. its permitted vagueness. Remember that RED is vague with respect to all kinds of different shades of this color and subsumes them all. Similarly, HIT is vague with respect to whether the action was performed with the left hand or the right hand. It can cover either one. As a result there is a lot of discussion in the philosophical and linguistic literature about what exactly the difference is between ambiguity (as with BACHELOR and, as we have just seen, SUBSTANTIALLY) and vagueness (as with RED and HIT). In both cases a number of distinct senses can be conveyed by one and the same word. This is not the proper context for a full discussion of this complex issue (see e.g. Ruth Kempson's 1977 *Semantic Theory*, Cambridge University Press, Cambridge, for a useful introduction), so let me give the reader my own basic understanding and a perhaps useful heuristic.

As I see it, the key difference between ambiguity and vagueness is more psycholinguistic in nature, rather than narrowly linguistic, and it lies in the fact that language users (both speakers and hearers/writers and readers) have to make a choice in all instances of ambiguity: You can't leave it unspecified whether you are talking about an unmarried man or a male animal without a mate during breeding time (for BACHELOR, recall §1.1), or talking about the booster or downtoner sense for SUBSTANTIALLY (in §2.1.1). You have to choose. But you can leave it vague and unspecified which shade of RED you intend when you assert that you saw a RED CAR drive by, or which hand was used by one person to HIT somebody else. Vagueness allows for this lack of specificity, though it is also possible that further details will be added later or in different contexts. But the crucial point is that you can use a vague term without necessarily selecting between its different senses, whereas with ambiguity it seems you do have to choose regularly from among its listed senses, and the number of choices is also typically much smaller.

2.2.1 *DISEASE*

In a medical insurance dispute (Upland, California, 1988) the precise meaning of the word DISEASE, and specifically DISEASE OF THE HEART, was central to the case. The insurance company excluded coverage of certain conditions during the first six months of the policy, and one of these was for a DISEASE OF THE HEART. The patient in question suffered a heart attack (technically a "myocardial infarction") within the first six months and sought payment for the treatment and costs. The insurance company refused on the grounds that these were expenses "for a condition in connection with disease of the heart," which was explicitly excluded in the policy.

So does DISEASE OF THE HEART cover a heart attack as part of its permitted vagueness, or not? I was asked to give my opinion. The answer is complicated, first of all, by the fact that the precise meanings assigned by medical practitioners to certain words of English can sometimes differ from their everyday meanings as understood by native speakers. More technical interpretations and definitions are often needed in medicine in order to establish precision among specialists who know the facts and the details in a way that the public at large does not. A difficulty in communication can then arise when technical interpretations diverge from everyday usage, by being more or less general, or having a different sense altogether, and this was, in fact, an issue in the present case.

This problem is not unique to medicine. Take legal terms. There are countless terms used by lawyers that are at variance with everyday understanding. Consider MALICE and MALICIOUS. A MALICIOUS ARREST in a legal context is one 'that proceeds without adequate justification.' For the man in the street, it would refer instead to 'a nasty or malevolent event, performed with evil intent.' Within linguistics, terms like AMBIGUITY and VAGUENESS are given more technical and precise meanings, as we have just seen, and everyday words like IMPLY are broken down into several more precise subtypes that must be regularly disambiguated in a way that everyday usage does not distinguish (see §1.5 and Chapter 5).

My role as an English language consultant was to try and give some clarity to the lawyers in this dispute about how DISEASE is understood in everyday English, since the insurance policy was written in English and average readers would bring their everyday understanding of DISEASE OF THE HEART to the reading process when deciding whether to buy this medical insurance or not. A challenge for medical professionals and insurance companies quite generally is that they need to interface with the public at large and use language that avoids misunderstandings or uncertainty.

The natural language and lay interpretation of DISEASE is captured by the various dictionaries of English, with different levels of detail depending on their overall size (recall §1.1). The *Merriam-Webster's Collegiate Dictionary* (11th edn) gives the following paraphrase:

> 'a condition of the living animal or plant body or of one of its parts that impairs normal functioning and is typically manifested by distinguishing signs and symptoms : SICKNESS, MALADY.'

In more detail, *The American Heritage Dictionary of the English Language* (5th edn) gives,

> 'An abnormal condition of a part, organ, or system of an organism resulting from various causes, such as infection, inflammation, environmental factors, or genetic defect, and characterized by an identifiable group of signs, symptoms, or both.'

And the *Random House Webster's Unabridged Dictionary* (2nd edn) includes,

> 'a disordered or incorrectly functioning organ, part, structure, or system of the body resulting from the effect of genetic or developmental errors,

infection, poisons, nutritional deficiency or imbalance, toxicity, or unfavorable environmental factors; illness; sickness; ailment.'

The critical issue in this case was, therefore, whether DISEASE, as captured in these definitions, and specifically DISEASE OF THE HEART, could refer to a heart attack (myocardial infarction). The lawyer for whom I consulted informed me that there was some ambiguity and uncertainty within the medical profession, based on his independent discovery and preparation for trial. The dictionary definitions, however, suggest that DISEASE OF THE HEART would not normally include a heart attack, but instead they pertain to conditions brought on by some kind of infection or environmental condition. Hence, if coverage for DISEASE OF THE HEART was excluded during the first six months of the policy, and if a heart attack is not such a disease, then it should not be excluded and the medical insurance company would have to pay up, regardless of whether there was any more technical sense of DISEASE, as used in a specialist medical context that would in fact subsume heart attacks.

In order to test the linguistic part of this opinion, I conducted a small experiment. There was insufficient time or money for a more systematic investigation (and back in 1988 there were no general or specialist and medical corpora such as we have today), so the law firm I consulted for was relying on dictionary definitions plus my testimony. Now, I was teaching a graduate class at USC at this time, with more than a dozen students, mostly specialists in English (within our Rhetoric, Linguistics and Literature Program in the English Department, or else they were specializing in applied linguistics within the Linguistics Department), all of whom had experience teaching and researching the English language. I conducted a survey among these students, and also among several of my faculty colleagues, and asked them the following question with the following lead-in:

> I would like you to think for a moment about the meaning of DISEASE in English. It is clear that there are lots of medical conditions that everybody would agree should be called DISEASES. Equally, if somebody, say, breaks a leg, everyone would agree that you would not describe that person as having a DISEASE OF THE LEG. Now, if somebody suffered a heart attack, would you say that that person had a DISEASE OF THE HEART?

The results were as follows. None of the (more than sixteen) respondents answered in the affirmative; i.e. nobody said that a heart attack should be considered a DISEASE OF THE HEART, as this phrase is used in plain English. One person pointed out that a HEART ATTACK could be caused by a DISEASE (but equally did not have to be), and that the two terms were quite separate. And one person said he had been doing a lot of thinking about diseases lately and wasn't sure.

I conclude from these pieces of evidence, the dictionary definitions, and the opinions of graduate and faculty specialists in English and applied linguistics that the natural language and everyday understanding of DISEASE OF THE HEART is narrower than it may possibly be in medical circles, and specifically it does not include within its range (and permitted vagueness) myocardial infarctions or heart attacks. Hence the cost of medical treatment for heart attacks should not be excluded by an insurance policy on the grounds that it is a DISEASE.

In effect, the linguistic and legal argument made by the medical insurance company in this case sought to extend the semantic range of DISEASE beyond what speakers of English normally understand it to mean. Their goal was to avoid paying for a particular treatment. They had a financial incentive, therefore, to try and expand the range of a meaning beyond what our lines of evidence indicated its meaning to be.

2.2.2 *APPROXIMATELY*

A 1993 real-estate contract dispute (in Los Angeles) involved the meaning of the word APPROXIMATELY and the extent of its permitted coverage and vagueness. The property being sold was described as consisting of APPROXIMATELY THREE HUNDRED (300) ACRES. It turned out subsequently that the acreage was only 202, and so we had a lawsuit and a disagreement about just how extensive the number of acres could be in the direction of 202 when using the phrase APPROXIMATELY 300. I was brought in to give my opinion about how everyday readers would understand this, and I was subjected to a grilling by lawyers for the defense in both a deposition and trial.

The word APPROXIMATELY is an adverb derived from the adjective APPROXIMATE. There is also a verb TO APPROXIMATE and a noun APPROXIMATION. They all derive ultimately from the Latin AD PROXIMARE, meaning 'to draw near to.' Dictionaries give very similar paraphrases for the meanings of the adjective and adverb that were central to this case. The *Oxford English Dictionary* (1st edn), for example, paraphrases the adjective APPROXIMATE as

> 'Very near, in position or in character; closely situated; nearly resembling.... Set very close together.... Nearly approaching to accuracy; fairly or reasonably correct.'

For the adverb APPROXIMATELY, the *OED* gives

> 'In an approximate manner, nearly; . . . with near approach to accuracy.'

The key concept that lies at the heart of APPROXIMATE and APPROXIMATELY is, therefore, that one thing is very near to, or nearly resembles, another. So is 202 very near to and does it nearly resemble 300? Obviously not! We can say that 295 is very near to and nearly resembles 300, perhaps 290, maybe even 285, and at a stretch 280. But 202 (as I testified) is "way out of line," and we don't even need to consider other numbers from 280 down to 202 and ask whether there is, or perhaps even test for whether there is, some gray area here as a result of which APPROXIMATELY 300 could refer to 202, using a psycholinguistic experiment with numerous native speakers. The lexical semantics of APPROXIMATELY in the phrase APPROXIMATELY 300 does not extend to 202. The lawyers for the defense were attempting to extend the semantic range of APPROXIMATELY way beyond its limit in order to justify an exaggerated and misleading property description in this real-estate contract.

There is, however, a complicating issue of "pragmatics" here, or everyday language usage, as opposed to the lexical semantics of dictionaries, which my deposition examiner was keen to exploit. There are some contexts of usage that appear to support the view that the meaning of APPROXIMATELY has much greater latitude than I have characterized it so far. Namely, there are contexts of usage in which precision does not matter and speakers can get away with what is technically a false approximation.

Let's say that I look out of the window of a downtown office into the town square and I utter (6),

(6) THERE ARE APPROXIMATELY 300 PEOPLE DOWN THERE.

Now, if there are only in fact 202, who cares? Nobody is going to know, nobody is going to find out, and it really doesn't matter. Or say I look into my fishpond at home and utter (7),

(7) THERE ARE APPROXIMATELY 300 MOSQUITO FISH IN MY POND.

Again, if there are only 202, who is counting? And how accurate would the count be anyway, given that one mosquito fish looks very much like another?

So these are contexts in which precision does not matter and speakers utter APPROXIMATELY 300 in a way that could refer to what ultimately turns out to be 202, if anybody bothered to check. There are no consequences; we don't know and we aren't terribly interested in the precise number. The basic point, however, is that it is not actually true under these circumstances to say that 202 is APPROXIMATELY 300, and if in these imprecise contexts the number is subsequently discovered to be 202, then APPROXIMATELY 300 would no longer be used to describe it.

A real-estate contract, by contrast, is a prime example of a linguistic context in which precision does matter, and there are real consequences of not adhering to the meaning of terms and of not being precise, as we see in the lawsuit currently under discussion. There are many such contexts where you cannot get away with an untrue description or a false approximation, and where there are consequences if you do and where accuracy and truth really matter.

Take the context of a university. Let's say that I have 300 students enrolled in my undergraduate class, and I am told by my teaching assistant that APPROXIMATELY 300 STUDENTS showed up for the midterm on a given day. If, in fact, there were only 202, then I have a major truancy problem on my hands and I have to deal with it.

Consider a second context, a medical one. A doctor is told by a medical researcher that there are APPROXIMATELY 300 RED BLOOD CORPUSCLES in a given unit of blood. If it turns out that there were only 202, this could be life-threatening.

Or take the more everyday example of baking a cake. You are following the recipe, and the recipe says, "ADD APPROXIMATELY 300 GRAMS OF BAKING POWDER TO THE CAKE MIX." If you add only 202, the cake will probably not rise.

These are contexts, therefore, where there are consequences if you do not follow the literal meaning of APPROXIMATELY, and do not refer to a number near or close to 300, and these consequences are detectable. The property contract in the present law case was of this type. There were real consequences for the buyer if he or she did not get what they thought they were buying, and a failure to adhere to the literal meaning of APPROXIMATELY 300 was detectable. The fact that there are other contexts of usage in which the precise number of people or of things referred to is unknown or irrelevant, and in which the literal meaning of APPROXIMATELY 300 is not put to the test, is no argument for disputing its literal meaning in a context such as the present one in which the literal meaning did matter and was subsequently put to the test.

2.3 Nonliteral and Extended Meanings

One fundamental fact about word meanings that is pervasive and has received significant discussion in the linguistic, philosophical, and lexicographic literature is that they can often be extended in interesting ways beyond their more literal, or basic, or invariant meanings as described in dictionaries. These extensions occur when words are used to refer to things and events that go beyond their core meanings in contexts that support this extension and make clear what it is.

Imagine that we have a mutual friend, Harry, who is very clumsy and awkward. I might say that HARRY IS AN ELEPHANT, meaning not that Harry is literally an animal in the local zoo but that he has elephant-like qualities. Similarly, HARRY IS A SNAKE predicates snake-like properties of Harry. Such nonliteral uses of ELEPHANT and SNAKE are referred to as "metaphor." Utterances such as THE SUN NEVER STOPS SHINING IN SOUTHERN CALIFORNIA are also not intended to be literally true: It does rain in Los Angeles, and the sun does not shine at night! What is being claimed is simply that Southern California has very good weather. These are cases of deliberate "hyperbole" or exaggeration for rhetorical effect. There are also cases when words can be used with deliberate falsehood in order to convey in context a meaning that is true, for example GRANDMA, THAT WAS A TERRIBLE MEAL uttered right after a dinner that everyone present knew to be fantastic. The intended meaning here is 'That meal was fantastic,' which everyone knows to be the case. This is called "irony."

The renowned philosopher Paul Grice was one of the first to systematize these nonliteral uses of language, as well as other related phenomena in everyday conversation, and he greatly clarified our understanding of how such processes work (in his 1975 paper "Logic and Conversation," in P. Cole and J. Morgan, eds., *Speech Acts*, Academic Press, New York, 41–58). He pointed out, first of all, that any time a word or phrase is used to convey some nonliteral meaning, it has to be the case that the hearer or reader can recognize the speaker's/writer's intention to convey some additional information in that context. In the metaphor examples of the previous paragraph, Harry is known to be a human being, not an elephant or a snake. Hence, to say that Harry is an ELEPHANT or a SNAKE is not literally true, and something else must be intended.

Second, it has to be clear to the hearer/reader, Grice argues, not just that some nonliteral meaning is intended, but what it is exactly. There is an act of reasoning, or inference, involved in all these nonliteral uses of language, to which he gave the technical term "implicature" (recall §1.5 and see Chapter 5). Essentially what the hearer/reader does is to figure out the intended nonliteral meaning on the basis of the literal meaning in conjunction with linguistic context, real-world knowledge, and certain conversational principles that Grice formulated (his so-called "maxims of conversation"). If Harry is not literally an elephant or a snake, what does the speaker/writer intend for me to understand? Answer – that he has certain properties that correspond to, or are like, the properties of an elephant or a snake, and hence that he is elephant-like or snake-like. Similarly, the hyperbole THE SUN NEVER STOPS SHINING IN SOUTHERN CALIFORNIA is known to be a ridiculous exaggeration in its literal meaning, and is converted by all parties to the closest available proposition that can reasonably be true based on our general knowledge of the world. And the intended interpretation of the ironic TERRIBLE MEAL is converted to its readily accessible 'fantastic meal' based on the recent experience and knowledge of those who attended the dinner.

With this much background we can consider some disputed meanings in lawsuits that center on whether the literal or nonliteral interpretation was intended, or that involved the precise delimitation between the two, i.e. what exactly the literal meaning was and what was extended.

2.3.1 FIGHTING, BATTLES, and WARS

A late 1990s case in which I was retained (for the defense) involved a company suing a group of workers for using militant language in their publications and flyers with the express purpose, it was claimed, of inciting violence against the company. The company claimed further that such acts of violence had indeed occurred as a direct consequence of this language. Specifically, the argument was made that the literal, military meanings of words like FIGHT, BATTLE, and WAR were at least partially responsible for the violence that ensued, as these words occurred in phrases such as FIGHT THE FIGHT, WAGE THE BATTLE, and WIN THE WAR.

The crucial issue in this case involved determining how exactly these words and phrases would be understood in the context of the publications and flyers in question. Were they being used in their literal, military senses? Such meanings would be readily assigned in the context of a text about World War II, for example. Or were they instead being used in a purely metaphorical and nonliteral sense in this present context?

Terms of war are among the most common metaphors in the English language and are widely applied to all kinds of situations that involve nonmilitary opposition (see George Lakoff and Mark Johnson's *Metaphors We Live By*, University of Chicago Press, Chicago, 1980). They are used to describe opposing parties in politics. For example,

(8) THE DEMOCRATS ARE FIGHTING THE REPUBLICANS FOR SENATE SEATS.

In debating and legal contexts,

(9) WE ARE GOING TO HAVE TO FIGHT THAT ARGUMENT TO WIN THE CASE.

In sports,

(10) THE HOME TEAM IS WINNING THE BATTLE AGAINST THE VISITORS.

And they can be used in numerous other cases as well. In all of these contexts a relevant, nonmilitary interpretation is assigned, and it would generally be ridiculous to claim that political commentators, debaters, lawyers, and sports newscasters were trying to incite violence through their use of such figurative language. The literal, military senses are immediately dismissed as irrelevant in these contexts, by both the speaker/writer and the hearer/reader.

In a similar way the larger context for FIGHT THE FIGHT, WAGE THE BATTLE, and WIN THE WAR in the publications and flyers at the center of this lawsuit did not support a literal, military interpretation. It focused instead on intellectual opposition, on the need for persuasion and argument, and on various peaceful means by which the workers could achieve their objectives. As a result, since the relevant language of the publications and flyers was clearly metaphorical and not militant, the claim that its purpose was to agitate and incite and encourage acts of violence, through the militant use of language, could not reasonably be made and was false, an opinion in which the trial judge concurred.

In this case the company in question seized upon the ambiguity of words like FIGHT (its literal and nonliteral interpretations) and attempted to make the legal and linguistic argument that its literal meaning was assigned in these written materials, despite all the contextual evidence to the contrary. This interpretation was then linked to the physical violence that occurred subsequently and was cited as a causal factor for it. But as I mentioned, there were no literal, militant meanings that would have been assigned in these publications and flyers in the first place; it was all metaphorical.

2.3.2 *CHEATING*

A 1994 case (in San Mateo, California) involved a libel suit against an individual who was quoted by a major national newspaper making a very negative claim about a public figure. The key sentence in this claim, given in quotation marks within the article, was (11)

(11) "HE CHEATS, AND HE HAS BEEN EXPOSED."

I was asked by the plaintiff's counsel, representing the person against whom (11) was directed, whether this statement, which was made in response to a question about the outcome of a legal proceeding, would be understood as "rhetorical hyperbole and/or as a statement of opinion which did not contain a provably false connotation." In other words, the issue here was again whether this context would lead to a literal or non-literal meaning being assigned, in this case a deliberately exaggerated nonliteral meaning. If the nonliteral meaning was assigned, then the reputational damage to the plaintiff would be much less since it would be unclear what the negative claim made against him was exactly.

The specific linguistic issues raised by (11) were accordingly first: What is the basic, literal meaning of the key negative word here, CHEATS, and also of EXPOSED? Second, is the context of the newspaper article in which (11) occurs compatible with an extended, nonliteral interpretation of CHEAT that could potentially weaken its (damaging) effect? And, third, if such a nonliteral meaning is assigned, does this render it not provably false? In other words, is CHEAT understood literally, or is this another example of a deliberately exaggerated implicature like THE SUN NEVER STOPS SHINING IN SOUTHERN CALIFORNIA, which could mitigate reputational damage?

The literal meaning of CHEAT is defined by major dictionaries in very similar terms. It is used both as a verb (TO CHEAT, HE CHEATS, etc.) and as a noun (THE CHEAT). The *Oxford English Dictionary* (1st edn) defines the verb as

> 'To defraud; to deprive of by deceit.... To deceive, impose upon, trick.... To deal fraudulently, practice deceit.'

The noun is defined as

> 'Applied to a person.... One who cheats; a swindler.... A deceiver, an imposter.'

Webster's Third New International Dictionary (1993) gives the verb as

> 'to deprive of something valuable by the use of deceit or fraud . . . to condition, influence, or lead by or as if by deceit, trick or artifice . . . to practice fraud or trickery . . . to violate rules dishonestly (as at cards) . . . to be sexually unfaithful . . .'

and the noun as

> 'the act or action of cheating or fraudulently deceiving . . . one that cheats esp. habitually . . . .'

These definitions make reference in their paraphrases to DEFRAUD and FRAUD. The *OED* defines DEFRAUD in turn as

> 'To deprive (a person) by fraud of what is his by right, either by fraudulently taking or by dishonestly withholding it from him; to cheat . . . To act with or employ fraud.'

And the noun FRAUD is defined by the *OED* as

> 'Criminal deception; the using of false representations to obtain an unjust advantage or to injure the rights or interests of another . . . An act or instance of deception . . . A method or means of defrauding or deceiving.'

For the verb EXPOSE meanwhile the *OED* gives the following paraphrases that are relevant in this context:

> 'To present to view, put forth . . . To exhibit openly; to display to the public gaze. To disclose . . . allow to be seen. To make known . . . To unmask, show up . . . to hold up to ridicule or reprobation . . . .'

And *Webster's Third New International Dictionary* gives similar paraphrases for it:

> 'to lay open to view : lay bare : make known . . . to disclose or reveal the faults, frailties, or unsoundness of : bring to light . . . UNMASK . . . .'

The literal meanings and concepts evoked by CHEAT and EXPOSE are clear from these definitions. To say that someone CHEATS is to say that this person 'defrauds, deceives, deprives by deceit, tricks, swindles,' and so on. It is a very strong claim. To say that the cheating has been EXPOSED is to say that it has been 'disclosed, made public, known, held up to reprobation,' and so on.

The critical issue raised in this libel suit was then whether this literal and very damaging meaning was the one that would be evoked by the quote (11) in the newspaper article, or whether instead readers would understand it as having an intentionally exaggerated and hyperbolic sense whose precise allegation could not be properly assessed. As I have mentioned, in this latter case the damage to the person's reputation and standing in the community would be much less.

Without going into details about the full contents of the article in this present summary it is sufficient to point out that the clear answer to this question about sentence (11) was "no," it would not have been understood in an intentionally exaggerated and hyperbolic sense, and for two reasons. First, and in contrast to our metaphors with FIGHTING in §2.3.1, there was nothing in the newspaper article itself, or in any general knowledge about the world that readers could bring to its interpretation, that would signal to them that CHEAT was being used, and should be understood, in anything other than its literal sense. And unless readers have some clear way of knowing that a nonliteral meaning is intended, as in HARRY IS AN ELEPHANT, THE SUN NEVER STOPS SHINING IN SOUTHERN CALIFORNIA, and THAT WAS A TERRIBLE MEAL (recall §2.3), then only the literal meaning will be assigned. CHEAT is therefore assigned its literal meaning in this article of 'to defraud, deceive, deprive by deceit, trick, swindle.'

Not only was there nothing in the context of the article or in real-world knowledge to suggest a nonliteral interpretation for CHEAT, but there were also facts and allegations reported in the article that were clearly compatible with, and that did support and underscore, the literal one. For example, we were told that a California arbitrator had ordered the person under discussion to pay $2.1 million to former employees. These employees claimed that they were deprived of compensation by unlawful means, and this claim was upheld by the state arbitrator after investigation. It was one of those employees who then uttered the words in (11). The literal meaning of CHEAT is fully consistent with the charges of these former employees, and these charges were upheld by an investigative body, so this meaning would be readily assigned by readers. This was not "rhetorical hyperbole," therefore.

With respect to the falsifiability question (Is (11) a statement "which did not contain a provably false connotation"?), the answer is that (11) is an example of what we call in linguistics and philosophy "a truth-conditional statement." It can indeed be potentially true or false. Truth-conditional statements differ from statements that are not truth-conditional, for example commands such as BRING ME THE APPLE. A command can be appropriately or inappropriately uttered (depending on who is speaking to whom), but it cannot be literally true or false. It is a linguistic instruction from one individual to another to perform a certain action. After the command has been uttered, we can determine whether or not the person in question complied, using the truth-conditional statement HARRY BROUGHT ME THE APPLE. This statement will be true if Harry did this and false if he did not, but the command itself, at the time of utterance, is not literally true or false; it is a "speech act" (see further John Searle's *Speech Acts*, Cambridge University Press, Cambridge, 1969).

Determining truth or falsity involves matching a given meaning with a set of circumstances in the world, in order to see which "truth value" (true or false) should be assigned. The meaning of CHEAT was defined previously as someone who 'defrauds, deceives, deprives by deceit, tricks, swindles,' and so on. Determining whether HE CHEATS is true will therefore be no different than determining whether numerous other sentences containing these paraphrases are true, such as HE DEFRAUDS, HE DECEIVES, and so forth. These are all truth-conditional, and hence they are all statements that are provably false.

Interestingly, there is a further set of circumstances in which it becomes problematic to assign truth values to a normally truth-conditional statement: namely when that statement is used with an implied nonliteral meaning or implicature. For example, what exactly are the truth conditions for HARRY IS A SNAKE used metaphorically? What precisely does Harry have to be like in order for us to say that this statement is true or false? The matter is complicated. It is also irrelevant in the present context since HE CHEATS in the newspaper article discussed here was not being used in any nonliteral way. Hence the quoted statement in (11) does have a literal interpretation and is provably (true or) false. The attempt by the defense to argue for a nonliteral meaning of CHEAT was designed to reduce the negative impact of this word within a libel suit. The nonliteral meaning was not supported by the larger context of the newspaper article, however.

2.3.3 *MURDER*

For some words, dictionaries will regularly list both their basic, literal meanings and certain extensions of these when they are particularly common. Such is the case with the word MURDER. This word was at the center of a defamation suit in a northwest city of the US (2017), filed against a local city councilor who had used it in a protest speech against the police in connection with the killing of an armed African American man. There were several linguistic issues raised by MURDER in this case, two of which I shall consider here. First, was the literal meaning the one that was intended and understood by those attending the protest speech and by those reading subsequent newspaper reports of it? The second concerned what the literal meaning is exactly, which became critical in a 2022 continuation of this case.

MURDER can be both a noun (A MURDER) and a verb (TO MURDER) in English. Both parts of speech have a literal meaning that basically involves 'a killing of a human being that is unlawful and premeditated.' Various extensions of this can range from 'something outrageous or blameworthy' to 'something very difficult,' as in THE TRAFFIC WAS MURDER. *Merriam-Webster's Collegiate Dictionary* (11th edn) gives the following definitions for the noun (abbreviated *"n"*) and the verb (*"vb,"* with *"vt"* being transitive and *"vi"* intransitive) and lists the following range of literal and nonliteral meanings:

> **murder** . . . *n* . . . '**1** : the crime of unlawfully killing a person esp. with malice aforethought . . . **2 a** : something very difficult or dangerous <the traffic was ~> **b** : something outrageous or blameworthy <getting away with ~>'
> **murder** *vb* . . . *vt* . . . '**1** : to kill (a human being) unlawfully and with premeditated malice **2** : to slaughter wantonly : SLAY **3 a** : to put an end to **b** : TEASE, TORMENT **c** : MUTILATE, MANGLE <~*s* French> **d** : to defeat badly ~ *vi* : to commit murder . . . '
> **murderer** . . . *n* . . . : 'one who murders; *esp* : one who commits the crime of murder.'

It is immediately apparent from these definitions that MURDER is a semantically loaded word in English. To claim MURDER is to assert not only that one individual killed another, but also that this was done in a way that is unlawful, premeditated, and with malicious intent. This is particularly damaging if the individual accused is a police officer, as it was in this case. The primary purpose of policing is to uphold the laws of the land and make sure that citizens behave in accordance with them. If police officers commit murder, they not only act unlawfully and are liable for criminal prosecution like any other individual, but this undermines their whole professional purpose and commitment. It is an extremely strong and damaging claim to make about the police and the police officers in question. And after they were named in person and identified in the local press, they filed the defamation suit.

The larger *Webster's Third New International Dictionary of the English Language Unabridged* (1993) gives more detailed entries and even refers to distinctions found in legal practice between "first-degree murder" and "second-degree murder," as well as documenting an original sense for the word found in English law:

> **murder** . . . *n* . . . '1 *early Eng law* : the killing of a person secretly or with concealment as opposed to an open killing **2** : the crime of killing a person under circumstances precisely defined by statute: as **a :** first-degree murder that deserves either capital or severe punishment because of being willful and premeditated, being committed with atrocity or cruelty (as by poisoning, starvation, mayhem or torture), being committed in the course of the commission of a serious felony (as arson, burglary, or kidnapping), or being committed after lying in wait for the purpose of killing the victim **b :** second-degree murder that in most states is all other murder not classified as first-degree murder **3 :** the killing of people in war <war is mass ~> **4 :** something extraordinarily difficult or dangerous <it'll be ~ on those roads up in the Sierras . . . > <in the more modest cafeteria . . . the crush is ~ . . . > **5 :** a parlor game . . . '
>
> **murder** . . . *vb* . . . *vt* '1 **:** to kill (a human being) unlawfully and with premeditated malice or willfully, deliberately, and unlawfully **2 :** to slaughter in a brutal manner esp. in war <bombs *~ed* people as they stood in the street> **3 a :** to put an end to : DESTROY <if ever he were in power would . . . ~ truth, freedom, and art . . . > **b :** to harass or depress grievously : TEASE, TORMENT <*~ed* this poor heart of mine . . . > **c :** to mutilate, spoil or deform by wretched performance : MANGLE <someone's difficult sonata was *~ed* on the piano . . . ><the average British traveler leads the world in *~ing* the French tongue . . . > ~ *vi* : to commit murder . . . .'

The first issue raised in this case was, therefore, which of these various meanings for the noun MURDER would actually be the one selected in the immediate context of the protest speech by the city councilor and in the larger context of the local newspaper reports describing it. Other terms that accompanied it and that were used by the councilor included allegations of RACIAL PROFILING, POLICE BRUTALITY, and the need for ACCOUNTABILITY. These, coupled with the fact that a killing had taken place, along with the general seriousness of the occasion and the anger expressed by both the councilor and those in attendance toward the police, made it clear that MURDER was being used and understood in its literal meaning and not in any of the more figurative extensions noted previously.

The second issue (raised by the defense counsel for the city councilor in the 2022 continuation) centered on what the literal meaning of MURDER was exactly, and whether the paraphrases given above in the Webster's dictionaries are fully accurate. The critical legal issue in this case, meanwhile, and the one that emboldened the police officers to file their lawsuit, was that an inquest was subsequently held into their actions in this killing, presided over by a judge and jury, and this inquest had cleared the officers of any wrongdoing. In other words, according to the inquest's findings these officers did not commit MURDER; they were not guilty of RACIAL PROFILING and they did not need to be held ACCOUNTABLE for criminal actions in this case. Instead the inquest found that the officers had been faced with a very difficult situation trying to arrest a man who had just recently been released from jail and who appeared to be resisting arrest and was holding a gun, contrary to the terms of his release. Crucially the inquest did not find evidence of police wrongdoing.

The defense accordingly argued that "most laypeople are not aware of the technical distinctions among different jurisdictions' treatment of the same conduct, and are invoking a more general cultural understanding that is moral and values-based when they use terms like 'murder.'" In other words, the defense was critical of whether a paraphrase such as sense 2 in the *Webster's Third New International Dictionary of the English Language*, with all of its references to technical distinctions in the law, was an accurate description of the meaning of MURDER that everyday users of English have in their minds. At issue was whether there is a "vernacular" use of MURDER that can be different from a more technical, legal one, and hence whether the city councilor and others were entitled to use MURDER in this weaker sense of something that was 'wrong' or 'immoral,' even if the inquest within a certain jurisdiction had found it to be within the law.

This point is interesting, and it does need to be conceded that the larger *Webster's* may be adding too much real-world and encyclopedic information about first- and second-degree murder into its definition for what is, after all, a word of the English language used by hundreds of millions of native and nonnative speakers around the world. Most of these speakers have no clue about such technical distinctions in the law, so what are these details doing in a language dictionary of word meanings anyway? I will return to this question later.

It is important, however, not to lose sight of the central concept that does characterize the everyday meaning of MURDER and that language users do have in their minds when they use this word, namely that it refers to a killing that is a 'crime' and 'unlawful.' This is highlighted in the two *Webster's* dictionaries noted previously. *The American Heritage Dictionary of the English Language* (5th edn) also refers to MURDER as a 'crime':

> '**1a.** The killing of another person without justification or excuse, especially the crime of killing a person with malice aforethought or with recklessness manifesting extreme indifference to the value of human life.'

The *Oxford English Dictionary* (3rd edn online) defines it as 'unlawful':

> '1. . . . a. The deliberate and unlawful killing of a human being, esp. in a premeditated manner.'

The basic meaning of MURDER accordingly involves more than an appeal to morals, values, and culture. It refers to a killing that is a crime and unlawful. But the inquest in this case found that the police officers did not act criminally and illegally. Hence the word MURDER, as defined by all the dictionaries we have considered, cannot and should not have been used to describe the killing in question, and since it is a highly loaded and negative term in English, to use it is to inflict severe reputational damage on the officers involved.

It is instructive to compare MURDER with the word KILL, which applies to all kinds of terminations of life, whether lawful or not, deliberate or not, by physical or other means, and so on. The *OED* (3rd edn) defines KILL as

> 'To put to death; to deprive of life; to slay, slaughter. In early use implying personal agency and the use of a weapon; later, extended to any means or cause which puts an end to life, as an accident, over-work, grief, drink, a disease, etc.'

The current and modern meaning of KILL is accordingly much more general than MURDER, and significantly for the present case it makes no reference to the law as the competent authority for deciding whether the word can be used. We can talk about the KILLING of the African American man, therefore, in a way that is semantically neutral and refers only to the fact that he was deprived of life, while leaving unspecified how exactly and whether this was 'lawful.' But MURDER is a loaded term semantically. It contains the additional meaning that the killing was a 'crime' and 'unlawful.' It would accordingly inflict immediate reputational damage, especially when directed at police officers whose whole purpose in society is to uphold the laws and make sure that people behave in accordance with them.

There is an important linguistic point here about what dictionaries are trying to do, or should be trying to do, when they define MURDER and lots of words like it that refer to complicated entities and distinctions in the world around us. What are they claiming exactly about word meanings, and what are they not claiming?

They are all trying to define, on the one hand, the general understanding of words like MURDER that all speakers of English have in their minds and that will be evoked every time speakers and hearers, and writers and readers, use this word. These definitions are given in the form of paraphrases, as we have noted (§1.1), using other words and phrases that capture the precise sense of the single word in question. In the case of MURDER the dictionaries tell us that there is an inherent appeal in its core meaning to the fact that the killing is unlawful, i.e. there is an inherent appeal to the law. This does not mean that dictionary writers expect users of English to know the relevant legal statutes and to know about legal distinctions made in different states or countries about different types of murder. On the contrary, these details are added in larger dictionaries like the larger *Webster's* for the benefit of those who are curious about how the law works, and who find it interesting, precisely because the core meaning of MURDER does refer to criminal conduct and the law. For the average user of English, however, the only meaning of MURDER that everybody is claimed to share is captured in its general definition: 'the crime of unlawfully killing a person esp. with malice aforethought . . .' (*Merriam-Webster's Collegiate Dictionary*, 11th edn). Hence there is an appeal within its core meaning to some legal body, or statutes, or set of findings that determine whether something is a MURDER or not.

MURDER is, therefore, one of a large class of words in English where there is a reference to what we can call a "competent authority" in its core meaning, i.e. to a body of experts who are recognized authorities in a particular field and who ultimately set the rules for how certain terms can be used. This is very common in areas of vocabulary such as medical and scientific terms. The recent pandemic was caused by a VIRUS, not by BACTERIA. The dictionary definition for VIRUS given in the *OED* (3rd edn) accordingly makes explicit reference to "*Medicine* and *Biology*" as the competent authorities for deciding that COVID-19 is a VIRUS, and hence for determining the applicability of this word to it. For those who are curious, it gives some additional medical details about the differences between a VIRUS and BACTERIA, just like the larger *Webster's* gives additional legal details for different kinds of MURDER.

But it is not obvious that dictionaries should be giving this kind of real-world information, since it blurs the distinction between a dictionary and an encyclopedia, and this can lead to some confusion, as we see in the present case, about what exactly it is that is "in a name" like MURDER and that is known by those who use the English language. Nonetheless, this is what the larger dictionaries do, and they do it for a reason: Because the word in question appeals to a competent authority and its usage depends on what that authority has determined.

Similarly, the *OED* definition for PLANET makes explicit reference to "*Astronomy*" and to the findings of the International Astronomical Union that Pluto is not a regular planet and hence the word PLANET no longer applies to it. In all of these examples everyday users of English do not generally have the technical expertise of the medical establishment and of biologists, or of astronomers, or of legal professionals, but they do know that these terms have a basic meaning that makes reference to a competent authority and that this authority will ultimately determine whether something is actually a VIRUS, a PLANET, or a MURDER, which then determines whether these words of English can accurately and fairly be applied to the relevant things and events in the world.

To conclude this section, note first that the context of utterance clearly selected a literal meaning for MURDER in this case, not an extended nonliteral one that would have attenuated the claim made by the city councilor and with it the libel accusation against this person. Second, this case raised questions about how much encyclopedic information should be present in a dictionary of word meanings, and more generally it led to questions about how accurate the dictionary definitions of a term like MURDER actually are. The argument made by the defense that there was a weaker "vernacular" sense of MURDER as something that is merely "wrong" or "immoral" and "values-based" is at variance with the definitions given by the major dictionaries I consulted that all define MURDER as a 'crime' and 'unlawful.' I accordingly opposed the view that MURDER appeals primarily to morals, values, and culture. What is highly relevant for the use of MURDER in the present case is precisely that the subsequent inquest by a legal body consisting of a judge and jury did clear the two officers of all wrongdoing, based on a full consideration of the facts in relation to the legal statutes of the state in question. Hence the word MURDER, as defined by all the dictionaries, could not and should not have been used to describe this shooting.

I return to the lexical semantics of MURDER and related words and to further consideration of the linguistic issues raised in the present case in §6.4.

2.4 Language in a Changing World

The linguistic and legal issue in the next case I shall discuss centered around the word TANGIBLE. It was at the basis of a lawsuit involving a very famous movie company in Los Angeles, and its affiliate in San Francisco, in connection with some very famous movies. The identities of these companies and their movies are not important in the present context with its focus on the English language; nor are numerous legal details. What is important is how an age-old question in the philosophy of language, and in the modern language sciences more generally, suddenly assumed huge real-world practical and financial significance in the context of the law.

The basic issue can be paraphrased as follows: When the world changes dramatically around us, and real-world objects like cars and trains look quite different today than they did 50, 100, and 150 years ago, do the words that refer to these entities, CAR and TRAIN, and the linguistic meanings they evoke in the minds of English language speakers, change as well? Clearly the world is changing, and as it does so our knowledge of the world changes, and with it the pictures and memories and associations that we have in our minds of real-world objects. When we use words like CAR and TRAIN, the corresponding real-world entities of the current era certainly spring to mind. When we visualize a car today we don't think of one from World War I (unless perhaps we've just been watching a silent-era movie), and when we mention TRAIN we don't think of an early nineteenth-century steam engine pulling some passenger compartments. But what about the language itself, i.e. the linguistic meanings of CAR and TRAIN and their basic "senses" as defined in dictionaries using paraphrases (recall §1.1)? Have they changed as well? Have their meanings shifted along with changes in the world? Or is it just the world that has changed, and the meanings of these words remain the same in a way that is general enough to be compatible with today's cars and trains, with yesterday's cars and trains, and with the cars and trains of tomorrow, whatever they might look like?

Let me set up the background to this case (Los Angeles and San Francisco, 2015) by mentioning a particular movie company, Disney, distinct from the ones in this case, and a particular movie, *Frozen*. I am partial to this movie because my (currently eight-year-old) youngest daughter watches it all the time, and because it is based on one of the fairy tales by Danish author Hans Christian Andersen that my own (Danish) mother used to read to me when I was a child of that age. In connection with this movie there are all kinds of merchandise items that can be bought and that children can play with and enjoy relating to the central characters and scenes in *Frozen*: plastic figures, hairclips, coloring books, and so on. Similarly in the 2015 case I am about to describe there was a lot of derivative merchandise relating to the characters and scenes in the movies, and this merchandise was produced by a "licensee" who was then obliged to pay a certain percentage back from the proceeds to the "licensor," the one holding the legal title to the creative work in question.

Now, the licensing agreements and contracts between the parties were written back in the 1960s, and they referred specifically to "TANGIBLE" items, more precisely to "ARTICLES OF TANGIBLE PERSONAL PROPERTY," in connection with the movies in question, on which the percentage from the proceeds had to be paid. In the 1960s the kinds of objects that were being produced, and that the contract writers and readers would have been thinking about when the relevant agreements were drafted, were very physical and "touchable" items, i.e. they were TANGIBLE in a very basic sense. But fast-forward to 2015, some fifty years later, and the derivative merchandise now included all kinds of computer-related and downloadable content that simply didn't exist back then. (Even computers barely existed at that time, outside of university departments that were busy developing them in places like Manchester.) So a lawsuit arose over how many items were now, in 2015, subsumed as TANGIBLE PERSONAL PROPERTY under the agreement from fifty years before, and on which the percentage needed to be paid. Was it just the very physical and touchable items of the kind that people had in mind in the sixties? Or were their modern electronic counterparts to be included as well, and could these still be regarded as TANGIBLE and covered by a legal contract from an era in which the world was different? In short, was the language different too? Did TANGIBLE refer only to items that people knew about and thought about back then? Or was its meaning, like the meanings of CAR and TRAIN, compatible with future and as yet unimagined types of things, as well as present ones? Depending on the outcome of this question, a significant amount of extra money would, or would not, need to be paid by the "licensee." The licensee accordingly had a financial incentive to construe the meaning of TANGIBLE as narrowly as possible, so as to avoid payment on numerous derivative items in the modern computer age; the licensor meanwhile had an incentive to construe it more broadly.

My role in this case was to advise one of the parties on this linguistic issue and specifically to write a rebuttal report critical of an opposing linguist's opinion (an experienced veteran, as it turned out, among expert witnesses in language and the law). This expert had argued that TANGIBLE, in the context of the 1960s agreement, had to be interpreted in the narrow 'touchable' and 'physical' sense that would have applied to the kind of merchandise that was being produced back then, and that its meaning was not compatible with computer-related and downloadable content showing the same images from films in 2015. Hence this later merchandise was not subject to the royalty payments in question. My contrary opinion, which I shall summarize in what follows, was that the meaning of TANGIBLE was already much broader than this, even back in the 1960s (think of "TANGIBLE BENEFITS," which don't have to be physical at all). The linguistic meaning here, I argued, was more like that of CAR and TRAIN, and could subsume corresponding objects existing in the past, in the present and in the future. In other words, computer images of objects in 2015 that existed in the physical world back in the 1960s could still be regarded as TANGIBLE and in accordance with the dictionary sense of this word both back then and now.

I shall leave it to readers of the present book to decide whether they agree with my rebuttal arguments in this case. The linguistic issues raised by this case were complex and subtle. They were also legally significant since there must be lots of contracts like this, where there have been rapid advances in science and technology and a contract written some years or decades before these advances were made. Do these old contracts still apply to the new inventions fifty years later? There were arguments made on both sides by the language consultants in this case. But there were some key points that my opposing expert failed to consider, and looking back on this case now as I replay it for the present book after almost ten years, I believe that my contrary opinion was correct. It was certainly helpful to the law firms that retained me.

2.4.1 *The Basic Grammar of ARTICLES OF TANGIBLE PERSONAL PROPERTY*

The grammar of ARTICLES OF TANGIBLE PERSONAL PROPERTY consists, as is usual in syntax, of phrases within phrases, each of which has a so-called grammatical "head" (see §1.3 and §4.1). The head is the key category syntactically that determines the grammatical nature and status of the immediately larger phrase within which it occurs. The presence of a noun like PROPERTY in the combination TANGIBLE PERSONAL PROPERTY makes this sequence a noun phrase (NP), i.e. [np TANGIBLE PERSONAL PROPERTY], with PROPERTY as the head noun. More precisely, PROPERTY combines first with PERSONAL to yield a 'compound noun' functioning as the head (see further §3.3), with TANGIBLE as the adjective that modifies this compound head, i.e. [np TANGIBLE [PERSONAL PROPERTY]]. This NP then occurs within a prepositional phrase (PP) whose head is the preposition OF, [pp OF [np TANGIBLE [PERSONAL PROPERTY]]], and this PP in turn occurs within a larger noun phrase headed by the noun ARTICLES. This gives the following grammatical structure for this phrase, with left and right square brackets around each phrase within a phrase, and with each phrase labeled on its left by the grammatical type in question, here NP or PP:

[np ARTICLES [pp OF [np TANGIBLE [PERSONAL PROPERTY]]]].

Within each of these phrases the meanings of the individual words, PROPERTY, PERSONAL, and so on, are combined together in ways that are either "compositional" or "noncompositional" (recall §1.2) to yield a combined semantic product, and this process is repeated phrase by phrase up what is in effect a hierarchical phrase structure tree diagram for the whole phrase, and eventually up to the whole sentence itself (see again §4.1 for further details and illustrations of such phrase structure groupings and tree diagrams in syntax). Now, the combinatorial semantic rules that determine the meaning of a whole phrase from its parts are subject to a number of technical issues in semantics that do not need to concern us, depending on the type of grammatical category and the type of combination in question and on details of the semantics, but one technical principle that was highly relevant in this case and that I discussed in my rebuttal (since the opposing expert did not mention it) was what can be called "the principle of adjective dependency." Basically, when an adjective like TANGIBLE has a range of possible meanings, as we shall see it does in the next section, selecting the appropriate one depends on the meaning of the head noun that it combines with, rather than vice versa. In other words, the meaning of the noun determines the meaning to be assigned to the adjective within the phrase in question.

Consider an adjective like FLAT in English. Its meaning can vary considerably. Compare FLAT ROAD (meaning 'a road that is horizontal'), FLAT TIRE ('tire without air'), FLAT BEER ('beer without bubbles'), FLAT NOTE ('note below the correct pitch in music'), FLAT VOICE ('monotonous'), FLAT SALES ('sluggish'), and so on. It is always the head noun, ROAD, TIRE, BEER, and so on, that determines the intended meaning of the adjective and of the whole combination. Similarly for the adjective TANGIBLE, the crucial determinant of its meaning is the meaning of the compound head noun PERSONAL PROPERTY that it modifies, and the selection of the appropriate sense of TANGIBLE will depend primarily on this head (see §2.4.3).

My own research in the field of linguistics has contributed to clarifying this relationship between semantic dependency and head-of-phrase status in grammatical structures like this. The interested reader is referred to chapter 2 of my 2004 book *Efficiency and Complexity in Grammars* (Oxford University

Press, Oxford) and to my more technical 1984 article "Modifier-Head or Function-Argument Relations in Phrase Structure: The Evidence of Some Word Order Universals," *Lingua* 63: 107–138.

2.4.2 *The Semantics of TANGIBLE*

The word TANGIBLE derives from the Latin "TANGIBILIS," meaning 'touchable,' and this is still a basic sense of the English word in modern usage. But TANGIBLE also has a range of further meanings going beyond this original Latin sense, and these are routinely captured in major dictionaries. For example, *Webster's Third New International Dictionary* (1969; abbreviated *"WTNID"* in this section) defines the original Latin sense as

> '**1 a :** capable of being touched'

and illustrates it with "a tangible separable thing like . . . salt or bread." With a slight weakening of this physical contact sense, *WTNID* adds to this first entry

> 'able to be perceived as materially existent esp. by the sense of touch'

and gives the example "wished he had a tangible reward for his efforts." With a further attenuation of the physical contact idea *WTNID* defines the following sense:

> '1 . . . **b :** substantially real : MATERIAL'

and exemplifies it with "the conquest of a territory meant a tangible advantage to the conqueror" and with "a tangible gain in money." Yet a further extension in meaning is given in

> '**2 :** capable of being realized by the mind : conceived or thought of as definable or measurable,'

exemplified by "I have never been in a community where happiness was so tangible" and by "the motives of action are quite tangible."

In fact, when one compares the definitions given in this and the other dictionaries that were discussed in the opposing expert's report and in my rebuttal (*Random House Dictionary of the English Language*, 1966, abbreviated *"RHD"*; *The American Heritage Dictionary of the English Language*, 1969, *"AHD"*; *Funk & Wagnalls Standard Dictionary of the English Language*, 1969, *"F&W"*), a clear picture emerged of a whole range of meanings for TANGIBLE from 'capable of being touched' (*WTNID*,

RHD, AHD) and 'perceptible by touch' (*F&W*) at the one end, through 'visible and appraisable' (*AHD*), to 'perceptible to the senses' (*F&W*), and further to 'capable of being apprehended by the mind' (*F&W*), 'capable of being realized by the mind' (*WTNID*), 'real or actual' (*RHD*), 'substantially real' (*WTNID*), and 'conceived of as definite or measurable' (*WTNID*).

Despite this range of meanings, defined in the dictionaries that were selected by the opposing expert and were all published in the 1960s, the period in which the movie agreements were written, the expert insisted that TANGIBLE PERSONAL PROPERTY had to have its original Latin meaning in the context of the agreements. That is, it referred, he claimed, only to objects that were available in the world at the time the contract was written and that were 'physical' and 'touchable.'

But whatever priority there was in the history of the English language for the physical sense of the Latin TANGIBILIS, speakers of Modern English (even in the 1960s) use TANGIBLE with a broad range of meanings from which the intended and appropriate sense is selected on different occasions of use. The first determinant of this selection, as I pointed out in connection with FLAT in the last section, is the head noun with which an adjective combines. This can be seen clearly in the example sentences given in the dictionaries, "tangible . . . thing, like . . . salt or bread" (*WTNID*), "tangible reward for his efforts" (*WTNID*), "tangible advantage" (*WTNID*), "tangible gain in money" (*WTNID*), "happiness was . . . tangible" (*WTNID*), "tangible evidence" (*F&W, AHD*), "tangible benefits of sunshine" (*RHD*), "tangible grounds for suspicion" (*RHD*), and so on. The selection of the appropriate meaning from the different senses of TANGIBLE that are commonplace in English depends crucially on the noun that follows: REWARD, ADVANTAGE, EVIDENCE, GROUNDS, and so on. The meaning of this noun determines the sense of TANGIBLE that is compatible with it. In the agreements that were at the center of this law case, TANGIBLE modifies the compound head noun [PERSONAL PROPERTY]. Its meaning accordingly varies with, and will be determined by, the meaning and reference of this compound head.

Before we consider the semantics of this compound, notice first that it is commonplace in English for words that have physical senses, like TANGIBLE, to have a range of other meanings that go well beyond the physical. This is of interest because it means that speakers and writers and readers of English are used to having to select from a broad range of meanings with words of this type. Consider the adjective PALPABLE. *WTNID* summarizes its range of meanings as follows:

> '**1 :** capable of being touched or felt : perceptible to the sense of touch . . . **2 :** easily perceptible by one or another of the senses other than touch . . . **3 :** easily perceptible by the mind . . . .'

Again we have the full gamut of senses for PALPABLE, just as we do for TANGIBLE, from 'touchable' through 'perceptible by one or another of the senses other than touch' to 'perceptible by the mind.'

Consider also the verb SEE in English. *WTNID* gives a range of possible senses for it, from '**1 a** perceive by the eye : apprehend through sight,' through

> '**3 a** to form a mental picture of : VISUALIZE . . . **b :** to perceive the meaning or importance of . . . **c :** to be aware of,' to e.g. '**6 a :** to regard as : CONSIDER, JUDGE.'

And for the verb FEEL in English, we have a similar range defined by *WTNID* from

> '**1 a** . . . **:** to perceive by tactile, muscular, integumental, or other sensation excited by some physical stimulus'

to

> '**4 a :** to be aware of (something objective) by instinct or inference rather than through actual experience or sensation <~ the presence of an intruder in the room> . . . **b :** to be persuaded or convinced of emotionally rather than intellectually <*felt* that the move would be unwise although she could give no positive reason> . . . **c :** BELIEVE, THINK, HOLD . . . <they *felt* that their own argument was as sound as that of their opponents>.'

For all these adjectives and verbs there is a broad range of meanings, including a direct perception and physical sense, but the meaning actually chosen from this range always depends primarily and crucially on the word or phrase with which the adjective and the verb combine within their respective phrases.

2.4.3 The Combinatorial Semantics of TANGIBLE PERSONAL PROPERTY

As pointed out above, PERSONAL PROPERTY is a "compound noun." It comprises two words, the adjective PERSONAL plus the noun PROPERTY, both functioning together as a tightly bound unit.

Compounds are not generally listed in dictionaries because there are too many of them, and their meanings are often clear from their component parts. When compounds do have distinctive non-compositional meanings (recall §1.2) or occur with especially high frequency, however, they are typically listed and defined. Such is the case with PERSONAL PROPERTY. Most dictionaries I consulted do list it and define it.

A particularly clear and succinct definition for PERSONAL PROPERTY comes from *Random House Webster's College Dictionary* (2000 edition):

> 'an estate or property consisting of movable articles both corporeal, as furniture or jewelry, and incorporeal, as stocks or bonds (disting. from *real property*).'

Included in this definition is the word PROPERTY itself, for which the same dictionary gives the following senses, inter alia:

> '**1.** that which a person owns; the possession or possessions of a particular owner. **2.** goods, land, etc., considered as possessions. **3.** a piece of land or real estate. **4.** ownership; right of possession, enjoyment, or disposal, esp. of something tangible. **5.** something at the disposal of a person, a group of persons, or the community or public . . . .'

The term ESTATE, which also appears in the definition of PERSONAL PROPERTY, is further clarified in the entry for PROPERTY as follows:

> 'ESTATE refers to property of any kind that has been, or is capable of being, handed down to descendants or otherwise disposed of in a will . . . It may consist of personal estate (money, valuables, securities, chattels, etc.) or real estate (land and buildings).'

The meaning of TANGIBLE, as defined in §2.4.2, combines with that of PERSONAL PROPERTY, as just defined, to yield a "compositional product" or combined meaning. Before we define it, there is a basic issue in semantics that needs to be clarified, because clarifying it was especially important in this case. It involves the distinction between what is called "sense" and "reference," a long-standing distinction that goes back to many foundational works in philosophy and linguistics. A convenient summary of the issues can be found in John Lyons's book *Semantics* (Cambridge University Press, 1977, see especially chapter 7).

Nouns like PROPERTY and compounds like PERSONAL PROPERTY have a certain meaning or "sense," which the dictionaries define using their paraphrases (recall §1.1). On the basis of this "sense" these nouns can then achieve "reference" to particular entities in the world. For example, THE PROPERTY could refer to 'the property that I own' or to 'my sister's property,' and so on (see further §6 on reference and identification). John Lyons then introduces a further distinction between "reference" and "denotation," and simplifying somewhat, by "denotation" is meant the full set of all possible things in the world that could ever be referred to by e.g. PROPERTY and PERSONAL PROPERTY, on the basis of their meaning and "sense." "Reference," by contrast, involves talking about and referring to particular items, at particular times, on particular occasions, by particular people. In other words, "denotation" means all the possible entities, actual or not, that can ever be "denoted" by a noun on the basis of its "sense," i.e. all the things that can possibly and conceivably be 'personal property,' whereas "reference" is to particulars.

The beauty of a natural language like English is that it consists of words and phrases that have general meanings and "senses" like this that we can use to talk about all kinds of things (their "denotation"), whether these things exist now or in the past or the future, whether they are actual or imagined or unimagined at the time of writing and speaking, as long as they conform to the "senses" of the relevant words. We have already mentioned this flexibility in "reference" with things like CAR (and AUTOMOBILE) and TRAIN. They each have a "sense" defined by the dictionary. But the kinds of things in the world that they made "reference" to in the past were quite different from the cars and trains that we see today, and yet we still call them CARS and TRAINS respectively, because their "sense" is general enough to subsume them all without us having to assume that there was any change in "sense" that accompanied these differences and changes in "reference."

In a parallel way the kinds of things that PROPERTY and PERSONAL PROPERTY can apply to now will be different than they were back in the 1960s, i.e. some fifty years before the 2015 lawsuit when the agreements were written and signed. These words will refer to things now that were unimaginable back then, but these things will still be covered by their basic "senses," just as cars in the past and also modern cars are covered by the word CAR, and so on. The world has changed dramatically in this time, with technology in particular. There were no widely available computers then, and thus no hardware and software items, no internet, no downloadable videos, and so on. The kinds of things that people could own and "refer" to as PROPERTY and PERSONAL PROPERTY would not have included these things, but they did include them in 2015. The world has changed, but the "senses" of these words has not. A legal contract containing the words PROPERTY and PERSONAL PROPERTY, therefore, is understood by users of English to include everything in the world today, yesterday, and in the future that matches the "senses" of these terms, whether or not those who drafted the contract and wrote the words in it ever used these words to "refer" to all these things at the time they were writing. Obviously they did not.

This important distinction between meaning or "sense" in language and the objects and changing objects in the world to which language "refers" is one that is frequently misunderstood, even by professional linguists who are not specialists in semantics, and it was not properly recognized in the expert report I was rebutting. There was no need to go back to contemporaneous dictionaries from the 1960s, as the expert did, because the English language and the meanings of the key terms ARTICLES, TANGIBLE, and PERSONAL PROPERTY have not changed since then: It is the world that has changed. There are different entities now that these words can refer to, based on their "senses," such as computer-related items.

When the adjective TANGIBLE combines with its compound head noun [PERSONAL PROPERTY], an appropriate and compatible meaning for TANGIBLE is selected from the broad range defined for it in the last section that is compatible with the head, by the "principle of adjective dependency" that I illustrated with FLAT. This range of possible "senses" and meanings for TANGIBLE went from 'capable of being touched' and 'perceptible by touch' at the one end, through 'visible and appraisable,' to 'perceptible to the senses,' and further to 'capable of being apprehended by the mind,' 'capable of being realized by the mind,' 'real or actual,' 'substantially real,' and 'conceived of as definite or measurable.' I gave dictionary definitions for the meanings of the head nouns PROPERTY and PERSONAL PROPERTY earlier in this section, and I pointed out that a changing technological world has had as one of its consequences that items to which linguistic expressions like PROPERTY and PERSONAL PROPERTY can now "refer" on the basis of their "senses" have expanded to include new products and inventions that are compatible with these senses. This same expansion in reference is true of the combination [TANGIBLE [PERSONAL PROPERTY]].

In the past, and also today, someone might own a novel or a story written in paper form, and this would be both PERSONAL PROPERTY and TANGIBLE in its original 'touchable' sense. Subsequently this novel or story might be made into a movie that could be privately owned in the form of a video or DVD and that could be played on a TV or computer screen. This DVD and its packaging would be 'touchable,' but the movie itself would be 'visible and appraisable' and 'perceptible to the senses' (see the sense definitions for TANGIBLE) rather than 'touchable.' One could certainly touch the TV or computer screen at this stage on which the photographic images were projected, but there would have been little point in doing so. Later still, and into the truly modern era of the internet, email, apps, Skype, Wi-Fi, and so on, it is possible to download movies where all you have before you is consecutive photographic images on a screen and there would be no plastic spool or packaging as there was before. Your computer can obviously be TANGIBLE PERSONAL PROPERTY, but what of its software and its downloaded contents? Are these suddenly not part of your TANGIBLE PERSONAL PROPERTY just because they are not readily 'touchable' or because the spool and the packaging for the video are no longer needed? Clearly not. The essential entity that is possessed when a video is possessed, namely the consecutive photographic images on a screen, remains as it was. More importantly, the linguistic meaning of TANGIBLE is clearly compatible with such modern products as these. The possible "senses" for TANGIBLE include 'visible and appraisable' and 'perceptible to the senses,' and it is these aspects of its meaning that are evoked when PERSONAL PROPERTY combines with TANGIBLE to refer to downloadable and modern technology items. Hence TANGIBLE PERSONAL PROPERTY can refer, by virtue of the combination of "senses" for these words as given in standard dictionaries, to a range of items that were not even imagined at the time the agreements were written, but that are now instances of it. They are natural extensions in "reference" but not in "sense" to new items in a modern virtual reality world that did not exist before but that fall within the "denotation" of TANGIBLE PERSONAL PROPERTY, i.e. the full set of things to which it can potentially refer. In a similar way, CAR and TRAIN can refer to items now that they did not refer to before, based on their "senses."

There is one further detail about modern technology that is worth mentioning in this context. With the invention of touchscreen computers, users can now actually touch the screens of their computers, and thereby give commands and interact with computer programs and with content downloaded from the internet in a very direct and physical way. For the purist who insists, as my opposing expert did, that TANGIBLE PERSONAL PROPERTY in the context of the agreements must refer to items that are 'touchable,' and only to these, the wheel has turned full circle. Purely downloadable content that lacks a plastic spool and packaging is again TANGIBLE in a 'touchable' sense, in addition to being 'visible and appraisable' and 'perceptible to the senses.' Hence such downloadable content is TANGIBLE PERSONAL PROPERTY even by the narrow 'touchable' criterion which, as I argued, is far too narrow anyway.

2.4.4 *The Semantics of ARTICLES*

When the noun ARTICLES and the preposition OF are added to [np TANGIBLE [PERSONAL PROPERTY]] we get the larger noun phrase, which I repeat:

[np ARTICLES [pp OF [np TANGIBLE [PERSONAL PROPERTY]]]].

ARTICLES is the head noun of this higher NP. The interesting semantic point about this head noun in this structure is that, in contrast to adjective + noun combinations where the head noun determines the meaning selection for the adjective (recall FLAT TIRE, FLAT NOTE, etc.), it is now the head noun itself that varies its semantic content with the accompanying PP. Compare e.g. ARTICLES OF CLOTHING with ARTICLES OF FAITH, ARTICLES OF THE CONSTITUTION, ARTICLES IN A SCIENTIFIC JOURNAL, and ARTICLES IN ENGLISH GRAMMAR. ARTICLE has numerous meanings, and which one is chosen in these phrases depends crucially on the relevant PP (headed by OF or IN here) that it combines with. We can use *The American Heritage Dictionary* to define this range of meanings for ARTICLE:

> '**1.** An individual thing in a class; an item: *an article of clothing.* **2.** A small thing. **3.** A particular section or item of a series in a written document, such as a contract, constitution, or treaty. **4.** A nonfictional literary composition that forms an independent part of a publication; a report or essay. **5.** *Grammar.* Any of a class of words used to signal nouns and to specify their application. . . . **6.** A particular part or subject; a point or specific matter.'

My opposing expert drew attention to the "ARTICLE OF CLOTHING" illustration in sense 1 and cited it as further evidence for the purely 'physical' and 'touchable' interpretation for the articles in question. But there is no such necessarily physical interpretation for ARTICLES OF TANGIBLE PERSONAL PROPERTY. We have seen (in §2.4.3) that TANGIBLE varies its meaning and adapts to whatever PERSONAL PROPERTY can refer to, whether physical or not, virtual or not, accessible or not through touchscreen interaction, and so on, as long as one or more of the possible meanings of TANGIBLE can be satisfied in the combination. Similarly, the meaning of ARTICLES depends on the meaning of its accompanying phrase, here the PP [pp OF [np TANGIBLE [PERSONAL PROPERTY]]], and this meaning then adapts to whatever TANGIBLE PERSONAL PROPERTY can refer to. If this latter refers to a physical entity like CLOTHING, then the ARTICLE in question will also be a physical item. But if the TANGIBLE PERSONAL PROPERTY is, say, a downloadable video or app that is owned and has been paid for, that is 'visible and appraisable' and 'perceptible to the senses,' and that is accessible via an icon on the computer's desktop, then the ARTICLE in question will be exactly that. And this latter possibility will comply with one or more of the "senses" of the dictionary definition for ARTICLE, namely as 'An individual thing in a class; an item . . . A small thing,' just as readily as the physical reference to ARTICLE OF CLOTHING does. Hence ARTICLES OF TANGIBLE PERSONAL PROPERTY has a broad "denotation" that includes and is not limited to items that are actually 'touchable.'

2.4.5 *The Linguistic Context of the Movie Contract*

Within the agreements that were at the center of this lawsuit, some concrete examples were mentioned of the kinds of things that could be "ARTICLES OF TANGIBLE PERSONAL PROPERTY" and that the writers drafting the agreements had in mind when they used this phrase. These included "PRINTED STATIONERY AND POSTERS" and other "MANUFACTURED" items. The agreements also made reference to the "SHIPMENT" of these items to customers. My opposing expert used these examples as a further argument for the necessarily 'physical' character of the articles in question, by drawing on the larger linguistic context in which the phrase appeared (recall §1.4).

But people would not have been thinking of downloadable computer content in the 1960s for one very simple reason: It did not exist at the time! And giving lots of examples from the past that did exist then does not shed light on what the general meaning of TANGIBLE PERSONAL PROPERTY is, and on whether and how it could refer to later items as well as earlier ones. The 'touchable' examples cited in the agreements exemplified some of the possible "referents" that this phrase could have (calendars, greeting cards, postcards, etc.). These examples did not eliminate other possibilities and references to nonphysical items; they merely exemplified the 'physical' and 'touchable' ones from the range of semantic possibilities that were in existence back then.

As a consequence, readers of these agreements now and in the future, who have different knowledge of the world, will find nothing in the language of these agreements to prevent assigning a nontouchable interpretation to ARTICLES OF TANGIBLE PERSONAL PROPERTY, based on the senses for these words that have existed all along. In short, my opposing expert's contextual analysis did not distinguish between "exemplification" and "elimination" of the semantic possibilities for this phrase. There was no elimination of a nonphysical and nontouchable interpretation in these agreements, merely examples that illustrated the physical and touchable interpretations that were commonplace in the past.

I conclude, based on all this evidence, that the meaning and reference of the phrase ARTICLES OF TANGIBLE PERSONAL PROPERTY was not limited in these agreements only to those that were necessarily physical and touchable. It can also refer, in ways that are fully consistent with word meanings defined at the time of the agreements and subsequently to items of personally owned downloaded computer content that are 'visible' and 'perceptible.' Hence, the licensing agreement at the basis of this lawsuit that employed this phrase should not be understood as having only the narrow semantic range for it that benefited the licensee legally and financially.

CHAPTER 3

Disputes over Word Combinations

We saw in §1.2 that when words combine together into different kinds of phrases, their meanings combine in ways that may be "compositional" or "non-compositional." In this latter case the combined meanings are not straightforwardly derivable from the meanings of the parts, and the whole combination can have a characteristic and distinctive meaning, over and above the meanings of its parts. These "non-compositional" meanings can sometimes be hard to pin down. They can also be at the center of lawsuits, whereupon linguistic analysis is required to clarify what exactly the meaning of the whole phrase is and how it will be understood by everyday users of English.

In this chapter I examine (in §3.1) the precise meaning and grammar of the WRENCH-ENGAGING SURFACE that occurred in the dental implant patent that was considered in §2.1, in connection with its positioning SUBSTANTIALLY ENTIRELY BELOW THE TOP OF THE ANCHORING MEANS. This is followed by the phrase REHAB FOR BILLY in a libel suit brought by a country music celebrity against a tabloid magazine (§3.2). In the third section (§3.3) I introduce the linguistics of trademark law with particular reference to word combinations of compound nouns [$Noun_1$ $Noun_2$]. The classification and assignment of these compounds to the different categories of trademark law is often in dispute. In this chapter I focus on "generic" and "descriptive" terms. Section 3.4 discusses APP STORE as a paradigm case of genericness, and presents the grammatical and empirical usage arguments that can be made, and were made, in support of this status. Section 3.5 does the same for descriptiveness, using the phrase HALF PRICE BOOKS. Generic terms can never be trademarks, while descriptive terms can be trademarks only if a "secondary meaning" can be proven whereby they are understood to refer to a particular producer. Subsequent chapters discuss "suggestive" terms (§5.5), which can be trademarks along with other strong identifiers of the unique source of the product or service in question (see again §3.3 and also §6.2).

3.1 WRENCH-ENGAGING SURFACE

The accused product in the 1996 patent infringement case for a dental implant (discussed in §2.1) used a WRENCH-ENGAGING SURFACE within its ANCHORING MEANS as a way of securing the artificial tooth within the jaw. At first sight the meaning of WRENCH-ENGAGING SURFACE is straightforward. This is 'a surface that engages with a wrench' or 'that can engage with a wrench.' But there is more to it. There is an additional non-compositional meaning in this construction, and this additional component turned out to be critical in describing the difference between the accused product and the accusing one.

Let's start with the grammar. WRENCH-ENGAGING SURFACE is a noun phrase (NP) consisting of a participial -ING form of the verb TO ENGAGE, immediately preceding and combining with the head noun SURFACE (recall §1.2 and §2.4 and see also §4.1 for further discussion of "heads" in syntax). WRENCH is in turn directly attached to the left of this participial verb ENGAGING and is also compounded with it. We saw in §1.2 that whenever you have left-attached compounds in English, like the [$Noun_1$ $Noun_2$] compounds FLOWER POT and PAPER CLIP, the modifying item on the left is severely restricted in its grammar compared with corresponding items attached to the right. There is no *FLOWERS POT, or *WITH FLOWERS POT, but you can specify these extra details with modifiers on the right of the head noun, POT WITH FLOWERS, POT FOR HOLDING FLOWERS, and so on. Correspondingly there are frequently non-compositional elements of meaning with these left-attached modifiers. A PAPER CLIP is not typically a 'clip of paper' or a 'clip made of paper'; it is a 'clip for holding papers together.' Right-attached modifiers, by contrast, are syntactically not compounds, and they are regularly compositional in their meaning.

The same left-right grammatical difference is found with Noun-Verb+ing compounds like WRENCH-ENGAGING. There is no *WITH-A-WRENCH-ENGAGING SURFACE, or *WRENCHES-ENGAGING SURFACE in English, and prepositions and other semantically clarifying material must be placed to the right of the verb not to its left, i.e. the surface in question is for ENGAGING WITH A WRENCH. Correspondingly, the meaning of WRENCH-ENGAGING SURFACE is not fully compositional. There is an added element of meaning in this construction that goes beyond the meanings of the individual words. What is it exactly? We can paraphrase it as follows: This is 'a surface that is designed to engage a wrench' or 'a surface for the purpose of engaging a wrench,' and this is how it will be understood by readers of the patent.

This 'design' or 'purpose' interpretation is very productive in English compounds with all kinds of leftward-occurring modifiers of head nouns. So, TREE-PRUNING SHEERS are those 'designed for the purpose of pruning trees.' POTATO-PEELING UTENSILS are 'utensils for the purpose of peeling potatoes.' COOKING UTENSILS (with a simple participial verb modifying UTENSILS and minus the attached noun to the left specifying what exactly is being cooked) receives the same interpretation: 'utensils for the purpose of, and designed for, cooking.' Similarly, FERTILITY PILLS with its [$Noun_1$ $Noun_2$] structure refers to pills whose 'purpose is to increase fertility.' The considerable productivity of this purposive interpretation is discussed in Judith Levi's (1978) monograph *The Syntax and Semantics of Complex Nominals*, Academic Press, New York.

These noun phrases with prenominal modifiers are all syntactically reduced compared to their more explicit postnominal paraphrases, therefore, and their semantics is correspondingly less explicit as well, with the result that in everyday language use the reader amplifies and enriches their interpretation in the appropriate way. The precise content of this enrichment can vary, depending on the basic meanings of the words combined and on our general knowledge of the world. So, an OIL-BURNING HEATER is designed for the immediate purpose of burning oil, but the real, higher purpose is to produce heat. OIL-PRODUCING COUNTRIES meanwhile are not actually countries designed for the purpose of producing oil, since countries, unlike utensils, are not designed by anyone for particular purposes. Instead an OIL-PRODUCING COUNTRY is one that 'has the property that it produces significant amounts of oil,' a paraphrase that is supplied by our knowledge of the world in conjunction with the meanings of these words. For nouns denoting tools, utensils, and other man-made devices, however, the 'purpose' or 'intended design' interpretation for compounds with participial verbs and with other prenominal modifiers is extremely productive and readily inferred, and the phrase WRENCH-ENGAGING SURFACE is accordingly understood as 'a surface designed for the purpose of engaging a wrench.'

Proof of the reality of this purposive meaning comes from the following consideration. If a given device is only optionally or incidentally usable for a certain purpose, then constructions with preposed participial verb modifiers in English cannot be used to refer to it. You could use COOKING UTENSILS if you want to beat your husband, for example, but this does not make them HUSBAND-BEATING UTENSILS! This is humorous precisely because they are still COOKING UTENSILS, designed and intended for cooking, even if the actual uses to which they are put by some people may include other purposes. The interpretation of these noun phrases in English is sensitive to their design features, or intended purpose, and the mere possibility of using cooking utensils for husband-beating does not lead us to call them HUSBAND-BEATING UTENSILS. That phrase would be reserved for utensils that really are designed for this purpose. Similarly, TREE-PRUNING SHEARS could conceivably be used to cut carrots, but that does not make them CARROT-CUTTING SHEARS! They are instead SHEERS THAT WERE USED TO CUT CARROTS WITH. Hence, when average readers encounter WRENCH-ENGAGING SURFACE they understand it to mean that this is 'a surface designed to engage with a wrench.' That is its purpose. They do not understand it to mean that this is just a possible or optional use of this surface. If it were, then the combination WRENCH-ENGAGING SURFACE would not have been used to describe it.

Now, in the patent infringement lawsuit the accusing product made use of a quite different means for inserting the prosthesis into the jawbone. The tooth was not screwed in with a small wrench but tapped in with a small hammer. The patent holder for the accusing product claimed that his invention was being infringed on the grounds that a surface described as a WRENCH-ENGAGING SURFACE in the accused patent did not necessarily have to be used with a wrench. Engagement with a wrench was just one way of inserting the tooth, and tapping it in with a hammer would be another, exactly as in the accusing product. But we have seen that a WRENCH-ENGAGING SURFACE is indeed one that is 'designed for the purpose of engaging with a wrench,' regardless of any unintended or incidental uses to which that surface is put. And since the accusing product inserted the tooth by tapping it in with a hammer (which would have been appropriately described as a HAMMER-TAPPING SURFACE), it was not designed for engagement with a wrench, and so once again (recall §2.1) there was no patent infringement here. The accusing device did not have a WRENCH-ENGAGING SURFACE as this word combination is commonly understood in English, whereas the accused device clearly did. The two products differed significantly from each other, therefore, and only one could be properly described by the non-compositional meaning of WRENCH-ENGAGING SURFACE. In effect, the lawyer for one side in this case was unaware of, or chose to ignore, this subtle non-compositional meaning when making the case for patent infringement against a product that differed precisely with respect to the design feature that was captured in this non-compositional meaning.

3.2 REHAB FOR BILLY

A 2016 libel suit was filed by a country music celebrity against a national magazine. In keeping with the policy of the present book I withhold his real name and also numerous legal details since our primary focus is on the English language. Let us call him "BILLY SCRANTON." The key offending phrase in the libel suit, appearing on the cover page in very large print, can be given here as REHAB FOR BILLY. Most of the remainder of the cover page was then filled with a large picture of Billy and the following sentences, (1) in large print, and (2)–(4) in smaller print:

(1) HE FINALLY HITS ROCK BOTTOM

(2) DRINKING VODKA BEFORE NOON & SLURRING HIS WORDS – IT'S WORSE THAN ANYONE KNOWS

(3) WHAT HE DID WHILE WASTED THAT DESTROYED HIS MARRIAGE

(4) HOW HIS FRIENDS BEGGED HIM TO STOP JOKING & GET HELP

I was asked what meaning readers would assign to REHAB FOR BILLY and to these accompanying sentences on the cover page. Billy was suing the magazine for "implying" that he was going into rehab, when this was not in fact the case. He had no intention of going into rehab. And I was asked also whether readers would understand that the magazine was making a statement of fact.

The linguistic question about whether a text makes "implications" beyond the literal meanings of the words and sentences within it, and the related issue of whether a statement of fact is presumed by a newspaper or magazine, was raised in §1.5 and will be the topic of Chapter 5, which is devoted entirely to these issues and in which numerous further examples are discussed. In the present section our primary focus is on the phrase REHAB FOR BILLY, more generally X FOR Y, which has some interesting semantic and pragmatic properties, as we shall see. Questions of implication and the presumption of truth are among them, so we shall raise them now in anticipation of later elaboration.

The complicating factual issue in this case was that, if and when readers looked inside the magazine and read the full three-page article that followed up on the cover page, they would learn that Billy Scranton had no intention of going into rehab. There were numerous further references to his excessive drinking in these pages, and also to other negative traits, but on the crucial issue at the center of the lawsuit about whether Billy was already in, or going into, rehab, readers were told that Billy was not already in rehab and that he had no intention of going there. Billy "WON'T LISTEN" to friends who had advised him to "CHECK ... INTO A FACILITY" and by "THROWING HIMSELF" into an upcoming TV series in which he was to feature as a judge he would be getting "THE BEST DISTRACTION AND ALL HE NEEDS." So does the cover page make a misleading claim about Billy going into rehab, and would readers understand this to be a factual one? If so, they would be surprised when they read the full article inside the magazine and discovered that Billy was neither in, nor going into, rehabilitation.

The opinion I rendered in this case was that the heading REHAB FOR BILLY on the cover page of the magazine does indeed convey the meaning that Billy is going into, or is already in, rehabilitation, on account of his drinking. This is how readers will understand this phrase of English, in the same way that they would understand a heading like "PRISON FOR THE THIEF" to mean that the thief in question is going to, or is already in, prison. The language of the remainder of the cover page, especially (1) and also (4), which refers to Billy's friends urging him to "GET HELP," strengthens the reader's understanding that Billy is going into or is already in rehab. Readers looking just at the cover page will therefore not understand (1–4) to mean that Billy has been advised by friends to go into rehab but has no intention of doing so. Similarly REHAB FOR BILLY on the cover page will indeed be understood as the words of the writer, as is usual in such headings, not as the words of Billy's friends, nor as those of anybody else. Readers will understand these words to be conveying the writer's intended meaning, for which he is presumed to have sufficient evidence, that Billy is going into or is already in rehab.

Let us consider the grammar and meaning of REHAB FOR BILLY in more detail. This is a commonly used phrase of English, of the form X for Y, where Y is a noun or proper name referring to a person, FOR is a preposition, and X is a noun describing the place or state or condition that the individual Y is going to enter into or will experience or has already entered and begun to experience. Some parallel examples are

PRISON FOR THE THIEF, LIFE FOR THE MURDERER, GUILLOTINE FOR THE KING OF FRANCE, DISMISSAL FOR THE CHELSEA MANAGER, AN A FOR THIS STUDENT, TOUCHDOWN FOR THE RAIDERS, and so on.

The fuller and more explicit meanings that these X for Y phrases convey can vary depending on the exact meaning of the X phrase. PRISON FOR THE THIEF corresponds to 'the thief is going to prison.' GUILLOTINE FOR THE KING OF FRANCE corresponds to 'the King of France is going to the guillotine,' i.e. Y is going to X where X is the location in which a certain action is carried out (confinement) or the location and the instrument of that action (beheading). LIFE FOR THE MURDERER means that 'the murderer is getting a life sentence,' and AN A FOR THIS STUDENT means 'this student is being awarded an A,' i.e. Y is getting or being awarded X (a negative life sentence or a positive grade in a class). The precise time frame referred to in these X for Y phrases can also vary. PRISON FOR THE THIEF, when uttered by the judge giving the sentence, will mean that the thief is going to prison in the future. By the time this is reported in the local newspaper as PRISON FOR THE THIEF, it will be understood to mean that the thief may already have started his sentence. DISMISSAL FOR THE CHELSEA MANAGER will mean that the manager has most likely already lost his position as manager and been sacked, past tense.

What cannot vary in these X for Y phrases is the clear link between the person Y and the location, condition, or state X. It is being claimed that Y is in the location, condition or state of X, and this gives rise to the paraphrases 'Y is going to X' or 'Y is entering a state of X' or 'Y is getting X.' In the current lawsuit, REHAB FOR BILLY can be paraphrased as 'Billy is going into rehab.' More precisely, given the possible variability in the time reference for this construction that we have just seen, the paraphrase should be 'Billy is going into, or is already in, rehab.'

There is a further aspect to the meaning of these X for Y phrases that involves their contexts of usage, or their "pragmatics." The examples we have given can be uttered as what are called "speech acts." A judge can utter "PRISON FOR THE THIEF" and "LIFE FOR THE MURDERER" and use these phrases to assign the punishment that he or she is authorized to set for them. The full speech act paraphrase for "PRISON FOR THE THIEF" would be 'I hereby make the judgement that the thief is going to prison.' Similarly a professor can assign grades to students and can do so by saying or writing "AN A FOR THIS STUDENT," for which the full speech act paraphrase would be 'I hereby determine that this student is getting an A.' A football referee can utter "TOUCHDOWN FOR THE RAIDERS" while raising both hands, and thereby determine that the play was indeed a touchdown, thus removing any uncertainty.

In his influential book on *Speech Acts* (Cambridge University Press, 1969) Berkeley professor John Searle discusses different types of speech acts in English, building on the insights of his Oxford mentor John Austin (in his book *How to Do Things with Words*, Clarendon Press, Oxford, 1962). Searle and Austin point out that all speech acts obey certain rules of usage. Only certain individuals can send thieves to prison, namely judges, and they have to use certain words and meanings when they do so. Only certain individuals can make decisions at football games, namely referees, and they have to express these decisions using certain words and/or signals. These rules are referred to as "appropriateness conditions" for the speech acts of judging, refereeing, and so on.

Asserting or declaring something when speaking or writing is also a speech act for Searle and Austin and is similarly subject to conditions of appropriate usage. If a speaker or writer declares e.g. "THE CHELSEA MANAGER HAS BEEN DISMISSED," the appropriateness conditions that Searle defines for asserting this proposition *p* include "[Speaker] has evidence (reasons, etc.) for the truth of *p*. . . . [Speaker] believes *p*. Counts as an undertaking to the effect that *p* represents an actual state of affairs" (Searle, *Speech Acts*, p. 66). In the event that the speaker lacks this evidence about the Chelsea Manager, or knows it to be untrue, it would be inappropriate, misleading, or lying to assert it. Hence there is a "presumption of truth" about assertions made in everyday language use (recall §1.5 and see further §5.4).

Sentences consisting of X for Y can be used to perform the same speech acts as their more explicit speech act paraphrases, and when they do so they are subject to the same conditions of appropriateness. "PRISON FOR THE THIEF" could be used by a judge to send the thief to prison. If uttered by an arbitrary bystander in the court, it would have no effect and there would be no consequences for the thief. In other words, it would be an inappropriate and failed speech act. "TOUCHDOWN FOR THE RAIDERS" must be uttered by a referee with the appropriate accompanying hand movements if it is to count. And "DISMISSAL FOR THE CHELSEA MANAGER" has exactly the same appropriateness conditions involving the presumption of truth by speaker or writer as the full sentence "I HEREBY DECLARE THAT THE CHELSEA MANAGER HAS BEEN DISMISSED" and will be just as misleading and inappropriate in the event that the speaker/writer has no evidence for the truth of this *p* or does not believe it.

To recap, the basic semantics of REHAB FOR BILLY on the cover of the magazine is 'Billy is going into, or is already in, rehab.' Moreover, it stands as a complete sentence, with the pragmatic speech act meaning of an assertion or a declaration, making this usage equivalent to the writer saying, 'I hereby declare that Billy is going into, or is already in, rehab.' Following the appropriateness conditions defined for assertions by Searle (*Speech Acts*, p. 66), whereby all assertions carry the presumption of truth, we can amplify the paraphrase for "REHAB FOR BILLY" as follows: 'I hereby declare as information known by me to be true that Billy is going into, or is already in, rehab.' This is how readers will understand this key phrase on the cover page of the magazine.

We can also use the theory and terminology of another famous Oxford philosopher of language, Paul Grice (see his "Logic and Conversation" in P. Cole & J. Morgan, editors, *Speech Acts*, Academic Press, New York, 1975, pp. 41–58), to describe the meaning of "REHAB FOR BILLY" on this magazine cover page in slightly different but related terms. Because of the presumption of truth and the meaning definition given in the last paragraph, REHAB FOR BILLY can also be said to "implicate" that 'Billy is going into, or is already in, rehab.' We saw in §1.5 that "implicate" (and its corresponding noun "implicature") is one of the technical terms that linguists and philosophers now use, following Grice, in order to give more precision to the nonspecialist and everyday terms "imply"/"implication" and "insinuate"/"insinuation." The key point is that REHAB FOR BILLY positioned on this cover page does indeed lead the hearer to understand that Billy is going into, or is already in, rehabilitation.

This "implicature" which was at the center of this lawsuit is supported by the other words and phrases on the cover page. Immediately above REHAB FOR BILLY is a highlighted circle containing the phrase "THE REAL STORY." This reinforces the reality and actuality of the writer's report. It makes explicit Searle's appropriateness condition that "[Speaker] believes *p* . . . [and] *p* represents an actual state of affairs" (Searle, *Speech Acts*, p. 66). In this context it reinforces and makes explicit the pragmatic force of the writer's intent, namely "I hereby declare as information known by me to be true . . . ." Billy Scranton is going into, or is already in, rehabilitation.

The additional words and phrases on the cover page of the magazine, (1)–(4) given above, provide further information that supports the meaning that will be assigned to REHAB FOR BILLY on its own. Our general knowledge of the world can regularly influence how particular words and phrases are understood in context, and in this context it is widely known that many people go into rehab when they have a severe drinking problem. Sentence (1) refers to Billy hitting "ROCK BOTTOM," (2) describes him "SLURRING HIS WORDS," and (3) says he was "WASTED" and this "DESTROYED HIS MARRIAGE." (4) States that his friends "BEGGED HIM . . . TO GET HELP." All of this reinforces the implicature that Billy is going into, or is already in, rehabilitation.

There is a simple test that was discussed in §1.5 involving possible and impossible continuations to a text in order to see whether our semantic and pragmatic analysis of how readers will understand the magazine's cover page is correct. Some continuations would be completely natural, given the meanings of the words and phrases that are there and the implicatures drawn from them. Other continuations would not be readily comprehensible and would be inappropriate and confusing. For example, it would be natural to follow REHAB FOR BILLY with the sentence HE STARTS NEXT WEEK. This follows naturally because readers have just been informed that Billy is going into or is already in rehab and now the next sentence provides relevant and more specific information that delimits the range of times permitted by 'is going into' and by the choice between the future option and 'is already in rehab.' The event in question begins next week. By contrast, it would not be natural to follow REHAB FOR BILLY with the sentence HE ISN'T GOING. This would leave the reader puzzled and wondering what is going on. This is because REHAB FOR BILLY implicates that Billy Scranton is indeed going into rehab, and what is left uncertain is not whether he is doing so but when. The first continuation HE STARTS NEXT WEEK clarifies this uncertainty and is highly informative in context. The second, HE ISN'T GOING, is confusing and inappropriate.

This explains why readers will be surprised when (and if) they move from the cover page to the fuller three-page article within the magazine itself, where they are told that Billy has no intention of going into rehab! He "WON'T LISTEN" to these friends who are apparently begging him and advising him to "CHECK . . . INTO A FACILITY," and instead he intends to get the distraction he needs from his drinking and other problems by "THROWING HIMSELF" into the new season of his upcoming TV program. This is "ALL HE NEEDS,' we are told, i.e. he does not need rehabilitation.

This linguistic test, and readers' surprise when they go beyond the cover page, confirms the semantic and pragmatic analysis we have given for REHAB FOR BILLY on the cover page. Namely, 'I (the writer) hereby declare as information known by me to be true that Billy is going into, or is already in, rehab.' Its pragmatic force in this context is, therefore, not 'I hereby declare as information based on hearsay that . . ., ' nor 'I hereby declare as information for which I lack adequate evidence . . ., ' nor 'I hereby declare as information that I have made no attempt to corroborate . . . .' On the contrary, the pragmatic force in this context is that this is information for which the writer has evidence, that is believed by him or her to be true, and that describes an actual state of affairs, exactly as defined in the appropriateness conditions for assertions in Searle's (1969) book. Quite generally, print media in our society have a responsibility to the public to provide accurate information, and the magazine in question conforms to this in the full article about Billy Scranton by making it clear that he is not going into rehab. But on the cover page readers will understand instead that Billy Scranton is either going into, or is already in, rehab, since this was clearly "implied," more precisely "implicated," and presented as a fact.

With respect to the legal issue of libel here, we can say that the cover page of the magazine does indeed make a negative impression, damaging to Billy Scranton, by leading readers to understand that he is going into, or is already in, rehabilitation on account of his excessive drinking.

3.3 Compounds in Trademarks

Word combinations, especially nominal compounds of the form [$Noun_1$ $Noun_2$], feature prominently in trademark disputes. The purpose of a trademark is to identify the source of the goods or services in question. Trademark law distinguishes (1) generic terms, which name a genus and which can never be trademarks (CUBE STEAK, TENNIS BALL); (2) descriptive terms, which describe the qualities and characteristics of the goods, and which can be trademarks as long as "secondary meaning" can be proven that identifies a particular provider (e.g. HOLIDAY INN motel); (3) suggestive terms that require imagination, thought, and perception in order to link the term with the goods (ROACH MOTEL insect trap, recall §1.5); (4) arbitrary terms (like APPLE for computers); and (5) fanciful terms (KODAK).

Distinguishing between these categories is often notoriously difficult, especially for terms that are not single words. Underlying the classification of a term and its assignment by the courts to one of the categories above are a number of subtle grammatical and lexical issues on the one hand, combined crucially with actual usage by members of the relevant (sometimes quite specialist) groups of consumers on the other. In this section

I summarize some of the linguistic issues and forms of evidence that ultimately determine whether a term can be a trademark or not, and how terms are classified in the hierarchy just summarized. The focus in this initial discussion will be on terms that are the least eligible for trademark status, generic and descriptive ones. I have personally argued (in a case against Apple Computers) that APP STORE is generic for a store that sells apps, just like COMPUTER STORE and PET STORE are generic for stores that sell computers and pets, respectively. APP STORE does not just refer, any longer at least, to Apple's product, despite vigorous efforts by Apple to claim it for their exclusive use as a trademark. By contrast, I have argued that HALF PRICE BOOKS is descriptive and not generic. The linguistic arguments for suggestive terms and other source identifiers will be considered in later chapters (see §5.5, §6.2, and §7.1). In this present context I shall focus on APP STORE as an example of genericness (§3.4) and on HALF PRICED BOOKS as an example of descriptiveness (§3.5), and give a summary of the kinds of linguistic evidence and arguments and counterarguments that can be, and were, presented to the courts in these cases. My bigger goal here is to draw attention to general issues of a linguistic nature that arise in this area of the law.

When talking about the classification of terms in trademark law, it is essential to begin with a summary of the work of the great legal scholar and grandfather of the whole field, Thomas McCarthy. His many editions of the multivolume *McCarthy on Trademarks and Unfair Competition* (Thomson/West) capture the legal decisions that have been made by the courts for American trademarks over the years in considerable detail, and with an admirable clarity and sophistication in matters of language. (He could have been a linguist!) His book, henceforth "*McCarthy*," is the necessary go-to volume for lawyers and linguists alike, and so we begin with it here in order to give some more background on the basic terms of trademark law and on genericness and descriptiveness in particular. The quotes (section and paragraph numbers) from *McCarthy* that I give below are from my own 2008 edition that I was using at the time when I was working on the APP STORE case of §3.4.

McCarthy writes that "a generic term is one that is commonly used as the name of a kind of goods" (§12:1 at 12–17), and he adds: "Generic designations tell the buyer what the product is, not where it came from." By contrast, a trademark (or just "a mark," as it is often called in trademark law) does tell the user "where [the product] came from." He continues: "A mark answers the buyer's questions 'Who are you? Where do you come from?' 'Who vouches for you?' But the name of the product answers the question 'What are you?'" In other words, a generic term is the common descriptive term or common name for something, and it does not identify a single source of origin.

McCarthy illustrates genericness using the example of THERMOS: "If the public chooses to call a product a "Thermos" bottle rather than a "THERMOS brand vacuum-insulated bottle," then "Thermos" is not serving as a mark – it is used as a generic name, regardless of the producer's intentions" (§12:1 at 12–17). Further examples of generic terms from McCarthy's illustrative list of terms held generic are ESCALATOR (moving stairway), DISCOUNT MUFFLERS (repair and replacement of auto mufflers), BABY OIL (mineral oil), and CUBE STEAK (tenderized steaks). These generic terms cannot be trademarks or service marks used by a particular provider to identify their product or service. In the event that some customers or providers do regard a term as a trademark, while others regard it as generic, then "Majority usage of the word is controlling" (McCarthy §12:6 at 12–21) and the principal or primary significance of the term in the minds of the consuming public must be determined, e.g. by surveys and other forms of linguistic evidence (as we will illustrate below for the trademark disputes in this chapter).

Terms that name a genus or a kind have, of course, been much discussed in linguistic theory, in lexicography, and in the language sciences generally. The quotes from McCarthy make it clear that "genericness" is what linguists understand as the basic and normal and literal meaning of a word or phrase. The semantic properties associated with individual words like ESCALATOR or COMPUTER, or with word combinations like CUBE STEAK and TENNIS SHOE, define classes of entities to which each of these terms can apply. The genus is defined by the semantic properties that are listed in the definitional sentences of dictionaries using their paraphrases (recall §1.1 in the present book). For example, COMPUTER is 'a device that computes, especially a programmable electronic machine that performs high-speed mathematical or logical operations or that assembles, stores, correlates, or otherwise processes information' (*The American Heritage Dictionary of the English Language*, 2011); a TENNIS SHOE is 'a low-cut shoe designed for playing tennis, typically having a rubber sole' (same dictionary); and so on. Note here that when McCarthy writes that a generic term is "the name" of something, he is not using "name" in the sense of "proper name." Quite the reverse, he means 'common name for the genus,' or the basic "sense" of a word, as this was discussed in §2.4.3.

A "descriptive" term is defined by McCarthy as follows: "A term is descriptive if it forthwith conveys an immediate idea of the ingredients, qualities or characteristics of the goods" (§11:67 at 11–148) and if it is descriptive of the intended purpose, function, or use of the goods, the size of the goods, the provider of the goods, the class of users of the goods, a desirable characteristic of the goods, the nature of the goods, or the end effect upon the user (§11:16 at 11–25 to 11–27). The crucial distinction between "genericness" and "descriptiveness" hinges (we will see in §3.5) on whether a term is the common and usual one for the entity in question (e.g. TENNIS SHOE), as opposed to some more roundabout and less frequently used but still descriptive phrase (e.g. SHOE FOR PLAYING TENNIS IN or simply SHOE FOR TENNIS). Descriptive terms cannot be protected as trademarks unless "secondary meaning" is proven (McCarthy §11:15 at 11–23). This means that there is another use for this descriptive term, and a distinct reference that it has, whereby it is clearly linked in the minds of consumers to a particular producer or service provider. Typical examples that McCarthy gives of descriptive marks that have acquired such secondary meaning are BEER NUTS salted nuts, CULTURE RIPENED coffee, and WORLD BOOK encyclopedia.

The remaining three terms on the trademark hierarchy can all serve as trademarks, since they identify the unique producer or source. For "suggestive," McCarthy writes, "A term is suggestive if it requires imagination, thought and perception to reach a conclusion as to the nature of the goods" (§11:67 at 11–148). Typical examples are GOBBLE GOBBLE processed turkey meat, HABITAT home furnishings, and SHEER ELEGANCE pantyhose (§11:72 at 11–163, 11–167). "Arbitrary" terms are those "that are in common linguistic use but which, when used with the goods or services in issue, neither suggest nor describe any ingredient, quality or characteristic of those goods or services" (§11:11 at 11–18). An example is JELLIBEANS for a roller-skating rink (§11:13 at 11–18) and of course APPLE for the computer company (§11:13 at 11–22). The "fanciful" category is exemplified by KODAK.

Before we look in more detail at the linguistic issues that arise in genericness and descriptiveness, it is worth mentioning a brief point about the title of McCarthy's book (*McCarthy on Trademarks and Unfair Competition*) that may be puzzling to some readers of the present book. Why is it "unfair competition" in the world of business if some terms, especially generic ones, are allowed to become trademarks for a particular company or service provider? The answer makes a lot of sense, both commercially and linguistically. Imagine that one firm manufacturing, say, tennis rackets, was allowed to trademark the compound TENNIS RACKET. That would have the effect that no other firm would be allowed to use it for their product, and every time a consumer went to a sporting goods store and asked for a TENNIS RACKET using this (hitherto) generic term, they would be given a racket from that one company only. In effect, TENNIS RACKET would no longer be available to English language speakers to use when they wanted to refer to this class of things or to individual instances of this class. And the firm that was allowed to (mis) appropriate it in this way would have an unfair advantage in the world of business. An unfair competitive advantage in business (which McCarthy stresses) would also be accompanied by an unfair linguistic imposition on all users of English since it would deprive them of their most frequent name for this class of things and force them to instigate a new generic term in the midst of miscommunications, errors, and relearning (a linguistic point that McCarthy does not mention!).

3.4 APP STORE

In 2012 I was asked to serve as expert witness and to prepare various reports for a major international law firm representing Amazon as the defending party against Apple in litigation over the term APP STORE. Apple claimed that it had been the first company to develop such a store, it wanted the term reserved for its own exclusive use as a trademark, it sought to prevent others like Amazon from using it, and it gave various arguments (through their lawyers and language experts) for why this was reasonable, including that APP was the first syllable of APPLE. The dispute, which subsequently played out in courts in Northern California, in Europe ("OHIM," the Office for Harmonization in the Internal Market), and in Australia, concerned the status of APP STORE in trademark law in these different jurisdictions with their sometimes partially different legal categories and definitions and different precedents. With respect to the North American litigation the crucial issue was whether APP STORE was a generic term, like PET STORE and COMPUTER STORE, in which case it could not be a trademark since it would be the common descriptive term that everyone should be entitled to use, regardless of who may have been the first to develop it. Amazon's lawyers and I argued that APP STORE was indeed a generic term. After various reports and rebuttals and a deposition on my part coupled with compelling legal counterarguments from Amazon, Apple finally withdrew its litigation attempting to prevent Amazon from using APP STORE (just days before the scheduled trial!).

In what follows I give a brief summary of the relevant linguistic arguments and evidence and a brief flavor of the dispute over genericness versus source identification that characterized this important case.

3.4.1 The Grammar and Meaning of English Compound Nouns

APP STORE is another example of a "compound noun" or a "complex nominal" (recall §1.2). Quirk, Greenbaum, Leech, and Svartvik use the former term in their *Comprehensive Grammar of the English Language* (Longman, Harlow, 1985, pp. 1330–1333), J. Levi uses the latter in *The Syntax and Semantics of Complex Nominals* (Academic Press, New York, 1978). Common to all analyses is the basic insight that combinations like APP STORE function as a unit, much like a single word. Within this unit, the righthand element, the noun STORE is the "head" (recall §1.2), while the noun APP, which is short for the full noun APPLICATION, "modifies" and immediately precedes the head. We can represent its syntactic structure as Noun[Noun_1 Noun_2], in which Noun_1 is the modifier, Noun_2 is the head, and the whole thing is a complex type of Noun.

The head of any compound is its most important part. It is the component that determines the syntactic status of the whole unit. If the head is a noun, so is the compound, regardless of the status of the modifier. WHITE HOUSE (referring to the president's residence in Washington, DC) is a noun compound because HOUSE is a noun. APP STORE is a noun because STORE is a noun, not because the modifier APP happens to be one as well. The head is also the most important element semantically, and the meaning of the modifier must adapt to, and be understood relative to, the head (again, recall §1.2 and also §2.4.1). A TENNIS SHOE is a certain type of shoe, as used in the game of tennis, as opposed to a BALLET SHOE, which is a shoe designed for ballet dancing. Similarly, an APP STORE is a certain type of store, one that provides applications or apps for download. It is not a type of app.

The orthography of English allows for different ways of writing these [Noun_1 Noun_2] compounds. There are three productive possibilities: the two nouns can be separate words, they can be joined by hyphenation, or they can occur in a single word. Occasionally all three are found with one and the same sequence. Quirk et al. (1985, p. 1569) give the example of FLOWER POT, FLOWER-POT, and FLOWERPOT, all of which occur productively. More generally, Quirk et al. write: "There is a progression [from separate words to hyphenation to single words] as a given compound becomes established, and hence widely recognized and accepted as a 'permanent' lexical item.'" In other words, there is a correlation between the frequency of usage for [$Noun_1$ $Noun_2$] sequences, and their compression into a single word. The single-word FOOTBALL and the two-word SOCCER BALL illustrate this overall correlation: The former is significantly more common and frequently used than the latter.

3.4.2 The Meaning and Usage of APP

The word APP is a fascinating word of modern English that came into being and then exploded in usage with the advent of today's internet and computer culture. Already back in 2010 it was voted "word of the year" by the American Dialect Society. It is an abbreviated form of APPLICATION and has been shortened by the same kind of reduction process that we see in words like TECH (from TECHNOLOGY and TECHNICIAN), BIKE (from BICYCLE), and EURO (from EUROCURRENCY and EUROPEAN).

Like the spelling conventions for single-word FOOTBALL versus two-word SOCCER BALL, reductions within single words are also highly correlated with frequency of usage. George Zipf was the first psychologist of language to draw attention to the inverse relationship between frequency of usage and word length (in his *Human Behavior and the Principle of Least Effort*, Hafner, New York, 1949), i.e. the more frequently used a word is, the shorter and less phonologically complex it is. He pointed out (p. 66) that this accounts straightforwardly for why longer words such as GASOLINE become reduced to GAS, and why shorter words like CAR gain in frequency over the longer AUTOMOBILE as usage increases. Other reductions that he discussed as part of his Law of Abbreviation for words included BUS for OMNIBUS and PARATROOP for PARACHUTE TROOPER. Zipf's mathematical insights about frequency and phonological size now form the basis for much subsequent work in the language sciences. My own 2004 book (*Efficiency and Complexity in Grammars*, Oxford University Press, Oxford) developed a principle of Form Minimization that built directly on Zipf's Law and used it to explain how languages actually change their words and word size over time as usage and frequency expand. The abbreviation of APPLICATION to APP follows from this very general pattern of language use and language change, therefore.

Even back in 2012 APP was already more frequently used than most of the other reductions cited in this section, judging from figures supplied by Google. A verbatim Google search for APP (conducted on July 22, 2012) returned 9.49 billion hits, for EURO it returned 8.68 billion, for TECH 7.3 billion, for BUS 4.59 billion, and for BIKE 3.34 billion. These enormously high figures for APP reflect the fact that there were already apps for almost everything, from games to dictionary downloads to tax-preparation guides, and that apps were visible and talked about everywhere. This frequency in turn explains why APP has been abbreviated from APPLICATION, in accordance with Zipf's Law.

APP is clearly a generic term of English. The *Oxford English Dictionary Online* (3rd edn) refers the reader to APPLICATION for its definition. The relevant sense of APPLICATION in a computer context is given as

> '*Computing.* A function performed by a computer to meet a specific user requirement; (now usually) a program or piece of software designed to perform such a function (as distinct from software which supports the operating system itself). Cf. *application program* . . . .'

The first attested use of APP in this sense is cited from 1985 by the *OED* 3rd edition:

> "At first look, the user sees only one new menu ('apps' for applications) at the top of the screen."

Interestingly the immediately preceding 2nd edition of the *OED*, from 1989, did not contain a separate entry for APP, despite the example just given. The first attested example for APPLICATION in this computer sense cited in the OED's 3rd online edition goes back as far as 1959, and numerous examples are given, frequently in compounds such as APPLICATION PROGRAM, APPLICATION SOFTWARE, and so on.

The *American Heritage Dictionary of the English Language*, 5th edition (2011), lists APP and defines it as 'A computer application. [Short for APPLICATION].' The relevant sense of APPLICATION (sense 7) is then defined as

> '*Computers* A computer program designed for a specific task or use . . . also **applications** *Computers* Of or being a computer program designed for a specific task or use: *applications software for a missile guidance system* . . . .'

The immediately prior edition of the *American Heritage Dictionary of the English Language*, the 4th from 2000, gives the same definition for APP as the 5th in 2011 but adds that this is an informal term. The edition immediately prior to that, the 3rd from 1992, contains no entry for APP in the computer sense but lists it only as an abbreviation for terms such as APPARATUS, APPENDIX, and APPLIED.

In addition to the *OED* and *American Heritage Dictionary*, I consulted numerous other dictionaries of English, and successive editions where these were available, in order to try and establish a timeline for the development and widespread use of APP as an abbreviation for APPLICATION in the computer sense. These included the *Merriam-Webster's Collegiate Dictionary*, 11th edition, 2011, which gives an entry and definition for APP in the computer sense and the year 1987 as the earliest recorded use, and the 10th edition from 1999, which gives no listing for APP at all; the *Random House Webster's Unabridged Dictionary*, 2nd edition of 1998, which lists and defines the computer APP in its "New Words Section" and dates its first appearance as occurring between 1985 and 1990; the *Random House Webster's Collegiate Dictionary* (Random House, New York) from 1995, which does define APP in the computer sense; the *Random House Compact Unabridged Dictionary* (Random House, New York) special 2nd edition 1996, which lists the computer APP in its "Addenda" section; the *Encarta World English Dictionary* (St. Martin's Press, New York), which lists it in 1999; and others.

Putting together all of these dictionary entries in an attempt to estimate when APP first became a productive term in English usage, it appears that the process of reducing APPLICATION to APP in the computer sense began around 1985, became increasingly common between 1985 and 1990, and then exploded in usage up until 2010 when it was named the American Dialect Society's word of the year. Since then its usage has expanded further still, but since subsequent figures are not relevant for the date of the lawsuits that I describe here and for documenting the transition from frequent use to dictionary listing, they will not be pursued further. The important point is that by 2012, the year of the litigation, APP in the computer sense had become even more frequently used than other common abbreviations such as EURO and TECH and BUS and BIKE (recall the figures noted above). Dictionaries began listing it meanwhile from 1995 to 1996, with almost all the dictionaries I surveyed recognizing its existence in a separate listing from the late 1990s or early 2000s onward. Based on this sampling we can say that it took between five and ten years from the time APP began to be frequently used for the first dictionaries of English to start listing it, and approximately ten years before most dictionaries listed it.

3.4.3 *The Meaning and Usage of STORE*

Dictionaries list several senses for STORE. The most general one defined by the *Oxford English Dictionary Online* (3rd edn) is

> 'A place where merchandise is kept for sale. **a.** Chiefly *N. Amer.* and elsewhere outside the U.K. . . . equivalent to the British use of SHOP . . . .'

The *American Heritage Dictionary of the English Language* (5th edn, 2011) defines this primary sense of STORE in almost identical terms:

> 'A place where merchandise is offered for sale; a shop.'

The *Merriam-Webster's Collegiate Dictionary* (11th edn, 2011) defines it as

> 'a business establishment where usu. diversified goods are kept for retail sale <a grocery ~> – compare SHOP.'

The kind of store to which APP STORE refers is that of an online retailer or service provider. In the modern era just about everything can be offered for sale and bought via the internet (books, DVDs, clothing, furniture, toys, food, etc.). It is no longer necessary to go to an actual physical location or building to buy these items, though this is still possible and indeed common. As the world of retail sales has expanded, so has the set of entities to which the word STORE has come to refer productively. Online retailers of books and their customers continue to use BOOKSTORE (or BOOK-STORE, BOOK STORE), combining BOOK with STORE, for new internet services that perform the same function of selling books. When the world changes and our technology evolves rapidly like this (recall our discussion of TANGIBLE in §2.4), words such as STORE are naturally extended to businesses that perform the same basic function of a store within the new technological environment. Online retailing establishments and service providers can be, and are, productively referred to as STORES, in the same general sense for STORE that characterizes business establishments that operate in physical premises.

The distinction between the basic concept or primary function of a store as a retailing establishment versus a possible physical location for it is reflected in the dictionaries when they give separate subentries for the physical sense as opposed to the general one. *The American Heritage Dictionary of the English Language* (5th edn, 2011) defines the physical sense in its fourth entry: 'A place where commodities are kept; a warehouse or storehouse.' The *Merriam-Webster's Collegiate Dictionary* (11th edn, 2011) likewise lists STOREHOUSE and WAREHOUSE as a distinct entry separately from the general sense summarized previously.

Clearly, the word STORE is not being used in this more specific physical sense when it refers to online retailing and services provided over the internet. But the general and primary meaning of STORE is still compatible with its use in this modern context, and users of English have routinely recognized this and have applied it productively to the online providers of products and services like BOOKSTORES and now APP STORES. If clarification is useful in a particular context it can be provided by the addition of a premodifier to the head noun, such as ONLINE STORE or PHYSICAL STORE or BRICK-AND-MORTAR STORE. These premodifiers serve to select among the different types of stores found in the world today, all of which are readily compatible with the general sense of STORE. There is nothing redundant or contradictory about adding such premodifiers to STORE, therefore. They simply give further details about the type of store in question, in the event that the speaker or writer wishes to give these details or wishes to refer to a particular subtype of store. Likewise, the addition of APP to STORE makes it clear that this is an online store, a particular subtype of such a store, one from which apps can be downloaded.

3.4.4 *The Meaning of APP STORE*

The first general point to make about the meaning of APP STORE, therefore, is that it combines the meanings of the generic nouns APP and STORE to make a compound noun in the same way that CLOTHING and STORE combine together to make what is clearly a generic compound CLOTHING STORE. COMPUTER STORE combines the generic single words COMPUTER and STORE to make this generic compound. FURNITURE STORE is a generic compound combining generic FURNITURE and STORE. LIQUOR STORE functions similarly; so does MUSIC STORE and so on. There are at least several hundred generic compounds like this with STORE that are currently used in English, and in all of them STORE is the head noun and the modifying noun that precedes it is understood to refer to the products or services that the store provides. A CLOTHING STORE is 'a store that sells clothing,' or equivalently 'a store for clothing'; a COMPUTER STORE is 'a store selling computers'; and so on. APP STORE functions the same way. It combines the generic word APP in the computer sense with the general sense of STORE to make a compound that is just as generic as these other examples. Its meaning can be paraphrased, as a first approximation, as 'a store that provides apps.' The definition can then be enriched to take account of the fact that this store is an online store from which apps are downloaded, and APP can be replaced by its fuller form, to give the following more complete definition: 'An APP STORE is an online store that provides applications for download' or 'an online store for downloading applications.'

This combined meaning of APP and STORE, derived by a productive compounding process, makes APP STORE as generic a term as these other combinations with STORE. They all refer to a certain class of entities in the world, namely the "genus" or type of store in question with its characteristic properties defined by the combined meanings of the two nouns, on the basis of which reference can be made to all or any members of the class. From the moment of their creation these English compounds were generic, CLOTHING STORE for 'stores providing clothing,' COMPUTER STORE for 'stores selling computers,' FURNITURE STORE for 'stores selling furniture,' and so on. Similarly, APP STORE has been generic from the very beginning in relation to the class of stores it describes.

So why was there any dispute over the legal and linguistic status of APP STORE? And how and why did Apple feel entitled to claim ownership and trademark status for this term? There were numerous specific arguments that their lawyers and language expert gave (see §3.4.9 for a summary), but let me just mention two linguistic issues at this point. First, the genus to which APP STORE refers only came into existence recently with the advent of the relevant technology, in contrast to CLOTHING STORES, FURNITURE STORES, and even COMPUTER STORES, which have been around for much longer. Second, Apple was one of the first companies to introduce the service, and at the time of litigation it was dominant in the marketplace, with as many as 25 billion downloads. Whenever a new service comes into being like this, with a new designation like APP STORE and a dominant initial provider, the linguistic situation will be atypical at first. Consumers and language users may only be aware of one provider of this new service, and they may only have name recognition for that company. But this situation is short-lived and is, in any case, irrelevant for a determination of "genericness" with this word combination.

It is an important principle of semantics that generic nouns and compounds in English define possible classes of entities, whether existing or imagined, numerous or rare – namely those that are described by the meanings of the words in question (recall the discussion of John Lyons' term "denotation" in §2.4.3). UNICORN is a generic noun, and its meaning defines a possible and readily imaginable class of such animals, even though there aren't any at all in the real world. The combination

X STORE is similarly available to users of English to describe a store selling any product or service X, whether it is one that came into existence only recently, like APP, or less recently like COMPUTER, whether that product is well established like CLOTHING and FURNITURE, and even if the store selling the relevant product is only imagined and a distant possibility. The fact that there were no app stores in the world until recently does not impact the linguistic status of APP STORE as the most natural and meaningful expression, formed by productive grammatical and lexical processes in English, for describing possible stores of this type.

Similarly, the first person who opened a FURNITURE STORE many years ago could draw upon and use a linguistic expression that had hitherto described only a possible store of this type, and this possibility became an actuality described by the English language once the store opened. As more and more competing furniture stores came into existence, their owners and customers naturally wished to make use of the most succinct and best descriptive term available to them in English. FURNITURE STORE is a generic compound of English, therefore, and has always has been so – an expression rich in meaning that readily describes both possible and actual stores of this type. In a parallel way, once APP became a generic noun abbreviating APPLICATION, it was available to combine with STORE to make APP STORE, a generic compound that speakers of English were free to use even before any such store came into existence, when there was only one, and when there were several. When other providers and competitors joined Apple in the marketplace, they and their customers naturally wished to make use of this generic term that so clearly and efficiently describes this class of services.

The further combination of the generic term APP STORE with Apple in "APPLE APP STORE" is analogous to "VIRGIN MUSIC STORE," which combines the generic compound MUSIC STORE with the brand name "VIRGIN." Virgin could not claim, and has not tried to claim, exclusive rights to MUSIC STORE, since that would have denied everybody else access to this generic compound when referring to these kinds of stores. Similarly, as other app stores entered the marketplace along with Apple's, they and their customers started to use the generic term APP STORE in reference to them.

3.4.5 *First Recordings of APP STORE*

The first recorded use of the term APP STORE appears to go back to 1998. In August 1998 Sage Networks filed an application with the US Patent and Trademark Office to register APPSTORE for

> providing computer software application hosting services by means of a global computer information network, where such services allow multiple users to rent software applications developed by applicant or third parties.

That application was later abandoned in November 2000. Another company, Salesforce, attempted a similar registration of APPSTORE in June 2006 for

> Application service provider (ASP) featuring computer software in the field of business project management, business knowledge, information and asset management, customer relationship management, sales, marketing, e-commerce, electronic messaging, and web site development.

That registration application was also abandoned in December 2008.

Apple's App Store meanwhile was launched in the summer of 2008 along with the iPhone 3G as an integral part of Apple's iTunes software. Many other retailers soon began to use the term APP STORE in addition to Apple, including "DIRECTV App Store," "White Label App Store," 'Shopify App Store," "Palm App Store," "Sentrion App Store," "MobiHand App Store," "Handango Mobile App Store," "Mobile2Day Appstore for Blackberry," and others. Amazon launched its "Amazon Appstore for Android" in March 2011.

Apple's insistence on exclusive rights to the term APP STORE, which more and more providers and customers were starting to use both generically and as a component of the names for these other app stores, created a period of uncertainty prior to 2012 that required legal resolution. From a purely linguistic perspective, however, the situation has always been quite clear: APP STORE is a generic term, regardless of how well-known the "Apple App Store" may have been.

Various online encyclopedias and online dictionaries available at the time were already beginning to list APP STORE prior to 2012. Widespread generic use was recognized, but so was Apple's particular version and its presence in the market. For example, the *Free Dictionary by Farlex* website gave two entries for APP STORE:

'(1) An online store for downloading applications. See online app store.
(2) Apple's online store for downloading free and paid iPhone, iPod touch and iPad applications from third-part developers. Launched along with the iPhone 3G in the summer of 2008, the App Store is accessible from the mobile device, and it is integrated into Apple's iTunes software.'

This online dictionary then added:

> 'This single point of focus for delivering smartphone apps was later followed with the debut of app stores for the Android, Blackberry and new Windows phone platforms (see online app store).'

The entry under ONLINE APP STORE was

> 'A Web site for downloading free and paid applications to smartphones as well as Mac computers. Launched with the iPhone 3G in 2008, Apple's App Store popularized the concept of a single point of contact for downloading applications and updates . . . .'

These entries from the *Free Dictionary by Farlex* capture both the generic nature of APP STORE (entry 1) and the role of Apple in developing the service (entry 2). The online *PC Magazine Encyclopedia* from 2012 gave almost identical entries to those in *Farlex*, containing both a generic definition (as in 1) and recognition of the pioneering role of Apple in developing this product (in 2).

APP STORE was accordingly listed and defined in these online encyclopedias and dictionaries in 2012, but this compound was not yet listed in any of the standard dictionaries whose definitions for APP and STORE were considered in §3.4.2 and §3.4.3. These latter dictionaries are compiled by professional lexicographers, and lexicographers try to follow certain criteria applicable to all areas of the English language when deciding whether to include or exclude compound terms.

3.4.6 The Absence of APP STORE from Standard Dictionaries

The absence of APP STORE from standard dictionaries at the time of this litigation in 2012 was not actually surprising, for several reasons. First, the meaning of the compound APP STORE is straightforwardly derivable from the meanings of APP and STORE alone, as we have seen (§3.4.4). Hence it was not necessary to list the combined form, and in these circumstances dictionaries regularly do not do so. Compounds involving STORE whose meanings are not straightforwardly derivable from their parts, on the other hand, are regularly listed. A CHAIN STORE is not one that sells chains and so this typically does have a separate listing and definition, e.g. as 'one of a number of retail stores operating under the same brand name and selling similar merchandise' (*American Heritage Dictionary*, 5th edn, 2011). A DEPARTMENT STORE also has a separate listing typically and is defined as 'a large retail store offering a variety of merchandise and services and organized in separate departments' (in the same dictionary). A PACKAGE STORE is also typically listed and defined as 'A store that sells bottles or cans of alcoholic beverages for consumption off the premises' (in the same dictionary), and so on.

Second, quite apart from the fact that it is unnecessary for dictionaries to list productive compounds with predictable meanings, it would be impractical for them to do so: There are simply too many. There are literally hundreds of sequences of Noun + STORE that are productively used in English and that have regular and predictable meanings, and the vast majority of them are not listed. Only the most frequently occurring ones will be listed when they are formed by productive combinatorial processes like this, and even then extremely frequent combinations are not listed. For example, the major dictionaries I consulted at the time of this litigation all listed GROCERY STORE, but none of them listed even common compounds such as JEWELRY STORE, PET STORE, FOOD STORE, and TOY STORE.

There is a third reason for not expecting APP STORE to be listed in these dictionaries, namely the recency of the service to which it refers. We saw in §3.4.2 that it took five to ten years from the inception of apps to the first dictionary listing of APP in the sense of APPLICATION, and approximately ten years before most general and nonspecialist dictionaries listed it. APP is a single word, and it stands a much greater chance of being listed than a compound. The time lag for listing a new compound should accordingly be even longer than for a new single word. The evidence from a LexisNexis search given in §3.4.8 suggests that APP STORE began to gain widespread recognition and usage around 2009. It was still much too early in 2012 for dictionary listings, based on this evidence. Today, by contrast, at the time of writing this chapter (July 2024), APP STORE is now listed and defined, for example, in the *OED* (3rd edn online).

3.4.7 Grammatical Evidence for the Genericness of APP STORE

Evidence for the genericness of APP STORE can come from its grammar and meaning, and from the kinds of syntactic environments in which it occurs and from the meanings assigned to them. Does APP STORE refer to a whole class of such stores in these cases, or does it just identify a particular one? The first test for genericness given in *McCarthy on*

Trademarks and Unfair Competition cited in §3.3 involved semantics: a generic term answers the question "What are you?" not "Who are you?"; it tells us what kind of thing the entity is, not who made it or who provided it.

Further tests for genericness can involve grammar and orthography. Since generic terms refer to a whole class of entities, we find them used productively in the plural, referring to more than one, e.g. SHOE STORES, CLOTHING STORES. We find them used with so-called universal quantifiers like ALL, referring to the totality of the class in question, e.g. ALL SHOE STORES, ALL CLOTHING STORES. We also find generic terms used productively with the indefinite article A(N) in English, A SHOE STORE, AN E-BOOK STORE, where they refer either to some arbitrary member of the class or to a member unknown to the hearer or reader (as in I'M LOOKING FOR A SHOE STORE). Singular terms with the indefinite article can also refer to the whole genus (A SHOE STORE IS A STORE WHERE YOU CAN BUY SHOES (see my own 2015 *Definiteness and Indefiniteness: A Study in Reference and Grammaticality Prediction*, Routledge, London, reprinted from 1978, and Quirk et al.'s 1985 *A Comprehensive Grammar of the English Language*, cited in §1.7 and §3.4.1). Generic noun phrases in English are generally written with small letters, e.g. "music store," as opposed to the initial capital letters typical of proper names such as "John" or "Virgin Music Store." Grammatical and orthographic diagnostics such as these can help us determine whether APP STORE is used generically to refer to a whole class of such stores, or as a proper name and a service mark referring to just one.

In one of my reports on APP STORE in 2012, I cited numerous examples from the media and industry press and by competitors and consumers showing how it was being used as a generic term, following these criteria. There were countless instances of APP STORE in the plural, i.e. APP STORES, referring to more than one and often many more than one of the genus. Examples also included AN APP STORE, with the indefinite article, referring to one among many. A small sampling of recorded examples from 2008 to 2011 is reproduced here (with APP STORE in small letters and the bold type added by me):

CNET.com, October 21, 2008

New mobile **app stores** launched by Apple, Google, and Research in Motion could shift the balance of power in the mobile market away from wireless operators and toward device and platform developers.

Wired.com, August 31, 2009
Since Apple introduced the iPhone App Store as a centralized clearing house for mobile applications in 2008, **app stores** have become an important part of the business strategy for most handset makers.

***New York Times*, November 26, 2009**
This year, the idea caught fire. New **app stores** opened for the Blackberry, Palm phones (the Pre and Pixi) and Windows smartphones. They join the existing stores for the iPhone/iPad Touch and phones that run on Google's Android phone software.

ReadWriteWeb, "Apple Says Other App Stores Can't Be Called App Stores," March 21, 2011
Intel has **an app store**, Samsung, Motorola and LG have **app stores**. My local public transit agency in Portland, Oregon has **an app store**. I bet you can think of some **app stores** too.

It is particularly notable that the former CEO of Apple, Steve Jobs, himself even used APP STORE generically by these grammatical and orthographic criteria. The following quote from Steve Jobs during an analyst call contains two generic uses of APP STORE in the plural (bold added):

> Amazon, Verizon and Vodaphone have all announced that they are creating their own **app stores** for Android. There will be at least four **app stores** on Android which customers must search through to find the app they want.

Their genericness is clear both from the plural morphology and from the linguistic context in which Steve Jobs introduces them. The first APP STORES links such stores explicitly to providers other than Apple, namely Amazon, Verizon, and Vodaphone. The second also refers to providers going beyond Apple. These competitors provide products that are instances of the genus APP STORE, and that is why speakers of English, including Steve Jobs, used APP STORES to refer to them.

APP STORES does not have any special or additional meaning in this context. For example, readers will not interpret this passage to mean that the app stores of Apple's competitors were so-called only because they were copying Apple's particular version of its app store or were imitations of it. Steve Jobs is using APP STORES as a generic term in this passage in exactly the same way that other speakers of English use it; i.e. he is referring to a plurality of the genus APP STORE that includes providers other than Apple. Apple was certainly a dominant force in this market at the time, and Steve Jobs may have held certain beliefs about the quality of his version of the app store compared with others. But such considerations are linguistically irrelevant and have no bearing on how readers of English will understand APP STORES in this quote by Steve Jobs. They will understand it to have the same generic meaning that it normally has whenever many members of the genus are being talked about.

Many more and similar generic uses of APP STORE were recorded in my reports by other employees of Apple and also by the subsequent CEO, Timothy Cook. Clearly it was impossible, even within the organization that was claiming APP STORE as a trademark, to avoid using it generically!

3.4.8 Corpus Evidence for Genericness

In §3.4.2 I gave some usage statistics from Google to show how massively frequent the references to APP had become at the time of this litigation. Google can also be used to show how the compound term APP STORE was being used throughout the English-speaking world, and to provide us with publicly available documents accessible via the Google search engine that make reference to it. In a Google advanced search (on February 24, 2012), I asked to see numerous attested examples of APP STORE occurring in the typical grammatical environments for generic terms summarized in the last section, namely APP STORES in the plural, ALL APP STORES with the universal quantifier, and AN APP STORE with the indefinite article. I then asked for the first 100 "hits" for each environment to be printed out, 300 in all, and I examined linguistic usage manually in each entry, both in the underlined heading and in the relevant text underneath. My goal was to check that these environments were indeed typically generic uses of APP STORE. If there was a genuine generic use of the noun phrase in question, I placed a tick ("√") alongside the entry (no more than one per entry). The semantics of the reference in the case of APP STORES had to be to at least two app stores, one of which must not be Apple's. For ALL APP STORES it had to be to a relevant totality that could include Apple but that included also other actual or possible providers, and for AN APP STORE it had to be to one among many that could include Apple but also others, or it had to refer to the whole genus. Sometimes the entry in question contained no example of the relevant phrase in the underlined heading or sample text. These cases were annotated with "no example" and were excluded from the count. The linked fuller text very likely did contain the relevant phrase, but this was not investigated for reasons of convenience and time. For AN APP STORE the indefinite article had to combine with APP STORE itself, not with some other head noun occurring to its right within a larger compound, such as AN APP STORE PRODUCT or AN APP STORE PASSWORD (which are paraphrases of 'a product from some app store or app stores' and 'a password for an app store,' i.e. with the indefinite article combining most closely syntactically and semantically with PRODUCT and PASSWORD respectively, not with APP STORE). There were numerous examples of this type, in many of which APP STORE could still be analyzed as generic, but they were excluded from the count in order to make the data consistent and were annotated with "compound." The remaining uses of APP STORES, ALL APP STORES, and AN APP STORE that were not clearly generic in the text sample available or that possibly referred only to Apple were marked with a cross ("x").

Typical examples of APP STORES, ALL APP STORES, and AN APP STORE found in these Google advanced searches were as follows:

> **App Stores Create 500,000 U.S. Jobs** . . .
> Almost half a million Americans can thank the rise of the "app economy" for their jobs, according to a Tech Net study.
>
> **Tips on submitting a mobile app to app stores**
> Once you create your mobile app, you should next think of submitting it to **app stores**. There are, as you know, many **app stores** in the market today, with newer . . . .
>
> **App Store Optimization – Search Engine Watch (#SEW)**
> **All app stores** require you to build an app according to their technical and ethical guidelines. Once your app has been added to an app store, ...
>
> **What site is available to show reviews from all app stores** . . .
> What site is available to show reviews from **all app stores**?
>
> **'We need an app store for root apps'**
> An Android developer is looking to provide a home for apps that are otherwise verboten on the Android market.
>
> **Nintendo 'plans Wii U app store' – *Telegraph***
> The new console will come with **an app store** that goes "far beyond" the current online stores that Nintendo provides for its DSi and Wii.

I then calculated the percentage of clear and robust generic uses ("√") for APP STORES, ALL APP STORES, and AN APP STORE, relative to unclear cases or references only to Apple ("x"; among the entries that had relevant examples and that were not part of larger compounds) according to the criteria just given for ticks and crosses. The figures were

APP STORES = 95% generic uses
ALL APP STORES = 88% generic uses
AN APP STORE = 96% generic uses

making an average of 93% generic uses for these environments. This provides strong confirmation for these environments being predominantly generic.

As more and more app stores entered the marketplace from 2008 and customers made use of their services, APP STORE expanded as a generic term and the clearly generic environments just illustrated gained in frequency from year to year. I pointed out in §3.4.4 that APP STORE was already born generic in relation to the service it describes, and that generic terms will have higher or lower frequencies of usage depending on how many entities there are in the world for them to refer to and depending on the number of occasions on which language users will choose to refer to them. As these entities and their popularity expand, so do their frequencies of occurrence.

This can be illustrated by plotting the expanding frequency of usage for the plural environment, APP STORES, over time. A different corpus, the LexisNexis MegaNews/US database, allowed me to do this since the news articles in question are clearly classified and searchable by year of publication. The following figures were collected from this database searching for the plural "app stores" with no capital letters, with "app" in the singular and "stores" in the plural, with both words written separately, and searching both in the heading of the article and in the body of the text. The goal was to quantify the increasing references to stores providing this service as their number expanded, by counting instances of the phrase "app stores," which has been shown to be typically generic in usage. The LexisNexis database covers a broad set of US media publications over the years.

References to "app stores" in LexisNexis MegaNews/US	
2008	37
2009	472
2010	1546
2011	2777

Back in 2008 plural uses of "app stores" without capitalization were therefore infrequent (37) but still occurring. They gradually became many times more frequent, growing to 2,777 by 2011, a seventy-five-fold increase. This confirms both the genericness of APP STORE, as revealed by plural usage, and the explosion in its frequency in the years prior to the 2012 litigation.

APP STORE was already generic from its first mention (§3.4.4). By 2012 it had clearly become one of the more frequent compounds with STORE in English usage. In order to quantify this comparative frequency for APP STORE with other Noun + STORE compounds, I made use of the largest electronic corpus of English that was available at the time, the "enTenTen12" corpus of 11.19 billion words derived, like Google, from documents accessible via the internet. This corpus was compiled specifically for lexicographic and linguistic research by the late Adam Kilgarriff, the director of Lexical Computing, Ltd., with whom I collaborated on this project.

The enTenTen12 corpus had fine-grained and sophisticated search capabilities. Using the "Phrase" setting I could count the relative frequency for these typically generic instances of APP STORE compared with other kinds of stores in their plural usage. For "app stores" the search returned 2,474 hits, or 0.2 per million within the 11.19-billion-word total of the corpus. This made "app stores" more frequent than the indisputably generic "computer stores" (at 1,048 hits) and "electronics stores" (1,278 hits). It made it also significantly more frequent than the equally indisputably generic "bike stores" (281 hits), "candy stores" (379 hits), "garden stores" (521 hits), "hat stores" (52 hits), "IT stores" (36 hits), and "paint stores" (309 hits). It made "app stores" comparable in frequency to the clearly generic "music stores" (2,644 hits), "shoe stores" (2,421 hits), and "toy stores" (2,421 hits), though its frequency was less than that of "clothing stores" (4,990 hits), "pet stores" (5,346 hits), "jewelry stores" (6,345), "food stores" (10,540), and the extremely frequent "grocery stores" (25,991 hits), i.e. stores with very long histories and traditions. Given the recency of the app store market at the time, the frequency of occurrence for APP STORE in this typically generic plural environment was actually remarkable and was already greater than or comparable to some of the most widely known and most widely referenced types of stores in English usage.

If Apple had succeeded in appropriating APP STORE and taking it out of common usage, it would have been just as logical (or rather "illogical") to assign each of these other common generic compounds to the highest bidder, giving Virgin exclusive rights to MUSIC STORE, Toys"R"Us exclusive rights to TOY STORE, See's Candies exclusive rights to CANDY STORE, and so on. Clearly, APP STORE is not only a generic term describing an online store for downloading apps (§3.4.4); it is the linguistically most appropriate and best term for it in English that people want to use, and this explains its explosion in usage, as seen in all these figures.

3.4.9 *Counterarguments to the Genericness of APP STORE*

Given all of this grammatical, semantic, and corpus evidence for the genericness of APP STORE, one might wonder how Apple (and especially their language experts) could possibly argue for trademark status and proprietary rights. We have already seen that the first online dictionaries and encyclopedias (in §3.4.5) did recognize Apple's early dominance in the field and its pioneering role in initiating this type of store, in addition to recognizing its genericness. But this is of no help if the name that a pioneering company chooses for its new product is a generic one! The fact that the first syllable in Apple's name happens to be APP does not help here either and lead users users to think uniquely of Apple, if the primary significance APP STORE is as a generic term.

One of Apple's language experts (a very distinguished one who has performed outstanding service for the field of forensic linguistics and for whom I have the greatest respect) did a good job with what I am sure even he would now recognize to be a weak case. He argued for the primary significance of APP STORE as a brand name rather than a generic term, and he gave four main lines of evidence. First, APP STORE did not appear in conventional dictionaries of the English language, as compiled by linguists and lexicographers, which he took to be an argument against genericness. Second, grammatical and semantic considerations involving this term in its totality were argued to support this. Third, he claimed that APP STORE had a special metaphorical interpretation, not a literal and generic one. And fourth, he presented various data sets for APP STORE, including from LexisNexis and Google, and concluded that "Apple did not appropriate a term that was already a generic term for services associated with the distribution of software programs."

The absence of a compound term like APP STORE from conventional dictionaries cannot be taken as evidence against its genericness, as I showed in §3.4.6. The vast majority of generic compounds in English consisting of Noun + STORE are not listed in traditional dictionaries. There are millions of possible and actual generic compounds in English with this same basic structure and with "head" nouns like STORE, yet only the tiniest fraction are ever listed in dictionaries, because there are simply too many, even for the largest and most scholarly dictionaries (cf. §1.1). Hence the absence of APP STORE from traditional dictionaries is no evidence against its genericness.

There is also an important difference here between single words and compound terms regarding dictionary listing. For single words like

STORE, JEWELRY, PET, FOOD, TOY, etc., dictionaries do generally try to list as many generic terms as possible, relative to their size and space constraints. The same is true for generic single words of recent origin, like APP, which emerged by form reduction from APPLICATION. Dictionaries try to keep up with new words like APP in their revised editions (recall §3.4.2). But for compounds, the practice of lexicographers and dictionary makers is of necessity different (recall again §3.4.6). Generic compounds with special meanings that are not predictable from the meanings of their component parts like CUBE STEAK and CHAIN STORE will often be listed, as will those with extremely high frequencies like GROCERY STORE (§3.4.8). Otherwise the vast majority of generic compounds in English, including those with the head noun STORE, are not listed.

The expert's second argument about the need to consider the meaning of APP STORE as a whole, including his point that two generic parts do not necessarily add up to a generic whole, is irrelevant in this context: I have shown in earlier paragraphs that APP is generic, so is STORE, and so is the combined APP STORE.

The third argument about the role of metaphor in this context is also a non-starter. There is nothing nonliteral or metaphorical in APP STORE (recall §2.3). APP has its literal meaning here, STORE has its literal and general meaning, and the combination APP STORE has a combined literal meaning derived from and compatible with both.

As his fourth (and perhaps strongest) argument, Apple's language expert presented various figures from the Corpus of Contemporary English, the LexisNexis database, and Google. He argued that "this research shows that Apple did not appropriate a term that was already a generic term for services associated with the distribution of software programs." His Google data, for example, showed 76 percent references to Apple (339 hits), 20 percent to other brands (91 hits), and 3 percent indeterminate references. Based on these and other statistics he argued that "APP STORE was not ... in general use ... prior to Apple's adoption of the term as a trademark."

This is a clever form of argumentation, but unfortunately the searches conducted were not sensitive to the kinds of subtle details of grammar and meaning that need to be recognized in this context. His searches for APP STORE did not control for capitalization, for example (e.g. "App Store" versus "app store"); nor did he control for the grammatical environment in which APP STORE occurs, e.g. following the indefinite article A(N) (i.e. AN APP STORE) or a genitive like APPLE'S APP STORE or a determiner plus superlative adjective like THE LARGEST APP STORE. There was no control either for whether APP STORE was part of a larger compound containing a following head noun, e.g. APP STORE EMPLOYEE. These searches were grammatically coarse, therefore, and insensitive to important differences in grammar, meaning, and orthography that are highly relevant for determining genericness versus non-genericness. In the searches reported in §3.4.8, I was careful to look for exact environments indicative of genericness such as AN APP STORE in the singular and APP STORES in the plural, using the Google advanced search capability, and I controlled for capitalization in my searches of the LexisNexis database and the enTenTen12 English corpus.

If a term is generic, then we expect to see it used productively in these diagnostic environments (§3.4.7) and without capitalization. Generic terms refer to a whole class of things, so they occur regularly in the plural (COMPUTER STORES), with universal quantifiers (ALL COMPUTER STORES), with superlative adjectives (THE LARGEST COMPUTER STORE), and with the indefinite article (A COMPUTER STORE). This was discussed in §3.4.7. Quantitative results involving APP STORES in the plural and AN APP STORE in the singular were presented in §3.4.8, taken from an advanced Google search, and were subjected to further manual checking. They showed 95 percent and 96 percent generic uses. Extensive and expanding plural usage from the LexisNexis database was also presented there. Plural APP STORES was compared with other plural generic terms consisting of Noun + STORES using the enTenTen12 corpus, and I showed that APP STORES was more frequently used than so many other clearly generic compounds of this sort, including COMPUTER STORES, TOY STORES, BIKE STORES, GARDEN STORES, and so on. Further illustrative generic uses (in §3.4.5) came from the media and industry press, from competitors and consumers, and even from Apple's own CEOs and personnel.

At the same time, however, there were many references to Apple when APP STORE was used in the singular, especially in the capitalized "App Store" but also in some uncapitalized uses. Apple's language expert cited data from LexisNexis, for example, showing 86 percent references to Apple, 13 percent to other brands, and 1 percent indeterminate (recall his 76 percent, 20 percent, and 3 percent, respectively, in the Google data summarized previously). How can we reconcile these references to Apple with the clear grammatical, semantic, and empirical evidence for genericness presented here?

I mentioned that searching only for APP STORE in the singular is grammatically coarse-grained. The focus has to be on diagnostic environments for genericness, such as APP STORES in the plural. But in addition to these, frequent references to Apple did occur precisely because Apple was one of the first companies to introduce an app store, and it was dominant in the marketplace after 2008. Apple chose to use APP STORE as the name of its store, so of course references to Apple's app store in advertising and the media would use the term "APP STORE" when referring to Apple's own. But as I noted in §3.4.4, APP STORE has always been generic, from the moment APP and STORE were first combined together to make the compound. It is formed by the same regular compounding process in English grammar that creates COMPUTER STORE, FURNITURE STORE, TOY STORE, and CLOTHING STORE out of their component parts and with their predictable meanings 'store that provides computers,' 'store that provides furniture,' and so on. Similarly, APP STORE is a 'store that provides apps.' This term was therefore born generic, it was still generic when Apple was the only significant provider, and its generic usage gained considerably in frequency as new app stores entered the marketplace.

The conclusion of Apple's language expert that "Apple did not appropriate a term that was already a generic term for services associated with the distribution of software programs" is not correct, therefore. Apple did exactly this. It attempted to make a trademark out of a generic term. At the same time the disproportionately frequent references to Apple's app store in the early usage of APP STORE, noted by the online dictionaries in §3.4.5, were simply a temporary and short-lived reflection of Apple's early dominance in the marketplace. As more and more providers developed their own app stores and started using APP STORE to describe them, Apple's share in the marketplace declined, and with it the linguistic references to their own app store compared with others. Apple's attempt to make a trademark out of APP STORE subsequently failed, and in 2012 Apple withdrew its legal actions against Amazon and against the claim that APP STORE was a source identifier for Apple and not a generic term.

3.5 HALF PRICE BOOKS

Having considered a paradigm example of genericness and arguments for and against it in the APP STORE case, let us turn now to descriptiveness, the second category on McCarthy's hierarchy of terms (§3.3). How exactly do genericness and descriptiveness differ?

In 2003 I consulted for a law firm in Dallas, Texas, in a trademark case brought by the plaintiff "Half Price Books, Records, Magazines Incorporated" (henceforth "HPBRM") against defendant "Barnes&Noble.com, LLC" (henceforth "BN.com"). The dispute involved the phrase HALF PRICE BOOKS. HPBRM claimed that this was a descriptive, not a generic, phrase and that it had acquired "secondary meaning" in the trade and among relevant consumers that clearly identified the plaintiff and the goods and services they provided using the mark HALF PRICE GOODS. They claimed that BN.com's use of HALF-PRICE BOOKS on its website to promote and advertise their book sales was an infringement of their trademark rights.

I was asked by plaintiff HPBRM to give my analysis and opinion on whether HALF PRICE BOOKS was generic or descriptive, and to address the arguments made for genericness by the lawyers for the defense and by an expert witness (not a linguist but a marketing expert) that they had recruited for this purpose. Clearly if the term was generic, it could no longer serve as a trademark and all attempted uses as a trademark would have to cease. If, on the other hand, the term could be assigned to the "descriptive" category in McCarthy's hierarchy, then it would be possible for HALF PRICE BOOKS to continue as a trademark, as long as secondary meaning was proven. That is, there would need to be a clear association in the minds of relevant consumers linking this term to the provider HPBRM. I was not personally involved with the proof of secondary meaning in this case. My role concerned the basic legal and linguistic status of the phrase HALF PRICE BOOKS on McCarthy's hierarchy. Was it descriptive or generic?

3.5.1 Separating Descriptive from Generic Terms in English

McCarthy points out (in *McCarthy on Trademarks and Unfair Competition*, recall §3.3) that the line between generic and descriptive terms in trademark law is not always easy to draw. There is actually a good reason for this. It is primarily and fundamentally a linguistic question having to do with the grammar, semantics, and everyday usage of words and phrases by the speech community in question. When can words or word combinations in English be said to name a "kind of goods" or a "genus" (McCarthy, §12.1), and when alternatively can they be said to be describing their "ingredients, qualities or characteristics" (McCarthy, §11.67) without actually naming them using the most common descriptive term? Depending on how this linguistic question is answered, there will be direct consequences for the law and for the assignment of words and phrases to the appropriate category on McCarthy's trademark hierarchy.

I pointed out in §3.4 that terms which name a genus or kind have been much studied in linguistics, as has the combinatorial semantics of phrases (this chapter) and of whole clauses (next chapter). Trademark law is trying to capture a very subtle linguistic distinction here, and it is not obvious that lawyers (and the law) should be trying to do so. It is a question of linguistic semantics. Interestingly, when I was consulting in London for the European arm of the Apple versus Amazon litigation over APP STORE, my reports originally written for the US litigation needed to be rewritten to reflect the fact that the two categories of generic and descriptive are collapsed into one broader "descriptive" category in that jurisdiction. That is, they do not make that legal distinction over there.

We have seen repeatedly that individual words like COMPUTER or word combinations like TENNIS RACKET name classes of entities to which these terms can refer, based on their meanings. These meanings are given in dictionaries and involve significant, permanent, and definitional properties of these entities, on the basis of which they can be distinguished from others. The properties define the genus, recall a COMPUTER, as 'a programmable electronic machine that performs high-speed mathematical or logical operations or that assembles, stores, correlates, or otherwise processes information' (*American Heritage Dictionary of the English Language*, 4th edn, 2000). A TENNIS RACKET is . . ., and so on.

The basic linguistic problem that underlies the generic/descriptive distinction in American trademark law, therefore, is that there are many other different ways in which items named by e.g. COMPUTER can be described in English, including the very paraphrases that are used in the dictionary definition itself! The generic name of the thing, on the other hand, is clearly "COMPUTER." Similarly, I can describe a tennis racket with "A RACKET FOR USE IN THE GAME OF TENNIS," or as "A RACKET THAT ONE CAN PLAY TENNIS WITH." But the generic name is TENNIS RACKET.

Word combinations pose a special problem for the generic/descriptive distinction, and McCarthy shows his own (and on this occasion also the Seventh Circuit's) linguistic sophistication when he offers some useful criteria for distinguishing them. For a word combination to be classified as generic it must be the case that a "kind" or "genus" is being named, or at least a significant "subcategory" within a kind or genus, as he makes clear in the following quote:

> In holding that TASTY for salad dressing is not generic, the Seventh Circuit said . . . that "tasty salad dressing" is "not a kind, sort, genus or subcategory

> of salad dressing.... It is not an adjective which in any way serves to classify the noun to which it is attached." Rather, the court viewed "tasty" ... as describing a quality found in many genuses of salad dressings. (McCarthy, §12:20)

McCarthy also stressed that composite terms must be considered as a whole in these cases.

Once again the precise manner in which words and phrases combine together with their resulting compositional or non-compositional meanings has been much studied in linguistics. This is ultimately and fundamentally a linguistic question, as I have stressed, and there is a science of language and a rich body of relevant work that needs to be consulted here that is directly relevant for resolving the generic/descriptive distinction.

For example, many phrases in English consisting of Adjective + Noun have two quite distinct meanings that can clarify, and serve as a diagnostic for, the crucial point that Professor McCarthy is making with respect to TASTY SALAD DRESSING. Consider the phrase CRIMINAL LAWYER. It can refer to a kind or type of lawyer, more precisely to a subcategory within the set of all lawyers (first meaning). Or it can refer to an individual lawyer whose behavior is described as CRIMINAL, whatever the type of law might be that he or she practices (second meaning). The first meaning is the generic one, since a genus or subcategory is being defined and the lawyer in question is not being described as CRIMINAL. The second meaning is the descriptive one. McCarthy's point about TASTY is that it combines with SALAD DRESSING in the manner of the second meaning and not in that of the first. The salad dressing is being described as TASTY, which is a "desirable characteristic of the goods" (McCarthy, §11:16), and the addition of this adjective to SALAD DRESSING does not define a new kind, genus, or subcategory.

Further examples of this ambiguity in English can be seen in THEATRICAL AGENT (a type of agent or someone who behaves in a "theatrical" way), and in BLUE BOOK (a certain type of book used as a 'price guide,' see §6.3.1, which may or may not have a blue cover, versus a book that is described as 'blue'). In all these examples the descriptive meaning can be revealed clearly by giving paraphrases in which the adjective is placed in a following predicate position, e.g. THIS LAWYER IS CRIMINAL (descriptive meaning only). In a parallel manner THIS AGENT IS THEATRICAL, THIS BOOK IS BLUE, and THIS SALAD DRESSING IS TASTY all have adjectives with descriptive meanings only.

These word combinations in English can be ambiguous like CRIMINAL LAWYER. They can be descriptive only, like TASTY SALAD DRESSING. Or they can be generic only, like HALF BROTHER, for which there is no descriptive paraphrase in predicate position: MY BROTHER IS HALF! Deciding the appropriate status of a disputed phrase like HALF PRICE BOOKS requires a careful analysis of its grammar and meaning, therefore, using criteria and tests such as these.

3.5.2 *The Grammar and Meaning of HALF PRICE BOOKS*

The phrase HALF PRICE BOOKS is a noun phrase (NP) in English consisting of the head noun BOOKS, and a modifier of this head, namely the phrase HALF PRICE. This modifier in turn consists of the adjective HALF and of the noun PRICE. The syntactic grouping of words is shown by the following bracketing: [np [HALF PRICE] BOOKS] (recall the discussion of phrasal groupings for word combinations in §1.3 and §2.4.1, and see §4.1).

Each of the words HALF, PRICE, and BOOKS has a lexical meaning that is defined in all dictionaries of English. The *American Heritage Dictionary of the English Language* (4th edn, 2000) gives the following definitions for HALF as a noun and as an adjective:

> *n.* . . . '**1a.** One of two equal parts that together constitute a whole. **b.** One part approximately equal to the remaining part . . . '
> *adj.* '**1a.** one of two equal parts. **b.** Being approximately a half . . . .'

The same dictionary defines the noun PRICE as follows:

> *n.* '**1.** The amount as of money or goods, asked for or given in exchange for something else. **2.** The cost at which something is obtained . . . .'

And the *American Heritage* definitions for the noun BOOK include the following:

> *n.* '**1.** A set of written, printed, or blank pages fastened along one side and encased between protective covers. **2a.** A printed or written literary work.'

The combination of HALF with PRICE in the modifier phrase HALF PRICE (or, with a hyphen, HALF-PRICE) occurs frequently in English, but was not actually listed in the majority of dictionaries that I consulted at the time of this litigation. It is listed in the *Oxford English Dictionary Online* (3rd edn) for 2003, which carries forward the definition from its earlier 2nd edition in 1989:

> '1. Half the usual or full price; esp. that at which children or poor people are admitted to an entertainment or the like, or that at which people are admitted to a theatre when the performance is half through . . . .'

It is also listed in the *Webster's Revised Unabridged Dictionary* (Dictionary.com) with the definition 'half the ordinary price; or a price much reduced.'

One reason why the combination HALF PRICE was not and is not generally listed in dictionaries is that its meaning is very transparent, i.e. the meaning of the whole phrase is clear from the meanings of its parts. HALF PRICE means that the 'cost at which something is obtained' (see the definition for PRICE given above) is just HALF, i.e. it is 'one part approximately equal to the remaining part' (see the definition for HALF). When meanings combine in such an obvious "compositional" way, dictionaries will typically not list them as we saw in connection with APP STORE (§3.4.6). Combinations of HALF with nouns whose meanings are not so obvious and transparent, by contrast, i.e. "non-compositional" ones, are generally listed. Thus the *American Heritage Dictionary* does give definitions for the following, in all of which the phrase has some meaning that is not entirely predictable from the meanings of its parts: HALF BACK, HALF BROTHER, HALF-CASTE, HALF-LIFE, HALF-MAST, HALF SISTER, HALF VOLLEY, HALF-WIT, and others.

When HALF PRICE combines in turn with the head noun BOOKS, the resulting meaning is again completely transparent and clear, and so the full combination HALF PRICE BOOKS was not listed in dictionaries of English that I consulted. The price reduction described by HALF PRICE is applied to the class of things that are described as 'written, printed, or blank pages fastened along one side and encased between protective covers' in the dictionary definition for the genus of BOOKS (discussed above). But does this addition of HALF PRICE to BOOKS result in a new genus or kind or subcategory of BOOKS, such that the combination of HALF PRICE BOOKS is a generic name, or is it instead a descriptive phrase?

My analysis supported a finding that HALF PRICE BOOKS was not a generic name. The issue here is the same one Professor McCarthy raised in his discussion of TASTY SALAD DRESSING (cf. McCarthy, §12:20). Is there a kind, sort, genus, or subcategory of books named by the phrase HALF PRICE BOOKS? My answer was no. HALF PRICE, when added to BOOKS, adds a descriptive property to the noun in the same way that TASTY adds a descriptive property to SALAD DRESSING. Both HALF PRICE and TASTY describe "a desirable characteristic of the goods"

(McCarthy, §11:16), and the resulting composite phrases are therefore descriptive by McCarthy's criteria and not generic names. The evidence for this is presented in the next section.

3.5.3 Diagnostic Linguistic Criteria for Descriptiveness

The descriptiveness of HALF PRICE BOOKS is supported by comparing it with the other composite noun phrases of English discussed previously. Does HALF PRICE combine with BOOKS to make a new kind or subcategory of books in the same way that CRIMINAL can combine with LAWYER to make the generic compound CRIMINAL LAWYER (in the 'type of lawyer' sense)? Or in the way that BLUE combines with BOOK to make the generic compound BLUE BOOK (again in the sense of 'a certain kind of book, one that gives price guides for certain products'; see further §6.3)? Clearly not. HALF PRICE combines with BOOK descriptively in the same way that TASTY combines with SALAD DRESSING, and in the way that CRIMINAL combines with LAWYER in its second descriptive meaning, and BLUE with BOOK in its second descriptive meaning referring to the color 'blue.' The linguistic test for descriptiveness is that in all of these phrases the adjective or modifier can be taken out of the noun phrase and placed in a following predicate phrase, preserving its descriptive meaning, i.e. THE SALAD DRESSING IS TASTY, THE LAWYER IS CRIMINAL, THE BOOK IS BLUE, and also THE BOOKS ARE HALF PRICE.

In addition to this grammatical or well-formedness test for descriptiveness, placing the modifier in predicate position, there is a semantic basis to the distinction between generic names and descriptive phrases. Crucial for genericness is that the meaning associated with a name must involve significant, permanent, and definitional properties of the genus or subcategory on the basis of which the members of the relevant class can be distinguished from other classes. There is no genus of DUSTY BOOKS, for example, because dustiness is not a significant, permanent, and definitional property of certain books. A book can be dusty one minute and clean the next; one person's copy of the same book can be dusty and another person's clean; and so on. DUSTY BOOK is a descriptive term, therefore. Similarly, one and the same book can be sold at half price at one store and full price at another. And whether one retailer happens to sell it at a different price from another is not a significant, permanent, or definitional property on the basis of which we would want to say that there is a different genus or subcategory of books when the prices differ. A BLUE

BOOK, on the other hand, can be, and is a separate genus or subcategory of books (§6.3). DUSTY BOOKS and HALF PRICE BOOKS, by contrast, are descriptive phrases.

I consulted the website for HPBRM ("HalfPriceBooks.com") at the time and noticed that HALF PRICE BOOKS was being used as a service mark to identify a company that sold books but that also sold records, magazines, and other related products. This is relevant evidence for the "secondary meaning" of HALF PRICE BOOKS as an identifier for a company providing much more than the literal meaning that the words in this phrase would describe, i.e. more than books. Crucially in this context HALF PRICE BOOKS is not a generic term for a kind or subcategory of books, and it is certainly not generic for a seller or service provider that sells lots of products that are not even books.

3.5.4 Counterarguments to Descriptiveness

BN.com's expert (a marketing one) opining on matters of language argued against the descriptiveness of HALF PRICE BOOKS as follows:

> The addition of the generic designation "books" to "half-price" refers to a well-recognized category of books, i.e. "half-price books" or books that are sold at 50% of the suggested retail price or some other substantial discount. The fact that the term "half-price books" is used so frequently in everyday language is persuasive evidence that the usage is common or generic rather than source indicating.

But frequency alone is not sufficient for genericness. HALF PRICE combines frequently with all kinds of nouns in everyday English usage, and the resulting composites are not necessarily generic names. The expert cited many examples occurring in connection with retail goods and services and domain names: HALF-PRICE AUTOMOTIVE SERVICES, HALF PRICE FIREWORKS, HALF PRICE CLEANERS, HALF PRICE PRINTING, HALFPRICECARS.COM, and others. But the crucial issue in all these examples is this: Is the composite whole defining a new genus or subcategory, or is the resulting phrase merely descriptive of a desirable characteristic of these goods or services? These examples are all descriptive by this criterion and do not define a kind or subcategory of e.g. automotive services. They also permit permutation of HALF PRICE into predicate position: THE AUTOMOTIVE SERVICES ARE HALF PRICE, and so forth. Similarly, HALF PRICE BOOKS does not define a kind or subcategory of books, and the permutation into THESE BOOKS

ARE HALF PRICE is well-formed. The expert's opinion that HALF PRICE BOOKS is a "well-recognized category of books" and generic is not sustainable, therefore. Being 'half price' is not a significant, permanent, and definitional property of books and frequency alone is not sufficient to establish genericness.

The linguistic criteria and evidence that I have illustrated and summarized here are crucial for distinguishing between descriptive and generic status. Not to consider them or to be unaware of them, as one side obviously was in this case, leads to unresolvable disputes over the semantic status of compounds like HALF PRICE BOOKS. If there is evidence for descriptiveness, as there was in this case, then the legal arguments can take over, following surveys of relevant consumers to see if there is also a so-called secondary meaning, more precisely to see if there is some additional and direct reference in the minds of consumers to a unique producer or service provider when they use the descriptive term in question. That is a separate issue, and it was not my role in this case to consider the evidence for or against secondary meaning. My role involved the distinction between descriptiveness and genericness, and my opinion on that has been summarized here.

CHAPTER 4

Disputes over Whole Clauses

When words and phrases join together to make whole clauses, there are different syntactic combinations that can result with often subtle meanings and meaning distinctions (recall §1.3). The precise meaning of a whole sentence can then be disputed and at the center of a lawsuit. In this chapter I discuss some examples of these types, beginning in §4.1 with attachment ambiguities involving the exact "phrase structure" of the words in the sentence, which resulted in some disputed differences in meaning. In §4.2 I consider the different meanings that can be assigned to clauses beginning with SUBJECT TO in English and the complications these caused in a real-estate contract, and in §4.3 I examine the precise meaning of the conjunction ALTHOUGH in subordinate clauses and how it impacted a libel suit.

4.1 Attachment Ambiguities

A false advertising suit (Washington, DC, 1998) centered on a sentence with a structure exactly like that shown in (1), in connection with hospitality services that were offered at a major national sporting event. (Names and details of this event have been changed in accordance with the present book's policy of focusing on the English language itself; sentence (1) is entirely parallel to the critical sentence in the lawsuit, which involved neither the Super Bowl nor Candlestick Park.)

(1) WE'RE ORGANIZING CORPORATE HOSPITALITY DURING THE SUPER BOWL AT CANDLESTICK PARK.

This was one of the opening sentences for a sales pitch used by the hospitality service company in question. The crucial issue involved where the services were being provided. They were actually located off the premises and at some distance from the sporting event itself. This was deemed to be misleading by the plaintiff, and so a lawsuit ensued against the hospitality company after the event itself and after the location of the hospitality services had been discovered.

English sentences with the grammatical structure of (1) permit an ambiguity with respect to where the phrase AT CANDLESTICK PARK is "attached." This results in different possible meaning assignments, and this in turn has consequences for the claim about where exactly the corporate hospitality was to be organized.

Let's start with the basic syntax. WE'RE is a contracted form of WE plus ARE, with a subject pronoun (abbreviated Pro) WE and the auxiliary verb (Aux) ARE. The portion of the sentence we are interested in then starts with the verb (V) ORGANIZING, which initiates a verb phrase (VP). This phrase contains CORPORATE HOSPITALITY, first of all, which is a noun phrase (NP) serving as the direct object of ORGANIZING. Next comes the prepositional phrase (PP) DURING THE SUPER BOWL, which comprises the preposition DURING and the NP, THE SUPER BOWL. In fact this is the first PP of two in this VP, so we label it PP_1. The second PP is AT CANDLESTICK PARK, which again comprises a preposition, AT, and a following NP, CANDLESTICK PARK. We label this second PP as PP_2.

The issue in this dispute was this: Where does PP_2 (AT CANDLESTICK PARK) go in the basic syntax of this sentence, what does it attach to, and how does this affect the meaning? There are two possibilities. PP_2 can attach to the verb ORGANIZING, which initiates the whole VP, in which case it semantically modifies this verb and its direct object NP with the basic meaning 'we're organizing corporate hospitality at Candlestick Park.' This event is then further modified semantically by PP_1 and occurs 'during the Super Bowl.' Or else PP_2 can attach to the immediately preceding NP, THE SUPER BOWL within PP_1, with the resulting meaning 'we're organizing corporate hospitality during the Super Bowl, which is at Candlestick Park.'

We can clarify this with some phrase structure groupings, corresponding to tree diagrams in syntax classes. The first possibility, in which PP_2 attaches directly to the VP and is a "sister" of the verb, along with its direct object NP and also PP_1, is shown in the square brackets given in (2) (with left and right brackets around each phrase, each phrasal type being shown on each left bracket, and brackets within brackets wherever there are phrases within phrases):

(2) PP_2 attachment to V within VP
WE'RE [vp ORGANIZING [np CORPORATE HOSPITALITY] [pp_1 DURING [np THE SUPERBOWL]] [pp_2 AT [np CANDLESTICK PARK]]]

This can be seen more clearly in tree diagram form in Linguistic Tree 4.1 (2'), which gives just the key words and phrases and their groupings, with PP_2 as a sister of V along with the direct object NP and PP_1, and which shows all of V, NP, PP_1, and PP_2 attached directly to VP:

(2')

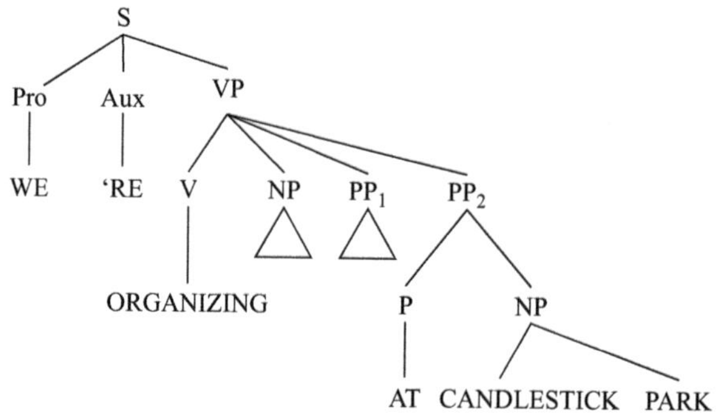

Linguistic Tree 4.1

The second attachment possibility is for PP_2 to attach to the NP within PP_1, as shown in (3):

(3) PP_2 attachment to the NP within PP_1
WE'RE [vp ORGANIZING [np CORPORATE HOSPITALITY] [pp_1 DURING [np THE SUPER BOWL [pp_2 AT [np CANDLESTICK PARK]]]]]

In tree diagram form, the basic phrase structure for this "lower" and "local" attachment of PP_2 to the NP within PP_1 can be seen more clearly in Linguistic Tree 4.2 (3'), which shows PP_2 attached directly to the immediately preceding NP THE SUPER BOWL, again giving just the key words and phrases and their attachments:

(3')

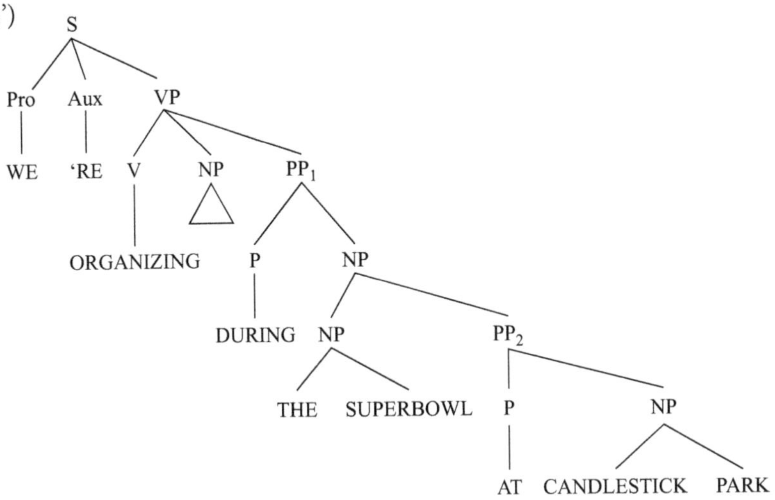

Linguistic Tree 4.2

We can refer to the first structural attachment in (2) and (2') as "verb modification," with the meaning that hospitality is being 'organized at Candlestick Park.' The second attachment in (3) and (3') involves "noun modification," whereby all that is being claimed semantically is that the NP, THE SUPER BOWL itself, is 'at Candlestick Park.'

So how do speakers of English actually understand a sentence like (1), when used as the lead-in to a sales pitch? I think the answer is pretty clear. They would normally understand that 'the corporate hospitality is being offered at Candlestick Park.' And it is indeed somewhat misleading to use this sentence, whether in a person-to-person sales pitch or in a TV or radio commercial, if the refreshments are going to be offered at some distance from Candlestick Park, say fifteen minutes away outside the gates of the stadium and with access only by bus. In other words, people viewing or hearing this commercial and sales pitch would reasonably conclude that they did not need to bring food and drink with them to Candlestick Park during the Super Bowl, because refreshments were going to be offered right there, and if it turned out that they needed to take a bus some way from the stadium in order to get to them, they would feel (and did feel) misled.

But how exactly do hearers and readers of sentence (1) reach this preferred interpretation, and which structure of the two options, (2)/(2') or (3)/(3'), do they select when assigning it? The answer is rather interesting linguistically and not completely straightforward. They will actually assign this preferred meaning in both cases, i.e. in both structural attachments, albeit in very different ways, and even though one of the options (structure (3)/(3')) does not strictly require it semantically!

If they choose structure (2)/(2'), with verb modification, then they will assign the meaning 'we're organizing corporate hospitality at Candlestick Park' directly to this sentence. And this structure is probably the preferred attachment because WE'RE ORGANIZING CORPORATE HOSPITALITY describes an activity that must of necessity take place in a certain location and AT CANDLESTICK PARK describes exactly the kind of location at which hospitality services can be, and are, offered. Hence the hearer understands in this reading that AT CANDLESTICK PARK is giving information of direct relevance to the verb, without which the activity described is incomplete, and so the verb modification attachment is readily made.

But the noun modification structure of (3)/(3'), with the meaning 'the Super Bowl is at Candlestick Park,' is also logically possible, and indeed because PP_2 (AT CANDLESTICK PARK) stands right next to the NP (THE SUPERBOWL) there is a strong tendency in language usage for items that stand together and are adjacent to be interpreted as belonging together as well (see e.g. my 2001 paper "Why Are Categories Adjacent?" in *Journal of Linguistics* 37:1–34). Now, this local adjacent attachment can also convey the same meaning as (2)/(2') to the effect that the hospitality services are offered at Candlestick Park where the Super Bowl is, but by a distinct process of contextual implication or "implicature" (recall §1.5). In technical discussions of semantics, the verb modification structure in (2)/(2') is said to "logically imply" or "entail" that 'we're organizing corporate hospitality at Candlestick Park,' whereas with noun modification in (3)/(3') this same meaning can also arise, but as we shall see presently does not necessarily always arise, from an implicature based on real-world knowledge. A hearer who assigns structure (3)/(3'), which requires logically only that the Super Bowl is taking place there and does not specify where the corporate hospitality is, could nonetheless understand the speaker to be implicating that the hospitality is offered there as well, if no other location for the hospitality is given. And indeed having both the game and the services at the same location makes sense and is the most natural state of affairs, and so this is a preferred interpretation as well for structure (3)/(3'), though not a logically required one, as it is for structure (2)/(2').

The bottom line is that the same meaning can be assigned in both attachments but by different semantic means, and because of this it is quite plausible to propose, in line with current psycholinguistic theories of "good enough parsing," that hearers will not necessarily bother to commit in actual usage to one attachment or the other but will simply draw the common basic meaning from both (see Fernanda Ferreira and Nikole D. Patson's 2007 article "The 'Good Enough' Approach to Language Comprehension," *Language and Linguistics Compass* 1/1–2: 71–83).

A further relevant consideration in the interpretation process for a sentence like (1), in addition to real-world knowledge, is whether the remainder of the text in the advertising pitch provided any further details about where exactly the hospitality services were being organized. Specifically, was any further information given about this, and was it mentioned anywhere that these services would be off-site? The answer is that no such further information was given. At no point did the larger text either state or implicate that the hospitality services were off-site. Hence, by the end of the advertising pitch, hearers would indeed understand that the corporate hospitality was being offered at the same location as the Super Bowl itself, whether through verb modification and entailment in (2)/(2') or through noun modification and implicature in (3)/(3'). Either way the result was a misleading description, but also as we have just seen a rather subtle one involving different phrasal attachments, and logical entailment meanings versus pragmatic implicatures. It is no wonder that a legal dispute arose involving the English language in this case, requiring some technical analysis in syntax, semantics, and pragmatics in order to sort it out.

In fact, disputes arising from attachment ambiguities are not uncommon. Another one, with a different grammatical structure, involved a (2017) insurance case that had the key wording KNOWINGLY COMMITTING OR PERFORMING ON MORE THAN ONE OCCASION ANY OF THE FOLLOWING UNFAIR SETTLEMENT PRACTICES. The issue was, Where does the initial adverb KNOWINGLY attach? Does it attach to the verb COMMITTING alone and modify this verb semantically to the left of OR, so that KNOWINGLY applies only to the COMMITTING, and not necessarily to the PERFORMING? In this case the performing of these unfair settlement practices on more than one occasion could in theory have been done unwittingly and unknowingly. This attachment is shown in (4) with local attachment of KNOWINGLY to COMMITTING only (to make a phrasal combination with this verb that we label here V') and with the semantic effect of KNOWINGLY applying only within the first VP up the tree and to the left of OR:

(4) [vp [vp [v' KNOWINGLY COMMITTING] OR PERFORMING] [pp ON MORE THAN ONE OCCASION] [np ANY OF THE FOLLOWING UNFAIR SETTLEMENT PRACTICES]]

The basic tree structure for the key words and phrases in (4) is given in Linguistic Tree 4.3 (4'), which shows the adverb KNOWINGLY attached locally to the first V, COMMITTING, within a higher V', which combines directly with OR and with the V PERFORMING under a higher VP, which combines in turn with the PP and NP that are all immediately dominated by the highest VP:

(4')

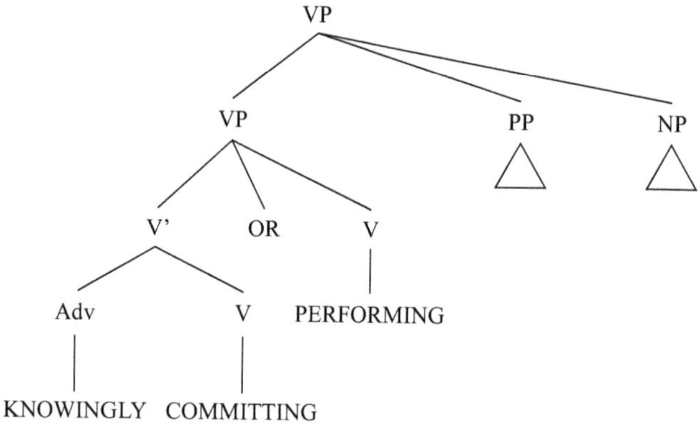

Linguistic Tree 4.3

Alternatively, does KNOWINGLY apply to both the COMMITTING and the PERFORMING ON MORE THAN ONE OCCASION . . ., in which case both must have been done 'knowingly'? This is shown in (5) with KNOWINGLY attached directly to the combined verbs COMMITTING OR PERFORMING (this combination occurring within a phrase labelled V') and modifying both semantically, or in more technical jargon "having scope" over the whole V' to its right and not just over the first verb COMMITTING:

(5) [vp [vp KNOWINGLY [v' COMMITTING OR PERFORMING]] [pp ON MORE THAN ONE OCCASION] [np ANY OF THE FOLLOWING UNFAIR SETTLEMENT PRACTICES]]

The basic tree structure for the key words and phrases in (5) is shown in Linguistic Tree 4.4 (5'), which has the adverb KNOWINGLY combining with the V' COMMITTING OR PERFORMING to make a VP, which then combines with PP and NP to make the highest VP:

(5')

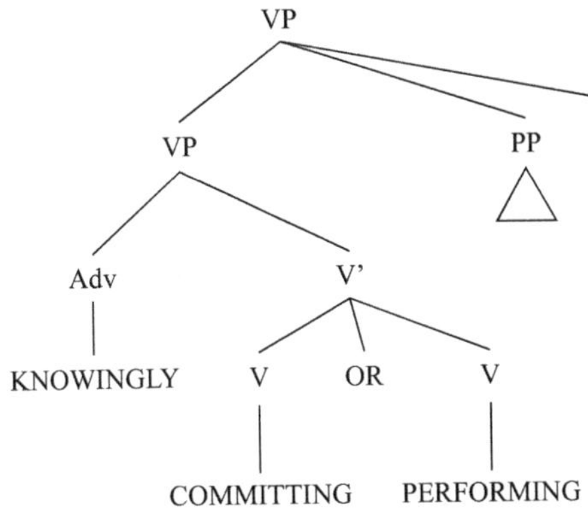

Linguistic Tree 4.4

The resolution of the ambiguity in this case, i.e. deciding which attachment the writer intended, involved considerations of linguistic semantics, on the one hand, and specialist real-world knowledge and plausibility, on the other, among those in the insurance industry.

First, the meaning of 'committing a certain act' and 'performing it' in this insurance context are practically identical. The disjunction OR here presents a paraphrase, therefore, indicating that one can refer to the acts in question linguistically one way or the other (just as I could say about your vehicle that it is called A CAR OR AN AUTOMOBILE). Hence, if KNOWINGLY is asserted to apply to the one, it applies by extension also to the other, which means that attachment (5)/(5') will be preferred.

But second, could the unfair settlement practices in question ever be performed 'unknowingly'? Real-world knowledge and plausibility suggested that this would be highly unlikely, so again structure (5)/(5') would be preferred when the larger context was taken into account. Or at least if for any reason the reader did make a local attachment of KNOWINGLY as in (4)/(4'), then there would be an implicature that the 'performing on more than one occasion ...' was also done 'knowingly,' for both semantic reasons having to do with the equivalence of COMMITTING and PERFORMING and for real-world knowledge reasons.

The attachment ambiguity for the adverb in (4) and (5) is reminiscent of the famous example discussed in linguistics textbooks involving the attachment of the adjective OLD in the noun phrase OLD MEN AND WOMEN. OLD can modify just the first noun, MEN, with the meaning 'old men and women of any age,' i.e. [[OLD MEN] AND WOMEN]. Or it can modify the combined phrase MEN AND WOMEN, i.e. [OLD [MEN AND WOMEN], in which case both men and women are claimed to be old, and under the scope of this adjective. And again, even when the former attachment is made and the age of the women is logically unspecified, there may be contexts in which it is implicated that they were old too, though there could be other contexts in which this was not implicated and the women could be younger or mixed in age or of unknown age.

Stepping back from the specific subtleties of these syntactic attachment ambiguities that have arisen in the law and can arise frequently, notice that we have here further examples of what I drew attention to in §1.1 and Chapter 2, in connection with individual words and their ambiguities and precise senses. Sentences like those we have seen in this section are challenging for linguistic analysis, both with respect to the proper semantic and pragmatic analysis of the meaning differences that go with the different syntactic attachments, and with respect to what the preferred interpretation will actually be in context. This is another case, therefore, of linguists facing certain challenges in their linguistic analysis, with the result that lawyers and their clients have challenges and possible problems too.

4.2 SUBJECT TO

A very different syntactic pattern and clausal type was at the center of a lawsuit stemming from a real-estate contract for the purchase of a property (Orange County, California, 2002). The key sentences were (6)–(8):

(6) BUYER HAS AGREED TO A 15 DAY DUE DILIGENCE PERIOD TO REVIEW ANY DOCUMENTS AND TO CONDUCT ANY SURVEYS OR OTHER INVESTIGATIONS.

(7) AFTER 15 DAYS FROM ACCEPTANCE, BUYER'S DEPOSIT SHALL BE NON-REFUNDABLE.

(8) BUYER AGREES TO CLOSE ANY TIME AFTER THE 15 DAY PERIOD SUBJECT TO SELLER BEING READY TO CLOSE (SUBJECT TO RELEASE OF LESSEE'S FIRST RIGHT OF PURCHASE).

The linguistic disagreement in this legal dispute involved the precise interpretation of the nonfinite clause (S) introduced by SUBJECT TO in (8), i.e. SUBJECT TO [s SELLER BEING READY TO CLOSE] (i.e.

'to close escrow'). A further SUBJECT TO occurs to the right of this clause and in parentheses. This second SUBJECT TO is "embedded," i.e. contained, within the first syntactically and semantically, and it precedes a noun phrase this time rather than a whole clause, SUBJECT TO [np RELEASE OF LESSEE'S FIRST RIGHT OF PURCHASE].

One side in this dispute, the buyer, argued that the SUBJECT TO clauses in (8) referred only to the date for closing escrow and allowed for a possible delay in that date depending on when the seller was ready to close. SUBJECT TO SELLER BEING READY TO CLOSE was accordingly interpreted as 'subject to when the seller was ready to close.' The other side, the seller, contended that the whole purchase agreement was made conditional on a first right of purchase or first right of refusal by the current LESSEE of the property, as a result of the second SUBJECT TO clause, SUBJECT TO RELEASE OF LESSEE'S FIRST RIGHT OF PURCHASE.

There is indeed an interesting ambiguity in clauses and phrases with SUBJECT TO in English. A phrase like SUBJECT TO DELIVERY OF THE VEHICLE can be understood in different contexts to mean 'depending on **when** the vehicle is delivered,' 'depending on **whether** the vehicle is delivered,' and even perhaps 'depending on **how** the vehicle is delivered.' The clause at the center of this lawsuit, SUBJECT TO SELLER BEING READY TO CLOSE (SUBJECT TO RELEASE OF LESSEE'S FIRST RIGHT OF PURCHASE), is similarly ambiguous. In some sentences and paragraphs it could indeed mean that the seller's readiness to close will 'depend on **whether** the lessee releases his or her first right of purchase.' But as it occurs in the sequence of (6)–(8) in this purchase agreement, the immediate context provided by the preceding sentences (6) and (7) eliminates this possible interpretation for (8) and only the meaning 'depending on **when** the lessee releases his or her first right of purchase' can be assigned. How exactly do (6) and (7) eliminate the 'whether' interpretation and reinforce the 'when' meaning?

The two occurrences of SUBJECT TO occur following BUYER AGREES TO CLOSE ANY TIME AFTER THE 15 DAY PERIOD . . . at the beginning of sentence (8). THE 15 DAY PERIOD is a definite noun phrase that refers back to the content of sentence (7), AFTER 15 DAYS FROM ACCEPTANCE, BUYER'S DEPOSIT SHALL BE NON-REFUNDABLE, which in turn refers back to BUYER HAS AGREED TO A 15 DAY DUE DILIGENCE PERIOD in (6). Sentence (7) introduces two pieces of information. First, there is a date at which the buyer's offer is accepted by the seller. Second, the buyer's deposit will be non-refundable after fifteen days from that date. In effect, after these fifteen days the buyer will have made a partial payment for the property, and the reader of the purchase agreement is told that the seller will not return the money after that point.

The meaning assigned to sentence (8) with its two occurrences of SUBJECT TO takes account of the preceding sentences (6) and (7). They provide the immediate context for interpreting the disputed sentence (8), therefore. Crucially, once the buyer's offer has been accepted, and once the property has already been partly paid for with a NON-REFUNDABLE DEPOSIT, as specified in (7), i.e. after the fifteen-day period described in (6), the reader has to assume that the sale is definitely going through. It would be unreasonable for the seller to take the buyer's deposit and extend the escrow past the fifteen days, whereupon the deposit becomes non-refundable, and then announce to the buyer that the seller could not actually close because the lessee had not released their first right of purchase, which would mean the deal was off, even though the buyer's partial payment was still non-refundable (according to (7)). This is obviously unreasonable and so the reader infers (in (8)) that the seller must have been in a position to make the sale by the end of the fifteen-day period, which means further that all conditions for making it would have been met, including the release of the lessee's first right of purchase. Because the existence of that release is now no longer in doubt in the reader's mind, a meaning will be assigned to SUBJECT TO RELEASE OF LESSEE'S FIRST RIGHT OF PURCHASE in (8), which is compatible with this contextual information. The only meaning for (8) that is compatible with the content of (6) and (7) is accordingly 'depending on **when** the lessee releases his or her first right of purchase,' not 'depending on **whether**' he or she does so.

General knowledge of the world supports the assignment of this 'when' meaning here. It is well-known that it takes a certain amount of time for all documents to be signed and completed in a complicated transaction like a property purchase. The lessee may be out of town or on vacation during the time frame in question, and the seller's possible need for some additional time is understandable, all of which makes the 'when' interpretation quite plausible.

The second SUBJECT TO in (8) is subordinate to and dependent on the interpretation given to the first SUBJECT TO, and because of the immediately preceding context and real-world knowledge this latter refers only to the date of closing escrow. It does not make the entire agreement dependent on any further conditions after the seller's acceptance of the offer, including the lessee's first right of purchase. The reader has to understand, therefore, that this first right of purchase has now been released as a prerequisite for the seller's acceptance and receipt of the buyer's non-refundable deposit, as a result of which the seller would now be ready to close escrow.

In effect, one side in this dispute argued for a **whether** interpretation of SUBJECT TO SELLER BEING READY TO CLOSE because it favored their legal argument for making the whole agreement dependent on the lessee releasing his or her first right of purchase. This is not what sentence (8) means in the context of this contract, however, i.e. following sentences (6) and (7), and given this context the other side was able to argue for the **when** interpretation.

4.3 ALTHOUGH Clauses

Complex syntax, involving finite subordinate clauses and the "subordinating conjunctions" that introduce them, can figure prominently in lawsuits involving language and can benefit from linguistic analysis regarding the precise meanings they convey. One such was part of a libel suit (Los Angeles, 1999) in which unprofessional conduct by a lawyer and drinking to excess were alleged, and the lawyer and his firm then sued the writer and publisher of the book in which the relevant language occurred. The meaning of the subordinating conjunction in question, ALTHOUGH, a so-called concessive conjunction, played a key role in the alleged libel.

We can describe and set up the background to this case as follows. A lawyer from a major Beverly Hills law firm, let's call him Smith (in line with this book's policy of removing people's names and focusing on the English language itself), represents a famous Hollywood actress; let's call her Felicity. At a private dinner party on New Year's Eve, Smith is seated opposite a gentleman, let's call him Jones, who is writing a book about Felicity. The two exchange brief words about Felicity, and a few months later the following sentences shown in (9) and (10) appear in an unauthorized biography of Felicity written by Jones:

(9) ALTHOUGH I HAD IDENTIFIED MYSELF AS FELICITY'S BIOGRAPHER, SMITH TOLD ME AFTER TWO BOTTLES OF MERLOT ON NEW YEAR'S EVE, "WHEN FELICITY WANTS SOMEONE, SHE RENTS A HOTEL ROOM AND TELLS HIM EXACTLY WHEN AND WHERE TO SHOW UP."

(10) "SHE MAKES IT CLEAR IT'S A ONE-TIME OPPORTUNITY.... SHE'S MADE THE MOVE ON SOME MAJOR NAMES."

Smith and Smith's law firm sued Jones and his publisher for libel.

These sentences are clearly damaging to the lawyer in question. They are not exactly flattering to Felicity either, who is portrayed as a sexual predator. As concerns the lawyer, it is clear that Smith should never reveal private and confidential information about a client to an outsider, especially not to someone who has explicitly stated that he is a biographer of this client and who can potentially pass on this less than positive information to hundreds of thousands of readers. The lawyer also appears to have been drinking to excess. Altogether this lawyer, Smith, is presented as engaging in unprofessional conduct. Smith, however (whose full and real name was given in the book), denied ever saying any of these things about Felicity at the dinner party in question, and he also denied drinking, let alone drinking to excess. Sentences (9) and (10) clearly put at risk his future as a prominent entertainment lawyer in Los Angeles, and they also put at risk the future of his whole firm.

Let us focus on the two parts of this case that I was asked to address, crucially involving the syntax and semantics of the language in (9), as they relate to excessive drinking on the one hand and unprofessional conduct on the other, by revealing confidential information about a client. What exactly does (9) assert or imply in these respects, and how are the relevant meanings created?

The prepositional phrase (PP) AFTER TWO BOTTLES OF MERLOT refers to a significant amount of wine. But who exactly was drinking it? It occurs within the verb phrase (VP) of a main clause (S), as shown in (11):

(11) [s SMITH [vp TOLD ME [pp AFTER TWO BOTTLES OF MERLOT]]]

The grammatical subject in (11), SMITH, is clearly understood to be drinking here, but what about ME, the indirect object of the verb TOLD and the writer of the passage? Was I drinking it too? Interestingly, (11) is vague in this respect (recall §1.1). This sentence could be true if Smith alone was the one drinking the two bottles of merlot. It could also be true if he and I (the writer) shared the two bottles. It could even be true in some contexts if I alone was the one doing the drinking in a sentence like (11), though in the present context it is implicated that

Smith was definitely drinking. But even if Smith was not alone in finishing off the two bottles, this amount of wine is still excessive for two people and more than sufficient to affect Smith's presence of mind and his ability to be discrete and professional.

And this is where the meaning of ALTHOUGH comes in and adds an important additional ingredient to the negative effect created by AFTER TWO BOTTLES OF MERLOT in (9) and (11). Consider first a simpler sentence with ALTHOUGH:

(12) ALTHOUGH IT WAS RAINING, THE BOYS PLAYED OUTSIDE.

Normally when it rains, one does not play outside. On this occasion we have an exception: The boys did something that went against the normal rule. Similarly consider (13):

(13) ALTHOUGH HE WAS SHORT, JOHNNY WAS A GREAT BASKETBALL PLAYER.

Normally you have to be tall to be a good basketball player, for obvious reasons so that you are closer to the high net and can score more points. On this occasion we have an exception to the rule. Johnny was great at basketball, despite being short.

In other words, ALTHOUGH signals that there is an unexpected departure from a normal state of affairs, and it is used appropriately when people know what these norms are and are told something that goes against them and that is exceptional (see Ekkehard König's 1986 chapter "Conditionals, Concessive Conditionals and Concessives: Areas of Contrast, Overlap and Neutralization," in E. C. Traugott, A. ter Meulen, J. S. Reilly, and C. A. Ferguson, eds., *On Conditionals*, Cambridge University Press, Cambridge). In the case of (9) the normal rule is that a lawyer does not reveal confidential information of any kind about a client, let alone information that is less than favorable. Similarly a doctor does not reveal confidential information about a patient to someone who is not involved with that patient's care. In (9) we have an exception. Smith did reveal confidential information about Felicity, information that would be construed negatively, and he even revealed it to someone who was a self-identified biographer of Felicity and who could then disseminate it further to lots of people.

But having introduced the meaning that there is going to be an exception to the normal rule, through the use of ALTHOUGH in the initial subordinate clause of (9), this provides the context for the full interpretation of AFTER TWO BOTTLES OF MERLOT in the immediately following main clause (11). This prepositional phrase is now understood to be providing the reason for this exception to the norm! It gives an explanation for the unusual conduct by the lawyer, Smith. It makes clear to the reader why Smith was doing this unusual thing and supplying information that he should not have supplied.

Consider a parallel example:

(14) ALTHOUGH I HAD IDENTIFIED MYSELF AS A CIA AGENT, THE RUSSIAN PREMIER TOLD ME AFTER TWO BOTTLES OF VODKA ON NEW YEAR'S EVE, "RUSSIA IS NOW SELLING WEAPONS TO IRAN."

Normally the Russian premier does not reveal state secrets to an outsider, especially not to an American CIA agent. On this occasion he did so. Why? Because the vodka loosened his tongue and he revealed things he should not have revealed.

Similarly, the phrase AFTER TWO BOTTLES OF MERLOT in (9) is understood to be giving a reason for why Smith did this unusual thing and supplied information, damaging information, that he should not have given, namely because the excessive alcohol led him to be indiscrete and unprofessional.

For those readers of the present book who are interested in how this case unfolded, I can reveal that there was disagreement among witnesses to the event on New Year's Eve at which sentences (9) and (10) were allegedly uttered, and hence there was disagreement about whether Smith actually said these words or not. Some said he did, some said he did not, and this compromised the plaintiff's case against Jones and the publisher of his unauthorized biography. What the court did agree on, however, was that sentence (9) did make a damaging allegation of excessive drinking leading to unprofessional conduct, as I have argued here. What was missing was conclusive proof that the relevant sentences were actually uttered.

CHAPTER 5

Disputes over Inferences

We have seen in earlier chapters that some of our disputed meanings are assigned by inferences that go beyond the literal meanings of words and constructions (recall the general discussion of inferential processes in §1.5). So, in the SUBJECT TO purchase agreement case (§4.2) the appropriate meaning given to it, of 'when' rather than 'whether' the seller would be ready to close the deal, was based on an inference from information given in the preceding sentences. These sentences made clear that the seller had already accepted the non-refundable deposit from the buyer after fifteen days and was prepared to close the deal. Hence the reader would reason that there was no longer a question of 'whether' the deal would go through after that, and this semantic possibility for SUBJECT TO was accordingly eliminated, by inference. Similarly, if the local attachment of AT CANDLESTICK PARK was made to DURING THE SUPER BOWL (§4.1), which asserts only that the Super Bowl takes place there, rather than attaching it to the verb and direct object ORGANIZING CORPORATE HOSPITALITY, there would still be an inference, based on real-world knowledge this time, that the hospitality services were going to be offered at the same place where the Super Bowl was, even though this was not strictly required semantically.

In cases such as these the relevant information is not literally said, and expressed directly by the meanings of the words, phrases, and clauses within a sentence, but it is nonetheless just as real in the minds of hearers and readers. I distinguished three subtypes of such inferencing in §1.5: (a) inferences that arise from information given in the immediate context of the text, which lead to an enrichment or a more precise specification of the information conveyed; (b) inferences that arise from what is called "the presumption of truth," whereby sentences are normally understood to be making a claim the speaker or writer believes to be true, unless this is explicitly qualified by e.g. IT MAY BE THAT . . ., IT HAS BEEN REPORTED THAT . . ., and so on; and (c) inferences that arise from real-world knowledge. The inferencing in the SUBJECT TO case was of the first type (a) involving immediately preceding sentences in the text. The preferred meaning for AT CANDLESTICK PARK when this phrase was assigned "locally" to THE SUPER BOWL (to the effect that the services in question were also offered there even though the sentence in this reading asserted only that the game itself was taking place at Candlestick Park) was a case of the third, (c). We will discuss a clear instance of (b) in §5.4 involving the presumption of truth and how to avoid inferences arising from it (see also §3.2).

What makes these legal disputes involving inference so interesting is that the inferencing procedures that underlie them are quite complex and subtle, and the precise manner in which they work and create these additional meanings or disambiguations is one of the hot topics that all the language sciences have been grappling with for some years now (traditional linguistics, philosophy of language, logic, psycholinguistics, and more recently computational linguistics). Once again, where there are challenges for linguistic analysis, there are challenges and potential problems for lawyers and their clients in the courtroom, or else there may be opportunities for lawyers and their clients to create a linguistic dispute, whether wittingly or unwittingly!

It is not just a question here of a certain context or piece of world knowledge selecting one meaning rather than another for ambiguous or vague words, as with SUBSTANTIALLY, DISEASE, APPROXIMATELY, and FIGHT (recall §1.4 and the relevant sections of Chapter 2). I will be dealing in this chapter often with a whole chain of reasoning derived from the collective information in a text (i.e. with a chain of "relevance implicatures" derived from previous sentences in a text; see Dan Sperber and Deirdre Wilson's 1995 *Relevance: Communication and Cognition*, 2nd edn, Blackwell, Oxford, and with the "presumptive meanings" of Stephen Levinson's *Presumptive Meanings*, MIT Press, Cambridge, Massachusetts, 2000). This means that any analysis of how readers understand a text, and its various parts, requires that we look carefully at the whole thing. We can't just cherry-pick some individual words and sentences. There may be some crucial information given in one sentence that sets off a chain of reasoning that affects the interpretation of a later word or phrase, as in the SUBJECT TO case. When general real-world knowledge rather than information in the text triggers the inference in question, we need to ask what exactly that knowledge is, how widespread it is among readers, whether different beliefs are held that can impact the inference, and so on.

Many of these inference-based lawsuits involve libel and defamation, though not all do (SUBJECT TO was a real-estate purchase agreement). In §5.1 I discuss one of my favorite cases, ZERO BANANAS, a libel suit against a tabloid magazine that relied crucially on an alleged inference derived by a chain of reasoning. ZERO BANANAS was the phrase I used, perhaps mischievously but effectively, when summarizing my analysis to the jury at the trial that ensued. SPATZ AND LATINOS in §5.2 was a similar inference-based case involving a political campaign mailer directed against Robert Spatz (name changed), who was claimed to be anti-immigrant. Section 5.3 discusses a defamation case involving the Foreign Corrupt Practices Act and the claim allegedly made by a speaker at a public hearing that a certain organization had violated it. In §5.4 I consider the interesting case of whether a tabloid magazine that was summarizing a book giving a new theory about the assassination of Bobby Kennedy did it in a way that would have led readers to believe that the magazine itself actually endorsed this theory and presented it as something that was true. And in §5.5 I turn to "suggestive" marks in trademark law, which typically derive their suggestiveness, as opposed to their descriptiveness, in relation to the product in question precisely from inferencing based on real-world knowledge. I discuss the trademark PERSONAL POST OFFICE for which I give an analysis in favor of its classification as a suggestive term legally.

5.1 ZERO BANANAS

A tabloid magazine presented a colorful two-page spread with five pictures featuring a Hollywood grandee. Let's call him Gary Fordham. In one he is seated in the lush garden of his home. In another he is shown indoors at his billiard table with numerous photographs from his long career in the background. In a third picture he is seen at his dining table with a young lady exchanging a toast using silver goblets. Both he and the lady are smartly and casually dressed. A fourth picture, the largest, shows him dressed quite formally now, with a tie, and in his garden again, with the imposing front façade of his house behind, and seated at his side is the same young lady as in the dinner table picture, who is also dressed quite formally. The fifth picture shows Gary with a young lady on his arm, a different one from pictures three and four, both leaning against a railing overlooking the sea. She is wearing a bikini, he is wearing a bathrobe, and it looks like they are on vacation somewhere and have both been swimming.

The accompanying text led the smartly dressed lady in pictures three and four to file suit against the tabloid on the grounds that it would lead readers to understand, in combination with the visual display, especially picture five, that Gary was having a sexual relationship with both of them. We'll call the lady filing the lawsuit Polly Keenan. Polly was accordingly the plaintiff in this case, and her lawyer recruited an English language consultant (Los Angeles, 1992) to make the case that the article suggested to readers, unmistakably, that Gary was having a sexual relationship with both ladies, and in fact with many more female visitors to his lush estate. Her expert conceded that no single word or sentence in the text taken out of context would necessarily lead to this "suggestive" inference, but taken together, one sentence after another, the average reader of the whole text would definitely understand, he argued, that Gary was using these young ladies for sex. I was recruited by the lawyers for the defense to give my opinion on the matter. I took on this case as an expert witness because I believed that the claim made by the plaintiff and her lawyers that readers would necessarily understand that Gary was using these ladies and many more like her for sex was exaggerated, and because it was an interesting linguistic case involving a putative chain of inference.

Notice by way of background, first of all, that tabloid newspapers are generally very careful and quite clever in the way they present their pictures and use language, precisely because they want to avoid expensive lawsuits. At the same time they want to entertain their readers, give them stories about the rich and famous, feed them insider gossip, and perhaps even shock and titillate them, and as a result sell more magazines! In the process they push the envelope of propriety to the limit, but generally not in a way that will lead to losing a libel suit. In the present case there was just one visual detail in picture four that readers might have found suggestive. In both pictures three and four Polly and Gary are shown fully and properly dressed. In picture four Polly is seated on what appears to be the remains of a large tree trunk; Gary and she are facing the camera with Gary standing on the right side of the tree trunk (to its left as readers see him in the picture), tilted slightly toward Polly but not at all close to her side, and leaning his left leg on the edge of the tree trunk. Polly's right arm makes slight contact with Gary's knee. The accompanying text makes clear, however, that Polly is not the bikini-clad lady in picture five who is arm in arm with Gary and on vacation by the sea.

With respect to the language of the text, a case such as this is fascinating because it can be an interesting test of whether the words and phrases used can really be said to be damaging to somebody's reputation and hence libelous. It can also be a test for whether current theories of language use and implicature are able to make sense of the reader's state of mind and beliefs after reading this text. As I mentioned previously, it is quite complex to make a solid argument that a particular inference can be drawn from a text, beyond the literal meanings of the words, phrases, and sentences it contains. Now we find a lawsuit where the dispute centers around exactly this analytical difficulty.

In the following discussion I present the heading for this article, first of all, and then the full text, so readers of the present book can judge for themselves whether they agree with my counteranalysis to the plaintiff's claims. At the very least this case brings to light, and enables us to make explicit, some general points about inferencing in libel suits. These points are subtle, almost never precisely and accurately discussed without guidance from language specialists, and they are frequently not well argued by language experts either, unless they have proper training in the more technical semantic, pragmatic, and grammatical areas of the language sciences (as opposed to, say, expertise in English literature or philology, as was the case with my opposing expert here).

The first and crucial point we need to appreciate by way of background to any analysis of the current case is that different readers can have very different beliefs about how things work in the world and about how people behave or should behave in it, over and above their shared knowledge of the fundamentals of human experience. And these different beliefs can then impact how different readers will react to a text and what inferences they will draw from it. Consider (1):

(1) GF, AN ACTOR, FREQUENTLY RECEIVES FEMALE VISITORS.

If you believe that all actors are invariably promiscuous and have sex on every possible occasion, you will indeed assume when reading (1) that GF has sex with his frequent female visitors. On the other hand, if you believe that actors are no different from the rest of us and may or may not have sex with frequent female visitors, then the reader will not necessarily assume that GF has sex with them, though it is not impossible that they will still understand this. And if you happen to believe, based on independent knowledge, that GF is happily married and an upstanding and moral person who respects his wedding vows to his wife, then no sexual interpretation will be assigned at all.

In other words, different readers can understand things differently based on their independent beliefs. Sentence (1) itself is semantically vague and noncommittal about the nature of the interaction between GF and his female visitors. In such circumstances, when readers hold different beliefs and the text says nothing more than what is given, it cannot be said to "imply" or "suggest" anything over and above its literal meaning. Similarly, if a reader is told that HARRY BOUGHT A NEW CAR he or she might (or might not) immediately think of their own favorite car, a Mercedes Benz, or they might know some things about Harry that lead them to believe that Harry would buy a Japanese import, or they may feel strongly that Harry would buy an American Ford, and so on. The point is that none of this is systematic, and the text cannot be said to be implying or suggesting any of these possibilities, because it is semantically vague and different readers may (or may not) assign more specific interpretations that are not contained in the literal meanings of the words and phrases themselves. The only time we can talk of a text implying or suggesting (i.e. "implicating," recall §1.5) some additional nonliteral meaning is when readers quite generally and systematically assign this additional interpretation, based on shared knowledge and beliefs, or when the text itself makes it clear that the additional interpretation should be assigned.

So how does a text do this (recall our brief discussion of this in §1.5)? Consider here the more elaborate sequence of sentences in the fictitious passage of (2):

(2) MALE ACTORS GENERALLY HAVE SEX WITH
FREQUENT FEMALE VISITORS TO THEIR HOMES.
GF IS A MALE ACTOR.
PK IS A FREQUENT FEMALE VISITOR TO HIS HOME.

This text does not actually assert that GF has sex with PK, but it does clearly implicate it in this context. If you read all the sentences of the text, then your knowledge of these word and sentence meanings leads you to draw this conclusion. If each of the sentences is true (and they are presented here as if they are, without any hedges or alternative lead-in sentences such as "SOME PEOPLE THINK THAT MALE ACTORS GENERALLY HAVE SEX WITH FREQUENT FEMALE VISITORS"; see §5.4), then the inference has to be true as well. That this is a clear implicature and psychologically present in the minds of readers can be seen in the fact that it can be cancelled appropriately with a cancelling clause, as shown in (2'):

(2') MALE ACTORS GENERALLY HAVE SEX WITH
FREQUENT FEMALE VISITORS TO THEIR HOMES.
GF IS A MALE ACTOR.

PK IS A FREQUENT FEMALE VISITOR TO HIS HOME – ALTHOUGH SHE IS NOT IN ANY SEXUAL RELATIONSHIP WITH GF. IT'S PURELY PLATONIC IN THIS CASE.

In effect, this cancelling clause makes explicit that we have an exception on this particular occasion to our understanding about the relationship between GF and PK based on the previous sentences of (2). The fact that this understanding can be denied appropriately and comes as no surprise to readers indicates that it was indeed there and present in their minds (recall the similar implicature cancellation discussed in §1.5).

Such inferencing and implicatures can also go through if the initial premise of the text is semantically weaker than MALE ACTORS GENERALLY HAVE SEX WITH FREQUENT FEMALE VISITORS TO THEIR HOMES in (2), but instead something like MALE ACTORS OFTEN HAVE SEX WITH FREQUENT FEMALE VISITORS TO THEIR HOMES. In this case the implicature will be more probabilistic ('GF is very likely or possibly having sex with them') than it is in (2). A cancellation along the lines of (2') can still be made appropriately even with this weaker premise, however.

So how does the text of the article at the center of this libel suit fare in this respect? Does it implicate that Gary Fordham was definitely, or even very likely, having sex with Polly Keenan, or does it not? I consider first (§5.1.1) the title and subtitle, and the claims made by the plaintiff and their language consultant about these, and I then give the text itself (§5.1.2) with the claims made by the plaintiff's language expert about that.

5.1.1 *The Title and Subtitle*

The heading of the text as presented in the tabloid, with its title (in large print and in red in the original) and the subtitle (in smaller black), is shown in (3):

(3) [GARY FORDHAM]: HOW DOES HIS GARDEN GROW? WITH PRETTY MAIDS IN A ROW.

The plaintiff alleged in her complaint that the average reader would take this to mean that PK was one of many young women in Gary Fordham's garden with whom he was having a sexual relationship. It was claimed further that the passage "suggests a methodical blossoming and deflowering of young maidens." The plaintiff's language expert elaborated by stating that (3) would lead many readers to imagine that Gary Fordham "painstakingly cultivated these young women for the sole purpose of deflowering them." He argued that the subtitle used phrases from a nursery rhyme that many or most readers would be familiar with, shown in (4):

(4) MARY, MARY, QUITE CONTRARY, HOW DOES YOUR GARDEN GROW? WITH PRETTY MAIDS IN A ROW.

He also pointed out that MAIDS here was a reduced form of the name for a certain type of flower, called MAIDEN-BLUSH or MAIDEN-ROSE in horticultural contexts.

My contrary opinion given to the court was that this was all exaggerated. The title and subtitle in (3) could not be said to be setting up any such inference about GF having a sexual relationship with PK and many other young women in his garden. Some readers, as I mentioned previously, may have had prior beliefs about male actors and their sex lives that led them to think this, but there was nothing in the language of (3) that would force them to this conclusion. The further claim that the title and subtitle would lead readers to infer that GF was cultivating these young women "for the sole purpose of deflowering them" was particularly extreme. We can assume, however, that many readers will recognize the nursery rhyme in (4), though many will not. For example, Latin Americans in the US (of whom there are tens of millions!) may not have grown up with English-language nursery rhymes. Some readers may indeed know that MAID is an ambiguous word in English (like BACHELOR in §1.1) and has different senses, 'a female maiden' and 'a type of flower,' but again many will not know this, and even if they do, most would have no clear idea about what type of flower it is and of the fuller horticultural names for it that MAID abbreviates.

The opposing language expert's claim that the 'flower' sense of MAID set up a psychological association with 'deflower,' and that readers would understand GF to be cultivating these young ladies for the purpose of "deflowering" them, was also quite implausible for several reasons. First, as I have said, some readers, possibly most, will not even know the 'flower' meaning of MAID. These readers could not begin to make any associations between 'flower' and 'deflower.' Second, even if some readers did know the 'flower' sense of MAID, they might not know the rather rare and literary word DEFLOWER and its meaning. Third, even among those who were aware of the ambiguity of MAID and who also knew the word DEFLOWER, the psychological distance between 'flower' and the 'deflowering of maidens' is considerable, and it is quite a stretch to assume that a systematic connection and psychological association between the two would be made in these people's minds in a text like this. There may be some individuals who think like this, perhaps those with experience and training in English literature, but it is far-fetched to claim that the average reader does.

In fact, we could make the stronger argument that PRETTY MAIDS has no sexual associations whatsoever, because MAID and MAIDEN convey the clear sense of 'innocence.' This is documented in the various entries for MAIDEN in the *Oxford English Dictionary* (all editions). One of its senses as an adjective modifier of nouns is 'virgin.' A MAIDEN NAME is a woman's name before marriage. MAIDEN SOIL is soil that has never been ploughed. MAIDEN-WAX is glossed as 'virgin wax.' A MAIDEN SPEECH is the first speech delivered by a member of Parliament, and so on. These different senses of the ambiguous MAIDEN, of which MAID is the reduced form, should more than offset any more distant associations with 'deflowering.' What is even more plausible, however, is that the average reader thinks of very little at the start of this text, beyond the literal meanings that can be assigned, and (depending on their cultural and ethnic background) beyond the existence of the nursery rhyme that these allude to.

5.1.2 *The Text Itself*

The article that followed the title and subtitle was short, and I reproduce it here in its entirety in (5):

(5) VETERAN ACTOR [GARY FORDHAM]'S GLAMOROUS BEVERLY HILLS MANSION IS LUSH WITH PLANTS, MEOMORABILIA AND PRETTY YOUNG GIRLS. [FORDHAM], WHO'S 74, DESIGNED THE $2.4-MILLION ESTATE THAT PROUDLY DISPLAYS HIS LOVE OF RARE PLANTS. ANTIQUES AND OTHER COLLECTIBLES GATHERED DURING HIS PRESTIGIOUS CAREERS IN BOTH THE MOVIES AND THE MILITARY. [GARY]'S STILL QUITE THE GALLIVANTER IN HOLLYWOOD CIRCLES, CONSTANTLY COLLECTING GORGEOUS YOUNG BLONDES, LIKE THESE TWO STUNNERS TO SHARE HIS SWINGING LIFESTYLE. ACTRESS [POLLY KEENAN] IS A FREQUENT VISITOR TO [FORDHAM]'S ABODE (PHOTOS RIGHT AND BOTTOM LEFT) AND

> BIKINI-CLAD MODEL [KJ] (LEFT) TRAVELS WITH THE DASHING ACTOR ON MANY OF HIS EXOTIC VACATIONS.

The plaintiff's language expert argued that there were as many as fifteen expressions here that confirm "the sexual relationship which the article as a whole clearly implies that [Gary Fordham] has on a continuing basis with a variety of women in general and with Plaintiff [Polly Keenan] in particular." He argued further that the article taken as a whole "unambiguously implies that [Gary Fordham] has several sexual playmates." I argued on the contrary that most of these fifteen completely lack any sexual associations whatsoever, while just four merit some further discussion, namely DASHING, GALLIVANTER, SWINGING LIFESTYLE, and MAID, which I have already mentioned. Even these four have more general or distinct senses, which I shall outline presently, and do not necessarily lead to the claimed sexual content or implicature in this context.

Among the expressions listed in the language expert's fifteen as implying a sexual liaison were LUSH, PRETTY YOUNG GIRLS, and LOVE OF ... OTHER COLLECTIBLES. But to describe a garden as LUSH, to refer to PRETTY YOUNG GIRLS, and to say that Gary Fordham's estate displays his LOVE OF ... OTHER COLLECTIBLES (in addition to rare plants and antiques) says nothing about any sexual relationship. This is not in the literal meanings of these words, nor is it implicated in context. The plaintiff's expert argued that LOVE OF ... OTHER COLLECTIBLES "refers transparently to the only subject in which the article is genuinely interested, [Fordham]'s habit of 'collecting gorgeous young blondes.'" But OTHER COLLECTIBLES is semantically compatible with a huge variety of things that can be collected. Even if we were to admit that gorgeous young blondes might be included among them here (normally they would not be since we generally collect things rather than people), it does not follow that Gary Fordham must be having sex with them.

Another of the fifteen expressions is FREQUENT VISITOR TO [FORDHAM]'S ABODE, in the sentence "ACTRESS [POLLY KEENAN] IS A ... ." The plaintiff's complaint contended that "in context, the average reader of the article would take this statement to mean that plaintiff is an actress who often visits [Gary Fordham's] home to have sexual liaisons with him." But this sentence is just like (1) above. It does not assert anything about a sexual liaison. It does not implicate it either in context, because although some readers may imagine that Gary

Fordham, being an actor, will seize every opportunity he can for sex with pretty women, other readers may think just the opposite, or they may have no opinion on the matter and will draw no inference about sex. There will be nothing systematic, therefore, in this alleged interpretation, and I previously pointed out that we can only talk about a text implicating a particular enriched meaning beyond its literal meaning if readers in general can be presumed to be drawing this inference, based on the previous text and/or on generally held beliefs. This is all quite unsystematic here, and all we can say about the average reader of ACTRESS [POLLY KEENAN] IS A FREQUENT VISITOR TO [FORDHAM]'S ABODE is that they will interpret it to mean what it literally says. It is not implicated that PK is visiting GF for the purpose of sex.

EXOTIC VACATIONS, STUNNERS, COLLECT(OR), and PRETTY MAIDS IN A ROW, four more expressions among the language expert's fifteen, are also quite harmless and neither assert nor implicate that there is a sexual relationship between Gary Fordham and the plaintiff.

The word DASHING occurs in the phrase THE DASHING ACTOR and is one that was argued to confirm the sexual relationship with the plaintiff. But the adjective DASHING is defined by the *OED* (2nd edn) as 'given to fashionable and striking display in manners and dress; that is a "dasher."' In other words, to describe Gary Fordham as a DASHING ACTOR is a comment about the way he dresses and about his manners, and it neither asserts nor implicates anything more. The people who get to see his appearance and experience his manners will undoubtedly include women, but this does not mean that Gary is having sex with them or that he is trying to do anything more than look fashionable and striking.

Gary Fordham is also described as a GALLIVANTER. The verb TO GALLIVANT is defined in the *OED* (2nd edn) as 'to gad about in a showy fashion, especially with persons of the opposite sex. Also merely = FLIRT.' On this occasion the word does make reference to being in the company of members of the opposite sex. But the *OED* is quite explicit that the nature of this interaction is quite harmless and equivalent to just 'flirting.' The primary thrust of the word is on being 'showy' and 'gadding about.' It occurs in the sentence "GARY'S STILL QUITE THE GALLIVANTER IN HOLLYWOOD CIRCLES . . . ." Whether anything more will be understood over and above the literal meaning would depend again on the reader's beliefs about Hollywood actors, and about Gary Fordham himself, and would be unsystematic from reader to reader. Nothing is literally asserted, or even implicated, about any sexual relations, therefore.

The most interesting word in the text, and the only one in fact for which a sexual meaning can be seriously proposed, is SWINGING. Gary Fordham is said to lead a SWINGING LIFESTYLE. What exactly does this mean in current English? SWINGING actually has several meanings and uses (i.e. it is an ambiguous word; recall §1.1 and §2.1), many of which would be described as "colloquial" or "slang" and hence limited in the range of users and the range of written and spoken styles in which they occur. The *OED* does not specialize in colloquialisms and slang, so we need to go to other dictionaries devoted to these kinds of words.

One such is Eric Partridge's (1984) *Dictionary of Slang and Unconventional English* (8th edn), which gives entries for SWING, SWINGER, and SWINGING. The adjective SWINGING is defined as 'lively and alert and progressive, with a connotation of success,' and the dictionary refers to an early association with jazz music. SWINGING also has the meanings of the verb TO SWING, which include 'to put to death by hanging . . . To play "swing" music . . . To have the basic feeling for jazz rhythms . . . as in "THESE TIMES ARE MORE SWINGING – livelier . . . whence the term THE SWINGING SIXTIES" . . . .' A further entry then gives the following additional meaning for SWING, SWINGER, and SWINGING: 'To indulge in group sexual activities'; it adds that these terms have 'tended to be applied to married couples (or those who might just as well be) interchanging partners, "wife-swapping."' SWINGING as a verbal noun can then refer to the 'swapping of marital partners in sexual activity.' Clearly, SWINGING does have at least one sense that is of an explicitly sexual nature.

A second dictionary confirmed this, Richard Spears's 1991 *Slang and Euphemism* dictionary (2nd edn), which specializes in "oaths, curses, sexual slang and metaphor, racial slurs, drug talk, homosexual lingo, and related matters." One of the senses of SWING he defines is 'to be involved with sexual fads, group sex, or the swapping of marital partners.' This dictionary also lists a second sexual meaning for SWING: 'To engage in homosexual activities.' This particular meaning seems to be less commonly known than the wife-swapping one, which will be familiar to average readers through magazines and newspapers that advertise wife- and partner-swapping opportunities. Other dictionaries of slang that I consulted in 1992 also gave the 'wife-swapping' sense, including *NTC's Dictionary of American Slang and Colloquial Expressions*, the *Dictionary of Jargon*, the *Third Barnhart Dictionary of New English*, and *The Dictionary of Contemporary Slang*.

It is therefore true, as the plaintiff's language expert noted, that SWINGING has "powerful sexual overtones." But let us examine them in more detail. Would either of the two sexual senses these dictionaries define be activated and appropriate in the Gary Fordham text? In other words, would the average reader understand that Gary was engaged either in homosexual activities or in wife-swapping? The homosexual meaning is clearly out of the question. But equally the text makes no reference to any marital partner that Gary has and that he could potentially be swapping, so even this sense is not strictly applicable in this context.

Richard Spears's *Slang and Euphemism* dictionary makes an important further point about these words. In addition to the wife-swapping sense, the word SWINGER has a very general and benign meaning, he writes, defined as 'a youthful, socially active, and knowledgeable person. Not necessarily with sexual connotations.' This makes it clear that SWINGER has much broader uses than the purely sexual meanings given, as reflected in all the other nonsexual entries defined in these dictionaries. But since the two explicitly sexual senses of SWING, SWINGER, and SWINGING are not directly relevant in this text, the context makes it more appropriate for SWINGING to be understood in a sexually neutral or nonsexual way. Hence Gary Fordham is not necessarily being claimed to have sex with many women in his garden. At most a meaning will be assigned that matches the meaning assigned to the other "suggestive" word used about him, GALLIVANTER, i.e. one who 'gad[s] about in a showy fashion, especially with persons of the opposite sex. Also merely = FLIRT.'

The *Dictionary of Contemporary Slang* makes a further useful observation that supports this weaker, 'gallivanter'-type interpretation for SWINGING, outside of the homosexual and wife-swapping contexts we have mentioned. This dictionary states that SWING can be used as a 'catch-all euphemism for promiscuity.' A "euphemism" occurs when a weaker term is used to suggest, or more technically to implicate, that a stronger one is intended. For example, I might say that I had an interesting INTERACTION with a young lady during the night after I met her at a party, implicating that I had sex with her. Euphemism is like metaphor and irony (recall §1.5) in that it implicates something distinct from the literal meaning of a word, albeit something that is clearly derivable from this meaning in the context in question.

Now, the fact that this dictionary refers to SWINGING as a "euphemism" for 'promiscuity' supports the point that it is generally a mild or vague expression without any necessarily sexual content in its various entries apart from 'homosexuality' and 'wife-swapping.' It gets its sexual explicitness in contexts other than these from the remainder of the text, just like INTERACTION can be enriched and used euphemistically in the example I just gave. So, will the context of the Gary Fordham article force a euphemistic implicature that he is being 'promiscuous' with the women who are visiting him in his garden? No, I argued, because the only word in the article that has any clear sexual meaning is SWINGING itself. Everything else is neutral, innocent, and noncommittal about the nature of Fordham's relationship with the plaintiff, and the two sexually explicit senses of SWINGING are not applicable in this context. If any reader thinks that sexual activity is going on between GF and PK, therefore, this will be because of their independent beliefs about Hollywood actors or about Gary Fordham in particular, or because the second lady in the pictures, not PK, is wearing a bikini and on vacation with Gary, and so on. But a text cannot be held to be offensive or libelous because of the beliefs and opinions that some readers may hold about its content, or because there are pictures not involving the plaintiff herself and not involving Gary Fordham's lush garden that lead them to draw conclusions that are not in, and do not follow from, the text itself. In such a situation it would be just as logical, or illogical, for the plaintiff to sue the readers as the writer!

5.1.3 At the Trial

The plaintiff's language expert did eventually concede in this case that none of their fifteen expressions considered on their own could be said to assert or implicate that there was a sexual liaison between Gary Fordham and Polly Keenan. But their primary argument then focused on "the article as a whole," and they claimed that the meanings and associations of these expressions in combination and in the sequence in (5) would "unambiguously imply" that Gary Fordham was having a sexual relationship with the plaintiff. This line of argumentation became the key point in the trial that ensued, and in the answers that their language expert gave under examination and cross-examination.

The argument that the text as a whole unambiguously implies something that each of its component expressions does not can be problematic, however. Only one of the fifteen expressions has any explicit sexual senses at all, SWINGING, and even these are not directly relevant to Gary Fordham's situation. It is certainly possible for words that are vague with respect to sex, or that have nothing to do with it (like INTERACTION in the example I gave), do implicate "euphemistically" in a particular context that sex is going on. But the context of the Gary Fordham article does not do this either. All these expressions are either innocent or irrelevant with respect to a sexual interpretation, and however many innocent or irrelevant words there are, the effect is still the same: The text as a whole does not suggest or implicate a sexual relationship between GF and PK. Some readers may, as I keep stressing, assign a less innocent interpretation, but this will not be because of the language in the text itself and the accompanying pictures. It will reflect their own personal beliefs. We can only talk of a text implicating some additional, nonliteral meaning when readers can be presumed to be interpreting it this way quite generally and systematically. And whereas some readers may indeed be suspicious of Gary Fordham with respect to Polly Keenan, others will not be, and others still will just not know and will take the text to mean simply what it literally says.

When it came to the trial, the plaintiff's expert appeared first and made his argument about the text as a whole "unambiguously implying" that Gary Fordham was having a sexual relationship with Polly Keenan and with many other women in his garden. I was then brought on to the witness stand by the defense. This was a trial by jury, rather than by a judge alone, and it took place in downtown LA where jury selection draws from a very mixed pool of people, in terms of educational level and standard of living. It is quite a different demographic from the one you would find in, say, Beverly Hills or Santa Monica (see §5.4). I walked up to the stand and was sworn in and before the questioning began I gave a long hard look in the direction of the jury. There was a mix of men and women, mainly men as I recall, several of them looking like they had just come in off the nearby building site. They seemed utterly bored, and tired, and their faces told me that they thought this whole thing was a waste of their time and they didn't want to be there.

For a moment I panicked. There was no way I could present my prepared answers on the differences between literal and nonliteral meanings, between logical entailments versus implicatures, on the role of individual beliefs in interpreting a text, on the precise semantics and lexical definitions for key words, and so on, like I have been presenting them in this book. Many of my students at the elite University of Southern California (USC), at Cambridge University, and at the University of California (Davis, Berkeley, and LA campuses), where I have taught, require several hours of instruction over several weeks to appreciate these kinds of subtleties. I could not possibly delve into these points before this audience, many of whom would not have had any further education beyond high school. In fact, when I think back on it, it is remarkable that something of this nature, involving technicalities from the language sciences, was ever tried before a jury, rather than before a judge, and even with a judge you would have needed one who had at least some background in linguistics or philosophy.

So what did I do? Luckily I was alert that morning and quick on my feet. I tore up my inner script, and in response to the key issue raised by the previous expert's testimony about the text as a whole "implying" a sexual relationship with PK, I thought of an analogy that would be close enough to the linguistic details to make my counterargument comprehensible. Situated in front of me, and clearly visible to the jury, was a small wooden table.

"Ladies and gentlemen of the jury," I said looking directly at them, unsure whether I should be addressing them like this, and indeed whether I should be addressing them at all. "You see this table in front of me, right?" That seemed to get their attention, and their eyes turned to the table.

"There is nothing on this table," I continued. "This table is empty, correct?" They suddenly looked rather puzzled, and I could see them wondering, "Who is this guy? Where is he going with this?"

"In particular," I said, "there are no bananas on this table, right? Zero bananas." A smile broke out on some of their faces, and a chuckle, and I could see they were starting to wake up and pay attention.

"Now," I continued. "You have all been to high school and have had some basic math. So if I add another zero bananas to the zero bananas on the table, how many bananas do we have? Still zero, right?" At this point I was getting their full attention and laughter.

"And if I add yet another zero bananas, it's still zero. In fact, I can go on adding zero bananas to zero bananas plus zero bananas, but it all amounts in the end to the same zero bananas, correct?" They all nodded their agreement, but their amusement became uncontrollable laughter when I added the punchline.

"OK. This is exactly what is going on in this trial. Zero reference to sex, plus zero reference to sex, plus zero reference to sex; it all makes zero reference to sex! There is no reference to sex in this article!"

The whole courtroom erupted at this point, not just the jury, but also my defense lawyers, and even the judge, a lady with an obvious sense of humor, almost fell off her chair. The only people who sat stone-faced and not amused at all were the two lawyers for the plaintiff. Looking back, the reaction I got was all the more extreme because trials like this are often so ponderous and slow-moving, and jurors, and even judges it seems, need a little entertainment and humor. Needless to say the defense won this case and the Gary Fordham article was not deemed libelous to the plaintiff Polly Keenan. When the jurors were interviewed after their verdict and asked why they had decided against her, I was told that they had produced, unanimously, just two words: "ZERO BANANAS."

I shall leave it to readers of the present book to decide whether they agree with my counteranalysis to the plaintiff and whether this analogy was entirely appropriate. It certainly won the case for the defense. It also taught me a lesson for future trial appearances: Try to establish some rapport with your audience, assess their mindset, adjust your testimony to it both in content and in how you present it, understand that their days in court have often been long and tedious, and don't be afraid, whatever the case may be about, to inject a little humor into it. Above all, try to find some parallel examples to the disputed meanings in question, most often parallel examples from the English language that will make clearer the point you are trying to get across (recall my use of INTERACTION above as a euphemism for sex), or give examples from everyday experience or from some subject matter that they do all know about like basic mathematics, as was done here.

The other moral of this story is that it is not straightforward linguistically to show whether a text does, or does not, implicate some additional meaning, over and above its literal meaning, in the minds of readers. The libel case here rested crucially on this additional meaning being of a sexual nature and potentially damaging to the plaintiff. But the linguists involved disagreed, and so we had both a linguistic dispute and a legal dispute. The linguistic dispute was not helped by the fact that one of the experts (my opponent) was not a specialist in any of the areas of the language sciences that were crucially needed in this case, namely in pragmatic meanings and the logic of conversation and inference. Some of the claims made about the associations between "flowers" and "deflowering" in the minds of average readers reflected the rich imagination of a literary critic, rather than a more measured analysis in terms of "relevance theory" (Dan Sperber and Deirdre Wilson's 1995 *Relevance: Communication and Cognition*, 2nd edn, Basil Blackwell, Oxford) and "presumptive meanings" (Stephen C. Levinson, 2000, *Presumptive Meanings*, MIT Press, Cambridge, MA), upon which I based my opposing opinion.

5.2 Spatz and Latinos

In 1998 a political campaign mailer was delivered to registered voters in Southern California who had Hispanic surnames in one of California's senate districts. The mailer was critical of a Democratic Party candidate running for reelection, Robert Spatz (real name changed), and it supported another, Ricardo Alcaraz (again name changed). At issue was whether

Spatz had identified too strongly with the Republican Governor of California at the time, Pete Wilson (real name), in pursuing policies perceived to be anti-immigrant and specifically anti-Latino. Spatz filed a libel suit against the people who had written and distributed the mailer, and I was hired by his lawyers, i.e. by the plaintiff, to give an analysis of how exactly the text would be understood and what it asserted and "implied." Specifically, I was asked to assess whether it conveyed the following information (A)–(C) to readers:

(A) 'Spatz participated in the Republican leaders' 1988 scheme to hire uniformed security guards in order to scare immigrants away from voting.'
(B) 'Spatz approves of and/or participates in Pete Wilson's tactics of scapegoating immigrants and Latinos in order to further his own political purposes.'
(C) 'Spatz was attempting or would attempt to scare or intimidate Latino voters away from voting in the [upcoming June] primary.'

If it did convey this content that would clearly be damaging to the reputation of Robert Spatz, a Democrat. He believed that it did so, the defense disagreed, and so I was brought in to give my assessment and analysis.

The campaign mailer began with the following two sentences, numbered here (6) and (7) (the numbering follows on from the five sentences of the previous section):

(6) [ROBERT SPATZ] ATTACKED THE FIRST LATINO TO BECOME SPEAKER OF THE ASSEMPLY.

(7) NOW SPATZ IS ATTACKING [RICARDO ALCARAZ].

Alcaraz was a prominent Latino politician and one of Spatz's main opponents, ultimately the successful one, in the election for the relevant Senate district seat. These two sentences set up the following clear implicature in the reader's mind (implicatures derived stepwise when reading the mailer sentence by sentence will be given here in roman numerals):

(i) 'Robert Spatz attacks Latino politicians.'

The mailer continues with two sentences that are supportive of Alcaraz, and it then provides the information shown in (8):

(8) TOGETHER, ROBERT SPATZ AND PETE WILSON . . . PUSHED 167,000 YOUNG PEOPLE OUT OF COLLEGE.

CUT AID TO DISABLED, BLIND AND ELDERLY.

From this the reader draws the clear general inference in (ii):

(ii) 'Robert Spatz and Pete Wilson have acted together in pursuing common policies.'

The reader will also recognize that the policies that Spatz and Wilson are claimed to have pursued jointly are of a single type. All the groups referred to, the disabled, the blind, the elderly, and young people in college, are needy and socio-economically underprivileged within our society. They all depend on society as a whole for their well-being. Spatz and Wilson have, we are told, acted against the well-being of these groups, and the language used to describe their actions is unusually forceful. Instead of saying simply that Spatz and Wilson REDUCED COLLEGE ENROLLMENTS, the writer asserts that they "PUSHED" young people out of college. In sentences (6) and (7) Robert Spatz has already been described as "ATTACKING" Latino politicians, rather than ARGUING AGAINST, CRITICIZING, or OPPOSING them. The more specific implicature that will be conveyed by sentence (8) in this context is therefore

(iii) 'Robert Spatz and Pete Wilson have acted jointly and forcefully against socio-economically underprivileged groups and minorities.'

The mailer now continues with

(9) ONE OF PETE WILSON'S REPUBLICAN LEADERS WAS GUILTY IN FEDERAL COURT OF HIRING GUARDS TO SCARE IMMIGRANTS AWAY FROM VOTING.

This sentence makes the claim that a Republican leader was found guilty in a scheme that would be well-known to Latino voters and very much in their collective memory and that involved hiring uniformed security guards to scare immigrants away from voting in the 1988 election, i.e. ten years before this campaign mailer and lawsuit. The Republican leader in question is described as "ONE OF PETE WILSON'S REPUBLICAN LEADERS." Pete Wilson is not standing for election in the year of this campaign mailer, however (1998). The topic of the mailer, i.e. the person against whom it is directed and the person that voters are being encouraged not to support, is Robert Spatz. And this fact alone will lead readers to look for some connection between sentence (9) and Robert Spatz, a member of the normally opposing Democratic Party.

That connection is not hard to find. Sentence (8) has already led to implicature (ii) that 'Robert Spatz and Pete Wilson have acted together in pursuing common policies' and to implicature (iii) that 'Robert Spatz and Pete Wilson have acted jointly and forcefully against socio-economically underprivileged groups and minorities.' Latino immigrants are an underprivileged group and a minority (even more so back in the 1990s than today in 2024). The reader has already drawn the inference that Robert Spatz attacks the leaders of Latino immigrant groups from sentences (6) and (7); see implicature (i). A plausible argument can be made, therefore, that sentence (9) in this context encourages readers to understand that Robert Spatz was also involved with the Republican leaders' 1988 scheme to scare immigrants away from voting.

This inference that Spatz participated in this now infamous and widely known scheme to scare immigrants away from voting is further supported by the last two sentences of the mailer:

(10) DON'T LET WILSON AND SPATZ WIN.

(11) DON'T BE AFRAID TO VOTE.

Sentence (10) reinforces implicatures (ii) and (iii) to the effect that Spatz and Wilson have identical policies and political practices. But Pete Wilson is not running for election in 1998, so the reader has to understand that a victory for Spatz now, who is running, would also be a victory for the policies and practices of Republican Pete Wilson. Sentence (11) then implicates that the people it is addressed to, namely Latino immigrants, have good reason to be afraid to vote, i.e. (iv):

(iv) 'Latinos and immigrants have reason to be afraid to vote.'

This implicature arises from one of the "appropriateness conditions" for the negative imperative speech act in (11) (see John Searle's 1969 *Speech Acts*, Cambridge University Press, Cambridge). Compare DON'T MAKE A NOISE, which is only appropriately uttered when the person it is addressed to is indeed making a noise, and it thereby implicates that this is the case. The speech act itself consists of telling the hearer to stop performing this action.

But why exactly should Latino immigrants be afraid to vote for Robert Spatz, a Democrat, when it was Republicans who were responsible for (and found guilty of) the earlier scheme to hire uniformed security guards to scare immigrants away from voting? The answer is that Robert Spatz is being strongly associated with Pete Wilson and his Republican leaders in this mailer, and he is also being implicated, through a chain of inference in the text, of having participated in this notorious Republican scheme. That is why voters need to be afraid of voting for him now. This inference is supported by the claimed identity between Spatz's policies and practices and those of Republican Pete Wilson (in implicature (ii)), by their common opposition to underprivileged groups and minorities of which the Latino community is one (implicature (iii)), and by Spatz's prior opposition to Latino politicians (implicature (i)). Anyone who has acted this way in the past may do so again, so there is a reason for Latino voters to be afraid, which is confirmed by the use of the negative imperative in (11) (and its implicature (iv)). Sentence (11) accordingly leads to implicature (v):

(v) 'One reason why Latinos and immigrants should be afraid to vote is because Robert Spatz was also involved in the Republican leaders' scheme to hire uniformed security guards in order to scare them away from voting in 1988, and he may do so again.'

In conclusion, we can now answer questions (A)–(C) that were posed at the beginning of this section, which I repeat. Does the campaign mailer convey the information given in (A)?

(A) 'Spatz participated in the Republican leaders' 1988 scheme to hire uniformed security guards in order to scare immigrants away from voting.'

I have argued that it does so, on the basis of implicature (v) that we have just discussed.

Does the mailer convey the information in (B)?

(B) 'Spatz approves of and/or participates in Pete Wilson's tactics of scapegoating immigrants and Latinos in order to further his own political purposes.'

Again I have argued that it does so, because they have been claimed to have a joint political agenda as captured in implicatures (ii), 'Robert Spatz and Pete Wilson have acted together in pursuing common policies,' and (iii), 'Robert Spatz and Pete Wilson have acted jointly and forcefully against socio-economically underprivileged groups and minorities.'

And does the mailer convey the information in (C)?

(C) 'Spatz was attempting or would attempt to scare or intimidate Latino voters away from voting in the [upcoming June] primary.'

Implicature (v) makes it clear that it does so. Hence I argued that all of (A)–(C) are indeed conveyed in this campaign mailer, on the basis of the sequence of implicatures that it leads readers to draw and that I have defined in (i)–(v).

5.3 The Foreign Corrupt Practices Act

A 2014 libel suit (San Francisco) in which I was a rebuttal witness for the defense (which means that my function was to argue against an expert opinion that had already been presented by the plaintiff) highlighted an important general point about the language of libel and defamation. Namely, in assessing whether a text, or in this case the transcript of a public talk, is damaging or not in what it asserts and "implies," you have to look at the whole thing. You cannot selectively pick certain words and sentences that appear to support one side, and ignore those that would cast doubt on, or even argue against, your analysis. The case in question involved a major casino operator, known nationally and internationally, with a presence in Macau. Let's call the casino operator "Moon and Moon Resorts" (name changed). At a public symposium in Berkeley, California, a "Mr. Konos" (again name changed) made certain statements about Moon and Moon Resorts in relation to the Foreign Corrupt Practices Act. According to the complaint filed by the lawyers for Moon and Moon Resorts, Konos "stated that [Moon and Moon Resorts] had violated the Foreign Corrupt Practices Act," and it added, "The Statement is defamatory per se in that it communicates the false message that [Moon and Moon Resorts] acted illegally and in contravention of criminal law by violating the Foreign Corrupt Practices Act."

The difficulty in this case was that, from a linguistic point of view, there was nowhere in the transcript from the symposium that the plaintiff could point to where Mr. Konos could be found actually stating this, i.e. using words and sentences whose literal meanings and logical entailments would amount to 'Moon and Moon Resorts have violated the Foreign Corrupt Practices Act in their Macau casino.' The most that could be said was that this was "implied" by some of the words and sentences that Konos did use, in context. And this was exactly the argument that the plaintiff's language expert used, who opined, "In the context in which they were uttered, the words of Mr. [Konos] would be understood as implying that [Moon] had violated the FCPA." He continued, "Mr. [Konos] implies that [Moon]'s Macau casino is involved in corruption sufficient to warrant indictment under the FCPA."

This lawsuit was another one, therefore, in which inferences and implicatures figured prominently, and this made it essential to look carefully at where these supposedly unstated meanings came from and what they were based on. For example, the plaintiff's linguist cited the following passage from Konos's transcript as supporting the implicature that 'Moon had violated the FCPA':

(12) "I MEAN, THE FACT OF THE MATTER IS . . . THE FOREIGN CORRUPT PRACTICES ACT. . . . IT'S A PRETTY BROAD LAW. ALMOST ANY COMPANY DOING MEANINGFUL AMOUNTS OF BUSINESS IN CHINA PROBABLY COULD BE FOUND IN VIOLATION OF THE FCPA."

But this is a very general, almost "hyperbolic" (i.e. exaggerated) and probability-based statement about the FCPA and its breadth, and the noun phrase ALMOST ANY COMPANY DOING MEANINGFUL AMOUNTS OF BUSINESS IN CHINA refers to a possibly huge number of foreign companies going beyond casinos to companies in general, and beyond Macau to China as a whole. It does not refer specifically to American casino operators such as Moon operating in Macau. The plaintiff's linguist then summarized remarks made by other participants at the symposium.

But what did Konos himself actually say about Moon and Moon Resorts and about US casinos like Moon, in relation to the FCPA and the law more generally? On searching through the transcript as a whole I found just two remarks by Konos that were relevant, and they were very revealing. When talking about US casino operators, including Moon Resorts, Konos produced the following subordinate clause with a subordinating conjunction WHILE in (13) (recall the discussion of subordinate clauses in §1.3 and §4.3), which was then followed by content that I shall comment on presently.

(13) "WHILE THEY [US CASINO OPERATORS, INCLUDING MOON] MIGHT BE ADHERING TO EVERY ASPECT OF LEGAL REQUIREMENTS IN WHAT THEY WERE DOING . . . "

The precise meaning of this WHILE subordinator in combination with the MIGHT modal verb in English is subtle. It sets up a contrast between the state of affairs described in the subordinate clause and some other state of affairs. Consider first a parallel sentence (14) in English:

(14) WHILE MODERN MEDICINE MIGHT BE KEEPING MOST OF US ALIVE FOR LONGER,
IT STILL HAS NOT ELIMINATED MANY FATAL DISEASES.

This conveys the meaning, on the one hand, that 'modern medicine is keeping most of us alive for longer.' But on other hand, all is not for the best: The following main clause asserts that 'there are still many fatal diseases that need to be eliminated.' This contrast results in an implicature that the content of the subordinate clause is true, and yet there is a qualification that needs to be made. The qualification leaves fully intact the truth of the subordinate clause on this occasion. On other occasions the force of the qualification given in the following main clause can be stronger. Consider (15):

(15) WHILE MODERN MEDICINE MIGHT BE BETTER THAN TRADITIONAL MEDICINE, THERE ARE SEVERAL OLDER TREATMENTS THAT WE HAVE FORGOTTEN ABOUT THAT WORK BETTER THAN MODERN PILLS.

The proposition in the subordinate clause here, 'modern medicine is better than traditional medicine,' is now partly denied by the contrasting proposition in the main clause, namely, 'several older treatments work better than modern pills.' The resulting implicature from the sentence as a whole is then that the proposition in the subordinate clause is true in general, but not in all respects, and it needs some qualification.

Back to (13), what exactly is Konos implicating about US casino operators including Moon in relation to their legality? And what is the qualification that follows and that he then says needs to be made? The subordinate clause of (13) considered on its own like this sets up the clear implicature that 'US casino operators, including Moon, are adhering to every aspect of legal requirements.' The qualification that he goes on to give is that they are also engaging in practices that he considers "QUESTIONABLE." And this brings me to the second relevant remark in the transcript in which he reveals why he is unhappy with them. He refers to their practices as "LEGAL FRAUD." FRAUD is a very negative term, a type of 'deception' (recall §2.3.2), and it is often illegal, though not always so as we see here. LEGAL FRAUD is not necessarily a contradiction, therefore. Konos makes it clear that he does not approve of some of the business practices of these US casinos in Macau, but he is quite clear in conveying that they are still "LEGAL." Hence the implicature of the subordinate clause in (13) to the effect that 'US casino operators including Moon are operating within the law' remains intact, in context, and is not impacted by the subsequent qualification.

Now, the present lawsuit was not about whether Konos liked or disliked what Moon and Moon Resorts were doing in Macau in the statements he made at the Berkeley symposium, and whether he approved or disapproved of their business practices (clearly he did not). It had a much narrower focus. It was about the law and the FCPA. At issue was whether "[Moon and Moon Resorts] acted illegally and in contravention of criminal law by violating the Foreign Corrupt Practices Act" (according to the plaintiff's complaint). Since Konos did not use language that actually asserted that 'Moon and Moon Resorts were in violation of the FCPA,' it was vital to look for language that he did use that could be said to implicate content of relevance to the law. One sentence that does this is (13); the phrase LEGAL FRAUD is another. They both make quite clear that Konos was not accusing Moon and Moon Resorts of acting illegally.

Neither of these linguistic points was mentioned in the plaintiff's expert report that I was rebutting. Yet they are clearly relevant to the central issue: Konos was implicating here not that "[Moon] had violated the FCPA," as their language expert claimed, but just the reverse, that 'Moon did not violate the FCPA and adhered to every aspect of legal requirements.'

The moral of this case: A language analyst must be careful not to omit key words and sentences from a text that are potentially relevant for any claimed inferencing process. Once again we had both a linguistic dispute between the language consultants on the two sides and a legal dispute.

5.4 Reporting a New Theory of Bobby Kennedy's Assassination

An interesting linguistic issue was at the center of a libel suit from 1994 (Santa Monica, California) against a tabloid magazine. It involved the "presumption of truth" in everyday speaking and writing, which we first introduced in §1.5 and again in §3.2, and whether the magazine was presenting the content that it was reporting as if it endorsed it and believed it to be true. The content in question was the review of a (then) new book about the assassination of Bobby Kennedy. (This assassination took place back in 1968 in a Los Angeles hotel.) The author of the book, Robert Morrow (real name), claimed that Bobby Kennedy's murderer was not the ultimately convicted Sirhan Sirhan, but the Iranian Secret Police Agency (SAVAK) acting on behalf of the mafia. The real assassin, according to Morrow, was someone posing as a campaign worker for Bobby Kennedy, and this individual was shown (with an arrow clearly pointing him out) standing behind Kennedy in a picture reproduced in the tabloid that was taken just moments before the shooting. Round his neck is what looks like a camera but, in reality, according to Morrow, is a gun. The individual so identified filed suit against the tabloid for presenting Robert Morrow's claims as if they were established fact and as if the magazine also believed them.

What was critical to this case was not whether Robert Morrow's theory was plausible and whether the facts could be said to support it, or whether it was well-argued and convincing and well-written. The book itself was not being sued; the tabloid magazine was. And the focus was on how the tabloid presented and summarized the book. One side in the dispute (the plaintiff) claimed that the tabloid was summarizing the book in such a way as to lead readers to believe that the tabloid writer also believed it and presented it as true. The other side (the defense) argued that the writer was being careful not to do this and was not endorsing it.

This all boils down again to a question of how the English language is being used. And as in the other lawsuits summarized in this chapter, there was nowhere in the text where the writer came flat out and said words to the effect of 'Robert Morrow has written this book and I believe his theory about the assassination of Bobby Kennedy is true' or 'Robert Morrow has written this book and I don't believe a word of it.' We are dealing with inferences again, and with implicatures, and specifically with the "presumption of truth," and with the manner in which the words and phrases selected in the article relate to this presumption. I first devote a subsection (§5.4.1) to the presumption of truth itself and what it means exactly, as a background to a summary of the text itself (§5.4.2). I then give my analysis, in which I present some facts and figures (§5.4.3) of relevance to the central issue: Did the tabloid present Robert Morrow's book in such a way that readers would infer that it was true and that the writer believed it? These facts and figures were presented to the Santa Monica jury in this trial when I was invited to give evidence there, at the request of the defense.

5.4.1 The Presumption of Truth

In John Searle's book *Speech Acts* (Cambridge University Press, Cambridge, 1969), which we first referred to in §2.3.2 and again in §3.2, he discusses different types of speech acts in English, building on John

Austin's *How to Do Things with Words* (Clarendon Press, Oxford, 1962). Searle and Austin pointed out that all speech acts obey certain rules of usage. A speech act like 'commanding someone to do something' (BRING ME THE APPLE) can be made appropriately by, say, a teacher to a student, but not vice versa. Only certain individuals can send thieves to prison, namely judges, and they have to use certain words and meanings when doing so (e.g. I FIND THIS MAN GUILTY). These rules of usage are the "appropriateness conditions" for the speech acts of commanding, judging, refereeing, and so on.

Asserting or declaring something when speaking or writing is also a speech act for Searle and Austin and is similarly subject to conditions of appropriate usage. If a speaker or writer declares e.g.

(16) THE ENGLAND FOOTBALL MANAGER HAS BEEN GIVEN THE SACK,

then the appropriateness conditions that Searle defines for asserting this proposition *p* include "[Speaker] believes *p*.... [Speaker] has evidence (reasons, etc.) for the truth of *p*.... Counts as an undertaking to the effect that *p* represents an actual state of affairs" (Searle 1969, p. 66). In the event that the speaker lacked this evidence about the England football manager, or knew it to be untrue, it would be inappropriate, misleading, or lying to assert it. This is what the "presumption of truth" means. The hearer or reader of (16) infers that it is true and that the speaker or writer believes it to be so.

Everyday statements that we make, whether spoken or written, like "I AM A PROFESSOR AT UC DAVIS" or "SHE HAS A PHD IN LINGUISTICS" or "SIRHAN SIRHAN SHOT BOBBY KENNEDY," are also intended by the speaker or writer, and presumed by the hearer or reader, to be true. And I mentioned in earlier chapters that it is because of this presumption of truth that we have such a thing as "lying." We call someone a liar when a statement is made that is not true and yet the speaker/writer presents it as if it is, simply by following, indeed exploiting, the presumption of truth! It is because there is such a presumption in the normal case that a liar can exploit it and say something that the audience presumes to be true while the speaker/writer knows it to be false.

Now, there are many occasions in everyday language use when we are not sure of the truth of "*p*" in Searle's appropriateness conditions, and we do not want to invoke the presumption and mislead the hearer/reader into believing that "*p*" is necessarily true. And fortunately the English language makes available to us many words and phrases that have precisely this effect of removing the presumption of truth. One such is "modal" verbs (more precisely "epistemic modal" verbs) like MAY, MIGHT, or COULD, exemplified in the sentences of (17):

(17) HE MAY BE A PROFESSOR AT UC DAVIS.
SHE MAY HAVE A PHD IN LINGUISTICS.
SIRHAN SIRHAN MIGHT HAVE SHOT BOBBY KENNEDY.
IT COULD BE THAT SIRHAN SIRHAN SHOT BOBBY KENNEDY.

Another is to use a verb of "reporting" like SOMEONE CLAIMS or MAINTAINS or simply SAYS, as shown in the examples of (18) and (19):

(18) HARRY CLAIMS THAT HE IS A PROFESSOR AT UC DAVIS.
HARRY CLAIMS THAT SUSAN HAS A PHD IN LINGUISTICS.
HARRY CLAIMS THAT SIRHAN SIRHAN SHOT BOBBY KENNEDY.

(19) HARRY MAINTAINS THAT SIRHAN SIRHAN SHOT BOBBY KENNEDY.
HARRY SAYS THAT . . . .
HARRY SUGGESTED THAT . . . .
HARRY ARGUED THAT . . . .
HARRY CHARGED THAT . . . .

These modal and reporting verbs can be called "disclaimers." It is presumed to be true that Harry did indeed claim or say these things (and the speaker/writer would be lying if Harry did not do so), but no claim is made about the content of the claim following MAY/MIGHT etc. and the subordinate clause after THAT. As far as the speaker/writer and listener/reader are concerned, Harry 'may or may not be a professor at UC Davis' in (17), Susan 'may or may not have a PhD in linguistics,' and Sirhan Sirhan 'may or may not have shot Bobby Kennedy' in (18) and (19).

Notice that these disclaimers do not necessarily assert that the content that is disclaimed is untrue. The subordinate clauses of (18) and (19), for example, merely report a claim to which the speaker presents himself or herself as being neutral, i.e. these sentences say nothing (and are "vague"; recall §1.1 and §2.2) about whether the speaker/writer believes the content of the claim in question. The hearer/reader accordingly understands that the speaker/writer is neutral and that the presumption of truth is no longer invoked.

In written English there is another important device, of punctuation this time, that can serve as a disclaimer, in addition to or instead of these verbs: "quotation marks."

(20) "I AM A PROFESSOR AT UC DAVIS," SAID HARRY.
"I AM A PROFESSOR AT UC DAVIS."

Quotation marks, verbs of reporting, and modal verbs are all "disclaimers," therefore, and they remove the presumption of truth. The speaker/writer is not lying if the content of the disclaimer, the subordinate clauses in (18) and (19), the material in quotation marks in (20), and the material under the "scope" of the modal verb in (17) turn out to be false. This is because the speaker/writer never claimed that it was true to begin with. But the speaker/writer would be lying if, for example, Harry never made the claims in (18) and (19) and the material in quotation marks in (20) was never uttered.

5.4.2 *The Text of the Disputed Article*

The article began with the title and subtitle shown in (21). The title was in bold, and the subtitle in large bold capitals, as reproduced here:

(21) **Former CIA agent claims: IRANIANS KILLED BOBBY KENNEDY FOR THE MAFIA.**

There were seventeen short paragraphs that followed, plus one that served as a caption for two photographs, the first (the larger one) showing Bobby Kennedy moments before he was shot with several campaign workers standing behind him, the second showing a picture of Sirhan Sirhan. I show the first four paragraphs in full here in (22)–(25), in order to give a flavor of the writing, and converting the words and sentences in these paragraphs from their normal mix of small and capital letters to consistently capital letters, as is done throughout this book:

(22) BOBBY KENNEDY WAS ASSASSINATED BY AN IRANIAN SECRET POLICE HIT SQUAD UNDER ORDERS FROM THE MAFIA, A FORMER CIA AGENT CHARGES.

(23) DRAMATIC NEW EVIDENCE REVEALS THAT CONVICTED KILLER SIRHAN SIRHAN WAS MERELY A DECOY, SAYS ROBERT MORROW, AUTHOR OF THE

SENATOR MUST DIE; THE MURDER OF ROBERT F. KENNEDY (ROUNDTABLE).

(24) MORROW CLAIMS THE MAFIA ENGINEERED THE MURDER OF PRESIDENT JOHN F. KENNEDY, THEN ORDERED HIS BROTHER KILLED FIVE YEARS LATER BECAUSE THEY FEARED HE WOULD RENEW JFK'S WAR AGAINST ORGANIZED CRIME IF HE BECAME PRESIDENT.

(25) "INCREDIBLY, THE MOB HIRED THE NOTORIOUS IRANIAN SECRET POLICE AGENCY, SAVAK, TO DO THE JOB," HE SAYS.

Thirteen further paragraphs in this vein then followed, elaborating on Morrow's theory about the murder of Bobby Kennedy and why and how it happened. These thirteen plus the four in (22)–(25), plus the title and subtitle in (21) and the caption to the pictures, made nineteen paragraphs in all.

It can be readily seen that the title and subtitle in (21) contains a verb of reporting, CLAIMS, i.e. there is a disclaimer right at the outset about what the former CIA agent is proposing in his book, and a neutral stance is taken by the tabloid to its truth or falsity. The first sentence of the text, (22), uses another verb of reporting, CHARGES, and again indicates a neutral stance. The second sentence, (23), gives a third verb of reporting, SAYS, and the third sentence, (24), uses CLAIMS again, both verbs corroborating the neutral stance of the writer. The fourth paragraph shown here, (25), puts quotation marks round the words of the author; plus it uses SAYS again.

In each of the sentences (21)–(25), therefore, the tabloid writer was careful to use either a verb of reporting or quotation marks or both when reproducing the words and claims made by author Robert Morrow. There was no sentence or wording here that was not embedded under or within one of these disclaimers that would lead the reader to think that these were the words and claims of the writer. If these paragraphs were typical of the full nineteen in the text, then the libel suit against the tabloid would have no basis in language usage: The writer would not be presenting these claims as claims that the tabloid endorsed. It turned out that all nineteen paragraphs were indeed of this nature. Every single one of them contained at least one disclaimer like this, and when a paragraph contained more than one proposition or claim, each one of them contained a disclaimer as well.

Hence the tabloid did not present any of the claims by Robert Morrow with the presumption of truth, in such a way that would lead readers to think that the tabloid was endorsing them.

5.4.3 *Facts and Figures*

Altogether, there were nineteen paragraphs in this article, as we have seen, including the heading (21) and the photo caption. Every single one of them contained either a verb of reporting or quotation marks, or both. In other words, the tabloid's neutrality to the claims made by Robert Morrow in his book was stressed in every single paragraph. The figures are given in (26):

(26)	Paragraphs containing a verb of reporting alone	=	12
	Paragraphs containing a verb of reporting plus quotes	=	5
	Paragraphs containing quotes alone	=	2
	Total	=	19

Some of these paragraphs were longer than others and summarized more than one claim made by Robert Morrow. So, in the first paragraph, (22), there is just a single claim being made about Bobby Kennedy being 'assassinated by an Iranian hit squad under orders from the Mafia.' But in the third paragraph (24) there were two claims being reported, the first about John F. Kennedy, and the second about his brother Bobby, as shown in (24'):

(24') MORROW CLAIMS THAT [1ST THE MAFIA ENGINEERED THE MURDER OF PRESIDENT JOHN F. KENNEDY], [2ND THEN ORDERED HIS BROTHER KILLED FIVE YEARS LATER BECAUSE THEY FEARED HE WOULD RENEW JFK'S WAR AGAINST ORGANIZED CRIME IF HE BECAME PRESIDENT].

Within the nineteen paragraphs there were now twenty-four propositions made in total like this, i.e. more than the number of paragraphs. Remarkably, every single one of these propositions was either qualified by (i.e. under the semantic scope of) a verb of reporting or in quotes, as shown in (27):

(27)	Propositions qualified by a verb of reporting alone	=	16
	Propositions qualified by a verb of reporting plus quotes	=	5
	Propositions containing quotes alone	=	3
	Total	=	24

Again, the tabloid's neutrality to the claims made in Robert Morrow's book was stressed in every single proposition made within the nineteen paragraphs of the article.

Among the verbs of reporting, the most frequently used was SAYS (ten times), followed by CLAIMS (four times), and then by the following occurring once each: CHARGES, REVEALS, ADDS, and EXPLAINS. The amount of text in quotation marks was considerable. There were ninety-four lines in total in the article, of which thirty-two were within quotation marks, i.e. a full third.

The linguistic details in this dispute were overwhelmingly in favor of the defense, therefore, i.e. the tabloid newspaper. This was not a case in which I needed to lose much sleep worrying about whether my analysis was right or not. Clearly the newspaper did not present Robert Morrow's claims in a way that would lead readers to believe that the tabloid was endorsing them: No presumption of truth about these claims was made in any of its paragraphs or propositions. I was also helped at the trial in Santa Monica by a very attentive and clearly committed set of jurors, mostly older women as I recall. They were all taking notes avidly, and nodding their agreement, as I presented these facts and figures. Needless to say, the defense prevailed.

5.5 Suggestive Terms in Trademark Law

Inferencing is an important part of the everyday understanding of terms in trademark law that are classified as "suggestive" (recall §1.5 and §3.4.1), as a result of which they can serve as an appropriate proper name for the product or service in question. In §1.5 I discussed a paradigm example, ROACH MOTEL, a "suggestive" trademark for an insect trap made by a particular manufacturer. (By the way, I have personally used these insect traps in my house in Northern California – I selected this brand precisely because it's a paradigm case of a suggestive trademark, and they work beautifully!)

The borderline between suggestive marks and descriptive ones is often legally contentious, especially for word combinations and compounds. A term can still be a trademark if descriptiveness with secondary meaning is proven, as we have mentioned, in which case the manufacturer is quite happy and can keep on using the term, regardless of its classification. But from a linguistic perspective we need more precision on the grammar, semantics, and processing mechanisms that are activated in these cases, and in particular we need to better understand what exactly makes a term "suggestive."

In the ROACH MOTEL compound, the head noun MOTEL is defined in dictionaries as an establishment that exists for humans only, not for animals and certainly not for insects. Hence MOTEL does not apply to roaches, and the combination ROACH MOTEL is semantically incongruous. By inference, we try to make sense of the incongruity, using our knowledge of the real world, on this occasion our knowledge about insects and pests and pest removal, and we reason that the establishment in question is one that does for roaches what we all want to do with them, namely get rid of them by trapping them. Hence, a contextual inference, involving knowledge of the world in combination with linguistic knowledge, enables us to apply the term ROACH MOTEL to something that it does not literally describe, namely an insect trap. The genius of suggestive terms lies precisely in this reasoning process.

In the remainder of this chapter I discuss the case of PERSONAL POST OFFICE brought before the Trademark Trial and Appeal Board (TTAB) first in 1999 and then again in 2007, both litigations in Los Angeles. The registration of this term as a trademark was first refused by the TTAB, but later this decision was reversed and the manufacturer was permitted to use PERSONAL POST OFFICE as a mark for its product: a small handheld scale for weighing letters up to four ounces that enabled users to know which postage stamps to put on their letters. I was a consultant and expert witness for the plaintiff, who wanted to carry on using this term as a trademark and who eventually succeeded in doing so. In what follows I first give a brief summary of suggestiveness in trademark law (§5.5.1). I discuss the linguistic arguments that can be made, and were made, for the suggestiveness of this mark (§5.5.2–3), and I then consider some of the counterarguments made to its registration by language experts for the defense (§5.5.4).

5.5.1 *Suggestiveness*

When considering trademark law (recall §3.4.1) we need to return once again to the grandfather of the field, Thomas McCarthy, this time using his 1999 edition of *McCarthy on Trademarks and Unfair Competition* (4th edn, West Group, Saint Paul, Minnesota). His basic pronouncement on suggestiveness is that "A term is suggestive if it requires imagination, thought and perception to reach a conclusion as to the nature of the goods" (McCarthy 1999, §11-110). Typical examples that he gave are GOBBLE

GOBBLE processed turkey meat, HABITAT home furnishings, and the ROACH MOTEL insect trap that we have just discussed (McCarthy 1999, §11-123/125).

McCarthy stresses that the borderline between suggestive and descriptive terms (recall §3.3) is highly significant legally, since source identification and trademark status is automatically guaranteed by the former but not by the latter, unless lawyers and linguists and professional survey consultants go through the sometimes elaborate and expensive procedure of proving "secondary meaning." And yet, McCarthy acknowledges, the linguistic basis for the distinction is sometimes difficult, and this is why outside linguistic expertise is frequently sought.

McCarthy, with his keen awareness of matters of language (remember I said he would have made a good linguist!), offers some helpful tests and guidelines for lawyers and linguists alike (McCarthy 1999, §11-109 through §11-120). One of these is the "degree of imagination" test: "The more imagination that is required on the customer's part, the more likely the term is suggestive, not descriptive" (McCarthy 1999, §11-109). "If one must exercise 'mature thought or follow a multi-stage reasoning process' to determine attributes of the product or service, the term is suggestive, not descriptive.... If the mental leap between the word and the product's attributes is not almost instantaneous, this strongly indicates suggestiveness, not descriptiveness" (McCarthy 1999, §11-111). It is precisely because of this multistage reasoning process that we are considering suggestive marks in this chapter on linguistic inferencing, and we shall give a detailed example of what exactly the different stages in reasoning are for PERSONAL POST OFFICE (in §5.5.3).

Any inherent "incongruity" in a phrase is a further "strong indicator of suggestiveness" (McCarthy 1999, §11-111), as in ROACH MOTEL again, which he mentions in this connection (McCarthy 1999, §11-111, footnote 7).

A further test is the competitors' need test:

> The more imagination that is required to associate a mark with the product, the less likely the words used will be needed by competitors to describe their products.... If, however, the message conveyed by the mark about the goods or services is so direct and clear that competing sellers would be likely to need to use the term in describing or advertising their goods, then this indicates the mark is descriptive. (McCarthy 1999, §11-112/113)
>
> A more realistic way to pose the question is to ask whether, without any prior knowledge of [the] mark, others would be likely to want to use it to describe their products? (McCarthy 1999, §11–119)

A related issue has to do with the generality or vagueness of a term and its compatibility with many kinds of entities (recall in this connection §1.1 and §2.2): "Even though the mark may tell something about the goods or services, is it just as likely to conjure up some other, purely arbitrary connotation? E.g. SUGAR & SPICE baked goods . . . " (McCarthy 1999, §11-120).

5.5.2 *The Grammar and Semantics of PERSONAL POST OFFICE*

PERSONAL POST OFFICE is grammatically a noun phrase in which PERSONAL is a modifying adjective and both POST and OFFICE are nouns. There are two phrasal groupings or attachments that are possible in principle (recall §4.1). In the first, POST and OFFICE combine together into a compound noun that is modified by PERSONAL, i.e. [PERSONAL [POST OFFICE]]. In the second, PERSONAL modifies POST, and that combination in turn modifies OFFICE, i.e. [[PERSONAL POST] OFFICE]. The meaning in this latter case would be 'an office for personal post.' Compare, for example, [[PERSONAL DIARY] SHOP], which means 'a shop selling personal diaries.'

The preferred word grouping that readers will assign is the first one, [PERSONAL [POST OFFICE]]. There are two reasons for this. First, the lexical combination POST OFFICE is extremely common in English and will be well-known to all readers since post offices are so numerous and such important parts of our everyday lives. This is reflected in the fact that dictionaries, which as we have shown previously list word combinations only when there is good reason to do so (because of their non-compositionality or high frequency), routinely give a separate entry for POST OFFICE. Second, although we do refer to our PERSONAL POST, we do not normally have a special office for it, and this greatly reduces the likelihood of the second parsing, [[PERSONAL POST] OFFICE]. Hence the first parsing is favored, the second is disfavored, and so the first will be selected. The meaning assigned to the whole phrase is accordingly the product of combining the meaning of PERSONAL with that of POST OFFICE.

The principal meanings of POST OFFICE are defined in the *American Heritage Dictionary of the English Language* (3rd edn, Houghton Mifflin Company, Boston, 1992) as follows:

‘1. The public department responsible for the transportation and delivery of the mails.. . .
2. A local office where mail is received, sorted, and delivered, and where stamps and other postal materials are sold.’

Webster’s Third New International Dictionary of the English Language Unabridged (Merriam-Webster, Springfield, Massachusetts, 1993) gives the following paraphrases and illustrative uses (in angled brackets <. . .>):

> ‘1a : a government department charged with regulating and handling the transmission of mail in a country . . .
> b : a section of a post office department handling the mail for a particular place (as a city or town) . . .
> c : (1) a building or a section of a building housing facilities and staff for carrying out all or some of the functions of a post-office department . . .
> d : a place where mail is handled for dispatch and delivery <a camp *post office*> <a university *post office*>.’

The principal meanings for PERSONAL are defined in the *American Heritage Dictionary* as

> ‘1. Of or relating to a particular person; private . . . ;
> 2 a. Done, made, or performed in person . . . b. Done to or for or directed toward a particular person . . .
> 3. Concerning a particular person and his or her private business, interests, or activities . . . .’

Webster’s Third New International Dictionary lists the following principal meanings for it:

> ‘1 : of or relating to a particular person: affecting one individual or each of many individuals: peculiar or proper to private concerns; not public or general . . .
> 2 a : done in person without the intervention of another . . . .’

There is a further semantic property of PERSONAL that is associated with its syntactic use as an adjective. Compare e.g. MY PERSONAL ZOO with THE ZOO I USE PERSONALLY (when I want to see wild animals). The former, with the adjective, means ‘the zoo for my exclusive private use’ or ‘the zoo that I own.’ The latter, with the adverb PERSONALLY, means only ‘the zoo that I use myself, whereas others may use a possibly different zoo.’ The meaning of the adjective is ‘exclusive,’ the meaning of the adverb is merely ‘comparative,’ comparing me as an individual and my practices to those of others, which may or may not overlap with my own.

The dictionary definitions and the syntactic point just mentioned about the adjective versus the adverb and their respective meanings make it clear that the meaning of PERSONAL as an adjective is 'private and not public,' and this explicitly contradicts the 'public' or 'government' aspect of the meaning of POST OFFICE. The combined phrase PERSONAL POST OFFICE cannot receive a normal literal interpretation, therefore, on account of this contradiction, and language users will need to apply what we will show presently is a multistage reasoning process in order to make sense of it and understand what it refers to. The chain of reasoning involves searching for relevant interpretations, or metaphorical extensions, that avoid the contradiction between the public and private components of these respective meanings.

The dictionary definitions for POST OFFICE also make clear that this compound evokes a building and a service. Everyone who enters a post office wants to send mail, or buy stamps in order to send mail, or sometimes receive mail. The handheld letter scale is neither a public institution nor a building; it does not provide these services, and it is not a personal substitute for a public institution that does. On the other hand, some customers in a post office will need to have their mail weighed, especially when they are sending parcels or other heavier items. The kind of large, flat surface scale that is generally used for this purpose is again different from the small handheld letter scale. And in order to apply the phrase PERSONAL POST OFFICE to the letter scale, language users will have to extend its meaning far beyond the physical characteristics of a post office, and beyond its functional characteristics, to an activity that is secondary to the primary task of sending mail. Applying the term PERSONAL POST OFFICE to the handheld letter scale with its weight limit of four ounces involves an abandonment or extension of the literal meaning of either PERSONAL or POST OFFICE, therefore, combined with reasoning and inference. The mental leap from these words to the product's attributes will be anything but instantaneous, all of which indicates suggestiveness rather than descriptiveness.

Another of McCarthy's criteria for suggestiveness, the generality or vagueness of the term and its compatibility with many other entities than the one that the suggestive term refers to, is also relevant here. In a LexisNexis and Westlaw search of periodicals (conducted in 1999) I found PERSONAL POST OFFICE being used in reference to answering machines for a telephone, to electronic mail servers that collect and distribute mail, and to private mailboxes at a post office. These are all attempts to make the primary function of a post office (viz. sending and receiving mail) compatible with an individual's mailing needs. Other metaphorical meanings of PERSONAL POST OFFICE included extensions to a car that performed postal services, even to a basket in a basketball game in which there was a player named "THE MAILMAN" who delivered lots of balls to it, and to a quarterback in football who delivered messages to the team. All these meanings involve thought, imagination, and reasoning to link the words with the entities they refer to. They are all attempts to give meaning and reference to words that are incongruous in combination, i.e. when considered as a whole (which is something that trademark law and the TTAB insist on). And their sheer diversity is evidence against mere descriptiveness, by McCarthy's criteria. PERSONAL POST OFFICE conveys no immediate idea of the "ingredients, qualities or characteristics of the goods" (recall §5.5.1).

5.5.3 *The Multi-Stage Reasoning Process*

We have seen that PERSONAL POST OFFICE has been used to refer to entities far removed from post offices, such as a basket in basketball and a quarterback in football. The plaintiff's product in this case, the small handheld letter scale, is also not a post office, but it is linked suggestively to what a real post office does. The chain of reasoning that is activated when PERSONAL POST OFFICE is used in relation to the plaintiff's product must try to make sense of this composite phrase in this usage, by linking it to the general functions that are performed by real post offices and to the properties of this particular product, the handheld letter scale.

The actual steps involved in this reasoning processing, when we make them explicit, are more numerous than one might think. I begin in (a)–(d) by enumerating the basic steps involved in assigning lexical meanings, grammatical structure, and combinatorial meanings to PERSONAL POST OFFICE. In other words, (a)–(d) define the initial "parsing" operations involved. For readers of the present book who want some general background to the grammar and semantics of English that underlies these parsings, consult a good introductory textbook to linguistics such as William O'Grady, John Archibald, Mark Aranoff, and Janie-Rees-Miller's 2001 *Contemporary Linguistics: An Introduction*, as listed in §1.7.

Then, in (i)–(xii) I set out no fewer than twelve stages that are required for language users to reason their way to the intended meaning and reference for PERSONAL POST OFFICE, given the initial parsings in (a)–(d). In defining these stages I follow standard rules of reasoning from classical logic, as summarized in any good logic textbook, such as

E. J. Lemmon's 1972 *Beginning Logic* (Hackett Publishing, Indianapolis), and as these are employed in pragmatic theories such as Dan Sperber and Deirdre Wilson's 1995 *Relevance: Communication and Cognition* (2nd edn, Basil Blackwell, Oxford). Sperber and Wilson incorporate logical reasoning into their theory of natural language use and conversation, thereby providing a particularly appropriate model for describing the mental inferencing that takes place in a case like this.

Users of English first assign the following lexical and grammatical properties to PERSONAL POST OFFICE in its initial parse:

(a) Recognize the individual words, PERSONAL, POST and OFFICE and assign grammatical parts of speech and lexically listed meanings to each: PERSONAL is an adjective, POST is a noun, OFFICE is a noun, [POST OFFICE] is a lexically listed compound noun; lexical meanings are those aspects of word and compound meaning defined in dictionaries, as illustrated in §5.5.2.
(b) Assign the overall phrase type Noun Phrase (NP) and the preferred syntactic parsing, namely PERSONAL combines with [POST OFFICE] to give the overall phrase [np PERSONAL [POST OFFICE]]. The preference for this parsing over [np [PERSONAL POST] OFFICE] was summarized in §5.5.2.
(c) Assign the additional semantic property to PERSONAL associated with its syntactic use as an adjective, 'unique to the individual in question,' recall MY PERSONAL ZOO in §5.5.2.
(d) Attempt to assign a meaning to the whole phrase [np PERSONAL [POST OFFICE]] by combining together ("compositionally") the meanings of the constituent parts [PERSONAL] and [POST OFFICE].

It is at step (d) in the parse that the multistage reasoning process begins, triggered by a failure to find a clear and literal combined meaning for [np PERSONAL [POST OFFICE]]. The nature of this product is not straightforward for language users, as a result of the contradiction between its parts. We can define the following mental steps that speakers have to go through, therefore, in order to link this phrase with this product:

[i] Recognize the contradiction between the 'public' component in the lexical meaning of POST OFFICE and the 'private,' 'non-public,' and 'exclusive' components of meaning in PERSONAL.
[ii] Reason that either POST OFFICE or PERSONAL does not have its literal meaning, and initiate the search for a possible and relevant interpretation.

[iii] Access what is known about the product, including

(1) it is a handheld letter scale that weighs items up to four ounces; and
(2) the handheld letter scale informs users of the appropriate postage amount by means of a separate information card containing postage rates.

[iv] Reason that such an entity is not a 'public department responsible for the transportation and delivery of the mails,' not a 'local office' of this public department, nor any 'place where mail is handled for dispatch and delivery,' as exemplified in English usages such as <a camp *post office*> and <a university *post office*>, and does not involve any 'transportation and delivery of the mails.'

[v] Conclude that none of the literal meanings of POST OFFICE given in §5.5.2 applies to this entity.

[vi] Reason that the literal meaning of PERSONAL given in the definitions of §5.5.2 may still apply to this entity.

[vii] Extend and/or amend the lexical properties of POST OFFICE to render them compatible with this entity and, if possible, with the literal meaning of PERSONAL.

[viii] Reason that some form of postal-related business and service may nonetheless be relevant for the interpretation of this phrase.

[ix] Access general and encyclopedic knowledge about the postal business and about postal services, including

(1) the collection, transmission, and distribution of mail requires payment for services;
(2) payment is indicated on postal items by means of stamps;
(3) selection of the appropriate payment requires weighing the items to be mailed;
(4) the weight must then be matched with a particular postage rate that is required in a particular place or country and at a particular time;
(5) stamps must then be purchased and affixed to the postal item.

[x] Apply knowledge of the particular features of the handheld letter scale in [iii] to the general and encyclopedic knowledge about the postal business and services in [ix]. Specifically, recognize the match between properties [iii] (1) and (2), pertaining to the letter scale, and properties [ix] (3) and (4) drawn from general and encyclopedic

knowledge. The match involves the need for weighing and calculation of the appropriate postage amount.

[xi] Infer that [np PERSONAL [POST OFFICE]] is used to suggest reference to the handheld letter scale, by a significant extension from the literal meaning of POST OFFICE and its adaptation to the properties of the small handheld letter scale.

[xii] Infer that the entity is indeed for private and exclusive use, in accordance with the literal meaning of the adjective PERSONAL; recall §5.5.2.

5.5.4 *Counterarguments to Suggestiveness*

In 1997 the manufacturer of the handheld letter scale had applied to register the term PERSONAL POST OFFICE with the TTAB. The registration was initially refused, as I mentioned previously, on the grounds that the term was "merely descriptive." This refusal was then reversed in 2004, citing inter alia a 1999 report of mine that included some of the arguments I have just summarized here in favor of suggestiveness. The TTAB now concurred that "several steps are required to move from the combined term PERSONAL POST OFFICE to an understanding of the nature of the applicant's goods," making this a term that is not merely descriptive. Items [i]–[xii], given above, lay out what these various steps are exactly.

It is instructive in the present context, where we are discussing the legal boundary between descriptiveness and suggestiveness, to consider the linguistic arguments that were made against (in 1997) and then for registration (in 2004). The 2004 TTAB reversal summarized the earlier refusal by the then Examining Attorney as being based on the argument that PERSONAL is "descriptive of the identified goods because applicant's scales are small in size and designed for home or small office use," while POST OFFICE is descriptive "because the use of scales to weigh letters and packages is a typical function of the U.S. Post Office." The identified goods were accordingly of a "personal nature" and "provide[d] a Post Office function." The Examining Attorney in 2004 argued against this stating that PERSONAL POST OFFICE was "an incongruous term" and required "a multistage reasoning process."

A second linguistic bone of contention in the refusal versus reversal arguments by the TTAB concerned whether PERSONAL POST OFFICE "falsely suggest[s] a connection with the U.S. Postal Service." The 1997 refusal argued that POST OFFICE was very similar to "United States Post Office" and that consumers would make this connection and would believe that the handheld letter scale was one of the many additional products that the US Post Office sells in addition to stamps. The 2004 reversal argued instead that POST OFFICE does not "uniquely identify the U.S. Postal Service." In support of this, linguistic evidence was presented showing website links to official POST OFFICE sites in sixty-two different countries, along with copies of six trademark registrations for other composite terms containing POST OFFICE, none of which referred to products made or authorized by the US Postal Service. Hence, "it cannot be said that POST OFFICE points uniquely to the U.S. Postal Service." And while

> "Post Office" . . . is highly descriptive or generic of registrant's services . . . the remaining parts of applicant's . . . mark are different and when these different components are combined with the term POST OFFICE, the marks in their entireties [i.e. POST OFFICE and PERSONAL POST OFFICE] are not so similar that they would be likely to cause confusion when used in connection with the respective goods and services. (TTAB 2004 reversal)

The Examining Attorney in 2004 accordingly reversed the earlier refusal from 1997, and PERSONAL POST OFFICE became a legitimate trademark for the handheld letter scale. This was not the end of the story, however. The reversal was challenged in 2007, and the US Postal Service became involved as well. The US Postal Service retained a language expert, and a further report of mine was written in 2007 critiquing their language expert's opinion, with my counterarguments presented in a deposition. The parties came to an agreement at the end of that year and before trial, with PERSONAL POST OFFICE remaining as a valid trademark. The linguistic arguments over POST OFFICE raised some interesting general issues about reference and the unique identification of entities, which is the topic of the next chapter, so I shall return to this aspect of PERSONAL POST OFFICE there (in §6.1) and conclude this section on suggestiveness in trademark law here.

CHAPTER 6

Disputes over Reference and Unique Identification

Lawsuits can arise over who or what exactly certain noun phrases refer to, which people or entities in the world they pick out and evoke in the minds of language users, and how they achieve this reference. We have already seen disputes in trademark litigation over whether a term like APP STORE refers uniquely to the product of one particular company or whether it refers to lots of similar products on the basis of its common descriptive (and legally "generic") meaning; recall §3.4. If a term like HALF PRICE BOOKS is classified as "descriptive," then a "secondary meaning" has to be proven for it to be a trademark, showing that there is a second usage that clearly identifies a unique provider separate from all the others being described (see §3.5). In fact, from a linguistic perspective the legal term "secondary meaning" is a misnomer: a better label would be "secondary reference," since in this secondary usage these terms function like proper names JOHN and SUSIE in relation to what they refer to, and proper names do not have meaning as such but they do have reference. The suggestive and other terms lower on McCarthy's hierarchy (recall §3.3) that qualify straightforwardly for trademark status achieve their unique and source-identifying reference either through inference and an extension of their literal meanings (§5.5), as with ROACH MOTEL, or by functioning like the proper names JOHN and SUSIE as with ("arbitrary") APPLE and ("fanciful") KODAK. All valid trademarks achieve their unique identification by these respective means. The invalid ones ("generic" terms and "descriptive" ones with no secondary meaning or reference) refer to more general classes of entities on the basis of their semantic properties.

In the language sciences a key distinction is made between "sense" and "reference," as we discussed this in §2.4.3. The sense of a term is its general meaning that makes it available to users so they can refer to people and entities that have the semantic properties associated with their dictionary definitions. This is how generic and descriptive terms operate and refer to classes of entities in the world and to more or fewer of them on different occasions, depending on how detailed the linguistic description is in the noun phrase in question and depending on the context of utterance. Unique identification of one particular entity, on the other hand, requires some special and different "mapping" (as we call it) between the forms of language and what they refer to in the world. In the extreme cases we have the arbitrary and fanciful links between APPLE and KODAK and their respective companies. These involve the greatest departures from any basic sense that these terms might have. (APPLE computers have nothing to do with APPLE 'the fruit,' and KODAK has no sense at all.) A less extreme departure from a basic and literal sense is the "suggestive" extension of ROACH MOTEL to its producer. And the least departure of all is seen in secondary references for descriptive terms like HALF PRICE BOOKS, for which one provider of the products so described may have achieved particular salience among consumers.

Linguistic issues that arise in distinguishing generic from descriptive, and descriptive from suggestive, can be quite subtle, as we saw in §3.3 and §5.5 respectively, and this then leads to legal disputes over the legitimacy of a trademark and unfair competition. The key linguistic issue is then: Is the reference that a linguistic term (word or phrase) has one of unique identification by one of the means we have seen with APPLE (computers), KODAK, ROACH MOTEL, and HALF PRICE BOOKS? Or is the reference a more general one to possibly multiple entities on the basis of the "sense" of this term?

There is often confusion, I have found, in the linguistic reasoning that has been invoked in trademark litigation to back up certain legal arguments. Recall e.g. the arguments over the unique identification of Apple versus generic usage in APP STORE (§3.4). I will argue in §6.1 that a similar confusion arose in the PERSONAL POST OFFICE case (recall §5.5) and in the US Postal Service's (USPS's) objection to the use of POST OFFICE in this mark on the grounds that POST OFFICE was supposedly a source identifier for the USPS. It is crucial here to establish what exactly the "sense" of POST OFFICE is and what it then refers to on the basis of this sense. This compound is not, in fact, a unique identifier of the USPS. By way of contrast I discuss in §6.2 the trademark ELASTIC, which can be readily shown, on overwhelming empirical grounds, to have a clear and unique identification of the service provider in question, which is quite distinct from the other senses and uses that are associated with this word (just like APPLE referring to 'the relevant company' is quite distinct from APPLE 'the fruit'). The next section (§6.3) examines the case of BLUE BOOK, which is shown on the basis of both dictionary and usage evidence to have lost its original and unique reference to the Kelley Blue Book Company Inc. and its periodically issued price list for used cars. Instead this term has undergone "genericide" (just like THERMOS and XEROX did) and is now widely used with the general meaning of any price list, not only for used cars but for all kinds of other objects and appliances as well.

In §6.4 I turn to a further aspect of reference that has been much discussed in linguistics and the philosophy of language involving certain linguistic devices, like the little word THE in combination with nouns, and how they achieve their reference and unique identification in different contexts of usage. In particular, a lawsuit can arise, and has arisen, over what exactly and who exactly a definite noun phrase like THE POLICE refers to, and over the role of the speaker's and hearer's "mutual knowledge" in understanding its reference. A distinction is made in the philosophy of language between "referential" and "attributive" uses of such phrases: They both involve "reference" on the basis of their "sense," but the former refers to individuals who are mutually known and identifiable to speaker and hearer, the latter to the police force in general and their members, whoever they might be. This can make a big difference when "THE POLICE" stand accused of certain crimes. Is it the police force in general that people are talking about (the attributive use), or are certain individuals, say Masters and James, who are known independently to speakers and hearers, being picked out and identified when "THE POLICE" is uttered (the referential use)? In this latter case these individuals would stand accused of the crimes in question and suffer reputational damage.

6.1 Sense and Reference in POST OFFICE

The litigation that I summarized at the end of the last chapter (§5.5) involving PERSONAL POST OFFICE resulted in a successful reversal by the TTAB in 2004 of its earlier refusal to grant trademark status to this term. Renewed litigation took place in 2007 when the parties were joined by the USPS, which objected to the inclusion of POST OFFICE within the composite PERSONAL POST OFFICE. The USPS hired a language expert who argued that "in the United States, the term 'Post Office' is synonymous with the USPS.... [It] *does* point uniquely to the USPS." Their expert in his report claimed that "the meaning of *post office* in American English is intrinsically in reference to the United States Postal Service" and that "within the United States . . . the term POST OFFICE is a source identifier that means intrinsically 'place of business or business product of the United States Postal Service' and is therefore not generic." The expert claimed further that extensions of POST OFFICE to "the postal authorities of other countries" involved "'figurative' use of language and a type of metaphor known in the literature as 'metonymy.'"

This USPS expert was not someone who had expertise and publications in the area of the language sciences that is most relevant here, namely the semantics and pragmatics of referential expressions, and I argued in my opposing report that there were confusions in his opinions. To claim that POST OFFICE is "synonymous with the USPS" and that its "meaning . . . is intrinsically in reference to" the USPS ignores the fundamental distinction in semantics between the "sense" or meaning of a term and its "reference." The USPS does not figure at all in the meaning of POST OFFICE, and POST OFFICE is not "synonymous" with the USPS. That is to say, there is no identity or similarity in meaning between them, and POST OFFICE is not a source identifier for the USPS. This can be seen in the dictionary definitions for POST OFFICE that were given in §5.5.2, which are even American dictionaries describing the English language as used in America. They define it as a common descriptive or generic term for any kind of post office, and they make no mention of the USPS.

To see why it is so important to make the distinction between "sense" and "reference" here consider a different term, PRESIDENT. It has a certain sense or meaning, of the kind that dictionaries define. This sense makes it available for use by speakers when they refer to individuals who have the semantic properties listed in the dictionary entry, like Donald Trump at the time of writing. But Donald Trump is no part of the sense or meaning of PRESIDENT, PRESIDENT is not synonymous with this individual, and its meaning is not intrinsically or inherently linked to him. There are lots of other individuals, at other times, in other places, and even in the United States, who satisfy the semantic requirements of being a president and to whom PRESIDENT can refer. Former presidents of the US were referred to by the term PRESIDENT in their time, and this reference can continue even after they leave office. Many other countries have presidents, and PRESIDENT is used to refer to each of them. American institutions like universities also often have presidents, and PRESIDENT is used in reference to these individuals as well. There is nothing special about Donald Trump, from a linguistic point of view, even though currently he is probably the most frequent "referent" of the term PRESIDENT in modern America and even though Americans will generally think most often of him when they hear this term.

The same is true of POST OFFICE. It has a certain sense or meaning that dictionaries define (§5.5.2), on the basis of which it can be used to refer to entities like the USPS in the US and to similar entities in other countries. However frequent the references to the USPS may be, in this country and at this point in time, the mental image that American speakers have in their minds of the meaning of POST OFFICE is, nonetheless, that which the American dictionaries of English are defining, and particular referents of this term, even commonly used ones like the USPS, are not a part of its meaning, are not synonymous with it, and are not intrinsically or inherently linked to it. Semantic confusion can only result, and did result in this case, from a failure to make the distinction between "sense" and "reference." The USPS and their language expert were arguing that the most common referent of POST OFFICE in the United States, the USPS, was somehow a part of its sense or meaning, and that POST OFFICE was "synonymous with the USPS" and was a source identifier for it. It is not.

Since this distinction is important and has legal consequences, I refer readers of the present book once again to relevant pages from the classic textbook on semantics by John Lyons, which explains the distinction between sense and reference more fully (and also the term "denotation," which was discussed in §2.4.3): John Lyons's 1977 *Semantics*, vol. 1, pp. 174–206 (Cambridge University Press, Cambridge). I also summarize in what follows the basic arguments and evidence for making the distinction between sense and reference as it applies to PERSONAL POST OFFICE, since this had a direct bearing on the legal dispute over whether this term was likely, or not likely, to cause confusion with the USPS and with its various products and services.

6.1.1 Dictionary Definitions of POST OFFICE

The first piece of evidence against the claim that POST OFFICE has a meaning that is "synonymous with the USPS" and involves "inherent reference" to it comes, as I mentioned previously, from dictionary definitions. The meanings defined in §5.5.2 make no reference to the USPS or to any intrinsic link to the USPS. They are careful to describe the sense or meaning of POST OFFICE, more precisely its senses and meanings (since more than one is listed), and they do not confuse these senses and meanings with entities in the world that POST OFFICE can refer to, as the lawyers and language expert for the USPS did in these quotes. These dictionaries are, moreover, American dictionaries that are designed to describe, and give priority to, American English usage. Their semantic definitions are nonetheless compatible with POST OFFICE being used for buildings and offices outside the US as well as within the US. The precise country is irrelevant to the sense or meaning of POST OFFICE, and there is no departure from its meaning when Americans use POST OFFICE to describe entities other than the USPS. The fact that POST OFFICE does frequently refer to the USPS and to its offices and buildings in this country is a fact about its "reference" at this point in time and in this place, not about its meaning or "sense."

I also consulted at least a dozen other dictionaries of English, and every single one defined senses for it that are essentially similar to the definitions given in §5.5.2, from the *American Heritage Dictionary* and *Webster's*. These dozen included additional dictionaries with a focus on American usage, such as *The Oxford American Dictionary of Current English* (Oxford University Press, Oxford, 1999), as well as the *Oxford English Dictionary*, 2nd edition (Clarendon Press, Oxford, 1989) with its focus on British English, and also dictionaries for Canadian, Australian, New Zealand, and South African English. They were all in substantial agreement over their definitions for POST OFFICE. This is a strong argument for the genericness of POST OFFICE and against the claim that it is a unique identifier for the USPS in the US. It is not.

6.1.2 Grammatical and Semantic Evidence against the Unique Identification of USPS

A second set of arguments that can be given against the semantic analysis of POST OFFICE by the USPS and their language expert comes from the grammar of English and from the meanings of noun phrases that contain this compound noun. Notice first that sentences with POST OFFICE on its own are often ungrammatical and must be accompanied by some other word, such as the indefinite article A (A POST OFFICE), or the definite article THE (THE POST OFFICE), or unless modified by plural inflection -S (POST OFFICES). Sentence (1) is ungrammatical (the asterisk "*" indicates ungrammaticality here):

(1) *I VISITED POST OFFICE.

But (2), (3), (4), and (5) are all grammatical:

(2) I VISITED A POST OFFICE.

(3) I VISITED THE POST OFFICE.

(4) I VISITED POST OFFICES.

(5) I VISITED SOME POST OFFICES.

The meaning of POST OFFICE combines with the meanings of A or THE or SOME and with plurality in these noun phrases, and can combine with many other noun phrase elements, such as the quantifiers ALL and EVERY (ALL POST OFFICES, EVERY POST OFFICE), adjectives like LOCAL (LOCAL POST OFFICES), and so on, to give an overall meaning for the noun phrase and sentence, which is a product of the meanings of its parts. (Recall the similar grammatical combinations with APP STORE discussed in §3.4.7 as evidence for the genericness of this latter.)

Let us remind ourselves of the precise claim that the USPS made about POST OFFICE. I give a further quote from their language expert:

> Because, in American English usage, the term *post office* refers intrinsically to the United States Postal Service, the trademark POST OFFICE cannot be considered a GENERIC term. As a term of art in linguistics . . . the word GENERIC has a meaning that is essentially the same as that of the law: a term applied to goods or services is generic in a person's vocabulary if the person thinks of the word as the name of the thing itself rather than the name of a particular brand of thing.. . . The evidence is clear that Americans think of the primary significance of *post office* as referring to The United States Postal Service, and POST OFFICE is therefore the name of a particular brand of letter-and-parcel delivery service that is operated under the authority of the federal government of the United States.

There are, in fact, some real differences in the use of the term "generic" between linguistics and the law (compare McCarthy's definition, which I gave in §3.3, with linguistic usage in Gregory N. Carlson and Francis Jeffry Pelletier, eds., 1995, *The Generic Book*, University of Chicago Press, Chicago), but a clear example of a sentence containing a noun phrase that is classified as "generic" by both disciplines would be

(6) A POST OFFICE IS AN OFFICE WHERE MAIL IS RECEIVED, SORTED AND DELIVERED

(see further Quirk et al. 1985, chapter 5, and my own 2015 *Definiteness and Indefiniteness: A Study in Reference and Grammaticality Prediction*, Routledge, New York, reprinted from 1978, for many more examples of "generic noun phrases" in English).

A POST OFFICE in (6) refers to the genus or class in question. This sentence is not restricted to post offices operated by the USPS. It is defining post offices in general and what they do, i.e. any post office, anywhere in the world, in the past, or the future, or in one's imagination, is claimed to have the property of being an office where mail is received, sorted, and delivered. Even when Americans utter or write this sentence, for example if a teacher in an American school uses it in answer to a question from a student, the set of entities he or she has in mind is not limited to post offices operated by the USPS. This generic sentence can be continued with ... SO WHEREVER YOU ARE IN THE WORLD YOU CAN TAKE YOUR LETTER TO A LOCAL POST OFFICE AND MAIL IT TO YOUR FRIEND BACK HOME. POST OFFICE here would be ungrammatical without the indefinite article in (7):

(7) *POST OFFICE IS AN OFFICE WHERE MAIL IS RECEIVED, SORTED AND DELIVERED.

It has a generic meaning in combination with A in (6), and its meaning in this usage is the one that the dictionaries are defining. If POST OFFICE were synonymous with USPS and were limited in its reference to the USPS, this generic usage and meaning would be unexpected.

POST OFFICE can also be used in noun phrases with "universal" quantifiers, like ALL and EVERY, as shown in (8) and (9):

(8) ALL POST OFFICES RECEIVE, SORT AND DELIVER MAIL.

(9) EVERY POST OFFICE RECEIVES, SORTS AND DELIVERS MAIL.

These sentences do not refer only to branches of the USPS. They refer to all members of the class of post offices, wherever they may be, even when these sentences are uttered by Americans in America. If POST OFFICE were really restricted to the USPS and its branches, combining this term with ALL and EVERY would simply result in a reference to all the branches of the USPS, but it does not.

POST OFFICE can be used in negative sentences such as (10) and (11):

(10) I'VE NEVER BEEN IN A POST OFFICE.

(11) I'VE NEVER BEEN IN ANY POST OFFICES.

These sentences are not making a limited claim about the USPS. They are not claiming merely that the speaker has never been in offices of the USPS. They are claiming instead that 'the speaker has never been in post offices anywhere.' An American, speaking in America, cannot truthfully utter (10) and (11) when that person has been in post offices in other countries, for example in Britain or Australia. These sentences would be false under these conditions. Once again, the meaning of POST OFFICE is in accordance with the dictionary definitions, not with the USPS's claims.

POST OFFICE can be combined with additional nouns to its right, as in (12):

(12) I'VE NEVER BOUGHT POST OFFICE MERCHANDISE BEFORE IN MY LIFE.

This sentence does not make the restricted claim that the speaker has never bought USPS merchandise only. It means that the speaker has never bought merchandise in any post office anywhere, and the sentence would be false in the event that he or she had bought merchandise in a post office outside the US.

POST OFFICE can be used in noun phrases that have "non-specific" reference. Consider

(13) I WANT TO WORK IN A POST OFFICE WHEN I GROW UP.

This sentence is ambiguous. There may be a "specific" post office that the speaker has in mind (e.g. the one down the road from where I live), but the more likely meaning assigned to it is the "non-specific" one in which the speaker does not have a particular post office in mind, and any one will do. The sentence in this non-specific reading does not claim that the speaker's wishes about the future are necessarily limited to a branch of the USPS. If the speaker ended up moving to Britain and got a job in a post office in that country, his or her wishes for the future would be fulfilled. (Equally in the "specific" reading, the particular post office an American speaker had in mind could be in Britain.) The dictionary definitions of POST OFFICE give the correct description for the meaning of A POST OFFICE in these uses; the semantic analysis of the USPS and their language expert did not.

These grammatical and semantic details were not considered in the legal and linguistic arguments given by the USPS, and as a result there was considerable imprecision in their claim that "the term 'Post Office' is synonymous with the USPS" and that "'Post Office' *does* point uniquely to the USPS." What syntactic forms were they talking about here? POST OFFICE on its own is often ungrammatical in English; recall (1) and (7). In such sentences it has no clear meaning at all, being unusable. Were they making their semantic claim about POST OFFICE when it occurs grammatically in combination with the indefinite article A, or with the definite article THE, or with plural -S, or with a universal quantifier, or an accompanying adjective, and so on? Depending on the choice of determiner or modifier, were they intending their semantic analysis to hold for all "generic" and "universal" uses or for "specific" and "non-specific" uses? Were they making their claim only for noun phrases that consist of POST OFFICE alone? This imprecision led them to overlook the kinds of details I have discussed here, and these details show clearly that POST OFFICE is not a source identifier for the USPS.

There was further imprecision when the USPS language expert gave the following quote from Wikipedia: "**The United States Postal Service** . . . *is generally referred to within the United States as 'the post office.'*" The addition of the definite article THE has a clear semantic and pragmatic effect when added to POST OFFICE, by linking this entity to a particular context or "universe of discourse," in a way I have discussed in detail in my 2015 (1978) book *Definiteness and Indefiniteness: A Study in Reference and Grammaticality Prediction*, referenced previously. THE POST OFFICE will be understood as 'the post office that speaker and hearer have been talking about,' or 'the post office of a particular town in a country like the USA or Britain,' or 'the post office of a particular institution like a university,' and so on.

But this does not support the claim that POST OFFICE (without THE) is inherently linked to the USPS, because PERSONAL POST OFFICE does not contain the phrase THE POST OFFICE; it consists only of POST OFFICE! The definite article is nowhere present in PERSONAL POST OFFICE, nor is it in any way psychologically understood or omitted, and hence semantic and pragmatic properties that are unique to "THE POST OFFICE" cannot be used to support a claim about the meaning of "POST OFFICE" occurring without THE. By failing to attend to such details, the USPS saw support for their analysis where there was none, and gave no attention to simple counterexamples of the kind we have considered in this section. The determiners and modifiers illustrated here combine with POST OFFICE in a way that supports the dictionary definitions for it as a generic term on McCarthy's hierarchy (§3.3).

6.1.3 Empirical Usage Evidence for the Genericness of POST OFFICE

The language expert for the USPS conducted various empirical searches for POST OFFICE in American newspaper headings using LexisNexis, and these were presented as evidence for its unique identification of the USPS. But these searches did not establish that the meaning of POST OFFICE was "synonymous" with the USPS. They merely showed that the referents of POST OFFICE were often skewed to the USPS in American publications. This is not surprising. PRESIDENT will also be skewed in its references to Donald Trump within current American newspapers and periodicals, KING will be skewed in its references to Charles the Third in current British publications, and so on. This does not warrant the conclusion that PRESIDENT is synonymous with Donald Trump and points uniquely to him, nor that KING is synonymous with Charles the Third. These are frequent references within their respective countries and national news media, but they are not part of the respective meanings of these terms. Similarly, POST OFFICE is not synonymous with and does not point uniquely to the USPS, even though this may be the most common referent that the term currently has in American newspapers and periodicals.

Once again it was unclear in the usage figures supplied by the USPS's language expert what exactly he was counting: A POST OFFICE, THE POST OFFICE, POST OFFICES, or just POST OFFICE, in any combination with other modifiers. (Recall that POST OFFICE on its own is ungrammatical.) I accordingly conducted my own Google search for noun phrases containing POST OFFICE in September 2007. To make the search more precise I targeted the phrases A POST OFFICE, POST OFFICES, THE POST OFFICE, and the general POST OFFICE separately. I counted the first 100 hits for each and calculated the percentage of these that were **not** references to the USPS. The results are shown in (14):

(14) References to entities other than the USPS in the first 100 Google hits:
A POST OFFICE = 62%
POST OFFICES = 80%
THE POST OFFICE = 49%
POST OFFICE = 39%

These figures show clearly that these phrases are used regularly to make reference to a wide range of entities other than to branches of the USPS, in accordance with the dictionary definitions for POST OFFICE. These references are found, moreover, in a medium, Google, that Americans frequently access and read. Many of the hits were written outside of the US. But Americans are regularly exposed to British and Australian English, through TV and other media, and through search engines such as Google. The lexical meaning of POST OFFICE does not differ across these countries, and the rules of English grammar as described by Quirk et al. 1985 and also Pullum and Huddleston 2002 (referenced in §1.7) are largely shared as well, at least for these noun phrase constructions. What does vary widely across the world is the set of referents, i.e. the entities to which A POST OFFICE, and so on, applies. But this is a question of "reference," not of "sense" or meaning (§6.1). The Google hits illustrate this diversity in reference, and they corroborate the general dictionary meanings for POST OFFICE that are compatible with this diversity.

Since POST OFFICE is not synonymous with. and cannot be linked uniquely to, the USPS, the conclusion by their language expert that "PERSONAL POST OFFICE ... will be understood by speakers of American English as meaning a 'United States Postal Service-branded product for use by only one individual at a time'" does not follow. The premise on which his reasoning was based (that POST OFFICE does refer uniquely and intrinsically to the USPS) is simply false. Instead, PERSONAL POST OFFICE has a nonliteral meaning and involves the chain of reasoning that I defined for it in §5.5.2–5.5.3. The TTAB also agreed in 2007 that "PERSONAL POST OFFICE does not falsely suggest a connection with the U.S. Postal Service."

6.1.4 Against the Metonymy in POST OFFICE

The misanalysis of POST OFFICE by USPS and their language expert then led to the further claim that when POST OFFICE does refer to "the postal authorities of other countries," this involves a "figurative" use of language and what is called "metonymy." But nothing of the sort is going on here. Figurative language is defined by Peter Matthews as "an extension of a basic or literal meaning" in his *Concise Oxford Dictionary of Linguistics* (Oxford University Press, Oxford, 1997, p. 128). Metonymy is a type of figurative language whereby a word or phrase with a certain literal meaning is used to refer to something else that is associated with it, as in I DRANK A GLASS TOO MANY (where GLASS is used to refer to the liquid in the glass, not to the literal glass container itself).

But there is nothing figurative or metonymic about using POST OFFICE in relation to the postal authorities of other countries. POST OFFICE is still being used in its literal sense in these cases. Applying PRESIDENT to the president of Pakistan would involve figurative language and metonymy, according to this mistaken logic, by extension from Donald Trump, and applying KING to the king of Denmark would involve figurative language and metonymy, by extension from Charles the Third. But these are not figurative and metonymic extensions! Using POST OFFICE for a post office in Australia, or PRESIDENT for the president of Pakistan, or KING for the king of Denmark involves no departure whatsoever from the literal sense or meaning of these terms, as defined in dictionaries of English, including American dictionaries. It involves only the selection of different referents in different contexts, while still maintaining the full and literal senses of POST OFFICE, PRESIDENT, and KING.

A further example of imprecision in the semantic analysis of PERSONAL POST OFFICE by the USPS language expert can be seen in the following quote: "The plain and easily understood meaning of the three commonplace words of the name Personal Post Office, taken together, directly conveys to consumers that the product is *personal*, that is, something an individual would use personally. . . ." I pointed out in §5.5.3 parsing step (c) that the adjective PERSONAL has a subtly different meaning from the adverb PERSONALLY. Compare MY PERSONAL ZOO with THE ZOO I USE PERSONALLY, the former being 'exclusive,' the latter merely 'comparative.' We can therefore talk without contradiction about THE POST OFFICE I USE PERSONALLY, with the adverb, but MY PERSONAL POST OFFICE with an adjective contains the contradiction that triggers the nonliteral suggestive interpretation that I defined in §5.5.3. Yet the adjective PERSONAL is loosely paraphrased with the adverb PERSONALLY in the quote from the USPS expert. These are not equivalent. The composite PERSONAL POST OFFICE poses a problem of interpretation for users of English and involves a chain of reasoning in order to resolve it. In the process PERSONAL POST OFFICE does not falsely suggest a connection with the USPS. It is inherently distinctive and eligible for trademark status, a finding with which the TTAB eventually concurred.

6.2 Source Identification in Trademarks

Having just seen this dispute over POST OFFICE and whether it can or cannot be said to identify the USPS uniquely (it cannot!), and a similar dispute earlier over APP STORE in §3.3 (it no longer identifies the Apple company alone), we turn in this next section to another mark, ELASTIC, whose status has been disputed, but which can be shown, on solid linguistic grounds, to be a unique identifier for the software provider in question.

6.2.1 ELASTIC as a Source Identifier

In 2020 I was invited to write a report (for a law firm in Palo Alto, California) about the use of the term ELASTIC in the context of computer software (downloadable and nondownloadable). The issue was, Had this term acquired distinctiveness as a unique identifier for the products and services of the Elastic Company (Elasticsearch BV)? This was in response to the Examining Attorney for the US Patent and Trademark Office calling for clear evidence showing that "the relevant public understands the primary significance of the mark as identifying the *source* of applicant's product or service rather than identifying the product or service itself" and stating that "in this case, a more descriptive term [like ELASTIC] requires more evidence."

And indeed there were a number of subtle linguistic issues that arose in this case, involving both lexical semantics and usage, and these merit a summary in the present context of reference and unique identification, both because they are linguistically instructive and because they illustrate how linguistic argumentation and evidence can be of considerable help to the "triers of fact" in the law. The Google search engine provided important evidence, both with respect to the mark ELASTIC used alone and within the large family of combinatorial marks that included ELASTIC as one component (ELASTIC STACK, ELASTIC LOGS, ELASTIC MAPS, etc.; see §6.2.2).

I examined the first 100 Google hits for each of fourteen such marks in which ELASTIC was the common characteristic. Remarkably, a full 100 percent of these searches (1,400 in all) referred to the Elastic Company! This is compelling evidence that the Elastic Company is consistently seen as the source of these terms. For ELASTIC alone I examined all the hits in all the pages returned by Google in response to a search for "ELASTIC," namely 430. Within these 430 hits many (175) were references to elastic, the rubber material, or figurative extensions of this in economics or in medicine; see §6.2.3. In other words they involved distinct "senses" of ELASTIC. Of the 247 hits that were clearly referring to computers or computer software, an impressive 210 (or 85 percent) referred to the Elastic Company, thus providing further support for the strong association between ELASTIC and the Elastic Company (§6.2.3). Finally, I discuss (in §6.2.4) an interesting potential complication for my analysis involving the phrase ELASTIC COMPUTING and its semantics.

6.2.2 The Family of Marks Containing ELASTIC

By 2020 the Elastic Company had adopted a number of ELASTIC-related brands using noun phrase combinations containing ELASTIC, in order to increase its brand awareness and reinforce the marketplace association with this company and its products and services. These included the following fourteen items:

(15) ELASTIC STACK
ELASTIC SITE SEARCH
ELASTIC APP SEARCH
ELASTIC ENTERPRISE SEARCH
ELASTIC LOGS
ELASTIC METRICS
ELASTIC APM
ELASTIC UPTIME
ELASTIC SIEM
ELASTIC ENDPOINT SECURITY
ELASTIC MAPS
ELASTIC CLOUD ON KUBERNETES
ELASTIC CLOUD ENTERPRISE
ELASTICSEARCH-HADOOP

The Examining Attorney had stated that in order to prove the existence of a family of combined terms such as this as trademarks, the applicant would have to show "that its putative family (1) has a recognizable common characteristic that is distinctive, and (2) has been promoted in such a way as to create "'recognition among the purchasing public that the common characteristic is indicative of a common origin of the goods or services.'"

The common characteristic of the family of marks in (15) is ELASTIC. And one way to test whether this family of word combinations is actually associated with the Elastic Company, i.e. as a source identifier, was to use an internet search engine. One of the most widely employed and respected of these was, and still is, Google, which I have used in other cases described in this book as well. Google finds and lists words and phrases that occur in texts and websites throughout the internet by the public at large, which includes potential consumers and actual consumers of the products and services of the Elastic Company. It therefore provides a window onto both product awareness in the community and onto English language usage more generally. In conjunction with lexical-semantic analysis, as carried out in linguistics, Google data can shed direct light on how certain words and phrases are used, what they refer to exactly, and with what frequency. In particular, in the current context Google can reveal whether certain words and word combinations are being used as "proper names" to identify a unique source or product, or whether they are used instead with more descriptive or generic meanings.

I accordingly conducted searches for all fourteen of the word combinations containing ELASTIC listed in (15). I examined the first 100 hits shown with blue headings for each of these combinations (in searches carried out in June 2020), resulting in 1,400 entries. I did not include any of the paid advertisements ("Ads") by any company in these searches, since that would have biased the results in favor of that company. I examined all of the entries carefully to see if they identified the Elastic Company or one of its products, on the one hand, or if they were used instead either descriptively or in reference to a different company. The analysis was surprisingly straightforward. As I mentioned previously, a full 100 percent of these Google hits (all 1,400!) referred to the Elastic Company and its products, and only to that company. This is strong proof that the Elastic Company is clearly seen as the source of these terms and of the products and services they name. Since ELASTIC is the common characteristic of this family of marks, and since each member of the family is so strongly and uniquely associated with the Elastic Company, this is clear evidence for a "recognition among the purchasing public that the common characteristic is indicative of a common origin of goods or services," which the Examining Attorney had called for.

In the next section I enumerate the kinds of descriptive meanings that the word ELASTIC can have when it is not referring to the Elastic Company, mainly in reference to rubber material and figurative extensions of this in economics or medicine, and also in computing.

6.2.3 ELASTIC Alone

For ELASTIC alone the Google search engine returned 430 hits, again excluding Ads. I analyzed all 430 carefully. Many of these (175) were references to elastic, the rubber material, or figurative extensions of this that had nothing to do with computing or software and that mainly involved economics ('elasticity in supply and demand') or medicine ('skin tone,' etc.). These literal and figurative meanings that I found are well-defined in dictionaries such as the *Oxford English Dictionary Online* (3rd edn). I summarize the key entries for ELASTIC from the *OED Online*:

elastic, adj. and n.

'3 a. Of material substances, whether solid, liquid, or gaseous: That spontaneously resumes (after a longer or shorter interval) its normal bulk or shape after having been contracted, dilated, or distorted by external force.... Also of motions, forces, etc....'

'4 a. (Partly attributive use of the noun.) In popular language, esp.: That can be stretched without permanent alteration of size or shape. Applied to fabrics, or articles made of them, containing threads or thin strips of rubber usually covered by a woven material.'

figurative. 'Of immaterial things: That can be 'stretched' or expanded to suit circumstances; flexible, accommodating.'

The 175 noncomputing meanings of this type in Google were accordingly irrelevant and would not be assigned by speakers of English to the word ELASTIC in any context involving computers and software, and hence they could be discounted here. Similarly the meaning of APPLE as 'a fruit' would be irrelevant for any assessment of Apple 'the company' on consumer awareness using a Google search like this.

A total of 247 of the 430 hits for ELASTIC did have a meaning or reference that involved computers or software, however, and of these 210 (or 85 percent) named the Elastic Company or its products and services. In other words, a full 85 percent of the Google searches that returned hits of relevance to computing and software identified the Elastic Company. This is again strong evidence of acquired distinctiveness, in addition to the 100 percent association between ELASTIC and the Elastic Company in the combinatorial marks containing ELASTIC in (15). The fact that as many as 210 of the 430 hits for ELASTIC referred to the Elastic Company (a full 49 percent of the total or almost half), even more than the 175 entries (41 percent) for all the other noncomputing meanings combined (rubber material, economics, medicine, etc.), is a striking reflection of just how widespread name recognition and product awareness of the Elastic Company had become.

6.2.4 ELASTIC COMPUTING

In 210 of the 247 uses of ELASTIC that referred to computers or software (85 percent), this word was being used as a proper name and source identifier for the Elastic Company. In the remaining 37 (15 percent), ELASTIC had a different and descriptive meaning that can be categorized linguistically as a figurative extension of one of its literal meanings within a computing context, as found in word combinations such as "ELASTIC COMPUTING." This phrase refers to the fact that overall computer resources are being expanded or decreased, i.e. balanced up or down, to meet changing external demands and increased or reduced computing needs.

This figurative meaning of ELASTIC in ELASTIC COMPUTING is quite different linguistically from ELASTIC when it refers to the Elastic Company in two respects, and these differences would be clearly recognizable and understood by purchasers in the field. First, ELASTIC as a proper name referring to the company has distinct patterns of grammar and lexical usage that are different from those of the descriptive adjective or noun ELASTIC, just as BAKER as a proper name is used differently when talking about people with that family name, as opposed to talking about professional bakers. There will generally be linguistic indicators that make clear whether we are talking about the Baker family (e.g. I talked with "BAKER" or "THE BAKERS") or about the profession (e.g. I went to "THE BAKER" for bread). Similarly, references to the Elastic Company and its products and services will be clearly recognizable as such, as in e.g. "Elastic offers free introductory training" or "What's the best thing about working at Elastic?," and these will be distinguishable from so-called descriptive uses.

Secondly, the meaning of ELASTIC in "ELASTIC COMPUTING" does not describe what the Elastic Company does, and so this meaning will again not be associated with, nor confusable with, the Elastic Company. This company is widely known to provide software that "offers solutions for searching and analyzing all types of data, including textual, numerical, geospatial, structured, and unstructured data" (to quote from one of the declarations in the legal proceedings). This software does not balance overall computer resources in response to an increase or decrease in computing needs in the figurative sense of the phrase ELASTIC COMPUTING, therefore. This semantic difference may seem small to an outsider, but to the purchasing public it is clearly significant and contributes further to distinguishing ELASTIC in the so-called descriptive "ELASTIC COMPUTING" sense from ELASTIC as a proper name identifying the Elastic Company.

In order to test for this distinct meaning of ELASTIC in "ELASTIC COMPUTING" and for a lack of confusion with the Elastic Company, I searched for the phrase "ELASTIC COMPUTING" as such on Google (in June 2020) and analyzed the first 100 hits, excluding Ads. Not a single one referred to the Elastic Company. This showed that purchasers in the field understand the term ELASTIC in ELASTIC COMPUTING to be quite different in meaning from the proper name and trademark ELASTIC, referring to the Elastic Company and its products and services.

We can conclude on the basis of quantitative and lexical-semantic evidence from these Google searches returning almost 2,000 entries in total that ELASTIC has indeed acquired clear distinctiveness as a name uniquely identifying the Elastic Company and its products and services.

6.3 Losing Source Identification and "Genericide"

Sometimes a term that once had clear distinctiveness as a trademark may lose this status and undergo what has been called "genericide." I referred in §3.3 to the definition of genericness (§12.1 in *McCarthy on Trademarks and Unfair Competition*, 4th edn, 2012): "A generic term is one that is commonly used as the name of a kind of goods" (§12.1). As a result McCarthy writes that "the concepts of 'generic name' and 'trademark' are mutually exclusive." So, if one seller uses a term as a trademark and as an identifier for that seller's company, but "a majority of the relevant public then appropriates [it] as the name of a product, the mark is a victim of 'genericide' and trademark rights may cease." I cited the example of THERMOS in §3.3 in this connection. XEROX is another. McCarthy makes the following comments on the causes of such genericides (with all these quotes from §12.1):

> Sometimes genericide occurs as a result of the trademark owner's failure to police the mark, resulting in widespread usage by competitors leading to a perception of genericness among the public, who sees many sellers using the same term.... Sometimes, a term intended by the seller to be a trademark for a new product is taken by the public as a generic name because customers have no other word to use to name this new thing.... Such was the fate under U.S. law of words like "aspirin," "cellophane," and "escalator."

In this section I summarize a legal dispute that arose (Century City, California, 2000) over the term BLUE BOOK. What was at issue was precisely whether it had undergone genericide or whether it still served as a source identifier for the Kelley Blue Book Company Inc. and its famous price guides for used vehicles. We shall see that there was good linguistic evidence that BLUE BOOK had indeed fallen victim to genericide.

6.3.1 The Grammar and Meaning of BLUE BOOK

BLUE BOOK is a noun phrase consisting of the adjective BLUE and the noun BOOK. The precise combinatorial relationship between the adjective and the noun admits of two possibilities, and there are two quite distinct interpretations. In the first, BLUE is an adjective modifier of the head noun BOOK, and it receives its literal and compositional meaning (see §1.2), i.e. the book in question has the color blue (most typically the cover alone will be blue, not the pages), and no additional claim is made about the book over and above its color. In the second, BLUE joins with BOOK to form a "compound" noun, both parts of which function collectively as the grammatical head of the noun phrase. In this parsing BLUE BOOK has a more specialized meaning, or more precisely set of meanings, and these meanings are not predictable from the meanings of BLUE and BOOK alone, i.e. they are non-compositional (see again §1.2). One of these is the 'price list' meaning that was at the center of this lawsuit, and often the book in question will not even be blue. Because the combination of BLUE with BOOK can convey specialized, non-compositional meanings, dictionaries regularly list BLUE BOOK in addition to entries for the individual words BLUE and BOOK, and they give semantic definitions for the compound, in addition to defining the meanings for each word alone.

The ambiguity here in BLUE BOOK is reminiscent of that in CRIMINAL LAWYER and THEATRICAL AGENT, which were discussed in §3.5 in connection with HALF PRICE BOOKS. The compositional meaning of BLUE BOOK permits the paraphrase THE BOOK IS BLUE, just like THE LAWYER IS CRIMINAL and THE AGENT IS THEATRICAL (and also THE BOOKS ARE HALF PRICE and THE SALAD DRESSING IS TASTY). The non-compositional meanings in CRIMINAL LAWYER, as a type of lawyer specializing in criminal law, and in THEATRICAL AGENT as a special type of agent, and HALF BROTHER as a certain type of brother, do not permit these paraphrases whereby the adjective is taken out of the noun phrase and placed in a predicate position following IS. BLUE BOOK has this same compositional/non-compositional ambiguity.

Interestingly, this ambiguity in structure and meaning with BLUE BOOK can also be distinguished in spoken English on the basis of stress patterns. In the non-compositional compound (referring to a certain type of book) the primary stress is on the initial word BLUE, while BOOK receives secondary stress and loses its pronunciation as an independent word (i.e. *BLUEbook*). In the modifier before head parsing with literal and compositional meaning ('The book is blue'), the stress is more even and the two words are pronounced as separate words (*BLUE BOOK*).

Dictionaries define several specialized senses for the non-compositional BLUE BOOK. In the next section (§6.3.2) I summarize the results of a survey of numerous dictionaries that I examined when preparing my report (in 2000). Dictionaries are highly relevant in this legal context (recall §1.1) because their entries and semantic paraphrases have generally been formulated after consulting a large database of actual usage instances to which lexicographers have access. These databases and the patterns of usage accordingly shed light on the crucial issue in the present case: What do speakers of English understand a term like BLUE BOOK to refer to? Does it identify just one particular producer, or is it used with a more general semantics that covers a certain type of book with certain inherent properties, regardless of the producer?

My survey of dictionaries revealed four distinct senses for the compound that were defined with some regularity, though dictionaries did differ in the precise wordings for defining each sense and also in the number of senses they defined. The *Merriam-Webster's Collegiate Dictionary* (10th edn, 1999) defined the four as follows:

> '**1 :** a register esp. of socially prominent persons **2 :** a book of specialized information often published under government auspices **3 :** a blue-covered booklet used for writing examinations **4 :** a periodically issued price list (as of used cars).'

The first of these meanings, which I shall refer to as the 'list of prominent persons' reading, is defined in very much this form by almost all the dictionaries. The second meaning, which I shall call the 'official publication' meaning, is given in variant forms, depending on whether reference is made to the British government or to the US government. For example, the *Random House Webster's College Dictionary* (2nd edn, 2000) defines this sense as 'a British government publication bound in a blue cover,' whereas the *American Heritage Dictionary* (3rd edn, 1992) defines it as 'an official list of persons in the employ of the U.S. government.' The third 'examination book' meaning is not known in Britain because these special books with blue covers that students bring to course examinations are not used in Britain, but they are widespread in America and in American language usage and in American dictionaries. The fourth meaning, the 'price list' sense, is the one most relevant to the current lawsuit. The *Merriam-Webster's Collegiate Dictionary* lists it along with the other three, thereby claiming that BLUE BOOK is commonly used with the general meaning of 'a periodically issued price list (as of used cars).' In so doing this dictionary defines this sense as a generic one. In §6.3.2 I shall consider other dictionaries that do so as well.

The order of the four meanings in the *Merriam-Webster's Collegiate Dictionary* reflects the historical order in which these meanings were attested in English. The 'list of prominent persons' and the 'official publication' senses were the first two recorded. The 'examination book' sense is later, it is semantically unrelated to the first two and is characteristic of American rather than British usage, as we have seen. The fourth and historically most recent meaning is the 'price list' one, and it can be seen linguistically as a semantic extension of the original two. The list of 'socially prominent persons' has been extended from a list of people to a list of things. At the same time, the 'official publication' sense has influenced this semantic extension by limiting it to the set of things for which an official listing is useful, namely those that require an authoritative statement as to their value, such as for used cars. This is a natural, and frequently observed, form of historical language change. It was set in motion by the fact that price lists for used cars did, and still do, often have blue covers, making them BLUE BOOKS in a literal sense as well. Since these price lists were blue, the term BLUE BOOK came to mean 'price list' in a nonliteral sense as well, by extending the nonliteral meanings of BLUE BOOK from the original 'list of prominent persons' and 'official publication' senses to the 'price list' for used cars. And once this happened, price lists could be called BLUE BOOKS, whether they had blue covers or not, since they were price lists.

This semantic extension in BLUE BOOK has taken place more productively in the United States than in Great Britain. Neither the 'examination book' nor the 'price list' senses are known in Britain, and these senses are not listed in the twenty-volume *Oxford English Dictionary* (2nd edn, 1989). This dictionary did give separate entries for the second 'official publication' sense, reflecting both British and American usage. Namely,

> 'a. A book bound in blue; spec. one of the official reports of Parliament and the Privy Council, which are issued in a dark blue paper cover; also in extended use. b. *U.S.* "A printed book containing the names of all persons holding office under the government of the United States, with their place of birth, amount of salary, etc."'

The extended use that is referred to here under 'a' is exemplified by a 1928 example from *The Daily Telegraph*: "The 'Blue Book,' the directory . . . of the electrical engineering and allied trades." This usage refers to a list of prominent people within a profession, which makes it similar to the first entry in the *Merriam-Webster's Collegiate Dictionary* above, i.e. the register of 'socially prominent persons.' Extensions beyond that to a price list for used cars were not motivated in the British context, since Kelley and other producers of price lists in the United States have not produced comparable price lists bound in blue covers for values of cars within the British market and in British pounds.

Given this brief history of usage for BLUE BOOK, and given the regional differences between American and British English, the issue that must be addressed regarding the trademark versus generic status of this term is this: Has BLUE BOOK actually attained the generic sense of 'price list' in American English, as claimed by the tenth edition of *Merriam-Webster's Collegiate Dictionary* cited previously, as opposed to referring uniquely to the Kelley Blue Book Company? Is the general 'price list' usage now sufficiently widespread to justify genericness, or are we dealing instead with a more limited phenomenon that might be better analyzed as a metaphorical extension of other senses in certain contexts and on certain occasions? In order to decide this we must consult other dictionaries, especially those covering American usage, and we must collect and examine actually attested examples of usage for evidence about the semantic status of BLUE BOOK. This is what the next two sections do (§6.3.2 and §6.3.3).

6.3.2 General Dictionary Evidence for Genericness

The *Merriam-Webster's Collegiate Dictionary* cited previously is, of course, a classic dictionary focusing on American English and a respected authority. The fact that even one major dictionary would list 'a periodically issued price list (as of used cars)' as one of the common meanings of BLUE BOOK must be taken as strong evidence for genericness. The lexicographers who compiled it have evidently encountered BLUE BOOK with sufficient frequency in this general sense in their database to justify its inclusion as a generic meaning. Hence, even though this meaning is the most recent one, and even though it began as a metaphorical extension from earlier uses applied to books that were literally blue, this dictionary has now concluded that the threshold has been crossed to justify listing it as a primary sense in current American English. By "primary sense" I mean that this is one that is accessed immediately by speakers of English, by virtue of knowing the lexical meanings of words. It does not need to be derived on different occasions of use from other senses by metaphorical inference (recall §1.5, §2.3, and Chapter 5). The context makes it clear which of the primary senses of BLUE BOOK is intended on each occasion of use (§1.4).

Dictionaries focusing on American English are especially revealing, given the differences in usage between British and American English with regard to BLUE BOOK. There are several Oxford dictionaries that specialize in American usage. The *Oxford American Dictionary and Language Guide* (1999) gives the same four entries of the *Merriam-Webster's Collegiate Dictionary* in §6.3.1, though in a different order and with two subentries for the 'official publication' reading:

> '1 a listing of socially prominent people. **2** a blank book used for college examinations. **3** . . . a reference book listing the prices of used cars. **4** . . . **a** a report issued by the government. **b** *Brit.* a report issued by Parliament or the Privy Council.'

These same entries are also given in identical form in the *Oxford Dictionary and Thesaurus, American Edition* (1996), and all but the last, 4b, are found in the *Oxford Illustrated American Dictionary* (1998). *The Oxford American Dictionary of Current English* (1999) has just three entries, the third of which is the 'price list' meaning:

> '1 a listing of socially prominent people. **2** a blank book used for college examinations. **3** a reference book listing the prices of used cars.'

The *Longman Dictionary of American English* (2nd edn, 2000) gives just two entries for BLUE BOOK, the second of which is the 'price list' one:

> '**1** a book with a blue cover that is used in colleges for writing answers to test questions **2** a book with a list of prices that you should expect to pay for any used car.'

The *Random House Webster's College Dictionary* (2nd edn, 2000) lists four entries for BLUE BOOK with some interesting wording differences, compared with the *Merriam-Webster's Collegiate Dictionary* entries in §6.3.1:

> '1. a register or directory, esp. of socially prominent persons. **2.** a blank book for taking college examinations, usu. with a blue cover. **3.** a manual listing the current market value of any of various consumer items, as appliances. **4.** a British government publication bound in blue cover.'

The 'price list' meaning, number 3, is now defined in a more general way and refers to any consumer item and not just to used cars. This represents a further semantic extension within the 'price list' meaning to include other items, though used cars are still subsumed, of course, under this more general sense. The *Webster's American Family Dictionary* (1998) is based on this *Random House Webster's College Dictionary* and includes its first three entries in identical form, but excludes the fourth British sense.

Finally, the *Langenscheidt's New College Merriam-Webster English Dictionary* (1998) has the same four entries as the *Merriam-Webster's Collegiate Dictionary* in §6.3.1.

Some dictionaries, especially those with earlier publication dates than the ones I have cited here, do not include the 'price list' meaning among their entries for BLUE BOOK. For example, the *Webster's Ninth New Collegiate Dictionary* from 1986 gives the first three senses of the tenth edition of the *Merriam-Webster's Collegiate Dictionary* (1999) in identical form, but does not contain the latter's fourth meaning, 'a periodically issued price list (as of used cars)'; nor does the *Webster's Third New International Dictionary of the English Language Unabridged* from 1993 and nor do the *Webster's New Universal Unabridged Dictionary* from 1989 and the first edition of the *Random House Dictionary of the English Language* from 1983.

Another American dictionary that does not include the 'price list' meaning is the *American Heritage Dictionary* in both its third edition from 1992 and fourth edition from 2000, which give only the following three senses:

> '**1.** An official list of persons in the employ of the U.S. government. **2.** A book listing the names of socially prominent people. **3.** A blank notebook with blue covers in which to write the answers to examination questions.'

Dictionaries published in Britain, such as the twenty-volume second edition of the *Oxford English Dictionary* from 1989, have only limited entries for BLUE BOOK, as I mentioned, and make no reference to the 'price list' sense (though the more recent third online edition of the *OED*, with its worldwide coverage, does give an entry for US usage with the meaning 'A reference book which lists current market prices for consumer items of a particular type, esp. used automobiles'). The *Cassell Concise Dictionary* for English from 1997, published in London, and the *Chambers Dictionary* from 1998, published in Edinburgh, do not include the 'price list' sense.

If we exclude the British dictionaries that are oriented primarily to British English usage, then most of the dictionaries I consulted for this case covering American English usage did include a separate entry for the 'price list' meaning. Those that did not were generally earlier editions. This is understandable because the 'price list' sense is the most recent one in

American English usage, and we have seen in §3.4.6 in connection with APP STORE that dictionaries tend to be conservative and that it takes some time for a new meaning to be reflected in a dictionary. The fact that so many of the dictionaries I surveyed, with their respective databases, did give the 'price list' meaning is strong evidence for the genericness of BLUE BOOK in this sense.

One American dictionary I surveyed was atypical in that it defined BLUE BOOK as a trademark, in reference to used cars, the *Random House Webster's Unabridged Dictionary* (2nd edn, 1998). It gave six entries in all:

> '1. A register or directory of socially prominent persons. **2.** any register or directory, as of major companies or officials. **3.** a blank book used in taking college examinations, usually with a blue cover. **4.** a British parliamentary or other publication bound in a blue cover. **5.** (*caps.*) *Trademark.* a reference manual listing the current market value of used cars by model and year of manufacture. **6.** a similar manual listing the market value of other items, appliances, etc.'

The classification of usage number 5 as a trademark in reference to used cars does not accord with any of the other dictionaries cited here. Nor does this classification within a single dictionary have any legal status, of course.

The collective evidence from all these dictionaries indicates that BLUE BOOK should be regarded as a generic term (as of the year 2000 at least) for used vehicle price guides in American English. It has become a common descriptive name for these price guides, occurring with sufficient frequency in the databases for most dictionaries of American English from the mid and late 1990s onward to list it as a primary meaning, along with other primary meanings for BLUE BOOK.

6.3.3 Usage Evidence for Genericness

Further corroboration for the genericness of BLUE BOOK in the 'price list' sense came in this case from a large database of uses that were collected directly from newspapers and magazines, the internet, and legal transcripts.

First, there were many examples in this database that supported the very general definition provided by the *Random House Webster's College Dictionary* (2nd edn, 2000) as 'a manual listing the current market value of any of various consumer items, as appliances.' This is more extensive than the definition referring to used cars alone, but it obviously subsumes used cars as well. In the internet data, for example, there were references to blue books for various kinds of vehicles, for mechanical appliances, musical instruments, collectors' items, cameras, guns, pool cues, apartments, and other categories as well. A selection is given in (15):

(15) THE OFFICIAL HELICOPTER BLUE BOOK
NATIONAL FARM TRACTOR AND IMPLEMENT BLUE BOOK
1990 LAWN MOWER TRADE-IN BLUE BOOK
BLUE BOOK SLOT MACHINE GUIDE
BLUE BOOK OF ELECTRIC GUITARS
BLUE BOOK OF ACOUSTIC GUITARS
SAXOPHONE BLUE BOOK
OFFICIAL BLUE BOOK OF UNITED STATES COINS (SERIAL)
CAMERA BLUE BOOK
BLUE BOOK OF GUN VALUES
BLUE BOOK OF POOL CUES
APARTMENT BLUE BOOK.

The compound BLUE BOOK could be replaced in all these examples by the words PRICE LIST or PRICE GUIDE, and is being used with a generic meaning.

Second, the generality of this 'price list' meaning is supported by numerous uses from American newspapers and magazines. In (16) I give a sample (I preserve the spelling conventions as used in the original, showing capital or small letters, etc.):

(16) "Golf has developed a Blue Book for the most recent and popular pre-owned clubs available . . . " (*Boulder County Business Report*, 2000).

"We do not yet have enough sales to create a Blue Book for electric generating facilities . . . " (*Electricity Journal*, 1999).

"Is there any good reference Web site out there for determining the 'blue book' resale value on a used computer?" (*The Fresno Bee*, 1999).

"Be sure to check mutual fund's blue-book value" (*The Fort Worth Star-Telegram*, 1999).

"There were more than 2 million slaves in America; their blue-book value was greater than a billion dollars . . . " (*The Village Voice*, 1998).

'The bomb's blue-book value is about $5" (*The Washington Times*, 1994).

"There needs to be a blue book value placed on PCs, just like in the automobile industry" (*PC Week*, 1988).

Again BLUE BOOK is being used generically in all these cases, with the last example illustrating how the automobile industry provided the model and impetus for extending car price guides to price guides in general.

Third, even in reference to cars BLUE BOOK can be found in a completely generic sense, and not as a trademark. In the internet data, for example, I saw references to a MID-WEST AUTOMOBILE BLUE BOOK going back as far as 1919, to a 1921 AUTO BLUE BOOK, and to a 1946 "BLUE" BOOK OF USED CAR PRICES, this latter being actually red in color. In American newspapers and magazines I found examples such as

(17) "I don't know where they found a Blue Book for non-functioning automobiles, but maybe one exists . . . " (*The Chronicle of Philanthropy*, 1999).

"Car donors frequently deduct the blue book value of the vehicle . . . " (*The Washington Post*, 1986).

"He was asking only what the 'blue book,' a catchall name for several used-car price guides, said the car was worth at retail" (*The U.S. News & World Report*, 1986).

The genericness of BLUE BOOK in reference to used cars is explicitly defined in the last quote from *U.S. News & World Report*, while the hypothetical and general nature of the references to used car price guides in the prior examples also involves generic usage.

Genericness is further supported by variation in the spelling of BLUE BOOK that can be seen in the examples just given. Since BLUE BOOK appears so frequently in book titles, the letter B often appears capitalized in both words. On the other hand BLUE BOOK is now a generic term, just like PRICE GUIDE and PRICE LIST, and such terms are not generally capitalized. This explains the variation in spelling. The occasional hyphen between BLUE and BOOK (and even a reduction to a single word) reflects its status as a compound term (recall §1.2) and is modeled on examples such as BLUE-CHIP and BLUEBIRD, which exist alongside BLUE BLOOD spelled with two words, all of which are compounds in modern English.

There was a further set of data that was collected in this case involving a telephone survey commissioned by the plaintiff of relevant consumers (car salespeople, car insurance claims adjusters, and car loan bank officers). These surveys are designed to elicit information about language usage, and they consist of various questions asked in a phone interview that are deemed relevant for assessing how consumers understand the term in question. In my experience of seeing such survey data in a number of cases, the results are very often problematic unless extreme care is taken, in how exactly the questions are formulated (they can be unclear or ambiguous, especially in this decontextualized telephone interview context) and in how the quantities are interpreted.

Such was the case in this survey. There was an ambiguity in the question that was supposed to yield information about whether BLUE BOOK referred uniquely to the Kelley Blue Book Company, but the way it was formulated asked only about whether people "associated" the name Kelley with BLUE BOOK, which is not the same thing. You can "associate" the name Webster's with dictionaries without necessarily believing that Webster's is the only company that produces them. A "yes" answer to whether Kelley was "associated" with BLUE BOOK was just as ambiguous as the question itself: People might think that Kelley was the only producer, or they might think that the term had more general reference and might even know the names of other producers. There was an ambiguity also in various other definite noun phrases used in the set of questions asked (e.g. sentences with supposedly similar noun phrases to THE BLUE BOOK using THE ENCYCLOPEDIA) over whether reference was made to the whole genus or to a particular instance, which would again affect the responses about whether there was one or more than one producer. Even with these semantic problems in the questions, there was more quantitative support for a generic interpretation of BLUE BOOK in the survey results than for a source-identifying one (identifying the Kelley Company), despite the plaintiff's claims to the contrary!

It is for reasons such as these that telephone surveys are now less common than they used to be and lawyers of my acquaintance prefer to use corpus data instead, as a better way of shedding light on, and quantifying, the usage and meaning of critical terms. Rich and increasingly large corpora are now available for this purpose, and the precise ways in which they can be exploited are illustrated elsewhere in this book, especially for the more recent cases in which I was involved (see e.g. §3.4 and §6.2 and §7.1). Even corpus data are not perfect data, however, and care must be taken in how they are searched and interpreted, as we saw and shall see in the chapters and sections of this book just cited.

6.4 Referential and Attributive Uses of THE POLICE in a Defamation Suit

A lawsuit can arise over what exactly and who exactly a definite noun phrase like THE POLICE refers to, and over the role of speaker and hearer's "mutual knowledge" in understanding the reference (see e.g. Herbert H. Clark and Catherine R. Marshall's 1981 "Definite Reference and Mutual Knowledge," in A. Joshi, B. Webber, and I. Sag, eds., *Elements of Discourse Understanding*, Cambridge University Press, Cambridge, 10–63). A distinction is made in the philosophy of language between "referential" and "attributive" uses of such phrases: The former refers to individuals who are mutually known and identifiable to both speaker and hearer, the latter to the police force in general and their members (see the important 1966 article by Keith Donnellan on "Reference and Definite Descriptions" in *The Philosophical Review* 75: 281–304, which first introduced this distinction). This can make a big difference when "THE POLICE" stand accused of certain crimes. Is it the police force in general that people are talking about (the attributive use), or are certain individuals, say Masters and James, who are known independently to speaker and hearer, being picked out and identified when "THE POLICE" is uttered (the referential use)? In this latter case these individuals would stand accused of the crimes in question and suffer reputational damage as individuals.

6.4.1 THE POLICE

This referential/attributive distinction came up in the 2017 lawsuit mentioned back in §2.3.3 when discussing the word MURDER. An African American man was shot dead by two police officers after allegedly resisting arrest. At a downtown protest following the shooting, a local city councilor, let's call her Katie Savant (name changed), gave a speech in which she used very negative language against "THE POLICE." She described the shooting by the police officers as "MURDER," "BRUTAL MURDER," "A BLATANT MURDER AT THE HANDS OF THE POLICE," and "RACIAL PROFILING."

When the speech and its contents were subsequently reported in the local press, the press revealed the identities of the two police officers involved in the shooting, John Masters and Steve James (names changed). Both men were white. These officers immediately became the individuals that the local public understood to be the alleged "POLICE MURDERERS." Because of the controversy caused by this shooting, an inquest was soon held presided over by a judge and jury. The inquest considered all the facts of the case: The man who was shot was just recently released from jail and was armed and dangerous, contravening the terms of his parole; video footage showed him reaching for his gun when the police arrived; and so on. The judge and jury concluded that the officers had good reason to act the way they did, and the inquest cleared Masters and James of wrongdoing. According to this judgement these officers did not commit "MURDER" and were not guilty of "RACIAL PROFILING." Masters and James then filed a lawsuit against the local councilor, Katie Savant, for reputational and financial damage as a result of the language she had used at the protest speech and apparently continued to use subsequently, despite the finding at the inquest.

There are two big linguistic issues that needed to be considered in this case. The first (in §6.4.2) picked up on the general issue raised in earlier chapters: What exactly do the key words and phrases mean here, as used by Katie Savant in her protest speech and subsequently? The second (in §6.4.3) is the new point of this chapter: How does reference to external individuals work when we use expressions like THE POLICE? Who was Katie Savant referring to and accusing of MURDER and RACIAL PROFILING, how was this reference understood, and how did it evolve over time as the case started to receive press coverage and the audience expanded from the protest speech to the whole local community?

6.4.2 *Key Terms and Their Meanings*

The word MURDER was discussed in §2.3.3 along with some of the issues that need to be addressed when defining its precise lexical semantics. The basic sense that all the dictionaries capture is that we are dealing with a 'killing' that is a 'crime' and 'unlawful.' This is summarized in the *American Heritage Dictionary of the English Language* (5th edn, 2011) as

> '**1a.** The killing of another person without justification or excuse, especially the crime of killing a person with malice aforethought or with recklessness manifesting extreme indifference to the value of human life'

and in the *Oxford English Dictionary* (3rd edn, online) as

> '1. . . . a. The deliberate and unlawful killing of a human being, esp. in a premeditated manner.'

I also mentioned in §2.3.3 that MURDER is one of a class of words that appeals to a "competent authority" in its core meaning, like a medical or scientific body, on this occasion the law and the courts who set the rules for what constitutes a 'crime.' This ultimately determines when the term MURDER can be used appropriately in its literal sense (as opposed to 'the traffic is murder' sense). And I pointed out that in a subsequent continuation of this defamation case in 2022 the defense had produced an expert report, arguing that there was also a weaker "vernacular" but still literal sense of MURDER, as something that was merely 'wrong' or 'immoral' and values-based. They argued further that Katie Savant and others were using MURDER in this weaker sense.

I opposed this view on the grounds that what is common to all the definitions from the major dictionaries I considered is that MURDER is a 'crime' and 'unlawful.' It involves more than an appeal to morals, values, and culture. The use of the word MURDER by Katie Savant in this case was problematic precisely because a subsequent inquest by a legal body consisting of a judge and jury cleared Masters and James of all wrongdoing, based on a full consideration of the facts in relation to the legal statutes of the state in question. Hence the word MURDER, as defined by all the dictionaries, could not and should not have been used to describe this shooting.

One could possibly argue against the law here as it is defined and practiced in a certain state (and the defense's legal expert did exactly that) and which, if certain statutes or precedents were changed, might then (or might not) have had consequences for the use of language in cases of this kind. But as it stood, the law had pronounced Masters and James not guilty, and hence MURDER was not a word that could be used appropriately against them, given its linguistic definition.

I did concede in §2.3.3 that some of the more detailed dictionaries, especially the large *Webster's Third New International Dictionary of the English Language* with its separate entries for "early English law," "first-degree murder," and "second-degree murder," were putting too much encyclopedic knowledge into the dictionary, thus blurring the boundary between them. But the basic emphasis on something 'criminal' and 'unlawful' remains in all the dictionaries I considered.

Another negative term used by Katie Savant in her speech was RACIAL PROFILING. This conveys the meaning that the police were 'racially prejudiced' and that they acted on the basis of this prejudice and not on the basis of the evidence before them. It is defined in the *American Heritage Dictionary* (2011) as follows:

> **racial profiling** *n.* 'The use of a generalized suspicion based on race rather than evidence specific to the individual in policing and law enforcement activities.'

Merriam-Webster's Collegiate Dictionary (2011) makes reference to this phrase in its entry under PROFILING:

> **profiling** *n.* . . . : 'the act or process of extrapolating information about a person based on known traits or tendencies <consumer ~>; *specif*: the act

> of suspecting or targeting a person on the basis of observed characteristics or behavior <racial ~>.'

Earlier dictionaries from before 2000 that I consulted had no entry for RACIAL PROFILING, most likely because this compound term was used much less frequently back then.

Katie Savant also used the phrase RACIST MURDERERS against THE POLICE. The word RACIST can be both a noun (someone is A RACIST) and an adjective (a RACIST PERSON), and it is closely related to the noun RACISM ('a racist' is someone who 'commits racism'). The essential meaning of these words is that the individual in question is guilty of racial prejudice or discrimination. This is again a particularly serious and negative allegation to make against police officers, whose job is to uphold the law equally among all citizens, regardless of their ethnicity or color. *Merriam-Webster's Collegiate Dictionary* (2011) defines RACISM as follows and refers to RACIST:

> **racism** . . . *n* . . . **1 :** 'a belief that race is the primary determinant of human traits and capacities and that racial differences produce an inherent superiority of a particular race **2 :** racial prejudice or discrimination – **racist** . . . ' *n or adj*

6.4.3 *Who Is Being Referred to and When?*

When Katie Savant made her allegations of MURDER and RACIAL PROFILING in the protest speech, who exactly was she making these allegations against? She refers to "THE POLICE" and "THE POLICE DEPARTMENT." She did not explicitly identify the two police officers by name who did the shooting, John Masters and Steve James. Her definite noun phrase THE POLICE would therefore have been understood by her audience at the original time of its utterance to refer to whoever the members of the police force happened to be who carried out the "BRUTAL MURDER" of the man killed. After her protest speech, however, the police officers in question were named in the local press and details about them were given. Their ages were thirty-four and thirty-eight, respectively; they were both hired in 2008, and both were white. This radically changed the whole linguistic context for the interpretation of THE POLICE, i.e. it changed the nature and number of the people involved in this linguistic exchange, and what they would understand THE POLICE to refer to based on their "mutual knowledge" (recall the Clark and Marshall reference provided previously).

The context of the original protest speech by Katie Savant consisted, therefore, of the speaker herself, her live audience at the time, their downtown location, the information given in other speeches at the protest, and the knowledge shared by these participants of relevant events in the world, especially about the shooting of the African American. When the protest and the speeches were reported in the local press, the context expanded significantly to include many more individuals in the community who now received this information, who read quotations from the speakers (including Katie Savant), and who learned pieces of information that were added to their shared community knowledge base, including, if they hadn't heard it before, about the shooting. They also learned details about the police officers who did the shooting. As the participants in this linguistic exchange expanded, so did their "mutual knowledge" and the amount of information that the speaker or writer could now assume that the hearer or reader shared with the speaker/writer.

For the wider community the allegations of "MURDER" and "RACIAL PROFILING" then became directed not just against THE POLICE in general but quite specifically against these two named police officers who carried out the shooting. All the allegations of "MURDER," "RACIAL PROFILING," and "RACISM" now became inextricably linked in people's minds to these two individuals, in addition to 'the police force in general.' Hence, as the discourse context expanded from the local protest march to the wider community, through the media, additional information was added to readers' knowledge base, there were many more readers than there were hearers originally, and the negative and damaging allegations made by Katie Savant against "THE POLICE" would have been extended specifically and inevitably to the two individuals named who carried out the shooting.

This is all relevant to Keith Donnellan's referential/attributive distinction for definite noun phrases (recall the citation given in §6.4). He gave the example sentence "SMITH'S MURDERER IS INSANE." In the attributive use the interlocutors know only that Smith has been murdered, but they don't know by whom, and it is asserted that whoever carried out this deed, the murder of Smith, must be insane. In the referential case, the interlocutors use "SMITH'S MURDERER" to refer to an individual who is known independently as, for example, HARRY or THE MAN NEXT DOOR, and it is asserted that this individual is insane, for reasons that could be quite distinct from his murder of Smith. The crucial basis for this difference in meaning and reference involves the degree of mutual knowledge shared by the interlocutors. If the identity of "SMITH'S

MURDERER" is not known, its meaning will be attributive. As soon as this person's identity becomes mutually known, it has to be understood referentially, i.e. as identifying that very person.

When Katie Savant first made her allegations of "MURDER" against "THE POLICE" and "THE POLICE DEPARTMENT," these definite descriptions were therefore understood attributively by her audience. They were understood to be directed against whoever the individuals happened to be who were members of the police force and who carried out this shooting, their precise identities being unknown. But as soon as these individuals were named in the press and identifying features were given in addition to their names, namely their ages, dates of hiring, and ethnicity, then the meaning became referential and hearers and readers could not avoid associating these individuals with THE POLICE and with the allegations made by Katie Savant. So her reference to "THE BRUTAL MURDER ... AT THE HANDS OF THE POLICE" was now understood, when uttered or reported later, not attributively as 'the African American was murdered at the hands of whoever the police officers happened to be.' It was understood referentially as 'this man was murdered by John Martin and Steve James, the particular police officers who carried out the killing.' They now stood accused of "MURDER," "RACIAL PROFILING," and "RACISM," and were understood in the minds of hearers and readers to be the perpetrators of the crime of unlawfully killing the man in question, even when more general terms such as "THE POLICE" were used to refer to them.

CHAPTER 7

Disputes over Spelling and Punctuation

This chapter considers some lawsuits in which spelling and punctuation were at the basis of the dispute. In §7.1 a classic example is discussed of how a small difference in spelling can make a big difference in language usage and the law. It involved the Salesforce Company, which uses the mark SALESFORCE written as a single word, as opposed to the two-word SALES FORCE. The former differs from the latter primarily by not having a single space between the two words, and also through frequent use of a capital "S" in "Salesforce." The latter two-word sequence does not evoke this association with the Salesforce Company and is generally used as a descriptive compound term for 'a group of salespeople responsible for selling the goods or services of a company,' i.e. any company. The linguistic and legal challenge raised in this case concerned whether the single-word SALESFORCE had indeed achieved this distinctiveness from its two-word counterpart as a source identifier. It is shown here, on the basis of various corpora that are sensitive to spellings and word separations, that SALESFORCE has indeed achieved unique reference and source identification.

The next section (§7.2) considers a case with a similar nominal compound involving Noun + Noun, but where the space between the two nouns could be shown not to be significant. This was the case for MOVIEGUIDE, in which the plaintiff claimed this single-word version as their trademark, just like SALESFORCE is a trademark. On this occasion, however, clear semantic and corpus evidence showed that the two-word MOVIE GUIDE and the one-word MOVIEGUIDE were used interchangeably, both as generic terms, and hence neither could be a source identifier and a trademark.

Finally in §7.3 a lawsuit is discussed in which the dispute centered around who exactly was being covered by insurance in the phrase "THE NAMED INSURED: X, Y" as a result of the comma punctuation between the entities listed as X and Y.

7.1 SALESFORCE versus SALES FORCE

A trademark dispute in which I was retained (2018–2019, Palo Alto, California) involved a small difference that had major consequences for language and the law. It involved SALESFORCE written as a single word, which now enjoys widespread recognition as an identifier and trademark for the Salesforce Company, as opposed to the two-word SALES FORCE. The legal issue that prompted my involvement was that the Salesforce Company had filed an appeal with the US Patent and Trademark Office to protect its mark, and specifically it was trying to prevent the registration of another mark by a different company that included the same single-word spelling for the compound, namely YOUR WORKFORCE IS YOUR SALESFORCE. My assignment was, first, to assess whether SALESFORCE was indeed associated with the Salesforce Company in American English usage at the time, and second to assess whether the two spellings were consistently differentiated from one another in their meaning and reference. My conclusion, based on quantitative corpus evidence combined with lexical-semantic analysis, was that they were quite distinct in usage and not interchangeable, and that using SALESFORCE within a mark that was registered to a different company would likely cause confusion.

The linguistic patterns in the usage data from this case were very interesting, and they merit a summary in the present context, as does the role of linguistic argumentation in resolving a dispute within the law. The case is especially revealing because it shows how what are often alternatives in English spelling for one and the same word combination with the same pronunciation are on other occasions not interchangeable at all (though we shall see below that the issue of whether they were interchangeable or not was disputed in this case). A small difference in spelling and punctuation can suddenly acquire enormous real-world significance, sufficient to trigger a lawsuit.

7.1.1 The Grammar and Orthography of SALESFORCE and SALES FORCE

SALESFORCE and SALES FORCE are further examples of "noun compounds" or "complex nominals" in English of the same general type that we discussed in connection with the APP STORE case (§3.4). (Recall that Quirk, Greenbaum, Leech, and Svartvik use the former term with "compound" in their 1985 *Comprehensive Grammar of the English Language*, Longman, London & Seminar Press, New York, pp. 1330–1333, while Levi uses the latter in *The Syntax and Semantics of Complex Nominals*, Academic

Press, New York, 1978). The noun FORCE is the "head" of this compound, while the noun SALES "modifies" and immediately precedes the head. Its syntactic structure is $_{Noun}$[Noun$_1$ Noun$_2$], with Noun$_1$ as the modifier and Noun$_2$ as the head.

It was pointed out earlier (recall §1.2 and §2.4.3) that the head of any compound is its most important part. It is the component that determines the syntactic status of the whole unit. If the head is a noun, so is the compound, regardless of the status of the modifier. SALESFORCE (also SALES FORCE) is a noun because FORCE is a noun, not because the modifier SALES happens to be a noun as well. The head is also the most important semantically, and the meaning of the modifier must adapt to, and be understood relative to, the head. In SALES FORCE the speaker is referring to a certain type of FORCE, understood in this context as 'an organized body of workers' (cf. the *New Shorter Oxford English Dictionary*, 1993), and the SALES modifier then limits the reference of FORCE to 'those workers who are responsible for selling goods and services.'

With respect to spelling, I mentioned in §3.4.1 there are three different ways of writing these [Noun$_1$ Noun$_2$] compounds: The two nouns can be separate words, they can occur in a single word, or they can be joined by hyphenation. Occasionally all three are found as alternatives. Quirk et al. (1985) gave the example of FLOWER POT, FLOWERPOT, and FLOWER-POT (p. 1569). More often, however, the spelling conventions of Modern English have settled upon just one variant as the only or preferred spelling form for each noun compound, and a major determinant of the compression of two words into a single-word spelling is frequency of usage. The single-word FOOTBALL is much more frequently used than the two-word SOCCER BALL.

For noun compounds containing SALES as the first element, the *OED* online (3rd edn) writes SALESMAN as a single word and gives a separate entry and definition for it, whereas SALES REPRESENTATIVE and SALES REP, which are also given separate entries and definitions, are written as two words. The former is much more commonly used than the latter two. More generally, the *OED* online lists and gives attested examples for many compounds with SALES as the first element. These are all judged by the dictionary to occur with sufficient frequency to merit inclusion, from among the much larger set that are grammatically and semantically possible in accordance with the productive rules of English grammar. The criterion of overall frequency of occurrence is used by all the dictionaries in this way to select which compounds to include and which to leave out. The *OED* online gives the most usual, or the only spelling form, for the noun compounds that it lists. When there are common alternatives (as with FLOWERPOT, FLOWER POT, and FLOWER-POT), these are also listed.

I summarize here, as background to the discussion of SALESFORCE and SALES FORCE that follows, a number of the compounds with SALES + Head Noun that are listed in the *OED* online (3rd edn). Single-word compounds are given first in (1), including any alternative spellings; then the hyphenated ones and their alternatives are shown in (2); and those written with two words are given in (3):

(1) SALESMAN, SALESWOMAN, SALESROOM (also SALES-ROOM, SALES ROOM)

(2) SALES-MANAGER (also SALESMANAGER), SALES-PERSON (also SALESPERSON), SALES-PEOPLE (also SALESPEOPLE, SALES PEOPLE)

(3) SALES CLERK, SALES DRIVE, SALES ENGINEER, SALES FIGURES, SALES FORCE, SALES OUTLET, SALES PITCH, SALES PRESENTATION, SALES PROMOTION, SALES REP, SALES REPRESENTATIVE, SALES SLIP, SALES TAX, SALES VOLUME.

The OED online (3rd edn) is now the largest worldwide dictionary of English, and it includes American English as well as the other major varieties. It lists SALES FORCE among the two-word compounds summarized in (3). The first example that it gives for it is from another dictionary, the 1934 edition of *Webster's New International Dictionary of the English Language*, and is in the form of a definition: 'the sales clerks or sales agents of an establishment.' An attested example from 1980 is

> "Soon the Bonnard's sales force would start clocking in, and . . . after that the customers."

The *OED* makes no mention of SALESFORCE written as a single word, however. Nor did any of the other dictionaries that I consulted in 2018–2019. Since both SALESFORCE and SALES FORCE were by then very frequently occurring in American English, I needed to go to a source of recent data that could provide quantitative and qualitative information about these two forms of the noun compound and answer the following questions: How frequently used is each of these terms in American English? And, crucially, is there a significant difference in meaning and reference between SALESFORCE and SALES FORCE, as was claimed by the plaintiff (the Salesforce Company), such that the former had trademark status in actual usage whereas the latter did not?

Large corpora of English language usage can now provide answers to these questions. One of the most widely used in linguistic research is the Corpus of Contemporary American English ("COCA") developed at Brigham Young University (BYU) as one of a suite of BYU corpora (accessible at https://corpus.byu.edu/coca/). I accordingly searched for the two spelling variants in this corpus, and I present the results in the next section.

7.1.2 Usage Figures in COCA

COCA consisted (in 2018) of 560 million words of texts divided equally between different genres of English, spoken, fiction, popular magazines, newspapers, and academic texts, and collected between 1990 and 2017 (20 million words from each year). This corpus, in contrast to some others, permits searches that are sensitive to the precise written form of the items being searched. COCA also has the capability to show the sentences surrounding the sentence in which the key word occurs, thus making it possible to assess how the word is being used in context, and what exactly it means and refers to in that context. The context can be accessed first in the single line of text in which the word occurs, and then in a much larger sequence of running text if more detail is needed.

In the 560 million words of COCA there were 326 occurrences of the two-word SALES FORCE and 58 occurrences of the one-word SALESFORCE. There were also five occurrences of the hyphenated SALES-FORCE. I analyzed all of these occurrences in order to see whether there was any difference between them, in meaning and reference, or whether they were just alternative spellings for the same compound, with the same meaning and reference. The results were quite striking.

All fifty-eight instances of the single-word SALESFORCE referred to the Salesforce Company. Not a single one referred to any other company, or to any other company's sales force, or to sales forces in general. They all referred to Salesforce, and they all used a capital "S." Typical examples were

> "Salesforce was expected to post earnings of 47 cents a share ... " (MarketWatch, 2018).

> "Overall, Salesforce's revenue was up 27 per cent year over year ... " (CNBC, 2018).

> "they have been meeting with companies including Uber and Salesforce to improve on a longstanding issue of underrepresented minorities . . . " (Ars Technica, 2017).

> "Salesforce shares fell more than 4 percent in extended trading . . . " (BloombergQuint, 2018).

The 326 occurrences of the two-word SALES FORCE, by contrast, were used quite differently. I examined their precise grammar and meaning, along with the linguistic context for all of them. A full 324 (or 99 percent) described a sales force or forces in general, or they referred to the sales force of a company other than Salesforce. In other words, the two-word SALES FORCE was used almost exclusively as a descriptive term. Grammatical indicators of this descriptive usage included the presence of the indefinite article "A" before SALES FORCE, as in

> "Knowland even has a sales force that will call that decision maker and woo the person for a hotel" (*Washington Post*, 2010).

> "it's pretty efficient to have a single sales force pitching toothpaste as well as laundry detergent" (NPR, *Talk of the Nation*, 2013).

> "musical numbers were performed by members of a rather unique sales force" (*Musical Educators Journal*, 2015).

A further grammatical indicator of descriptiveness was the use of a possessive adjective like "THEIR" linking the reference of SALES FORCE to a term such as SALES EXECUTIVES (referring to 'sales executives in general'), as in

> "sales executives usually espouse one or two techniques that they want their sales force to follow" (*Reference & User Services Quarterly*, 2014).

Possessive adjectives, or possessive noun phrases with a genitive "S," also served to link the reference of SALES FORCE to a company or companies other than Salesforce, as in

> "Microsoft is restructuring its global sales force to refocus the group . . . " (*Business Insider*, 2017).

> "GE has ordered up thousands for its sales force . . . " (*Mother Jones*, 2011).

> "AOL's sales force will also have the right to sell some display advertising" (*New York Times*, 2005).

The definite article THE before SALES FORCE also served to link the reference to a different company, as in the following in which THE SALES FORCE refers back to Gilead:

> "Gilead's sales material reminds doctors of the drug's toxicity, and reps urge them to prescribe Genvoya.... To prove its case, the sales force is armed with head-to-head studies" (*Los Angeles Times*, 2016).

Another common indicator of descriptive usage was when SALES FORCE was both preceded by THE and followed by a prepositional phrase like IN AMERICA or OF A DIFFERENT FIRM that described which sales force was being referred to:

> "the pharmaceutical sales force in America doubled ... " (*The Atlantic*, 2006).

> "to seek employment in the sales force of a different firm" (*Fortune*, 2005).

Of the two examples in COCA that did use separate words and referred to the Salesforce Company, one used both capital "S" and capital "F," i.e. "Sales Force," and the other from a *CBS: This Morning* computer-generated transcript used small letters throughout, i.e. "sales force." The five instances of hyphenated SALES-FORCE in COCA were all descriptive terms and were used like the two-word SALES FORCE.

I also searched for plural uses of these different written noun compounds, i.e. with the head noun in the plural, FORCES. I reasoned that if SALESFORCE as a single word referred productively to the Salesforce Company, whereas SALES FORCE with two words was descriptive and legally "generic" for sales forces in general or for those of different companies, then we would expect this latter to occur in the plural as well as the singular in English, since there could be many such. The single-word SALESFORCE, on the other hand, should not be found in the plural, given its strong association with the Salesforce Company, of which there is only one. (Recall the similar reasoning and test for genericness in the APP STORE case, §3.4.7–3.4.8.) I accordingly checked in COCA, and the results bore this out. There were zero occurrences of SALESFORCES in the plural but thirty-four instances of SALES FORCES, all of them descriptive of sales forces in general or of sales forces linked to companies other than Salesforce. Typical examples were

> "Some drug companies have cut their sales forces ... " (*The Atlantic*, 2006).

> "Super Bowl Sunday is the first holiday created solely by sales forces without ties to religion, heritage or history in America ... " (*Denver News*, 2008).

These data from 2018 pointed to a clear partitioning in American English between the single-word SALESFORCE and the two-word SALES FORCE. The former was clearly associated with the Salesforce Company, and COCA provided evidence for the public's strong familiarity with it, whereas the latter was used as a descriptive term that did not refer uniquely to Salesforce. There was one respect, however, in which COCA underrepresented the true frequency of usage for SALESFORCE and the strength of its association with the Salesforce Company. COCA at that time covered data collected evenly (20 million words per year) from American sources between 1990 and 2017. But the Salesforce Company was only founded in 1999. So for the first nine years, or almost one-third of the total time frame of twenty-eight years covered by COCA, there could be no examples of SALESFORCE referring to the Salesforce Company, because this company did not yet exist! And had it existed, we could have expected far more than the fifty-eight instances derived from the later time frame. I accordingly consulted a second corpus from BYU, the News on the Web (or "NOW" corpus), consisting of many more words, 6 billion, and derived from web-based newspapers and magazines from a later period, 2010 to the time of this litigation, i.e. a time frame during which Salesforce was already in existence. NOW is a constantly expanding web-based database (accessible at https://corpus.byu.edu/now/), and the figures provided in the following section were based on searches conducted in September 2018.

7.1.3 Usage Figures in NOW

As expected, the number of occurrences of single-word SALESFORCE relative to two-word SALES FORCE increased significantly in the NOW corpus. The absolute numbers were also higher, of course, because NOW in 2018 was more than ten times the size of COCA. The 58 SALESFORCE to 326 SALES FORCE tokens in COCA became as many as 10,121 SALESFORCE tokens to 3,137 SALES FORCE in NOW (with 23 hyphenated instances of SALES-FORCE), i.e. SALESFORCE rose from 15.1 percent of the total for both in COCA (excluding the hyphenated examples) to 76.3 percent in NOW, a fivefold increase. These NOW corpus results, coupled with the COCA findings, provided prima facie evidence for an extremely strong association in the public's mind between the single-word SALESFORCE and the Salesforce Company, as reflected in newspapers and magazines since 2010.

I performed a linguistic analysis of the meaning and reference of the different spelling variants in NOW, similar to that conducted for COCA. Since the number of items in NOW was so much larger, I selected a sample. I chose the first 300 occurrences of SALESFORCE, the first 300 of SALES FORCE, and all 23 instances of SALES-FORCE. As a result a total of more than 1,000 occurrences of SALESFORCE, SALES FORCE, and SALES-FORCE in the two corpora received detailed qualitative analysis, in addition to the overall quantities cited.

Of the first 300 occurrences of the single-word SALESFORCE in NOW, all but 9 referred to the Salesforce Company, i.e. 291 out of 300 (or 97 percent). Typical examples were

> "On May 2, the second day of the quarter, Salesforce closed on its $6.5 billion acquisition of MuleSoft . . . " (MarketWatch, 2018).

> "A previous version of this story compared Salesforce's EPS number with a Thompson Reuters estimate . . . " (CNBC, 2018).

> "So far the Transbay neighborhood – home to Salesforce, Trulia, LinkedIn, DocuSign, Fitbit and many other companies . . . " (*San Francisco Chronicle*, 2018).

This 97 percent association between SALESFORCE and the Salesforce Company is all the more remarkable because the newspapers and magazines of NOW are taken from the web, and a considerable number of its publications originate in English-speaking countries outside of the US, including Asia and Africa. The Salesforce Company had clearly achieved worldwide recognition, based on this evidence, along with people's knowledge that the single-word SALESFORCE referred to it.

For the first 300 occurrences of the two-word SALES FORCE in NOW I found exactly the same pattern as in COCA: All but two were used descriptively, i.e. 298 out of 300 (or 99 percent). Typical examples were

> "Purdue Pharma says in a written statement the company 'vigorously' denies that its sales force acted improperly . . . " (WPLN, 2018).

> "the risk that we may not be able to successfully maintain an effective sales force to commercialize ZILRETTA" (MarketWatch, 2018).

> "the upstart hired a massive sales force, sponsored a Tour de France team . . . " (*Toronto Star*, 2018).

The two examples that used SALES FORCE to refer to the Salesforce Company (both written with capital "S" and capital "F"; i.e. "Sales Force") originated in Jamaica and Singapore, respectively. Clearly, the two-word SALES FORCE was used almost exceptionlessly as a descriptive term, whereas the single-word word SALESFORCE referred in 97 percent of instances to the Salesforce Company. The twenty-three hyphenated instances of SALES-FORCE in NOW were all descriptive as well and did not refer to the Salesforce Company.

These figures from COCA and NOW, and the results of my linguistic and contextual analysis, revealed a clear pattern in the spelling conventions of contemporary American English, and indeed in English writing worldwide. The single-word SALESFORCE refers to the Salesforce Company; SALES FORCE with two words and the hyphenated SALES-FORCE refer to a sales force or sales forces in general or to companies other than Salesforce.

7.1.4 *The Rebuttal and the iWeb Corpus*

Despite this seemingly overwhelming evidence from COCA and NOW regarding the difference between SALESFORCE and SALES FORCE, the defense responded by arguing that the two different spellings were nonetheless both descriptive and interchangeable variants. They also produced a report by an expert (in business) arguing that SALESFORCE was a generic term, based on his many years of professional experience in this area. Some of the linguistic counterevidence cited by the defense to my usage figures from COCA and NOW were collected from a third and even larger BYU corpus, the iWeb corpus of 14 billion words (see https://corpus.byu.edu) that had just been developed at that time. I was accordingly invited to respond in a rebuttal report, in which I conducted a usage analysis of SALESFORCE and SALES FORCE in iWeb, similar to the one I had conducted in COCA and NOW. Needless to say, iWeb provided the same overwhelming association between the single-word term and the Salesforce Company as the other corpora. But because of the sheer size of the iWeb corpus, the small percentage of exceptions in the usage patterns for each became a larger number of actual occurrences in which SALESFORCE was not a trademark and SALES FORCE did refer to the Salesforce Company. These examples combined with other attested exceptions were cited by the defense as support for the interchangeability of the two variants and for the genericness of SALESFORCE.

In effect, what the defense did was to focus on the exceptional uses of the single-word term that did not refer exclusively to the Salesforce Company. At the same time they did not look for, and so withheld, all the evidence showing that SALESFORCE does normally refer to Salesforce. In fact, a full 98.5 percent of instances of SALESFORCE in iWeb referred to Salesforce (see below). There are bound to be handfuls of exceptions in a corpus as large as this, and interestingly many of these arose as simplifications and shortenings of the two-word SALES FORCE when combined with other words within a larger and more complex noun phrase (see §7.1.6), i.e. in phrases like SALESFORCE INCENTIVE, SALESFORCE EFFECTIVENESS, SALESFORCE MANAGEMENT, and FIELD SALESFORCE. Meanwhile, the two-word SALES FORCE was used in almost 98 percent of the examples in iWeb as a descriptive term referring to any group of people who sell the goods or services of a company.

7.1.5 Usage Figures in iWeb

In 2018 iWeb was a new web-based corpus developed by the corpus linguistics team at BYU with 14 billion words and was their largest corpus of English. The web pages that supplied these words were taken from the top 1 million websites worldwide in 2017 (based on numbers of users) and were restricted to those that originated in mainly native English-speaking countries (US, Canada, Ireland, UK, Australia, and New Zealand), with some further restrictions to avoid repetitions.

There were 73,144 instances overall of the single-word SALESFORCE in iWeb, and again the vast majority of these (some 98.5 percent) did refer to the Salesforce Company, based on the sample I selected for qualitative analysis (as discussed below). The exceptional examples cited by the defense that did not refer to the Salesforce Company, mostly in phrasal combinations, fell within the other 1.5 percent. They gave the following figures for uses of SALESFORCE that did not refer to "the Opposer," i.e. the Salesforce Company, shown here in (4) (see also the figures in (5)):

(4) 1 occurrence of SALESFORCE INCENTIVE ("not referring to Opposer");
16 occurrences of SALESFORCE EFFECTIVENESS ("most of which did not refer to Opposer");
20 occurrences of SALESFORCE MANAGEMENT ("most of which did not refer to Opposer");
14 occurrences of FIELD SALESFORCE ("none of which referred to Opposer");
22 occurrences of DIRECT SALESFORCE ("most of which did not refer to Opposer").

I return to these and other exceptions in the discussion that follows. In addition to the 73,144 occurrences of SALESFORCE (in August 2019), there were also 12,110 instances of the two-word SALES FORCE in iWeb.

I analyzed a large sample of these 73,144 and 12,110 instances, respectively, and examined their meaning and reference. My aim was, first, to test the finding from the other corpora that the single-word SALESFORCE was either exclusively associated with the Salesforce Company (COCA) or overwhelmingly so (at 97 percent in NOW), whereas the two-word term was almost always descriptive, referring to any group of sales people. Second, I hypothesized that the relatively small number of instances of the single-word SALESFORCE in iWeb not referring to Salesforce would fall within the exceptional 0–3 percent of such instances found in COCA and NOW, and that the exceptional numbers would be roughly what we would expect for a corpus the size of iWeb. I also expected that almost all the uses of the two-word SALES FORCE would again be descriptive.

I began by analyzing the first 2,000 of the 73,144 single-word instances of SALESFORCE in iWeb (in August 2019) and found that all but 26 referred to the Salesforce Company. That is, 1,974 of these 2,000, or 98.7 percent, referred to Salesforce, almost all with a capital "S," and just 26 did not and were descriptive and not limited to Salesforce. This supported the hypothesis that the descriptive uses of SALESFORCE cited by the defense were indeed taken from the 1–2 percent of exceptions. In order to check this further I examined the next 6,000 instances of SALESFORCE in iWeb, making 8,000 in all. The results were almost identical: 7,883 of these first 8,000, or 98.5 percent, referred to the Salesforce Company, and just 1.5 percent did not.

For the two-word SALES FORCE I analyzed the first 2,000 (of 12,110) in iWeb, making a combined 10,000 searches overall for the single- and two-word terms in this corpus. All but 42, 1,958 out of 2,000, or almost 98 percent of instances of SALES FORCE were used descriptively, almost all with a small initial "s," and did not refer to the Salesforce Company. This was the same pattern we found in COCA (§7.1.2) and NOW (§7.1.3).

These figures confirm the clear contrast between the single-word SALESFORCE, which refers overwhelmingly to the Salesforce Company, and the two-word SALES FORCE, which is almost always descriptive. What the defense did, in effect, was to cherry-pick from the 1–2 percent of exceptional uses of SALESFORCE in iWeb, while making no mention of the vastly greater number of single-word uses that do refer to Salesforce and that undermined the claim of interchangeability. The raw number of descriptive uses of SALESFORCE that were cited might seem, at first, to be not insignificant, but this false impression was created by the vast size of the iWeb corpus. Statistically the number of exceptions was very small. The single-word SALESFORCE referred in 98.5 percent of instances to the Salesforce Company; the two-word SALES FORCE was the common descriptive term in almost 98 percent of uses. These relative quantities in iWeb indicated further that all the other attested examples of the single-word term used descriptively and cited by the defense from various books and articles were indeed exceptional, and that the overwhelming (98.5 percent) usage of SALESFORCE in English does refer to the Salesforce Company.

7.1.6 The Single-Word SALESFORCE within Larger Noun Phrases

The exceptional uses of single-word SALESFORCE used descriptively and cited by the defense occurred especially within larger noun phrases consisting of many words. There is a tendency in written English to reduce the overall numbers of words within larger noun phrases whenever possible, for reasons of simplicity and brevity, and this results in occasional instances of shortening a descriptive term such as SALES FORCE INCENTIVE (three words) into SALESFORCE INCENTIVE. The latter contains just two words and has shorter overall length on account of the reduction of two intervening word spaces to just one. These reductions of SALES FORCE to SALESFORCE are not nearly as common, however, as the retention of the original two-word spelling for SALES FORCE in larger noun phrases, precisely because the two-word and single-word terms are generally different in meaning and reference, and writers avoid simplification most of the time. The defense failed to mention that the two-word SALES FORCE was still much more common in these combinations than the single-word SALESFORCE, and they only gave examples of the latter.

In order to show this I examined (August 2019) the frequencies of occurrence in iWeb for these exceptional larger noun phrase combinations containing the single-word SALESFORCE when it does not refer to the Salesforce Company, as cited by the defense, and I compared them with corresponding noun phrases consisting of the two-word SALES FORCE within exactly the same larger word combinations. I also checked and confirmed that the two-word term in all these otherwise identical combinations was being used descriptively. The comparison was quite striking:

(5) 1 occurrence of SALESFORCE INCENTIVE (“not referring to Opposer”), 8 of SALES FORCE INCENTIVE;

16 occurrences of SALESFORCE EFFECTIVENESS ("most of which did not refer to Opposer," I counted all 16 as not referring to Salesforce), 212 of SALES FORCE EFFECTIVENESS;

19 occurrences of SALESFORCE MANAGEMENT ("most of which did not refer to Opposer," I counted 7 that did not), 98 of SALES FORCE MANAGEMENT;

13 occurrences of FIELD SALESFORCE ("none of which referred to Opposer," I counted 11 that did not), 138 FIELD SALES FORCE;

22 occurrences of DIRECT SALESFORCE ("most of which did not refer to Opposer," I counted 19 that did not), 443 DIRECT SALES FORCE.

In other words, even in these larger noun phrases in which there is an independent tendency to shorten three-word into two-word sequences, we see that this tendency is resisted most of the time and that the two-word SALES FORCE is not generally reduced to single-word SALESFORCE, precisely because, I argued, the two are quite distinct in meaning and reference, and this distinction is maintained even here. So, SALES FORCE INCENTIVE was eight times more frequent in descriptive usage than the reduced two-word counterpart SALESFORCE INCENTIVE (8 to 1 occurrences). SALES FORCE EFFECTIVENESS was thirteen times more frequent than its two-word counterpart in descriptive usage (212 to 16). SALES FORCE MANAGEMENT was fourteen times more frequent in descriptive usage (98 to 7), FIELD SALES FORCE thirteen times more frequent (138 to 11), and DIRECT SALES FORCE twenty-three times more frequent (443 to 19).

These comparative figures show that even in longer and more complex noun phrases that are occasionally shortened and from which the defense drew their purported evidence for the descriptiveness of SALESFORCE, writers do not generally perform the shortening but instead preserve the clear distinction between single-word SALESFORCE and two-word SALES FORCE that is overwhelmingly evident throughout the iWeb corpus.

7.1.7 Against Genericness and Interchangeability

The defense in this case produced an expert report by a business consultant who argued, based on his long experience in the field, that SALESFORCE and SALES FORCE were "used interchangeably" and that SALESFORCE was a "generic term for individuals who sell the goods or services of a company."

In my rebuttal I summarized the empirical evidence set out in the previous sections of this chapter showing the clear difference in meaning and reference between the single-word SALESFORCE and the two-word SALES FORCE. The single-word SALESFORCE clearly answers the questions that McCarthy (*McCarthy on Trademarks and Unfair Competition*, 2008) set as a test for trademark status (see §3.4.1): "Who are you?," "Where do you come from?," and "Who vouches for you?" SALESFORCE refers either exclusively (in COCA) or almost entirely (in the NOW and iWeb corpora) to the Salesforce Company. It does not answer McCarthy's question "What are you?" and so is not "generic" by McCarthy's criteria. It is not the common descriptive term or common name for something, but instead identifies, and has clearly identified for many years, a single source of origin.

Nor is the single-word SALESFORCE even properly "descriptive" in McCarthy's terms (recall §3.3 and 3.5) in relation to the Salesforce Company. It does not describe the goods and services that this company actually provides. These are and were at the time quite numerous and included many different computer services for business management and marketing, designing, developing, and maintaining computer software for clients, consulting and technical support, hosting websites for others, social networking services, sales support management, and so on. SALESFORCE does not begin to describe any of these activities. The two-word SALES FORCE does not do so either. It describes only 'a group of salespeople responsible for selling the goods or services of a company.'

The expert's claim that SALESFORCE was interchangeable in usage with SALES FORCE and generic was incorrect, therefore. Despite the small orthographic difference between it and the two-word SALES FORCE, the one-word version is used as a trademark that clearly identifies a single source of origin. The two-word SALES FORCE is a common descriptive and generic term, but even this does not describe the goods and services of the Salesforce Company. Hence, both SALESFORCE and SALES FORCE are neither generic nor descriptive in relation to the actual goods and services provided by Salesforce, and SALESFORCE does refer to the Salesforce Company.

7.2 MOVIEGUIDE versus MOVIE GUIDE

Having just seen a case in which the space between words in a nominal compound really matters, let us now examine a parallel case, with an almost identical grammatical structure, in which it can be shown not to. This was the case of MOVIEGUIDE, in which Good News Communications, Inc., as the plaintiff claimed this single-word version as their trademark. For the two-word MOVIE GUIDE, they claimed no proprietary rights. I was retained by the defense (Los Angeles, 2008), representing a company that routinely used the two interchangeably. The defense had preliminary evidence that both versions were generic terms, and interchangeable, and hence that neither could be a source identifier and a trademark, and they wanted to make a legal argument to this effect.

I was asked to address two linguistic questions of relevance to this legal determination: first, whether MOVIE GUIDE was a "generic term for compilations of data that instruct or direct readers regarding movies"; second, if so, whether the elimination of the space between MOVIE and GUIDE, in MOVIEGUIDE, would mean that this latter ceased to be generic and acquired instead a source-designative function, in particular "in the context of computer-mediated communication such as an internet browser's address box, as in www.movieguide.xxx."

My opinion, based as usual on grammatical, lexical, orthographic, and usage evidence that I will summarize briefly below, was that MOVIE GUIDE is indeed a generic term in American English for compilations of data that instruct or direct readers regarding movies. Furthermore, eliminating the space between MOVIE and GUIDE, this evidence showed, in the context of computer-mediated communication, did not add any source-designative function such that MOVIE GUIDE ceased to be generic. The writing conventions for website addresses quite generally require all spaces between symbols to be eliminated, and so MOVIE GUIDE is consistently written as MOVIEGUIDE and is used productively with a generic meaning in this context. There is also evidence outside of this particular context for the increasing frequency of the single-word term MOVIEGUIDE as a generic alternative to the two-word MOVIE GUIDE.

7.2.1 *The Grammar and Pronunciation of MOVIE GUIDE and MOVIEGUIDE*

MOVIE GUIDE and MOVIEGUIDE are further examples of the "noun compounds" and "complex nominals" in English like SALES FORCE and SALESFORCE (recall §7.1.1 and the references therein to Quirk, Greenbaum, Leech, and Svartvik, 1985, and to Levi, 1978). The noun GUIDE is the "head" of this compound unit, and the noun MOVIE "modifies" and immediately precedes the head. Its syntactic structure is again $_{\text{Noun}}[\text{Noun}_1\ \text{Noun}_2]$, with Noun_1 as the modifier and Noun_2 as the head.

In addition to the grammatical properties of these nominal compounds summarized in §7.1.1, and also earlier in §3.4 in connection with APP STORE, which has the same basic structure, there was a further property of compounds that was of interest in this case and involved the assignment of stress or phonetic prominence (recall the discussion of stress assignment to BLUE BOOK in §6.3.3). Using italic letters to indicate such prominence, the pronunciation of MOVIE GUIDE is *MOVIE* GUIDE, with greater stress on the first noun and less on the second. Similarly, we say *MOVIE* STAR, *MOVIE* THEATER, *TENNIS* BALL, *SOCCER* BALL, *CUBE* STEAK, and also *DISH* CLOTH and *MOTOR* HOME, and so on. There is another competing stress pattern for [$Noun_1$ $Noun_2$] sequences in English, however, involving a more even stress on the two nouns. Quirk et al. (1985, p. 1330) give examples such as *IRON ROD* and *LIFE IMPRISONMENT* for this second pattern.

The rule for assigning initial prominence to sequences such as *MOVIE* GUIDE reflects, according to Quirk et al. (1985, p. 1330), "the degree to which a sequence is 'institutionalized' as a lexical item, *ie* a compound." Putting this another way, [$Noun_1$ $Noun_2$] sequences in English that are very commonly used and that function like single words generally have a stress pattern with one peak of prominence, just like single words do.

7.2.2 *The Compositional Meaning of MOVIE GUIDE*

The two nouns MOVIE and GUIDE are commonly used in modern American English, and they are each listed in all the major dictionaries I consulted. Both are generic or common descriptive nouns. The meanings defined for them do not differ significantly across the dictionaries that I relied on primarily for this case (*The American Heritage Dictionary of the English Language*, 3rd edn, 1992; *The Random House Webster's Unabridged Dictionary*, 2nd edn, 1997; and *Webster's Third New International Dictionary of the English Language Unabridged*, 1993).

For **MOVIE**, the *American Heritage Dictionary* gives the following entries:

> '**1.a.** A sequence of photographs projected onto a screen with sufficient rapidity as to create the illusion of motion and continuity. **b.** A connected cinematic narrative represented in this form. **2.** A theater that shows movies. **3. movies. a.** A showing of a movie. Often used with *the.* **b.** The movie industry . . . .'

The word **GUIDE** occurs both as a noun and a verb in English. For GUIDE as a noun, the *American Heritage Dictionary* gives the following entries, among others:

> '**1.a.** One who shows the way by leading, directing, or advising. **b.** One who serves as a model for others, as in a course of conduct. **2.** A person employed to conduct others, as through a museum, and give information about points of interest encountered. **3.a.** Something, such as a pamphlet, that offers basic information or instruction: *a shopper's guide*. **b.** a guide-book. **4.a.** Something that serves to direct or indicate . . . .'

The combined meaning for MOVIE plus GUIDE, i.e. for MOVIE GUIDE, is straightforwardly derivable from the meanings of these two words separately, i.e. "compositionally" (§1.2). Following the definitions just given, we can define this composite meaning as 'something, such as a book or pamphlet or service, that offers basic information or instruction about movies.' Quirk et al. (1985, p. 1330) point out that [Noun_1 Noun_2] combinations with a "premodifying" Noun_1 generally correspond semantically to more explicit phrases in which Noun_1 occurs as a "postmodifier" within a prepositional phrase. Thus a MOVIE GUIDE corresponds straightforwardly to a GUIDE TO MOVIES. An INVESTMENT GUIDE (cited by the *Random House Webster's Dictionary*) is a GUIDE TO INVESTMENTS, a MUSEUM GUIDE is a GUIDE TO MUSEUMS or TO A PARTICULAR MUSEUM, a CITY GUIDE is a GUIDE TO A PARTICULAR CITY or TO CITIES, a DVD GUIDE is a GUIDE TO DVDS, a TV GUIDE is a GUIDE TO TV (PROGRAMS), and so on. This pattern of Noun_1 + GUIDE is very common in English, therefore, with the meaning 'a guide to the things referred to by Noun_1, or to a particular instance of Noun_1.'

I conducted a Google search (in June 2008) for numerous English compounds with GUIDE as the head. The following is a small sample of those that yielded at least half a million hits, which is indicative of very common usage: ART GUIDE, CITY GUIDE, DVD GUIDE, FASHION GUIDE, INSURANCE GUIDE, INVESTMENT GUIDE, MONEY GUIDE, PHOTO GUIDE, PRICE GUIDE, SHOPPING GUIDE, and TV GUIDE. All these compounds carry stress on the first noun, like MOVIE GUIDE; they all have a corresponding postmodifier in a prepositional phrase, e.g. a GUIDE TO MONEY; and they all have a transparent compositional meaning, namely 'something, such as a book or pamphlet or service, that offers basic information or instruction about X.'

The use of MOVIE as a "premodifier" within compounds is also extremely common in American English. The *American Heritage Dictionary* comments on this explicitly stating that MOVIE is "Often used to modify another noun," giving as examples MOVIE

PRODUCER and MOVIE STARS. It also lists the single-word ($Noun_1$ +$Noun_2$) compounds MOVIEGOER and MOVIEMAKER. The *Random House Webster's Dictionary* lists MOVIE THEATER and MOVIE HOUSE, as well as the single-word MOVIEGOER, MOVIEMAKER, and also MOVIELAND. Common examples of two-word sequences containing MOVIE as the first noun that yielded at least half a million hits in a Google search (again conducted in June 2008) included MOVIE ACTOR, MOVIE AWARD, MOVIE BUSINESS, MOVIE CAMERA, MOVIE CRITIC, MOVIE EXTRA, MOVIE LISTING, MOVIE RENTAL, MOVIE SET, MOVIE SITE, MOVIE STUDIO, MOVIE TICKET, and MOVIE TRAILER. They all carry stress on the first noun, like MOVIE GUIDE. They all have paraphrases with a corresponding prepositional phrase postmodifier, the selection of the appropriate preposition depending on the rightmost head noun, namely an ACTOR IN A MOVIE or IN MOVIES (for MOVIE ACTOR), a CRITIC OF MOVIES (for MOVIE CRITIC), a TICKET TO A MOVIE (for MOVIE TICKET), a TRAILER FOR A MOVIE (for MOVIE TRAILER), and so on. And their semantics is readily derivable from the meanings of the two nouns alone, in either their premodifier (e.g. MOVIE CRITIC) or postmodifier orders (CRITIC OF MOVIES).

There are hundreds of sequences in English like these that combine either MOVIE or GUIDE, to yield common descriptive compounds, like the ones just illustrated. Since there are so many, and since they are semantically transparent, it is not necessary for dictionaries to list them all, and it would be impractical for them to do so. Every dictionary lists just a small number of two-word and one-word compounds and omits the great majority, even the commonly used ones, as we have seen repeatedly in this book. Neither the *American Heritage Dictionary* nor the *Webster's Third New International Dictionary* lists MOVIE THEATER, which is among the most frequently used compounds with MOVIE as the first element (10.5 million hits in the Google search). Nor do the *Random House Webster's* and the *Webster's Third New International Dictionary* list MOVIE STAR (11 million hits in the Google search). None of these three dictionaries lists MOVIE TRAILER (with 18.5 million hits in the Google search). And none of them lists the compound CITY GUIDE, which had as many as 63.7 million hits in the Google search.

For MOVIE GUIDE itself, none of these three dictionaries gave a separate entry for it or made reference to it in their definitions for MOVIE and GUIDE. We see now that this is not surprising. First, because it would be impractical for any dictionary to list all the compounds containing MOVIE and GUIDE, since there are so many. Second, even though MOVIE GUIDE is frequently used (scoring 12.9 million hits in the Google search), this is not a sufficient reason for dictionaries to include it. Compounds with higher scores (MOVIE TRAILER and CITY GUIDE) are regularly omitted, while some with lower scores are included, such as MOVIE HOUSE (with 1.4 million hits) and MOVIE PRODUCER (with less than a million), suggesting that the selection made by dictionaries among the illustrative compounds containing MOVIE or GUIDE can be somewhat arbitrary, despite the general rule of sensitivity to high frequency. Third, and most significantly, the meaning of the compound MOVIE GUIDE is straightforwardly derivable from the meanings of MOVIE and GUIDE alone, i.e. it is compositional. Hence, it is not necessary to list the combined form, and in such circumstances dictionaries regularly do not do so (recall §3.4.6). The absence of MOVIE GUIDE from dictionaries does not provide any evidence for its non-genericness, therefore. McCarthy also notes in his book (recall §3.4.1) that a number of compound terms have been found to be in wide generic usage that are not listed in dictionaries.

7.2.3 Usage of MOVIE GUIDE in Corpora

In order to determine whether MOVIE GUIDE is indeed a generic term, we must examine actual usage by speakers and writers of English. I accordingly examined a large number of its uses, in Google searches, in book titles and periodicals, and in a LexisNexis search. They all supported the conclusion that MOVIE GUIDE is a generic or common descriptive term in English, meaning 'something, such as a book or pamphlet or service, that offers basic information or instruction about movies.'

In Google I made use of the "advanced search" tool, which enabled me to search for MOVIE GUIDE written as two words, and to exclude the single-word MOVIEGUIDE. I then reversed the process and searched for and examined the single word only (see §7.2.4). Examples supporting the genericness of the two-word MOVIE GUIDE included, for example: "LEONARD MALTIN'S MOVIE GUIDE." Here the use of the proper name LEONARD MALTIN serves as a "possessive premodifier" to link the generic concept of MOVIE GUIDE to a particular individual who is providing the particular product that falls within this semantic genus. Its meaning is 'a book or pamphlet or service that offers basic information or instruction about movies as supplied by Leonard Maltin.' In "SUMMER MOVIE GUIDE" the generic concept of a MOVIE GUIDE is premodified by the noun SUMMER, just as the generic term VACATION can be modified by SUMMER in SUMMER VACATION. A SUMMER MOVIE GUIDE is a guide to movies shown during a particular season, just as a SUMMER VACATION is a vacation taken during this same season. A "WEEKEND MOVIE GUIDE" restricts the genus of MOVIE GUIDE to movies that can be watched during the weekend. Similarly, a WEEKEND VACATION limits the VACATION genus to those instances that occur during a weekend. The "SAN DIEGO MOVIE GUIDE" is a guide to movies in the San Diego area. A "GERMAN MOVIE GUIDE" is a guide to movies in which the German language is used, and so on.

Further supporting the genericness of MOVIE GUIDE are uses in premodifier position before a generic head noun such as REVIEW, as in LEONARD MALTIN MOVIE GUIDE REVIEW. MOVIE GUIDE is a generic premodifier of REVIEW here, yielding a generic compound, just as the generic terms MUSIC or CLASSICAL MUSIC can combine with REVIEW to yield MUSIC REVIEW and CLASSICAL MUSIC REVIEW, respectively. The generic compound MOVIE GUIDE REVIEW is then linked to Leonard Maltin again. In LOS ANGELES 1938 RAGSDALE'S MOVIE GUIDE MAP the generic head noun MAP is premodified by MOVIE GUIDE to give a larger generic compound MOVIE GUIDE MAP.

In all these examples from Google, MOVIE GUIDE is used as a generic term of English. Its generic meaning can be combined with the meaning and reference of other terms occurring in premodifier position, with proper names (LEONARD MALTIN), time expressions (SUMMER, WEEKEND), places (SAN DIEGO), nationalities (GERMAN), and so on, in exactly the same way that other generic terms can have their meaning and reference further specified and linked to particular individuals or to particular times or particular nationalities.

The genericness of MOVIE GUIDE is further supported by its productive usage in book titles and periodicals used by competitors selling products that fall within the same genus, which I examined in 2008. These included "LEONARD MALTIN'S FAMILY MOVIE GUIDE," "ROGER EBERT'S FOUR-STAR MOVIE GUIDE," "MOVIE GUIDE FOR PUZZLED PARENTS," "MOVIE GUIDE FOR LEGAL STUDIES," "THE ESSENTIAL MONSTER MOVIE GUIDE," "THE LAUGH AND CRY MOVIE GUIDE," "THE MOVIE GUIDE," "THE ANIMATED MOVIE GUIDE," "VIDEO MOVIE GUIDE," and many others. These titles use the English generic term MOVIE GUIDE, occasionally with the definite article THE alone, with exactly the kinds of premodifiers and postmodifiers that English generic nouns normally allow, and with exactly the kinds of combinatorial meanings that follow from the rules of English grammar and semantics. Thus MOVIE GUIDE FOR PUZZLED PARENTS and MOVIE GUIDE FOR LEGAL STUDIES restrict the genus to the set of movie guides that are appropriate for puzzled parents and for those engaged in legal studies, respectively. In THE ESSENTIAL MONSTER MOVIE GUIDE, the restrictive premodifier MONSTER defines a certain subset of movies for which this publication offers a guide, and THE ESSENTIAL provides a further qualitative restriction relative to that. VIDEO premodifies MOVIE in VIDEO MOVIE GUIDE, just as it does in VIDEO MOVIE alone, and this in turn premodifies GUIDE and restricts its reference. In all of these titles, competitors in the MOVIE GUIDE market are making use of the generic term MOVIE GUIDE and combining it in productive ways with other words and concepts of English, in exactly the manner that the grammar of English permits for generic nouns and compounds generally. Clearly MOVIE GUIDE is generic. Now, what about the single-word MOVIEGUIDE?

7.2.4 *Against Source Identifiability in the Single-Word MOVIEGUIDE*

Let us begin with MOVIEGUIDE in "computer-mediated communication," the particular linguistic context that I was asked by the defense to address in this case. There is an important writing convention in this context, especially in the spelling of website addresses, which was of particular significance in this lawsuit. "Computer-mediated communication" was understood to refer primarily to such internet addresses and to printed references to them. This writing convention involves the requirement that these addresses should be written as connected sequences of letters or symbols. Thus we find two or more words in normal English orthography compressed into a single word in "CARINSURANCE.COM," "SPEEDINGTICKET.COM," "BIBLESTUDY.COM," "QUALITYPAPER.COM," "REDAPPLE.COM," "WANTARIDE.COM," and countless others. As soon as the reader opens the website for "REDAPPLE.COM," he or she immediately encounters RED APPLE written as separate words in the normal way. Similarly, WANT A RIDE is found when opening the web page for "WANTARIDE.COM." Even in the absence of these normal written cues and prompts, readers know that e.g. "BIBLESTUDY.COM" corresponds to BIBLE

STUDY written as two words, based on their knowledge of normal English writing conventions.

What this means is that average readers in this electronic age who access websites have learned to compress multiple words into connected sequences. When they encounter "WANTARIDE.COM," they recognize the word boundaries and parse them as if they were written in normal orthography. When the space is eliminated between the nouns of a noun compound that is normally written as two words, the connected sequence will be converted into its two-word equivalent. Thus "CARINSURANCE.COM" will be recognized as CAR INSURANCE, and "QUALITYPAPER.COM" as QUALITY PAPER. Similarly, "MOVIETHEATRE.COM" will be converted into the two-word equivalent, MOVIE THEATER, and "MOVIEREVIEW.COM" will be converted into MOVIE REVIEW.

At the center of the lawsuit under discussion was MOVIEGUIDE. The plaintiff claimed that the single-word term was their trademark and that the company represented by the defense was using this trademark "to lure and redirect the general viewing public, . . . away from MovieGuide's web site" to their own domain website. The linguistic issue here was therefore whether eliminating the space between MOVIE and GUIDE in the context of computer-mediated communication, i.e. MOVIEGUIDE, acquired any source-designative function (recall §6.2).

Notice first that it is impossible in the context of website addresses for any trademark to rely solely for its distinctiveness on the elimination of spaces between words, when the writing conventions expressly forbid the use of spaces. There is no formal distinction any more between the single word MOVIEGUIDE and the two-word compound MOVIE GUIDE, and any distinctiveness that might be claimed in normal orthography disappears in this medium.

In the last section I gave numerous examples from English usage supporting the genericness of the two-word compound MOVIE GUIDE. The same and similar examples could be found in websites and in computer-mediated communication generally in connected form, with the space eliminated. These showed that MOVIEGUIDE did not cease to be generic when written as a single word in this context. For example, I pointed out that the generic meaning of MOVIE GUIDE can be combined with the meaning and reference of other terms occurring in premodifier position, such as time expressions (SUMMER, WEEKEND) and places (SAN DIEGO), in the same way that generic terms can quite generally have their meaning and reference further specified by premodifiers. MOVIE GUIDE can itself occur as a premodifier before e.g.

REVIEW in MOVIE GUIDE REVIEW. These examples are formed using the productive rules of English syntax and semantics, and they support the conclusion that MOVIE GUIDE is a generic term (recall §7.2.3).

Examples identical or similar to these could be found in connected form in web addresses. Thus we find "SUMMERMOVIEGUIDE.COM," "WEEKENDMOVIEGUIDE.COM," "SANDIEGOMOVIEGUIDE .COM," and "MOVIEGUIDEREVIEW.COM" (spelled "movieguidereview.com" and "MovieGuideReview.com"). Similarly, we find "ADULTMOVIEGUIDE.COM" standing for ADULT MOVIE GUIDE, "PARENTSMOVIEGUIDE.COM" standing for PARENTS MOVIE GUIDE (spelled "parentsmovieguide.com" and "Parentsmovieguide.com"), and "KIDSMOVIEGUIDE.COM" standing for KIDS MOVIE GUIDE (spelled "KidsMovieGuide.com"). The connected sequence "MOVIEGUIDE.COM" accordingly stands for, and is understood as, the generic compound MOVIE GUIDE in the context of a website address.

In 2008 it was also possible to document the increasing use of the single-word MOVIEGUIDE more generally as an alternative to MOVIE GUIDE, i.e. not just in single-word web addresses. In order to show this, I conducted an advanced Google search (June 2008) for MOVIEGUIDE as a single word and excluded the two-word MOVIE GUIDE. There were large numbers of hits, such as "Leonard Maltin's 2005 MovieGuide Palm/Pocket PC," and in which the associated website contained both MOVIEGUIDE and MOVIE GUIDE spellings. The meaning of both was clearly the generic one linking the generic concept of a MOVIE GUIDE to this particular individual, Leonard Maltin, providing this service. Further hits for the single-word MOVIEGUIDE with generic meaning included "MovieGuide Features," "movieguide poll," and "MovieGuide Forums."

The single-word term could also be shown in 2008 to be increasingly used in website addresses for providers other than the plaintiff in this case. So in addition to the contentious "www.movieguide.org" and "www.movieguide .com" that figured in this lawsuit, addresses such as "www.movieguide.com .au" and "www.movieguide.co.nz" were also found that clearly referred to other providers. All of this was sufficient and compelling evidence of the need that competitors had, and still have, to make use of both the two-word MOVIE GUIDE and the single-word MOVIEGUIDE as generic compounds, especially in the context of computer-mediated communication but also more generally. And this evidence enabled me to answer the linguistic question I had been asked to address about whether MOVIEGUIDE ceased to be generic and instead identified a particular source when compressed from MOVIE GUIDE, especially "in the context of computer-mediated communication such as an internet browser's address box." My answer was that the single word clearly did not lose its genericness when compressed from two words into one, and in particular it did not do so in the context in question.

7.3 THE NAMED INSURED

The last lawsuit to be discussed in this chapter involved a case of punctuation, specifically the use of the comma in English spelling. In an insurance policy taken out by a company providing containers for transportation and storage, let's call it "Manzini Containers" (not the real name, in accordance with the anonymity policy of this book), there was a vagueness in the policy regarding what exactly was being covered by the insurance in question. The "named insured" was listed using an overall phrase that consisted first of MANZINI CONTAINERS, followed by a comma, followed by another phrase that we can render in parallel form here as EMPLOYEE PENSION PLAN. The named insured were accordingly given, following a colon, in the form "X, Y" as shown in (6):

(6) THE NAMED INSURED: MANZINI CONTAINERS, EMPLOYEE PENSION PLAN

The container company alleged, in response to and following certain crimes committed by its employees involving employee dishonesty, that it was entitled to compensation from the insurance company since Manzini Containers was explicitly listed as the named insured in the policy and coverage for the financial losses in question was covered by language elsewhere within it. The insurance company refused to pay up, however, on the grounds that only the employee pension plan was covered as the named insured, and not any other financial losses incurred by Manzini Containers that were not strictly related to the pension plan itself, and so we had a lawsuit filed by Manzini Containers against the insurance company (in Pasadena, California, 2000). I was retained by the plaintiff to give expert testimony in both a deposition and a trial.

In essence, one side in this dispute (the defense) was claiming that in the phrase X, Y only Y (the employee pension plan) was being covered by the insurance policy, and any other claims made by X (Manzini Containers) going beyond this were not included. The positioning of Y after the comma, the defense claimed, had the effect of excluding any claim made by X that did not relate to Y. The other side (the plaintiff) claimed that the policy did cover items pertaining to X that were in addition to Y, and that other relevant items were specifically mentioned later in the policy. Hence Y did not have this exclusive effect on X in (6) as it occurred at the beginning of the policy.

The key linguistic issue I was asked to address was accordingly: What is the exact meaning of "X, Y" in structures such as (6) and how do X and Y relate to one other? I was not involved with legal issues, of course, nor with a detailed examination of the remainder of the insurance policy and what it covered. The central question that the plaintiff asked of me was, What is the semantics of the comma in a listing of the form X, Y?

As usual, matters of interpretation, especially for a question of punctuation like this, are less straightforward than they appear to be at first. The sequence X, Y can have a number of different interpretations and is actually vague with respect to which one will be relevant in a given case. Selecting the intended one will depend on the semantics of each of X and Y on the one hand, and on the wider context on the other. One interpretation that is possible in principle is one in which Y is equivalent to X, as shown in (7):

(7) USC, THE UNIVERSITY OF SOUTHERN CALIFORNIA

The Y here gives a fuller elaboration and clarification of X. Clearly this is not a relevant interpretation for (6) since there is no equivalence between Manzini Containers and their employee pension plan.

Another possible interpretation is one in which Y gives a description, or predicates something, of X, as in (8):

(8) USC, A PRIVATE UNIVERSITY IN CALIFORNIA

Again this possibility is not relevant for (6) since EMPLOYEE PENSION PLAN does not describe Manzini Containers and what this company is or does.

A third option is one in which Y is understood as being in addition to X. This can be seen in an X, Y sequence such as (9), which could occur in a real-estate contract or in a home-insurance policy referring to the sale or protection of

(9) THE MAIN BUILDING, SURROUNDING HILLSIDE

The surrounding hillside (Y) is clearly in addition to the main building itself (X) here. If this interpretation is applied to (6), then both Manzini Containers in general (X) and their employee pension plan (Y) would be covered by the insurance in question. This was the interpretation that the plaintiff argued for in this case, claiming that the remaining language of the insurance policy covered potential losses incurred by Manzini Containers that went beyond coverage of the pension plan alone.

But there is a fourth possibility, namely one in which Y is included in X and thereby rules out certain possibilities within X that are not Y. Consider (10), discussing someone who studies

(10) MUSIC AT USC, VIOLIN

Most probably this will be interpreted as "implicating" (recall §1.5) that the student is not studying other instruments (cello, trumpet, etc.) that are also offered as part of a music degree, i.e. the addition of Y here (VIOLIN) following the comma excludes some things that are potentially included in X. At the same time it does still remain true, and this sentence asserts that 'the student is studying music (X).' It is this fourth possible interpretation that the defense seized upon when arguing that the EMPLOYEE PENSION PLAN (Y) in (6) ruled out other possible claims relating to MANZINI CONTAINERS (X), even though this X was indeed the company that was insured and listed in the named insured, but only, it was alleged, with respect to the Y in question, its employee pension plan, just as (10) has the effect of excluding other instruments (by implicature) offered by USC other than the violin.

In effect, the plaintiff in this case favored and argued for the third interpretation (Y in addition to X), the defense for the fourth (Y excludes items in X apart from Y itself). So which interpretation would average readers select? Well, once again the larger context of the insurance policy would need to be examined to see which interpretation was favored (recall §1.4). It was not my brief to do this, but my understanding was that there were other things that were mentioned in the insurance policy as being covered in addition to the employee pension plan, and hence when readers processed the full language of the policy and then returned to (6) at the beginning, they would have to resolve its vagueness in favor of the 'Y in addition to X' meaning exemplified by (9), rather than in favor of 'only Y applies within X' exemplified by (10). So, the paraphrase that I gave to the plaintiff for the sentence parallel to (6) at the beginning of their insurance policy was 'The named insured is Manzini Containers, also including their employee pension plan.'

A further relevant linguistic consideration that I gave to the plaintiff in this case was that if the intent of the insurance policy had indeed been to cover only the employee pension plan and to exclude other items pertaining to Manzini Containers, then other constructions and spellings of

English would have been far more natural and appropriate as summary descriptions at the outset of the policy. These included

(11) THE NAMED INSURED: MANZINI CONTAINERS' EMPLOYEE PENSION PLAN

i.e. "X's Y". Also (12):

(12) THE NAMED INSURED: THE EMPLOYEE PENSION PLAN OF MANZINI CONTAINERS

i.e. "the Y of X." Even (13):

(13) THE NAMED INSURED: THE MANZINI CONTAINERS EMPLOYEE PENSION PLAN

i.e. "the X Y." Instead of using unambiguous formulations like these that make clear that only the employee pension plan is being insured, and by using the vague X, Y with its many possible interpretations, it was difficult for the defense to argue that the interpretation had to be the one in which Y was exclusive of other items in X (along the lines of (10)), rather than additional to these (as in (9)). First because of the inherent vagueness in the X, Y listing of (6) and second because the remainder of the policy did specifically refer to other relevant items in X as being included in the coverage, and hence the larger context of the policy did resolve this uncertainty in favor of the 'X, also including Y' interpretation in (9), thereby eliminating the other possible interpretations as in (7), (8), and (10).

CHAPTER 8

Conclusions

We have seen that disagreements have arisen between the parties in many lawsuits over the meanings of English words, phrases, and sentences, with serious legal and financial consequences. The disputed meanings I have witnessed personally have been in contract interpretations, patent infringements, advertising, trademarks, libel, and defamation, and in all of them certain words and phrases of English, and their uses in context, were critical. In effect, the English language was "on trial" in these cases.

In this concluding chapter I first give a summary of the book itself (§8.1), and then I try to capture, succinctly, the general lessons learned (§8.2).

8.1 Summary of the Book

This book has stepped back from the legal specifics and their outcomes, and has analyzed and classified these disputes from the perspective of the language sciences, especially semantics and pragmatics in linguistics and philosophy, and language comprehension in psycholinguistics. My goal has been to better understand how, where, and why these lawsuits have arisen among speakers who do not normally miscommunicate or disagree with one another over the meanings they assign to their words and phrases. In contrast to other books on linguistics in relation to the law (see the titles given in the section immediately following these conclusions), which are generally concerned with the intersection between these two fields and describe actual lawsuits in considerable detail, the focus of the present book has been on English itself. What parts of the English language, and what aspects of English language usage, have given rise to these disputed meanings among lawyers and their clients, and why?

The chapters and sections were therefore arranged according to the level of linguistic analysis that was crucially involved in each dispute (single words, word combinations, whole clauses), the type of grammatical structure (nominal compounds, referring expressions), processes of interpretation (conversational inference versus conventional meaning), and aspects of spelling and punctuation. This enabled me to give a classification, first of all, of the disputed meanings in terms of well-established distinctions made in linguistic analysis. Did they crucially involve an individual word (Chapter 2), a word combination (Chapter 3), or the phrasal groupings of whole clauses and different clause types in syntax (Chapter 4)? Were there inferential processes going beyond the literal and conventional meanings of words, phrases, and sentences (Chapter 5)? Did the disputes involve nominal reference to external entities with or without unique identification (Chapter 6)? And were there orthographic issues of spelling and punctuation (Chapter 7)? Within each of these general areas of English lexis, grammar, usage, and orthography, I could then delve more deeply into the disputed meanings and try to identify general patterns and descriptive issues that would help us better understand, ultimately, how and why these disputes arose.

So, in Chapter 2 involving individual words, I classified the disputed meanings into four subtypes: those that involved lexical ambiguity between the distinct senses of a word (§2.1, exemplified by the booster and downtoner senses of SUBSTANTIALLY), those that involved vagueness in the full extent of a single word sense (§2.2, as with DISEASE and APPROXIMATELY), nonliteral versus literal meanings (§2.3, in e.g. FIGHTING, BATTLES, and WARS), and word meanings in a changing world (§2.4 and the case of TANGIBLE). In each of these four the nature of the dispute was slightly different. In §2.1 it involved one party selecting one of the ambiguous meanings (the downtoner one) and the other party selecting the other (the booster). In §2.2 the parties disagreed over the full extent of the meaning of DISEASE and APPROXIMATELY. In §2.3 they disagreed over whether the FIGHTING was literal or metaphorical. And in §2.4 they disagreed over whether the meaning of a word like TANGIBLE could still apply to new entities in a changing world of advancing technology, in addition to those that were envisaged at the time the relevant contract was written.

With the added clarity that this taxonomy gave us (and notice that we were in effect adding precision here to the highly ambiguous term "AMBIGUITY" as it is used in so many lay and legal discussions of language), we could raise deeper questions of causality into why these disputes arose in the law. These questions were asked, and relevant answers have been given, throughout the chapters of this book. With respect to individual words, we could say that the English language clearly does allow different possibilities of interpretation, of these four general types at least. But why didn't English writers and readers then just do what they normally do in these cases when they create and select meanings in everyday language use, as summarized in §1.4? That is, why didn't they reach the same interpretation and resolve the ambiguity or vagueness of the word in the usual way, by consulting the linguistic or visual context and allowing it to eliminate meanings possible to these words that were excluded by that context (recall the useful quote by Dell Hymes in §1.4: "The context eliminates from consideration the meanings possible to the form other than those the context can support")?

In the case of SUBSTANTIALLY in §2.1 and of FIGHTING in §2.3, I showed that this is exactly what language users would have done. There would have been no actual ambiguity in the minds of language users in the contexts in which these words were used, therefore (assuming that readers were unbiased and actually read the whole text properly!). The visual context of the patent (i.e. the drawings) showed clearly that the booster meaning of SUBSTANTIALLY was the one intended (i.e. 'the surface in question was to a considerable extent below the anchoring means'), not the downtoner one ('most of it was below') that the plaintiff argued for. And the linguistic context for FIGHTING clearly selected its metaphorical and nonliteral meaning in that case. These lawsuits arose, first, because there was a lexical ambiguity in principle in these words. But second and crucially they arose because one party in the dispute was unaware of, or chose to ignore, a fundamental principle of disambiguation by context in the everyday understanding of English. In short, they arose because of a faulty linguistic analysis about how meanings are selected in everyday language use. And this in turn, I argued, was motivated and ultimately caused by the fact that the eliminated downtoner meaning for SUBSTANTIALLY conferred a legal and financial benefit for the party in question (this party could now claim patent infringement by the accused product), as did the inapplicable literal meaning of FIGHTING to the party arguing for that (this meaning was invoked as the cause for subsequent violence).

The ultimate causes underlying the vagueness disputes in §2.2 (with DISEASE and APPROXIMATELY) and the disputed language in a changing world in §2.4 (TANGIBLE) were, I argued, different. It was not a question here of one side ignoring the clear role of context in disambiguation. It was rather, as I pointed out in §1.1, that there are real challenges in all of dictionary writing and lexicography over how exactly we define certain word meanings, how many distinct senses we list, and what the full extent or semantic coverage of each sense is. Some of these challenges for lexicographers are then reflected in disagreements and disputes that we find in courtrooms over how exactly a word like DISEASE is understood, whether its borders are clear, whether there are differences in interpretation between average language users and specialists in the medical profession, and so on (see §2.2.1). In other words, linguistic difficulties in lexicography were being played out in the courtroom here. A similar issue of vagueness arose with APPROXIMATELY, though I argued that the area of semantic indeterminacy was moot in this case since there was no way that 202 acres could fall within the range permitted by APPROXIMATELY 300 ACRES (in §2.2.2), despite the attempt by one party in the lawsuit to argue that it did. The case of TANGIBLE in §2.4 raised profound and long-standing philosophical issues about how closely linguistic meanings track the real world, as well as general linguistic issues involving the differences between "sense," "reference," and "denotation" (see §2.4.3 and §6.1).

In these cases of indeterminacy in §2.2 and §2.4, there were also legal and financial incentives driving the different interpretations, therefore, as there were in the SUBSTANTIALLY and FIGHTING cases of §2.1 and §2.3. A broader interpretation of DISEASE (§2.2.1) meant that the insurance company could expand the exclusions in its coverage and not pay for treatment of the heart attack, a narrower interpretation benefited the patient and entitled him to coverage. A broader interpretation of APPROXIMATELY (§2.2.2) benefited the seller of the property, the narrower interpretation benefited the buyer and his lawsuit against the seller. A broader interpretation of TANGIBLE (§2.4) benefited the movie company issuing the relevant contract, the narrower contract interpretation benefited the licensee paying royalties to the movie company. So while there were genuine issues of linguistic analysis underlying the cases of §2.2 and §2.4, as opposed to erroneous linguistic arguments ignoring the role of context in disambiguation by one of the parties as in §2.1 and §2.3, the disputes in all these cases were ultimately driven by the respective legal and financial benefits for the parties concerned, arguing for their preferred interpretations.

In Chapter 3 I examined word combinations, and as in Chapter 2, I began by distinguishing some different subtypes on linguistic grounds as a background to achieving greater clarity on what the disputed meanings were exactly, so that we could address how and why they had arisen. One distinction of significance for word combinations involves compositionality: Do the meanings of the parts combine together simply and transparently to yield a combined meaning for the whole, or is there some component of meaning that characterizes the whole that is not present in the parts? We see this distinction in the ambiguity of combinations like CRIMINAL LAWYER. It can refer to someone who is 'a lawyer' and also 'criminal' (compositional), or else it refers to a certain type of lawyer ('one who practices criminal law as opposed to other types of law'), which is the non-compositional meaning.

So, in the patent infringement litigation of §3.1, involving a WRENCH-ENGAGING SURFACE in a dental implant, it was precisely this non-compositional meaning of the word combination that was critical to the case. One side had a product where this surface was clearly designed for engagement with a wrench; the product on the other side used a hammer to tap the relevant surface into the anchoring means. The non-compositional meaning of WRENCH-ENGAGING SURFACE can be paraphrased as 'a surface that is designed to engage a wrench' or 'a surface for the purpose of engaging a wrench,' just like an OIL-BURNING HEATER is one that is 'designed for the purpose of burning oil so as to make heat' and a HUSBAND-BEATING FRYING PAN, if it existed, would be a frying pan with the design or for the purpose of beating your husband! In this lawsuit one party (the defense) clearly had a WRENCH-ENGAGING SURFACE with the design and purpose feature that matched its non-compositional meaning, and the other party (the plaintiff) did not, so there was no actual patent infringement in this respect. The plaintiff's argument that the accused product with its WRENCH-ENGAGING SURFACE could also describe the accusing product that didn't use a wrench at all (and which would have been more appropriately described as a HAMMER-TAPPING SURFACE) was linguistically implausible. Making this argument was again ultimately motivated by legal and financial considerations. But there was now a more subtle linguistic issue underlying this dispute: It involved an elusive and almost hidden non-compositional aspect of meaning concerning the design or purpose feature of this word combination that the lawyers (on both sides) were unaware of until it was brought to their attention through linguistic expertise, whereupon it did enter the legal discussion and could become part of the judge's decision-making about whether there was a patent infringement or not.

In §3.2 I examined the word combination REHAB FOR BILLY on the front page of a tabloid and argued that its meaning would be enriched by average readers to 'I hereby declare as information known by me to be true that Billy is going into, or is already in, rehabilitation,' which was neither flattering to Billy nor in accordance with the information given in the fuller article later within the tabloid that he had no intention of doing this.

In the remaining sections of this chapter, §3.3–3.5, I discussed compound nouns in trademark law, and the general distinction between the top-two items on Thomas McCarthy's hierarchy of terms, "generic terms" exemplified by APP STORE (which can never be trademarks), and descriptive ones that can be trademarks as long as "secondary meaning" is proven. I argued that HALF PRICE BOOKS was such a descriptive term. For both these terms I gave a number of grammatical diagnostics that we can apply in order to prove their generic or descriptive status, as opposed to the source-identifying meanings and uses that clearly identify a unique producer as discussed later in §5.5, §6.2, and §7.1. I exemplified the diagnostics for genericness using APP STORE (in §3.4.7) and the diagnostics for descriptiveness using HALF PRICE BOOKS (in §3.5.3).

The actual distinction between genericness and descriptiveness is, I argued, a rather subtle one from a linguistic perspective. It involves trying to distinguish a common or the most common descriptive term for a product, e.g. TENNIS RACKET, from all the other words and phrases that can be used to describe it, e.g. RACKET FOR TENNIS, RACKET FOR PLAYING TENNIS WITH, and so on. I argued that this is ultimately a linguistic question involving semantics, grammar, and language usage, and it is not obvious that lawyers should be trying to make this kind of distinction, and I noted that in some jurisdictions this distinction is not in fact made in trademark law. (For example, in London and Europe generally, there is just a single descriptive category for both generic and descriptive terms at the top of McCarthy's hierarchy.)

In Chapter 4 I gave examples of disputed meanings that involved larger combinations of words and phrases into whole clauses. A common source of disagreement involves the precise bracketing and grouping of words within clauses, so-called attachment ambiguities, and the different interpretations that can then result. An example was discussed in §4.1 involving the attachment of the prepositional phrase AT CANDLESTICK PARK (in WE'RE ORGANIZING CORPORATE HOSPITALITY DURING THE SUPERBOWL AT CANDLESTICK PARK) with respect to where exactly the hospitality services were being provided. In one meaning this phrase attaches directly to the verb ORGANIZING, and it is logically entailed that the services are being 'organized at Candlestick Park,' where the Super Bowl is taking place. In the other meaning the prepositional phrase attaches to the immediately adjacent THE SUPER BOWL, and it is no longer entailed that the hospitality services are necessarily offered there and on-site. Instead the sentence in this reading entails merely that the Super Bowl is being played there, and it is left unspecified, or vague, where the hospitality services are exactly. In this latter case, I argued that there would nonetheless be a conversational implicature to the effect that the hospitality services were also being offered in the same general location as the Super Bowl rather than some miles away, on account of our real-world knowledge and experience about where such services are normally provided. Despite the different syntactic attachments, therefore, and subtly different logical meanings, the net effect (and the outcome of a "good enough parsing" operation here) would be the same: The hospitality services would be understood as being offered at the same place as the game itself, at Candlestick Park.

The different parties in this lawsuit therefore seized on different syntactic attachments with their different logical entailments. One interpretation (with local attachment of the prepositional phrase to THE SUPER BOWL) was used by the defense to justify the fact that the services in question were offered some way away from the Super Bowl itself. The plaintiff, on the other hand, argued for the meaning in which the services would be on-site at Candlestick Park. But the subtle interplay between pragmatic implicatures and logical entailments, and the role of good enough parsing, meant that the overall impact on how this advertising sales pitch would be understood was actually the same in both attachments! Both possibilities would lead readers to understand that the hospitality services were offered on-site, where the Super Bowl was being played. This kind of analysis was not something that the lawyers alone could have appreciated and discussed without linguistic expertise. In effect, this dispute arose from faulty linguistic reasoning by one party to the effect that a local attachment of AT CANDLESTICK PARK to THE SUPER BOWL would necessarily mean that only the Super Bowl was being claimed to take place there and that the sentence in this reading made no claim about where the hospitality services themselves were offered. This was not the case, however, and it ignored the basic fact that the meanings that are created and selected from in everyday language use can arise from different sources that include both "logical entailments" and "pragmatic implicatures" (as summarized in §1.5).

In the contract dispute of §4.2 involving the precise interpretation of clauses beginning with SUBJECT TO, the different interpretations possible in principle over 'when' or 'whether' the sale in question could go through were resolved in context in favor of 'when.' In effect, one side in this dispute paid insufficient attention, again, to the role of context in the form of the immediately preceding sentences eliminating the 'whether' interpretation when they argued for their legally and financially preferred outcome. In the libel suit of §4.3 the concessive subordinating conjunction ALTHOUGH played a key role in setting up the implicature that the lawyer in question was drinking too much merlot and that this led to his indiscretion in this case. This linguistic analysis was apparently convincing to the court. What was disputed, and ultimately not established beyond a reasonable doubt, was whether the lawyer actually uttered the damaging and indiscrete words that were at the basis of the libel.

For the processes of conversational inference (or "implicature") that were discussed in Chapter 5, I made a distinction between three major subtypes (see also §1.5), each of which led to different kinds of disputes involving so-called implications and required different kinds of linguistic analysis. The central issue in all these cases, however, was whether there was (or was not) some additional meaning that would be present in readers' minds, over and above the literal and conventional meanings of the words and phrases in question. And if there was, what was this additional meaning exactly? The first subtype involved the linguistic context, i.e. the other sentences of a text, and whether they would lead to an enrichment in the meanings conveyed. The cases discussed in all of §5.1–5.3 crucially involved the effect of the overall text, with one party arguing that there was such an additional meaning and the other side arguing that there was not. These three cases were all libel suits. The case discussed in §5.4, also a libel suit, involved a different basis for the implicature in question, going back to the so-called presumption of truth whereby speakers and writers are presumed to be uttering and writing sentences that they believe to be true and for which they have evidence, unless they use a disclaimer of some kind. And in §5.5 I discussed trademarks having a "suggestive" versus "descriptive" status, with the basis for the implicature and enrichment involving not the linguistic context but, crucially, knowledge of the world in addition to linguistic knowledge.

The ZERO BANANAS case of §5.1 raised the issue of whether there was, or was not, an implicature made by the totality of the article plus pictures in the tabloid magazine to the effect that the plaintiff was being used for sex by the veteran actor in question. I argued that the claim made by the plaintiff's language expert that there was such an implicature was exaggerated. Not only did this expert not apply any well-established theory of conversational inference from the language sciences in order to support this, but the arguments that he did make were clearly far-fetched and revealed a literary and philological training that was simply unhelpful in a case such as this. It was implausible of him to suggest that average readers in this day and age and in America would necessarily know that MAIDS was a type of flower and short for MAIDEN-BLUSH and MAIDEN-ROSE, and even more implausible to suggest that this 'flower' sense of MAID would set up a psychological association with the word DEFLOWER, which even fewer readers would have heard of. And even if some readers did know that MAID was a flower, and also knew the word DEFLOWER, to claim that the one led to a direct association with the other, and that this in turn set up the background for an implication of sexual exploitation throughout the whole article defied rational belief! When we ask how and why this dispute over meaning ultimately arose, we see that there was both a potential financial benefit for the plaintiff, had the case been won, but also there was erroneous reasoning by her language consultant, which was not ultimately helpful to her.

Whereas the alleged implicature in §5.1 could not be supported (either by me or by the court), the Spatz and Latinos case in §5.2 was more subtle, and here I argued that the collective sentences of the political flyer in question did set up the enriched meanings that were alleged by the plaintiff. For the case discussed in §5.3 involving the implied allegation by a speaker at a public event that the Foreign Corrupt Practices Act had been violated by the company in question doing business in Macau, I argued in my rebuttal that the implicature did not go through. There were key words and phrases in the text of the transcript that the opposing linguist ignored that contradicted the claim of illegality. Hence 'illegality' would not have been implicated.

What characterized all of §5.1, §5.2, and §5.3, therefore, were alleged damages to the reputations of the plaintiffs on the basis of enriched meanings and implicatures that were claimed to be set up by the collective texts in question. For the first and the third of these, I argued that the reasoning for an implicature was not convincing and would not have been present in readers' minds. For the second, the reasoning leading to the implicature was supported more strongly and hence it was plausibly present in readers' minds.

The presumption of truth case in §5.4 involved a dispute over whether the magazine in question did, or did not, present this new theory of who shot Bobby Kennedy in a way that would lead readers to believe that the magazine endorsed it, and by doing so, it was alleged, the magazine made the claim that the plaintiff, identified in one of its photographs, was the murderer. I argued, on the contrary, that there was no implicature to this effect since the magazine was extremely careful to use verbs of reporting and other disclaimers when presenting the theory in question. In fact, every single sentence and every single proposition contained within the article removed the presumption and any inference that could be derived from it about the magazine endorsing this theory.

Suggestive terms in trademark law are highly relevant in the context of inference and implicature since one of the characteristics that has been defined for them is that they involve a "multistage reasoning" process. This process draws crucially on real-world knowledge in reaching a particular interpretation, often deriving from some inherent incongruity in the component parts of the suggestive term (see §5.5.1). In §1.5 I outlined what such reasoning would look like for the suggestive mark ROACH MOTEL. In §5.5.2–5.5.4 I discussed PERSONAL POST OFFICE and defined in detail the multistage reasoning that would be required to reconcile the public nature of a post office with the private nature of the device in question (the handheld letter scale), which was designed for someone's personal use. These arguments for suggestiveness illustrate the contrast between it and descriptiveness, which is crucial for the law because the former automatically guarantees trademark status whereas the latter requires proof of secondary meaning. PERSONAL POST OFFICE is interesting and revealing in this context because the Trademark Trial and Appeal Board (TTAB) first classified it as descriptive, and then changed its classification to suggestive later, citing inter alia the multistage reasoning process given in my declaration and summarized here. Hence this case exemplifies nicely the kind of dispute that takes place at the suggestive/descriptive boundary, with the former appealing to reasoning that is based ultimately on real-world knowledge combined, of course, with lexical meanings.

In Chapter 6 I discussed the general question of how words refer to entities and people in the world, and specifically whether they refer to large classes of entities and people on the basis of their "sense" (as "generic" terms do in trademark law), or whether they provide instead unique identification of some particular entity or company or person by a variety of linguistic means (proper names and definite descriptions in language, and the suggestive, arbitrary, and fanciful terms of trademark law). I began in §6.1 by returning to the PERSONAL POST OFFICE case and discussed the objection made by the US Postal Service (USPS) and their language consultant to the use of POST OFFICE in this term on the grounds that it suggested a false association with the USPS. Their expert claimed more generally that POST OFFICE as used in America was "synonymous with" the USPS, was a source identifier for it, and referred uniquely to it. He claimed further that when POST OFFICE was used to refer to the post offices of other countries, this involved a process of semantic extension, so-called metonomy, from the literal meaning of POST OFFICE that was supposedly synonymous with the USPS in America. I showed instead that none of this is correct, or even reasonable or well-informed. Every dictionary I consulted, even American dictionaries, defines POST OFFICE as a completely general term, directly applicable to the post offices so-defined of any country (see §6.1.1), none of them made any special mention of the USPS (see §6.1.2), and actual usage evidence supported the generality and genericness of this term (§6.1.3). Invoking "metonymy" in this context was particularly far-fetched (see §6.1.4). In short, when we ask how and why this particular dispute ultimately arose, we have the usual legal and financial incentives of the respective parties, but we also had, as in the ZERO BANANAS case (§5.1), meanings and inferences being proposed by the consultant for one of the parties that were simply unreasonable, and needed to be argued against with no basis in reality and in the everyday understanding of POST OFFICE by language users, as revealed by dictionaries and language corpora.

Whereas POST OFFICE has a general sense that does not uniquely identify the USPS, the next section (§6.2) discussed ELASTIC and the family of marks containing it, which clearly do have strong source identification, referring to the Elastic Company, which provides software for different types of data analysis. The corpus evidence for this was quite overwhelming. ELASTIC makes a clear and unique reference to this company in a way that is recognizably distinct from the other senses and uses associated with this word, just like APPLE (the company) is clearly distinct from APPLE (the fruit). The following section (§6.3) examined BLUE BOOK, which was shown on the basis of both dictionary and usage evidence to have lost (by 2000, the date of this litigation) its original and unique reference to the Kelley Blue Book Company, Inc., and its periodically issued price list for used cars. Instead this term had undergone "genericide" (just like XEROX and THERMOS did) and was and is now widely used with the general meaning of a price list, not only for used cars but for all kinds of other objects and appliances as well. The meaning disputes in all these trademark cases therefore revolved around unique identification of a particular company versus a more general and legally "generic" meaning, with grammatical, dictionary, and crucially usage evidence being presented in order to make the right determination regarding how English language users understand these terms.

In §6.4 a further aspect of nominal reference was at the center of the lawsuit, one that has been much discussed in linguistics and philosophy.

Who exactly does a definite noun phrase like THE POLICE refer to, and how is this reference impacted by the speaker and hearer's "mutual knowledge"? A distinction is made in the philosophy of language between "referential" and "attributive" uses of such phrases: They both involve "reference" on the basis of their "sense," but the former refers to individuals who are mutually known and identifiable to speaker and hearer, the latter to the police force in general and their members, whoever they might be. This makes a big difference when "THE POLICE" stand accused of certain crimes. Is it the police force in general that people are talking about (the attributive use), or are certain individuals, say Masters and James, who are known independently to speaker and hearer, being picked out and identified when "THE POLICE" is uttered (in the referential use)? In this latter case these individuals would stand accused of the crimes in question and suffer reputational damage. I plotted the shift from attributive to referential use of THE POLICE in this case and its consequences for the individuals concerned.

In Chapter 7 I considered some lawsuits in which spelling and punctuation were at the basis of the dispute. One involved the Salesforce Company, which uses the mark SALESFORCE written as a single word, as opposed to the two-word SALES FORCE. This latter differs in the single space between the words; it does not refer to the Salesforce Company and is generally used as a common descriptive term for 'a group of salespeople responsible for selling the goods or services of a company', i.e. any company. The issue in this case concerned whether the single-word SALESFORCE had indeed achieved this distinctiveness as a source identifier. It was shown, on the basis of various corpora sensitive to spellings and word separations, that SALESFORCE had indeed, and quite clearly, achieved this unique reference and source identification. The next section (§7.2) considered a case with a similar Noun + Noun compound where the space between the two nouns could be shown not to be significant. This was the case of MOVIEGUIDE, in which the plaintiff claimed this single-word version as a trademark, just like SALESFORCE. But on this occasion clear semantic and corpus evidence showed that the two-word MOVIE GUIDE and the one-word MOVIEGUIDE were used interchangeably, both as generic terms, and hence neither could be a source identifier and a trademark.

Finally, in §7.3 a lawsuit was discussed in which the dispute centered around who and what exactly was being covered by insurance in the phrase "THE NAMED INSURED: X, Y" as a result of the comma between X and Y. One side argued that reference to Y here (the employee pension plan of the company in question, X) had the effect of excluding coverage of other items pertaining to X apart from Y itself. I showed, however, that the relationship between X and Y in listings of this type was actually highly ambiguous, or vague, and that sequences of X, Y could also include cases where Y was being covered in addition to whatever X referred to. The disambiguation here, as with the other disambiguations discussed in §1.4 and elsewhere in this book, would be determined by the larger text in question, here an insurance policy, and the meanings that were supported or eliminated in that text.

8.2 General Lessons Learned

Stepping back from all of this, we can now answer our general question posed throughout this book about why these disputes in language interpretation have arisen in American courts, as follows.

First, in cases of ambiguity and multiple interpretations, one side in the dispute paid insufficient attention to, or chose to ignore, the disambiguating role of context (see e.g. SUBSTANTIALLY in §2.1 and FIGHTING in §2.3).

Second, and perhaps most significantly from the perspective of English linguistics, at the heart of the dispute there was often a subtle and complex aspect of the unconscious knowledge of language that users of English bring to their everyday speaking and writing, and which the language sciences are trying to describe and make conscious and explicit. By applying the theories and empirical methods from the language sciences to these disputed meanings, we can understand better how they have arisen and why they have arisen, and we can give helpful analyses and empirical data to the triers of fact and so give relevant linguistic information for legal decision-making and the pursuit of justice that would not have been incorporated without linguistic expertise. These subtleties and complexities included lexicographic challenges involving the full extent of a word meaning (DISEASE in §2.2.1), clarifications over lexical ambiguity (e.g. SUBSTANTIALLY in §2.1), philosophical issues involving the relation between linguistic meaning and a changing world (TANGIBLE in §2.4), non-compositional meanings (e.g. WRENCH-ENGAGING SURFACE in §3.1), phrasal attachments in syntax and their semantic and pragmatic consequences (e.g. AT CANDLESTICK PARK in §4.1), different kinds of inference and implicature (from the immediate context, from the presumption of truth and from real-world knowledge, in §1.5 and Chapter 5), differences between sense and reference and denotation (e.g. POST

OFFICE in §6.1), grammatical criteria for proving genericness (e.g. APP STORE in §3.4) and criteria for descriptiveness (HALF PRICE BOOKS in §3.5), and the referential versus attributive distinction (for THE POLICE in §6.4).

Third, we have seen that there were regularly legal and financial advantages and benefits that were motivating each of the parties: The downtoner meaning of SUBSTANTIALLY supported the plaintiff's patent infringement argument, the booster meaning supported the defense (in §2.1); a narrower interpretation of DISEASE supported the plaintiff's claim for medical coverage, the broader interpretation allowed the defense to exclude coverage (in §2.2); a local attachment of AT CANDLESTICK PARK to THE SUPER BOWL, rather than to ORGANIZING, was at the basis of the argument by the defense that their advertising pitch did not specify where exactly their hospitality services were being provided but stated only where the Super Bowl was, while the plaintiff argued that average readers would understand these services to be at the same place as the Super Bowl (in §4.1). The implicature claimed by the plaintiff about being exploited for sex by the veteran Hollywood actor was potentially beneficial to her financially and legally, the argument that the implicature did not go through and was not necessarily present in readers' minds benefited the tabloid as the defending party (in §5.1), and so on.

Fourth, we have seen that the opinions of language consultants have not always been helpful to the triers of fact when those "experts" had little expertise and scholarly publications in relevant areas of the language sciences (see especially ZERO BANANAS in §5.1 and the POST OFFICE case in §6.1). As a result the meanings proposed by one party in the dispute were exaggerated and required what should have been unnecessary counterarguments.

One of my goals in writing this book, as I explained in the Preface, was to share these disputed meanings that I have witnessed personally with the language science community and especially with English language specialists. Another goal was to bring these analyses to the attention of legal scholars and of practicing lawyers and judges and to other interested parties. There are many high-profile cases of language interpretation that I have seen discussed in legal circles and that are summarized in the media and in the Further Readings that I give immediately following these conclusions, involving constitutional amendments, firearms, abortion, voting rights, marriage, and so on. The lawyers, judges, and Supreme Court justices discussing these issues use labels like "originalism," "textualism," "practical interpretation," and so on. They are clearly grappling with similar issues of natural language understanding of the type I have been presenting here in my more run-of-the-mill lawsuits involving various contract interpretations, patent infringements, libels, and so on. But whether the legal cases are high-profile or low-profile, the English language is the same in both, and the kinds of disputed meanings that arise in both are the same or similar. Discussions by lawyers, in both academic contexts and actual lawsuits, have not made, in my experience, nearly as much use of the insights and methods of the language sciences as they could in order to clarify and add precision to their language-based arguments. There is a growing interest among linguists, especially sociolinguists and applied linguists, in exploring the general relevance of linguistics to the law (see the Further Readings). The present book is more focused on the English language itself, and on the theories and methods of the language sciences that can shed light on where and why the disputes involving language interpretation have actually arisen. It is my hope that the examples of English "on trial" that I have witnessed personally and tried to explain in the chapters of this book may have wider applicability for, and may be helpful to, lawyers and linguists discussing other cases of language in the law, including the high-profile ones that have such social and legislative significance.

Finally, let me remind the reader that since the primary focus of this book is on English, rather than on legal outcomes or on the people involved, it has given only background information about the law itself, sufficient for understanding the lawsuits and the role of language within them. It has also removed all references to celebrities and other individuals and to many specific companies in the main text, and used pseudonyms or a simple omission of names. Some critical sentences have been converted into parallel ones that do not reveal the participants in question. I have also not named any of the lawyers or expert witnesses giving their arguments and opinions. The main exception to this practice of anonymity has been when discussing trademarks, where identification is unavoidable. It is not important for our purposes who was actually using English and who or what is being referred to in these cases. What is important is the language itself, the word, the construction, the ambiguity, and the analytical issues that these disputes raised over meaning. Plus I don't want people reading this book for the wrong reasons, in order to follow up on the often damaging allegations made against Hollywood celebrities and American country music stars, or against specific individuals. This book is a contribution to English and general linguistics, therefore, using a revealing and interesting set of data from American courts. Readers wanting more background information on the language sciences can consult §1.7, in which I give a reading sampler. Those wanting further references on linguistics in relation to the law can go to the Further Readings following the conclusions here. And for those who want to delve more deeply into the legal cases that I have drawn on in this book, I give information in the Appendix that will enable them to find these cases in the public domain.

Further Readings in Language and the Law

There is a growing interest in applications of linguistics to the law, and a number of books have appeared in recent years that discuss the general relationship between these two fields and describe lawsuits involving testimony by linguists. These other books give numerous details about the law, the companies and individuals involved, and the trials themselves, and they largely take as given the fact that there was a lawsuit and a dispute. The present book is different. It has asked fundamental questions about the language side of all this arising from lawsuits I have witnessed personally: What areas and properties of English give rise to these disputes? Can we expect them in some areas and not in others (and if so which)? Can we explain through our theories, analytical techniques, and corpus searches why we are getting these disagreements among language users who do not normally disagree in their unconscious use and understanding of English? Are there aspects of word meaning and phrasal meaning that are hard to define, that lexicographers and semanticists have difficulties with as well, and are these inherent difficulties ultimately responsible for the disagreement? Are some linguists who give testimony better informed about semantic and pragmatic theories than others, and better able to explain the unconscious thought processes going on in the minds of readers? Are legal and financial considerations interfering with the proper analysis of ambiguity resolution in context? These questions have taken center stage in the present book with its focus on the English language, English linguistics, and the theories and analytical tools of the language sciences.

Among the complementary books on language and the law are several by one of the biggest names in the field, the sociolinguist Roger Shuy. He has written on the intersection between these fields and given lively and excellent accounts of many lawsuits in which he was retained by one side or the other. For example, one of his books focuses on trademarks:

Shuy, Roger (2002) *Linguistic Battles in Trademark Disputes*, Palgrave Macmillan, New York.

Another covers defamation:

Shuy, Roger (2010) *The Language of Defamation Cases*, Oxford University Press, Oxford.

An earlier book had a strong focus on courtroom practices and on cases involving spoken language:

Shuy, Roger (1993) *Language Crimes: The Use and Abuse of Language Evidence in the Courtroom*, Wiley-Blackwell, Oxford.

A further book was designed to help linguists who have been asked by lawyers to consult and testify on matters of language:

Shuy, Roger (2006) *Linguistics in the Courtroom: A Practical Guide*, Oxford University Press, Oxford.

There have been similar books by other authors who use the label "forensic linguistics" to describe applications of linguistics to criminal and civil law cases. (Roger Shuy himself dislikes this term and doesn't use it.) For example, there is

Gibbons, John (2003) *Forensic Linguistics: An Introduction to Language in the Justice System*, Blackwell, Oxford.

Also the following two:

Olsson, John, and June Luchjenbroers (2014) *Forensic Linguistics*, 3rd edn, Bloomsbury Academic, London.

Coulthard, Malcolm, Alison Johnson, and David Wright (2017) *An Introduction to Forensic Linguistics: Language in Evidence*, 2nd edn, Routledge, New York.

One book that gives more attention to the language and linguistic analysis side of things, while also presenting numerous legal details, is the following:

Kaplan, Jeffrey (2019) *Linguistics and the Law* (Routledge Guides to Linguistics series), Routledge, New York.

This book discusses lexical semantics, syntax, and pragmatics, and includes chapters on police interviews, Miranda rights, and also trademarks. It has some overlap with the present one, therefore, but does not have its central goal of trying to explain why, and where, in English and in the analysis of English these disputes have arisen.

A valuable general resource for language and the law is

Tiersma, Peter, and Lawrence Solan (2012) *Oxford Handbook of Language and the Law*, Oxford University Press, Oxford.

These are all useful references for readers of the present book who wish to explore the intersection between language and law further. There is also a valuable whole series of books currently being developed on Foundations in Language and Law, published by De Gruyter Mouton and edited by Dieter Stein, which covers a range of relevant topics. One of their volumes, for example, is

Engberg, Jan (2024) *Between Text, Meaning and Legal Languages: Linguistic Approaches to Legal Interpretation*, De Gruyter Mouton, Berlin.

All of these books are highly recommended for readers of the present book who may be intrigued by some of the issues I have raised with respect to applications of language science to the law and who wish to pursue them further.

Appendix: Cases Discussed in This Book

Pseudonyms used in the main text are preserved here in square brackets.

1988	Bowman *v.* Gary Appel et al.: On the meaning of the term DISEASE OF THE HEART in a medical insurance contract; consultant for the Plaintiff's counsel, Althouse & Bamber, Upland, California; report September 1988.
1992	[Polly Keenan] *v.* Globe International, Inc.: Libel suit on the language of an article in the *Globe Special*; consultant and expert witness for the Defendant's counsel, Glassman & Browning, Beverly Hills, California; deposition September 1992 in Los Angeles, trial September 1992 in Los Angeles.
1993	Belease Investment Co. *v.* Braemar: On the meaning of the phrase APPROXIMATELY 300 ACRES in a property purchase agreement; consultant and expert witness for the Plaintiff's counsel, Kramer & McShane, Los Angeles; deposition September 1993 in Los Angeles, trial December 1993 in Los Angeles.
1994	McGovern *v.* Bunnell: Libel suit on the language of an article in the *Wall Street Journal*; consultant and expert witness for the Plaintiff's counsel, Bartko, Tarrant & Miller, San Francisco; declaration February 1994, deposition March 1994 in San Francisco.
1994	Khawar *v.* Robert Morrow, Round Table Publishing and Globe International, Inc.: Libel suit on the language of an article in *The Globe*; consultant and expert witness for the Defendant's counsel, Glassman & Browning, Beverly Hills, California; trial March 1994 in Santa Monica.
1995–1996	Core-vent *v.* Calcitek: Patent dispute involving the language describing a dental implant; consultant and expert

witness for the Defendant's counsel, Lyon & Lyon, Los Angeles; declaration November 1995, rule 26 expert report September 1996, deposition November 1996 in Los Angeles.

1998 United States Golf Association *v.* The Hospitality Group: On a prepositional phrase attachment ambiguity in a sales pitch within a false advertising suit; consultant for the Plaintiff's counsel, Trattner & Associates in Washington, DC, and Orrick, Herrington & Sutcliffe, LLP, in San Francisco; declaration October 1998.

1998 [Robert Spatz] *v.* Richard Polenco and Richard Ross: Libel suit involving the language of an election campaign mailer in Los Angeles; consultant for the Plaintiff's counsel, Glassman, Browning & Saltsman, Beverly Hills, California; declaration November 1998.

1999 Rosenfeld, Meyer & Susman, LLP, and [Smith] *v.* Carol Communications, Inc., Carol Publishing Group, and [Jones]: Libel suit involving a passage in a book about a Hollywood celebrity; consultant and expert witness for the Plaintiffs' counsel, Glassman, Browning & Saltsman, Beverly Hills, California; deposition May 1999 in Beverly Hills; trial September 1999 in Santa Monica, California.

1999 Luppen Holdings, Inc. *v.* Pitney Bowes, Inc., and Staples, Inc.: On the trademark status of PERSONAL POST OFFICE; consultant for the Plaintiff's counsel, Lyon & Lyon, Los Angeles; declaration October 1999.

2000 [Manzini Containers] *v.* Hartford Insurance: On the meaning, grammar and punctuation of entities designated as NAMED INSURED in an insurance policy covering crime and employee dishonesty; consultant and expert witness for the Plaintiff's counsel, Ernster Law Offices, Pasadena, California; deposition August 2000 in Los Angeles; trial September 2000 in Long Beach, California.

2000 Kelley Blue Book Company *v.* Primedia Intertec National Market Reports, et al.: On the trademark status of BLUE BOOK; consultant and expert witness for the Defendant's counsel, Leopold, Petrich & Smith, Century City, California; rule 26 expert report October 2000, deposition December 2000 in Century City, California.

2002 Ruben Fernandez *v.* Fullerton San Diego Enterprises, et al.: Linguistic analysis of a disputed clause containing SUBJECT TO in a real estate purchase agreement; consultant for the Plaintiff's counsel, Goldstein & Ward, Inc., La Habra, California; report September 2002.

2003 Half Price Books, Records, Magazines, Inc. *v.* Barnesandnoble.com, LLC: On the trademark status of HALF PRICE BOOKS; consultant for the Plaintiff's counsel, Akin, Gump, Strauss, Hauer & Feld, LLP, Dallas, Texas; declaration January 2003.

2007 Luppen Holdings, Inc. *v.* Pitney Bowes, Inc., and Staples, Inc.: On the trademark status of PERSONAL POST OFFICE; consultant for the Plaintiff's counsel, Zuber & Taillieu, LLP, Los Angeles; declaration July 2007, declaration October 2007; deposition July 2007 in Los Angeles.

2008 Good News Communications, Inc. *v.* Hollywood Media Corp.: On the trademark status of MOVIE GUIDE and MOVIEGUIDE; consultant for the Defendant's counsel, Leopold, Petrich & Smith, Los Angeles; rule 26 expert report July 2008.

2012 Apple, Inc. *v.* Amazon.com, Inc. and Amazon Digital Services, Inc.: On the trademark status of APP STORE; consultant for the Defendant's counsel, Arnold & Porter, LLP, San Francisco and Arnold & Porter, LLP, London; rule 26 expert report August 2012, rule 26 expert rebuttal report August 2012, expert report to the Office for Harmonization in the Internal Market (Europe), November 2012, deposition October 2012 in San Francisco.

2014 [Moon and Moon Resorts] *v.* [Konos]: Defamation suit relating to the description of the business practices of a company doing business in Macau in relation to the Foreign Corrupt Practices Act and made at a UC Berkeley public event; consultant for the Defendant's counsel, Arnold & Porter, San Francisco, California; rebuttal declaration November 2014.

2015 Fourth Age Limited et al. *v.* Warner Bros. Digital Distribution, Inc. et al. and the Saul Zaentz Company: Movie contract dispute centering on the phrase

ARTICLES OF TANGIBLE PERSONAL PROPERTY; consultant for the Defendants, O'Melveny & Myers LLP, Los Angeles, California, counsel for Warner Bros., and Arnold & Porter LLP, San Francisco, California, counsel for The Saul Zaentz Company; rebuttal declaration April 2015.

2016 [Billy Scranton] *v.* Bauer Publications Company et al.: Libel suit brought against *In Touch* magazine centering on the phrase REHAB FOR [BILLY] appearing on the cover page; consultant for the Plaintiff's counsel, Liner LLP, Los Angeles, California; declaration March 2016.

2017 [John Masters and Steve James] *v.* [Katie Savant]: Defamation case against a city council member for the language used to describe the actions of the police following a local shooting; consultant for the Plaintiffs' counsel, Williams, Kastner & Gibbs PLLC, Seattle, Washington; declaration September 2017.

2018–2019 Salesforce.com, Inc. *v.* Molly Wendell: On the trademark status of SALESFORCE; consultant for the Opposer's (Salesforce.com) counsel, Wilson Sonsini Goodrich & Rosati, San Francisco, California; expert report September 2018, rebuttal report September 2019.

2020 Elasticsearch BV trademark application before the United States Patent and Trademark Office (Serial No. 88564719): On the trademark status of ELASTIC; consultant for Elasticsearch BV and Wilson Sonsini Goodrich & Rosati, San Francisco, California; declaration July 2020.

2022–2023 [John Masters and Steve James] *v.* [Katie Savant]: Defamation case against a city council member for the language used to describe the actions of the police following a local shooting; consultant for the Plaintiffs' counsel, Williams, Kastner & Gibbs PLLC, Seattle, Washington; rebuttal report December 2022, declaration January 2023.

Index of Names

Subject Index

For EU product safety concerns, contact us at Calle de José Abascal, 56–1°, 28003 Madrid, Spain or eugpsr@cambridge.org.

www.ingramcontent.com/pod-product-compliance
Ingram Content Group UK Ltd.
Pitfield, Milton Keynes, MK11 3LW, UK
UKHW020445160626
472263UK00010B/300

* 9 7 8 1 0 0 9 6 8 2 8 2 4 *

CONTENTS

*Invited Paper

ADVANCES IN SCANNING PROBE MICROSCOPY FOR MULTIMODAL IMAGING AT THE NANOSCALE

*Invited Paper

ADVANCES IN MATERIALS EXPLORATION WITH NEUTRONS AND X-RAYS—THE STATE-OF-THE-ART IN THE INTERNATIONAL YEAR OF CRYSTALLOGRAPHY

*Invited Paper

*Invited Paper

PREFACE

Symposium OO, "In Situ Characterization of Dynamic Processes during Materials Synthesis and Transformation;" Symposium PP, "Advances in Scanning Probe Microscopy for Multimodal Imaging at the Nanoscale;" Symposium QQ, "Advances in Nanoscale Subsurface, Chemical and Time-Resolved Studies of Soft Matter;" and Symposium TT, "Advanced Materials Exploration with Neutrons and X-Rays—The State-of-the-Art in the International Year of Crystallography," were held November 30–December 5 at the 2014 MRS Fall Meeting in Boston, Massachusetts.

With the emergence of nanoscale dimensions in material science, the needs to advance metrology such as for time-resolved, spatially-resolved and material specific signatures have become more and more demanding. This symposium proceedings volume represents the recent advances relevant to these aspects of material and process discoveries. The papers have been organized to convey advances in: (1) *in situ* characterization of dynamic processes, (2) scanning probe microscopy for multimodal imaging at the nanoscale and (3) neutrons and X-rays for material science. Manuscripts in this volume explore various aspects of the most recent developments in metrology and characterization of materials at the most fundamental level, with spatial resolution down to the nanometer range. Our team has organized these reports in a way that, we hope, highlights the rich scientific advances taking place in the field of characterization and illustrates the importance of this field for materials research.

Dongsheng Li
Vassilia Zorba
Laurene Tetard
Klaus-Dieter Liss

October 2015

Materials Research Society Symposium Proceedings

Volume 1717E–	Organic Bioelectronics, 2015, M.R. Abidian, C. Bettinger, R. Owens, D.T. Simon, ISBN 978-1-60511-694-5
Volume 1718–	Multifunctional Polymeric and Hybrid Materials, 2015, A. Lendlein, N. Tirelli, R.A. Weiss, T. Xie, ISBN 978-1-60511-695-2
Volume 1719E–	Medical Applications of Noble Metal Nanoparticles (NMNPs), 2015, X. Chen, H. Duan, Z. Nie, H-R. Tseng, ISBN 978-1-60511-696-9
Volume 1720E–	Materials and Concepts for Biomedical Sensing, 2015, X. Fan, L. Liu, E. Park, H. Schmidt, ISBN 978-1-60511-697-6
Volume 1721E –	Hard-Soft Interfaces in Biological and Bioinspired Materials—Bridging the Gap between Theory and Experiment, 2015, J. Harding, D. Joester, R. Kröger, P. Raiteri, ISBN 978-1-60511-698-3
Volume 1722E–	Reverse Engineering of Bioinspired Nanomaterials, 2015, L. Estroff, S-W. Lee, J-M. Nam, E. Perkins, ISBN 978-1-60511-699-0
Volume 1723E–	Plasma Processing and Diagnostics for Life Sciences, 2015, E.R. Fisher, M. Kong, M. Shiratani, K.D. Weltmann, ISBN 978-1-60511-700-3
Volume 1724E–	Micro/Nano Engineering and Devices for Molecular and Cellular Manipulation, Simulation and Analysis, 2015, D.L. Fan, J. Fu, X. Jiang, M. Lutolf, ISBN 978-1-60511-701-0
Volume 1725E–	Emerging 1D and 2D Nanomaterials in Health Care, 2015, P.M. Ajayan, S.J. Koester, M.R. McDevitt, V. Renugopalakrishnan, ISBN 978-1-60511-702-7
Volume 1726E–	Emerging Non-Graphene 2D Atomic Layers and van der Waals Solids, 2015, M. Bar-Sadan, J. Cheon, S. Kar, M. Terrones, ISBN 978-1-60511-703-4
Volume 1727E–	Graphene and Graphene Nanocomposites, 2015, J. Jasinski, H. Ji, Y. Zhu, V. Nicolosi, ISBN 978-1-60511-704-1
Volume 1728E–	Optical Metamaterials and Novel Optical Phenomena Based on Nanofabricated Structures, 2015, Y. Liu, F. Capasso, A. Alù, M. Agio, ISBN 978-1-60511-705-8
Volume 1729–	Materials and Technology for Nonvolatile Memories, 2015, P. Dimitrakis, Y. Fujisaki, G. Hu, E. Tokumitsu, ISBN 978-1-60511-706-5
Volume 1730E–	Frontiers in Complex Oxides, 2015, J.D. Baniecki, N.A. Benedek, G. Catalan, J.E. Spanier, ISBN 978-1-60511-707-2
Volume 1731E–	Oxide semiconductors, 2015, T.D. Veal, O. Bierwagen, M. Higashiwaki, A. Janotti, ISBN 978-1-60511-708-9
Volume 1732E–	Hybrid Oxide/Organic Interfaces in Organic Electronics, 2015, A. Amassian, J.J. Berry, M.A. McLachlan, E.L. Ratcliff, ISBN 978-1-60511-709-6
Volume 1733E–	Fundamentals of Organic Semiconductors—Synthesis, Morphology, Devices and Theory, 2015, D. Seferos, L. Kozycz, ISBN 978-1-60511-710-2
Volume 1734E–	Diamond Electronics and Biotechnology—Fundamentals to Applications, 2015, C-L. Cheng, D.A.J. Moran, R.J. Nemanich, G.M. Swain, ISBN 978-1-60511-711-9
Volume 1735–	Advanced Materials for Photovoltaic, Fuel Cell and Electrolyzer, and Thermoelectric Energy Conversion, 2015, S.R. Bishop, D. Cahen, R. Chen, E. Fabbri, F.C. Fonseca, D. Ginley, A. Hagfeldt, S. Lee, J. Liu, D. Mitzi, T. Mori, K. Nielsch, Z. Ren, P. Rodriguez, ISBN 978-1-60511-712-6
Volume 1736E–	Wide-Bandgap Materials for Solid-State Lighting and Power Electronics, 2015, R. Kaplar, G. Meneghesso, B. Ozpineci, T. Takeuchi, ISBN 978-1-60511-713-3
Volume 1737E–	Organic Photovoltaics—Fundamentals, Materials and Devices, 2015, A. Facchetti, ISBN 978-1-60511-714-0
Volume 1738E–	Sustainable Solar-Energy Conversion Using Earth-Abundant Materials, 2015, Y. Li, S. Mathur, G. Zheng, ISBN 978-1-60511-715-7
Volume 1739E–	Technologies for Grid-Scale Energy Storage, 2015, B. Chalamala, J. Lemmon, V. Subramanian, Z. Wen, ISBN 978-1-60511-716-4
Volume 1740E–	Materials Challenges for Energy Storage across Multiple Scales, 2015, A. Cresce, ISBN 978-1-60511-717-1
Volume 1741E	Synthesis, Processing and Mechanical Properties of Functional Hexagonal Materials, 2015, M. Albrecht, S. Aubry, R. Collazo, R.K. Mishra, C-C. Wu, ISBN 978-1-60511-718-8
Volume 1742E–	Molecular, Polymer and Hybrid Materials for Thermoelectrics, 2015, A. Carella, M. Chabinyc, M. Kovalenko, J. Malen, R. Segalman, ISBN 978-1-60511-719-5
Volume 1743E–	Materials and Radiation Effects for Advanced Nuclear Technologies, 2015, G. Baldinozzi, C. Deo, K. Arakawa, F. Djurabekova, S.K. Gill, E. Marquis, F. Soisson, K. Yasuda, Y. Zhang, ISBN 978-1-60511-720-1

Materials Research Society Symposium Proceedings

Volume 1744– Scientific Basis for Nuclear Waste Management XXXVIII, 2015, S. Gin, R. Jubin, J. Matyáš, E. Vance, ISBN 978-1-60511-721-8

Volume 1745E – Materials as Tools for Sustainability, 2015, J. Abelson, C-G. Granqvist, E. Traversa, ISBN 978-1-60511-722-5

Volume 1746E – Nanomaterials for Harsh Environment Sensors and Related Electronic and Structural Components—Design, Synthesis, Characterization and Utilization, 2015, P-X. Gao, P. Ohodnicki, L. Shao, ISBN 978-1-60511-723-2

Volume 1747E – Flame and High-Temperature Synthesis of Functional Nanomaterials—Fundamentals and Applications, 2015, E. Kruis, R. Maric, S. Tse, K. Wegner, X. Zheng, ISBN 978-1-60511-724-9

Volume 1748E – Semiconductor Nanocrystals, Plasmonic Metal Nanoparticles, and Metal-Hybrid Structures, 2015, M. Kuno, S. Ithurria, P. Nagpal, M. Pelton, ISBN 978-1-60511-725-6

Volume 1749E – 3D Mesoscale Architectures—Synthesis, Assembly, Properties and Applications, 2015, H.J. Fan, S. Jin, M. Knez, B. Tian, ISBN 978-1-60511-726-3

Volume 1750E – Directed Self-Assembly for Nanopatterning, 2015, D.J.C. Herr, ISBN 978-1-60511-727-0

Volume 1751E – Semiconductor Nanowires—Growth, Physics, Devices and Applications, 2015, G. Koblmueller, ISBN 978-1-60511-728-7

Volume 1752– Carbon Nanotubes—Synthesis, Properties, Functionalization, and Applications, 2015, P.T. Araujo, A.D. Franklin, Y.A. Kim, M. Krueger, ISBN 978-1-60511-729-4

Volume 1753E– Mathematical and Computational Aspects of Materials Science, 2015, C. Calderer, R. Lipton, D. Margetis, F. Otto, ISBN 978-1-60511-730-0

Volume 1754– State-of-the-Art Developments in Materials Characterization, 2015, R. Barabash, L.G. Benning, A. Genc, Y. Kim, A. Lereu, D. Li, U. Lienert, K.D. Liss, M. Ohnuma, O. Ovchinnikova, A. Passian, J.D. Rimer, L. Tetard, T. Thundat, R. Zenobi, V. Zorba, ISBN 978-1-60511-731-7

Volume 1755E– Scaling Effects on Plasticity—Synergy between Simulations and Experiments, 2015, S. Van Petegem, P. Anderson, L. Thilly, S.R. Niezgoda, ISBN 978-1-60511-732-4

Volume 1756E– Informatics and Genomics for Materials Development, 2015, A. Dongare, C. Draxl, K. Persson, ISBN 978-1-60511-733-1

Volume 1757E– Structure-Property Relations in Amorphous Solids, 2015, E. Ma, J. Mauro, M. Micoulaut, Y. Shi, ISBN 978-1-60511-734-8

Volume 1758E– Recent Advances in Reactive Materials, 2015, D. Adams, E. Dreizin, H.H. Hng, K. Sullivan, ISBN 978-1-60511-735-5

Volume 1759E– Bridging Scales in Heterogeneous Materials, 2015, H.B. Chew, Y. Gao, S. Xia, P. Zavattieri, ISBN 978-1-60511-736-2

Volume 1760E– Advanced Structural and Functional Intermetallic-Based Alloys, 2015, I. Baker, M. Heilmaier, K. Kishida, M. Mills, S. Miura, ISBN 978-1-60511-737-9

Volume 1761E– Hierarchical, High-Rate, Hybrid and Roll-to-Roll Manufacturing, 2015, M.D. Poliks, T. Blaudeck, ISBN 978-1-60511-738-6

Volume 1762E– Undergraduate Research in Materials Science—Impacts and Benefits, 2015, D.F. Bahr, ISBN 978-1-60511-739-3

Volume 1763E– Materials for Biosensor Applications, 2015, R. Narayan, S.M. Reddy, T.R.L.C. Paixão, ISBN 978-1-60511-740-9

Volume 1764– Advances in Artificial Photosynthesis: Materials and Devices, 2015, H.A. Calderon, O. Solarza-Feria, P. Yang, C. Kisielowki, ISBN 978-1-60511-741-6

Volume 1765– Advanced Structural Materials—2014, 2015, J. López-Cuevas, F.C. Robles-Hernandez, A. García-Murillo, ISBN 978-1-60511-742-3

Volume 1766– Structural and Chemical Characterization of Metals, Alloys, and Compounds—2014, 2015, A. Contreras Cuevas, R. Campos, R. Esparza Muñoz, ISBN 978-1-60511-743-0

Volume 1767– New Trends in Polymer Chemistry and Characterization—2014, 2015, L. Fomina, G. Cedillo Valverde, M.P. Carreón Castro, J.A. Olivares, ISBN 978-1-60511-744-7

Volume 1768E– Concrete with smart additives and supplementary cementitious materials to improve durability and sustainability of concrete structures, 2015, L.E. Rendon-Diaz-Miron, L.M. Torres-Guerra, D.A. Koleva, ISBN 978-1-60511-745-4

Volume 1769E– Materials for Nuclear Applications, 2015, A. Díaz Sánchez, E. López Honorato, ISBN 978-1-60511-746-1

Prior Materials Research Symposium Proceedings available by contacting Materials Research Society

In Situ Characterization of Dynamic Processes

Mater. Res. Soc. Symp. Proc. Vol. 1754 © 2015 Materials Research Society
DOI: 10.1557/opl.2015.587

SAXS and *in-situ* SAXS to follow the structural evolution in hybrid materials

Silvia Pabisch[1], Harald Rennhofer[2], Nicola Hüsing[3] and Herwig Peterlik[2]
[1]University of Vienna, Faculty of Physics, Boltzmanngasse 5, Vienna, Austria
[2]University of Natural Resources and Applied Life Sciences Vienna, Institute of Physics and Material Science, Peter-Jordan-Strasse 82, Vienna, Austria
[3]Paris-Lodron University Salzburg, Materials Chemistry, Hellbrunnerstrasse 34, Salzburg, Austria

ABSTRACT

The paper focuses on the evolution of oriented nanostructures: An orientation in real space leads to scattering intensities with a preferred orientation with respect to the azimuthal angle in reciprocal space. Thus, the macroscopic orientation of nanostructures can be obtained from SAXS patterns. The additional advantage of *in-situ* SAXS is that one can directly follow the development of orientated nanostructures during thermal treatment, under extreme conditions or during processing. This is shown in the following for an orientational change of pores in two very different systems, the first being the formation of pores within carbon fibers during loading at high temperatures up to 2000 °C and the second is the development of macroscopically aligned pores in mesostructured silica in the sol-gel process during shear.

INTRODUCTION

Orientation of elongated structures or pores can result in multiple influences on material's properties, including the mechanical behavior as well as several functional properties, i.e. nature optimizes the crack resistance by orientation of mineral crystals and collagen fibrils [1]. As an example for technical materials, mechanical properties, among others, are controlled by the orientation of fibers [2]. Mechanical tensile stretching during production increases the orientation of crystallites within carbon fibers [3-5]. Another method to orient nanostructures is shear, which induced oriented crystallization in polymers [6]. Orientation of the structure often leads, as a consequence, to long and oriented pores: Considering carbon fibers, the structure is formed by stacks of graphene layers, which form long and elongated crystallites. These crystallites are ribbon-like shaped and form a network preferentially oriented with respect to the fiber axis. These ribbons consist of multi-layer graphene. Within the network, pores are enclosed between the crystallites. Because the boundaries are long and elongated ribbons with a high preferential orientation, the pores are usually needle- or slit-like and incline only a small angle with the fiber axis [7]. The degree of orientation controls the mechanical properties: The Young's modulus depends mainly on the orientation of the crystallites [8] and can be calculated for different structural organisations of the material, such as the series or parallel elements, the undulating ribbon, zigzag or the mosaic model [9]. The ultimate tensile strength, however, is dependent not only on the pores and their size, but also on the misalignment and entanglement of crystallites [10]. For carbon fibers, the intention to increase the orientation of pores and crystallites in the mesoregime is therefore mainly driven by the requirement to enhance the mechanical properties. This is different for functional materials such as mesoporous silica, for which an orientation of the pores should improve functional properties such as catalytic activity or flux. Different approaches were chosen to macroscopically align mesopores in silica-based materials, including magnetic field alignment [11,12], confined spaces or smart substrates [13] and mechanical shear [14]. To get a deeper insight, it is advantageous to directly follow the process of alignment of pores and its dynamics by *in-situ* techniques.

In-situ small-angle X-ray scattering (SAXS) is one of the methods, which fulfills the above requirements: From the oriented distribution of scattering intensities, one obtains the orientation of pores in dependence on different processing parameters: This was shown for pores within carbon fiber bundles [15] and also single carbon fibers with a diameter of only 7 microns [16], where the crystallite orientation was followed under load at high temperatures up to 2000 °C. Pores in carbon fibers are usually modelled as dilute system of microvoids [17,18]. In the following we present data for the alignment of pores in carbon fibers as well as for macroscopically oriented hexagonally arranged pores in mesoporous silica, where the nanostructure was subjected to shear during sol-gel processing.

IN-SITU X-RAY SCATTERING OF CARBON FIBERS

Test equipment

Figure 1 shows the test equipment for *in-situ* X-ray scattering of carbon fibers under load at high temperatures. The carbon fibers are fixed in a vacuum vessel (not shown in the scheme) and directly heated. Two different types of carbon fibers were chosen: One type of fiber origins from a polyacrylonitrile (PAN) precursor. The fibers (HTA5131, TohoTenax) were either taken as-received or heat treated at 1800 °C for one hour. The second type of fiber originated from a mesophase pitch (MPP) precursor (K321, Mitsubishi).

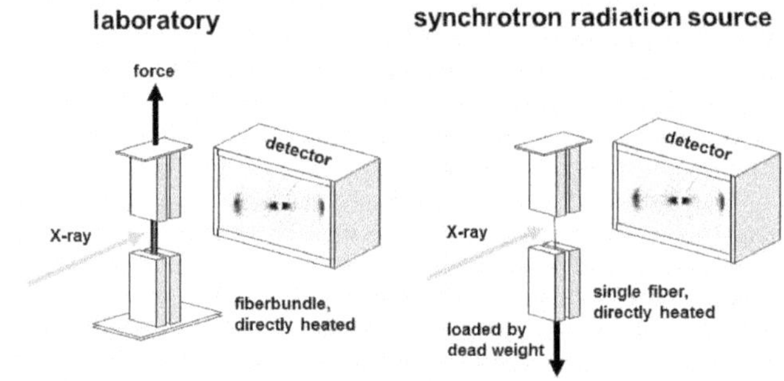

Figure 1. Scheme of the *in-situ* X-ray scattering equipment to determine the structural change of carbon fiber bundles (left image) and of single fibers (right image).

While in the laboratory SAXS set-up a carbon fiber bundle with at least some hundreds of carbon fibers is necessary for data collection, synchrotron radiation sources allow for single fiber measurements. In the laboratory equipment (Rigaku R200, rotating anode generator with X-rays from copper Kα-radiation, X-ray energy 8 keV and wavelength 0.1542 nm, equipped with a 2D position sensitive gas-filled detector, HighStar from Bruker AXS), carbon fibers were loaded in a tensile test set-up, whereas at the synchrotron radiation source (μ-spot beamline at BESSY II [19]), single carbon fibers were loaded by a dead weight. The time required to take a pattern is about 600 seconds in both cases, however, in the synchrotron radiation source the multi-read mode was used to eliminate the background from cosmic rays. This leads to an effective measurement time of 300s for one pattern. The beam size at the μ-spot beamline at BESSY II is about 10 to 15 microns, realized by a set-up with Bragg-Fresnel lenses, and has a flux of about 10^9 photons [19]. This allows the measurement of single carbon fibers with a size of 6 to 10 microns. The X-ray energy chosen for the experiment was 15 keV, corresponding to a wavelength of 0.08266 nm. For the signal detection at the μ-spot beamline, a Mar Mosaic 225 CCD is available.

To determine the orientation of the pores, the scattering intensities in the SAXS regime were background corrected and integrated in a regime of the scattering vector from 1.2 to 2.2 nm^{-1} to obtain the scattering intensity in dependence on the azimuthal angle. These intensities were then fitted with a Gaussian function and the Gaussian half-width is denoted as mean misalignment angle. A scattering vector in the regime from 1.2 to 2.2nm^{-1} was chosen for integration.

Results and Discussion

In the first experiment, the time dependence of the orientation of pores was investigated: The fibers were heated to a certain temperature and the mean pore misalignment angle χ was determined in dependence on time (Figure 2). Data measured at room temperature are denoted by open symbols, high temperature measurements by filled symbols. The data were then normalized to their initial value χ_0 (open hexagon) and the relative decrease in misalignment (increase in orientation) is shown in Figure 2. The mean misalignment angle decreases with time rather with the same rate for a single fiber (gray symbols) and for fiber bundles (black symbols). After about one hour, the process of structural change is nearly finished. The main remarkable difference is the strong decrease of the misalignment angle in the first heating step, which is much more pronounced for the fiber bundle in comparison to the single fiber. A possible interpretation is that the temperature control in the case of fiber bundles is much more difficult: Inner fibers are shielded by outer fibers, which leads to a distribution of different temperatures within the bundle. Another reason could be the loss of weak fibers in the fiber bundle during heating, as the mechanical strength of carbon fibers has a strong variation. It should be noted that the decrease of the misalignment angle of the pores (as shown in Figure 2) closely corresponds to the one of the crystallites, which was obtained from the (002)-reflection (data given for fiber bundles in [15] and for single fibers in [16]).

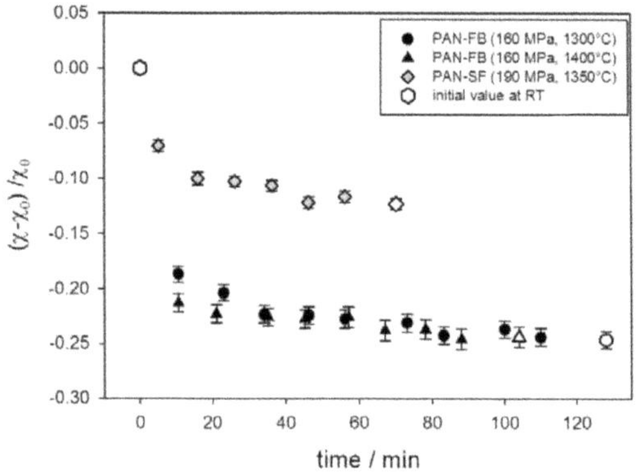

Figure 2. Decrease of mean misalignment angle of pores (increase in orientation) in carbon fibers in dependence on time. Values measured at room temperature are denoted as open symbols, measured at high temperature as filled symbols. The main difference between single fibers (gray symbols) and fiber bundles (black symbols) is the much higher decrease of the misalignment angle (increase in orientation) at the first heating cycle.

Figure 3 shows the temperature dependence: The mean misalignment angle decreases at a certain temperature, depending on the processing conditions of the fibers. Again, there is a stronger decrease for the fiber bundle (black circles), which is interpreted as a consequence of the less controlled temperature conditions in this experiment. There is no considerable difference between the PAN fiber (light gray circles) and the MPP single fiber (dark gray diamonds): The initiation point of the decreasing misalignment angle is similar, probably due to similar heat treatment conditions during processing. However, a previous heat treatment of the fibers without load leads to stability: The heat treated PAN fiber (medium gray squares) exhibits nearly no change of the orientation within the observed temperature regime. Only a slight decrease in the misalignment angle for the highest test temperature of 1900 °C, above the heat treatment temperature without load of 1800 °C, is observed.

The stability of heat treated fibers suggests that crystallites could rearrange in a stable position, whereas a heat treatment under load leads to a continuous change of the orientation [15]. This process might be enhanced by splitting off residual nitrogen from the polymeric precursor, which typically takes place at 1400 °C, and enhances the formation of new covalent cross-links between crystallites [15]. Crystallite growth and rearrangement can happen by growth from crystallites facing the edges of the graphene layers, the planes or by a process similar to dislocation glide and annealing [15]. An increasing orientation of the pores as observed in this work is probably a consequence of the increased orientation and growth of the crystallites: As the pores are located between crystallites, the pores grow and align with the fiber axis concomitantly with the crystallites.

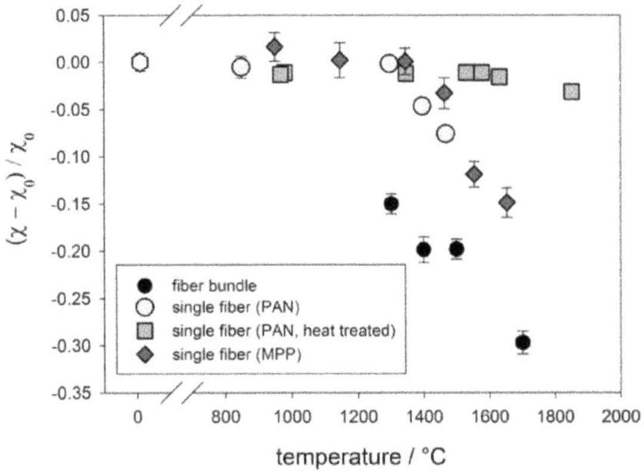

Figure 3. Decrease of mean misalignment angle of pores in carbon fibers in dependence on temperature. At a certain temperature, the misalignment angle decreases (orientation increases) for PAN fiber bundles (black circles), PAN single fibers (light gray circles) and MPP-based fibers (dark gray diamonds). Heat treatment leads to stability (medium gray squares). The data in the figure were taken from [15] and [16].

IN-SITU X-RAY SCATTERING OF MESOPOROUS SILICA

Test equipment

The macroscopic alignment of mesopores is followed by SAXS measurements in transmission mode using a laboratory equipment (Bruker Nanostar, equipped with a pinhole camera, rotating anode generator with Cu Kα-radiation). A self-developed shear device allows following the orientation of the porous structure by evaluating the oriented scattering signal measured by a 2D position sensitive detector (Vantec 2000). Typical measurement times are between 180 and 300 seconds for one image. The sample to detector distance is 108 cm, which leads to a range of the scattering vector from q=0.1 to 3 nm^{-1}. The orientation of the pores was determined from Gaussian fits of the azimuthal spread of the scattering intensity of the first strong reflection (originating from distance d_{10} of the mesopores, which are arranged in a 2D hexagonal system [20]).

Figure 4 shows a sketch of the device: The distance from the center (by positioning the device into the X-ray beam) can be varied and the rotational speed of the rotor can be adjusted to control the shear velocity. The sol-gel precursor paste is put between the stator and the rotor and the orientation of the liquid crystalline (LC) template structures during the gelation process with additional superimposed shear can be followed *in-situ*. As an additional parameter one has to consider that the sol-gel paste is changing with time from a pasty state to a “wet” solid gel. One goal was to limit the shear forces so that the macrostructure of the material is not completely destroyed: Still one should be able to obtain a monolithic material, even after applying the shear forces. The basic components of the sol-gel material used were an ethylene glycol modified silane as the silica precursor and Pluronic P123 / HCl mixture as the structure directing agent according to ref [21]. For this system the formation of well organized mesopores in a macroscopically phase separated matrix has been reported previously [21]. An *in-situ* SAXS experiment to determine the dynamics and the activation energy of the material, but without shear forces, is found in [22].

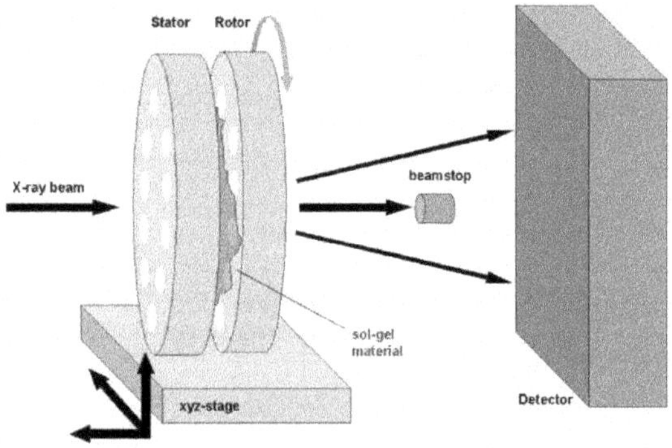

Figure 4. Scheme of *in-situ* X-ray scattering equipment to determine the alignment of mesopores during processing.

Results and Discussion

Shear has a considerable influence on the orientation of the nanostructure: In Figure 5, the orientation for two different shear velocities is shown. The black curve, with a shear at a lower velocity, is clearly more oriented than the gray curve, which is the material after shear at a higher velocity (upper part). The degree of orientation is calculated from the half-width of fits with Gaussian functions of the scattering intensities, shown in Figure 5 in dependence on the azimuthal angle. The amount of the oriented phase is obtained from the ratio of the scattering intensity of the oriented phase (peaks) to the total scattering intensity (total curve). As statistical average, it turns out that there is only a weak tendency for an increase of the oriented phase with increasing shear velocity (lower right part in Figure 5). However, the shearing time is much more decisive: If the shear rotation is stopped after 60 or 90 min, the samples exhibit nearly no orientation. An optimum regarding the orientation was reached by shear for 120 min during processing, whereas the amount of the oriented phase decreases again for higher times (150 min), lower left in Figure 5. The samples turn opaque about roughly 120 minutes (this is also true for samples without shear) indicating macroscopic phase separation. Thus one can conclude that the macroscopic orientation can only be optimized by shear during/after phase separation. A further shear of the sample, beyond the gelling point and during development of the mesostructure, leads to a decrease of the macroscopic orientation.

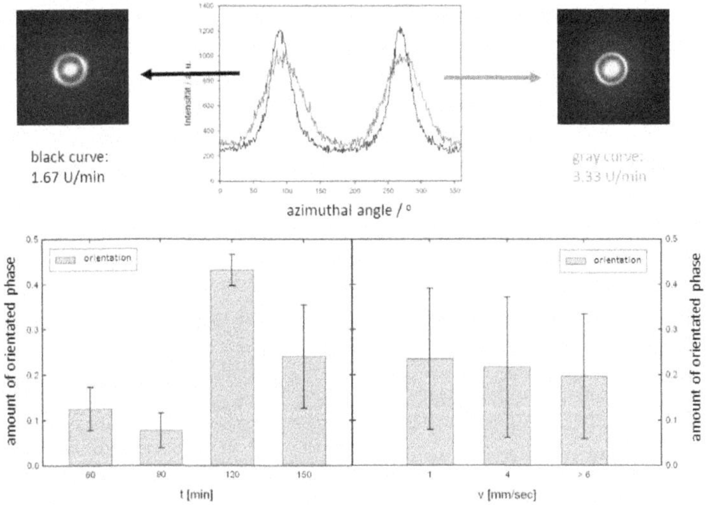

Figure 5. Upper part: The scattering intensity is oriented, slightly different for different shear velocities. The influence of the shear velocity is relatively small (lower right image), but much larger for the time, when the shear process is stopped (lower left image). For a shear up to 120 min (the time of macroscopic phase separation, before gelling and development of mesostructured, an optimum is reached.

To get a deeper insight, *in-situ* experiments were performed with permanently following the development of the mesostructure and its orientation (Figure 6). The amount of the oriented phase is visible in the upper left part of Figure 6: The oriented phase increases from 70 min on and has a maximum at about 130 min during the sol-gel process. If the sample is sheared further, the amount of the oriented phase decreases and vanishes after about 170 min of shear. The mesostructure, however, starts to develop during the sol-gel process not before 150 min, visible by the decrease of the half-width Δq of the (10)-reflection of the hexagonally ordered mesophase (indicating crystallite growth, lower right part of Figure 6) and the increase of the peak amplitude of this reflection (upper right image in Figure 6). The typical distance, obtained from the position of the first strong peak, exhibits a complicated behaviour (lower left figure). First, a decrease of the distance is observed, indicating a shrinkage of the repeating unit distance of the liquid crystalline phase. After about 120 min, the fit is dominated by the strong reflection of the evolving hexagonally arranged LC composite mesostructure. This reflects now a growth of the mesostructure and also an increase of the pore distance, as material is taken up during phase separation. Finally, after about 200 min, the mesostructure also shrinks, probably due to evaporation of alcohol. This *in-situ* experiment shows that the moment where the shear forces are stopped is decisive, and there is a subtle interplay between the development of the mesostructure and the effectivity of the application of shear forces to macroscopically orient the pores.

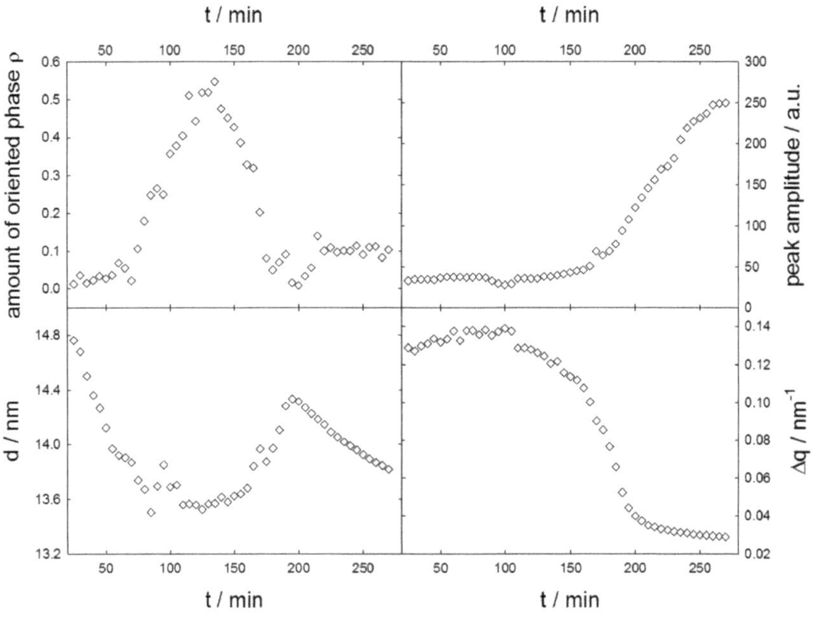

Figure 6. Typical *in-situ* experiment to follow the development of the orientation of the mesostructure: The amount of the (macroscopically) oriented phase increases and then decreases during shear (upper left figure), whereas the mesostructure usually evolves later (upper figure, right), with an increasing peak amplitude of the (10)-reflection indicating the growth of the hexagonal mesophase. The crystallite growth is also visible in the lower right figure by the decreasing half-width Δq of the (10)-reflection. The original distance of the units (only short range order) decreases, increases by uptake of material during the development of the mesostructure and finally shrinks again due to evaporation of alcohol (lower left figure).

CONCLUSIONS

In-situ SAXS allows following the development of nanostructures in an extreme variety of environments or at extreme conditions, and synchrotron radiation sources allow time resolved experiments down to the millisecond range [23]. *In-situ* SAXS was used in this work to study the alignment of pores in two completely different systems: In the first system, carbon fibers, an increasing orientation of the voids is found during loading at high temperatures up to 2000 °, whereas fibers, which were previously treated without load, are stable. In the second system, the development of macroscopically aligned pores in mesostructured silica during the application of shear forces in the gelling system was investigated. It could be shown that the timing of the application of shear forces to a gelling, phase separating system and time of the development of the hexagonal mesostructures is decisive: Applying shear forced prior to phase separation gives a low degree of macroscopic orientation of the mesopores, while shear forces well after phase separation are also not beneficial for an alignment.

ACKNOWLEDGMENTS

The financial support from the Austrian Science Funds, DACH Project Nr. I449, is gratefully acknowledged. We acknowledge beamtime at the μ-spot beamline at the BESSY II storage ring. We also are indebted to O. Paris for many intense discussions, and S. Siegel and C. li for their support during the stay at BESSY II.

REFERENCES

1. H. Peterlik, P. Roschger, K. Klaushofer and P. Fratzl, *Nat. Mater.* **5**, 52 (2006).
2. S.Y. Fu and B. Lauke, *Compos Sci Technol* **56**, 1179 (1996).
3. D.D. Edie, *Carbon* **36**, 345 (1998).
4. E. Fitzer, *High Temp.–High Press.* **18**, 479 (1986).
5. X. Zhang, Y.G. Lu, H. Xiao and H. Peterlik, *J. Mater. Sci.* **49**, 673 (2014).
6. L. Yang *et al.*, *Macromolecules* **37**, 4845 (2004).
7. A. Oberlin, *Carbon* **22**, 521 (1984).
8. L. Fischer and W. Ruland, *Coll. Polym. Sci.* **258**, 917 (1980).
9. M. Shioya, E. Hayakawa, and A. Takaku, *J. Mater. Sci.* **31**, 4521 (1996).
10. W.N. Reynolds and J.V. Sharp, *Carbon* **12**, 103 (1974).
11. S.H. Tolbert, A. Firouzi, G.D. Stucky and B.F. Chmelka, *Science* **278**, 5336 (1997).
12. Y. Yamauchi *et al.*, *J. Mater. Chem.* **15**, 1137 (2005).
13. K. Ariga *et al.*, *Bull. Chem. Soc. Jpn.* **85**, 132 (2012).
14. Z. Qiang *et al.*, *Carbon* **82**, 51 (2015).
15. H. Rennhofer, D. Loidl, S. Puchegger and H. Peterlik, *Carbon* **48**, 964 (2010).
16. H. Rennhofer *et al.*, *Carbon* **80**, 373 (2014).
17. R. Perret and W. Ruland, *J. Appl. Cryst.* **2**, 209 (1969).
18. A.F. Thünemann and W. Ruland. *Macromolecules* **33**, 1848 (2000).
19. O. Paris *et al.*, *J. Appl. Cryst.* **40**, S466 (2007).
20. W. Ruland and B. Smarsly, *J. Appl. Cryst.* **38**, 78(2005).
21. D. Brandhuber *et al.*, *Chem. Mater.* **17**, 4262 (2005).
22. M. Weinberger *et al.*, *Silicon* **1**, 19 (2009).
23. W. Bras and A.J. Ryan, *Adv. Colloid Interfac.* **75**, 1 (1998).

Mater. Res. Soc. Symp. Proc. Vol. 1754 © 2015 Materials Research Society
DOI: 10.1557/opl.2015.636

Evolution of Carbon Fiber Microstructure During Carbonization and High-Temperature Graphitization Measured In Situ Using Synchrotron Wide-Angle X-ray Diffraction

Michael Behr[1], James Rix[2], Brian Landes[1], Bryan Barton[1], Eric Hukkanen[1], Jasson Patton[1], Steven Weigand[2], Denis Keane[2]
[1]Core Research and Development, The Dow Chemical Company, Midland, MI 48667
[2]DND-CAT Synchrotron Research Center, Northwestern University, APS/ANL 432-A004, 9700 S. Cass Avenue, Argonne, IL 60439

ABSTRACT

This paper will discuss the structure-property model developed that correlates the tensile modulus to the elastic properties and angular distribution of constituent graphitic layers for carbon fiber derived from a polyethylene precursor. In addition, a high-temperature fiber tensile device was built to enable heating of carbon fiber bundles at a variable rate from 25 °C to greater than ~2300 °C, while simultaneously applying a tensile stress. This capability combined with synchrotron wide-angle x-ray diffraction (WAXD), enabled observation in situ and in real time of the microstructural transformation from different carbon fiber precursors to high-modulus carbon fiber. Experiments conducted using PAN- and PE-derived fiber precursors reveal stark differences in their carbonization and high-temperature graphitization behavior.

INTRODUCTION

The extraordinary combined properties of carbon fiber are a direct consequence of its constituent highly-oriented graphitic microstructure, which is typically obtained commercially through controlled pyrolysis of either polyacrylonitrile (PAN) or mesophase pitch-based precursor fiber, but can also be produced from non-traditional relatively inexpensive precursors, including polyethylene (PE). The fundamental building block of carbon fiber, a two-dimensional sheet of hexagonally-arranged sp^2-bonded carbon atoms, is similar to that of graphene, which exhibits incredible mechanical properties. Specifically, a single sheet of graphene exhibits ~1010 GPa tensile modulus, 107 GPa tensile strength, and 20% strain at failure [1]. In a carbon fiber, these graphitic sheets are intertwined, well-connected, and preferentially aligned along the fiber axis, as observed in transmission electron microscopy (not shown). It is well-accepted that the degree of preferred orientation governs the tensile modulus of the resulting carbon fiber [2-10].

Measurement of the characteristics of the graphitic microstructure, such as orientation, crystalline domain size, and interlayer spacing as a function of processing conditions is thus critical to understand structure-property-process relationships for these very different starting materials.

This paper will discuss the structure-property model that relates the tensile modulus to the elastic properties and angular distribution of constituent graphitic layers for carbon fiber derived from polyethylene precursors, and will present in situ WAXD characterization obtained in real time of the development of this graphitic microstructure during carbonization and graphitization processes.

THEORY

The relationship between tensile modulus and the orientation distribution of the constituent graphitic layers for the well-oriented microstructure of a carbon fiber can be interpreted using a uniform stress, or series model, as first described by Ruland [8]. In this model, the fiber is considered to be built up of a parallel array of fibrils which are well connected in the fiber direction, but weakly in the perpendicular direction; applied tensile stress is thus distributed uniformly across these fibrils. In such a model, the tensile modulus is governed by the orientation distribution of graphitic layers relative to the fiber axis and the shear modulus for shear between adjacent layers through the equation

$$\frac{1}{E}=\frac{1}{e_1}+\frac{\langle\cos^2\varphi\rangle}{g} \qquad \textbf{Equation (1)}$$

where E is the tensile modulus, e_1 is the in-plane modulus of graphite (1060 GPa), g is the shear modulus for shear between adjacent graphitic layers (4-5 GPa in graphite), and $\langle\cos^2\varphi\rangle$ is the orientation distribution or average orientation of graphitic layers, as shown in Figure 1.

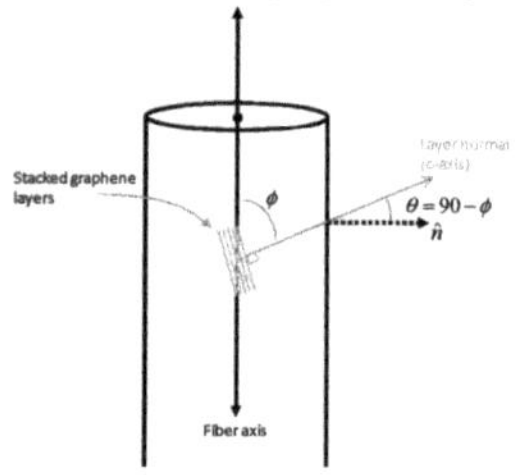

Figure 1. Schematic diagram of a stacked graphitic layer domain within a carbon fiber, with orientation angles defined. Adapted from [11].

EXPERIMENT

Carbon fibers examined in this study were produced from Dow Chemical internal polyethylene resins. Oriented precursor fibers ~10 microns in diameter were produced through melt spinning with and without subsequent hot draw processes, and then combined to form fiber tows of approximately 1500 filaments. These precursor fiber tows were then stabilized with and without tension in a continuous process using various combinations of sulfuric acid strengths and temperatures. Stabilized fibers were then converted to carbon fiber at temperatures ranging from 900 to 2400 °C in an inert atmosphere.

Tensile modulus, tensile strength, and elongation at break of individual carbon fiber filaments selected from larger fiber tows were measured using an Instron 5956 with Bluehill 2 software. The specific methodology used was according to the ASTM D2256 (Tensile Test for Single Strand Yarn).

The microstructure of individual carbon fiber filaments was investigated using WAXD measurements conducted at the Advanced Photon Source (APS), DND-CAT, 5-ID-D beamline. Single fibers previously tensile-tested were measured in vacuum in transmission-normal geometry using the standard APS Undulator A x-ray source at 17 keV ($\lambda = 0.7293$ Å). Two-dimensional diffraction patterns were collected on a Rayonix MarCCD 2k x 2k camera with acquisition times set at 3 – 5 minutes. Angular calibration and instrumental broadening correction was obtained using a LaB_6 powder standard.

Orientation parameters were numerically evaluated using Dow-developed SCATTER data visualization and analysis package [12]. Additional microstructural parameters, including interlayer spacing (d_{002}), and crystal sizes L_c and L_a were also calculated from the (002) and (100) peak half-widths, respectively using the Scherrer equation.

To observe in real time the development of graphitic microstructure during heat treatment, a high temperature fiber tensile device was designed and built, as shown in Figure 2. Briefly, fiber bundles are held by graphite clamps in a controlled inert atmosphere. The bottom clamp is moveable to enable application of stress to the fiber bundle and allow for fiber elongation. Fiber heating is achieved via one of two modes: directly heating the fiber bundle resistively by passing direct current through the fiber bundle, or by passing direct current through a pair of surrounding tungsten coils to radiatively heat the middle section of the fiber bundle. Temperature of the fiber bundle is monitored with a digital pyrometer focused at a location coincident with the x-ray beam. Kapton windows located on opposite sides of the outer chamber enable the x-ray beam to enter and scattered x-rays to exit the chamber for real-time investigation of fiber microstructure during heat treatment.

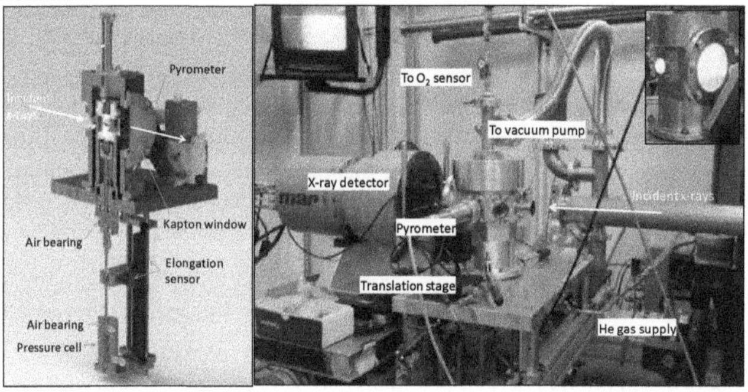

Figure 2. (Left) Schematic and (right) picture of high-temperature fiber tensile device.

RESULTS AND DISCUSSION

Structure-property relationship

Figure 3 shows data for ~140 single carbon fibers measured in this study, plotted as fiber compliance (1/E) as a function of orientation parameter, $<\cos^2\varphi>$. Also included for comparison in this plot are data for PAN- and pitch-derived carbon fiber compiled from numerous sources in the published literature [2-8]. All data were fit using the uniform-stress model as described above. From this plot, it is evident that the relationship between orientation and modulus is dependent on the precursor type. Fibers produced from PAN exhibit the highest shear modulus, g = 98 +/- 17 GPa while both pitch- and PE-derived carbon fiber exhibit significantly lower shear moduli, g = 35 +/- 1 GPa and g = 24 +/- 1 GPa, respectively, as calculated by Equation 1 and corrected for porosity. This trend ($g_{PAN} > g_{pitch}$) is consistent with that observed previously by both Northolt et al. and Sauder et al. [2, 11]. Observed shear moduli greater than that of bulk graphite (~4-5 GPa) have been interpreted as evidence for the presence of covalent sp^3-sp^3 crosslinks between adjacent graphitic layers. Indeed, TEM images (not shown) show the presence of intertwined and stacked graphitic carbon layers that exhibit spacing greater than that of bulk graphite. Thus, one possible hypothesis is that the graphitic layers present in these PE-derived carbon fibers, are on average less cross-linked than those present in PAN- and pitch-derived fibers.

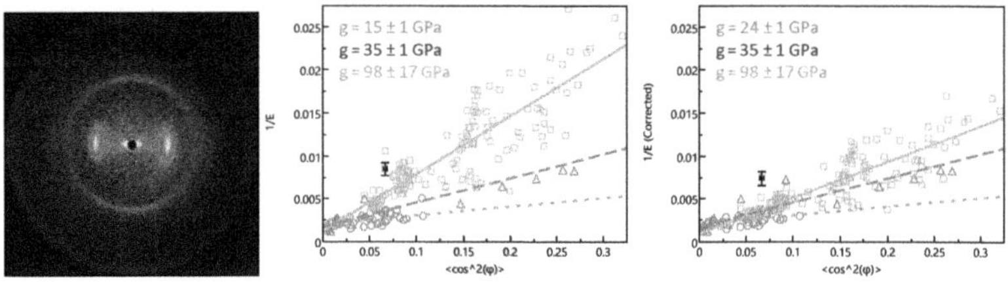

Figure 3. Representative WAXD pattern, and plots of compliance (1/E) vs. orientation parameter for PE- (squares), PAN- (circles), and pitch- (triangles) derived carbon fiber. Calculated shear moduli for each type are listed in the same order. Tensile moduli for the PE-derived carbon fiber are corrected for porosity and shown in the right plot. Error bars were estimated from replicated measurements of the same fiber.

These fundamental differences have important consequences on the resulting mechanical properties and carbonization behavior of the fibers. For example, for an equal degree of microstructure orientation, PAN-derived fiber is expected to exhibit a higher tensile modulus than pitch- or PE-derived carbon due to its higher shear modulus. However, as will be discussed, the ability to change this microstructure orientation at a given temperature is very different for these precursor types.

Microstructure transformation during heating

The data shown in Figure 4 reveal the gradual evolution of microstructure with increasing temperature for sulfonated polyethylene (open blue) and a comparative oxidized PAN (solid black) precursor fiber. The sulfonated PE precursor fiber was heated resistively, whereas the comparative oxidized-PAN fiber was heated using the heated tungsten coils. At low temperature, the constituent graphitic-based microstructure of sulfonated PE is relatively unoriented after stabilization. By comparison, oxidized PAN microstructure is much more aligned along the fiber axis after the stabilization (oxidation) process. Both materials are also initially characterized as having small crystal sizes, L_c and L_a, and large spacing between adjacent layers, d_{002}, which yield a relatively porous structure.

As temperature is increased, changes in all microstructural characteristics are observed as both materials transform to the oriented graphitic microstructure of high-modulus carbon fiber. However, the rate, onset temperature, and overall magnitude of microstructural changes are not the same for these two materials. For comparison, the microstructural characteristics of two commercially-available carbon fibers, Torayca® T300 (PAN) and Thornel® P-25 (pitch), are indicated on each plot [13,14].

The average misorientation of graphitic layers, described by $\langle \cos^2\varphi \rangle$, rapidly decreases for the oxidized PAN fiber from its initial value of ~0.145 at 500 °C to ~0.1 at 1100 °C. Above ~1100 °C, however, the average orientation of layers remains largely unchanged. This plateau is consistent with the higher observed shear modulus of PAN-derived fibers, hypothesized to result from a higher level of covalent crosslinks present connecting adjacent layers. Concomitant with this decrease is an observed sharpening of both the (100) and (200) peaks, indicating that average in-plane graphitic layer size, L_a, and the number of stacked layers, characterized by L_c, slowly grow with temperature. L_a and L_c reach values of ~3 nm and ~2 nm, respectively, by 1750 °C.

In contrast, the onset of microstructural changes observed for sulfonated (stabilized) PE precursor fiber was significantly delayed to higher temperatures. In fact, $\langle \cos^2\varphi \rangle$ does not begin to change until ~1300 °C, a temperature much higher than that observed for PAN. The rate of change of the orientation begins to accelerate above ~1800 °C, and does not reach a final equilibrium value even at ~2100 °C, exceeding values obtained by the PAN precursor fiber. Growth of both in-plane (L_a) aromatic structure and the number of stacked sheets (L_c) is observed, reaching values of ~ 4.5 nm and ~3.75 nm, respectively, by 2100 °C. Whereas the increase in L_a tracks quite closely in temperature with the changes in orientation, the increase in L_c is delayed; significant changes begin to occur for temperatures greater than ~1700 °C. This observed increase in L_c indicates the formation of larger graphitic domains in three dimensions. It is interesting to note that for a given level of microstructural orientation, the PE-derived fiber exhibits larger crystal sizes compared to the PAN-derived fiber, indicating a higher quality 3-D graphitic structure.

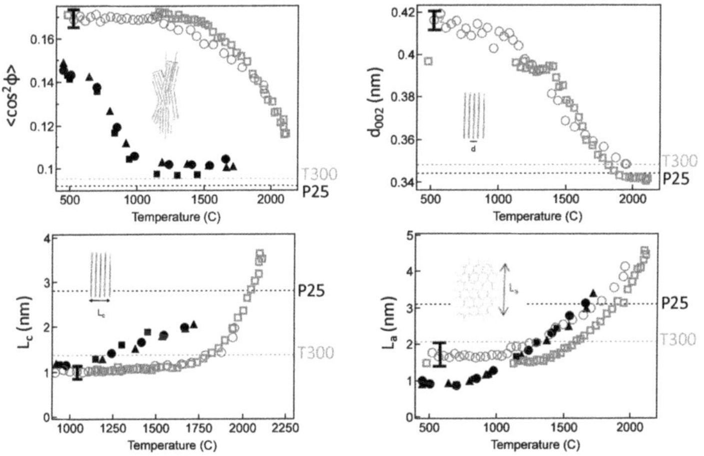

Figure 4. Microstructural parameters plotted as a function of temperature from in situ direct and tungsten coil heating experiments of oxidized PAN (solid symbols, coil heat), sulfonated polyethylene (open symbols, direct heat). The different symbols indicate replicated experiments. Error bars were estimated from the maximum deviation between replicates.

The evolution of interlayer spacing, d_{002}, provides further evidence for this three-dimensional ordering of graphitic sheets. As temperature is increased, the average spacing begins to decrease sharply from its initial value of ~0.42 nm at ~1400 °C, and continues to decrease linearly with temperature to ~0.35 nm by ~1800 °C; thereafter, the spacing continues to decrease at a lower rate, approaching the 0.335 nm spacing of bulk graphite. That d_{002} approaches that observed in bulk graphite suggests that many adjacent layers are in registry and exhibit a similar AB stacking found in a three dimensional graphite crystal. This appears to indicate that many of the carbon sp^3 cross-link bonds between adjacent layers have been eliminated, resulting in a lower overall shear modulus, as discussed above.

It is also interesting to note that the onset of these changes in d_{002} appear to slightly precede the observed changes in orientation. This is likely an indication that elimination of cross-links between adjacent layers during formation of extended graphitic layers facilitates the movement and gliding of adjacent layers, a process that is necessary to significantly impact the overall orientation of the fiber microstructure.

These results also suggest that extremely high-modulus carbon fiber may be produced at more moderate temperatures (<2500 °C) from sulfonated-PE precursors than can be produced using PAN precursors. A lower shear modulus in PE-derived fibers results in a microstructure that is more graphitic and enables microstructure to be more easily oriented, whereas the high shear modulus in fibers derived from PAN make it more difficult to orient the microstructure at moderate temperatures, requiring temperatures approaching ~3000 °C [6].

CONCLUSIONS

In conclusion, it was found that carbon fiber derived from sulfonated PE precursor exhibits a microstructure that is more similar to graphite than that found in either PAN- or pitch-derived carbon fiber. The low shear modulus exhibited between adjacent graphitic layers enables more extensive microstructural ordering during carbonization and graphitization processes compared to an oxidized PAN precursor fiber.

ACKNOWLEDGEMENTS

Portions of this work were performed at the DuPont-Northwestern-Dow Collaborative Access Team (DND-CAT) beamline line located at Sector 5 of the Advanced Photon Source (APS). DND-CAT is supported by E.I. DuPont de Nemours & Co., The Dow Chemical Company and Northwestern University, as well as U.S. Department of Energy under Contract No. DE-AC02-06CH11357.

REFERENCES

1. H. Zhao, K. Min, and N.R. Aluru, *Nano Letters*, **9**, 3012-3015 (2009).
2. M. Northolt, L.H. Veldhuizen, and H. Jansen, *Carbon*, **29**, 1267-1279 (1991).
3. L. Fischer, and W. Ruland, *Colloid and Polymer Science*, **258**, 917-922 (1980).
4. D. Loidl, et al., *Carbon*,. 41, 563-570 (2003).
5. T. Hino, H. Kurodo, International Patent 4983457 (1991).
6. D.H. Isaac, S. Ozbek, and J.G. Francis, *Materials and Manuf. Processes*, **9**, 179-197 (1994).
7. P. Morgan, *Carbon fibers and their composites*. Taylor & Francis (2005).
8. W. Ruland, *ACS Polymer Preprints*, **9**, 1368-1375 (1968).
9. Y. Huang, and R.J. Young, *Carbon*, **33**, 97-107 (1995).
10. R. Bacon, W.A. Schalamon, *Journal of Applied Polymer Science*, **9** (1969).
11. C. Sauder, J. Lamon, and R. Pailler, *Carbon*, **42**, 715-725 (2004).
12. P. Rudolf, B. Landes, *Spectroscopy*, **9**, 22-33 (1994).
13. Torayca® is a registered trademark of Toray Carbon Fibers America, Inc.
14. Thornel® is a registered trademark of Cytec Industries.

Mater. Res. Soc. Symp. Proc. Vol. 1754 © 2015 Materials Research Society
DOI: 10.1557/opl.2015.198

A Novel In-Situ Nanoindentation Characterization of Phase Transforming Materials

A. Alipour Skandani[1], R. Ctvrtlik[2] and M. Al-Haik[3]

[1] Department of Industrial Engineering, University of Pittsburgh, Pittsburgh, PA 15261, USA.
[2] Joint Laboratory of Optics of Palacky University and Institute of Physics of Academy of Science of the Czech Republic, Olomouc, Czech Republic.
[3] Department of Engineering Mechanics, Virginia Tech, Blacksburg, VA 24061, USA.

ABSTRACT

Materials with different allotropes can undergo one or more phase transformations based on the changes in the thermodynamic states. Each phase is stable in a certain temperature/pressure range and can possess different physical and mechanical properties compared to the other phases. The majority of material characterizations have been carried out for materials under equilibrium conditions where the material is stabilized in a certain phase and a lesser portion is devoted for onset of transformation. Alternatively, in situ measurements can be utilized to characterize materials while undergoing phase transformation. However, most of the in situ methods are aimed at measuring the physical properties such as dielectric constant, thermal/electrical conductivity and optical properties. Changes in material dimensions associated with phase transformation, makes direct measurement of the mechanical properties very challenging if not impossible. In this study a novel non-isothermal nanoindentation technique is introduced to directly measure the mechanical properties such as stiffness and creep compliance of a material at the phase transformation point. Single crystal ferroelectric triglycine sulfate (TGS) was synthetized and tested with this method using a temperature controlled nanoindentation instrument. The results reveal that the material, at the transformation point, exhibits structural instabilities such as negative stiffness and negative creep compliance which is in agreement with the findings of published works on the composites with ferroelectric inclusions.

INTRODUCTION

The concept of materials and structures with negative stiffness although not too recent but still requires further clarifications in terms of both definition and quantification. It is well established that a constrained bi-stable structure such as a buckled beam can exhibit negative stiffness under certain circumstances[1]. From negative stiffness one may expect the material/structure to displace opposite to the direction of the applied force. The importance of such materials/structures can be expressed in extremal vibrational damping [2], composites with elevated stiffness [3] and acoustical absorbers [4]. Even more application is being thought ranging from meta-materials to seismic protection of structures[5] and strings with negative stiffness and hyperfine structures[6]. The design and evaluation of bi-stable structures as negative stiffness elements has been touched in several cases whereas investigation for materials with negative stiffness remains limited to the proof of the concept by Lakes et al. [7]. They showed that materials undergoing certain structural changes- namely phase changes-, when embedded in a constraining matrix can show negative stiffness. They also showed that the concept of the negative stiffness varies fundamentally from negative passion ratio materials. The overall mechanical properties of the resultant composites changes dramatically when the stimulating factors (temperature in terms of a phase change) reaches the threshold. Lake et al. reported an infinitely stiff composite of VO_2 1% –Sn around the phase change temperature of VO_2 (66 °C). Also based on their observation the damping coefficient (tan δ) showed a peak at the same temperature range with a value much greater than best naturally damping materials such as rubber. This opened a plethora of methods to the already existing ones for improving the viscoelastic and damping properties of structural materials [8-11]. The extraordinary material responses in the temperature range where inclusions show abnormalities arises from their material constants switching from regular behavior (positive) to an irregular unstable mood (negative). In this study for the first time we showed an in-situ method to directly measure the negative stiffness of a ferroelectric material, quantitatively, rather than the traditional indirect approximation with respect to a stiff matrix. Depth sensing indentation is a contact based technique widely used for the evaluation of mechanical properties at small scales. During a typical test a diamond tip of known geometry is pressed into the sample surface, while the indentation load and depth are continuously recorded. Hardness and elastic modulus are measured in most cases, but other phenomena like pressure-induced phase transformations[12,13], incipient plasticity [14] or time dependent effects [15] can be studied by analyzing the indentation curve. Furthermore, it is possible to perform such test at elevated temperatures and study temperature stability of the material [16,17] or temperature related phenomena. The novelty of our approach resides in performing nano mechanical testing while sweeping the temperature within a range, rather than at a set point stabilized temperature, and compensating for the alteration in the dimension of sample and test setup due to constant temperature change. Triglycine sulfate crystal exhibits a typical second-order ferroelectric phase transition at temperature $T_C = 322$ K from ferroelectric phase with the non-centrosymmetric monoclinic point group P21 to the paraelectric phase with P21/m symmetry [18]. The crystal lattice remains monoclinic for both the ferroelectric ($T < T_C$) and parraelectric ($T > T_C$) phase. The nature of the ferroelectric transition is an order/disorder type[19]. The description of the phase transition is out of the scope of the present paper and can be found elsewhere[20]. There is no change in lattice parameters of the TGS crystal at the Currie point. However, the coefficient of thermal expansion is changing its sign [21,22]. Information on the change of the lattice parameters of the TGS crystal can be found e.g. in [21].

EXPERIMENT

Triglycine sulfate (TGS) with a formula $(NH_2CH_2COOH)_3 \cdot H_2SO_4$ was chosen over other ferroelectric materials such as VO_2 because of its rationally higher stability in presence of the oxygen and none toxicity whereas VO_2 is toxic and tends to convert to its higher order oxides in atmospheric environment. Moreover, TGS has a reported Curie temperature around 47°C which is one of the lowest transforming temperatures among other ferroelectric materials 23. The dielectric, optical and thermal properties of TGS have been studied extensively [24, 25]. Single crystal TGS was grown from an aqueous solution of sulfuric acid, containing a greater than three-fold excess of glycine [26]. Nanoindentation experiments were performed using a fully calibrated NanoTest instrument (from MicroMaterials, Ltd., UK) with a diamond sphero-conical Rockwell indenter with a nominal radius of 50 μm in load controlled mode. TGS crystal with edge dimensions of ~5 mm and thickness of 2 mm was mounted onto a heated ceramic hot block. Specimen temperature was monitored and controlled using two thermocouples mounted beneath the sample and on the samples surface. The nanoindentation experiments were employed to explore the mechanical response of the material to external loading. The TGS single crystal phase transition temperature is reported approx. 49 °C. Therefore the nanoindentation was performed as the hot stage experiment in the temperature range from 50.5 to 39.5 °C to include the phase transition temperature. Prior to the indentation experiment; the sample was heated up to 50.5 °C at a rate of 2.3 °C/min and stabilized for at least one hour upon reaching the target temperature. The experiment was set up as indentation test with short 10 s loading part, 60 s long dwell period at peak load and prolonged unloading part lasting 480s. The indenter was pressed into the surface along the [001] crystallographic direction of the TGS crystal. Since the abnormal behavior of the TGS is expected when it passes through the transition temperature the sample was cooled transiently after 60s of unloading; until that the temperature was held constant at 50.5 °C.

DISCUSSION

The typical as-measured (uncorrected) indentation hysteresis is shown in Fig.1. During the isothermal loading cycle, the recorded nanoindentation depth comprises elasto-plastic deformation; the corresponding loading curve is of regular shape. On the other hand the unloading/cooling part of the indentation curve is very different from the typical isothermal one. The unusual shape of the unloading curve stems from the synergy of the regular isothermal elasto-plastic indentation response and temperature induced effects [27]. These include deformations due to nonlinear thermal drift, change in the sign of coefficient of thermal expansion and ferroelectric phase transition of order/disorder type. Note that coefficient of thermal expansion for TGS crystal is negative bellow and positive above the Currie point [21, 22]. Therefore, the standard methods [28, 29] to evaluate the indentation response of TGS as it undergoes these phenomena are not readily applicable without appropriate corrections. Regular indentation tests are fundamentally performed at constant temperature and any thermal drift correction is based on the assumption of its linear and monotonous character. This does not hold for the case when the temperature is changed nonlinearly in a wide range. Moreover, coefficient of thermal expansion of TGS crystal possesses a different sign below and above transition temperature. In order to compensate for the above mentioned affects, and to isolate the deformation due to phase transition from the other types, the nanoindentation experiment at very low load with prolonged dwell period was carried out during the temperature sweep from 50.5°C to 39.5 °C analogically to the unloading/cooling experiment. However, in this case the cooling took place during the 480 s lasting creep period and started after 60 s after its beginning. The peak load of 0.5 mN and relatively large radius of the used spherical indenter of 50 μm ensure that the recorded depth change represents exclusively the TGS crystal volume changes during the temperature sweep, in lieu of the time dependent low load creep effects. Considering this record as reference data, one can subtract it from the uncorrected unloading/cooling data, see Fig.1. The corrected unloading curve comprises only the elastic deformation, and deformation due to phase transition can be further analyzed using the standard methods [28, 29]. The corrected indentation curve together with appropriate temperature with respect to time is depicted in Fig. 2, since the phase transition is temperature-dependent. It is apparent that the initial part of the corrected unloading curve exhibits the regular shape with positive slope until the beginning of the negative sloped part (see Fig.1). This singularity represents the onset of the TGS phase transition taking place at temperature of approx. 47 °C as can be seen from Fig. 2. Note that this temperature agrees well with the literature data. Using the conventional analysis of nanoindentation data based on approximation of the unloading curve by power law fit (Oliver and Pharr 28) or linear fit (Doerner and Nix 29) the contact stiffness can be estimated using the slope of the upper portion of the fitted unloading curve. Providing that the indentation contact area A is known the reduced elastic modulus E* can be deduced from its relationship with contact stiffness $S = 2E^* \sqrt{\frac{A}{\pi}}$.

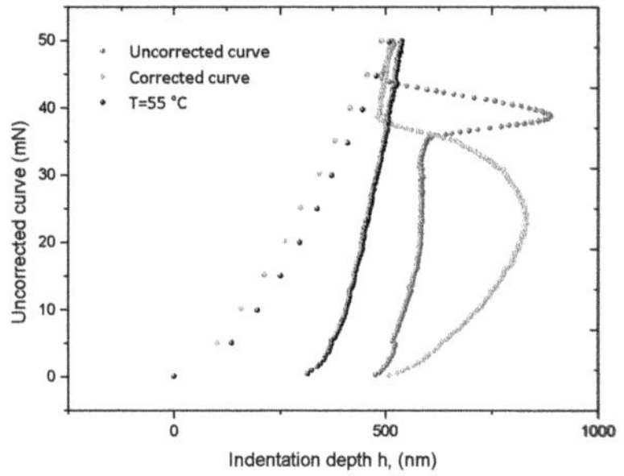

Figure 1. Indentation curve before and after correction. The experiment was performed in the temperature range of 50.5-39.5 °C. The isothermal curve measured at T=55 °C is shown for comparison.

In order to extract the values of the mechanical properties from the corrected indentation curve, the linear approximation of the upper part of the unloading curve was employed as can be seen from Fig.3. The linear fit in the range 99%–80% of maximum depth (indentation load of 50–40 mN) gives a contact stiffness of 0.350 mN/nm that corresponds to a reduced modulus of 26.4 GPa.

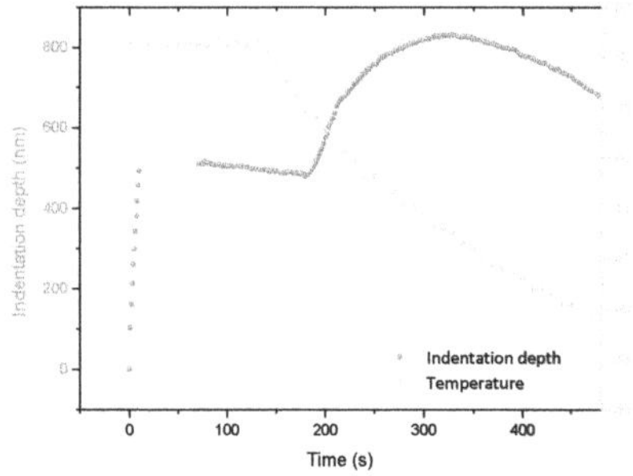

Figure 2. Corrected indenter penetration depth and crystal temperature as a function of temperature during the indentation experiment performed in the range of 50.5-39.5 °C.

The interaction of the diamond indenter with the TGS crystal undergoing the temperature induced phase transition results in a change in slope of the unloading curve from positive to negative. Using the approach utilized for analyzing the upper portion of the unloading curve, the slope of the negative portion of the unloading curve corresponds to 37–35 mN which yields a contact stiffness of 0.017 mN/nm. This change of slope suggests that the magnitude of the negative stiffness is approximately 5% of the regular (i.e., positive) contact stiffness. Using the power law fit for the analysis of the upper portion (99-80%) of the corrected curve yields a contact stiffness of 0.339 mN/nm that corresponds to reduced modulus value of 25.8 GPa. Comparison of results of both fits suggests a very good feasibility of the linear approximation and justifies its application in this particular case. In both cases, the actual diamond area function was used. Note that the isothermal curve measured at T=55°C gives almost the same value of contact stiffness and elastic modulus like the corrected curve in Fig.1.

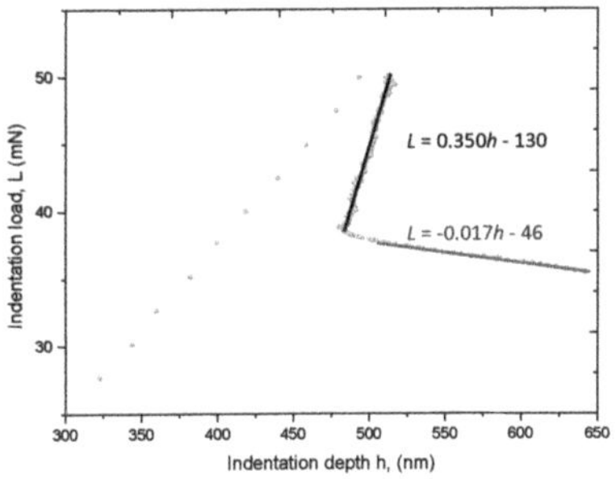

Figure 3. Upper part of the corrected indentatino curve with the linear fit of its positive and negative sloped sections.

Various experiments were performed under different experimental conditions (temperature range, duration of the unloading). The calculated values stay close when the sphere was replaced by the three-sided Berkovich indenter. Using the outlined approach the magnitude of the negative stiffness is (5.0±0.5) % and (5.1±1.9) % of the regular (i.e. positive) contact stiffness for Berkovich and Rockwell indenter, respectively.

CONCLUSIONS

The outlined approach can be utilized for quantification of negative stiffness for other materials without the need to embed them in a matrix. In our approach the diamond indenter, as the stiffest material available, plays the role of constraining matrix. Hence absolute comparison of materials exhibiting negative stiffness can be made.

ACKNOWLEDGMENTS

This work has been supported by the National Science Foundation (NSF) awards CMMI-0846589 and CMMI-1200506. The authors gratefully acknowledge this support.

REFERENCES

1. J. Prasad and A. R. Diaz, J. Mech. Design. **128**, 1298 (2006).
2. T. Mizuno, T. Toumiya and M. Takasaki, Int. J. Jap. Soc. Mech. Eng. **46** (3), 807-812 (2003).
3. R. S. Lakes, T. Lee, A. Bersie and Y. C. Wang, Nature. **410**, 565-567 (2001).
4. L. Kashdan, C. Seepersad, M. Haberman and P. S.Wilson, Rapid Prototyping J. **18** (3), 194-200 (2012).
5. A. A. Sarlis, S. M. A. D. T. R. Pasala, M. A. M. C. Constantinou, F. A. A. M. Reinhorn, M. A. S. Nagarajaiah and D. P. Taylor, J. Struct. Eng. **139**, 1124-1133 (2013).
6. M. C. Diamantini and H. Kleinert, Physical review letters **82** (2), 267-270 (1999).
7. T. Jaglinski, P. Frascone, B. Moore, D. S. Stone and R. S. Lakes, Philosophical Magazine **2011**, 4285-4303 (2006).
8. A. A. Skandani, A. Y. Boroujeni and M. Al-Haik, presented at the ASME 2013 Int. Mech. Eng. Cong. and Exp., San Diego, (2013).
9. A. A. Skandani, A. Y. Boroujeni, R. Kalhor, S. W. Case and M. Al-Haik, Polymer Composites (2014).
10. A. A. Skandani, N. Masghouni and M. Al-Haik, *Superior Damping of Hybrid Carbon Fiber Composites Grafted by ZnO Nanorods*. (Springer, New York, 2014).
11. A. A. Skandani, N. Masghouni, S. Case, D. Leo and M. Al-Haik, Applied Physics Letters **101** (7), 073111 (2012).
12. A. Kailer, Y. G. Gogotsi and K. G. Nickel, Journal of Applied Physics **81** (7), 3057-3063 (1997).
13. V. Kulikovsky, V. Vorlíček, P. Boháč, M. Stranyánek, R. Čtvrtlík and A. Kurdyumov, Thin Solid Films **516** (16), 5368-5375 (2008).
14. S. Suresh, Nat Mater **5** (4), 253-254 (2006).
15. L. Shen, W. C. D. Cheong, Y. L. Foo and Z. Chen, Mater. Sci. Eng. A, **532** (0), 505-510 (2012).
16. N. M. Everitt, M. I. Davies and J. F. Smith.
17. R. Ctvrtlik, M. S. Al-Haik and V. Kulikovsky, Journal of Materials Science (2014).
18. A. Cizman, T. Antropova, I. Anfimova, I. Drozdova, E. Rysiakiewicz-Pasek, E. B. Radojewska and R. Poprawski, *Size-driven ferroelectric-paraelectric phase transition in TGS nanocomposites*. (2013).
19. S. Hoshino, T. Mitsui, F. Jona and R. Pepinsky, Physical Review **107** (5), 1255-1258 (1957).
20. R. B. Lal and A. K. Batra, Ferroelectrics **142** (1), 51-82 (1993).
21. S. Iwao and H. Sadao, Japanese Journal of Applied Physics **1** (5), 249 (1962).
22. K. Deguchi and E. Nakamura, Physics Letters A **60** (4), 351-352 (1977).
23. B. T. Matthias, C. E. Miller and J. P. Remeika, physical review **104**, 849-850 (1956).
24. B. Andriyevsky, N. Esser, A. Patryn, C. Cobet, W. Ciepluch-Trojanek and M. Romanyukc, Physica B **373**, 328-333 (2006).
25. K. Deguchi and E. Nakamura, Phys. Let. **60A**, 351-352 (1977).
26. H. V. Alexandru and C. Berbecaru, Cryst. Rex Technol. **30** (3), 307-315 (1995).
27. A. A. Skandani, R. Ctvrtlik and M. Al-Haik, Appl. Phys. Let. **105** (8), - (2014).
28. W. C. Oliver and G. M. Pharr, J. Mat. Research **7**, 1564-1583 (1992).
29. M. F. Doerner and W. D. Nix, J. Mat. Research **1** (04), 601-609 (1986).

Mater. Res. Soc. Symp. Proc. Vol. 1754 © 2015 Materials Research Society
DOI: 10.1557/opl.2015.584

In-Situ Scanning Electron Microscope Observations of Strain-Confined Lithium Nucleation at Electrode/Electrolyte Interfaces in All-Solid-State-Lithium Battery

Munekazu Motoyama[1,2], Makoto Ejiri[1,2], and Yasutoshi Iriyama[1,2]
[1]Department of Materials, Physics and Energy Engineering, Nagoya University, Furo-cho, Chikusa-ku, Nagoya, 464-8603, Japan
[2]JST-ALCA, 5 Sanban-cho, Chiyoda-ku, Tokyo 102-0075, Japan

ABSTRACT

We have studied electrochemical Li deposition/dissolution processes at amorphous solid electrolyte (LiPON) interfaces with 30-nm-thick-Cu-current collectors at different current densities by *in-situ* scanning electron microscopy (SEM). When the current density is smaller than 300 μA cm^{-2}, Li islands continue to grow under a Cu film without coalescing with their neighbors. Consequently, they produce small cracks in the Cu film leading to isolated Li rod growth from the cracks. On the other hand, a current density of 1.0 mA cm^{-2} provokes the nucleation of Li islands with a higher number density. They rapidly coalesce under a Cu film in all lateral directions before cracking the Cu film. High current density conditions therefore suppress Li rod growths.

INTRODUCTION

A great deal of attention has been paid to the development of next-generation-rechargeable batteries such as metal-air, Li-S, and Li metal batteries that can store several times more energy than commercial Li-ion batteries. The research on all-solid-state-lithium batteries (SSLB) has been significantly propelled by advancements in techniques to decrease solid/solid interface resistivity and new discoveries of solid Li^+ ionic electrolytes [1-3]. Inorganic solid electrolyte can block Li dendrite growth even if Li metal is used as the anode. Undoubtedly, this feature is quite attractive because the theoretical specific capacity of Li metal anode (3860 Ah kg^{-1}) is much greater than that of graphite anode (372 Ah kg^{-1}). There are also other advantages of using ceramic electrolyte: (1) non-flammability; (2) simplified battery pack design due to no risk of electrolyte leakage; (3) longer cycle and calendar life compared to organic liquid electrolyte. However, Li rapidly grows to penetrate through solid electrolyte during charging if there are percolated gaps between grains like in a ceramic-powder pellet. Hence, the Li anode easily touches the cathode even with solid electrolyte in some cases. Amorphous electrolyte thus plays a key role in blocking Li growth from the Li metal anode in SSLB. Hence, it is important to study how Li metal grows and dissolves through amorphous solid electrolyte interfaces during charging and discharging. Extensive studies of electrochemical Li deposition and dissolution in solid electrolyte systems have not been reported [4-7].

Previous work studied the electrochemical Li deposition and dissolution using an amorphous electrolyte of lithium phosphorous oxynitride (LiPON) [8-10]. Li deposition invokes non-uniform nucleation that leads to whisker-like growths on a LiPON layer. Hence, this study reports on the growth and dissolution of Li islands/whiskers through solid electrolyte interfaces coated with a Cu current collector using *in-situ* scanning electron microscopy (SEM).

EXPERIMENTAL

Figure 1 shows a two electrode-type-electrochemical cell for *in-situ* SEM observation. The majority of the electrolyte (1.25 cm × 1.25cm) is a mirror-polished $Li_{1.3}Al_{0.3}Ti_{1.7}(PO_4)_3$ (LATP) sheet (OHARA Co.) with a thickness of 150 μm. It was subsequently coated with LiPON layers with thicknesses of 2.5 μm on the upper and bottom surfaces by radio frequency (RF) magnetron sputtering. The details are described elsewhere [8-10]. The working electrode is a Cu film deposited onto a circular area with a diameter of 5.0 mm in the center of the LiPON-coated upper surface of the electrolyte by pulsed laser deposition (PLD). Cu is a typical current collector material for lithium ion battery [11]. The counter electrode is a Li film with a thickness of 3–4 μm and an area of $(0.45)^2 \times \pi$ cm^2 evaporation-deposited onto the bottom of the electrolyte. This trilayered ceramic electrolyte sheet with the electrodes is clamped with thick Cu and brass plates to obtain electric contacts as presented in Fig. 1. There is a viewport with a diameter of 3.0 mm in the center of the top Cu plate. This viewport is aligned within the area of a Cu working electrode. *In-situ* observations of Li electrodeposition and dissolution were conducted through the viewport. The brass plate is attached to a Li counter electrode on the bottom. An electrochemical cell is assembled on a custom-made sample stage in an Ar-filled glove box. It is carried into a Keyence VE-9800 SEM without being exposed to air. The observations were conducted with an acceleration voltage of 10 kV. One frame during *in-situ* SEM observation is taken for less than one second. A potentiostat was installed outside a SEM. Galvanostatic Li electrodeposition and dissolution were conducted at current densities from 50 μA cm^{-2} to 1.0 mA cm^{-2}, which were calculated using the overall area of the PLD Cu film. Electrochemical impedance spectroscopy was performed with voltage amplitude of 10 mV at an open circuit voltage.

RESULTS & DISCUSSION

Figure 2(Left) shows voltage transients during Li electrodeposition at 50, 100, 300 μA cm^{-2}, and 1.0 mA cm^{-2}. The total charges are 180 mC cm^{-2} for all the current densities. This charge amount corresponds to a plating of a 242-nm-thick Li film if the plated film formed a contiguous solid thin film. Hence, the total duration (3600 s to 180 s) is shorter with a larger current density. The absolute values of the voltages in Fig. 2(Left) are the sum of the relative potential difference of a Cu working electrode to a Li counter electrode and the ohmic drop across the electrolytes. The Li^+ ionic conductivities of LATP and LiPON are approximately 1×10^{-4} S cm^{-1} [12] and 2×10^{-6} S cm^{-1} [13], respectively. The total electrolyte resistance is thus approximately 2.0×10^3 Ω if a uniform cross-section with the same area as the working electrode [= $(0.25)^2 \times \pi$ cm^2] is considered for Li^+ ionic conduction between the electrodes. All the voltage transients show the negative peaks in the early stages of electrodeposition. The negative peak appears sooner as the current density increases. The peak height measured from the flat voltage in the following stage slightly increases with increasing current density. The meaning of those negative voltage peaks is discussed elsewhere [14].

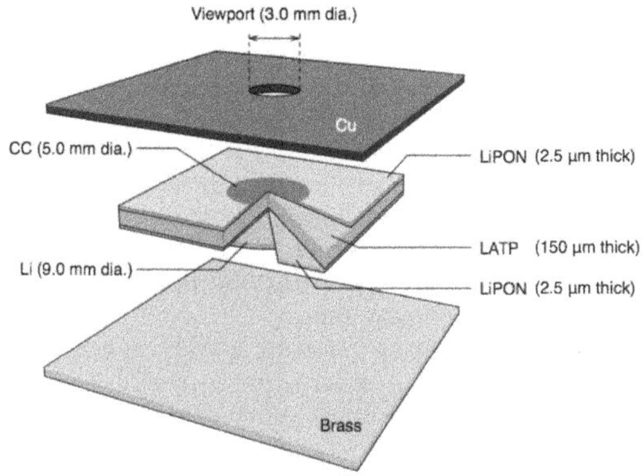

Figure 1. Electrochemical cell for *in-situ* observation by SEM (CC: current collector). A Li counter electrode is deposited onto the lower LiPON surface. A trilayer electrolyte sheet with electrodes are clamped with Cu and brass plates. There is a viewport hole with 3.0 mm in diameter in the center of the Cu plate.

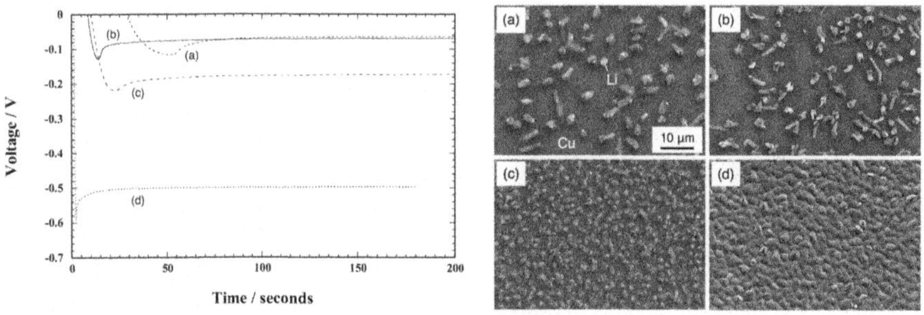

Figure 2. (Left) Voltage transients during Li electrodeposition with Cu current collectors of 30 nm in thickness. (Right) SEM images of Cu surfaces after Li electrodeposition after 180 mC cm^{-2} was passed. All images were taken with tilt angles of 10°. (a) 50 μA cm^{-2}, (b) 100 μA cm^{-2}, (c) 300 μA cm^{-2}, (d) 1.0 mA cm^{-2}.

Figure 2(Right) shows SEM images of PLD Cu film surfaces after Li electrodeposition at different current densities with 180 mC cm^{-2} charges. Li rods with diameters of approximately 1–2 μm appear to grow from a Cu film as reported in previous work [8-10]. The number densities of Li rods do not show further increases after certain times. Some Li rods eventually attain lengths of approximately 10 μm. The Li nucleation densities increase as the current density increases. The deposition amount per site decreases as the nucleation density increases because the total charges are the same for all the current densities (= 180 mC cm^{-2}). At a current density of 1.0 mA cm^{-2}, Li rod growths are therefore not observed due to their high nucleation density. After each *in-situ* experiment, the displayed magnification of a SEM was lowered to observe surrounding regions outside the field of view exposed to electron beams for 180 to 3600 s. There were no clear differences in Li nucleation density and morphology between regions with and without a long exposure to electron beams.

Impedance spectroscopy measurements revealed direct current (DC) resistance values of 2.5 to 3.0 × 10^3 Ω for the entire electrolyte region (not shown). These values are close to the electrolyte resistance estimated above. Hence, electrolyte ohmic drops were 20 to 400 mV that need to be taken into account in Fig. 2(Left). We assume that the overpotentials for a Li counter electrode are negligibly small in the present study.

We measured the nucleation density transients at different current densities (50, 100, 300 μA cm^{-2}). The nucleation density cannot be accurately measured at 1.0 mA cm^{-2} because of the rapid coalescence of Li nuclei. A transient nucleation density variation is often considered by the following equation [15,16].

$$N_{(t)}/N_0 = 1 - \exp(-k_n t) \tag{1}$$

where $N_{(t)}$ is the nucleation density at a time of t, N_0 is a saturation nucleation density, k_n is a nucleation rate constant. The nucleation rate at $t = 0$ equals k_n in Eq. (1). The theory behind Eq. (1) assumes that nucleus-centered exclusion zones, which radially extend with time, deplete the free zones for subsequent nucleation resulting in the saturation of nucleation density [15]. The k_n values for our results were 4.2 × 10 cm^2 s^{-1}, 5.5 × 10^2 cm^2 s^{-1}, and 2.4 × 10^3 cm^2 s^{-1} at 50, 100, and 300 μA cm^{-2}, respectively. Although, further studies are necessary to conclude that the above nucleation theory can be sound for Li growth in a solid electrolyte system in the present study, the nucleation rate constant, k_n, increases with increasing current density as expected.

The series of SEM images in Fig. 3(Left) show the time evolution of a Li nucleation site at 50 μA cm^{-2}. The Cu surface slightly swells after approximately 8 minutes suggesting that a Li island initiated its growth beneath the Cu. A crack in the Cu surface starts to be significant after 15 minutes. A straight Li rod with a diameter of 1.4 μm appears from the crack and grows toward the left of the field of view. The growth rate of this Li rod is roughly estimated to be 2.0 nm s^{-1}. This means that the local current densities for the growth of Li rods are approximately 1.5 mA cm^{-2}. When electrochemical Li dissolution is performed at a current density of 50 μA cm^{-2}, the Li rod gradually hollows resulting in the creation of a cavity while surface layers remain undissolved as presented in Fig. 3(Left). Nevertheless, the coulombic efficiency on dissolution was 85% (cutoff voltage: 1.5 V).

Numerous circular holes in a Cu current collector remained after all Li rods and islands were dissolved completely (not shown). Those diameters were 1 to 2 μm, which were the same lengths as the diameters of Li islands or rods. These observations help understanding of how Li rods grow to appear as in Fig. 3(Left). We think that Li nuclei deform the top Cu layers by growing until the stress in deformed Cu reaches the fracture point. Eventually, Li escapes through a crack to grow. A rod-shape Li consequently grows as illustrated in Fig. 3(Right).

Figure 4(Left) shows sequential SEM images during Li electrodeposition at 1.0 mA cm^{-2}. Deformations of Cu layers due to Li nucleation are observed in all places. Isolated Li islands at 50 seconds laterally grow to coalesce at 120 seconds as delineated with dotted lines. On dissolution, the coulombic efficiency was 84% (cutoff voltage: 1.5 V). This means that the elec-

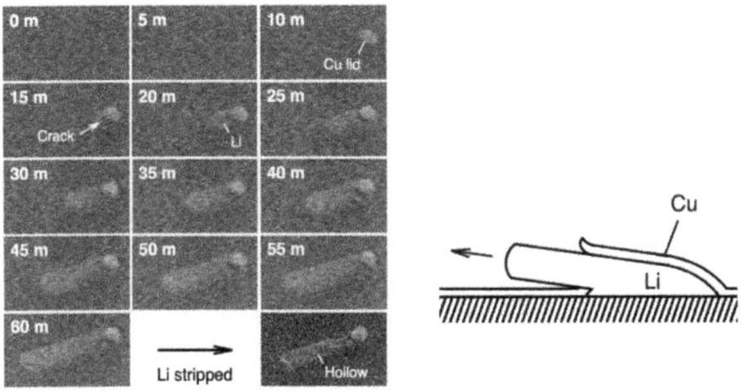

Figure 3. (Left) SEM images (width: 7.7 μm) at 5.0-minute intervals for the growth of a Li rod at 50 μA cm^{-2}. The lower-right-corner image is taken at the same location after Li is dissolved by anodic dissolution. (Right) Growing Li rod from LiPON surface coated with a Cu layer.

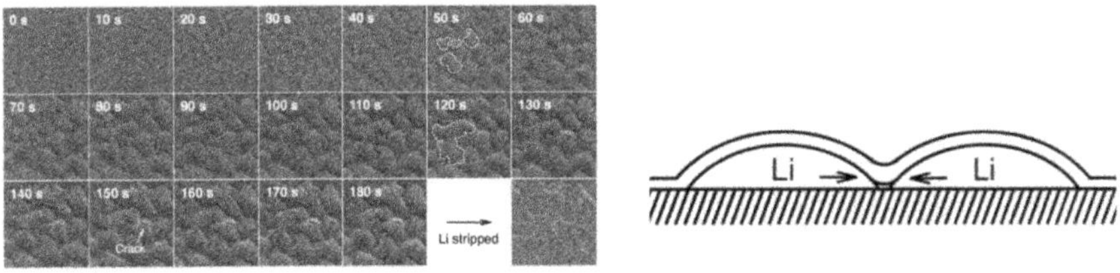

Figure 4. (Left) SEM snapshots (width: 8.7 μm) at 10-second intervals of Cu surface during Li electrodeposition at 1.0 mA cm^{-2}. The lower-right- corner image is taken at the same location after Li is dissolved by anodic dissolution. (Right) Li islands on LiPON surface with top Cu lids. Adjacent islands coalesce beneath the Cu layer.

trochemical reversibility with this all-solid-state cell has been proven.

When the current density is smaller than 300 μA cm^{-2}, rod-shape Li grows as shown in Fig. 3. This is because the nucleation densities are so small that Li islands continue to separately grow to the critical sizes (i.e. 1–2μm in diameter) that produce cracks in a Cu film. On the other hand, adjacent Li islands rapidly coalesce under Cu layers at 1.0 mA cm^{-2} [Fig. 4(Right)]. This island coalescence functions to level the Li surface. Consequently, the local stress concentrations in a Cu film are suppressed compared to the case that individual Li islands continue to grow separately. A small crack is observed at 1.0 mA cm^{-2} when the charge amount is 150 mC cm^{-2} in Fig. 4(Left). On the other hand, the cracking occurs when the charge amount is only 40 mC cm^{-2} at 50 μA cm^{-2} in Fig. 3(Left). The leveling effect due to the high-number-density nucleation delays the cracking.

CONCLUSIONS

We have observed transient behaviors of Li electrodeposition and dissolution that occur across LiPON electrolyte interfaces coated with a Cu current collector using an *in-situ* SEM technique. The use of an amorphous electrolyte without grain boundaries effectively prevents Li growth toward the cathode. Moreover, the use of a non-volatile solid electrolyte offers the unique benefit that an electron microscope can be coupled with electrochemical experiments without substantial efforts to modify sample cells. At lower current densities ($\leq 300\ \mu A\ cm^{-2}$), Li nucleation densities are small enough for individual Li islands to continue to grow separately. Consequently, Li islands initiate cracks in Cu films. Li rods begin to grow through those cracks. The Li nucleation rate at Cu/LiPON interfaces increases with increasing current density. On the other hand, Li nucleation events take place in the entire region of Cu/LiPON interfaces at 1.0 mA cm^{-2}. Li islands readily coalesce under a Cu film to laterally extend in all directions. Li rod growths are therefore effectively prevented.

ACKNOWLEDGMENTS

This work was financially supported by JST-ALCA and JSPS, 26870272.

REFERENCES

1. R. Murugan, V. Thangadurai, and W. Weppner, *Angew. Chem., Int. Ed.,* **46,** 7778 (2007).
2. N. Kamaya, K. Homma, Y. Yamakawa, M. Hirayama, R. Kanno, M. Yonemura, T. Kamiyama, Y. Kato, S. Hama, K. Kawamoto, and A. Matsui, *Nat. Mater.,* **10,** 682 (2011).
3. A. Sakuda, A. Hayashi, and M. Tasumisago, *Sci. Rep.,* **3,** 2261 (2013).
4. J. Corish and C. D. O'Brian, *J. Mater. Sci.,* **6,** 252 (1971).
5. M. Lee, R. O'Hayre, F. B. Prinz, and T. M. Gür, *Appl. Phys. Lett.,* **85,** 3552 (2004).
6. M. Rohnke, C. Rosenkranz, and J. Janek, *Solid State Ionics,* **177,** 447 (2006).
7. T. Hasegawa, K. Terabe, T. Tsuruoka, and M. Aono, *Adv. Mater.,* **24,** 252 (2012).
8. K. Okita, K. Ikeda, H. Sano, Y. Iriyama, and H. Sakaebe, *J. Power Sources,* **196,** 2135 (2011).
9. F. Sagane, R. Shimokawa, H. Sano, H. Sakaebe, and Y. Iriyama, *J. Power Sources,* **225,** 245 (2013).
10. F. Sagane, K. Ikeda, K. Okita, H. Sano, H. Sakaebe, and Y. Iriyama, *J. Power Sources,* **233,** 34 (2013).
11. S. C. Nagpure, R. G. Downing, B. Bhushan, and S. S. Babu, *Scripta Mater.,* **67,** 669 (2012).
12. S. Hasegawa, N. Imanishi, T. Zhang, J. Xie, A. Hirano, Y. Takeda, and O. Yamamoto, *J. Power Sources,* **189,** 371 (2009).
13. X. Yu, J. B. Bates, J. E. Jellison, Jr., and F. X. Hart, *J. Electrochem. Soc.,* **144,** 524 (1997).
14. M. Motoyama, M. Ejiri, and Y. Iriyama, *to be submitted.*
15. M. Avrami, *J. Chem. Phys.,* **7,** 1103 (1939); M. Avrami, *J. Chem. Phys.,* **8,** 212 (1940); M. Avrami, *J. Chem. Phys.,* **9,** 177 (1941).
16. G. Oskam, J. G. Long, A. Natarajan, and P. C. Searson, *J. Phys. D: Appl. Phys.,* **31,** 1927 (1998).

Mater. Res. Soc. Symp. Proc. Vol. 1754 © 2015 Materials Research Society
DOI: 10.1557/opl.2015.585

Observations of Magnetic Domain Structure Change in $Nd_2Fe_{14}B$ Magnets at Elevated Temperature with External Magnetic Field by Lorentz Microscopy

Toshimasa Suzuki[1], Koichi Kawahara[1], Haruka Tanaka[1] and Kimihiro Ozaki[2]
[1] Materials Research and Development Laboratory, Japan Fine Ceramics Center (JFCC), Nagoya, 456-8587, Japan.
[2] Materials Research Institute for Sustainable Development, National Institute of Advanced Industrial Science and Technology (AIST), Nagoya, 463-8560, Japan.

ABSTRACT

In this study, we conducted the in-situ observations of the magnetic domain structure change in $Nd_2Fe_{14}B$ magnets at elevated temperature by transmission electron microscopy (TEM) / Lorentz microscopy. The in-situ observations in $Nd_2Fe_{14}B$ magnets revealed that the magnetization reversal easily occurred at the elevated temperature. At more than 180°C, the magnetic domain wall motion could be observed by applying the magnetic field of less than 20 mT. The motion of the magnetic domain wall was discontinuous and the domain wall jumped to one grain boundary to the neighboring grain boundary at 180°C. On the other hand, the continuous domain wall motion within grain interior as well as discontinuous domain wall motion was observed at 225°C, and some grain boundaries showed still strong pinning effect even at 225°C. The temperature dependence of the pinning effect of grain boundaries would not uniform.

INTRODUCTION

$Nd_2Fe_{14}B$ magnets with excellent properties have extended the applications in the field of motors for Hybrid Electric and Electric Vehicles. The permanent magnet motors are often used at elevated temperature as high as 200°C. It is well known that the $Nd_2Fe_{14}B$ magnets without dysprosium (Dy) show the decrease of coercivity at elevated temperatures. In order to attain high coercivity of sintered $Nd_2Fe_{14}B$ magnets even at high temperature, various methods have been employed [1-3]. However, the coercivity of developed $Nd_2Fe_{14}B$ magnets were worse than the coercivity of $Nd_2Fe_{14}B$ with Dy [4]. Therefore, in order to reduce deterioration of coercivity of $Nd_2Fe_{14}B$ magnets at elevated temperatures, it is important to observe generating sites of reverse magnetic domains and pinning sites against magnetic domain walls motion in $Nd_2Fe_{14}B$ magnets. In this study, we observed the magnetic domain structure change in fine-grained $Nd_2Fe_{14}B$ magnets at elevated temperatures by transmission electron microscopy (TEM) / Lorentz microscopy.

EXPERIMENT

Fine-grained sintered $Nd_2Fe_{14}B$ magnets without Dy were prepared using Hydrogenation-Disproportionation-Desorption-Recombination (HDDR) processed $Nd_2Fe_{14}B$ powder. Details of preparation of sintered magnets were described in ref. 5. The average grain size of sintered $Nd_2Fe_{14}B$ magnet was about 380 nm (Fig. 1). A coercivity of the sintered

$Nd_2Fe_{14}B$ magnet is 1.2 T. Prior to preparation of thin foils suitable for TEM observations, the sintered $Nd_2Fe_{14}B$ magnet was thermally demagnetized in Ar atmosphere at 350°C.

Thin foils with dimensions of ca. 10 μm x 10 μm x 100 nm were prepared by a focused ion beam (FIB) thinning method (Hitachi FB-2100). The thin foils were supported on Mo grids. In order to observe the thermal demagnetization process in TEM, the prepared foils were magnetized using an electromagnet with applying an external magnetic field of 2.0 T. Then, foils were subjected to TEM observation. A Hitachi HF-3300EH was used in this study with acceleration voltage of 300 kV. In-situ observation of the magnetic domain wall motion at high temperatures was carried out using a double-tilt heating holder at the temperature range from room temperature to 225°C.

Magnetic domain walls were observed by the Lorentz TEM microscopy with Fresnel mode. In-situ observation of domain wall motion was conducted by applying a magnetic field from condenser lens in TEM. The applied magnetic field was set to 0 - 100 mT, and the direction of the applied magnetic field was parallel to the incident beam. During observation, the sample was tilted by 30°, so that the effective magnetic field, that was the magnetic field component parallel to the easy magnetization direction, was the range of 0 - 30.9 mT.

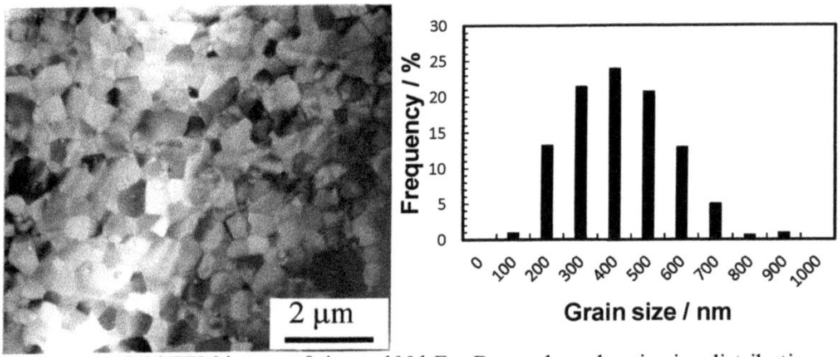

Figure 1 Bright field TEM image of sintered $Nd_2Fe_{14}B$ sample and grain size distribution evaluated from TEM images.

DISCUSSION

Figure 2 shows the Lorentz microscope images of sintered $Nd_2Fe_{14}B$ observed at different temperatures. At room temperature (Fig.2 (a)), no magnetic domain wall was observed. This result indicated that the magnetization directions in the observed area would be the same because the thin foil sample was magnetized before observation under the magnetic field of 2.0 T. As increasing the temperature up to 150°C, no clear change was observed (Figs. 2 (b) and (c)), indicating that the magnetization reversal was not occurred. As further increasing the temperature up to 180°C, a bright line-contrast, which corresponds to the magnetic domain wall, appeared as indicated by the arrow in Fig.2 (d). Moreover, the observation temperature was further increased up to 225°C (Figs.2 (e) and (f)). As shown by the arrows 2 and 3 in Fig.2 (f), bright and dark line-contrasts appeared in the observed area at 225°C. The domain between the bright and dark line-contrasts is the reverse magnetic domain occurred by thermal demagnetization process. These observations suggest that magnetization reversal easily occurs at elevated temperature higher than 225°C in $Nd_2Fe_{14}B$ magnet used in this study.

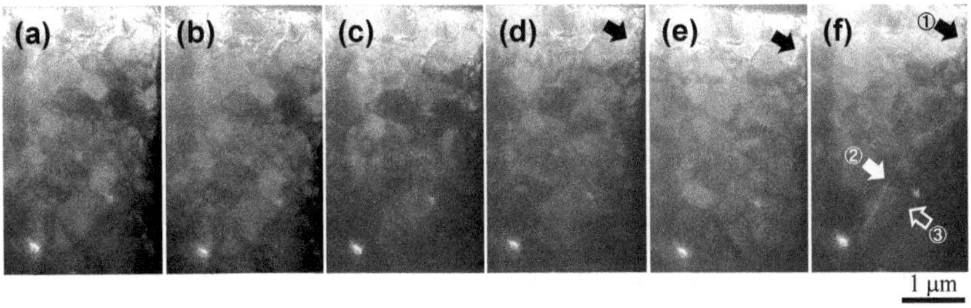

Figure 2 Lorentz microscope images of the thin foil sample of sintered $Nd_2Fe_{14}B$: (a) After magnetization at room temperature, (b) 100°C, (c) 150°C, (d) 180°C, (e) 200°C, (f) 225°C. The arrows show the magnetic domain walls.

The magnetic domain wall motion was observed by applying the magnetic field to the foils during the Lorenz TEM observation. Figure 3 shows the Lorentz TEM images observed at the same area but under the different applied magnetic field. The observation temperature was room temperature. The magnetic domain walls were observed to locate along grain boundaries, resulting in a zigzag shape domain wall configuration. As shown in Fig.3, the motion of the domain wall was not observed though the magnetic field strength was increased up to 30.9 mT. Since the strength of the magnetic field applied here was as weak as 30.9 mT, the magnetic domain structure did not change at room temperature. As mentioned above, the magnetization reversal easily occurred at elevated temperature, then, we conducted the in-situ observations of the magnetic domain wall motion at elevated temperatures.

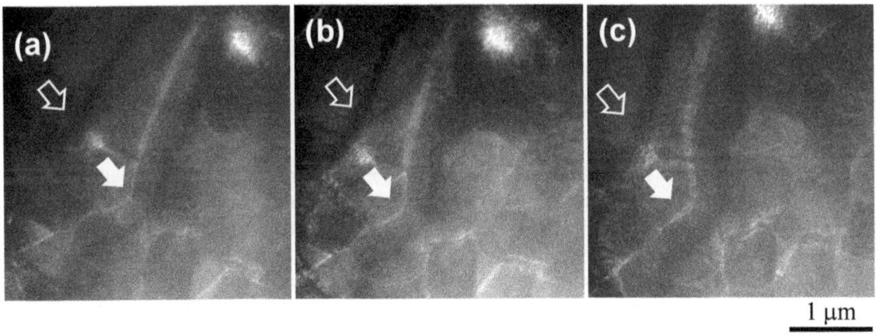

Figure 3 Lorentz microscope images observed at room temperature with different strength of the applied magnetic field: (a) 0 mT, (b) 17.7 mT, (c) 30.9 mT. The arrows show the magnetic domain wall.

Figure 4 demonstrated the in-situ observation of the motion of the magnetic domain walls at 180°C. Each schematic illustration inserted in the figures shows the grain boundary and domain wall configurations at the area indicated by the white square in Fig.4 (a). The solid and dotted lines represent the grain boundaries and magnetic domain wall, respectively. The inset of Fig.4 (a) show only grain boundaries. As shown in Fig. 4, the magnetic domain wall moved toward the left direction with increasing the applied magnetic field (Figs.4 (b)-(f)). The magnetic domain wall motion was not observed as increasing the magnetic field up to 8.8 mT (Fig.4 (b)), however, a part of the magnetic domain wall abruptly jumped to the neighboring grain boundary when the applied magnetic field was increased to 11.0 mT (Fig.4 (c)). The location of the domain wall scarcely changed when the applied magnetic field was increased up to 15.4 mT (Fig.4 (e)), then, the magnetic domain wall jumps to the next neighboring grain boundary (Fig.4 (f)). At 180°C, the motion of the magnetic domain wall was discontinuous; the domain wall jumped from a pinning site to the other pinning site. These in-situ observation results revealed that the motion of the magnetic domain wall was discontinuous by the interaction between the domain wall and the pinning sites, and that main pinning sites observed here were grain boundaries.

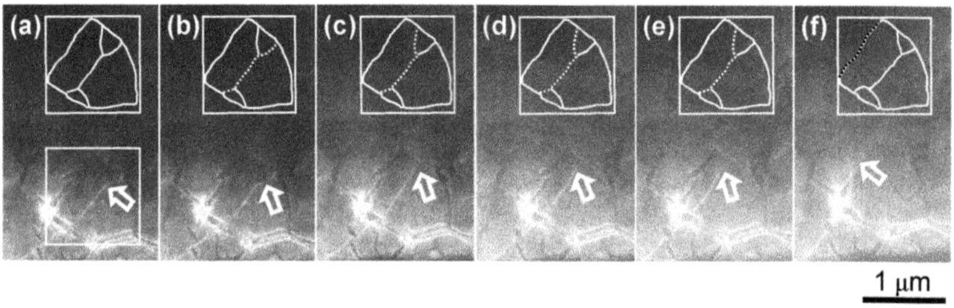

Figure 4 Lorentz microscope images observed at 180°C with different strength of the applied magnetic field: (a)6.6 mT, (b)8.8 mT, (c)11.0 mT, (d) 13.2 mT, (e)15.4 mT, (f) 17.7 mT. The arrows show the moving magnetic domain wall with increasing the applied magnetic field. Each schematic illustrations of inset show the square area in Fig.4 (a). The solid and dotted lines represent the grain boundaries and magnetic domain wall, respectively. The inset of Fig.4 (a) show only grain boundaries.

Figure 5 is the in-situ observation showing the motion of the magnetic domain walls at 225°C. The magnetic domain wall was not observed in the observation area (Fig.5 (a)). When the magnetic field was increased from 0 to 4.4 mT, the magnetic domain wall (bright line-contrast, indicated by the arrow in Figs.5 (b) and (c)) moved from right-lower area toward the left upper direction. Unlike the observations at 180°C, the magnetic domain wall moved rather continuously; the magnetic domain wall moved rather slowly even within the grain interior. However, when the magnetic field was increased up to 6.6 mT, the domain wall was pinned by the grain boundary (Fig.5 (d)). As further increasing the magnetic field up to 8.8 mT, the domain wall abruptly jumped to the other grain boundary (Fig.5 (e)). It should be noted that there were at least two grain boundaries between pinning sites observed in Figs.5 (d) and (e). This result indicates that all grain boundaries do not act as pinning sites against the domain wall motion. As further increase the magnetic field, the pinned part of domain wall (as shown by the arrows 1 in Fig.5 (e), (f) and (g)) did not move, however, the unpinned part of domain wall (as shown by the arrows 2 in Fig.5 (e), (f) and (g)) went into the grain interior. When the pinned part of the domain wall unpinned, the domain wall jumped to the next pinning site (Fig.5 (h)). The pinning sites shown by the arrow 1 in Figs.5 (g) were grain boundaries, however, some grain boundaries did not act as a pinning site.

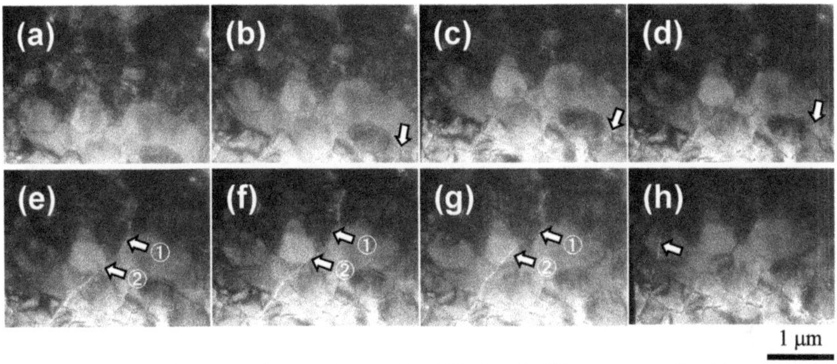

Figure 5 Lorentz microscope images observed at 225°C with different strength of the applied magnetic field: (a)0 mT,(b)2.2 mT, (c)4.4 mT, (d)6.6 mT, (e)8.8 mT, (f)11.0 mT, (g)13.2 mT, (h)15.4 mT. The arrows show the moving magnetic domain wall. The arrows 1 in Fig.5 (e), (f) and (g) show the pinned part of domain wall and the arrows 2 in Fig.5(e), (f) and (g) show the unpinned part of domain wall.

The in-situ observations in $Nd_2Fe_{14}B$ magnets revealed that the magnetization reversal easily occurred at the elevated temperature, particularly, at more than 180°C, the magnetic domain wall motion could observed by applying the magnetic field of less than 20 mT. The motion of the magnetic domain wall was discontinuous and the domain wall jumped to one grain boundary to the neighboring grain boundary at 180°C. This result indicates that almost the all grain boundaries would act as a pinning site against the domain wall motion at 180°C. On the other hand, the continuous domain wall motion within grain interior as well as discontinuous domain wall motion was observed at 225°C. This result indicates that the pinning effect of grain boundaries would decrease with increasing temperature. However, some grain boundaries showed still strong pinning effect even at 225°C. Thus, the temperature dependence of the pinning effect of grain boundaries would not uniform, i.e., the temperature dependence of the pinning effect of grain boundaries would depends on the grain boundary characters such as misorientation angle, grain boundary plane orientation, etc. In the future work, in order to propose a guideline of design for thermally stable magnets, we need to clarify these grain boundary characters that show strong pinning effect even at higher temperatures.

CONCLUSIONS

Magnetic domain structure change in $Nd_2Fe_{14}B$ magnets with fine grain size was observed at elevated temperature by transmission electron microscopy (TEM) / Lorentz microscopy. Obtained results are summarized as follows;

(1) The magnetization reversal easily occurred at elevated temperature higher than 225°C in $Nd_2Fe_{14}B$ magnet used in this study.
(2) The in-situ observations in $Nd_2Fe_{14}B$ magnets revealed that the motion of magnetic domain walls easily occurred at elevated temperature, particularly, at more than 180°C, the magnetic domain wall motion could observed by applying the magnetic field of less than 20 mT.
(3) The motion of the magnetic domain wall was discontinuous and the domain wall jumped to one grain boundary to the neighboring grain boundary at 180°C.
(4) Though the pinning effect of grain boundaries would decrease with increasing temperature, some grain boundaries showed still strong pinning effect even at 225°C.
(5) The temperature dependence of the pinning effect of grain boundaries was suggested to depend on the grain boundary characters.

ACKNOWLEDGMENTS

This work has been supported by Future Pioneering Projects /Development of magnetic material technology for high-efficiency motors from Japanese Ministry of Economy, Trade and Industry.

REFERENCES

1. 1. R. Ramesh, G. Thomas, and B. M. Ma, J. Appl. Phys. **64**, 6417 (1988).
2. H. Sepehri-Amin, T. Ohkubo, T. Nishiuchi, S. Hirosawa, and K. Hono, Scr.Mater. **63**, 1124 (2010)
3. T. Akiya, J. Liu, H. Sepehri-Amin, T. Ohkubo, K. Hioki, A. Hattori, K.Hono, J. Appl. Phys. **115**, 17A766 (2014).
4. K.Hono, H. Sepehri-Amin, Scr.Mater. **67**, 530 (2012)
   K. Takagi, M. Ishii, R. Soda, K. Ozaki, in *The 23rd International Workshop on Rare Earth and Future Permanent Magnets and Their Applications (REPM 2014) Processing*, edited by G. C. Hadjipanayis pp.148..

Mater. Res. Soc. Symp. Proc. Vol. 1754 © 2015 Materials Research Society
DOI: 10.1557/opl.2015.586

A Differential Scanning Calorimetric Study of Carbide Transition in 10Cr Tempered Martensitic Steels

H.C. Wang
Ruhr-Universität Bochum, Institute für Werkstoffe, Universitätsstr. 150,
44801 Bochum, Germany

ABSTRACT

The process and kinetics of carbide precipitation upon tempering of an Fe-10Cr-0.15C (wt.%) alloy fabricated from high-purity components has been studied. Differential scanning calorimetry reveals three exotherms in a temperature range of 100-700°C. Using advanced electron microscopy and Kissinger analysis, the exothermic processes have been interpreted. Cementite precipitated first upon tempering at temperatures as low as 200°C; M_7C_3 and $M_{23}C_6$ appear at higher temperatures, precipitating at approximately the same time but on different sites (M_7C_3 within grains and laths and $M_{23}C_6$ on grain and lath boundaries). Subsequently, the more stable $M_{23}C_6$ coarsens at the expense of M_7C_3, which dissolves. The first exotherm was interpreted as being related to the precipitation of cementite whilst the other two overlapping exotherms were interpreted as relating to the concurrent precipitation and coarsening of M_7C_3 and $M_{23}C_6$, respectively. In-situ SEM and TEM observation is being conducted in order to obtain a more precise understanding and further validate the interpretation of the DSC results.

INTRODUCTION

Ferritic-martensitic 9-12 wt.% Cr heat-resistant steels with alloying additions are widely used in steam power plant owing to their satisfactory creep and oxidation resistance, high thermal conductivity, low thermal expansion coefficient and low susceptibility to thermal fatigue. The void swelling resistance of these steels also makes them particularly attractive for use in nuclear power generation[1, 2]. In the dislocation creep regime in which these alloys are used, one of the main contributions to creep strength comes from the presence of a variety of fine precipitates such as carbides, nitrides, carbonitrides and intermetallic phases[2-6].

Precipitation reactions during tempering may take various forms depending on the initial as-quenched state, the temperature and the chemical composition. Tempering of alloy steels typically introduces one or more types of transient carbides within the martensite laths, at lath boundaries and/or at prior austenite grain boundaries. After further exposure to high temperature, these metastable carbides are replaced by more stable carbides. Particularly, in higher-chromium steels (higher than 7 wt.%)[7], the normal carbide precipitation sequence during tempering is: Supersaturated martensite → Cementite → M_7C_3 → $M_{23}C_6$. This sequence can be modified by alloying additions; typically M_2C will precipitate after cementite if molybdenum is added, while $M_{23}C_6$ is unstable with respect to M_6C in steels containing tungsten[8, 9]. The coarsening of the lath boundary carbides, and the recovery and recrystallization of ferrite may follow depending on the conditions applied. Various mechanisms of carbide nucleation such as in-situ nucleation within pre-existing carbides and separate nucleation have been reported[10].

Although research activity into precipitation processes during tempering is intensive, it has mainly been focused on commercial steels, and there is also a lack of kinetic data relating to the tempering process. Due to the complexity of commercial steels, it is difficult to elucidate the decomposition mechanisms explicitly. Studies of binary or ternary systems made from high-purity components can offer a more fundamental understanding of the precipitation processes and the underlying mechanisms. In the present work, precipitation at various temperatures in a high-purity Fe-10Cr-0.15C (wt.%) alloy is examined; to our knowledge, precipitation studies on this system have not been previously reported in the literature. The main experimental technique used is differential scanning calorimetry (DSC), which has been used successfully for the kinetic study of precipitation reactions in other systems[11-18]. The DSC results were interpreted by means of scanning electron microscopy (SEM) and transmission electron microscopy (TEM).

EXPERIMENT

Sample preparation

The alloy used in this study was produced by arc-melting electrolytic iron (99.99 wt.% purity) and chromium (99.99 wt.% purity) and an iron-carbon pre-alloy (2.15 wt.% C) under vacuum. The fabricated ingot is button-shaped with a diameter of 30mm and weighs approximately 50g. In order to avoid compositional inhomogeneity, the ingot was flipped and remelted for 10 times under high vacuum in the arc-melter. The results of chemical analysis of the ingot, using a spark emission spectrometer measurement, are given in Table I.

Table I Chemical analysis results of the fabricated alloys

	Cr	C	Si	Mn	S	Ni	Mo
wt.%	9.98±0.01	0.15±0.01	0.038	0.021	0.0097	0.029	0.012
	Cu	V	Co	Zr	N	others	Fe
wt.%	0.013	0.019	0.013	0.006	0.0159	<0.001	bal.

In order to obtain martensitic microstructure and further ensure the compositional homogeneity in the initial microstructure, the ingots were austenitized at 1150°C for 4 h and then water-quenched. Part of the austenitized and water-quenched (hereafter denoted WQ) ingot was retained for use in differential scanning calorimetry. From the remainder, samples were cut and isothermally tempered at 400, 600, 750°C for 1h (denoted as T400, T600 and T750 respectively), followed by air cooling.

SEM and TEM bright-field micrographs showing the microstructure after austenization at 1150°C for 4 hours and water quenching are depicted in Figure 1. The as-quenched microstructure was determined to be fully martensite with characteristic features including prior austenite grain boundaries (PAGB), and packet and block boundaries (sub-boundaries). In Figure 1(b), dense dislocation network was observed and there is no evidence of carbides even at the fine scale of the TEM micrograph, so it can be concluded that no auto-tempering has occurred.

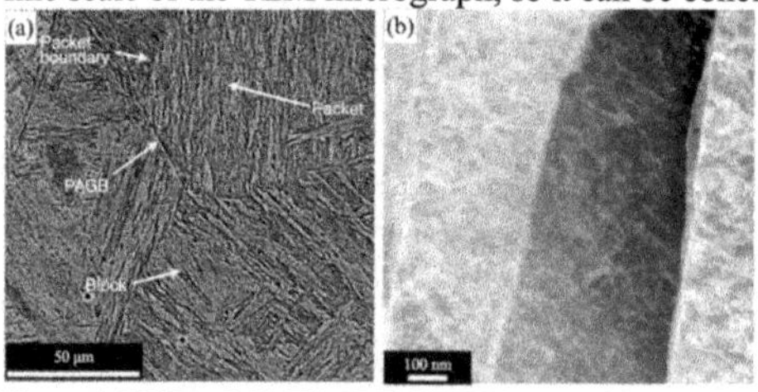

Figure 1 SEM and (b) HAADF-STEM image of the microstructure of the alloy after quenching. Important microstructural features are indicated by white arrows in (a).

TEM observation of isothermally tempered samples

The morphology and crystallographic characteristics of carbides found in the sample of T400, T600 and T750 are shown in Figure 2. The different carbides that appear at different temperature were identified by selected area diffraction pattern (SADP). Cementite was observed in T400 sample. It has also been observed that the cementite precipitates have an average length of 61±13 nm and width of about 15±5 nm and grow as lamellae aligned in specific directions within the former martensite laths. Analysis found it follows the familiar Bagaryatski orientation relationship with the ferritic matrix ($M_3C[001]//\alpha$-Fe[011]) and this is in agreement with literature[19, 20]. The microstructure of T600 sample is decorated by two types of carbides: elongated larger $M_{23}C_6$ found preferentially on grain and lath boundaries (indicated by white arrows in Figure 2(b)), and the smaller M_7C_3 (indicated by black arrows in Figure 2(b)) and more spheroidal in morphology lying within the grains and laths. Figure 2(c) shows the microstructure of T750, the carbides found inside the grains and laths after tempering at 600°C, namely M_7C_3, are now no longer identifiable, and all the remaining particles are lying along grain boundaries, which were identified as $M_{23}C_6$.

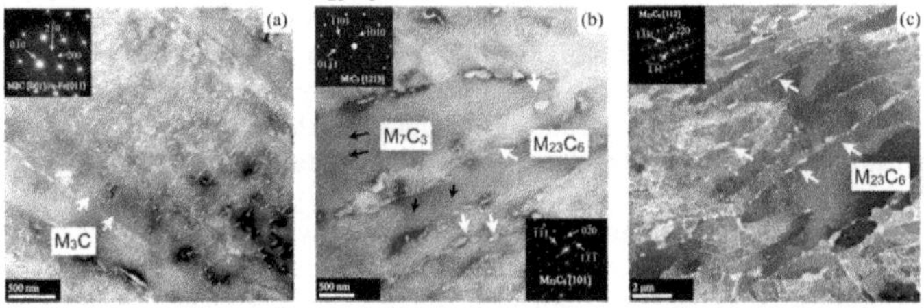

Figure 2 HAADF-STEM image of microstructure of (a) T400, (b) T600 and (c) T750. The microstructure is decorated with different carbides (indicated by arrows in the figure) at different tempering temperature.

Differential scanning calorimetry

DSC measurements were conducted using a Netzsch 204F calorimeter on the WQ material using different heating rates. In order to avoid temperature gradients, while preserving a good signal-to-noise ratio, the specimens were machined into discs of diameter 5 mm and thickness less than 0.5 mm (giving a mass of about 80mg). During DSC measurement, the specimens were protected by dynamic argon gas with a flow rate of 27 ml min^{-1}. The temperature of the DSC machine was calibrated against the melting point of pure aluminum. Platinum crucibles were used, and a high purity of Fe-10Cr alloy with similar size and weight with the sample was placed in the reference crucible.

Figure 3 shows typical DSC traces (signal divided by respective heating rate) obtained with heating rate of 5, 10 and 20°C min^{-1}. As peak positions vary depending on the heating rates, in the following context we take 10°C min^{-1} heating rate result as example. Exothermic reactions are readily detectable at temperature about 270 and 600°C. However, as can be seen in the figure, the exothermic part at about 600°C in the DSC trace shows a complex shape with two shoulders. This suggests that the peak consists of two overlapping exotherms and the results have been interpreted assuming this to be the case.

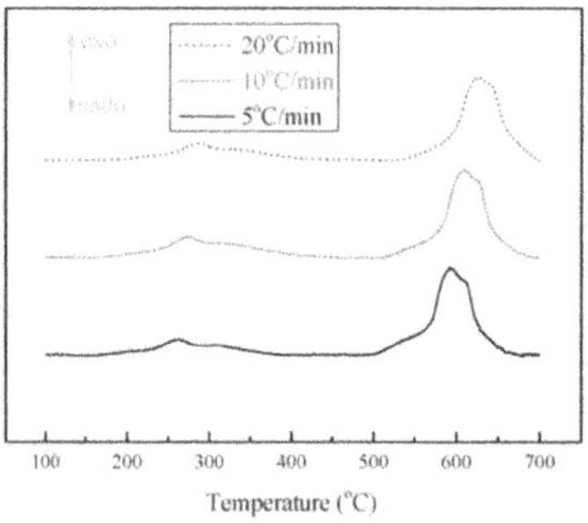

Figure 3 Typical DSC curves (an offset plot) obtained in the current study with different heating rates.

DISCUSSION

The combination of electron microscopy and DSC results allows us to infer the precipitation sequence and coarsening processes upon tempering. The metallic element content of the cementite is very similar to that of the matrix, because the primary rate-controlling element is carbon when the predominant precipitates are cementite. Cementite particles grow by a paraequilibrium mechanism[21, 22] in which the boundary conditions at the ferrite/cementite interface are such that the cementite inherits the metal composition of the matrix. When the temperature increases to 600°C, nucleation of more stable carbides at the various types of boundaries is to be expected because these are energetically favorable sites which also provide paths for relatively rapid diffusion of solutes[23, 24].Consequently, the aging effect is usually more advanced in these regions and the precipitates are more massive. In Figure 2(c), it can be seen that the particles on the boundaries are much larger than those inside the grains and laths. It is evident in the current study that precipitation of $M_{23}C_6$ occurs preferentially at grain and former lath boundaries. By contrast, precipitates of M_7C_3 are found within the grains and laths. This observation is in agreement with that of Inoue et al.[10], who suggested that M_7C_3 nucleates at the interface between cementite and matrix and grows by an in-situ mechanism. Thus, the nucleation and growth of M_7C_3 and $M_{23}C_6$ should be two separate processes taking place at different sites. The disappearance of M_7C_3 after tempering at 750°C for 1 h implies a competition between M_7C_3 and $M_{23}C_6$ at this stage: the latter grows at the expense of the former, which eventually vanishes from the microstructure.

From TEM observation, it can be concluded that the first peak reveals in the DSC curve is related to the cementite precipitation in the current investigated alloy system. From 400°C to 600°C, it is clear that cementite were replaced by thermodynamically more stable M_7C_3 as well as $M_{23}C_6$. Since the latter two types of carbide precipitate at approximately the same time[25], it is difficult to separate them easily from the DSC curve. However, the DSC peak which appears at about 600°C shows a shoulder shape, which indicates a complex reaction occurring. It is well known that the activation energies of the exothermic reactions appearing in the DSC curve can be calculated using the Kissinger plot method[26], i.e., an analysis of the dependence of the peak position, expressed in terms of the temperature of the peak maximum, T_p, on the applied heating rate, β, which is assumed to be constant. The apparent activation energy, E_A, is given by:

$$\ln\left(\frac{\beta}{T_p^2}\right) = \ln\left(\frac{k_0 R}{E_A}\right) - \left(\frac{E_A}{RT_p}\right)$$

where R is the gas constant and k_0 is the pre-exponential factor in the Arrhenius expression for the rate constant of the reaction. Although the Kissinger equation was developed initially to solve the simplest processes, namely the first-order homogeneous reactions, because its ease to utilize during a thermal analysis, its general capability of application has been largely verified and generalized to apply to solid reactions without concerning the reaction mechanisms, a number of original papers are available in the literature, such as[27-32]. The temperatures of each peak was determined by the second derivative method and Kissinger plots were then made and least-squares fitting was used to obtain apparent activation energy values for the three peaks of 123 ± 13 kJ/mol, 274 ±15 kJ mol^{-1} and 324 ±15 kJ mol^{-1}, respectively.

The activation energy of the first peak at about 270°C is close to the carbon diffusion energy in bcc iron which is well understandable since the peak is related to the cementite precipitation and the rate-controlling factor is the carbon diffusion as we discussed before. The other two exothermal processes at about 600°C are more complex since they overlap with each other and have significant activation energy difference. From Figure 2, it suggests that cementite was replaced by thermodynamically more stable M_7C_3 and $M_{23}C_6$ at 600°C. M_7C_3 was eventually consumed by $M_{23}C_6$ at 750°C in competitive coarsening. Several processes involved here including the precipitation (and growth) of both M_7C_3 and $M_{23}C_6$, coarsening of each carbide, as well as the competitive growth (or coarsening) between M_7C_3 and $M_{23}C_6$. The complex peak shape in the DSC curve at 600°C is a good indication to the complexity. Both M_7C_3 and $M_{23}C_6$ are Cr-rich carbides and Cr-diffusion could probably be the rate-controlling factor for the precipitation of them. Chromium is a fast substitutional diffuser in steels and it has been reported that the activation energy for its diffusion in ferritic steel[7, 33-34] is between 240 and 279 kJ mol^{-1}. The activation energy of the reaction related to the second peak is well within this range and it can thus be assumed that the rate of the associated exothermic reaction is controlled simply by Cr diffusion. Therefore, the current result and analysis suggest that the second peak may be related to the concurrent precipitation of both carbides.

The third reaction requires considerably higher activation energy to proceed, indicating a slower process which nonetheless has some continuity with the former one, since it overlaps the second peak over a wide temperature range. Bhattacharyya and Russell[27] theoretically evaluated compound precipitates of type $A_\alpha B_\beta$ growing in a matrix of a third element M and concluded that coarsening is a much slower process than precipitate growth, the activation energy for coarsening being in general considerably greater than that for diffusion. This evaluation is intuitively reasonable since the particle growth only involves mass transport from the matrix to the growing particles, while coarsening occurs by cannibalization of other particles. It is not enough to diffuse Cr from small particles to large in order to effect coarsening. It is also necessary to diffuse Fe out of the way so that Cr will have a place to re-precipitate. Hence, the current observation from DSC is in agreement with their theoretical evaluation and the third peak in the DSC traces can be related to the carbide coarsening process of M_7C_3 and $M_{23}C_6$.

In summary, a fundamental understanding of the precipitation processes in a high-purity 10Cr steel was obtained by the current study. This may be instructive to the future alloy designing work in order to further improve this type of steels. Moreover, results that yield from high-purity alloy system may also serve as ideal input data for computational modeling to predict steel properties.

CONCLUSIONS

The precipitation sequence in the current investigated alloy was confirmed to be cementite → M_7C_3 + $M_{23}C_6$ → $M_{23}C_6$. The precipitation processes revealed by DSC were interpreted as to be related to the cementite precipitation, concurrent precipitation and coarsening of M_7C_3 and $M_{23}C_6$ respectively. The activation energy of each process was calculated by Kissinger method as to be 123 ± 13 kJ/mol, 274 ±15 kJ mol^{-1} and 324 ±15 kJ mol^{-1}, respectively. *In-situ* TEM observation is being conducted in order to obtain a more precise understanding and further validate interpretation of the DSC results and more results will be disclosed in future.

REFERENCES

1. S. Saroja, A. Dasgupta, R. Divakar, S. Raju, E. Mohandas, M. Vijayalakshmi, K. Bhanu Sankara Rao and B. Raj, J. Nucl. Mater. **409**, 131-139 (2011).
2. R. L. Klueh and D. R. Harries, *High chromium ferritic and martensitic steels for nuclear applications*. (ASTM International, 2001).
3. F. Abe, Mater. Sci. Eng., A **319–321**, 770-773 (2001).
4. K. Maruyama, K. Sawada and J.-i. Koike, ISIJ International **41**, 641-653 (2001).
5. F. Masuyama, ISIJ International **41**, 612-625 (2001).
6. H. C. Furtado, L. H. de Almeida and I. Le May, Mater. Charact. **58**, 72-77 (2007).
7. A. F. Smith, Met. Sci. Tech. **9**, 375-378, 425-429 (1975).
8. H. K. Danielsen and J. Hald, in *Energy Materials: Materials Science and Engineering for Energy Systems* (Maney Publishing, 2006), Vol. 1, pp. 49-57.
9. A. Golpayegani, H.-O. Andrén, H. Danielsen and J. Hald, Mater. Sci. Eng., A **489**, 310-318 (2008).
10. A. Inoue and T. Masumoto, Metall. Trans. A **11**, 739-747 (1980).
11. J. M. Park, W. S. Ryu and Y. H. Kang, J. Nucl. Mater. **209**, 221-225 (1994).
12. K. Das and T. K. Bandyopadhyay, Scr. Mater. **44**, 2597-2603 (2001).
13. L. Cheng, C. M. Brakman, B. M. Korevaar and E. J. Mittemeijer, Metall. Trans. A **19**, 2415-2426 (1988).
14. P. V. Morra, A. J. Böttger and E. J. Mittemeijer, J. Therm. Anal. Calorim. **64**, 905-914 (2001).
15. N. Dudova and R. Kaibyshev, ISIJ International **51**, 826-831 (2011).
16. P. Adler and R. Delasi, Metall. Mater. Trans. A **8**, 1185-1190 (1977).
17. G. W. Smith, Thermochimica Acta **313**, 27-36 (1998).
18. M. P. Jackson, M. J. Starink and R. C. Reed, Mater. Sci. Eng., A **264**, 26-38 (1999).
19. N. J. Petch, Acta Crystallogr. **6**, 96–96 (1953).
20. D. V. Shtansky, K. Nakai and Y. Ohmori, Acta Mater. **48**, 969-983 (2000).
21. M. Hillert and J. Ågren, Scr. Mater. **50**, 697-699 (2004).
22. D. V. Shtansky and G. Inden, Acta Mater. **45**, 2861-2878 (1997).
23. A. Bjärbo and M. Hättestrand, Metall. Mater. Trans. A **32**, 19-27 (2001).
24. H. K. D. H. Bhadeshia, in *Encyclopedia of Materials: Science and Technology (Second Edition)* (Elsevier, Oxford, 2001), pp. 5203-5206.
25. E. C. Bain and H. W. Paxton, *Alloying elements in steel.* (American Society for Metals, 1961).
26. H. E. Kissinger, Journal of Research of the National Bureau of Standards **57**, 217 (1956).
27. S. K. Bhattacharyya and K. C. Russell, Metall. Trans. **3**, 2195-2199 (1972).
28. L. V. Meisel and P. J. Cote, Acta Metall. **31**, 1053-1059 (1983).
29. J. P. Elder, J. Therm. Anal. **30**, 657–669 (1985).
30. P. Budrugeac and E. Segal, J. Therm. Anal. Calorim. **88**, 703-707 (2007).
31. R. Svoboda and J. Málek, J. Therm. Anal. Calorim. **115**, 1-7 (2014).
32. C. Huang, X. Mei, Y. Cheng, Y. Li and X. Zhu, J. Therm. Anal. Calorim. **116**, 1153-1157 (2014).
33. M. Sugihara, Y. Yamazaki, S. Takaki, K. Abiko and Y. Iijima, Mater. Trans. **41**, 87-90 (2000).
34. R. Braun and M. Feller-Kniepmeier, Phys. Status Solidi A **90**, 553–561 (1985).

Mater. Res. Soc. Symp. Proc. Vol. 1754 © 2015 Materials Research Society
DOI: 10.1557/opl.2015.343

Translocation of N-acetyl Cysteine Capped Fluorescent Quantum Dots in Plant Tissue: Confocal Imaging Studies

Smruti Das[1], Jeremy Tharkur[1,2], Laurene Tetard[1,3] and Swadeshmukul Santra[1,2,4,5,*]

[1]NanoScience Technology Center, [2]Burnett School of Biomedical Sciences, [3]Department of Physics, [4]Department of Materials Science and Engineering and [5]Department of Chemistry, University of Central Florida, 12424 Research Parkway, Suite 400, Orlando, FL 32826.

*Corresponding Author

ABSTRACT

Semiconductor fluorescent quantum dots (Qdots) are popularly used as bioimaging taggants in live cell imaging and spectroscopy. In recent years, Qdots taggants are emerging in agricultural applications. Studies are primarily focused on nanotoxicity of ultra-small size water-soluble Qdots in plant systems. Nanotoxicity is correlated with Qdot core composition and surface coating. However, Qdots with certain chemical composition and surface coating may boost plant growth. In this study, we report that N-acetyl cysteine (NAC) capped ~3.5 nm size ZnS:Mn/ZnS Qdots (NAC-Qdot) are efficiently uptaken by the snow pea (*Pisum sativum L.*, a model plant) vascular system, enhancing the root growth at a dose level of 80 μg/mL. Fluorescence microscopy studies confirmed localization of NAC-Qdots in the intercellular regions. Germination and growth of the snow pea seeds were found to be strongly dependent on Qdot dosage and incubation time with Qdots. Seed germination reached 100% within 48 hours of NAC-Qdot exposure. Based on our preliminary findings, it is suggested that NAC-Qdot can be used as systemic plant nutrient material for boosting the seed germination and plant growth.

INTRODUCTION

Zinc is the second most abundant transition metal that plays vital role in many biological processes in natural environment[1, 2]. Most of the plant enzymes involved in carbohydrate metabolism, protein synthesis, pollen formation and regulation of auxin synthesis are activated in the presence of Zn[3]. However, it is difficult to follow the non-destructive analytical in-situ methods to monitor the presence of intercellular Zn^{2+} optically due to absence of its optical properties[4].

ZnS is a most common and remarkable semiconductor that can be doped with a suitable dopant such as Mn to produce doped Qdots with outstanding optical properties[5]. Moreover, ZnS is considered as an attractive material for biological applications as it exhibits low toxicity compared to its surrogate CdS (or CdSe) based Qdots[6-8]. To stabilize Qdot core and its optical properties, a wide band-gap epitaxially-matched shell layer is generally applied around the core, thus producing a core-shell Qdots[9, 10]. The Mn^{2+} dopant serves as the luminescence center, emitting characteristic orange fluorescence at around 590 nm due to its ${}^4T_1 \Rightarrow {}^5A_1$ transition[11].

Qdot surface coating agent impacts not only overall solubility in biological medium but also influence on their uptake potential (i.e. bioavailability). NAC is a thiol containing biomolecule. Thiol group of N-acetylcysteine (NAC) is readily deacetylated in the cells to form L-cysteine enhancing intercellular glutathione production. Glutathione plays crucial role in maintaining homeostasis in any living organism and helps to protect the cells from reactive oxygen species

(ROS), toxic compounds or any DNA damaging agents[12, 13]. NAC is therefore an important biocompatible material to be considered as surface coating agent for Qdots. Moreover, NAC is an antioxidant which makes it more attractive for agricultural applications[14]. However, the biocompatibility of NAC has not yet tested in plant cells. Moreover, the impact of ultra-small size (<5 nm) NAC coated inorganic particles (such as Qdots) on plant growth has not been fully studied.

In this proof-of-concept study, we have shown via fluorescence imaging that ultra-small size (~3.5 nm) NAC coated ZnS:Mn/ZnS Qdots are capable of penetrating through seed coats and translocating into intercellular regions. To the best of our knowledge, this is the first ever study introducing a non-heavy metal containing fluorescently active Qdot based NAC delivery system to monitor impact of such delivery system on plant growth.

EXPERIMENT

Materials

All reagents were purchased from commercial vendors and used without any further purification unless stated specifically. Manganese acetate tetrahydrate, N-acetyl-L-cysteine (NAC) and dioctyl sulfosuccinate sodium salt (Aerosol OT, AOT) were purchased from Acros Organics (New Jersey, US). Zinc acetate dihydrate and sodium sulfide was purchased from Sigma-Aldrich (St. Louis, MO). HPLC grade heptane and ethanol (95%; V/V) were obtained from Fisher Scientific (Pittsburgh, PA) and acetone was obtained from VWR (Radnor, PA). Purified deionized Water (DI) was obtained from Nanopure (Barnstead Nanopure Diamond purifier; model # D11931).

Instrumentation

Quantum dot fluorescence was visualized using a hand-held UV excitation source (Mineralight®, multiband UV 254/365nm lamp, Model UVGL-58). All UV-Visible absorption and fluorescence emission spectra were recorded at room temperature using a Cary 300 UV-VIS Spectrophotometer and a NanoLog Spectrofluorimeter (SPEX, Jobin Yvon Horiba), respectively. HRTEM of Qdot was done using a FEI Technai F30 High-Resolution Transmission Electron Microscopy (HRTEM).

UV-Visible and Fluorescence Spectroscopy

Quartz cuvette (1cm path length) was used for all UV-Vis and fluorescence measurements. For UV-Vis measurements, the instrument was calibrated against DI water in the wavelength range 200 – 800 nm. Sample was appropriately diluted to obtain absorbance value less than 0.1 at 320 nm. Fluorescence emission spectrum was recorded at 320 nm excitation keeping slit width (both excitation and emission) fixed at 5 nm and scan rate at 1nm/0.5sec.

High Resolution Transmission Electron Microscopy (HRTEM)

Carbon coated copper grids with 400 mesh (Electron Microscopy Sciences) were submerged in NAC-Qdot solution (in DI water) for 20-30 min and then placed on a kimwipe in a plastic petri dish to dry overnight. Grids were carried for HRTEM analysis for measuring crystal size and visualizing the crystallinity.

Synthesis of NAC Coated CdS:Mn/ZnS Qdots

ZnS:Mn Qdots were synthesized via a reverse micelle method following a published protocol[15, 16] with some modifications as stated below. Three stock solutions (A, B and C) of salts (zinc acetate dihydrate, manganese acetate and sodium sulfide) were separately prepared. Stock solution "A" contains a mixture of 219 mg (0.1 mol) of zinc acetate and 4 mg of manganese acetate (1.8 mol % with respect to metallic Zn) in 10 mL of DI water. Stock solution (5 mL; DI water) of "B" and "C" contain 257.5 mg of sodium sulfide and 285.3 mg of zinc acetate dehydrate (0.26 mol), respectively. Then three separate AOT/heptane/water water-in-oil (W/O) microemulsion solutions, 1 , 2 and 3 were prepared containing 0.9 mL of stock solution "A", 2.7 mL of stock solution "B" and 2.7 mL of stock solution "C", respectively. Microemulsion 1 contains 2.23 g AOT and 25 mL heptane whereas microemulsions 2 and 3 contain 6.69 g AOT and 75 mL heptane. Microemulsion 1 was added to 2 followed by magnetic stirring for 15 minutes (mins). Thereafter, microemulsion 3 was added to the combined mixture of 1 and 2 dropwise. After 24 hrs of stirring, bright orange-red color emission was seen when the microemulsion solution was exposed to a hand-held UV lamp confirming formation of CdS:Mn/ZnS Qdots. Post-coating with NAC was done while Qdots were present in W/O microemulsion. NAC coating procedure involved the following steps. A W/O microemulsion containing NAC was prepared by combining 175.0 mL of heptane, 15.61 g AOT and 0.55 mg NAC solution (prepared in 6.3 mL of DI water). Next, NAC containing microemulsion was added dropwise to Qdot microemulsion followed by stirring 24 hrs. NAC coated Qdots (NAC-Qdots) were then recovered by first destabilizing the microemulsion using a solvent mixture of acetone and ethanol (95% V/V) followed by centrifugation (11,000 rpm for 10 mins). The NAC-Qdot pellet was then re-dispersed in 10 mL of acetone followed by centrifugation (11,000 rpm, 5 mins), sonication (5 mins) and vortexing (2-3 mins). This washing procedure was repeated using acetone (2x), heptane (2x) and acetone (1x). Finally, the NAC-Qdot palette was dried at 60 ^{0}C for 4 mins to obtain the product in powder form.

Preparation of Seeds and Plant growth condition

Snow Pea (*Pisum sativum L.*) seeds were purchased from Lucas Nursery (Orlando, FL) and stored in a dry opaque packet at room temperature. Prior to use, seeds were soaked in DI water for 30 min to soften the seed coat. Thereafter, surface sterilization was performed by washing the seeds with 70% ethanol and 1% sodium hypochlorite for 1 min respectively. Seeds were then washed five times with DI water to ensure the removal of additional sterilizing solutions possibly sticking to the surface. The sets of Qdot treated and untreated seeds were sown in cups containing potting mixture at a constant day/night temperature (70/65°F) to see the effect of Qdot on seedling growth (roots and shoots length).

Plant Germination Tests

Different concentrations of NAC- Qdots (0, 2, 5, 10, 20, 40, 60, 80, 100 μg/mL) were prepared in DI water to study their effect on seed germination and growth of seedling of snow pea (*Pisum sativum L.*). Seeds were soaked under different concentrations of freshly prepared NAC-Qdot for 24 hrs. Seed germination was tested on moist filter paper (Whatman ^{TM} filter paper size 41; GE Healthcare Life sciences). In each Petri dish (85 mm diameter), 20 seeds were randomly placed on the filter paper, then 5ml of NAC-ZnS Qdot solution was added (i.e. treated seed samples). The controls were maintained by similarly treating seeds with 5 ml of DI water. Seeds were germinated for five days under dark in a controlled environmental condition (25 °C and 50% Relative Humidity, RH). Germination was considered successful when the coleoptiles were longer than 2 mm. Three replicates were carried out for each treatment. Germination rate is the average number of seeds that germinate over the five-day time period.

$$Germination(\%) = \frac{Number\ of\ seeds\ germinated}{Total\ number\ of\ seeds\ in\ petri\ dish} \times 100\%$$

Sample Preparation for Microscopy

For the microscopic studies, cross sections (<0.5 mm thick slice) of cotyledons (treated and untreated) were prepared manually using a single edge blade (~ 230 μm thickness; American Safety Razor Company; Catalogue # 66-0392; Verona, VA) and mounted on microscope slides (Fisherbrand®; Size 12x75x1 mm; Catalogue # 12-550-003). Samples were observed under phase contrast (Olympus 1X71, Japan) and processed using ImageJ software (National Institutes of Health).

Statistical analysis

Each treatment was conducted with three replicates, and the results were presented as mean±SD (standard deviation). The statistical analysis of experimental data was done through two way annova. Experimental values were found to be significant at $P < 0.05$.

RESULTS AND DISCUSSION

Characterization and microscopic study of NAC-Qdot

Fig. 1a depicts uv-visible spectra of NAC-Qdot compound with an absorption peak of 320 nm. Again the intensity has increased with increasing concentration of NAC-Qdot from 2μg/mL-100μg/mL. The fluorescence intensity of the NAC-Qdot was observed at 590 nm, the peak emission wavelength (Fig. 1b). The fluorescence of the Qdots is attributed to the Mn dopant. Researchers have reported in previous work that ZnO Qdot fluorescence can be used as cancer cell biomarker[17]. Absorbance and fluorescence spectra were used to select appropriate filters for phase contrast imaging to detect the uptake and localization of NAC-Qdot in plant cells. FTIR spectra of NAC, NAC-ZnS (1M NAC:1M ZnS), Qdot and NAC-Qdot is shown in Fig. 1c. The characteristic NAC S-H peak at 2552 cm^{-1} was not observed in NAC-Qdot, indicating NAC capped to the Qdot surface through the formation of Zn-S bonds. Thiol ligand makes NAC an ideal stabilizer for Qdots. After surface coating, NAC improves solubility of Qdots. This is due to the presence of hydrophilic carboxyl (–COOH) and acetamide (–$NHCOCH_3$) groups in NAC structure[18]. Therefore, NAC-Qdot exhibits excellent water solubility. Previous work suggests that ZnS:Mn Qdots with surface modification improves water solubility and luminescence[19]. HRTEM images of NAC-Qdots are shown in Fig. 2a. Despite a few clusters, Qdots (dark contrast) were fairly monodispersed as seen in the high-magnification image. High magnification HRTEM

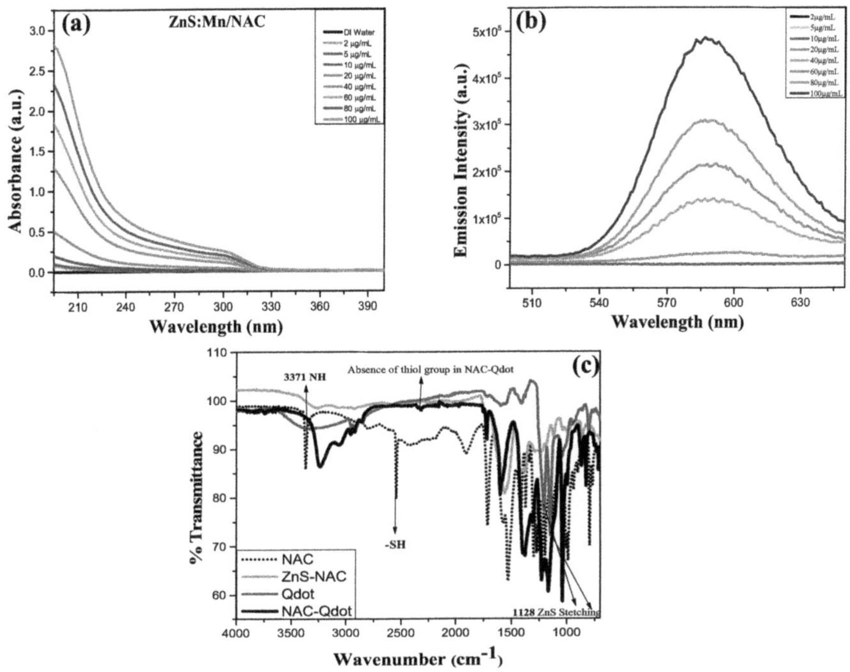

Fig. 1. Characterization of NAC-Qdot. (a) UV-Vis and (b) steady-state fluorescence emission spectra of NAC, bare Qdot and NAC-Qdot and (c) FT-IR spectra of NAC, bare Qdot and NAC-Qdot.

imaging revealed crystal lattice plane 110 for ZnS. HRTEM therefore confirmed that the Qdot surface coating with NAC did not compromise the particles crystallinity (Figure 1a(iv)).

To localize NAC-Qdot in the treated seeds, phase contrast microscopy techniques was performed. A cross section of the treated seed (about 5 mm diameter) was mounted on a microscope slides for imaging. Fig. 2b shows phase contrast images in transmission (phase) and fluorescence mode. Presence of NAC-Qdots in the seeds is represented in overlay of phase and fluorescence images as false blue-color transmission background and red color fluorescence of the NAC-Qdots. Interestingly, Qdots were mostly populated in the intercellular regions and the cell walls (false red colored areas). This microscopic study indicates the translocalization of ultra small size NAC-Qdots, with sizes around 3.5 nm, within intercellular regions of the tissue.

These finding draws an attention to study further the uptake, presence and fate of that NAC-Qdot into other plant parts including stems and leaves during various growth stages.

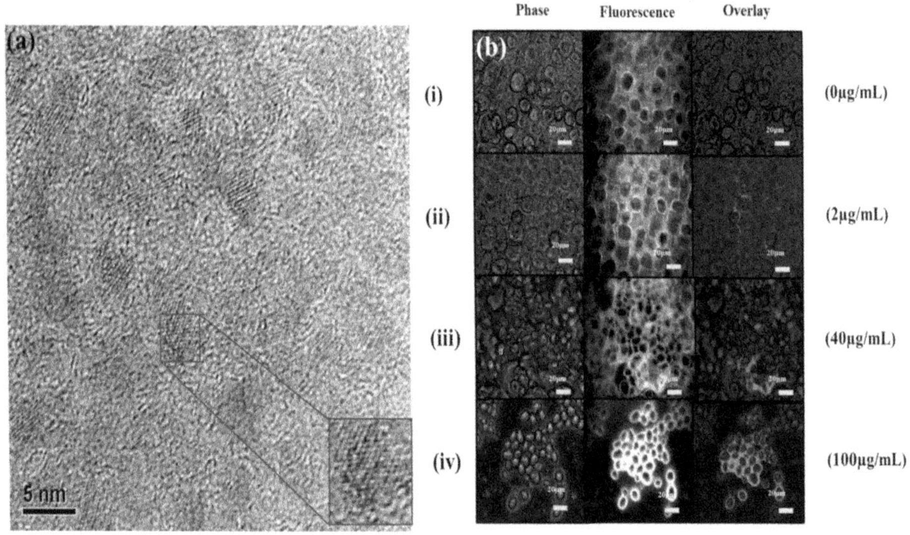

Fig. 2. Characterization of NAC-Qdot. (a) HRTEM of NAC-Qdots; high magnification image (inset) showing scattered dark contrast confirming the presence of electron-rich material of NAC coated ZnS:Mn/ZnS Qdots and (b) Image showing phase contrast, fluorescence and phase-fluorescence overlay depicting absence of quantum dot in untreated seeds (0 µg/mL) and presence of NAC-Qdot at the intercellular regions of cells (2-100 µg/mL) of snow pea (*Pisum sativum*)

NAC-Qdot mediated growth

Fig. 3 shows schematic representation of the plant growth under normal and NAC-Qdot treated conditions. As shown on the right is the digital image of bright colored fluorescent NAC-Qdot was taken using hand hand UV light lamp (366nm multiband UV excitation source). The red colored dots along the vascular system of the snow pea (*Pisum sativum*) plant represents probable path of transport and localization of the NAC-Qdot. It can be inferred from this study that ultra small size NAC coated Qdots can indeed boost the plant growth if used under suitable concentration.

Effect of NAC-Qdot on root growth

The impact of different concentration of NAC-Qdot (0, 2, 5, 10, 20, 40, 60, 80 and 100 µg/mL) was monitored for the radicle and root growth in snow pea (*Pisum sativum*) seeds. The observation was taken on 3rd, 6th, 9th, 12th and 15th day. We observed a steady increase in growth at dosage of 80μg/mL which then reduced and remained constant with further increase in

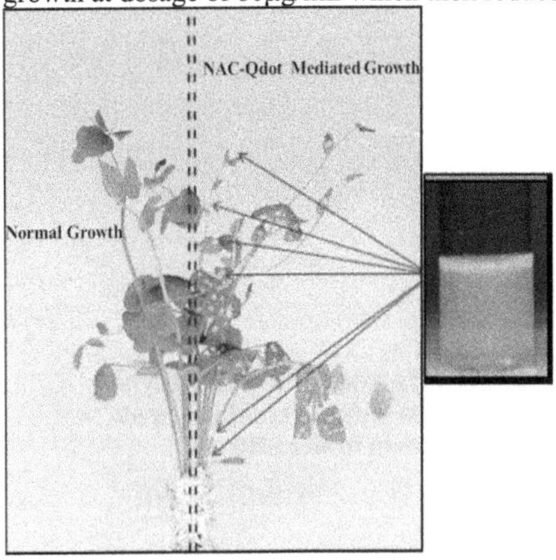

Fig. 3. Schematic showing (a) normal growth and (b) NAC-Qdot boosted growth of snow pea (*Pisum sativum*). Inset (Figure3b) is a digital image of glass vial containing NAC-Qdot solution in DI water showing characteristic bright emission when exposed to a hand-held 366 nm multiband UV excitation source.

dosage upto 100μg/mL (Fig. 4). Highest root length observed ranged in between 17.6cm to 31.33cm from 3rd day to 15th day of treatment the variety, concentration and interactions of variety-concentration were found to be significant at 0.1% confidence level. All treated seeds attained 100 percent germination on 2nd day of treatment as compared to untreated seeds. Interestingly, hypocotyl appeared only in NAC-Qdot treated seeds. Previous work stated growth in roots of higher plant species due to effect of rare earth oxide nanoparticles, nano-CeO2, nano-La2O3, nano-Gd2O3 and nano-Yb_2O_3[20].

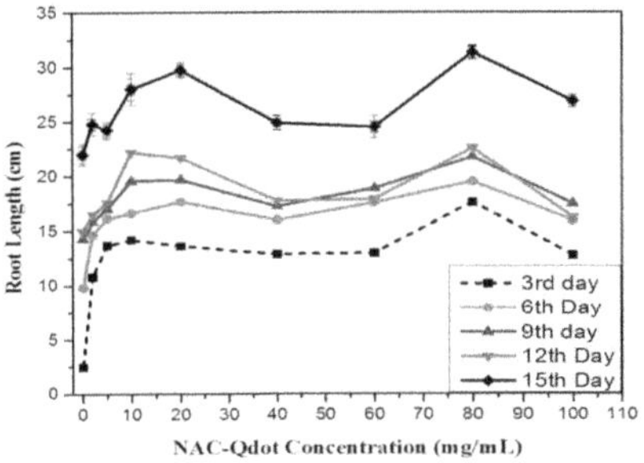

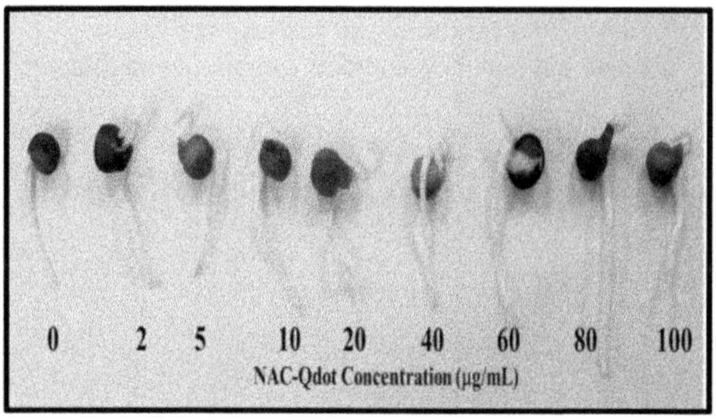

Fig. 4. Effect of different concentration of NAC-Qdot on (a) growth of root length on different days of snow pea (*Pisum sativum*) at different levels of NAC-Qdot based on Duncan test P≤0.05 and (b) digital image displaying the growth under different concentrations of treatment.

CONCLUSION

For the first time, we have demonstrated uptake and translocalization of fluorescently active NAC coated semiconductor ZnS:Mn/ZnS Qdots by plant cells using snow pea (*Pisum sativum*) model system. The efficiency of Qdot uptake through seed coat is dose dependent. Translocalization of particles in inter-cellular regions was confirmed by fluorescence imaging which exploited outstanding optical properties of Qdots. NAC-Qdot did not exhibit any phytotoxicity to plant cells. This is possibly due to incorporation of a biocompatible NAC (an antioxidant, free-radical scavenger) and Zn ion (a plant micronutrient). This paper also suggests that ultra-small size biocompatible particulate system could be developed to deliver cargoes such as NAC into plant vasculature system.

ACKNOWLEDGEMENT

Authors acknowledge in kind support from Dr. Andre Gesquiere (UCF NanoScience Technology Center, Department of Chemistry and CREOL College of Optics and Photonics) for phase contrast microscopy. Authors acknowledge in kind support from Dr. Helge Heinrich (UCF Department of Physics) with HRTEM. Authors also acknowledge UCF-Advanced Materials Processing and Analysis Center (AMPAC)-Materials Characterization Facility (MCF) for the electron microscopy facility. Authors acknowledge partial financial support from the Citrus Research and Development Foundation Inc. grant # 907.

REFERENCES:

1. J. M. Berg and Y. G. Shi, Science **271** (5252), 1081-1085 (1996).
2. S. Frassinetti, G. Bronzetti, L. Caltavuturo, M. Cini and C. Della Croce, Journal of Environmental Pathology Toxicology and Oncology **25** (3), 597-610 (2006).
3. D. T. Clarkson and J. B. Hanson, Annual Review of Plant Physiology and Plant Molecular Biology **31**, 239-298 (1980).
4. H. B. Ren, B. Y. Wu, J. T. Chen and X. P. Yan, Analytical Chemistry **83** (21), 8239-8244 (2011).
5. J. D. Bryan and D. R. Gamelin, in *Progress in Inorganic Chemistry, Vol 54*, edited by K. D. Karlin (2005), Vol. 54, pp. 47-126.
6. N. Chen, Y. He, Y. Y. Su, X. M. Li, Q. Huang, H. F. Wang, X. Z. Zhang, R. Z. Tai and C. H. Fan, Biomaterials **33** (5), 1238-1244 (2012).
7. M. Cirillo, T. Aubert, R. Gomes, R. Van Deun, P. Emplit, A. Biermann, H. Lange, C. Thomsen, E. Brainis and Z. Hens, Chemistry of Materials **26** (2), 1154-1160 (2014).
8. H. Li, M. Y. Li, W. Y. Shih, P. I. Lelkes and W. H. Shih, Journal of Nanoscience and Nanotechnology **11** (4), 3543-3551 (2011).
9. D. Bera, L. Qian, T. K. Tseng and P. H. Holloway, Materials **3** (4), 2260-2345 (2010).
10. S. Verma, S. Kaniyankandy and H. N. Ghosh, Journal of Physical Chemistry C **117** (21), 10901-10908 (2013).
11. J. Beltran-Huarac, M. J. F. Guinel, B. R. Weiner and G. Morell, Materials Letters **98**, 108-111 (2013).
12. M. L. Circu and T. Y. Aw, Free Radical Research **42** (8), 689-706 (2008).
13. C. E. Presnell, G. Bhatti, L. S. Numan, M. Lerche, S. K. Alkhateeb, M. Ghalib, M. Shammaa and M. Kavdia, Current Neurovascular Research **10** (2), 185-194 (2013).
14. S. D. Flora, A. Izzotti, F. D. Agostini and R. M.Balansky, Carcinogesis **22** (7), 999-1013 (2001).
15. S. Santra, H. Yang, J. T. Stanley, P. H. Holloway, B. M. Moudgil, G. Walter and R. A. Mericle, Chemical Communications (25), 3144-3146 (2005).
16. S. Santra, H. S. Yang, P. H. Holloway, J. T. Stanley and R. A. Mericle, Journal of the American Chemical Society **127** (6), 1656-1657 (2005).
17. F. Liu, Y. Zhang, C. C. Chu, J. J. Lu, J. H. Yu and X. R. Song, Monatshefte Fur Chemie **145** (1), 121-127 (2014).
18. D. Zhao, Z. K. He, W. H. Chan and M. M. F. Choi, J. Phys. Chem. C **113** (4), 1293-1300 (2009).
19. B. H. Zhang, L. Qi and F. Y. Wu, Microchimica Acta **170** (1-2), 147-153 (2010).
20. Y. H. Ma, L. L. Kuang, X. He, W. Bai, Y. Y. Ding, Z. Y. Zhang, Y. L. Zhao and Z. F. Chai, Chemosphere **78** (3), 273-279 (2010).

Mater. Res. Soc. Symp. Proc. Vol. 1754 © 2015 Materials Research Society
DOI: 10.1557/opl.2015.470

Polyelectrolyte brushes: Water Content, Zeta Potential and Mechanical Properties

Joseba Irigoyen[1], Jagoba Iturri[1], José Luis Camacho[2], Edwin Donath[2], Sergio Moya[1]
1CIC biomaGune, Paseo Miramón 182 C, 20009, San Sebastián, Spain. Tel: +34 943 00 53 11 ; E-mail: smoya@cicbiomagune.es
2 Institute of Medical Physics and Biophysics, Leipzig University, Härtelstrasse 16-18, D-04107, Leipzig, Germany

ABSTRACT

Polymer brushes of poly[2-(methacryloyloxy)ethyl]trimethylammonium chloride (PMETAC) and poly(sulfo propyl methacrylate) (PSPM) were synthesized by Atomic Transfer Radical Polymerization from planar and colloidal surfaces. Polymer brush growth was followed by QCMD and the water content determined by combined QCMD and elipsometry. From the water content the percentage of water lost during the brush collapse with the ionic strength could be obtained.

Highly charged PSPM brushes were indented by Atomic Force Microscopy at different ionic strengths. The force response was fitted to a phenomenological equation analogous to the equation of state of a compressible fluid. Internal energy and brush compressibility were obtained as a function of ionic strength.

Spherical brushes of PMETAC and PSPM display an invariance of the zeta potential with ionic strength in the range from 20 mM to 200 mM NaCl, the zeta potential remains almost constant. This invariance can be explained applying a hairy surface approach.

INTRODUCTION

Polyelectrolyte brushes are monolayers of polyelectrolyte chains tethered by one end of the chain to a surface while the other end remains free[1,2]. Brushes are very appealing for the functionalization of surfaces and colloids, and have possible applications in surface lubrication, as barriers, nanoactuators or as model systems for the glycocalix[3].

Polyelectrolyte brushes also offer an interesting physical chemistry resulting from the spatial arrangement of the polymer chains, the charge of the monomeric units and the cooperative and supramolecular character of the brush. This interdependency means that changes in the individual chains of the brush induce a response of the brush as a whole. This is the case for the response of the brush to the ionic strength. Increasing the ionic strength causes the chain of the brush to acquire more coiled conformation and the brush reduces thickness, the so called collapse. These conformation changes with the ionic strength are a consequence of the screening of the brush charges as the ionic strength increases[4,5].

In this proceeding we want to present some results from our laboratories related to the physics associated to the cooperative response of the brush. Polyelectrolyte brushes are composed of the polyelectrolyte chains and water, which is associated to the charged monomers and entrapped between chains. Water is lost in a reversible manner during brush collapse. The water content is fundamental in defining chain friction and brush mechanics. We will show that it is possible to determine the water content of a polyelectrolyte brush using a combination of Quartz Microbalance with Dissipation (QCMD) and Ellipsometry in a single device. Brushes will be synthesized in situ in the QCMD chamber and the whole synthesis will be followed with the QCMD and the ellipsometer. Wet mass of the brush will be obtained from the QCMD measurements while the dry mass or polymer mass will be obtained from the ellipsometry data[6,7].

The response of a polyelectrolyte brush under compression with Atomic Force Microscopy (AFM) will be studied at different ionic strength. We will show that the force vs distance curves can be fitted applying a model analogous to that of a compressive fluid where force and distance display an equivalent relation as pressure and volume in a gas. From these fitting thermodynamics variables of the brush will be obtained[8,9].
Finally, we will present the response of thin spherical brushes in presence of an external field. We will show that the brush displays an almost constant zeta potential independently of the ionic strength of the media, differing from the classical Schmoluchowski behavior. This particular response of the spherical brushes can be explained by the field penetration in the brush applying the theory of hairy soft interfaces[10].

Results

Water content of polyelectrolyte brushes

The combination of QCMD and ellipsometry in a single device was applied to study the growth of polyelectrolyte brushes of poly [2-(methacryloyloxy) ethyl] trimethylammonium chloride (PMETAC) and poly (potassium sulfopropyl methacrylate) (PSPM). Both brushes brushes were synthesized by means of Atom Transfer Radical Polymerization (ATRP) from monolayers of thiol initiators grafted to gold surfaces. From the QCMD data we can follow the frequency variations due to the synthesis of the polymer brush which can be converted in mass by application of the Sauerbrey equation. For the hydrated polyelectrolyte brushes in aqueous media, the spectroscopic ellipsometry will provide a value for the solvent-free mass of the polymer. By comparison of the masses obtained by QCM-D and ellipsometry the water content in the film can be obtained. The mass measured by ellipsometry, called optical mass (mopt) corresponds to the polymer free of solvent. The mass obtained from the QCMD or acoustic mass (mQCM) corresponds to the mass of polymer and water included in the brush. Brush hydration can be calculated as follows:

$$\mathrm{Hydration}(\%) = \frac{(m\mathrm{QCM} - m\mathrm{opt})\mathrm{x}100}{m\mathrm{QCM}} \qquad (1)$$

In the Figure 1 we can observe the in situ growth of a PMETAC brush monitored by the QCM-D/ellipsometry combined set up. The brush was synthesized from a monolayer of previously assembled thiol iniciator, ω-mercaptoundecyl bromo isobutyrate.
The variations in the acoustic parameters, frequency and dissipation, as recorded by the QCM-D device are shown in Figure 1a. Frecuency follows a continuous decrease along the polymerization as the mass grows on top of the sensor. The brushes display a low ratio of dissipation to frequency, allowing the application of the Sauerbrey equation to calculate *m*QCM . By applying Equation 1 we calculated the water content or hydration of the brushes. For PMETAC brushes, the water content was the highest observed, around 67%. For PSPM water was observed to represent approximately 45% of their total mass[6].
From the water content of the brush it becomes possible to measure the percentange of water loss during brush collapse. Water loss during collapse can be measured by QCMD. At 100 mM and 1 M NaCl, the water mass in the PMETAC brush decreased by 0.54 and 0.81 mg/cm, equivalent to the loss of a 26% of the mass at 1 M NaCl. For the PSPM brush, there is a negligible mass loss at 0.1 M NaCl but at 1 M NaCl it releases over 1.7 μg/cm^2 of water, 32% of its content[6,7].

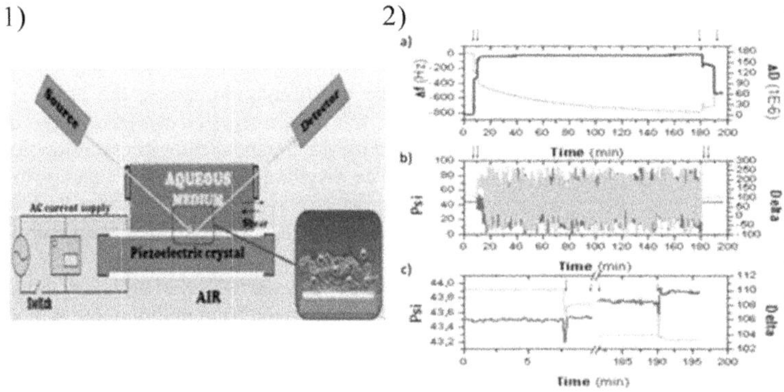

Figure 1 1) Scheme of the combined QCMD and ellipsometry set up. 2)Synthesis of the PMETAC brush from a monolayer of 100% thiol initiator assembled on top of a gold surface followed in situ by the combined QCM-D/ellipsometry device. (a) QCM-D response, i.e., Δf and ΔD vs. time for a selected overtone ($i = 3$). (b) Ellipsometric response, i.e., Ψ and Δ vs. time for a selected wavelength ($\lambda = 632.5$ nm). (c) Magnification of the ellipsometric response before and after the polymerization. The starting time of each solution injected is indicated by solid arrows.

Brush indentation and Equation of State

Dense PSPM brushes were indented with an AFM tip as well as with an 8 μm silica colloidal probe at different ionic strengths ranging from Millipore water to 1M NaCl. The force response during indentation was fitted to a phenomenological equation analogous to the equation of state of a compressible fluid. In this way, internal energy and brush thickness were obtained as a function of ionic strength. The brush indentation was analyzed from a thermodynamical perspective. The brush indentation curves showed an outward semblance to the behavior of a compressible liquid, when instead of pressure and volume, force and brush height are used as the state variables. This led to the idea to fit the indentation curves with a phenomenological equation similar in structure to the equation of state (EOS) of a compressible liquid.

In the equation of state of a compressible fluid, equation 2, p, V, and T are pressure, volume and absolute temperature, respectively. a can be interpreted as the cohesive pressure, which in a first

$$(p + a) \cdot (V - V_0) = c \cdot T \tag{2}$$

approximation does not depend on volume. V_0 represents the finite volume achieved at infinitely high pressure, and c is a constant proportional to the number of molecules. For the one-dimensional situation of a brush probed with an AFM we may use the force, F, instead of pressure and, correspondingly, the brush thickness, h, instead of the volume.
h_o represents the minimal brush thickness reached at infinite compression. The parameter $\boldsymbol{a}$, in

$$(F + a) \cdot (h - h_0) = c' \cdot T \tag{3}$$

analogy to the EOS of compressible liquid, would be equivalent to a force reducing the opposing force of brush exerted on the indentor. It has to be emphasized that Eq. 3 is not an EOS of the brush, because the force F is not a state variable as it depends on the size and shape of the indentor. Eq. 3 is only meaningful in the range of indentation, where the brush is really compressed by the indentor. The obtained fits of the experimentally measured force distance curves were used as regularization tools for obtaining the brush swelling pressure or 'force per unit area' as a function of brush compression. The swelling pressure as a function of brush thickness, h, followed over a wide range a power law close to $\sim h^{-2}$. This approach allowed deriving fundamental brush parameters on a thermodynamical basis like the compressibility as a function of thickness[9].

The thickness of a PSPM brush was determined by Atomic Force Microscopy imaging as function of the loading force at different ionic strengths, ranging from milliQ water to 1 M NaCl. Imaging was also performed both with a sharp tip and a colloidal probe. We observed brush thickness strongly depends both on the applied load and on ionic strength. A brush thickness of 150 nm is measured in Millipore water when applying the minimal loading force. Imaging with an 8 μm silica particle as a colloidal probe, results in a thickness 30 nm larger than the measured with the tip. Increasing the ionic strength causes the well known reduction of the thickness of the brush. The maximal thickness reduction is 65 nm at 1 M NaCl [8].

Figure 2 displays the response of the brush to the loading force during the AFM scan. To generate a reference a stripe of brush was removed and the brush thickness was determined as the vertical distance between the reference stripe and the brush surface. The figure 2 shows for the case of the AFM tip the best fits (solid lines lines) together with the experimentally measured thickness on approach for different ionic strengths. .

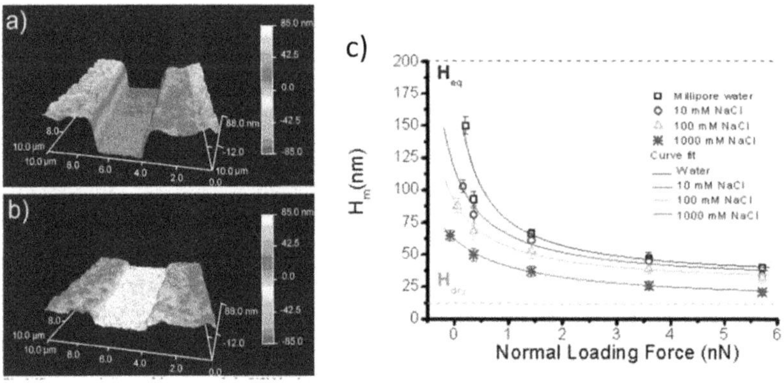

Figure 2. a) 3D contact mode images of the response of PSPM brush to imaging loading forces with the AFM Tip in millipore water with minimal loading force b) with a loading force 5.7 nN. Same z scale for both images. c) Brush thickness versus force curves measured with the AFM tip at different salt concentrations. The salt concentrations employed were 1000, 100 and 10mM NaCl and Millipore water. The solid black lines represent the least square fits of the experimental data to Eq. 2.

Zeta potential of spherical brushes

The ζ-potential of spherical brushes of PMETAC and PSPM synthesized from silica particles was measured as a function of ionic strength. The ζ-potential for bare SiO_2 particles follows an expected trend. The potential is negative and decreases in absolute value continuously from approximately -70 mV at 10 mM NaCl to about -25 mV as the concentration increases to 200 mM NaCl. We observe that at 50 mM the absolute value of the ζ-potential has decreased already to less than -40 mV. In the case of the SiO_2 particles coated with a PMETAC brush the ζ-potential has reversed to positive values as result of the presence of the PMETAC, bearing quaternary amine monomers with a positive charge. For PMETAC brushes the potential at 10 mM NaCl is about +30 mV, in absolute value significantly smaller than that for the bare silica. More surprisingly, the potential decreases very slowly with increasing ionic strength. At 50 mM NaCl it has only decreased to 25 mV, 5 mV less than the initial values. Increasing the ionic strength up to 200 mM NaCl only reduces the potential to + 20 mV. On total a reduction of the potential of 10 mV could be observed while for the bare SiO_2 particles the potential varies in 40 mV for the same range of NaCl concentrations.A similar situation is observed for the PSPM spherical brushes. The potential remains negative as the PSPM brushes bear negatively charged sulfonate groups but it has a value of only -30 mV at 10 mM NaCl. The absolute value of the potential decreases with the ionic strength even more slowly than for the PMETAC remaining at values between -30 mV and -25 mV for the whole range of the employed NaCl concentrations.

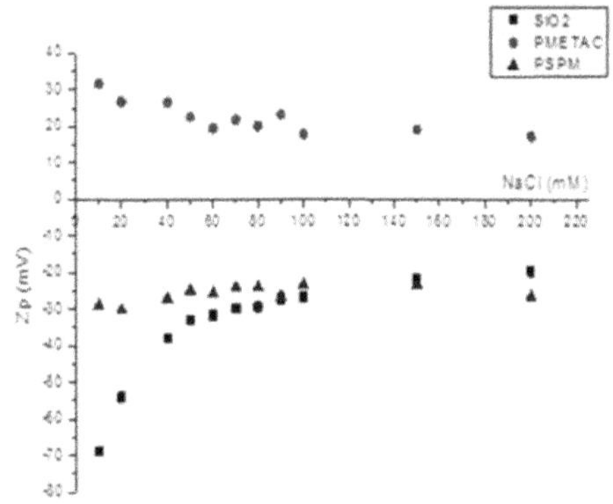

Figure3. ζ-potential of bare SiO_2 particles (squares), spherical brushes of PSPM (triangles) and spherical brushes of PMETAC (circles) measured as a function of the ionic strength.

This unusual weak dependence of the ζ-potential on ionic strength can be quantitatively explained on the basis of the responsiveness of brushes toward changes in the ionic strength as well as taking into account the specific hydrodynamics of the hairy brush solution interface. The electric potential distribution could be described in the framework of the the Debye-Hückel approximation[10].

CONCLUSIONS

Water content and percentage of water release of polyelectrolyte brushes during collapse could be measured by combining QCMD and ellipsometry. Brushes are highly hydrated and at 1 M NaCl a maximal loss of a 30 % of the mass could be measured for dense brushes.

Indentation curves of PSPM brushes measured by AFM could be fitted using an equation analogous to the state equation of a compressible fluid using Force and Thickness at the place of

Pressure and Volume. Thermodynamic parameters and thickness of the brush could be obtained from the fittings.
Thin spherical brushes showed an usual constant of the ζ-potential in a large range of salt concentrations. This can be explained by a combination of brush thickness response to ionic strength, and by flow penetration into the brush.

Acknowledgments
This work was financially supported by the Marie Curie project"Transport Studies on Polymer Based Nanodevices andAssemblies for Delivery and Sensing" (TRASNADE; Grant 247656).

REFERENCES

1. M. Ballauff and O. Borisov , Curr. Opin. Colloid Interface Sci. ,11 , 316 (2006).
2. S. G. Boyes , A. M. Granville , M. Baum , B. Akgun ,B. K. Mirous , W. J. Brittain Surf. Sci. , *570* , 1 (2004) .
3. O. Azzaroni Journal of Polymer Science, Part A: Polymer Chemistry 50, 16, 3225 (2012).
4. T Chen , R. Ferris , J. Zhang , R. Ducker , S. Zauscher , Prog. Polym.Sci. 35 , 94 (2010) .
5. S. E. Moya , O. Azzaroni , T. Farhan , V. L. Osborne , W. T. S. Huck , *Angew. Chem. Int. Ed. 44* , 4578 (2005) .
6.J.J.Iturri Ramos, S.E. Moya Macromolecular Rapid Communications 32, 1972 (2011).
7. J.J.Iturri Ramos, S.E. Moya Macromolecular Chemistry and Physics 213, 549 (2012).
8. J.L.Cuellar, I..Llarena, S. .E.Moya, E..Donath 9. J. Luis Cuellar, I..Llarena, J.J.Iturri, S. E. Moya, E. Donath Nanoscale 5, 11679 (2013).
9. J.L.Cuellar, I..Llarena, S. .E.Moya, E..Donath Macromolecules 46,6, 2323 (2013).
10. J. Irigoyen, Valeri Arekalyan, Z. Navoyan, J. Iturri, E. Donath, S.E. Moya Soft Matter 9, 11609 2013).

Advances in Scanning Probe Microscopy for Multimodal Imaging at the Nanoscale

Mater. Res. Soc. Symp. Proc. Vol. 1754 © 2015 Materials Research Society
DOI: 10.1557/opl.2015.217

Investigation of Polymer Dendritic Growth in Composite Material using Contact Resonance Method

Ravi Gaikwad[1], Xunchen Liu[1], Priyesh Dhandharia[1], Thomas Thundat[1]

[1] *Department of Chemical and Materials Engg, University of Alberta, Edmonton*

ABSTRACT

A special class of polymer called dendrons which are repeatedly branched polymers linked together by a network of cascade branched monomers. A composite of these dendritic polymers with linear polymers may have unique physical and chemical properties. Using contact resonance mode of atomic force microscopy we are able to detect the viscoelastic properties of the dendritic formation of the polyethylene oxide (PEO) mixed with Polyvinylpyrrolidone (PVP). PEO is known to form nanometric crystallites due to the diffusion limited aggregation process. However, the dendritic formation in the mixture has not been reported before. The amplitude and phase of the contact resonance shows a clear dendritic growth of PEO in the composite material. The extent of the polymer crystallization can be several nanometers thick within the composite material. Additionally, the intrinsic properties of such polymers to form denrimers can be explored for fabricating polymer composites having numerous potential applications in chemical sensing, drug-delivery, energy applications and many more.

INTRODUCTION

One of the key challenges in producing macromolecules composites of high durability is to investigate whether the individual polymers have blended together. It will be of great importance to locate with high spatial resolution and exact morphology of the individual polymers that constitute the composite polymer material. Atomic force microscopy[1] has been one such advanced tool that have shown promising detection of the mechanical properties of the polymers with high resolution. Most importantly, mechanical properties detected using static modes like Force spectroscopy have been proposed. The major limitation with these techniques is that the substrate under investigation should be complaint with the cantilever specifications. However, dynamic modes where the cantilever is oscillated at its resonance frequency can provide quantitative measurements of mechanical properties of complex systems like polymer composites. A number of such techniques like phase imaging[2,3], ultrasonic atomic force microscopy[4], heterodyne force microscopy[5], atomic force acoustic microscopy (AFAM)[6] are used to determine quantitatively the mechanical properties of materials. The contact resonance mode basically originated from the acoustic microscopy and has been used successfully to study a wide range of materials like polymer nanotubes[7], polymer blends[8], biomolecules like DNA[9] and metal surfaces[10].
Here, we investigate the blend of polyethylene oxide (PEO) (M.W=1,00,000) mixed with polyvinylpyrrolidone (PVP)(M.W=1,30,000) in water using contact resonance microscopy. PEO is known to form dendritic structures and lot of research has been done in understanding its crystallization growth and its dynamics[11,12]. Our mail goal is to understand (1) how the two polymers are phase separated in the polymer blend and (2) Using the contact resonance

technique, can we determine qualitative viscoelastic properties of the individual polymer phases. In contact resonance, when the AFM tip comes in contact with a surface, the resonance frequency is shifted to higher values relative to its frequency in free space. This change is caused due to mechanical properties like the stiffness of the surface and can be used to determine the Young's modulus of the material using appropriate elasticity models. Once properties like viscoeleasticity, fracture, stress and strain relaxation of polymeric blends are determined, it will help in the proper design of materials having numerous potential applications in chemical sensing, drug-delivery and energy applications.

EXPERIMENTAL DETAILS

The polymer sample used was 10:10 by weight percent blend of polyethylene oxide (PEO) and Polyvinylpyrrolidone (PVP) dissolved in deionized water. The blend was spin coated on a for Zinc selenide circular disc (4cm diameter) prewashed with ethanol to remove any contaminants. For the AFM imaging, the sample was mounted on a stage and held in place with vacuum. The data was collected using the contact resonance mode available with Bruker icon system (Santa Barbara, CA). The measurements were performed using standard triangular contact mode tip (SNL-A, Bruker probes), resonance frequency (f_0=60 kHzhz) and spring constant of 0.58 N/m. The tip was modified by coating gold thin film ~100 nm to increase its conductivity for simultaneous kelvin force spectroscopy imaging. The high speed contact resonance (HS-CR) phase, amplitude, and data were collected simultaneously with the topography image in the contact mode. The contact force was held constant around 15 nN to minimize the sample deformation and achieving high quality contact resonance imaging. We also used the peak-force kelvin force microscopy (PF-KPFM) to collect the topography, deformation, adhesion and surface potential (KPFM) of the polymer blend. The contact resonance data was collected at a tip scan rate of 1Hz, while the KPFM data at 0.5Hz. The data was collected with optimized gain parameters for achieving good HS-CR images.

RESULTS AND DISCUSSION

Figure 1 shows a collage of the topography (A), deformation (B), adhesion (C) and the surface potential, KPFM (D) of the PVP and PEO polymer blend. The graphs on the right are the corresponding cross sections. The blend shows a continuous PVP phase with discrete dendritic structures of PEO about 5-10 nm in height. PEO dendritic structures have been reported earlier[12–14] which makes the domains easy to identify in this blend of polymer. The cross section of the topography is shown in figure 1E where the PEO domain heights are clearly seen. However, in addition to these higher domain heights of PEO, we also have about a nanometer thick layer of PEO layer which is revealed in the deformation, adhesion and the KPFM images. The crystallization of flexible polymers like PEO results in highly branched lamellar crystals[15,16] which is explained by the diffusion limited aggregation (DLA) process[17]. PEO due to its crystalline structure is deformed less as seen Figure 1B as compared to continuous PVP matrix in the background. The deformation image shows with a high resolution the boundaries of the dendritic structures and the monolayer of the PEO phase below and around it. The adhesion force (Figure 1C) between the tip and the polymer blend shows a significant contrast between the two polymers. Since adhesion is directly proportional to the surface tension, a viscoelastic property it is obvious to observe such a clear distinct contrast between the two polymers.

Adhesion force between the AFM tip and the two phases of PEO does not show a significant change and hence it is around 30nN while PVP has about 40nN as seen from the cross section profile (Figure 1G). The quantitative determination of the viscoelastic property is however difficult from these adhesion maps. The KPFM image (Figure 1D) shows the distribution of surface charge on the polymer blend. It is interesting to note that the surface potential for the two phases of PEO has varying charge distribution where the dendritic structure of PEO have a potential of about 150-200 mV (Low potential PEO) while the matrix of PEO on where it resides have a potential of about 600 mV (High potential PEO). PVP on the other hand has a potential of around 300 mV. The difference in the potential of PEO phases may arise due to the orientation of the PEO molecules during crystallization which is explained by the DLA mechanism.

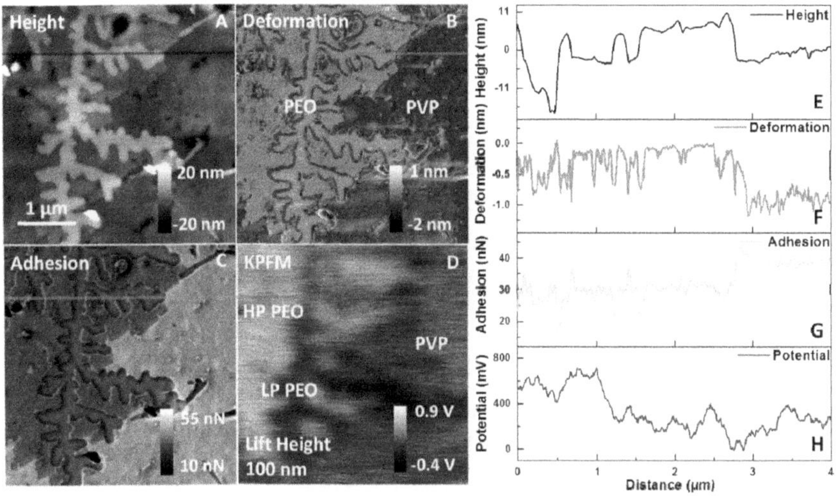

Figure 1: AFM collage of topography (A), deformation (B), adhesion (C) and KPFM (D) while the corresponding cross section profiles are plotted as E, F, G and H respectively.

Figure 2 shows the histogram of the quality factor of the tip when measured on the three distinct regions (two phases of PEO and one phase of PVP) of the polymer blend. The quality factor is lower for PVP as compared to the two phases of PEO. Figure 2B shows the first flexural contact resonance for lower potential PEO, higher potential PEO and PVP. Depending on the stiffness of the polymer, the contact resonance changes from 193.22 kHz for high potential PEO to 204.88 kHz for PVP. The change in the contact resonance phase of the different phases of polymer is plotted in figure 2C. Please note a similar trend in the phase as observed in figure 2B.

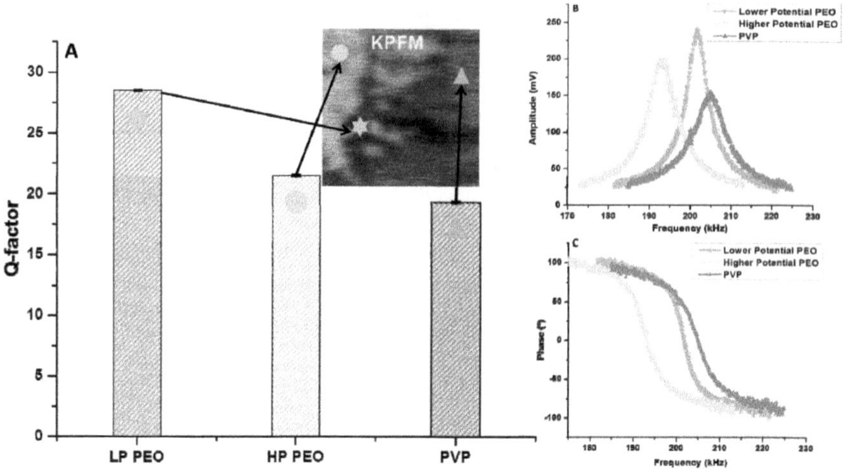

Figure 2: The histogram (A) of the quality factor of the tip obtained by fitting a Lorentzian function to the frequency spectrums of shown in B. This histogram is taken at the three distinct phases of the polymer blend which is observed in the surface potential map as shown in the inset of (A). The plots B and C show the first order flexural contact resonance and phase obtained on the three polymer phases.

The contact resonance amplitude image of the polymer blend for the PVP, Low potential (LP) PEO and high potential (HP) PEO at first flexural contact frequencies of 204.88 kHz, 201.57 kHz and 193.22 kHz respectively is shown in Figure 3 A-C respectively. The contrast in each image shows that during the scanning of the image with its relative contact resonance frequency, the amplitude is changing accordingly. The plots on the right are the corresponding cross sections of the amplitude images for PVP (D), LP PEO (E) and HP PEO (F). The variations as measured from the cross-section profiles clearly show the amplitude is the smallest for the PVP. The amplitude variation for the LP PEO is lower than 75 mV while that for the HP PEO is around 100 mV. When a tip oscillating at the contact resonance frequency interacts with a soft material its amplitude decreases due to an increase in the viscoelastic effects between them. Hence the amplitude for PVP is reduced as compared to the two phases of PEO and can be seen from the cross section images of Figure 3D, 3E and 3F.

It is known that at room temperature polyethylene (PEO) is a flexible solid consisting of some solid crystalline (high degree of structural order and rigidity) and melted amorphous domains (lower degree of structural order). The PF-KPFM technique is sensitive enough to detect the change in the surface potential in these domains due to its molecular arrangements. As seen in

Figure 1D, the amorphous domains have a much higher surface potential (~600mV) as compared to the crystalline domains having comparatively lower surface potential (~200mV) for the PEO while that for PVP is ~300mV. These surface potential values are determined relative to each other when the tip potential is set to 100 mV. It is quite interesting that the contact resonance mode differentiates the different phases of PEO and PVP with high contrast as seen in the surface potential map (Figure 1D). This is due to the fact that when the tip comes in contact with the different components of the blend, the energy dissipated at the higher order contact mode frequencies into the system is very sensitive to the different degrees of structural order and rigidity of the polymer blend. This dissipation is reflected in the change of amplitude (Figure 3) and phase (Figure 4) of the contact resonance frequency allowing a direct correlation between the surface potential maps and the contact resonance data.

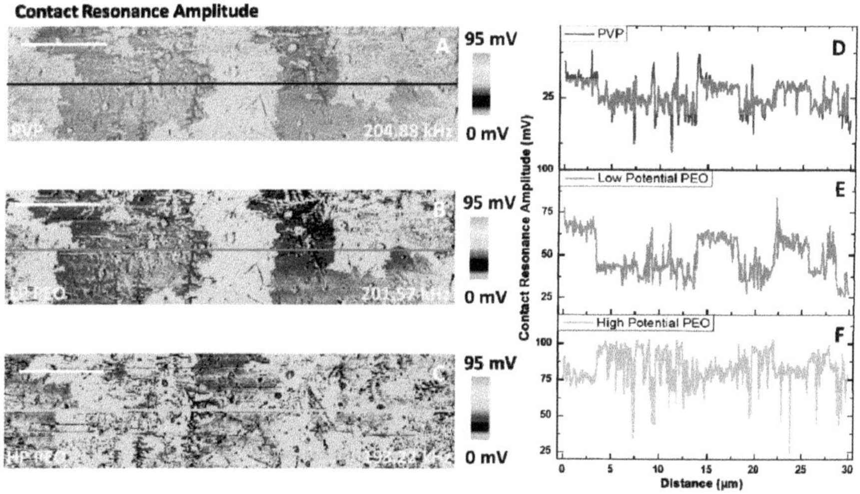

Figure 3 shows the contact resonance amplitude for the PVP (C) and two phases of PEO: LP PEO (B) and HP PEO (A). The corresponding cross sectional analysis is shown in D, E and F respectively. The scale bar in all the above images 5 □ m

The two different phases of PEO is difficult to differentiate from the deformation and adhesion images in Figure 1B and 1C respectively. However, the contact resonance phase seem to amplify this difference with a high contrast as seen in Figure 4A, 4B and 4C. All the images are taken at the corresponding first flexural contact frequencies of 204.88 kHz, 201.57 kHz and 193.22 kHz for the PVP, low potential (LP) PEO and high potential (HP) PEO respectively. The high contrast in the phase of LP PEO (figure 4B) and HP PEO (Figure 4C) qualitatively suggest that even though PEO have two phases with similar elastic stiffness, they have different damping and dissipative characteristics. The high contrast images in Figure 4 are a proof of the sensitivity of the contact resonance technique to differentiate between two phases of the same polymer (PEO).

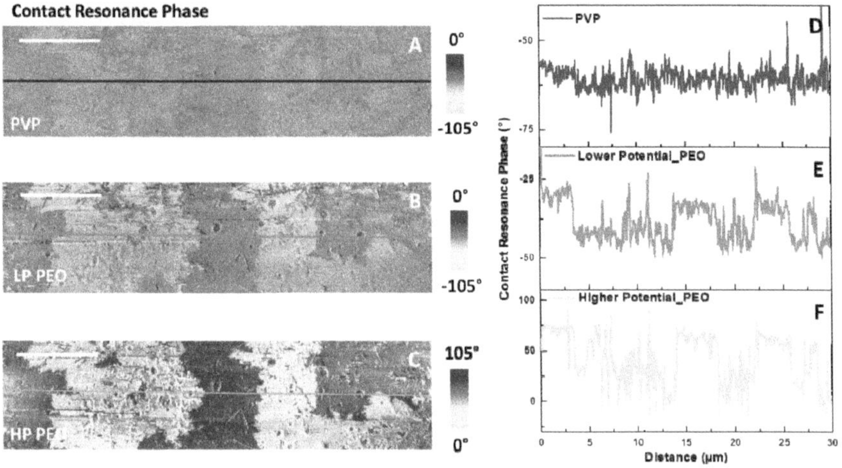

Figure 4 shows the contact resonance phase for the PVP (C) and two phases of PEO: LP PEO (B) and HP PEO (A). The corresponding cross sectional analysis is shown in D, E and F respectively. The scale bar in all the above images is 5 □ m.

CONCLUSIONS

We have demonstrated contact resonance images for a blend of PVP and PEO polymer. The contrast observed in the first flexural mode contact resonance of the individual polymer was observed with high quality. A clear and distinct phase of PEO other than the dominant dendritic feature is also observed in the phase and amplitude of the contact resonance images. Additionally, the adhesion and deformation maps of these blends clearly show the two phases of PEO and one continuous phase of PVP. Depending on the material to be investigated, appropriate tip parameters were chosen to get simultaneous contact resonance data for phase and amplitude. These maps although qualitative in nature can provide more precise information about viscoelastic properties of the materials exhibiting the stress and dissipative properties of the polymers. Using proper models for elasticity and approximation, we can determine the young's modulus of the materials. The contact resonance study can reveal with great significance the material properties of heterogeneous material. The study from this work may aid in the development of composite materials for applications in bio-sensing, drug-delivery and energy applications.

ACKNOWLEDGMENTS

We are grateful to the support of Canadian excellence research chair program for this project

REFERENCES

[1] G. Binnig, C. Quate, C. Gerber, *Phys. Rev. B* 56 (1986) 930.

[2] D. Platz, E. a Tholén, C. Hutter, A.C. von Bieren, D.B. Haviland, *Ultramicroscopy* 110 (2010) 573.

[3] G. Bar, Y. Thomann, R. Brandsch, H. Cantow, N. Carolina, *Langmuir* 7463 (1997) 3807.

[4] K. Yamanaka, Y. Maruyama, T. Tsuji, K. Nakamoto, *Appl. Phys. Lett.* 78 (2001) 1939.

[5] M.T. Cuberes, H.E. Assender, G.A.D. Briggs, O. V Kolosov, *J. Phys.D Appl. Phys.* 33 (2000) 2347.

[6] U. Rabe, W. Arnold, *Appl. Phys. Lett.* 64 (1994) 1493.

[7] S. Cuenot, C. Frétigny, S. Demoustier-Champagne, B. Nysten, *J. Appl. Phys.* 93 (2003) 5650.

[8] J.P. Killgore, D.G. Yablon, A H. Tsou, A Gannepalli, P. A Yuya, J. A Turner, R. Proksch, D.C. Hurley, *Langmuir* 27 (2011) 13983.

[9] A. Gannepalli, D.G. Yablon, A H. Tsou, R. Proksch, *Nanotechnology* 22 (2011) 355705.

[10] G. Stan, R.F. Cook, *Nanotechnology* 19 (2008) 235701.

[11] S.G. Street, M.S.S. Ia, *Polymer* (Guildf). 33 (1992) 432.

[12] J.K. Hobbs, C. Vasilev, A.D.L. Humphris, *Polymer* (Guildf). 46 (2005) 10226.

[13] X.-S. Feng, D. Taton, E.L. Chaikof, Y. Gnanou, *J. Am. Chem. Soc.* 127 (2005) 10956.

[14] M. Wang, H.-G. Braun, E. Meyer, *Polymer* (Guildf). 44 (2003) 5015.

[15] G. Reiter, J.-U. Sommer, *Phys. Rev. Lett.* 80 (1998) 3771.

[16] G. Reiter, J.-U. Sommer, *J. Chem. Phys.* 112 (2000) 4376.

[17] J.-U. Sommer, G. Reiter, *J. Chem. Phys.* 112 (2000) 4384.

Mater. Res. Soc. Symp. Proc. Vol. 1754 © 2015 Materials Research Society
DOI: 10.1557/opl.2015.258

Determination of the Physical Properties of Oil Sands Components using Scanning Probe Microscopy

Ravi Gaikwad[1], Tinu Abraham[1], Aharnish Hande[1], Fatemeh Bakhtiari[1], Siddhartha Das[2], Thomas Thundat[1]

[1] Department of Chemical and Materials Engg, University of Alberta, Edmonton, [2]Department of Mechanical Engg, University of Maryland, Baltimore

ABSTRACT

Atomic force microscopy is employed to study the structural changes in the morphology and physical characteristics of asphaltene aggregates as a function of temperature. The exotic fractal structure obtained by evaporation-driven asphaltene aggregates shows an interesting dynamics for a large range of temperatures from 25^0C to 80^0C. The changes in the topography, surface potential and adhesion are unnoticeable until 70^0C. However, a significant change in the dynamics and material properties is displayed in the range of 70^0C - 80^0C, during which the aspahltene aggregates acquire 'liquid-like' mobility and fuse together. This behaviour is attributed to the transition from the pure amorphous phase to a crystalline liquid phase which occurs at approximately 70^0C as shown by using Differential Scanning Calorimetry (DSC). Additionally, the charged nature of asphaltenes and bitumen is also explored using kelvin probe microscopy. Such observations can lead to the development of a rational approach to the fundamental understanding of asphaltene aggregation dynamics and may help in devising novel techniques for the handling and separation of asphaltene aggregates using dielectrophoretic methods.

INTRODUCTION

The major problem associated with the underground recovery of heavy oil is the high viscosity of the bitumen for which petroleum asphaltenes are mainly responsible[1]. Petroleum asphaltene mainly consists of high molecular weight hydrocarbons of predominantly aromatic character with low hydrogen content (around 8%) formed by condensation and dehydrogenation from aromatic-naphthenic hydrocarbons of lower molecular weight[1,2]. Asphaltenes are readily soluble in liquid aromatics like benzene and toluene. This makes the separation of polymeric ashpaltene chemically possible but it consists of a wide range of chemically different structures. Although there has been extensive research on asphaltenes, the exact chemical composition for this solubility class is not well understood and it varies depending on the sources from where it is obtained. Hence it is extremely important to precisely investigate the reasons for its aggregation and flocculation. Such information will aid in the easy separation and removal of asphaltenes and upgrading of heavy oil.

A plethora of attempts are made at understanding the aggregation using advanced technique like atomic force microscopy (AFM)[3] where the thickness[4] and morphology of adsorbed asphaltene aggregatges[5–9] on mica and silicon wafers are determined. The influence on the asphaltene aggregates on mica substrate on the addition of resins and demulsifiers is also studied[10]. In our studies, we determine the effect of temperature on the morphologies of asphaltene nano-aggregates. We observed a transition from self-assembled fractal structures to substantially larger fluid domains that show interesting self-coalescence behaviour using AFM[11]. Hence it is important to understand the nature of nucleation sites on a given surface which facilitates deposition of aggregates. By understanding the aggregation dynamics via the topography, surface potential maps, adhesion, overall surface charge density and dielectric property of asphaltenes at the nanoscale, it may help in devising strategies/methods to prevent aggregation and subsequent flocculation.

EXPERIMENTAL DETAILS

Crude asphaltene sample was obtained from the Institute for Oil Sands Innovation (IOSI) Laboratory, University of Alberta. The impure asphaltene contained about 50% heptane-insoluble materials and was initially precipitated by adding n-pentane to Athabasca bitumen originally obtained from the Nexen plant. We extracted 100% pure asphaltene from this impure asphaltene in a procedure explained in ref 11. This pure chemically separated asphaltene sample was dissolved by sonication in High Performance Liquid Chromatography (HPLC) grade toluene to make 0.005 wt% asphaltene solution. A drop (volume ~10μL) of this asphaltene solution was cast deposited on $1cm^2$ piece of SiO2 wafer (Nanofab, University of Alberta) which was prewashed with ethanol. The drop was then allowed to dry (i.e., the toluene evaporated) at ambient room temperature conditions for 30 minutes to ensure that all the toluene has been evaporated. The substrate with asphaltene was subsequently mounted on a stage installed under atomic force microscope probe. In this configuration, topographic, surface potential and adhesion maps were collected using the Peak-force KPFM mode. For all the AFM imaging, we used Bruker Icon AFM (Santa Barbara, CA) system and conducting SCM-PIT probes (Bruker, Santa Barbara, CA) with resonance frequency about 75 KHz, spring constant of 2.8N/m and radii of curvature of 20nm.

RESULTS AND DISCUSSION

The typical self-assembly of asphaltene nanoaggregate is about 6 nm in height and about several microns in lateral dimensions and resembles a fractal like structure. The topography (Figure 1A-1D), surface potential (Figure 1E-1H) and the adhesion image Figure (1I-1L) at various temperatures is shown below. Such topographies were previously observed for asphaltene aggregates when were dispersed on glass[12] and mica[5] substrates. Our hypothesis is that these structures are formed due to the evaporation driven process of asphaltene dissolved in toluene solution. Although there has been studies reported on the dynamics of the aggregation process, we are mainly interested in the physical and material properties of asphaltene as function of temperature. The self-assembled asphaltene aggregates are adsorbed in its most thermodynamically stable state at room temperature. The asphaltene aggregates form fractal structures at the ambient temperature condition and its fractal dimension is found to be 1.76. This value was observed to remain more or less constant for a wide temperature range (from 25^0C to 70^0C). The most interesting changes in the topography of the asphaltene aggregates are observed when the temperature is increased beyond 70^0C. We observed intriguing variations in the morphology at 80^0C where the asphaltene aggregates attain a “liquid-like” fluidity allowing the domains to coalesce and leading to the formation of larger uniform domains of asphaltene aggregates. This temperature mediated coalescence of asphaltene aggregates is irreversible and no fractal structure similar to one observed before heating was observed on cooling the sample back to the room temperature.

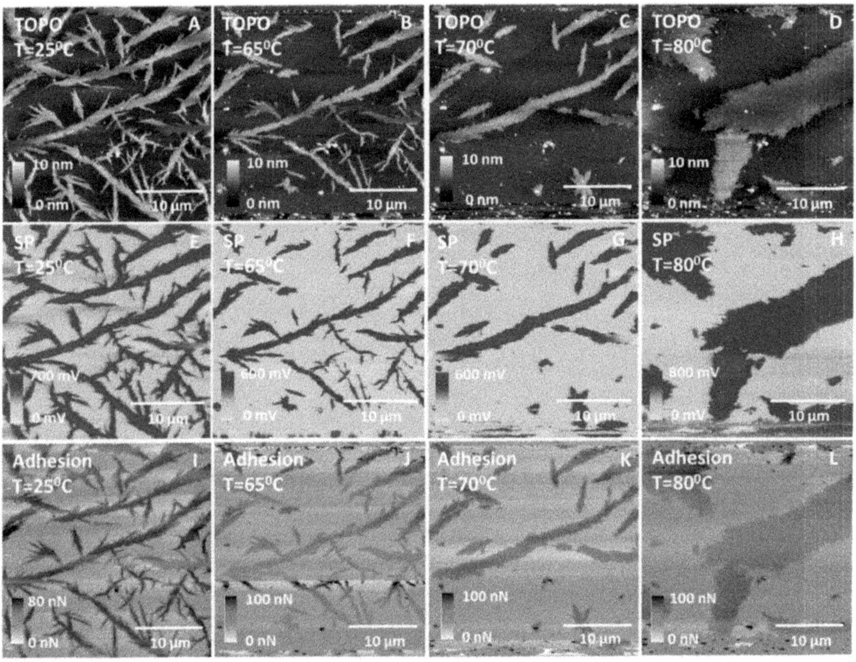

Figure 1: Asphaltene nanoaggregate dynamics as a function of temperature. The topography (A, B, C and D), surface potential (E, F, G and H) and adhesion (I, J, K and L) at temperatures 25^0C, 55^0C, 65^0C and 80^0C respectively.

In order to understand the coalescence mechanism of asphaltene aggregates at higher temperatures (>70^0C), we studied the variation of heat capacity of the asphaltene as a function of temperature by performing Differential scanning calorimetry (DSC) experiments[11]. The DSC thermogram clearly shows multiple glass transition temperatures (T_G) for the asphaltene sample for the first heating cycle. For the temperature range of our studies (25^0C to 80^0C), we get $T_{G1}=41^0$C and $T_{G2}=60^0$C. Most important is the third glass transition temperature $T_{G3}=75^0$C where there is exothermic phase transition across a small temperature window of 10^0C.
This phase transition T_{G3} intersects with the continuous endothermic phase transition that is observed in the entire temperature range considered for the thermogram. Such exothermic behaviour is a signature of the presence of small liquid crystalline domains that melts in the observed temperature range.

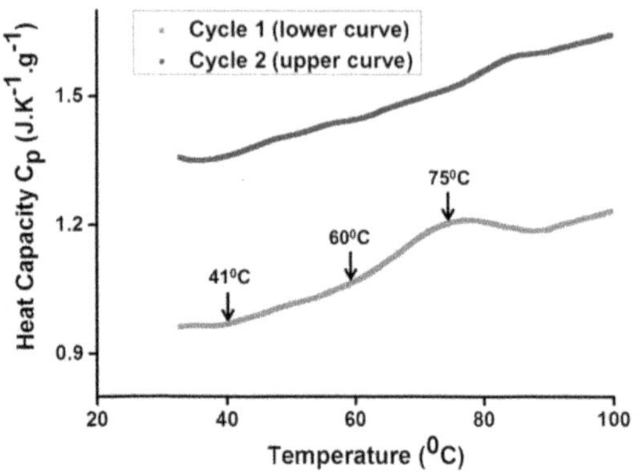

Figure 2: The variation of the heat capacity of asphaltene as a function of temperature by using differential scanning calorimetry. The first heating cycle (lower curve) shows multiple glass temperatures noted by arrows above while the second heating cycle (upper curve) shows the transitions are irreversible.

The asphaltene aggregation dynamics observed in Figure 1 can be clearly related to this glass transition temperature where the asphlatene exhibits liquid-like behaviour at temperatures exceeding 70^{0}C. The second heating cycle represented by the upper curve in Figure 2 shows that the phase transitions are irreversible and that no significant glass transition temperatures are observed in the studied temperature range with the exception at 85^{0}C.

The height, adhesion and surface potential distribution as a function of temperature of the asphaltene aggregates is shown in Figure 3a, 3b and 3c respectively. It is clearly seen from the height distribution that as the temperature is increased, the asphaltene domain heights decrease and becomes more flat due to the increased fluidity of the domains.

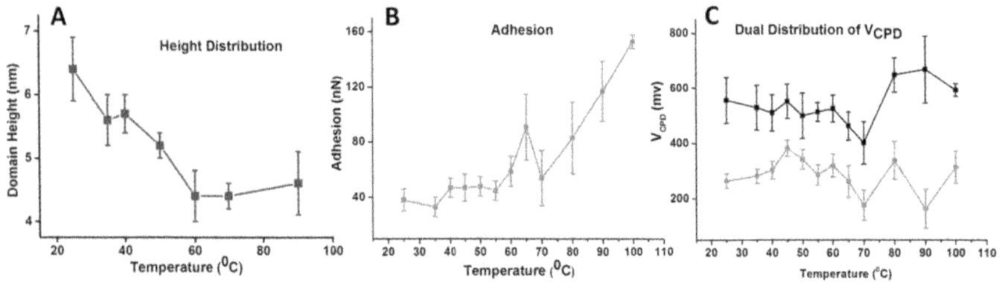

Figure 3 shows the distribution of height (A), adhesion (B) and the surface potential (C) of the asphaltene aggregates as a function of temperature.

The data for the above graph was measured across the asphaltene domains using the cross sectional analysis of the Nanoscope analysis software V1.40 (Bruker nano, Santa Barbara, USA). Each data point is an average value of atleast 10 cross-section lines along the horizontal axis and approximately around 50 data points. A slight high variation is observed in the measured data after around 70^0C due to the increased entropy of the system. The domain dynamics is very rapid around the temperature 70^0C where the phase transformation occurs, however the variations are reduced once equilibrium is achieved at 100^0C. The force of adhesion between the AFM tip and asphaltene aggregates increases and shows a peak around 65^0C after which it decreases and increases linearly for higher temperatures. Since the force of adhesion is directly proportional to the surface tension of the asphaltene aggregartes, it is trivial to deduce that the surface tension of the aggregates is also increased. In order to prove the dependence of temperature on the surface tension, a controlled study on the contact angle measurements will be performed in our future experiments. The surface potential (V_{CPD}) graph (Figure 3C) also shows interesting behaviour in the intrinsic property of surface charges originating from the chemical species of the asphlatene itself. The dual distribution as observed can be hypothesized due to the heterogeneity involved in the chemical species of asphaltene. If asphaltene was composed of homogeneous chemical specie, the surface potential may not show so much of variation. We plan to investigate this variation using specialized techniques to determine the chemical composition of the asphaltene aggregates.

CONCLUSIONS

We studied the effect of temperature on chemically separated asphaltene nanoaggregates. We observed a fascinating new aggregation dynamics occurring purely in the absence of any solvent. The aggregation is driven due to the fluid-like coalescing tendency of the asphaltene aggregates and it is well supported through systematic DSC thermograph that such behaviour stems from the transition of a purely amorphous phase to a liquid crystalline phase. The adhesion and surface potential variations in the asphaltene nanoaggregates also show some interesting phenomena due to the presence of varied chemical species present in pure chemically separated asphaltene nanoaggregates. By understanding the substrate repelling and coalescing dynamics of the asphaltene aggregates, the present study can open up new possibilities of separating and handling asphaltene.

ACKNOWLEDGMENTS

We are grateful to the support of Canadian excellence research chair program for this project

REFERENCES

[1] O.P. Strausz, Fuels 22 (1977) 171.

[2] L.N.V. De Bataafsche, P. Maatschappij, in:, Sixt. Colloid. Symp., 1939, pp. 139–149.

[3] G. Binnig, C.. Quate, C. Gerber, Phys. Rev. B 56 (1986) 930.

[4] H.W. Yarranton, D.P. Ortiz, D.M. Barrera, E.N. Baydak, L. Barre, D. Frot, J. Eyssautier, H. Zeng, Z. Xu, G. Dechaine, M. Becerra, J.M. Shaw, A.M. Mckenna, M.M. Mapolelo, C. Bohne, Z. Yang, J. Oake, Energy & Fuels 27 (2013) 5088.

[5] H. Toulhoat, C. Prayer, G. Rouquet, Colloids Surfaces A Physicochem. Engg Asp. 91 (1994) 267.

[6] L.Y. Zhang, S. Lawrence, Z. Xu, J.H. Masliyah, J. Colloid Interface Sci. 264 (2003) 128.

[7] C. Drummond, J. Israelachvili, J. Pet. Sci. Eng. 45 (2004) 61.

[8] L.Y. Zhang, P. Breen, Z. Xu, J.H. Masliyah, Energy & Fuels 21 (2007) 274.

[9] S. Sabbaghi, M. Shariaty-Niassar, S. Ayatollahi, A. Jahanmiri, J. Microsc. 231 (2008) 364.

[10] M.H. Ese, J. Sjoblom, J. Djuve, R. Pugh, Colloid Polym. Sci. 278 (2000) 532.

[11] M. Mehranfar, R. Gaikwad, S. Das, S.K. Mitra, T. Thundat, Langmuir 30 (2014) 800.

[12] E.D. Sourty, a Y. Tamminga, M. a J. Michels, W.-P. Vellinga, H.E.H. Meijer, J. Microsc. 241 (2011) 132.

Mater. Res. Soc. Symp. Proc. Vol. 1754 © 2015 Materials Research Society
DOI: 10.1557/opl.2015.199

Comprehensive Characterization of Neat Polymers and Compositional Imaging Heterogeneous Polymer Systems with AFM Based Mechanical, Electric and Spectroscopic Methods

Marko Surtchev, Sergey Belikov, Ivan Malovichko and Sergei Magonov
NT-MDT Development Inc., 7910 S. Kyrene Road, Tempe, AZ 85284, U.S.A.

ABSTRACT

Comprehensive characterization of materials suggests measuring their different properties for optimal use in technological applications and this task becomes more challenging as size of related structures decreases and their complexity increases. At smaller scales Atomic Force Microscopy (AFM) enables visualization of structures and quantitative measurements of their mechanical and electric properties. So far, several properties such as elastic modulus and work of adhesion, surface potential and dielectric permittivity can be extracted from the results obtained in various AFM modes. More complicated are the AFM experiments and their analysis in case of viscoelastic, piezoelectric and thermoelectric properties. Several examples of quantitative characterization of neat polymers will be given. In many cases the dissimilarity of the components' properties is employed for their recognition in heterogeneous systems such as polymer blends, block copolymers and metal alloys. The confined geometries, which are common for small-scale structures, might restrict such identification and a combination of AFM with spectral methods such as Raman scattering will be helpful. Achievements and challenges of compositional mapping will be illustrated on several complex materials.

INTRODUCTION

In last decades AFM applications are developing in the contact and oscillatory modes, which complement each other in high-resolution imaging, where these modes provide visualization of molecular-scale features and measurements of materials properties at scales down to nanometers. The contact mode is used for current, piezoresponse and contact resonance studies, whereas the oscillatory resonant mode – Amplitude Modulation (AM) is applied for local magnetic or electric measurements in single- or multi-frequency methods. In the oscillatory non-resonant mode such as HybriD mode [1] the probe deflection – the attribute of the contact mode - is applied for surface tracking. (Similar modes are used by Nanotec Electronica, JPK Instruments and Bruker.) This happens in every cycle while the probe-sample separation periodically changes from a non-contact to contact state at a frequency much smaller than that of the probe. This mode, in which the tip-sample forces fall in between the most gentle AM operation and stronger forces (particularly, lateral) of the contact mode, is useful for nanomechanical and electric studies. All three modes are successfully applied for quantitative examination of the elastic modulus of various materials and the analysis of the force curves in these modes will be demonstrated on samples of poly(vinyl acetate) (PVAC), polystyrene (PS) and low density polyethylene (LDPE). The different time scale of the tip-sample interactions in the above modes offers the access to the time-dependent mechanical properties especially when the measurements at various temperatures can be added to the data pool. Such experiments were initiated on neat polymers and related questions will be raised in studies of PVAC described below.

The AFM-based electric studies were initiated shortly after the invention of this method [2] and they can be realized in different ways. The most sensitive measurements of surface potential and capacitance gradient dC/dZ with a spatial resolution of few nanometers are performed in single-pass multi-frequency approach, in which the electrostatic force gradient is nullified [3]. The difference of surface potentials of metals, which was determined in this way, matches the difference of their tabulated work functions, and this supports quantitative nature of these measurements. These studies can be used for polymers with rich dipole moieties. Furthermore, the dC/dZ measurements of thin films of PVAC and PS on a conducting substrate have been utilized for finding the dielectric permittivity of these polymers [4].

In the following, we will demonstrate the local measurements of materials properties on a number of samples and provide the example of compositional imaging of multi-component systems, which is based on differences in the properties and chemical nature of the constituents. The chemical nature is determined with Raman spectrometer combined with AFM and the maps of chemically-sensitive Raman bands were recorded simultaneously with sample topography.

EXPERIMENT

The AFM experiments were performed in air with NTEGRA Prima and Titanium scanning probe microscopes made by NT-MDT. The NTEGRA Spectra instrument and the combination of Thermo Fisher Raman microscope DXR with NTEGRA Spectra unit were applied for AFM-Raman studies. The measurements were conducted in contact mode, Hybrid mode and AM mode with commercial Si probes with different size of the tip apex and with a conducting Pt coating. The studies in Hybrid mode were performed at frequency of 1.5 kHz and amplitudes in the 30-100 nm range. In some cases the measurements were performed at elevated temperatures. The samples were prepared from polymers and solvents supplied by Polymer Source Inc and Sigma Aldrich. The polymer solutions with different concentrations were deposited by spin-casting on several substrates: Si, mica and ITO glass, which were purchased from Ted Pella. Polymer samples in a form of 1-2 millimeters thick blocks were prepared by hot-pressing between two Si substrates. Quantitative AFM measurements require knowledge of the probe stiffness, optical sensitivity, as well as the tip shape and size. Thermal tune method is used for finding the spring constant of the probe and optical sensitivity of the microscope. A characterization of the probe dimensions is done with electron microscopy imaging or the shape calculation from the images of sharp surface features.

RESULTS AND DISCUSSION

The results of our studies are assembled according to the application areas and they include the data recorded in studies of samples of neat polymers and immiscible polymer blends.

Quantitative nanomechanical studies

In the contact mode the deflection-versus-distance (DvZ) curves, which are obtained in the zigzag motion of the vertical piezo scanner with the 0.1 -100 Hz rates, are used for the extraction of elastic modulus and the work of adhesion using solid state elastic deformation models (Hertz, Sneddon, JKR, DMT, etc). The DvZ curves obtained on PVAC block at different forces (Figure 1a) is the example of such studies. The loading and unloading curves almost match each other in the experiment at 50 nN load and they exhibit a hysteresis at higher load. In principle, the elastic deformation models can be applied only for the analysis of the low-force curve. The JKR analysis, which incorporates the conversion of the DvZ to the force-versus-deformation dependence, gives the elastic modulus (E_{el}) 2GPa close to its macroscopic value.

In the case of the Hybrid mode, the basic information is obtained in the deflection temporal plot (Dvt) and it can be also transformed to DvZ curve using the sinusoidal Z-motion of the sample placed on a scanner. Curves of both types (Figure 1b) can be used for quantitative analysis as shown in the case of PS where the experimental curve with both loading and unloading parts was fitted with DMT theoretical curve to get the elastic modulus for this sample. The theoretical curve precisely fits the experimental Dvt profile, which is symmetric with respect to its maximum when the deformation is elastic. The dashed line in the DvZ reflects the deflection response when the hard sample is used. The good fit is also seen in the DvZ curves where the loading and unloading traces coincide with each other and with the theoretical line. We have performed similar studies on other polymers with E_{el} from several MPa to 10GPa and found a reasonable correspondence between their moduli obtained in Hybrid mode and in macroscopic mechanical measurements.

In the AM mode the amplitude and phase of the probe are used for surface tracking and property-related contrast but the mechanical studies are complicated by the complex relation of these parameters and the tip-sample forces. This relationship can be derived from theoretical analysis of the probe behavior [5] and applied for quantitative AM experiments at different peak forces and deformations. This approach enables also the extraction of E_{el} from amplitude-versus-distance (AvZ) curves. For this purpose a series of theoretical AvZ curves for materials with different E_{el} was generated and the experimental curve was matched to one of the theoretical curves. This is seen in Figure 1c where the insert magnifies the AvZ curve dependence on E_{el} in the curves' part where the force and deformation are the largest. The experimental curve obtained on LDPE, which is shown with a dashed line is close to the curves for E_{el} of 200 MPa and 300 MPa that is in line with the macroscopic modulus of this polymer.

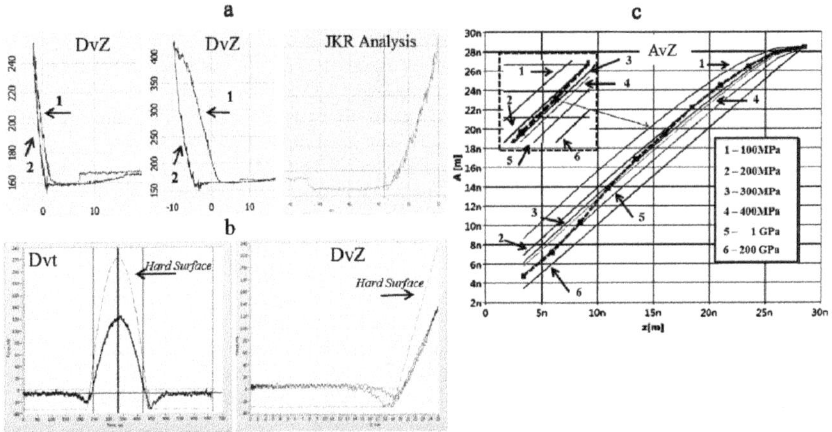

Figure 1a-c. (a) DvZ curves (1 – loading, 2 – unloading) on PVAC at 50nN and 150nN. The analysis of the loading curve – on the right. (b) Dvt and DvZ curves on PS. (c) Calculated AvZ curves for samples with different moduli. Dashed line - AvZ curve on LDPE.

The described above analysis in the contact and Hybrid modes can be performed off-line as well as on-line at large number of locations (up to 1024x1024 points). In the on-line measurements the maps of elastic modulus and other parameters calculated from the force curves (work of adhesion, deformation, etc) can be constructed simultaneously with the height image. The height and E_{el} map of PS/LDPE blend in Figure 2 show that the blend morphology is characterized by a stiffer matrix (E_{el} ~ 3 GPa) and softer spherical inclusions (E_{el} ~ 300 MPa), which can be assigned respectively to PS and LDPE, whose moduli are close to the measured ones. This assignment is also consistent with findings of lamellar structures of semicrystalline LDPE inside the spherical inclusions. This example of compositional mapping using E_{el} maps is superior to the indirect assignment of the components in the AM phase images commonly used for studies of microphase separation in polymer blends and composites.

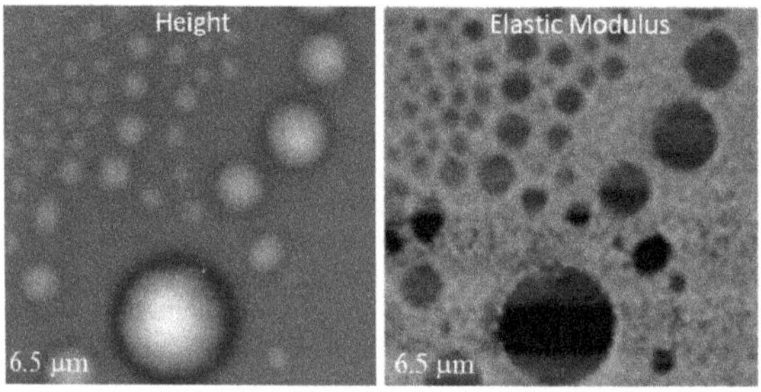

Figure 2. Height and elastic modulus map in Hybrid mode on a blend of PS and LDPE. The contrast of the height image covers the surface corrugations in the 0-100 nm range; the contrast of the map covers the modulus variations in the 0.3–3 GPa.

AFM-based electric studies

Surface potential and dielectric permittivity are the electric properties, which can be measured at the local scale with AFM. They have been examined on various materials. These properties can be also applied for compositional mapping of polymer blends and other heterogeneous materials. Particularly, the dielectric permittivity determined for thin films of neat PS and PVAC were used for clarification of the dC/dZ contrast in the PS/PVAC blend, which depends not only on the variations of permittivity but also on the thickness of the material inside the space between the tip and the conducting substrate. An example of the compositional mapping of a film of PS/PVAC blend with surface potential map is given in Figure 3. The film was scratched to open the conducting ITO glass, and the latter is recognized by a particular morphology in the right part of the height image. The polymer film on the left is ~ 60 nm in height as seen from the cross-section profile, which was taken along the film step and the substrate. The film morphology is characterized by the circular domains, which are slightly elevated over the matrix. The clear differentiation of the sample components is seen in the surface potential image. The potential contrast of the substrate is quite different from that of the film. Inside the film, the circular domains have ~ 200 mV higher potential than the matrix. These domains can be assigned to PVAC-rich locations, which have more charged groups than PS. The assignment was also supported by the fact that hydrophilic PVAC phase swells in vapors of methanol and water that leads to the expansion of circular domains [3].

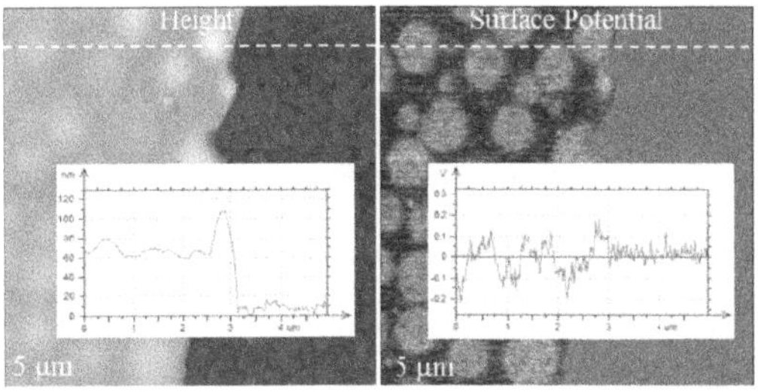

Figure 3. Height and surface potential images of PS/PVAC blends obtained in the single-pass Kelvin force microscopy. The inserts show the profiles along the white dashed lines.

Compositional imaging with AFM/Raman measurements

A combination of AFM with Raman spectroscopy enhances the compositional imaging by providing chemical-specific recognition in heterogeneous materials. Practically all polymers have specific Raman scattering bands for their identification. In the compositional mapping of PVAC and PS blend one can use the polymer-specific C-H bands for recognition of the components as seen from Figure 4. The height image of the blend shows the perforated protrusions embedded into a matrix. Such morphology hints on microphase separation.

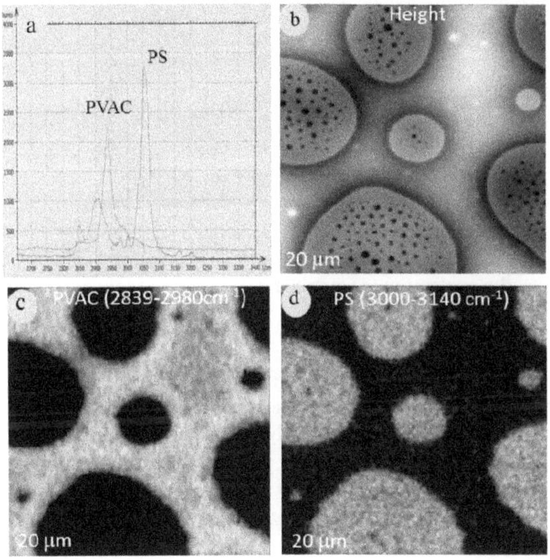

Figure 4. (a) Raman spectra of PS and PVAC in the region of C-H vibrations. (b) – (d) Height image of PS/PVAC blend and Raman maps of intensities of PVAC- and PS-specific scattering bands. The contrast in (b) is in the 0-50 nm range, in (c) and (d) – in the 0-40 counts/sec range.

The assignment of the particular locations to the individual components was based on differences of their shapes/dimensions and dissimilarities of their mechanical or electric properties. However, only the Raman maps provide a direct recognition of the constituents of complex materials based on their spectroscopic detected chemical nature. The intensity maps of the PS- and PVAC-specific bands (Figure 4c-d) indicate that the matrix is enriched in PVAC and the perforated protrusions are enriched in PS. A comparison of the nanoscale details of the height image and Raman maps shows that the spatial resolution of the maps are not high and typically limited by several hundreds of nanometer due to the diffraction limit. The ongoing developments in tip-enhanced Raman scattering will allow bringing the spectral resolution to the tens of nanometer range and with the optimal probes such imaging will become routine in the future.

Another example of the compositional imaging with AFM/Raman approach is even more valuable, Figure 5. The Hybrid mode study showed that the E_{el} map of the ultrathin film of PS/poly(butadiene) - PBD blend on Si (with a scratch on the left) indicates that the inclusions are softer than the matrix and E_{el} of the components are close to 2GPa matching E_{el} of PS. This result is puzzling because E_{el} of neat PBD is in tens of MPa. The Raman maps indicate that the "softer" inclusions are enriched in PS and the matrix - in PBD. The relative softness of the elevated PS domains can be explained by stronger enforcement of thinner PBD matrix lying directly on the rigid substrate.

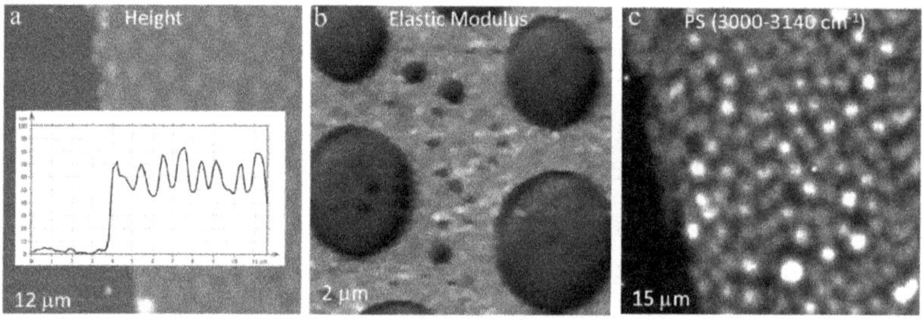

Figure 5. (a) Height image of PS/PBD film with the profile across the scratch and film step. (b) Map of the elastic modulus of the film location. (c) Raman map of PS-specific band. The contrast in (b) is in the 0.02-3GPa range; the contrast in (c) is in the 0–10 counts/sec range.

CONCLUSIONS

Advances in AFM characterization were demonstrated on several polymer samples. Further expansion in the quantitative nanomechanical and electric measurements is expected with increasing role of local spectroscopic methods in chemical analysis at the nanoscale.

REFERENCES

1. S. Belikov, J. Alexander, C. Wall, and S. Magonov, *MRS Proceedings* 1527 (2013) mrsf12-1527-uu02-042.
2. Y. Martin, D. A. Abraham, and H. K. Wickramasinghe *Appl. Phys. Lett. 52*, 1103, (1988).
3. S. Magonov, and J. Alexander, *Beilstein Journal of Nanotechnology 2*, 15-27 (2011).
4. S. Belikov, J. Alexander, S. Magonov, and I. Yermolenko, *Amer. Control Confer.* 3228 (2012)
5. S. Belikov, and S. Magonov, *Amer. Control Confer.* 979 (2009).

Mater. Res. Soc. Symp. Proc. Vol. 1754 © 2015 Materials Research Society
DOI: 10.1557/opl.2015.256

Nanometer Thermal Conductivity Mapping Using Laser-based Scanning Thermal Microscopy

Jeremy Goeckeritz[1], Gary Aden[1], and Ami Chand[1]
[1]Applied Nanostructures, 415 Clyde Ave. Suite 102, Mountain View, CA 94043, U.S.A.

ABSTRACT

A new measurement technique using a cantilever probe with an integrated thermal sensor is investigated for measuring thermal conductivity at the nanometer scale. The probe is used in a configuration wherein the laser from an atomic force microscope (AFM) heats the tip of the probe above ambient temperature. Heat is transferred from the probe to a sample based on the thermal conductivity of the sample. The heat flow creates a temperature change, as small as 0.01 °C, which is detected by the thermal sensor. The measurement technique presented offers a simple and effective method for mapping the thermal conductivity of a number of materials. We explore the ability of the technique to map silicon oxide on silicon, carbon fibers and gold nanoparticles. Analysis shows that the technique can be used to produce images with a thermal resolution surpassing 25 nm.

INTRODUCTION

A large number of physical, biological and engineered materials and phenomena require thermal imaging at high spatial resolution. In recent years, scanning thermal microscopy (SThM) has attracted considerable attention as a promising nanoscale thermal imaging technology. In SThM, a thermal probe consisting of a cantilever with a sharp tip is scanned over a sample while a temperature-sensing element near the tip measures thermal properties at the sample surface. The temperature sensor may be, for example, a thermistor, thermocouple, or Schottky diode [1-3]. Typically, an atomic force microscope (AFM) is used to scan the probe enabling simultaneous topography and thermal imaging.

The thermal probe may be operated in passive or active mode [4], [5]. In passive mode, the sample heats the tip while a temperature-dependent tip property is monitored. In active mode, the tip is heated above ambient temperature. The tip is then brought in contact with a sample and heat is transferred from the probe to the sample based on the thermal conductivity of the sample. For example, a resistive heater may be used to elevate the tip temperature while the temperature-dependent resistance of the heater is monitored during the scan. Such active mode SThM requires precise current control to heat the probe and electronics to monitor the temperature-dependent tip property.

Here, we present an alternative method for mapping thermal properties without a high-precision current controller or custom readout electronics. The setup requires only the feedback laser of an AFM to heat a thermal probe. The probe uses a thermocouple junction at the tip which produces a temperature-dependent voltage response when the tip is brought in contact with a sample. The voltage is amplified and sent to the AFM controller input for display. The setup does not require active current heating thus allowing the same probe to be used in passive or active modes by simply moving the AFM laser slightly away from the tip.

EXPERIMENT

Experiments were carried out using a Dimension 3100 AFM (Digital Instruments). As typical in AFM, an optical beam reflecting off the back of the cantilever and onto a segmented diode was used to detect cantilever deflection and a XY piezoelectric scanner was used to control the position of the probe on the sample surface. A thermocouple probe (Vertisense VTP-200, Applied Nanostructures) was used for thermal sensing. The probe had a spring constant of 24.9 N/m, a width of 50 μm and a length of 200 μm. A block diagram of the thermal measurement setup showing the topography and thermal data pathways is shown in Figure 1a. The probe's thermocouple sensor, in response to heat, produced a voltage that was amplified and sent to the AFM computer via a coaxial input. In all scans, the thermocouple output voltage was amplified by 10,000 to produce a useable voltage for the AFM. The AFM software (Nanoscope v5) used two input channels to display topography and thermal images simultaneously. All AFM scans were 512 samples/line and 512 lines. Post processing of images was performed with Nanoscope Analysis 1.5.

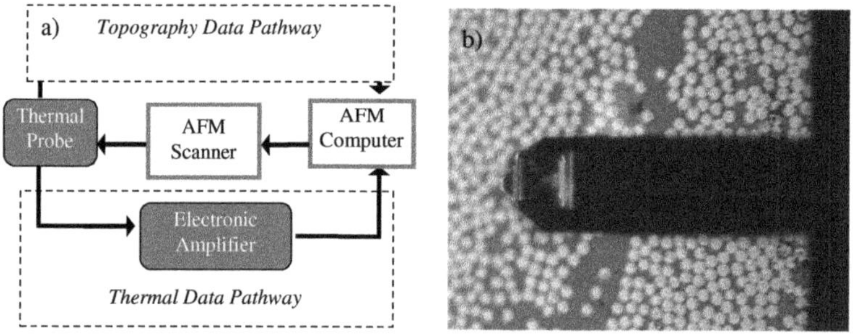

Figure 1. a) Block diagram of the thermal measurement setup. b) Optical image of a probe showing the cantilever/probe tip and the position of the AFM laser for heating the tip.

Before thermal imaging, the sensitivity of the probes was measured. The probes were brought in contact with a sample having a known temperature and the output voltage for several temperatures was measured. Here, the heated sample was a commercial K-type thermocouple embedded in a high temperature ceramic. The sample surface was polished such that only a small area of the K-type thermocouple (about 200 μm diameter) was exposed. A NiCr wire heater was mounted under the thermocouple. With this setup, the thermal probes can be calibrated from about 20 °C to 500 °C. The voltage response for several thermal probes is shown in Figure 2. The probes gave an average thermal sensitivity of about 10 μV/°C.

For thermal conductivity mapping, the AFM laser was positioned on the back of the tip (see Figure 1b. Typically, the laser was capable of heating the probe tip about 30 °C above ambient when the laser was positioned directly over the thermocouple. The laser output power for the AFM was 1 mW.

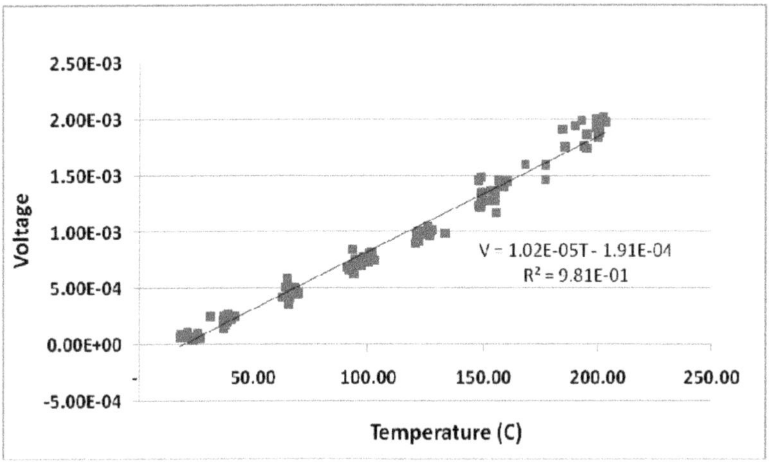

Figure 2. Voltage response of the thermocouple probes. The thermocouple sensor behaves linearly with an R^2 coefficient of 0.98 over the investigated temperature range.

DISCUSSION

Silicon oxide layer on silicon substrate

To demonstrate the feasibility of laser-based SThM, a silicon wafer with a silicon oxide step was scanned. Figure 3 shows the topography and thermal image of a 186 nm thick oxide layer. Crystalline silicon is an excellent thermal conductor and as a result, more heat was transferred from the tip to the silicon than from the tip to the oxide. The AFM interpreted the low voltage (conducting material) as a darker color and the higher voltage (thermally insulating material) as a lighter color. The thermocouple output voltage was measured along the lines shown in the thermal image of Figure 3. The average output voltage while scanning silicon was 3.19 V and the average voltage output was 3.29 V while the tip was in contact with oxide. Dividing these voltages by the amplifier gain and then dividing by probe sensitivity gave a tip temperature of 31.9 °C and 32.9 °C when the probe was on silicon and oxide respectively. The AFM used a 16 bit analog to digital converter over a voltage scale of 20 V corresponding to 65,536 discrete voltage values. Given a 10,000 gain and a 10 μV/°C sensitivity, relative temperature variations as small as 0.003° C could be encoded and displayed.

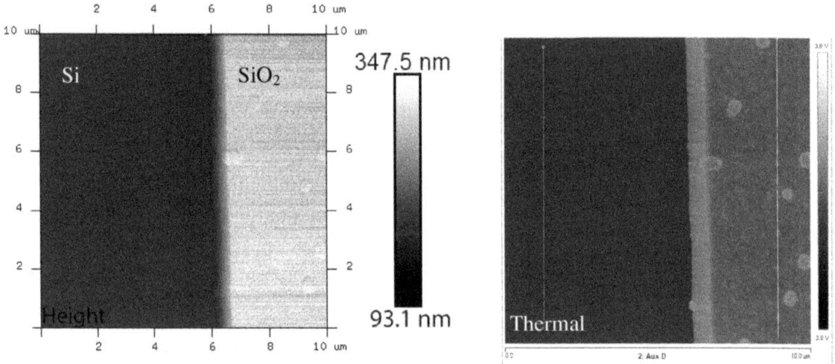

Figure 3. AFM topography image of an oxide step on a silicon substrate (left); scan area is 10x10 µm. The darker region is silicon and the lighter region is oxide. Thermal image showing the difference in heat transfer from the tip to the silicon and oxide (right). Silicon has a thermal conductivity about 100 times greater than silicon oxide; as a result, there is a significant difference in thermal transport from the tip to each of the materials.

<u>Carbon fibers embedded in epoxy</u>

To test image resolution, a sample consisting of carbon fibers embedded in epoxy was scanned. The sample was cross sectioned and polished to give a flat surface. The fibers are thermally conductive and the epoxy is thermally insulating. Figure 4 shows the SThM scan. Within the carbon fiber sample were small lines created during polishing. These lines were about 50 nm wide. Moreover, the spacing between the carbon fibers in certain areas was quite small. Figure 4c shows a thermal scan of a 3x3 µm area with fiber spacing of about 20 nm.

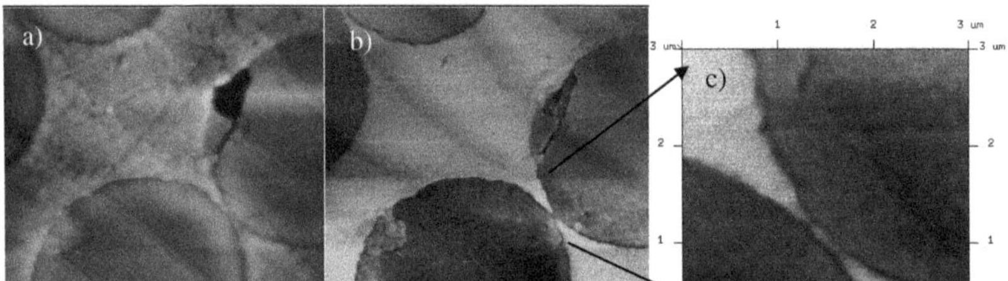

Figure 4. SThM scan of carbon fibers embedded in epoxy. a) Topography image (10x10 µm) showing the circular fibers. Small polishing lines can be seen in the scan. b) Thermal image showing the difference in thermal conductivity between the fibers (dark) and epoxy regions (light). c) 3x3 µm thermal scan showing a separation distance between fibers of about 20 nm.

Gold nanoparticles on glass

The SThM setup can also be used in tapping or semi-contact AFM mode. The thermal probe cantilever had a resonant frequency of 158 kHz. Figure 5 shows the thermal conductivity map of gold nanoparticles (GNPs) immobilized on a glass surface. The GNPs (nanoComposix) had an average diameter of 100 nm with a size distribution less than 15%. The particles were immobilized using (3-Mercaptopropyl)trimethoxysilane as a linker molecule [6], [7]. In tapping mode, heat transfer occurs only intermittently thus reducing the signal strength in the thermal image. This can be seen in Figure 5d where the difference in maximum and minimum voltage is only about 3 μV (before amplification).

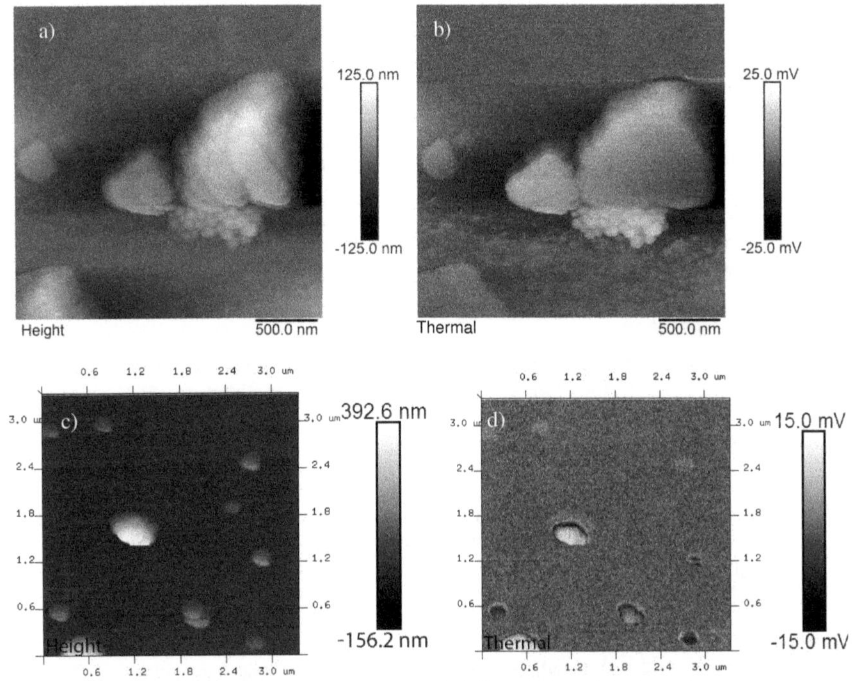

Figure 5. a) and c) show the topography scans of GNPs and b) and d) show the thermal scans. The GNPs are about 100 nm in diameter. The thermal scans show that many of the particles are not conducting heat from the tip. This phenomenon may be due to poor surface contact between the tip and particle or due to residual linker solution coating the particles.

The gold particles were dispersed in both clumps and individually. Interestingly, the thermal images show some of the GNPs as a lighter color meaning there was little heat transport from the tip. This result seems to be counterintuitive as a larger conductive metallic mass should sink more heat from the tip than the glass substrate. The reduced heat transport may be explained by the shape of the GNP grouping. For taller GNP groups, the tip comes off the surface resulting in less contact area and subsequently less heat transport. This phenomenon was only seen on slightly pointed or steeply sloped groups of particles. It is believed that the probe tip had less contact area with the particles as the tip moved up the side of the clump. Figure 5d shows that the tallest GNP groups are light colored, while the smaller particle groups or individual particles are darker supporting this idea. It is also possible that some of the particles were coated in the linker solution which interfered with heat transfer from the tip to the particles. Further investigation is needed to interpret these findings.

CONCLUSIONS

A laser SThM method was presented for mapping thermal properties with nanometer resolution. In this method, a thermocouple probe is heated using the laser from an atomic force microscope, thereby eliminating the need for a probe with a built-in heater or a current controller. For the particular model of AFM used in the experiments, the thermocouple probe could be heated tens of degrees above ambient temperature which was sufficient to image a diverse number of materials.

The thermal images showed high resolution as demonstrated in scans of carbon fibers and gold nanoparticles. The ability to qualitatively map thermal conductivity depends significantly on surface contact area between the probe tip and the sample. Interpretation of thermal images must be done carefully as increased surface roughness and sharp edges can alter heat transport from the tip to the sample.

ACKNOWLEDGMENTS

Support for this research was provided by the National Science Foundation grant number IIP-1256640.

REFERENCES

1. R.C. Davis, C. C. Williams, P. Neuzil, Appl. Phys. Lett. 66, 2309 (1995).
2. T. Leinhos, M. Stopka, E. Oesterschulze, Appl. Phys. A 66, S65 (1998).
3. J. R. Barnes, R. J. Stephenson, C. N. Woodburn, S. J. O'Shea, M. E. Welland, T. Rayment, J. K. Gmzewski, Ch. Gerber, Rev. Sci. Instrum. 65, 3793 (1994).
4. Y. Yue, X. Wang, Nano Rev. 3, 11586 - DOI: 10.3402/nano.v3i0.11586 (2012).
5. G. Jóźwiak, G. Wielgoszewski, T. Gotszalk, L. Kępiński, Ultramicroscopy 133, 80 (2013).
6. H. Weinrib, A. Meiri, H. Duadi, and D. Fixler, Journal of Atomic, Molecular, and Optical Physics, 2012, 683830 (2012).
7. J. Tseng, M. Lin, L. Chau, Colloids and Surfaces A: Physicochemical and Engineering Aspects, 182, 239-245, (2001).

Mater. Res. Soc. Symp. Proc. Vol. 1754 © 2015 Materials Research Society
DOI: 10.1557/opl.2015.286

Tip Enhanced Laser Ablation Sample Transfer for Mass Spectrometry

Kermit K. Murray, Suman Ghorai, and Chinthaka A. Seneviratne

Louisiana State University, Department of Chemistry, Baton Rouge, LA, 70803

ABSTRACT

Mass spectrometry is one of the primary analysis techniques for biological analysis but there are technological barriers in sampling scale that must be overcome for it to be used to its full potential on the size scale of single cells. Current mass spectrometry imaging methods are limited in spatial resolution when analyzing large biomolecules. The goal of this project is to use atomic force microscope (AFM) tip enhanced laser ablation to remove material from cells and tissue and capture it for subsequent mass spectrometry analysis. The laser ablation sample transfer system uses an AFM stage to hold the metal-coated tip at a distance of approximately 10 nm from a sample surface. The metal tip acts as an antenna for the electromagnetic radiation and enables the ablation of the sample with a spot size much smaller than a laser focused with a conventional lens system. A pulsed nanosecond UV or visible wavelength laser is focused onto the gold-coated silicon tip at an angle nearly parallel with the surface, which results in the removal of material from a spot between 500 nm and 1 μm in diameter and 200 and 500 nm deep. This corresponds to a few picograms of ablated material, which can be captured on a metal surface for MALDI analysis. We have used this approach to transfer small peptides and proteins from a thin film for analysis by mass spectrometry as a first step toward high spatial resolution imaging.

INTRODUCTION

Mass spectrometry imaging uses mass spectra obtained at regular intervals on an object such as a section of tissue with images formed by displaying the signal intensity for a particular mass at each position.[1-4] Under vacuum, mass spectra are obtained by bombarding the sample with a focused beam of ions for secondary ion mass spectrometry (SIMS).[5-7] or ablating and ionizing with a pulsed laser for laser desorption ionization (LDI) or matrix-assisted laser desorption ionization (MALDI).[5, 8] SIMS can image at spatial resolution down to 50 nm, but the harsh ionization conditions limit the detectable species to atomic and small molecular ions.[5, 9] The use of cluster ions for sample bombardment is gentler and can be used to ionize biomolecules up to approximately 1000 Da, but the spatial resolution is in the μm range.[10, 11] With MALDI, a light absorbing matrix is deposited on the tissue, which serves as an energy absorber and promotes ionization of biomolecules larger than 10 kDa without fragmentation.[12, 13] However, the spatial resolution of MALDI imaging is limited by the laser focus and is typically 50 to 100 μm, although specialized optics can bring this down to 5 μm.[14, 15]

Mass spectrometry imaging under ambient conditions allows for additional sampling options.[16, 17] For example, desorption electrospray ionization (DESI) uses a spray of highly charged droplets directed at the sample, wetting it and extracting of the components for imaging at a spatial resolution of about 500 μm.[18, 19] Surface sampling probes use solvent delivery and extraction capillaries that deliver liquid to the surface for extraction followed by transport of the extracted sample to the ion source.[20, 21] The nanospray desorption electrospray ionization (nano-DESI) source is a miniature liquid microjunction extraction source.[22] Ambient laser-based methods have a spatial resolution between 20 and 200 μm[23-26] and the ablated material can be ionized directly[27-30] or post-ionized by inductively coupled plasma,[31-33] chemical ionization,[34, 35] photoionization[36] or electrospray ionization.[37] Capture of the ablated material allows further processing prior to ionization with MALDI[38, 39] or electrospray ionization.[39, 40] Furthermore, the captured material can be separated by liquid chromatography[40-42] or capillary electrophoresis.[43]

The resolution of laser-based mass spectrometry imaging is constrained by the diffraction limited laser spot size, which is approximately 200 nm, half of the wavelength a UV laser. The best resolution is obtained in transmission mode where the laser irradiates the backside of the sample to eject material from the front side. An objective lens can focus the laser to a spot size below 1 μm,[44, 45] but the drawback to transmission mode is that it requires extremely thin samples of 1 μm thickness or less. In reflection mode, a standard high numerical aperture objective cannot be used because the low working distance means that the ablated material or ions are blocked by the objective. A unique solution to this problem is an objective lens with a central hole through which the desorbed ions pass. This approach has been used to produce focused spots of 600 nm and imaging resolution of 1 μm under vacuum[46] and a 25 μm spot for atmospheric pressure MALDI.[47] Long working distance Schwarzschild objectives have been used for laser desorption ionization imaging at 1 μm spatial resolution with at a working distance more than 10 cm.[48, 49]

There are two laser-based mass spectrometry imaging modes that are not limited by the ability to focus the laser. The first of these is microscope imaging mode in which ions are created from a large spot but are mapped to a two-dimensional detector at high resolution. This approach has been used to obtain 4 μm spatial resolution with a 200 μm laser spot,[50] which is below the diffraction limit for the IR laser used.[51, 52] A second approach is near-field desorption and ablation: aperture near-field uses a reflective-coated optical fiber probe and apertureless near-field uses a sharp conductive tip.[51] Direct ionization by laser desorption ionization has been accomplished by aperture near-field in vacuum[53] or under ambient conditions with the ions directed into the mass spectrometer.[54] Electron ionization has been used in conjunction with ambient aperture near-field ablation where molecules desorbed at atmospheric pressure were sampled into vacuum through a capillary tube and directed into the ion source.[55, 56] Apertureless near-field ablated material has been sampled into inductively coupled plasma mass spectrometry (LA-ICP-MS) with sub-micron spatial resolution.[57] In our group, we have used 355 nm apertureless near-field ablation to transfer small molecules for direct LDI and transfer of peptides and small proteins for MALDI.[58] With the apertureless approaches, there appears to be a tip enhancement effect for the ablation, but there has been some question as to whether it is truly a near-field effect.[58, 59]

In this work, we have extended our UV near-field laser ablation capture approach to visible wavelengths. A 532 nm pulsed nanosecond Nd:YAG laser was used to ablate peptide and protein samples from deposited thin films. The collected material was collected, mixed with a matrix and ionized in a MALDI time-of-flight mass spectrometer. The ability of the visible laser to transfer biomolecules without fragmentation was tested and the effect of laser polarization on the efficiency of material removal was studied.

EXPERIMENTAL DETAILS

The experimental setup has been described in detail previously.[58] An atomic force microscope (afm+, Anasys, Santa Barbara, CA) was used to image the sample surface and position the AFM tip for ablation. The AFM is modified with an exposed sample stage to allow direct laser illumination of the AFM tip. Gold-coated silicon AFM probes with a tip radius of 30 nm (ACCESS-NC-GG, Applied Nanostructures, Mountain View, CA) were used for the laser ablation and imaging experiments. The triangular pyramidal probe is tilted outward at an angle of 17° from vertical for direct optical access the tip while scanning, which allows tip-enhanced ablation. The probes have a nominal spring constant of 78 N/m and a resonant frequency of 300 kHz.

Materials were deposited from solution onto a glass coverslip mounted on a circular metal disc. Typically, a 50 µL volume of solution was deposited and the film was formed by slow evaporation. In this work, insulin and a peptide mixture were studied. The mixture of peptides was prepared by mixing solutions of bradykinin fragments (1-7), angiotensin II, angiotensin I, and renin substrate tetradecapeptide (porcine) in 3:4:5:6 molar ratio. It was possible to form thin films of insulin, however, the peptide mixture tended to segregate into separate crystals after slow evaporation. The AFM images of the sample surface are obtained in tapping mode. All AFM images shown in this work were obtained using the same experimental conditions.

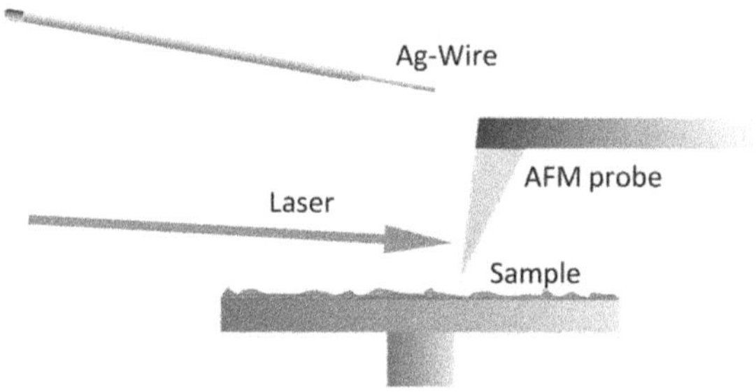

Figure 1. Diagram of the near-field laser ablation setup (not to scale); the laser irradiates the AFM probe that is held at an average height of 15 nm above the sample surface in tapping mode; ablated material is captured on a flattened silver wire 300 µm above the ablation spot.

The AFM tip was irradiated by a pulsed nanosecond Nd:YAG laser (Powerlite 8000, Continuum, San Jose, CA) that was frequency doubled to 532 nm wavelength. The laser was directed down onto the AFM tip at a shallow angle of approximately 10° from horizontal. The angle between the cantilever and the laser beam in the plane of the AFM table was approximately 45°. The laser was focused using a 25 cm CaF_2 lens to a spot size of approximately 600 µm and was attenuated using a variable neutral density filter. The polarization of the beam was adjusted with a rotating half-wave plate. Ablation was accomplished by irradiating the AFM tip while it was engaged with the surface in tapping mode at a height of approximately 15 nm. A flattened silver wire positioned ~300 µm above the sample surface was used to capture the ablated material. A schematic of the near-field setup is shown in Figure 1.

Mass spectra were obtained using a MALDI time-of-flight mass spectrometer (UltrafleXtreme, Bruker Corporation, Billerica, MA). Samples were prepared by washing the capture wire with 5 μL of a saturated solution of α-cyano-4-hydroxycinnamic acid (CHCA, Sigma-Aldrich, St. Louis, Missouri) matrix in a 50:50 (v/v) solution of acetonitrile (99.8%, EMD Chemicals, Gibbstown, New Jersey) and 0.1% aqueous trifluoroacetic acid (TFA, 99.0%, Fischer Scientific, Fairlawn, New Jersey). Blank mass spectra of the bare wire yielded silver and small silver cluster ions and matrix plus wire yielded only matrix ion peaks. The peptide and protein standards (Sigma) were used as received. The sample in matrix solution was deposited on a stainless steel MALDI target (MTP 384 massive, Bruker Corporation, Billerica, MA). Mass spectra were obtained from an average of 500 laser shots using the 355 nm laser in the MALDI instrument. The laser spot diameter in the MALDI mass spectrometer was 100 μm and 500 shots were used to obtain the spectrum from each spot. To enhance the signal, exhaustive sampling of the deposit performed and the sum of the spectra is reported.

RESULTS AND DISCUSSION

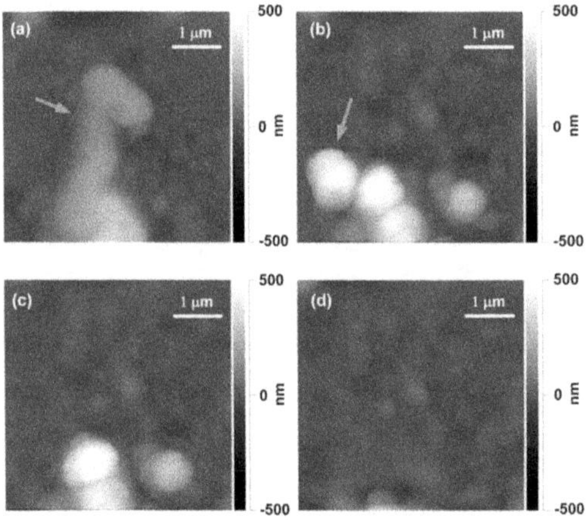

Figure 2. AFM images of (a) 5 μm x 5 μm region of a deposited peptide mixture; the light region indicated by the arrow corresponds to the sample; (b) material removal is observed after ablation from the top half of the sample and the arrow indicates the material targeted for ablation; (c) removal of some of the remaining material; (d) sample region after complete material removal.

The goal in this work was to compare the efficiency of ablation at 532 nm laser wavelength with that at 355 nm previously reported.[58] The working conditions were optimized for 532 nm ablation of peptides. The first sample analyzed was a peptide mixture created by mixing four peptide solutions. Figure 2a shows the sample region scanned prior to ablation. The ablation was performed with a single laser shot at every ablation spot with a laser fluence of 1 kJ/m^2. After selective ablation of material removal from the top half of the targeted sample region, the sample appeared shown in Figure 2b. Additional material was selectively ablated and captured and the resulting images are shown in Figure 2c and 2d. The ablated materials are captured on the flattened Ag wire and analyzed by MALDI.

The material captured from four regions similar to that shown in Figure 2 were dissolved in 5 µL of CHCA matrix solution by extensive washing of the tip of the Ag wire. Then, the solution was deposited on the MALDI target for analysis. Figure 3 shows the mass spectrum of the ablated and captured peptide mixture. As shown in Figure 3, peaks at *m/z* of 757, 1046.6, 1296.6 and 1759.1 were observed for bradykinin fragments (1-7), angiotensin II, angiotensin I and renin substrate, respectively. Due to the low sample quantity, spectrum was obtained by exhaustive sampling of the MALDI target spot. The intensities of the peptide peaks do not match the peptide concentration in solution, particularly for bradykinin (1-7), which has a low signal. This is most likely due to separation of the peptides on the target prior to near-field ablation and capture.

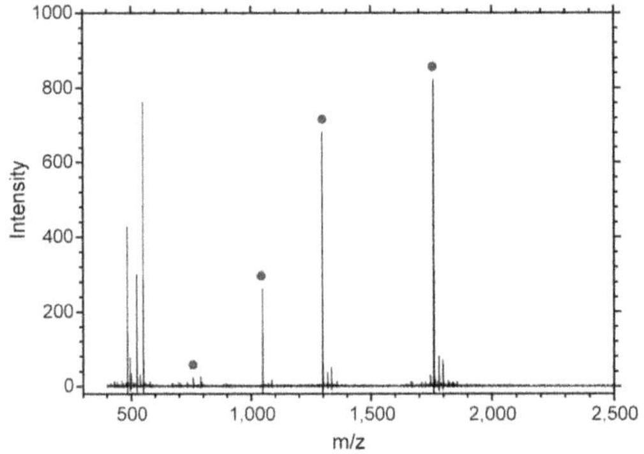

Figure 3. Mass spectrum of a peptide mixture ablated and captured for MALDI analysis; the circles indicate the protonated peptide peaks.

In previous work with a 355 nm ablation laser,[58] the protein insulin was detected by near-field laser ablation. Similar experiments were performed in this work at a 532 nm laser wavelength. A thin film of insulin sample was prepared and ablation was performed. Figure 4 shows a representative image of an ablation crater obtained on the insulin thin film at 532 nm wavelength. With a single laser shot at a fluence of 1.3 kJ/m^2, it was possible to create ablation crater 1 µm in diameter and 400 nm in depth. Comparable spots using the 355 nm laser wavelength required on the order of 30 laser shots.

A MALDI mass spectrum of insulin obtained using 532 nm tip-enhanced laser ablation transfer is shown in Figure 5. The protein was transferred from 10 individual ablation spots, dissolved in matrix, and deposited on the MALDI target for analysis. The most intense peak in the mass spectrum is the protonated insulin molecule at *m/z* 5734. The doubly protonated insulin molecule is also observed at *m/z* 2868. In contrast to laser ablation transfer at 355 nm,[58] additional fragmentation peaks were not observed. The gentler material transfer at 532 nm as compared to 355 nm is attributed to the stronger plasmon absorption expected at this wavelength for the 30 nm gold coated AFM tip.[60]

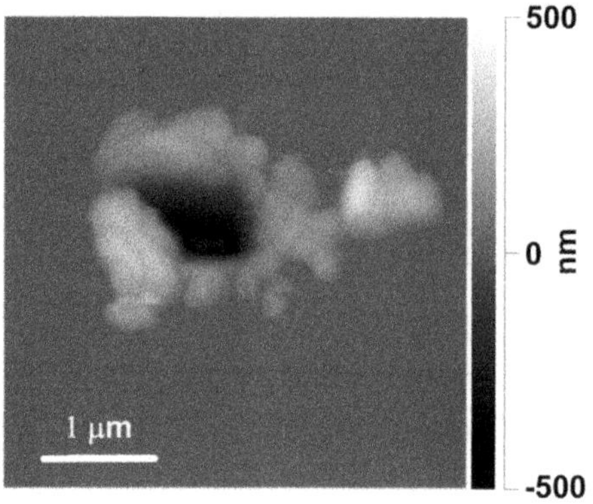

Figure 4. Insulin ablation crater from 532 nm tip-enhanced laser ablation.

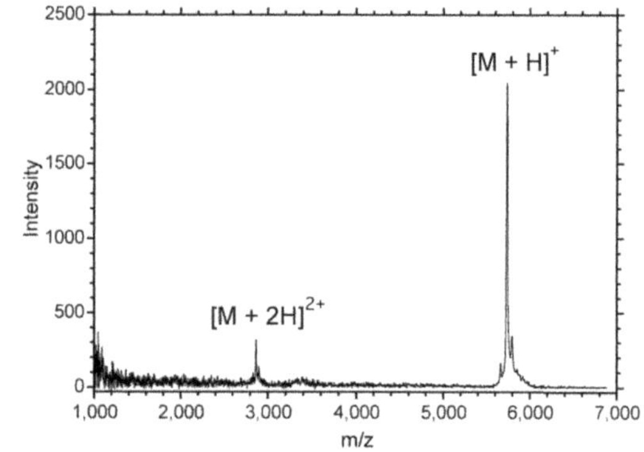

Figure 5. MALDI mass spectrum of the protein insulin using AFM tip enhanced ablation and capture.

One of the most significant differences between 532 nm near-field laser ablation and 355 nm ablation is the laser polarization dependence. At 355 nm it was found that s-polarization with the laser electric field parallel to the sample surface gave the best ablation.[58] The optimum polarization for apertureless near-field ablation is expected to be perpendicular to the surface and parallel to the optical antenna axis.[60] Figure 6 shows AFM images of craters formed with s-polarization (Figure 6a) and p-polarization (Figure 6b). A cross-section plot of the craters is shown in Figure 6c. With 532 nm radiation, p-polarization is favored and removes more than five times as much material as s-polarization, consistent with a near-field effect.

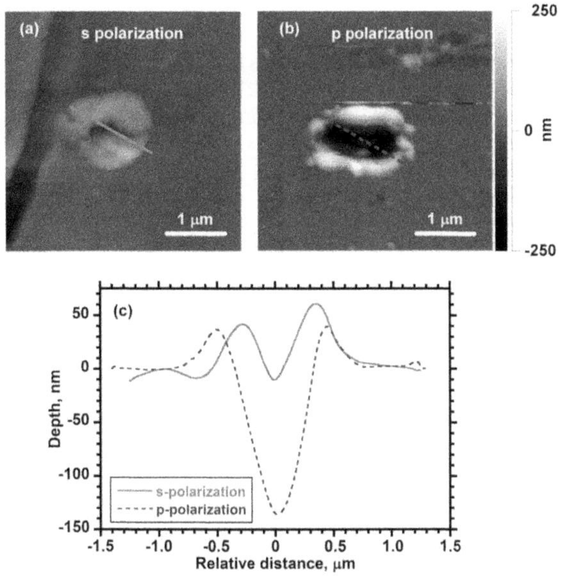

Figure 6. Near-field laser ablation of an insulin thin film with laser polarization a) perpendicular and b) parallel to the tip axis with c) crater depth profile.

CONCLUSIONS

In this work, 532 nm nanosecond pulsed laser tip enhanced laser ablation and capture was investigated as a means of transferring biomolecules from surfaces at submicrometer spatial resolution for mass spectrometry analysis. It was found that 532 nm ablation is significantly more efficient than UV ablation using a 355 nm laser.[58] More significantly, it was observed that the optimum laser polarization was p-polarization (perpendicular to the surface and parallel to the AFM tip). These observations are consistent with near-field ablation at a wavelength near the surface plasmon resonance of the gold AFM tip. The ablation transfer mechanism appears to be similar to that observed previously for gold quantum dot MALDI matrix.[61] The laser wavelength is resonant with the gold AFM tip, and this is sufficient for transfer of protein molecules from the surface with no fragmentation. Experiments are underway that will use near-field ablation capture to develop a system in which individual cells or tissue sections are imaged, ablated for MS analysis by ESI or MALDI, and then inspected by AFM after ablation.

ACKNOWLEDGMENTS

This work was supported by the National Institutes of Health Grant Number R21DA035504. The authors thank R. Shetty and K. Kjoller of Anasys for helpful discussions.

REFERENCES

1. K. Chughtai and R. M. Heeren, *Chem. Rev.* **110**, 3237-3277 (2010).
2. J. L. Norris and R. M. Caprioli, *Chem. Rev.* **113**, 2309-2342 (2013).
3. M. M. Gessel, J. L. Norris and R. M. Caprioli, *J. Proteomics* **107**, 71-82 (2014).
4. R. M. A. Heeren, *Int. J. Mass Spectrom.* **in press DOI:10.1016/j.ijms.2014.04.021**, 1-9 (2014).
5. L. McDonnell and R. M. Heeren, *Mass Spectrom. Rev.* **26**, 606-643 (2007).
6. S. S. Rubakhin and J. V. Sweedler, *Methods Mol. Biol.* **656**, 21-49 (2010).
7. E. R. Amstalden van Hove, D. F. Smith and R. M. A. Heeren, *J. Chrom. A* **1217**, 3946-3954 (2010).
8. A. Walch, S. Rauser, S. Deininger and H. Höfler, *Histochem. Cell Biol.* **130**, 421-434 (2008).
9. K. L. Moore, E. Lombi, F.-J. Zhao and C. R. M. Grovenor, *Anal. Bioanal. Chem.* **402**, 3263-3273 (2012).
10. M. K. Passarelli, A. G. Ewing and N. Winograd, *Anal. Chem.* **85**, 2231-2238 (2013).
11. C. Bich, D. Touboul and A. Brunelle, *Mass Spectrom. Rev.*, 442-451 (2014).
12. S. A. Schwartz and R. M. Caprioli, *Meth. Mol. Biol.* **656**, 3-19 (2010).
13. K. Schwamborn and R. Caprioli, *Mol. Oncol.* **4**, 529-538 (2010).
14. A. Zavalin, J. Yang and R. Caprioli, *J. Am. Soc. Mass Spectrom.* **24**, 1153-1156 (2013).
15. A. Zavalin, J. Yang, A. Haase, A. Holle and R. Caprioli, *J. Am. Soc. Mass Spectrom.*, 1-4 (2014).
16. A. L. Dill, L. S. Eberlin, D. R. Ifa and R. G. Cooks, *Chem. Comm.* **47**, 2741-2746 (2011).
17. C. Wu, A. L. Dill, L. S. Eberlin, R. G. Cooks and D. R. Ifa, *Mass Spectrom. Rev.* **32**, 218-243 (2013).
18. R. G. Cooks, Z. Ouyang, Z. Takats and J. Wiseman, *Science* **311**, 1566-1570 (2006).
19. G. J. Van Berkel, S. P. Pasilis and O. Ovchinnikova, *J. Mass Spectrom.* **43**, 1161-1180 (2008).
20. G. J. Van Berkel, A. D. Sanchez and J. M. E. Quirke, *Anal. Chem.* **74**, 6216-6223 (2002).
21. M. S. Elnaggar, C. Barbier and G. J. Van Berkel, *J. Am. Soc. Mass Spectrom.* **22**, 1157-1166 (2011).
22. P. J. Roach, J. Laskin and A. Laskin, *Analyst* **135**, 2233 (2010).
23. B. Shrestha and A. Vertes, *Anal. Chem.* **81**, 8265-8271 (2009).
24. P. Nemes and A. Vertes, *Meth. Mol. Biol.* **656**, 159-171 (2010).
25. A. S. Galhena, G. A. Harris, L. Nyadong, K. K. Murray and F. M. Fernandez, *Anal. Chem.* **82**, 2178-2181 (2010).
26. J. T. Shelley, S. J. Ray and G. M. Hieftje, *Anal. Chem.* **80**, 8308-8313 (2008).
27. V. V. Laiko, M. A. Baldwin and A. L. Burlingame, *Anal. Chem.* **72**, 652-657 (2000).
28. V. V. Laiko, N. I. Taranenko, V. D. Berkout, M. A. Yakshin, C. R. Prasad, H. S. Lee and V. M. Doroshenko, *J. Am. Soc. Mass Spectrom.* **13**, 354-361 (2002).
29. Y. Li, B. Shrestha and A. Vertes, *Anal. Chem.* **79**, 523-532 (2007).
30. Y. Coello, A. D. Jones, T. C. Gunaratne and M. Dantus, *Anal. Chem.* **82**, 2753-2758 (2010).
31. A. L. Gray, *Analyst* **110**, 551-556 (1985).
32. R. E. Russo, X. Mao, H. Liu, J. Gonzalez and S. Mao, *Talanta* (2002).
33. R. E. Russo, X. Mao, J. J. Gonzalez, V. Zorba and J. Yoo, *Anal. Chem.* **85**, 6162-6177 (2013).

34. J. J. Coon, K. J. McHale and W. W. Harrison, *Rapid Commun. Mass Spectrom.* **16**, 681-685 (2002).
35. L. Nyadong, A. S. Galhena and F. M. Fernandez, *Anal. Chem.* **81**, 7788-7794 (2009).
36. A. Vaikkinen, B. Shrestha, T. J. Kauppila, A. Vertes and R. Kostiainen, *Anal. Chem.* **84**, 1630-1636 (2012).
37. J. Shiea, M.-Z. Huang, H.-J. Hsu, C.-Y. Lee, C.-H. Yuan, I. Beech and J. Sunner, *Rapid Commun. Mass Spectrom.* **19**, 3701-3704 (2005).
38. M. Z. Huang, S. S. Jhang, C. N. Cheng, S. C. Cheng and J. Shiea, *Analyst* **135**, 759-766 (2010).
39. S.-G. Park and K. K. Murray, *J. Am. Soc. Mass Spectrom.* **22**, 1352-1362 (2011).
40. O. S. Ovchinnikova, V. Kertesz and G. J. Van Berkel, *Anal. Chem.* **83**, 1874-1878 (2011).
41. M. Lorenz, O. S. Ovchinnikova and G. J. Van Berkel, *Rapid Commun. Mass Spectrom.* **28**, 1312-1320 (2014).
42. S.-G. Park and K. K. Murray, *J. Mass Spectrom.* **47**, 1322-1326 (2012).
43. S.-G. Park and K. K. Murray, *Rapid Commun. Mass Spectrom.* **27**, 1673-1680 (2013).
44. F. Hillenkamp, E. Unsold, R. Kaufmann and R. Nitsche, *Appl. Phys.* **8**, 341-348 (1975).
45. F. Hillenkamp, E. Unsold, R. Kaufmann and R. Nitsche, *Nature* **256**, 119-120 (1975).
46. B. Spengler and M. Hubert, *J. Am. Soc. Mass Spectrom.* **13**, 735-748. (2002).
47. A. Römpp, K. C. Schäfer, S. Guenther, Z. Wang, M. Köstler, A. Leisner, C. Paschke, T. Schramm and B. Spengler, *Anal. Bioanal. Chem.* **405**, 6959-6968 (2013).
48. M. R. Savina and K. R. Lykke, *Anal. Chem.* **69**, 3741-3746 (1997).
49. J. Behm, J. Hemminger and K. R. Lykke, *Anal. Chem.* **68**, 713-719 (1996).
50. S. L. Luxembourg, T. H. Mize, L. A. McDonnell and R. M. A. Heeren, *Anal. Chem.* **76**, 5339-5344 (2004).
51. S. Luxembourg, L. McDonnell, T. Mize and R. M. Heeren, *J. Proteome Res.* **4**, 671-673 (2005).
52. J. Soltwisch, G. Göritz, J. H. Jungmann, A. Kiss, D. F. Smith, S. R. Ellis and R. M. A. Heeren, *Anal. Chem.* **86**, 321-325 (2014).
53. D. A. Kossakovski, S. D. O'Connor, M. Widmer, J. D. Baldeschwieler and J. L. Beauchamp, *Ultramicrosc.* (1998).
54. J. A. Bradshaw, O. S. Ovchinnikova, K. A. Meyer and D. E. Goeringer, *Rapid Commun. Mass. Spectrom,* **23**, 3781-3786 (2009).
55. R. Stockle, P. Setz, V. Deckert, T. Lippert, A. Wokaun and R. Zenobi, *Anal. Chem.* **73**, 1399-1402 (2001).
56. T. A. Schmitz, G. Gamez, P. D. Setz, L. Zhu and R. Zenobi, *Anal. Chem.* **80**, 6537-6544 (2008).
57. M. V. Zoriy and J. S. Becker, *Rapid Commun. Mass. Spectrom,* **23**, 23-30 (2009).
58. S. Ghorai, C. A. Seneveratne and K. K. Murray, *J. Am. Soc. Mass Spectrom.* **26**, 63-70 (2015).
59. L. Zhu, G. Gamez, T. Schmitz, F. Krumeich and R. Zenobi, *Anal. Bioanal. Chem.* **396**, 163-172 (2010).
60. L. Novotny, *Prog. Optics* **50**, 137-184 (2007).
61. J. A. McLean, K. A. Stumpo and D. H. Russell, *J. Am. Chem. Soc.* **127**, 5304-5305 (2005).

Mater. Res. Soc. Symp. Proc. Vol. 1754 © 2015 Materials Research Society
DOI: 10.1557/opl.2015.257

Practical Realization of Apertureless Scanning Near-field Optical Microscopy Using Hybrid Mode Atomic Force Microscopy

Sergey Zayats[1,3], John Alexander[1], Sergei Magonov[1] and Dmitry Kazantsev[2]
[1]NT-MDT Development Inc. 7910 S. Kyrene Rd. Tempe 85284 USA
[2]Institute for Theoretical and Experimental Physics, 25 Bolshaya Cheremushkinskaya Str., Moscow 117218, Russia
[3]Moscow Institute of Physics and Technology, 9 Institutskiy per., Dolgoprudny, Moscow Region, 141700, Russia

ABSTRACT

The local detection of optical response at the sub-wavelength scale on a materials' surface is an invaluable characterization capability of apertureless scanning near-field optical microscopy (ASNOM). The technique is traditionally realized in amplitude modulation (AM) AFM mode. We have expanded this method by employing an alternative scheme for the detection of the near-field and far-field responses with the use of Hybrid (HD) AFM mode. In HD mode the sample is brought to the intermittent contact with the tip in a periodic oscillation at a frequency (1-2 kHz) much smaller than the probe resonance. In every oscillation cycle the probe deflection to a set-point value is used for surface profiling. For optical measurements the metal coated AFM tip was top-illuminated by visible laser. Simultaneously with surface profiling the light scattered from tip-sample junction was collected by a sensitive photomultiplier (PMT). The homodyne optical signal detection scheme was applied to discriminate near- and far-field optical components. Our method was verified by the studies of various materials (semiconductors, metals, polymers, etc.). The presented results show that the contrast of ASNOM images can be used for compositional mapping of heterogeneous systems.

INTRODUCTION

ASNOM [1] is a powerful tool for optical surface characterization of materials because it provides lateral resolution down to a few nanometers [2,3] which is well beyond the diffraction limit. This method is based on the detection of scattered light arising from evanescent field interaction between a sample surface and the sharp tip of the conductive AFM. Practically, the dipole at the tip apex is periodically perturbed by the contact with a sample surface and the scattered light carries the signature of the optical properties of the sample. Different experimental setups are applied for extraction of a small near-field contribution "contaminated" by the strong far-field background signal. ASNOM technique with different excitation laser wavelength regions (visible, IR, THz, etc.) [4,5,10] was successfully used in studies of different multicomponent materials [6-8,11] based on semiconductors, metals, polymers, bio-materials [3,9].

Typically ASNOM applications are performed in AM AFM Mode. In this operation the tip-sample interaction takes place at the resonance frequency f_{tip} of the AFM probe [1] which is usually in the 50-300 kHz range. It has been commonly accepted [13–16] that a strong non-linearity of the tip-surface near-field interaction dependency is reflected in the higher harmonics nf_{tip} of the probe resonance [5,8,12]. Detection of higher order harmonics implies the need of costly high-frequency range detectors. In addition shorter signals' acquisition rates impose time limitations on the processing algorithms and signal analysis.

In contrast to conventional high frequency ASNOM operations, the use of ASNOM/HD approach requires measurements at much lower frequencies. This facilitates the better signal-to-noise ratio and improved sensitivity. Furthermore, the increased optical signal accumulation time provides a more flexible choice for signal analysis. Particularly, the dependence of optical response on tip-sample separation in every point of a chosen sample area can mapped during real-time scanning and analyzed by a proper theoretical model. This is better than the simplified analysis based on the single frequency lock-in amplifiers detection of higher harmonics [2, 17, 18]. One additional analysis possibility is the use of the Fourier transform and its proceeds. In practice, we have performed the detection of optical signal by these different approaches on a variety of materials (semiconductors, metals, polymers, etc.) and the results confirmed the high-spatial resolution of optical detection. Implementation of ASNOM/HD approach enhances the capabilities of comprehensive studies of materials at small scales as we demonstrate by the following examples.

EXPERIMENTAL PART

The experiments were performed using NTEGRA Spectra Upright microscope (NT-MDT). For optical excitation of the sample 532 nm and 632.8 nm (HeNe) lasers were used. Gold coated top access probe (VIT_P/IR/Au, NT-MDT) was illuminated with the laser through a 100x, 0.7 NA objective lens (Mitutoyo) from the top. Laser positioning on the cantilever was done by piezo-scanning mirror with capacitance sensors. Reflected light was collected with the same objective and focused onto Hamamatsu PMT detector.

Cantilever was approached to the surface using soft approach algorithm in which the cantilever engage is controlled by the variation of phase of its oscillations. AFM topography measurements were performed in HD AFM Mode. 1.5 kHz vertical oscillations were provided to the sample in every scan point. When location of interest was found on the sample surface, excitation laser was aligned on the end of the cantilever by the scanning piezo mirror with capacitance sensors. During the alignment procedure we collected optical force-volume maps of total, far- and near-field optical signals in every scan point. Optical curves (Figure 1) which reflect optical response when the tip is approached to the sample surface and retracted from it, collected for one cycle of sample oscillation were recorded.

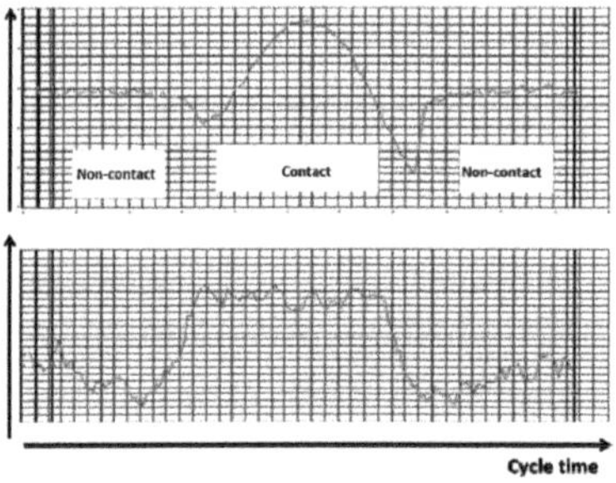

Figure 1. The temporal Deflection curve (top) and photomultiplier signal (bottom) during the cycle of Hybrid Mode operating at 1.5 kHz frequency.

Based on the shape of optical approach curve laser is placed on specific position on the cantilever to get the steepest slope on the curve. Collected optical signal is detected and processed by two approaches. Lock-in signal detection is done by means of Px AFM controller. In the mean time the use of HD controller enabled processing of total optical signal by means of FFT during the oscillation cycle as result giving single harmonics of oscillation. Furthermore, the use of HD mode enabled to record the difference between the total optical signal and the optical signal collected when the sample is in contact with the tip. The results collected on different types of samples illustrating the mentioned approach are represented below.

RESULTS AND DISCUSSION

The applications of ASNOM/HD are illustrated by the images obtained in studies of semiconductors, metals and polymer materials. All the scan frames are 512x512 pixels and obtained with a regular AFM scan rate (~ 12 minutes for the frame). The same AFM tip could be used for investigation of several samples producing multiple data frames with no quality compromise. In the first example, we are considering the results of the ASNOM/HD measurements of CMOS (complimentary metal-oxide semiconductor) structure, which was prepared in a cleaved-edge geometry, are combined with the examination of the same sample area with single-pass Kelvin force microscopy (KFM) mode and with HD mode, Figure 2.

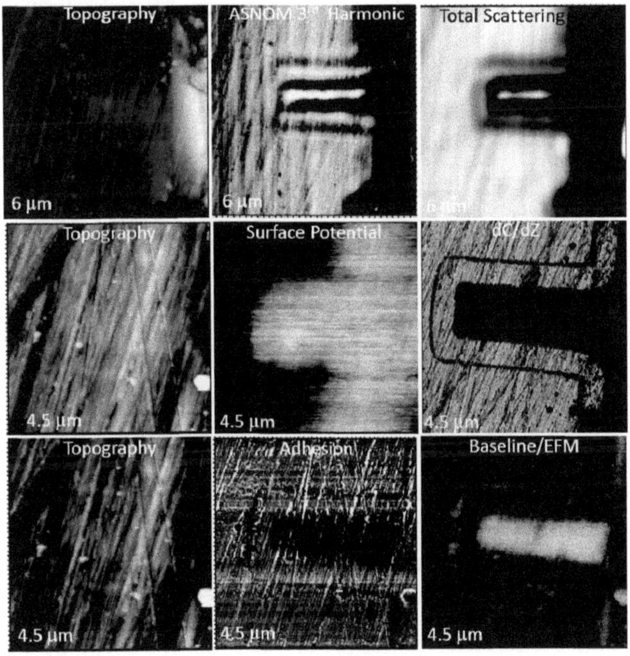

Figure 2. Images of CMOS structure in different modes: top – in ASNOM/HD; middle – in single-pass KFM; bottom – in HD mode with 3V bias voltage.

Such multi-mode analysis of the samples is the basis of comprehensive material characterization. In all three modes, the topography images show a relatively smooth surface with multiple polished grooves and few contamination particles. The total scattering map exhibits spatial intensity variations of the signal comprising the far-field and near-field components whereas the map of 3rd harmonic can be assumed exclusively to the near-field effect. In general, both maps (Figure 2, top) reflect the doped structure, which is not distinguished in the height images, yet the spatial resolution of the near-field map is much higher. The CMOS structure is also reflected but with a different pattern in the surface potential and capacitance gradient (dC/dZ) maps registered in KFM operation (Figure 2, middle). A presence of electrostatically active locations on the sample surface can be detected in the HD mode by recording the adhesive map or the variations of the baseline – the locations when the conducting probe is the non-contact parts of the oscillation cycle (Figure 2, bottom).

Recognition of individual constituents in the multi-component materials is one of the main AFM applications and the related images exhibit the contrast that reflects the variations of the local properties of the constituents. In incomplete metal alloys the compositional mapping can be provided by KFM because the difference of work functions of metals are visualized in the surface potential maps. We have examined an alloy of Bi and Sn and an optical view on the tip and a sample surface is shown in Figure 3 (left). The optical contrast reflects the difference of dielectric properties of these metals. The images of a smaller area show the sample topography and the map of 2nd harmonic with the later having a binary contrast corresponding to the alloy's composition.

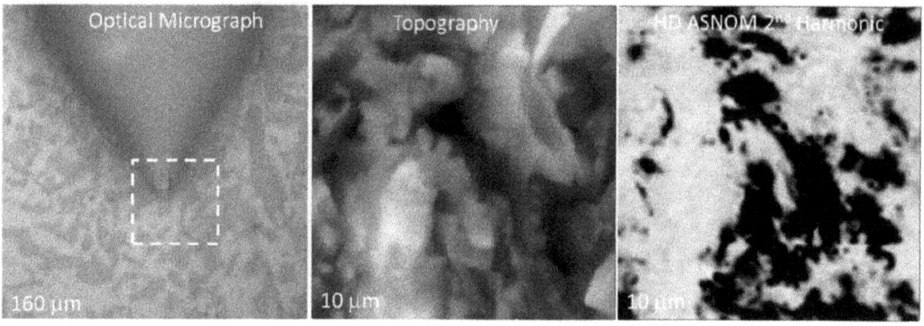

Figure 3. Left – optical micrograph of incomplete Bi/Sn alloy; middle and right – images in ASNOM/HD mode obtained within an 40-µm area marked with a dashed square in the optical micrograph.

Another sample with a binary composition was a blend of polystyrene (PS) and polybutadiene (PBD) as a film on Si substrate. The related images are shown in Figure 4. The contrast variations in all ASNOM images are consistent with the composition of the blend. In a different studies with AFM/Raman microscope we have demonstrated that the elevated circular domains seen on the topography image are enriched in PS and the matrix in between the domains is enriched in PBD. The different contrast observed in the ASNOM images, which are presenting the near-field scattering effects, can be explained by the variations of the polymers' dielectric properties in the visible range.

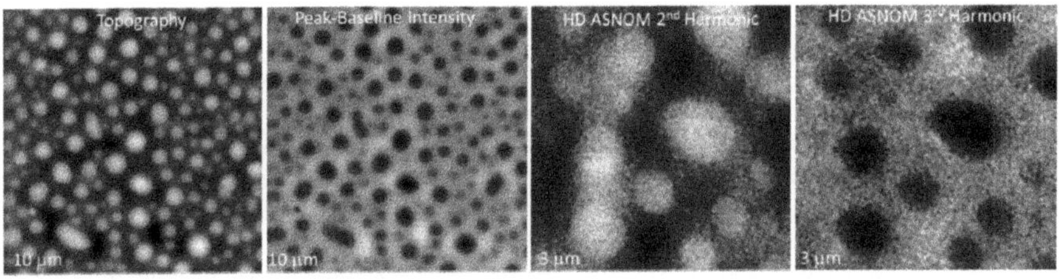

Figure 4. Topography and ASNOM images of PS/PBD blend on Si substrate, which were taken at different scales. The peak-baseline map present the contrast mostly related to near-filed scattering.

In the earlier paper [19] the results obtained in visible ASNOM on Au/Si/PS composition were interpreted in such way that is also applicable to the analysis of the data in Figures 3 and 4.

CONCLUSIONS

The visible ASNOM operation in HD mode was introduced and verified on several practical examples. The maps of the optical near-field response, which were extracted from the overall scattering signals, exhibit the contrast reflecting a composition of binary systems and doped semiconductor structures. The origin of this contrast is tentatively explained by variations of dielectric properties of the components in the visible range. The comparison of the ASNOM imaging with the result of other techniques which are used for compositional mapping of heterogeneous systems shows that this local optical technique becomes a valuable addition for the comprehensive characterization of materials.

REFERENCES

[1] F. Zenhausern, M. P. O'Boyle, and H. K. Wickramasinghe, "Apertureless near-field optical microscope," Applied Physics Letters 65, 1623–1625 (1994).
[2] F. Zenhausern, Y. Martin, and H. K. Wickramasinghe, "Scanning interferometric apertureless microscopy: Optical imaging at 10 angstrom resolution," Science 269, 1083–1085 (1995).
[3] Y. Martin, F. Zenhausern, and H. K. Wickramasinghe, "Scattering spectroscopy of molecules at nanometer resolution," Applied Physics Letters 68, 2475–2477 (1996).
[4] B. Knoll, F. Keilmann, A. Kramer, and R. Guckenberger, "Contrast of microwave near-field microscopy," Applied Physics Letters 70, 2667–2669 (1997).
[5] R. Hillenbrand, B. Knoll, and F. Keilmann, "Pure optical contrast in scattering-type scanning near-field microscopy," Journal of Microscopy 202, 77–83 (2001).
[6] B. Knoll and F. Keilmann, "Near-field probing of vibrational absorption for chemical microscopy," Nature 399, 134–137 (1999).
[7] G.Wurtz, R. Bachelot, and P. Royer, "A reflection-mode apertureless scanning near-field optical microscope developed from a commercial scanning probe microscope," Review of Scientific Instruments 69, 1735–1743 (1998).
[8] Markus Brehm, Heinrich G. Frey, Reinhard Guckenberger, Rainer Hillenbrand, Dimitri Kazantsev, Fritz Keilmann, Nenad Ocelic and Thomas Taubner, "Consolidating Apertureless SNOM", Journal of the Korean Physical Society, Vol. 47, August 2005, pp. S80↑ S85

[9] M. Brehm, T. Taubner, R. Hillenbrand, and F. Keilmann, "Infrared spectroscopic mapping of single nanoparticles and viruses at nanoscale resolution," Nano Letters 6, 13071310 (2006).
[10] Fritz Keilmann, Andreas J. Huber, Rainer Hillenbrand, "Nanoscale Conductivity Contrast by Scattering-Type Near-Field Optical Microscopy in the Visible, Infrared and THz Domains", J Infrared Milli Terahz Waves (2009) 30:1255–1268
[11] Andreas J. Huber, Dmitry Kazantsev, Fritz Keilmann, Jesper Wittborn and Rainer Hillenbrand, "Simultaneous IR Material Recognition and Conductivity Mapping by Nanoscale Near-Field Microscopy", Advanced Materials, 19, 2209-2212 (2007)
[12] M. Labardi, S. Patan`e, and M. Allegrini, "Artifact-free near-field optical imaging by apertureless microscopy," Applied Physics Letters 77, 621–623 (2000).
[13] L. Novotny and N. van Hulst, "Antennas for light," Nature Photonics 5, 83–90 (2011).
[14] R. Esteban, R. Vogelgesang, J. Dorfm¨uller, A. Dmitriev, C. Rockstuhl, C. Etrich, and K. Kern, "Direct near-field optical imaging of higher order plasmonic resonances," Nano Letters 8, 3155–3159 (2008).
[15] J. M. Stiegler, Y. Abate, A. Cvitkovic, Y. E. Romanyuk, A. J. Huber, S. R. Leone, and R. Hillenbrand, "Nanoscale infrared absorption spectroscopy of individual nanoparticles enabled by scattering-type near-field microscopy," ACS Nano 5, 6494–6499 (2011).
[16] M. Esslinger, J. Dorfm¨uller, W. Khunsin, R. Vogelgesang, and K. Kern, "Background-free imaging of plasmonic structures with cross-polarized apertureless scanning near-field optical microscopy," Review of Scientific Instruments 83, 033704 (2012).
[17] N. Maghelli, M. Labardi, S. Patan`e, F. Irrera, and M. Allegrini, "Optical near-field harmonic demodulation in apertureless microscopy," Journal of Microscopy 202, 84–93 (2001).
[18] A. Bek, R. Vogelgesang, and K. Kern, "Apertureless scanning near field optical microscope with sub-10 nm resolution," Review of Scientific Instruments 77, 043703 (2006).
[19] T. Taubner, R. Hillenbrand and F. Keilmann, "Performance of visible and mid-infrared scattering-type near-field optical microscopy", Journal of Microscopy, Vol. 210, Pt 3 June 2003, pp. 311-314.

Mater. Res. Soc. Symp. Proc. Vol. 1754 © 2015 Materials Research Society
DOI: 10.1557/opl.2015.255

Dynamic photo-induced force microscopy

Junghoon Jahng[1] and Eric O. Potma[2]
[1]Department of Physics and Astronomy, University of California at Irvine, Irvine CA 92697, U.S.A.
[2]Department of Chemistry, University of California at Irvine, Irvine CA 92697, U.S.A.

ABSTRACT

We provide a general description of the operating principle of the photo-induced force microscope (PiFM), which probes the optically induced changes in the dipolar interactions between a sharp polarizable tip and the sample, in terms of classical fields and forces. We rigorously calculate the photo-induced force behavior and compare the predicted profile with experimental results obtained from a gold nanowire.

INTRODUCTION

Recent developments in combining optical excitations in molecules with mechanical force detection seek to add chemical selectivity to atomic force microscopy (AFM). A successful example in this category of techniques is photo-induced force microscopy (PiFM), which probes the optically induced changes in the dipolar interactions between a sharp polarizable tip and the sample [1, 2]. In this paper, we provide a general theoretical description of the characteristics of the force-distance curve in PiFM, and compare the predicted profile with experimental results obtained from a gold nanowire. Our study identifies the distance regimes in which attractive gradient forces are dominant and points out under which conditions molecular selective signals are optimized.

THEORY

We consider the dynamics of the cantilever-tip system in the presence of the photo-induced force F_{PiF} [1]. The cantilever motion is modeled as a set of independent point-mass harmonic oscillators, with motion confined to the z coordinate only [3, 4]. In practice, two mechanical resonances are of relevance to the PiFM experiment, namely the first- and second-order mechanical eigenmode of the cantilever-tip system. The first mechanical resonance is excited by the external driving force F_1 with angular frequency ω_{01}, whereas the second-order resonance at ω_{02} is actively driven by F_{PiF}. Since the beam intensity is modulated at $I_0(1+\cos(\omega_2 t))$ by using an acousto-optic modulator (AOM), where I_0 is the incident beam intensity, then the photo-induced force is acting on a cantilever with $F_{PiF}(1+\cos(\omega_2 t))$ at the second-order resonance [1]. In addition, the cantilever tip is subject to the interaction force F_{int}, which includes all relevant van der Waals, electrostatic, magnetic, chemical, and Casimir forces. In this model, when we assume the motion of a cantilever is a superposition of eigenmodes, the equations of motion for the displacement of the first- $z_1(t)$ and 2nd-order $z_2(t)$ mode are found as

$$m\ddot{z}_1 + b_1\dot{z}_1 + k_1 z_1 = F_1\cos(\omega_1 t) + F_{\text{int}}(z(t)) + F_{PiF}(z(t)), \qquad (1)$$

$$m\ddot{z}_2 + b_2\dot{z}_2 + k_2 z_2 = F_{PiF}(1+\cos(\omega_2 t)) + F_{\text{int}}(z(t)), \qquad (2)$$

where m is the effective mass of the cantilever; k_i and b_i are, respectively, the force constant and the damping coefficient of the *i*-th eigenmode [3, 4]. Note that the resonance frequency ω_i and the external driving force F_1 can be expressed as $\omega_i = k_i / m$ and $F_1 = k_1 A_{01} / Q_1$, respectively, where A_{01} is the free oscillation amplitude of the driven first eigenmode of the cantilever, and Q_i is the quality factor of the *i*-th eigenmode. In addition, the damping coefficient can be expressed as $b_i = m\omega_i / Q_i$. The instantaneous tip-surface distance is represented by

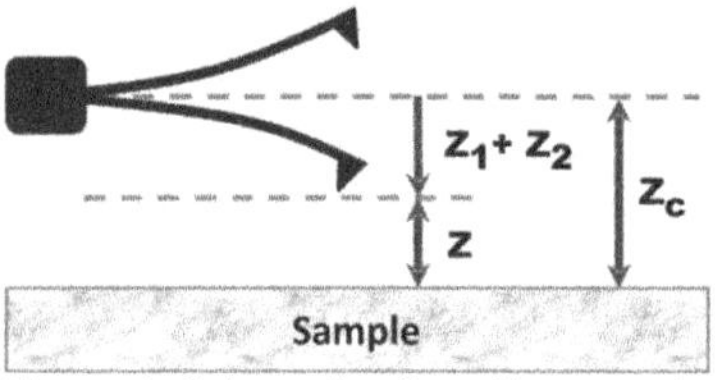

Figure 1. Schematic of cantilever motion

$$\begin{aligned} z(t) &= z_c + z_1(t) + z_2(t) + O(\varepsilon) \\ &\approx z_c + A_1\sin(\omega_1 t + \theta_1) + A_2\sin(\omega_2 t + \theta_2) + O(\varepsilon) \end{aligned} \qquad (3)$$

Where $z_c(t)$ is the equilibrium position of the cantilever, A_i is the amplitude and θ_i is the phase shift of the *i*-th eigenmode, and O(ε) is a term that carries the contribution of the other modes and harmonics [4]. In general, F_{int} is a nonlinear function of the tip-sample distance z and contains both conservative and dissipative (i.e., nonconservative) forces, $F_{\text{int}} = F_c(z) + F_{nc}$. The conservative term F_c, by definition, depends only on the distance z. For our description here, we assume that the nonconservative force can be written as $F_{nc} = -\Gamma(z)\dot{z}$ [5], where represents the effective damping coefficient of a given dissipative interaction. Since the $F_{PiF}(z)$ shows a z^{-4} dependence [1], the offset PiF can be included in the conservative force F_c as:

$$F_c(z) + F_{PiF}(z) + F_{nc} = \overline{F}_c(z) + F_{nc} = \overline{F}_{\text{int}}, \qquad (4)$$

where $\overline{F}_{\text{int}}$ is the effective tip-sample interaction force. Substituting Eq. (3) and Eq. (4) into Eqs. (1) and (2) by multiplying both sides of the resulting equation by $\sin(\omega_i t + \theta_i)$ and $\cos(\omega_i t + \theta_i)$, followed by an integration over the oscillation period, the following general relations for amplitude, phase, mechanical interaction force, and PiF are obtained:

$$(k_1 - m\omega_1^2)\frac{A_1}{2} = \frac{F_1}{2}\sin\theta_1 + \frac{1}{T}\int_0^T \overline{F}_{\text{int}}\sin(\omega_1 t + \theta_1)dt, \qquad (5)$$

$$\frac{b_1\omega_1 A_1}{2}=\frac{F_1}{2}\cos\theta_1+\frac{1}{T}\int_0^T \bar{F}_{\text{int}}\cos(\omega_1 t+\theta_1)dt, \tag{6}$$

$$(k_2-m\omega_2^2)\frac{A_2}{2}=\frac{1}{T}\int_0^T[\bar{F}_{\text{int}}+F_{PiF}\cos(\omega_2 t)]\sin(\omega_2 t+\theta_2)dt, \tag{7}$$

$$\frac{b_2\omega_2 A_2}{2}=\frac{1}{T}\int_0^T[\bar{F}_{\text{int}}+F_{PiF}\cos(\omega_2 t)]\cos(\omega_2 t+\theta_2)dt, \tag{8}$$

To simplify the description, we assume that the tip displacement is small such that the force at z can be obtained through a Taylor expansion of the force at the equilibrium position Z_c [5]. Under these conditions, the mechanical interaction force and the PiF can be expressed by

$$\bar{F}_{\text{int}}(z)=\bar{F}_c(z)-\Gamma(z)\dot{z}\ \approx \bar{F}_c(z_c)+\left.\frac{\partial \bar{F}_c(z)}{\partial z}\right|_{z_c}(z-z_c)-\Gamma(z_c)\dot{z} \tag{9}$$

$$F_{PiF}(z)\approx F_{PiF}(z_c)+\left.\frac{\partial F_{PiF}(z)}{\partial z}\right|_{z_c}(z-z_c) \tag{10}$$

By putting the Eqs. (9) - (10), including the relations $z-z_c=z_1+z_2$ and $\dot{z}(t)=\dot{z}_1(t)+\dot{z}_2(t)$ $=A_1\omega_1\cos(\omega_1 t+\theta_1)+A_2\omega_2\cos(\omega_2 t+\theta_2)$, into Eqs. (5) – Eqs. (8) the equations are recast as

$$(k_1-m\omega_1^2)\frac{A_1}{2}=\frac{F_1}{2}\sin\theta_1+\frac{1}{T}\int_0^T[\bar{F}_c(z_c)+\left.\frac{\partial \bar{F}_c(z)}{\partial z}\right|_{z_c}(A_1\sin(\omega_1 t+\theta_1)+A_2\sin(\omega_2 t+\theta_2))$$
$$-\Gamma(z_c)(A_1\omega_1\cos(\omega_1 t+\theta_1)+A_2\omega_2\cos(\omega_2 t+\theta_2))]\sin(\omega_1 t+\theta_1)dt \tag{11}$$

$$\frac{b_1\omega_1 A_1}{2}=\frac{F_1}{2}\cos\theta_1+\frac{1}{T}\int_0^T[\bar{F}_c(z_c)+\left.\frac{\partial \bar{F}_c(z)}{\partial z}\right|_{z_c}(A_1\sin(\omega_1 t+\theta_1)+A_2\sin(\omega_2 t+\theta_2))$$
$$-\Gamma(z_c)(A_1\omega_1\cos(\omega_1 t+\theta_1)+A_2\omega_2\cos(\omega_2 t+\theta_2))]\cos(\omega_1 t+\theta_1)dt \tag{12}$$

$$(k_2-m\omega_2^2)\frac{A_2}{2}=\frac{1}{T}\int_0^T[\bar{F}_c(z_c)+\left.\frac{\partial \bar{F}_c(z)}{\partial z}\right|_{z_c}(A_1\sin(\omega_1 t+\theta_1)+A_2\sin(\omega_2 t+\theta_2))$$
$$-\Gamma(z_c)(A_1\omega_1\cos(\omega_1 t+\theta_1)+A_2\omega_2\cos(\omega_2 t+\theta_2))+(F_{PiF}(z_c)+\left.\frac{\partial F_{PiF}(z)}{\partial z}\right|_{z_c}$$
$$\times(A_1\sin(\omega_1 t+\theta_1)+A_2\sin(\omega_2 t+\theta_2)))\cos(\omega_2 t)]\sin(\omega_2 t+\theta_2)dt \tag{13}$$

$$\frac{b_2\omega_2 A_2}{2}=\frac{1}{T}\int_0^T[(\bar{F}_c(z_c)+\left.\frac{\partial \bar{F}_c(z)}{\partial z}\right|_{z_c}(A_1\sin(\omega_1 t+\theta_1)+A_2\sin(\omega_2 t+\theta_2))$$
$$-\Gamma(z_c)(A_1\omega_1\cos(\omega_1 t+\theta_1)+A_2\omega_2\cos(\omega_2 t+\theta_2)))+(F_{PiF}(z_c)+\left.\frac{\partial F_{PiF}(z)}{\partial z}\right|_{z_c}$$
$$\times(A_1\sin(\omega_1 t+\theta_1)+A_2\sin(\omega_2 t+\theta_2)))\cos(\omega_2 t)]\cos(\omega_2 t+\theta_2)dt \tag{14}$$

The integration of Eq. (5)-Eq.(8) is calculated with the period $T = p_1 2\pi / \omega_1 = p_2 2\pi / \omega_2$ where p_1 and p_2 is integer. For this it is required that the eigenmode frequencies, ω_1 and ω_2, are commensurable; i.e., $\omega_2 / \omega_1 = p_2 / p_1$ for a certain pair of integers p_1 and p_2, this is always possible with high accuracy [4]. By time-averaging over one period, a set of integrals is obtained that take on the following form:

$$\frac{1}{T}\int_0^T [\sin(\omega_1 t+\theta_1)\times\sin(\omega_1 t+\theta_1)]dt = \frac{1}{2},\quad \frac{1}{T}\int_0^T [\sin(\omega_2 t+\theta_2)\times\sin(\omega_2 t+\theta_2)]dt = \frac{1}{2},$$
$$\frac{1}{T}\int_0^T [\cos(\omega_1 t+\theta_1)\times\cos(\omega_1 t+\theta_1)]dt = \frac{1}{2},\quad \frac{1}{T}\int_0^T [\cos(\omega_2 t+\theta_2)\times\cos(\omega_2 t+\theta_2)]dt = \frac{1}{2},$$
$$\frac{1}{T}\int_0^T [\sin(\omega_2 t+\theta_2)\times\cos(\omega_2 t)]dt = \frac{\sin\theta_2}{2},\quad \frac{1}{T}\int_0^T [\cos(\omega_2 t+\theta_2)\times\cos(\omega_2 t)]dt = \frac{\cos\theta_2}{2}.$$

By making use of the time integrals above, equations (11) – (14) can be simplified to:

$$(k_1 - m\omega_1^2)\frac{A_1}{2} = \frac{F_1}{2}\sin\theta_1 + \left.\frac{\partial \bar{F}_c(z)}{\partial z}\right|_{z_c}\frac{A_1}{2}, \tag{15}$$

$$\frac{b_1\omega_1 A_1}{2} = \frac{F_1}{2}\cos\theta_1 - \frac{1}{2}\Gamma(z_c)\omega_1 A_1, \tag{16}$$

$$(k_2 - m\omega_2^2)\frac{A_2}{2} = \frac{F_{PiF}}{2}\sin\theta_2 + \left.\frac{\partial \bar{F}_c(z)}{\partial z}\right|_{z_c}\frac{A_2}{2}, \tag{17}$$

$$\frac{b_2\omega_2 A_2}{2} = \frac{F_{PiF}}{2}\cos\theta_2 - \frac{1}{2}\Gamma(z_c)\omega_2 A_2 \tag{18}$$

By integrating Eq. (15), we retrieve the conservative force as:

$$\bar{F}_c(z_c) = \int_{z_c}^{\infty}[\frac{F_1}{A_1(z)}\sin\theta_1(z) - (k_1 - m\omega_1^2)]dz \tag{19}$$

With the help of Eq. (16), the non-conservative force can be derived as:

$$\Gamma(z_c) = \frac{F_1}{A_1(z_c)\omega_1}\cos\theta_1(z_c) - b_1 \tag{20}$$

By substituting Eq. (17) into Eq. (18) and using the trigonometric identity $\cos^2\theta + \sin^2\theta = 1$, the reconstructed F_{PiF} is found as:

$$|F_{PiF}(z_c)| = A_2(z_c)\sqrt{m^2(\bar{\omega}_2^2 - \omega_2^2)^2 + \bar{b}_2^2\omega_2^2}\,, \tag{21}$$

where $\bar{\omega}_2 = \sqrt{(k_2 - \left.\frac{\partial \bar{F}_c(z)}{\partial z}\right|_{z_c})/m}$ and $\bar{b}_2 = b_2 + \Gamma(z_c)$.

Eqs. (19)-(21) show that if A_1, A_2, θ_1 can be experimentally identified, the photo-induced force and the effective mechanical interaction force can be reconstructed.

DISCUSSION

We validate the theoretical description above with PiFM measurements on a gold nanowire. A 20 nm radius gold coated silicon tip whose f_{01}, Q_1, k_1 and f_{02}, Q_2, k_2 are 58.73kHz, 181.93, 1.61N/m and 372.41kHz, 561.36, 52.24N/m, respectively, is used in the experiement. The 200 fs pulsed laser beam with a center wavelength of 809 nm is focused to a glass microscope cover slide by an oil immersion objective NA = 1.40. The gold nanowire is electro-deposited on the glass cover slide with an average height of 25nm. Figure 2 shows the amplitude (a) and phase (b) of the first resonance and the amplitude of second resonance (c), which are recorded simultaneously while the tip is positioned on the gold nanowire. The amplitude of the second resonance A_2 shows the characteristic peak, followed by a shallow dip and a plateau at longer distances. At shorter tip-sample distances, A_2 settles at ~ 75 pm, as the tip enters the hard-contact mode, indicated by the blue data points. As expected, in this regime A_1 and θ_1 remain invariant. In this region the thermal expansion of sample can be characterized. Figure 2(d) depicts the reconstructed force from the measured amplitude and phase curves (black squares). The reconstructed force curve can be fitted by $|F_{PiF}(z_c)| = \left| -\frac{\beta}{z_c^4} + F_{sc} \right|$ from Ref. [1], which is shown by the red line in Figure 2(d). Based on the fit, an estimated value for the scattering force can be extracted as F_{sc} = 6.13 pN, and the gradient force pre-factor β is found as $2.26\times10^{-40} N\cdot m^4$.

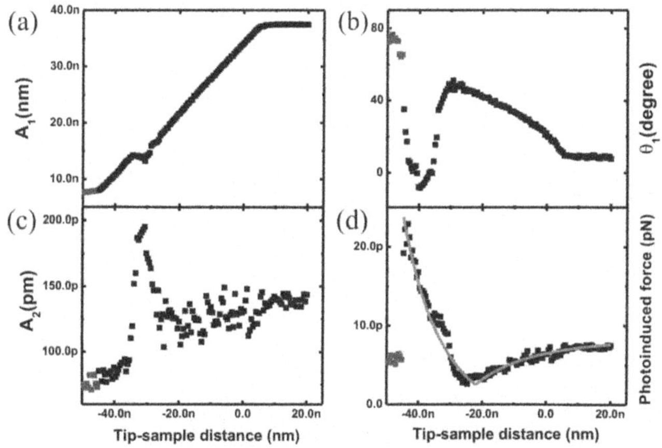

Figure 2. The characteristic behavior of a cantilever with respect to tip-sample distance. (a) amplitude and (b) phase of fundamental resonance. (c) amplitude of 2nd resonance (d) reconstructed photo-induced force

CONCLUSIONS

In this work, we have provided a theoretical description of the cantilever dynamics in the presence of F_{PiF}, which is the photo-induced force to that drives the second resonance of the cantilever with incident beam, and $\overline{F}_{int}$, which is the effective mechanical interaction force between the tip-sample. The presence of these forces resulted in a frequency shift and loss of first and second mechanical resonances. The photo-induced force is conveniently reconstructed from the measured total force by extracting the mechanical interaction forces. The framework developed here makes it possible to quantitatively extract the photo-induced force from scanning force measurements, which is essential for interpreting the image contrast related to molecular spectroscopic information.

ACKNOWLEDGMENTS

This work was supported by the National Science Foundation, Grant No. CHE-0802913.

REFERENCES

1. J. Jahng, J. Brocious, D. A. Fishman, F. Huang, X. Li, V. A. Tamma, H. K. Wickramasinghe, and E. O. Potma, Phys. Rev. B **90**, 155417 (2014).
2. I. Rajapaksa, K. Uenal, and H. K.Wickramasinghe, Appl. Phys. Lett. **97**, 073121 (2010).
3. R. Garcia and E. T. Herruzo, Nat. Nanotechnol. **7**, 217 (2012).
4. J. R. Lozano and R. Garcia, Phys. Rev. B **79**, 014110 (2009).
5. M. Lee and W. Jhe, Phys. Rev. Lett. **97**, 036104 (2006); J. E. Sader and S. P. Jarvis, Appl. Phys. Lett. 84, 1801 (2004); J. E. Sader et al., Nanotechnology 16, S94 (2005); B. Anczykowski et al., Appl. Surf. Sci. 140, 376 (1999).

Advances in Materials Exploration with X-Rays—The State-of-the-Art in the International Year of Crystallography

Mater. Res. Soc. Symp. Proc. Vol. 1754 © 2015 Materials Research Society
DOI: 10.1557/opl.2015.146

The European Spallation Source And Future Opportunities For Materials Science

Oliver Kirstein[1,2]

[1]European Spallation Source, Visiting address: Tunavägen 24, 22363 Lund, Sweden
[2]School of Engineering, The University of Newcastle, Callaghan, NSW 2308, Australia

ABSTRACT

The European Spallation Source is Europe's next generation high-power neutron source utilising a linear accelerator and a rotating tungsten target to produce neutrons that will be used for fundamental research and industrial applications. The facility is co-hosted by the states of Denmark and Sweden, and while the main site will be placed in Lund, Sweden, the Data Management and Software Centre will be located in Copenhagen, Denmark. The facility will cover a broad range of scientific applications in the fields of physics, chemistry, biology, or life sciences. A focus will also be materials science and engineering, and dedicated instruments will gradually become available to the user community once neutrons will be produced neutrons from 2019 onwards.

INTRODUCTION

The European Spallation Source (ESS) will be a major user facility at which researchers from academia and industry will investigate scientific questions using neutron beams, which provide insights about the molecular building blocks of matter not available by other means. The use of proton-driven neutron sources, generated by cyclotrons, synchrotrons, or linear accelerators, was beginning to be explored in the late 1970s and early 1980s. Pioneering work at Argonne National Laboratory and Los Alamos National Laboratory in the USA and in Tsukuba in Japan indicated that pulsed proton sources held out a significant technological advantage over the most intense research reactors. This was because the spallation reaction employed in proton machines generates significantly less heat per useful neutron than does a fission reactor, which culminated with the commissioning of the high flux reactor at the Institute Laue-Langevin (ILL) which retained a scientific lead even 40 years after the reactor became critical. In addition, the generation of neutrons in pulses provides peak brightnesses that far exceed those available from reactors, Figure 1. In the late 1970s, construction began on Europe's first proton spallation source, ISIS, which was built close to Oxford, UK, and produced a first beam in 1984. Despite having a design power of only 180 kW, ISIS demonstrated that world-class science could be carried out very effectively on such sources. ISIS was the birthplace of many new instrument concepts, some of which had been prototyped on other neutron sources. ISIS also provided a degree of support to the user community that surpassed the contemporary accepted relationship between the central facility and its user community, and the success of ISIS culminated in a new second target station (TS-II, first neutrons in December 2007) including many new and integrated state-of-the art neutron scattering instruments.

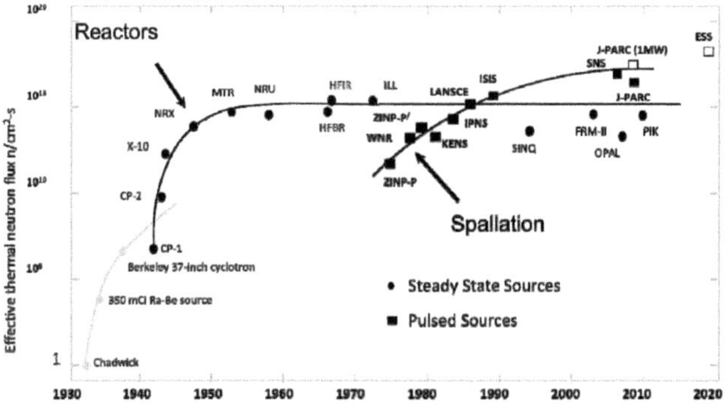

Figure 1. Development of neutron sources world-wide, pulsed and steady-state, since the discovery of the neutron by Chadwick in the 1930s. The ILL first started operating in 1971, ISIS started operating its first target station in 1984 [1].

Having the two most powerful neutron sources by the late 1990, which were complemented by a network of medium and low intensity neutron sources throughout Europe, lead to a growth of the European research community who used neutrons for a significant part of their research. A survey made by the European Neutron Scattering Association (ENSA), which represents scientists from a multidisciplinary community of physicists, chemists, of materials, life, earth, and engineering scientists, indicates this number to be around 6000 [2,3]. However, the need for a next generation spallation source in Europe was emphasised within the global neutron strategy that was put forward by the OECD Megascience Forum in 1998 [4,5], which was endorsed by the OECD Ministerial Conference in 1999. The recommendation resulted in a 2002 design study for ESS that comprised a 10 MW spallation source with two targets and that was furnished with more than 40 neutron instruments [6-8]. The concept from 2002 was updated during 2003 comprising a 5 MW proton linear accelerator delivering a 2 to 3 millisecond-long pulse to a single target station surrounded by a suite of 20 to 25 neutron instruments, Table 1.

Table I. High-level parameter defining the ESS facility, approved by the ESS Steering Committee on 18 April 2011 [9].

Parameter	**Unit**	**Value**
Average beam power	MW	5
Number of target stations		1
Initial number of public instruments		22
Number of beam ports		48
Number of moderators		2
Separation of ports	degrees	5
Proton kinetic energy	GeV	2.5
Average pulse current	mA	50
Pulse length	ms	2.86
Pulse repetition rate	Hz	14

Maximum accelerating cavity surface field	MV/m	40
Annual operating period	hrs	5000
Reliability	%	95

It is this concept from 2003, which was endorsed by the user community in Europe, that will deliver first neutrons in 2019, and which also will satisfy the initial OECD global neutron strategy and provide Europe with a world-leading neutron source that will stay at the forefront of neutron scattering in the 21st century.

THE ESS PROGRAM

Legally and administratively ESS is a Limited Company (Swedish Aktiebolag) under Swedish law and the CEO reports to a governing Board populated by Swedish and Danish members reflecting the 3:1 shareholding of the two countries and their status as co-hosts. The nature of ESS will change into an international organization by becoming a European Research Infrastructure Consortium (ERIC) in 2015 [10]. A second line of governance, the Steering Committee (STC), was established to represent the scientific institutes and Research Ministries of the various partner countries. At the time of writing the STC includes representatives from 17 partner countries: *Sweden, Denmark, Norway, Latvia, Lithuania, Estonia, Iceland, Poland, Germany, France, the United Kingdom, the Netherlands, Hungary, the Czech Republic, Switzerland, Spain*, and *Italy*. The STC is supported by an Administrative and Finance Committee (AFC), which is formally a sub-committee of the STC, populated by national delegates. Two further advisory committees exist that are directly related to the ESS organization itself and are the source of independent advice. These are the *Scientific* and *Technical Advisory Committees* (SAC and TAC, respectively). They are populated by international scientific and technical experts and are nominated by the ESS organization itself and do not map onto the 17 ESS partner countries.With 17 European partners committed to construct ESS, with a construction cost of 1.843B€ (in 2013 Euro), it is inevitable that a significant source of revenue will be components manufactured and supplied as in-kind contributions. The significant fraction of in-kind contributions brings with it particular challenges though it not only maximises the involvement of partners and capitalises on the existing experience and expertise but is even more important as there is no existing infrastructure on site in Lund; in-kind makes ESS a truly European project.

ESS PROJECTS

Four different ESS Directorates (Infrastructure, Machine, Science, Administration) are responsible for realising different projects that in summary will deliver the ESS Program. In the following the Accelerator Project, the Target Project and the Neutron Scattering Systems Project (NSS), which includes the neutron scattering instruments and supporting infrastructure, will be described briefly. It is clear however, that the Conventional Facilities, the Integrated Control System or the Administrative Support are equally important but outside the scope of this paper.

The Accelerator Project – Machine Directorate

ESS is an accelerator-driven neutron source with the role of the accelerator being straightforward. The accelerator creates protons at the ion source, accelerates them to an appropriate energy and steers them onto the target to create neutrons via the spallation process. A proton kinetic energy of 1–3 GeV is optimal for practical target and moderator designs, and to keep the shielding requirements reasonable. The ESS energy of 2.5 GeV requires an average macro-pulse current of 50 mA to reach a beam power of 5 MW. This current is consistent with the need for high reliability, but leaves some leeway for a potential energy (and thus power) upgrade. The current limit is mainly set by space charge effects at low energy, by the power that can be delivered to the beam in each cavity at medium and high energies, and by beam losses.

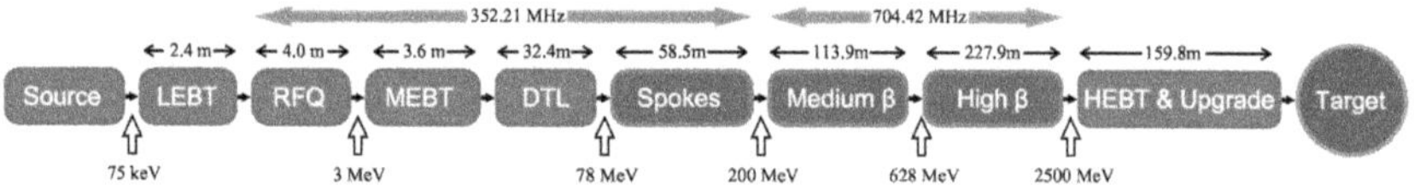

Figure 2. Block diagram of the accelerator lattice described in [9]. The items such as the radio frequency quadrupole (RFQ) and the drift tube linac (DTL) are normal conducting, while the spoke resonators (Spokes) and the medium and high-β elliptical cavities (Medium β and High β, respectively) are superconducting.

Figure 2 shows a block diagram of the accelerator, some of the high-level accelerator parameters are given in Table I, and a detailed description of the accelerator can be found in [9].

The Target Project – Machine Directorate

The main function of the target station is to convert the high-energy proton beam from the accelerator into low-energy neutron beams with the greatest possible efficiency, safety and reliability. The proton beam window, the rotating target wheel system, the moderator-reflector assembly and the beam extraction system will interact directly with protons and/or neutrons. The target material will transform high-energy protons to fast neutrons. The moderator-reflector system surrounding the target will transform the fast neutrons into slow neutrons, which will be guided to neutron scattering instruments via the beam extraction system. The baseline technology chosen for the target is a rotating tungsten wheel cooled by inert helium gas, and two moderators, which will slow down the neutrons created via spallation to thermal and cold energies, are located above and below the target wheel.

At the time of writing, the baseline of the angular beam port separation is 5° but there are discussions between the Target Project and the NSS Project to optimise the exact angular separation in the different sectors depending on the instruments chosen. The target design is described in detail in [9].

The Neutron Scattering Systems Project – Science Directorate

ESS will push the frontiers of neutron science due to its capabilities in two key areas: Its unique characteristics as a neutron source, and state-of-the-art neutron scattering instruments, which are complemented by an integrated computing and scientific infrastructure. The user infrastructure will include sample preparation, characterisation, and specialised synthesis laboratories, and will follow the best-practice employed at leading facilities such as ILL, ISIS, J-PARC or SNS to support users carrying out experiments at ESS. This combination will allow to study a broad range of structures and time scales, offering neutron beams of unparallelled brightness, delivering more neutrons than the world's most powerful reactor-based neutron source with higher peak intensities than other spallation sources, Figure 3.

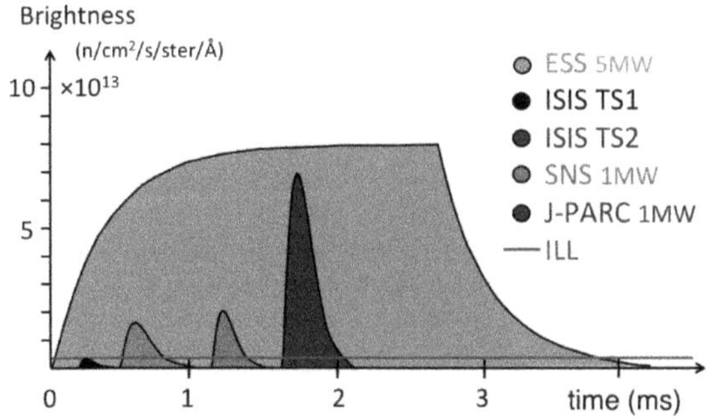

Figure 3. Single-pulse source brightness as a function of time at a wavelength of 5Å at ESS, ILL, SNS, J-PARC and ISIS target stations 1 and 2. In each case, the cold moderator with the highest peak brightness is shown.

The designs of instruments at ESS will be less limited by the time-structure of their long-pulse source than are instruments at short-pulse sources. They will benefit from a substantially higher peak brightness, combined with a time-average brightness which is much higher than that at any short-pulse source, while retaining much of the flexibility of continuous-source instruments, Figure 3. Many of the instruments will be substantially longer than their counterparts at short-pulse sources. The underlying reason is the requirement for good wavelength resolution; the pulse length at the source represents the uncertainty in the emission time of the neutrons, which can be reduced compared to their time-of-flight by making the instrument longer. However, the instrument length also directly affects the bandwidth; that is, the longest wavelength that can be measured from a particular source pulse before it overlaps in time with the shortest wavelength emitted from the following pulse. Pulse-shaping choppers are an alternative method of improving wavelength resolution. Placed close to the source, they effectively reduce the pulse length, and hence the resolution, without making it necessary to increase instrument length. A large part of the optimisation of the instrument suite consists of balancing resolution and bandwidth considerations through appropriate combinations of instrument lengths and chopper systems. As indicated in Table I a total of 22 public instruments will be built at ESS to serve the neutron user community, with the initial instruments foreseen to move into a hot commissioning phase using spallation neutrons in 2019. The choice of instruments to build will take place as an ongoing process in which a number of concepts are selected every year [11]. This staged approach will allow ESS to remain engaged with the European neutron community and to choose instrument designs that are state-of-the-art and scientifically relevant when they enter user operation. The process of selecting instruments started in 2013 and the evaluation criteria include expected scientific impact, user base and demand, instrument performance, strategy and uniqueness, technical maturity and costing. Out of 4 proposed instrument concepts the SAC, and finally the STC, endorsed to move 3 instruments into a preliminary engineering design phase [12]. In 2014 a total of 16 instrument concepts were submitted out of which 14 were evaluated by the SAC. The process resulted in 9 instrument concepts that were endorsed by the SAC and the STC [13] covering the areas of spectroscopy, SANS, diffraction and reflectometry to ensure an early scientific impact. At the time of writing it is expected that about 10 instrument concepts will be evaluated by the SAC in 2015.

INSTRUMENTS FOR MATERIALS AND ENGINEERING RESEARCH

The grand challenges of modern society originate in the priorities of a sustainable development of modern technologies and our interest in the improvement of everyday life including e.g. computers, batteries, food, medicine, transportation, and energy. Technological progress was, is and will be largely based on the improvement of materials. The development of materials with high performance and tailored functionality is based on fundamental understanding of the relation between the microstructure and properties of a material. This also requires development of new and improved experimental tools for precise and reliable characterisation of materials. Development, fabrication, optimisation and degradation monitoring of modern engineering materials is essential for the production of more efficient, more environmentally friendly and more durable engineering components. To achieve such ambitious goals, employment of scientifically based approaches towards material design and development as well as adoption of new methods for production, thermomechanical processing, testing and characterisation of materials is required. Among novel multiphase engineering materials and composites are e.g. materials for lightweight engineering components: *high-strength dual, multi-phase, TRIP, TWIP and superbainite steels as structural materials in transport, energy and defense applications; magnesium, aluminium and titanium alloys for consumer electronics and □transport; fiber-reinforced and metal/polymer matrix composites; □high temperature and corrosion resistant intermetallics and precipitation-hardened alloys □for energy conversion, turbo-machinery, aero-engines and space applications; □shape memory alloys (SMA) and foams for morphing structures, large-extension actuators,vibration dampers, sensors; high temperature SMAs for heat engines and □superelastic Ni-free biomedical components.* □

Neutron diffraction has become a well-established experimental tool for microstructure characterisation in materials and engineering sciences and industrial applications during the last 10 to15 years. Conventional use of neutron diffraction lies in the field of phase analysis, residual stress, and texture analysis, as well as defect and nanostructure analysis. However, the complexity of materials as well as the kind of experiments has changed significantly in recent years, with *in-situ* and *in-operando* experiments becoming more important. The reason is that not only the microstructure but also the processing techniques for production of modern materials have become increasingly more complex but further progress can often only be made when the time-dependent processes are studied under production-like conditions in real time. To this end, the NSS Project will provide two instruments, briefly described in the following sections, which will certainly attract the material science and engineering community.

ODIN – A Multipurpose Imaging Beamline

Neutron imaging is a real-space technique examining the inner structure of potentially highly complex components by studying at the transmitted beam. The multi-purpose imaging beamline ODIN will be designed to push spatial resolutions down to the micron range coupled with ongoing advances in detector technology, thanks to the high brightness of ESS. The pulsed nature of the source will give access to wavelength-resolved information, yielding a qualitative informational advance over state-of-the-art instruments available today. The instrument offers its future users a variety of imaging techniques for the characterisation of objects, covering cultural heritage, energy materials, magnetic phenomena and fuel cells as well as inspection of engineering components. Different imaging techniques, from traditional attenuation-based imaging to advanced dark field or Bragg edge imaging will be available with unprecedented efficiency and detail. The instrument concept takes full advantage of the flexibility made possible by the ESS time structure, allowing wavelength resolution, bandwidth and collimation to be tuned for each application [14].

Single-Pulse Measurements: As an example Figure 4 shows the instrument being used in single-pulse mode, with a variable wavelength resolution ranging from 3.8%-10.6%. This set-up will allow for conventional imaging with high spatial and temporal resolution, qualitative textures and microstructure imaging, or quantitative dark-field (DF)/2D resolved SANS measurements.

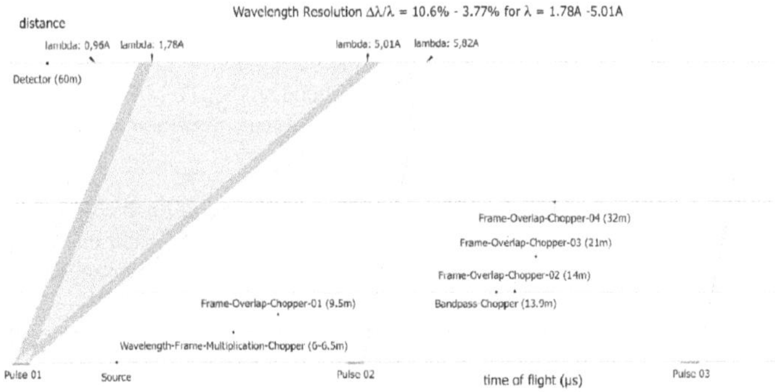

Figure 4. Time-distance diagram showing the ODIN chopper system set-up for single pulse measurements. The distance from the ESS source to the detector is 60m. The positions of the different chopper systems are indicated. Such a configuration would allow to access a wavelength range from 1.78-5.01Å with a variable resolution of about $\Delta\lambda/\lambda$=10.6%-3.8%.

Wavelength-Frame Multiplication: The unique long pulse of the ESS of 2.86msec allows selecting more than one shorter pulse. If the chopper system is designed accordingly this

"Wavelength-Frame Multiplication" (WFM) [15] allows to 1) extend the dynamic range of the instrument by suppressing subsequent pulses and 2) to maintain a constant resolution within the individual "frames". Such a set-up would be well suited to e.g. study texture and microstructures in transmission imaging mode; resolve crystalline phases and observe phase transitions; map strains in time-of-flight transmission imaging mode. This is schematically shown in Figure 5.

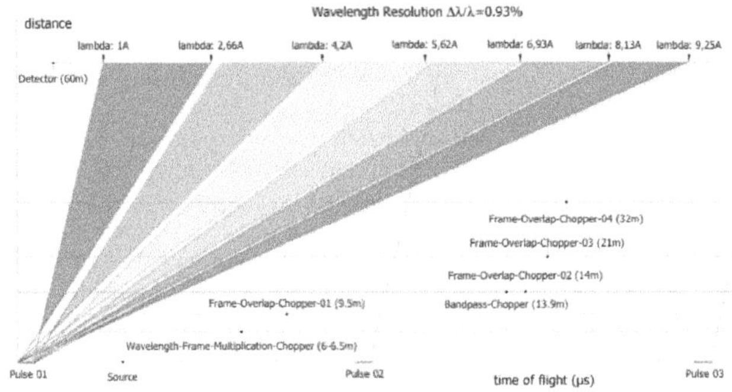

Figure 5. Time-distance diagram showing the ODIN chopper set-up in WFM mode. By suppressing every second pulse coming from the ESS source the dynamic range covers almost 10Å with a constant wavelength resolution of about 1%.

Performance: Comparing instruments from different facilities with each other, whether they are existing or planned, is largely based on estimates unless gold-foil measurements were done. However, the Table II indicates, for a defined collimation ration of L/D= 500 how ODIN will compare with other instruments that are currently available at PSI, TUM/FRM-II or planned in case of IMAT at ISIS. ODIN will be one of the first instruments at ESS and is expected to move into hot commissioning towards the end of 2019.

Table II. Comparison between different imaging instruments for a defined collimation of L/D=500. The neutron flux, in units of 10^6 n/s/cm^2, is indicated for different instrument modes of operation. Instruments in *italic* are either currently under construction and numbers are based on simulations. Values marked (*) are estimated at a nominal wavelength of 6.2Å.

Instrument - Facility	**Conventional white beam**	**DF/2D SANS Δλ□λ□10% Nominal λ: 4.5Å**	**Texture / polarised Δλ□λ□1% Nominal λ: 4.5Å**	**Strain Δλ□λ□0.3 % Nominal λ: 4.5Å**
NEUTRA – PSI	4.8	0.15	0.15	0.005
ANTARES – FRM2	70	5.0	0.50	0.12
IMAT - ISIS	*25*	*25(*)*	*2.5(*)*	*1.5*
ODIN - ESS	*75*	*60*	*7.5*	*2.5*

BEER – Beamline for European Materials Engineering Research

While ODIN was endorsed by the SAC and STC already in 2013, the second instrument that will attract the European, and international, material science community is BEER, the "Beamline for European Materials Engineering Research". With respect to analogous instruments such as VULCAN at SNS, TAKUMI at J-PARC or ENGIN-X at ISIS, the proposed instrumental concept can be characterised by its high performance in terms of intensity and resolution, and high flexibility by having tuneable instrumental parameters, unique sample environments and excellent time resolution to study dynamical processes. Similar to the ODIN instrument the exploitation of the unique 2.86msec pulse opens the possibility to increase the instrument's capabilities by e.g multiplexing the source pulse.

Single pulse measurements: The high peak intensity combined with the possibility of tailoring the resolution defined by the first chopper system will allow for single peak measurement. This is schematically shown in Figure 6. The integrated intensity for BL9 is 9.3 times lower than the integrated intensity of the 'rectangular' pulse defined by the BEER chopper system (both pulses centred around 0 μsec).

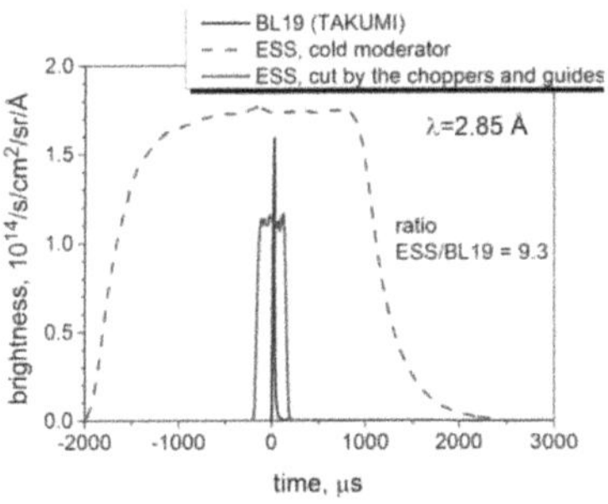

Figure 6. Brightness and time structure of BL19 at J-PARC and ESS at 2.85Å. the difference in integrated intensity is 9.3.

In 2010 an *in-situ* hot compression test of 2Mn-0.2C steel was done at TAKUMI with J-PARC operating at 120kW beam power. The instrument was used in high-flux mode with an incident slit of 5mm without radial collimators between the specimen and the detectors. The data shown in Figure 7 (top) represent a 10 s time slice collected after hot compression and holding the sample at 700°C, which resulted in 25.5 % ferrite (74.5 % austenite) content. Figure 7 (bottom) shows a simulated experiment with the same sample at the proposed BEER instrument in the medium resolution mode, with a wavelength band centred at λ=2.0Å. The simulation does not include texture, intrinsic peak broadening and anharmonic terms in the Debye-Waller factor. However, both data sets reveal the same peak widths Δd/d = 0.4 %, and sufficient accuracy in peak position of < 50 με, indicating that similar single-pulse experiments will be feasible on BEER.

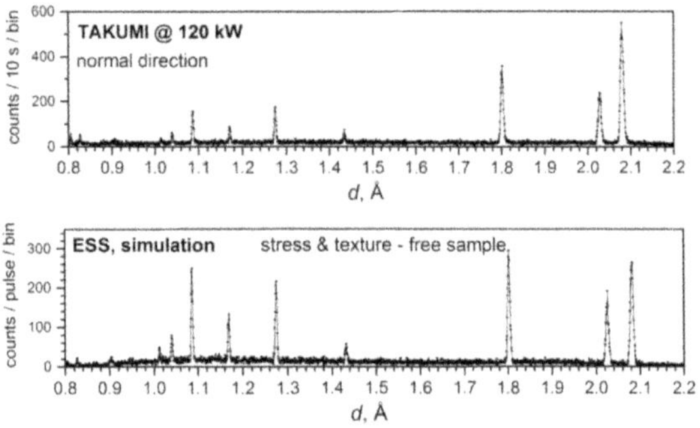

Figure 7. Top: Experimental diffraction pattern of the normal strain direction obtained on TAKUMI for a 2Mn-0.2C sample. Note on the y-axis that the units are **counts/*10sec*/bin**. Bottom: Simulated diffraction pattern of the normal strain direction for a 2Mn-0.2C sample using BEER. Note on the y-axis that the units are **counts/*pulse*/bin**.

Performance: Figure 8 shows a comparison between instruments at SNS, J-PARC and FRM-II including the BEER beamline at ESS.

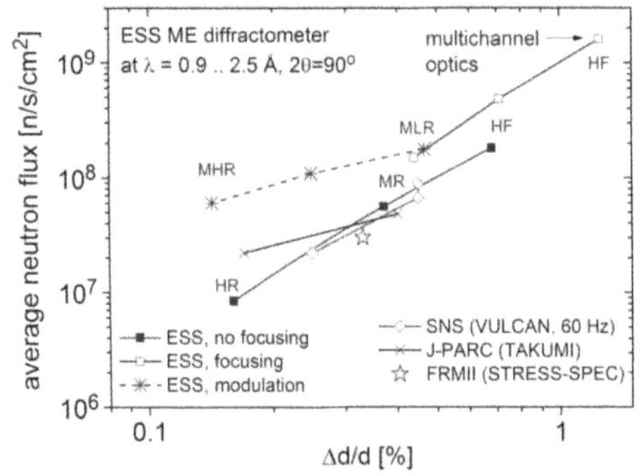

Figure 8. Comparison of the BEER instrument at ESS with instruments at SNS, J-PARC and FRM-II. *HR, MR, HF* as well as *MHR, MLR* refer to different modes of operations and chopper system settings in case of BEER[1].

The instrument can be operated in different modes and a detailed description is unfortunately beyond of the scope of this paper; details are given in e.g. [16,17]. However, it is clear that BEER will offer not only a much larger range of resolutions but also gains in intensity,

[1] Different modes of operating the chopper system of BEER: HR=high-resolution, MR=medium-resolution, HF=high-flux, MHR=multiplexing at 280Hz, MLR=multiplexing at 70Hz

which are around one order of magnitude. Such intensity gains, in combination with sophisticated sample environments such as load frames, dilatometers or physical simulators of materials processing devices that will allow for *in-situ* and *in-operandi* experiments to be carried out, will change the way the material science and engineering community will do experiments from 2023 onwards.

SUMMARY

The ESS project, the largest research infrastructure project in Europe, has started after more than 2 decades since being discussed first, by breaking ground on the 2nd September 2014 followed by laying the foundation stone on the 9th October 2014. Construction on-site in Lund has also started and the first neutrons are expected to be produced by the Target in 2019. This will allow the initial instruments to start hot commissioning using neutrons and instruments will successively become available covering all areas of science over the next decade. The peer-reviewed user program is expected to start in 2023. In terms of material science and engineering present dedicated neutron diffraction instruments and methods have reached their limits, imposed by a lack of brilliance of neutron sources. The engineering and materials science community is impatiently waiting for a stronger neutron source and new instruments with much higher flux on the sample to be able to tackle important problems with new and improved methods once the instruments will become available. The journey has begun.

ACKNOWLEDGMENTS

The author gratefully acknowledges and thanks all the colleagues in the ESS team, which includes not only staff at the ESS headquarter in Lund but all staff working for ESS at labs throughout Europe; without their effort and contributions such a project would not be possible.

The author also wishes to thank the ODIN project team and the BEER project team for the supporting documentation. Both projects are prime examples of how different laboratories across different countries can work together to build world-leading and state-of-the-art neutron scattering instruments.

BEER team: A. Schreyer[1], P. Lukáš[2], R. Kampmann[1], J. Fenske[1], G. Nowak[1],□M. Rouijaa[1], P. Staron[1], H.-G. Brokmeier[1,4], M. Müller[1];□J. Šaroun[2], J. Pilch[2,3], P. Šittner[3], P. Strunz[2], P. Beran[2], V. Ryukhtin[2], L. Kadeřávek[2,3]; [1]Helmholtz-Zentrum Geesthacht, Geesthacht, Germany, [2]Nuclear Physics Institute, Řež, Czech Republic, [3]Institute of Physics, Praha, Czech Republic, [4]Technical University of Clausthal, Clausthal-Zellerfeld, Germany

ODIN team: M. Strobl[1], B. Schillinger[2], E. Lehmann[3], [1]European Spallation Source, Sweden, [2]Forschungs-Neutronenquelle Heinz Maier-Leibnitz (FRM II), Germany, [3]Paul-Scherrer Institut (PSI), Switzerland

REFERENCES

1. K. Sköld and D.L. Price (eds), *Neutron Scattering*, Academic Press, 1986.

2. European Neutron Scattering Association (ENSA). *Survey of the Neutron Scattering Community and Facilities in Europe*, 1998.

3. European Science Foundation (ESF) and European Neutron Scattering Association (ENSA). *Survey of the Neutron Scattering Community in Europe*, 2005.

4. D. Richter and T. Springer. *A twenty years forward look at neutron scattering facilities in the OECD countries and Russia.* Technical report, European Science Foundation, Organisation for Economic Co-operation and Development Megascience Forum, 1998.

5. Final Report OECD Megascience Forum Working Group on Neutron Sources (1997), http://www.OECD.ORG//dsti/sti/s_t/ms/prod/online.htm

6. F. H. Bohn et al., *'European source of science'. In The ESS Project, volume 1.* European Spallation Source, May 2002.

7. D. Richter, *'New science and technology for the 21st century'. In The ESS Project, volume 2.* European Spallation Source, May 2002.

8. F. H. Bohn et al, *'Technical report'. In The ESS Project, volume 3.* European Spallation Source, May 2002.

9. S. Peggs (ed), *ESS Technical Design Report*, ESS-2013-001, April 23, 2013, ISBN 978-91-980173-2-8

10. Council Regulation (EC) No 723/2009 of 25 June 2009 on the Community legal framework for a European Research Infrastructure Consortium (ERIC), OJ L 206, 8.8.2009, p. 1.

11. http://europeanspallationsource.se/proposing-instruments-ess

12. http://europeanspallationsource.se/constructing-instruments-and-science-support

13. http://europeanspallationsource.se/ess-instrument-suite-taking-shape

14. http://europeanspallationsource.se/sites/default/files/
odin_imaging_instrument_construction_proposal.pdf

15. M. Russina, G. Káli, Z. Sánta, F. Mezei, *First experimental implementation of pulse shaping for neutron diffraction on pulsed sources*, Nucl. Instr. Met. A, Vol. 654, Issue 1, DOI: 10.1016/j.nima.2011.05.077

16. http://europeanspallationsource.se/sites/default/files/beer_pdf.pdf

17. http://europeanspallationsource.se/building-europes-next-flagship-engineering-diffractometer-future-beer

Mater. Res. Soc. Symp. Proc. Vol. 1754 © 2015 Materials Research Society
DOI: 10.1557/opl.2015.145

Texture evolution in metals under mechanical stress: Application of a tensile stage on a laboratory X-ray system

J. te Nijenhuis, N. Dadivanyan and D.J. Götz
PANalytical B.V., Lelyweg 1, 7602 EA Almelo, the Netherlands

ABSTRACT

The evolution of texture in copper has been studied *in situ* as a function of the applied mechanical stress. A uniaxial tensile stage was integrated onto a Eulerian cradle in a laboratory X-ray diffraction system, providing a platform for pole figure measurements on samples under an externally applied mechanical load. Thin strips of rolled copper were investigated at various stages of elongation. The pole figures were of good quality such that the orientation distribution function could be well determined. Changes in the orientation distribution function as a function of strain along the β-fiber could be clearly observed; the initial main component S is replaced by the Copper component at higher stages of elongation.

INTRODUCTION

Macroscopic properties of solid materials, such as metals and ceramics, are determined by the intrinsic material properties and the orientation of each of the crystallites in the sample. In general the crystallites are not distributed randomly like in an ideal powder specimen. In most cases a preferred orientation of the crystallites, so-called texture, is present. This preferred orientation is a result of the history of the manufacturing process. In materials research it is therefore not only interesting to study the final texture of a sample but also to follow the texture evolution during the formation or deformation processes. Knowledge of the evolution of preferred orientations provides valuable information in order to optimize the manufacturing and (de)formation processes.

A well-known method to study deformation processes is recording the stress-strain curve of a sample. In this method the sample material is clamped between two vises and elongated by stretching it with a constant applied force. The relationship between the applied mechanical load and the amount of deformation (elongation) reveals the elastic and plastic characteristics of the material. During the deformation process the preferred orientation of the crystallites will change as a result of the applied mechanical stress. X-ray diffraction is a widely used technique to determine preferred orientations. Orientation distribution functions (ODFs) of worked pieces of material can be obtained from a set of measured pole figures.

In practice often large equipment is required to deform worked materials, making it virtually impossible to investigate the stress-strain behavior and the texture evolution simultaneously. With the integration of a compact tensile stage onto a Eulerian cradle on a laboratory X-ray diffraction system we have investigated the possibility to measure pole figures *in situ* as a function of the elongation of the sample. In the present study we describe the first results of texture evolution studies on rolled copper samples.

EXPERIMENT

Tensile tests

Mechanical deformation studies have been performed with the use of a Deben 300N tensile stage. This stage has been designed to investigate samples under well defined strain and stress conditions. Samples are clamped with a pair of jaws and supported on stainless steel sliding bearings. The stress or strain are computer controlled. Extension rates can be set between 0.1 mm/min and 1.5 mm/min. The compact design allows integration of this sample platform onto a three-axes cradle.

X-ray diffraction texture analysis

X-ray diffraction measurements were performed on a PANalytical Empyrean system equipped with a Deben 300N tensile stage mounted onto a Eulerian cradle. In the incident beam an X-ray lens was used that provides a quasi-parallel beam. A parallel plate collimator with an equatorial acceptance angle of 0.27° and a sealed proportional point detector were employed in the diffracted beam path. The absence of defocusing effects over a large tilt range in this geometry greatly improves the quality of the texture data.

Pole figures were measured in reflection geometry, according to the Schulz reflection technique [1] with complete circles over the rotation angle φ (0° - 360°) and fixed tilt angles χ over a range between 0° and 75°. The φ–rotation integration interval and the step size of the χ-tilt-angle were 3°. The measurement time per pole figure was 68 minutes.

A full representation of the texture over all crystal directions is given by the ODF, which can be calculated from a set of experimentally determined pole figures. The orientation distribution function was calculated using the Williams-Imhof-Matthies-Vinel (WIMV) method [2].

Sample material

As an example of the method a rolled copper strip with length of 25 mm, width of 15 mm and an initial thickness of 0.02 mm was analyzed. The sample was clamped in the tensile stage with the rolling direction (rotation angle $\varphi = 0°$) parallel to the direction of the tensile stress. The sample area analyzed was 10 mm x 15 mm initially. Pole figures of the {220}, {222}, {311} and {400} reflections of the face-centered cubic (FCC) structure of copper were measured on the sample in the initial status (extension 0 mm) and subsequently at eight different extensions up to 7 mm. During the pole figure measurements the elongation was kept constant for about four and a half hours.

The elongation rate was set to 0.2 mm/min for the first four measurements and then increased to 1.0 mm/min for the other measurements.

RESULTS AND DISCUSSION

Fiber analysis in FCC metals

In texture analysis of rolled FCC metals, the ODF is often represented by a set of specific orientations (texture components) [3] as shown in figure 1 and table I. These components are connected by fibers, where a fiber is a path of orientations through the ODF space. Most common fibers in FCC metals are the β- and α-fibers. The β-fiber runs from the Copper to the Brass component via S, whereas the α-fiber connects the Brass with the Goss component [3, 4]. Figure 2 shows the β- and α-fibers in the ODF obtained from the initial rolled copper strip (extension = 0 mm).

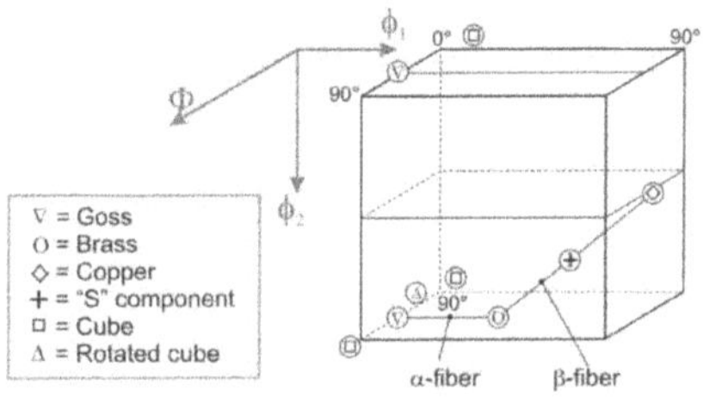

Figure 1. Overview of fibers and components in ODF orientation space (after [3]).

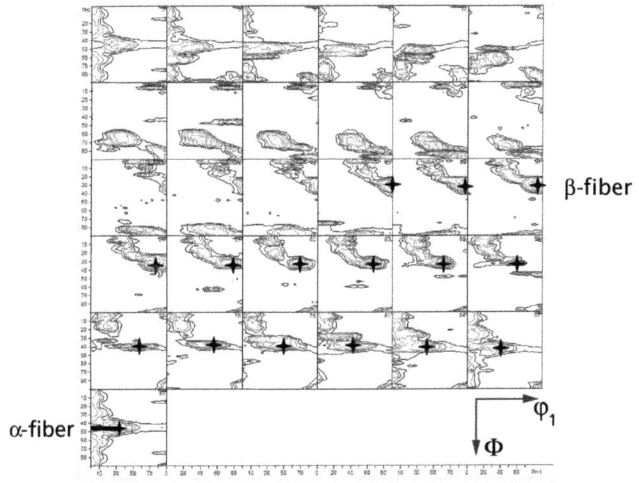

Figure 2. Orientation distribution function (φ_2= constant sections) of the initial copper strip. The β- and α-fibers are indicated by the stars and the black line respectively.

Table I. Texture components in rolled FCC metals [2].

Name (symbol)	Miller indices	Euler angles (Bunge) (φ_1,Φ,φ_2)
Copper (◇)	{211}<111>	(90, 35, 45)
S (+)	{321}<436>	(35, 65, 35)
Brass (O)	{110}<112>	(35, 45, 90)
Goss (∇)	{110}<001>	(0, 45, 90)
Cube (□)	{100}<001>	(0, 0, 0)
Rotated cube (Δ)	{520}<001>	(0, 25, 0)

Deformation experiments and ODF component analysis

Figure 3 shows the force required to extend the copper strip as a function of the elongation. After an initial slight increase of the force in the lower extension range up to ca. 1.5 mm the force flattens and steeply decreases above 2 mm until it reaches a steady state above 4 mm.

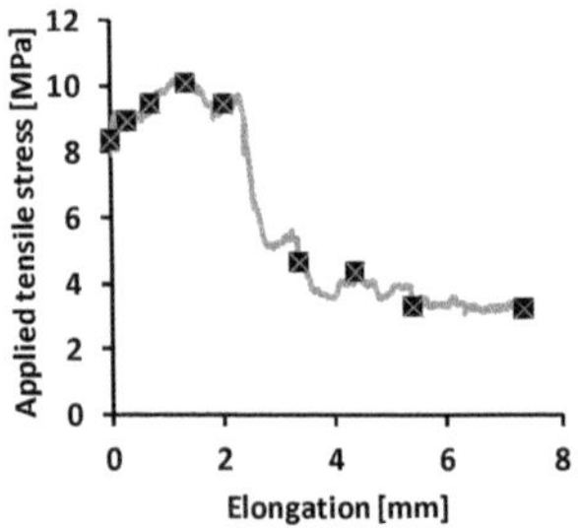

Figure 3. Applied tensile stress as a function of the elongation of the sample. The squares on the curve indicate the extensions at which the pole figures were measured.

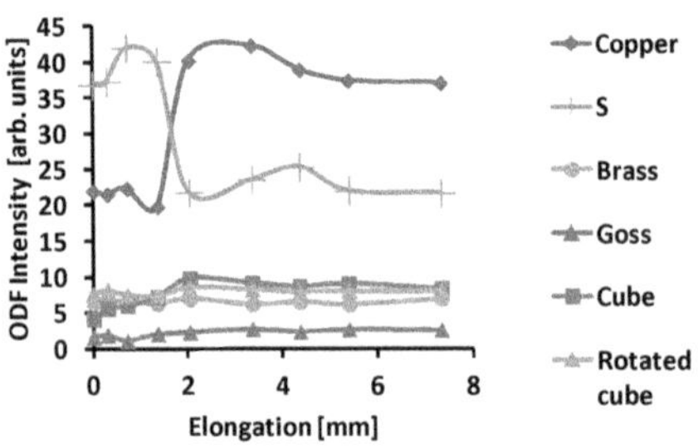

Figure 4. Intensity of the main texture components as a function of the elongation of the sample.

Figure 4 shows the ODF intensity of the main components in FCC metals for the rolled copper strips at the various stages of deformation. The intensity of most of the components is more or less independent of the elongation with two exceptions: the Copper and S components show a strong change in intensity. Whereas the Copper component strongly increases at an extension between 1.4 mm and 2.0 mm, the S component strongly decreases in the same interval. After these transitions the intensities remain constant. The position of the intensity cross-over coincides more or less with the steep decrease in force in the elongation curve in figure 3. Less clear but still visible is the slight increase of the cube component.

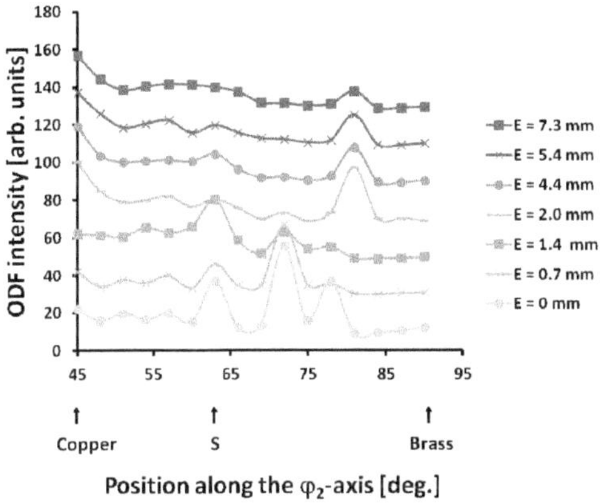

Figure 5. Intensity of the β -fiber as a function of position along the φ_2-axis in the ODF at different elongations. NB: The intensities have been offset to facilitate the analysis.

Analysis of the (generalized [5]) β-fibers as shown in figure 5 reveals that the intensity of the S-components along this fiber decrease with increasing extension of the sample, whereas the Copper component at a φ_2 position of 45° becomes the most important above an elongation of 2.0 mm.

Initially the rolled copper specimen exhibited a strong β-fiber texture, which is in accordance with literature [3]. The β-fiber itself is not a thin line but extends over several degrees in the orientation space [5]. The intensity distribution along the fiber is not flat, but shows maximums of S-components at the first stages of the deformation process. The β-fiber texture remained to be present, but the intensity distribution along the fiber changed at later stages. The Copper component becomes more prominent at the cost of the S-components; the Cube component only slightly increases in intensity. Copper is known to show a {111} (Copper-related) and a {100} (Cube-related) double fiber texture when it is placed under tensile stress [6]. The ratio of these two components depends on the initial texture of the sample. In our case of rolled copper it is clearly demonstrated that the initial S-components move towards the Copper component.

CONCLUSIONS

We have shown the possibility of measuring complete pole figures using X-ray diffraction under the application of external tensile stresses. ODF analysis of measurements on a thin rolled copper strip with various extensions showed a change from the initial main component S to Copper along the β-fiber.

ACKNOWLEDGMENTS

Dr. Gary Edwards, Deben UK Ltd., Woolpit, United Kingdom is gratefully acknowledged for providing the tensile stage used in this study.

REFERENCES

1. L.G. Schulz, *J. Applied Physics* **20**, 1030 (1949).
2. S. Matthies and G.W. Vinel, *Phys. Stat. Sol. (b)* **112**, K111 (1982).
3. A.D. Rollett and S.I. Wright, in *Texture and anisotropy*, edited by U.F. Kocks, C.N. Tomé and H.-R. Wenk (Cambridge University Press, Cambridge, UK, 1998), Chapter 5.
4. S.-H. Kim, S.Z. Han, C.J. Kim, I.-Y. Hwang and F. Yin, *Materials Transactions* **50,** 537 (2009).
5. J. Hirsch and K. Lücke, *Acta Metall.* **36,** 2863 (1988).
6. O. Engler and V. Randle, *Introduction to texture analysis: macrotexture, microtexture, and Orientation mapping*, 2nd ed. (CRC Press, Boca Raton, FL, 2009).

Mater. Res. Soc. Symp. Proc. Vol. 1754 © 2015 Materials Research Society
DOI: 10.1557/opl.2015.401

Comparative High-Resolution X-Ray Diffraction Analysis of GaN/AlGaN Heterostructure on Al_2O_3 and Si (111) Substrate Grown by Plasma Assisted Molecular Beam Epitaxy

Sanjay Kr. Jana[1, (a)], Saptarsi Ghosh[1], Syed Mukulika Dinara[1], Apurba Chakraorty[2], and D. Biswas[1, 2]
[1]*Advanced Technology Development Centre, IIT Kharagpur, Kharagpur 721302, India*
[2]*Department of Electronics & Electrical Communication, IIT Kharagpur, Kharagpur 721302, India*
[(a)]*E-mail: skjiit@gmail.com*

Abstract

The work presents a comparative study on GaN/AlGaN type-II heterostructures grown on c-plane Al_2O_3 and Si (111) substrates by Plasma Assisted Molecular Beam Epitaxy. The in-depth structural characterizations of these samples were performed by High-Resolution X-Ray Diffraction, X-ray Reflectivity and Field Emission Scanning Electron Microscopy. The in-plane and out-of plane strains were determined from measured c- and a-lattice parameters of the epilayers from reciprocal space mapping of both symmetric triple axis (002) and asymmetric grazing incidence (105) double axis mode. The mosaicity parameters like tilt and correlation lengths were also calculated from reciprocal space mapping. Moreover, the twist angle was measured from skew symmetric off axis scan of (102), (103), and (105) planes along with (002) symmetric plane. The defect density were measured from the full width at half maxima of skew symmetric scan of (002) and (102) reflection planes. Also, the strained states of all the layers were analyzed and corresponding Al mole fraction was calculated based on anisotropic elastic theory. The thicknesses of the layers were measured from simulation of the nominal structure by fitting with X-ray Reflectivity experimental curves and also by comparing with cross sectional Field Emission Scanning Electron Microscopy micrographs.

Introduction

III-V semiconductors have promising potential applications in the field of electronics and optoelectronics devices. The wide band gap nature of AlN (6.2 eV) and GaN (3.41eV) and their alloy, AlGaN, makes it possible to fabricate high power, and high frequency devices [1]. On the other hand, low band gap material InN (0.7 eV) and related ternary alloys (InGaN, InAlN) can be grown for generations of devices operating in the UV to IR wavelength spectrum. So, due to its enormous possibility of applications, lot of works has already been carried out in this field [2-4]. However, it is still a great challenge to grow defect free epitaxial nitride layers on foreign substrate like Al_2O_3 and Si due to the unavailability of native one [5]. The lattice and thermal mismatch is primarily responsible for defects in the epitaxy. On the other hand, material characterization is another challenging job due to mosaicity of the III-nitrides which means that layers are misoriented with respect to the substrate [6]. So, in this report comparative analysis of AlGaN/GaN heterostructures on both Al_2O_3 and Si (111) were investigated by High-Resolution X-Ray Diffraction (HRXRD) which is a fast and nondestructive characterization technique with high resolution. Notably, both the samples were grown by Plasma Assisted Molecular Beam Epitaxy (PAMBE).

Experiment

The Ga(Al) terminated GaN(cap)/AlGaN/GaN layers were grown on Sapphire (Al_2O_3) and Si (111) substrate by PAMBE. 6N pure solid sources were used for Al and Ga and RF plasma source was used for active nitrogen element. The ex-situ cleaning of both the substrates were performed by acetone, and 2 % HF solution to remove organic compounds and native oxides, respectively. Then the substrate was loaded immediately into the load lock chamber. Before growth, the substrates were heated at very high temperature (750 °C) for further removal of oxides from the surface. The real-time reconstruction of surface (e.g. Kikuchi pattern) was observed by RHEED operated at 15 KV and 1.5 Amps. First, AlN nucleation layer was deposited on either Al_2O_3 and Si substrate which initiates the formation of subsequent nitride layers and helps to improve quality of GaN/AlGaN layer. The HRXRD and X-ray Reflectivity (XRR) analyses were performed by BEDE D1 (Jordon Valley) diffractometer equipped with Cu $K\alpha_1$ (1.54056 Å) line source with the minimum step size of Omega (ω) and 2Theta (2θ) axis being 0.16 arc sec. Furthermore, the thicknesses of the layers were confirmed by means of cross sectional sectional Field Emission Scanning Electron Microscopy (FESEM) experiment (Carl Zeiss SMT).

Results and discussion

Figure 1 shows the (ω-2θ) scan of triple axis (TA) (002) plane which indicates the nominal structure of samples grown on Al_2O_3 (MN1) and Si (MN2) substrate, respectively. The individual peak signifies the presence of GaN, AlGaN and AlN layer. The full width at half maxima (FWHM) values of the peaks (as fitted by pseudo-voight function) i.e. 0.0072, 0.186 and 0.175° for MN1; 0.016, 0.206 and 0.052° for MN2 indicates that excellent quality epilayers were grown by PAMBE. All kind of defects and mosaicity effects were found to influence the FWHM of omega rocking curves (Figure not given) for both the samples.

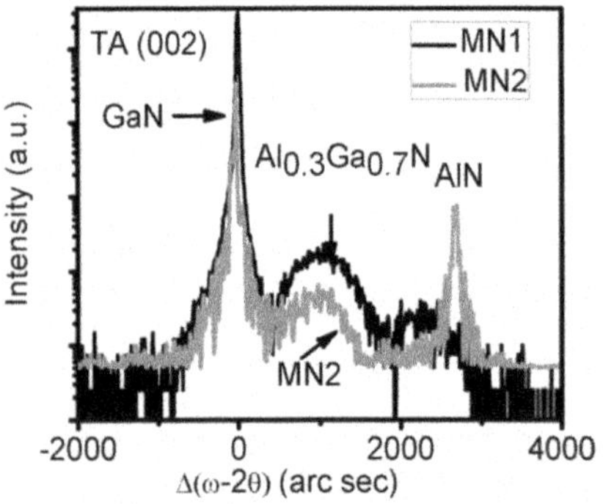

Figure 1 TA (002) diffraction plots of sample MN1 and MN2.

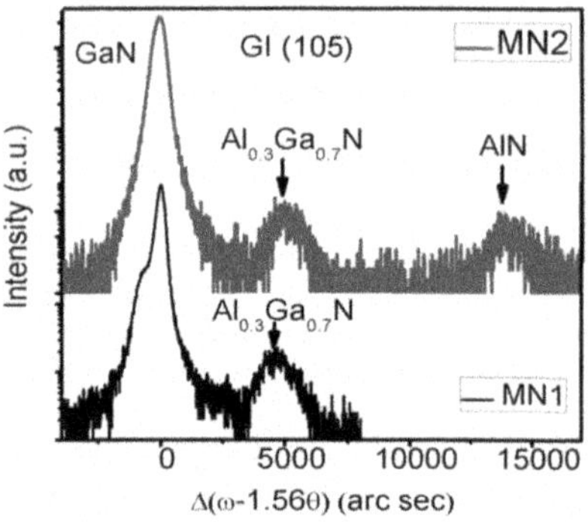

Figure 2 DA GI (105) diffraction plots of MN1 and MN2.

The measured FWHM of sample MN1=0.041° and MN2= 0.358° indicates that the AlGaN/GaN heterostructure quality is better for Al_2O_3 substrate than for Si. Moreover, asymmetric grazing incidence (GI)(105) (ω-1.56θ) scan also indicates the existence of AlGaN and GaN layer as shown in Figure 2. Here, the scan ratio (coupling coefficient) was taken 1.56 instead of 2 due to strained AlGaN layer on the GaN buffer and hence, calculations were performed on the basis of mole fraction and relaxation of the barrier. The FWHM of GaN, AlGaN and AlN in asymmetric double axis (DA) GI (105) scan are 0.354°(0.051°), 0.363° (0.130°) and 0.0447° for MN2 (MN1) which ensures the high quality of the grown epilayers. Notably, the AlN peak for the thin NL layer was not observed for MN1 sample in GI (105) mode. On the other hand, MN2 sample consist a stack of GaN/AlN layers for minimizing the threading dislocation (TD) density and also for providing insulation between active layer and Si substrate which in turn helps to accurately measure the transport properties. Figure 3 and 4 shows the reciprocal space mapping (RSM) of (002) and GI (105) respectively. Elliptical nature of the maps indicates the mosaicity of the layers. The lattice constants and plane spacings (d) were also measured from GI (105) RSM using the following expressions, $a = \frac{\sqrt{\frac{4(h^2+hk+k^2)}{3}}}{Q_x}$, $c = \frac{l}{Q_z}$ and $d^{-1} = \sqrt{Q_x^2 + Q_z^2}$, where a and c are the lattice constant, Q_x and Q_z are the reciprocal space coordinates [7]. The tilt angle and coherence lengths were measured by change of reciprocal space coordinate (ΔQ_z, ΔQ_x) and given in Table I following ref. 8. Figure 5 shows the FWHM values for skew scan of asymmetric (105), (103), (102) along with symmetric (002) plane. The twist angle of MN1= 0.38° and MN2=1.68° were measured by fitting with Shrikant model [9]. Analysis shows that mosaicity of MN2 sample is larger than MN1. It had occurred due to the larger lattice mismatch between GaN and Si substrate as compared to between GaN and Al_2O_3 substrate. However, due to optimized growth conditions and AlN/GaN/AlN buffer stack the quality of the MN2 sample is still quite suitable for device application in spite of the high mismatch between GaN and Si. The Al mole fraction is 30 % for both structures which was measured from lattice constants of strained AlGaN based on anisotropic elastic theory [10]. The details of HRXRD analysis show from RSM that the AlGaN layer is pseudomorphic in nature. The reciprocal lattice points (RLP) of the AlGaN layer for both the samples are same as the GaN layer in Q_x direction which ensures that its in-plane lattice constant is same as GaN layer and the AlGaN layer itself is fully strained. On the other hand, due to thick AlN relaxed buffer layer in sample MN2, the RLP of AlN is not same as GaN layer as shown in Fig. 4. On the other hand, GaN layer is nearly relaxed, and only residual strain is present in the same owing to the different thermal expansion coefficients between the epilayers and the substrates.

Table I. Measured lattice constant, tilt, twist angle and coherence length of sample MN1 and MN2.

Sample		**Lattice constant (Å)**		**Tilt angle (arc sec)**	**Twist angle (deg.)**	**Coherence length (μm)**	**In-plane strain (10^{-4})**	**Out-of plane strain (10^{-4})**
		'a'	**'c'**					
MN1	GaN	3.1898	5.1867	250	0.38	0.09	2.51	4.04
	AlGaN	3.1898	5.1020				76.44	-42.15
MN2	GaN	3.1885	5.1506	146	1.68	0.014	-1.57	-67.30
	AlGaN	3.1843	5.0992				59.07	-47.62

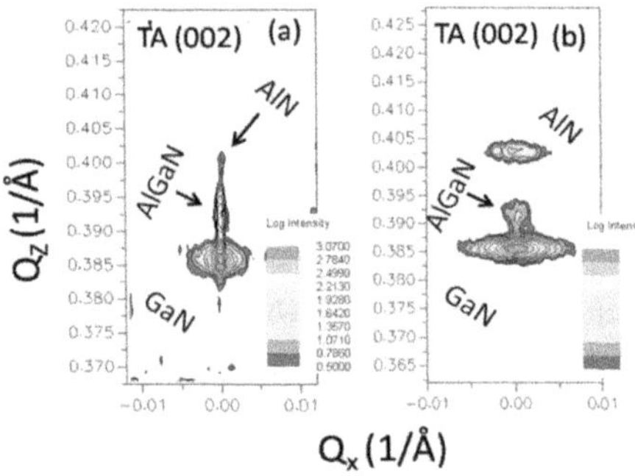

Figure 3 symmetric TA RSM of (002) plane of sample (a) MN1 and (b) MN2

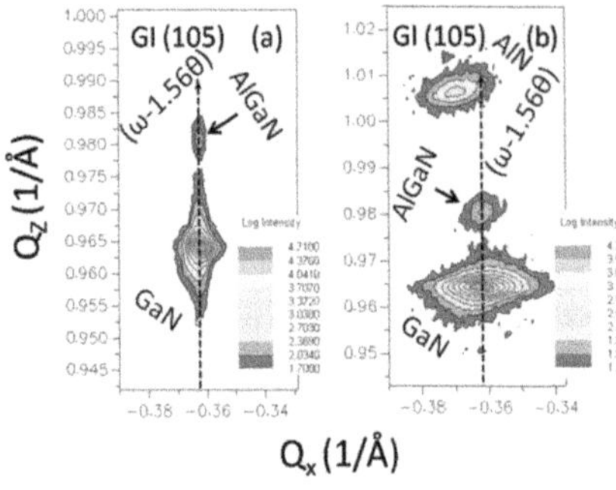

Figure 4 DA RSM of asymmetric GI (105) RSM of (a) MN1 and (b) MN2.

The screw and edge defect density were measured from the FWHM of skew symmetric scan of (002) and (102) plane respectively using the following equations, $D_{screw} = \frac{\beta^2_{(0002)}}{4.35b^2_{screw}}$, $D_{edge} = \frac{\beta^2_{(10\bar{1}2)}}{4.35b^2_{edge}}$, where D_{screw} is the screw type TD density, D_{edge} is the edge type TD density, β is the FWHM of X-ray reflections and b is the Burgers vector length ($b_{screw} = 5.1855$ Å, $b_{edge} = 3.1890$ Å) [11].

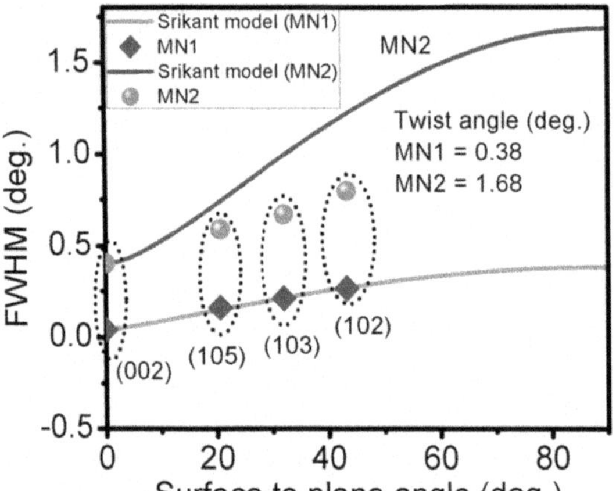

Figure 5 skew symmetric plot with Srikant model of MN1 and MN2

Thus the defect densities of MN1 and MN2 samples using FWHM values of (002) and (102) scans in the above expression were estimated as 3.71×10^8, 3.20×10^9 and 3.34×10^9, $4.29 \times$

$10^{10}cm^{-2}$ for screw and edge type , respectively. The high density of edge dislocations may have originated because of the low angle grain boundary. Figure 6 and 7 shows the XRR of both the samples with corresponding REFS fit and cross sectional FESEM micrograph [12], respectively.

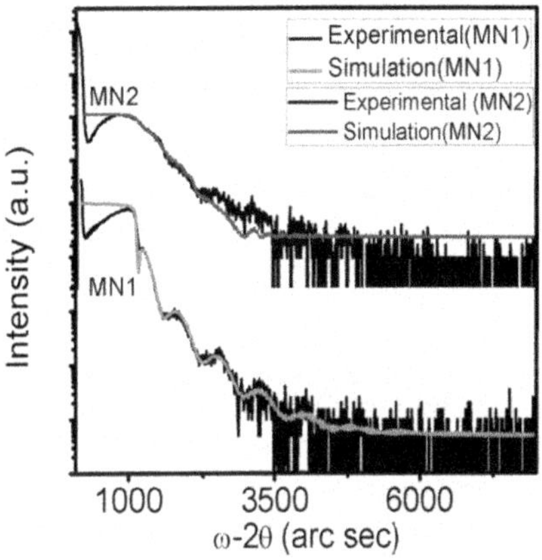

Figure 6 XRR plot with REFS fit of sample MN1 and MN2.

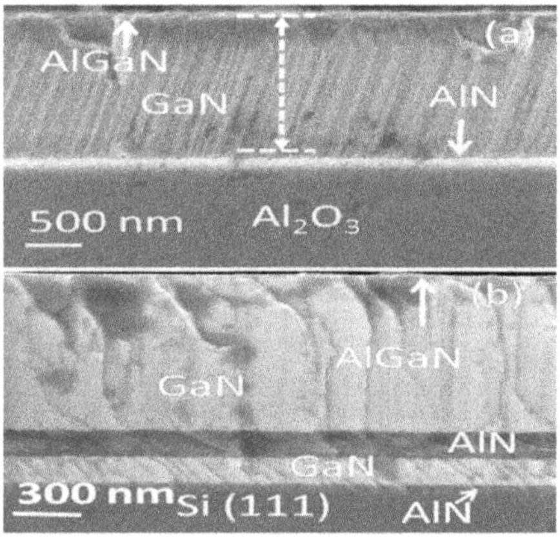

Figure 7 Cross sectional FESEM image of (a) MN1 and (b) MN2.

Table II: Measured thickness and roughness from XRR and FESEM.

Sample	Layers	XRR		FESEM
		Thickness (nm)	Roughness (nm)	Thickness (nm)
MN1	GaN (cap)	2.50	1.43	-
	AlGaN	18.26	0.20	20
	GaN	1349.97	0.90	1200
	AlN (NL)	18	0.15	20
MN2	GaN (cap)	2.7	1.7	-
	AlGaN	21.70	2.8	20
	GaN	1220.80	0.10	1200
	AlN	214.90	0.21	230
	GaN	276.17	0.10	270
	AlN	52.20	0.76	50

The Kiessing fringes of the XRR profile arises due to reflection at the smooth interfaces. Thus, the thicknesses of the individual layers were measured from distinguishable fringe spacing of the XRR scan. The measured thickness and roughness of all the layers as measured from XRR and FESEM are given in Table II. It is to be noted that the slight variation between thickness values evaluated from the two different techniques may have arose from the uncertainty in pinpointing the exact interface between layers having widely varying thicknesses or similar imaging contrast in FESEM analysis.

Conclusion

In this report, an attempt was made to carry out in-depth structural analysis of nitride heterostructures by HRXRD. The comparative analysis confirmed that AlGaN/GaN heterostructure can be grown on Si (111) substrate for electronics device applications in spite of large thermal and lattice mismatch between the GaN layer and the Si substrate. The AlN/GaN/AlN buffer layers for MN2 sample strategically restricts the propagation of threading dislocations. The measured FWHM of both symmetric (002) and asymmetric (105) plane ensured that high quality epitaxy was indeed achieved by PAMBE.

Acknowledgment

We thankfully acknowledge the financial support received from DST, INDIA (Sanction No. 100/IFD/196/2010-11, dated: 03/06/10). We also thank SVTA (USA) for their technical help during epitaxial work.

References

1 O. Amacher, B. Foutz, J. Smart, J. R. Shealy, N. G. Weimann, K. Chu, M. Murphy, A. J. Sierakowski, W. J. Schaff, and L. F. Eastman, J. Appl. Phys. 87, 334 (2000)

2 C. Wang, X. Wang, G. Hu, J. Wang, J. Li, and Z. Wang, Appl. Surf. Sci. 253, 762 (2006)

3 S. Keller, G. Parish, P. T. Fini, S. Heikman, C. -H. Chen, N. Zhang, S. P. DenBaars, U. K. Mishra, and Y.-F. Yu, J. Appl. Phys. 86, 4520 (1999).

4 H. Angerer, D. Brunner, F. Freudenberg, O. Ambacher, M. Stutzmann, R. Höpler, T. Metzger, and E. Born, G. Dollinger, A. Bergmaier, S. Karsch, and H. –J. Körner, *Appl. Phys. Lett.* 71, 1504-1506, (1997).

5 C Sukwon , H Eric, D Donald, V Ramakrishna, and G Samuel ,, J. Appl.Phys. 113, 093510, 2013.

6 E. Arslan, M. K. Ozturk, A. Teke, S. Ozcelik, and E. Ozbay, J. Phys. D: Appl. Phys. 41, 155317 (2008).

7 B. Poust, B. Heying, S. Hayashi, R. Ho, K. Matney, R. Sandhu, M. Wojtowicz, and M. Goorsky, J. Phys. D: Appl. Phys. 38, A93-A98, (2005).

8 Takuji Arauchi, Shotaro Takeuchi, Kunihiko Nakamura, Dinh Thanh Khan, Yoshiaki Nakamura, Hideto Miyake, Kazumasa Hiramatsu, and Akira Sakai, Phys. Status Solidi A, 211, 731-735 (2014).

9 V. Srikant, J. S. Speck, and D. R. Clarke, J. Appl. Phys. 82, 4286, (1997).

10 F. M. Morales, D. González, J. G. Lozano, R. García, S. Hauguth-Frank, V. Lebedev, V. Cimalla, O. Ambacher, Acta Materialia, vol. 57, pp. 5681-5692, (2009).

11 S. Cörekci, M. K. Öztürk, H. Yu, M. C¸akmak, S. Özcelik, and E. Özbay, Semiconductors 47(6), 820–824 (2013).

12 Bede Scientific, Inc., USA.

Mater. Res. Soc. Symp. Proc. Vol. 1754 © 2015 Materials Research Society
DOI: 10.1557/opl.2015.114

Hard X-ray beam damage study of monolayer Ni islands using SX-STM

Nozomi Shirato[1,*], Marvin Cummings[1], Heath Kersell[2], Yang Li[2], Dean Miller[3], Daniel Rosenmann[3], Saw-Wai Hla[2, 3], Volker Rose[1, 3,**]

[1] Advanced Photon Source, Argonne National Laboratory, Argonne, IL 60439, USA.
[2] Nanoscale and Quantum Phenomena Institute, Physics & Astronomy Department, Ohio University, Athens, OH 45701, USA.
[3] Center for Nanoscale Materials, Argonne National Laboratory, Argonne, IL 60439, USA.

Corresponding authors: [*](N.S.) nshirato@anl.gov; [**](V.R.) vrose@anl.gov

ABSTRACT

X-ray beam-induced damage in nanoscale metal islands was investigated. Monolayer-high Ni islands were prepared on a Cu(111) substrate. High brilliance X-rays with photon energies between 8.45 and 8.85 keV illuminated the sample for about 11 hours. In order to track changes in the morphology of the islands, the synchrotron X-ray scanning tunneling microscopy (SX-STM) technique was utilized. The result shows that X-ray illumination onto Ni islands does not induce noticeable damage. The study demonstrates that local beam-induced changes can be studied using SX-STM.

INTRODUCTION

High brilliance X-ray beams produced by third generation synchrotrons are a powerful source for sample analysis. The high flux density enhances signal-to-noise ratios and reduces data acquisition times. However, typically a sample irradiated by a high radiation dose tends to exhibit beam-induced damage, e.g., modifications of the chemical compositions of organic molecules or changes in the surface structure due to thermal annealing. It is necessary to monitor and quantify beam-induced damages for efficient data acquisition and sample preservation purposes. Various types of studies have been carried out to quantify beam-induced damage. Measuring changes in diffraction peaks intensity [1–3] and X-ray absorption near edge structure (XANES) spectroscopy [4, 5] are commonly used methods to observe X-ray beam damage. However, these techniques provide information about changes of the chemical composition and structure averaged over the entire area that is illuminated by the beam. They do not provide any direct localized information about changes in the surface chemistry or topography. Nevertheless, it is essential to characterize localized beam damage during X-ray illumination, in order to obtain a better understanding of complex systems, such as biological cells, batteries and nanostructures [6]. This goal can be achieved when a scanning tunneling microscope (STM) is used to image a sample surface during X-ray illumination [7].

Over the last decade, groups around the world have been developing instruments combining synchrotron X-ray illumination and STM [8–11]. Recently, synchrotron X-ray scanning tunneling microscopy (SX-STM) showed the capability to measure two-dimensional real space information of monolayer thick metal islands during X-ray illumination [12]. Here we present a study of potential hard X-ray beam-induced damage of monolayer Ni islands on a Cu(111) substrate using SX-STM. The technique allows us to track changes of the Ni islands' surface topography during continuous X-ray illumination. The results indicate the absence of beam-induced damage on the Ni islands even after almost half a day of continuous X-ray illumination at photon energies between 8.45 and 8.85 keV.

EXPERIMENTAL DETAILS

To examine the potential beam damage induced in metal islands, measurements were carried out at the hard X-ray nanoprobe beamline 26-ID of the Center for Nanoscale Materials and the Advanced Photon Source at Argonne National Laboratory [13]. The experimental schematic is shown in Figure 1. The entire experiment, from the sample preparation to the characterization of beam damage, was performed at room temperature and under UHV (<10^{-9} Torr) conditions. When the sample is illuminated by synchrotron X-rays, photoelectrons can be generated [14]. Because photoejected electrons from the sample can interfere with the conventional tunneling conditions of the STM [15], a nanofabricated "smart tip" was utilized, covered with layers of insulating and conductive coatings [12]. The smart tip focuses electron detection solely near the apex region of the scanning tip where the main interaction with the sample occurs, minimizing the background electrons collected at the sidewalls of the tip [16,17]. Additionally, the incoming X-ray beam was chopped at 3 kHz in order to achieve stable tunneling conditions through a filter that separates photoexcited currents from the topographic signal used in the feedback system of the STM [18].

A clean Cu(111) substrate was prepared by several cycles of sputtering with Ar^+ ions and e-beam annealing for 30 minutes at 600 Celsius. For the sample preparation, a submonolayer of Ni (Alfa Aesar 99.995 %) was deposited onto the clean Cu(111) substrate. The Ni islands were grown using an electron beam evaporator with a controlled deposition rate of 0.2 ML/min for 60 seconds, while the substrate was kept at room

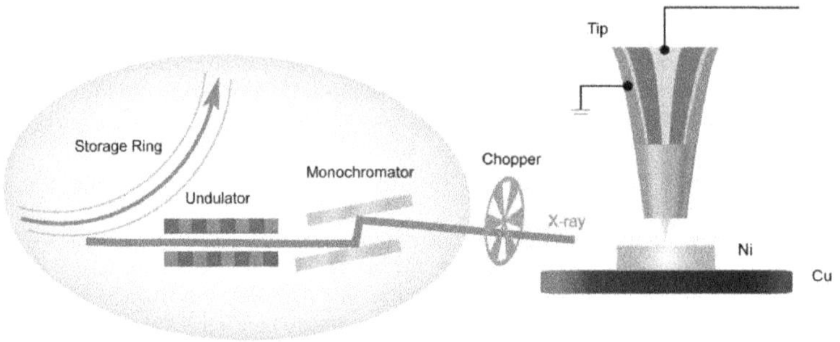

Figure 1. Schematic of the experimental setup. Electrons path through an undulator to generate high brilliance X-rays. A monochromator selects a specified photon energy. The chopped X-ray beam illuminates the sample, which is simultaneously imaged by a nanofabricated tip.

temperature. Immediately following the deposition, the sample was transferred to the STM head.

Before starting the measurement, the tip and sample were carefully aligned with respect to the incoming beam. Then the sample was continuously illuminated for about 11 h with X-ray photon energies between 8.45 and 8.85 keV. The X-ray flux density was about 3×10^{13} photons s^{-1} mm^{-2} $(0.01\%\ \text{bandwidth})^{-1}$ in the utilized photon energy range. In order to evaluate beam damage, an isolated Ni island was continuously imaged while the sample was irradiated by an X-ray beam with a spot size of around 100 µm. During the irradiation the tip scanned across the surface to monitor changes in shape and volume of the Ni islands.

DISCUSSION

In Figure 2a-e, we present a time series of STM topography images recorded over a single Ni cluster with a diameter of about 20 nm. The time value at the top-right corner of each image indicates the duration of continuous X-ray illumination. The initial height of the island was measured as 201±16 pm, which indicates single-atomic height. The series of images was obtained at a fixed bias voltage of -1 V and a constant tip current of 1 nA. The integrity of the Ni islands on Cu(111) was carefully monitored in order to inspect the sample for potential radiation damage. Despite a continuous illumination with high energy X-rays, the Ni cluster appeared rather stable for the entire measurement time. Only after a long scanning period exceeding several hours, a slight change in the island shape was observed, while the island height remained stable. However, such small changes of the island shape can also occur due to room temperature thermal diffusion of Ni atoms at island step edges without X-ray illumination. In addition to the topographic images, chemical contrast images [12] were obtained simultaneously. Figure 2f shows a

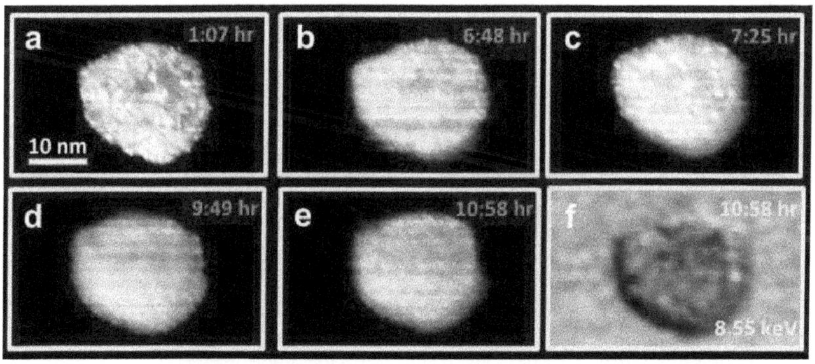

Figure 2. **a-e,** STM topography images of a Ni cluster upon continuous X-ray illumination with photon energies between 8.45 and 8.85 keV. The respective elapsed illumination time is indicated in the images. **f,** Chemical contrast image obtained at 8.55 keV photon energy after 10 hr and 58 min X-ray illumination.

chemical contrast image at a photon energy of 8.55 eV, obtained after 10 hours and 58 minutes of continuous illumination. It likewise confirms the stability of the Ni cluster.

The island volume calculated from the topography information is plotted as a function of illumination time (Figure 3). There are no significant changes in the island volume observed during the illumination. The results prove inertness and stability of Ni island on the Cu(111) substrate at room temperature. Considering that the island consists of just one monolayer of Ni atoms, the result is encouraging for future studies, e.g., X-ray spectroscopy of adatoms or organic molecules on a metal substrate.

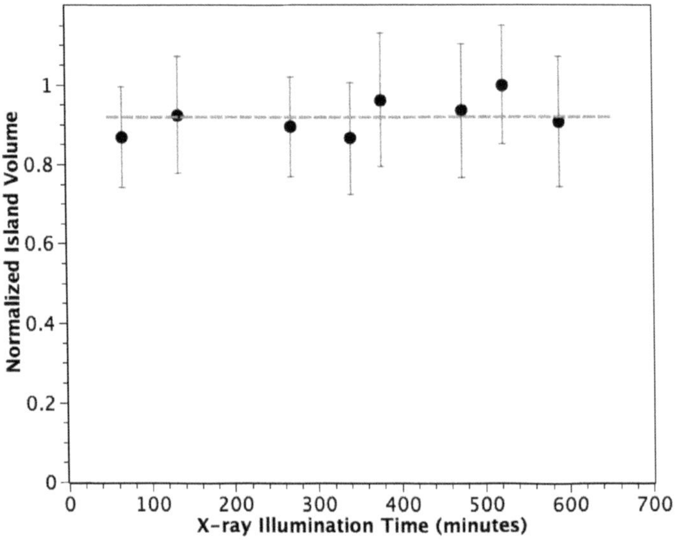

Figure 3. Normalized Ni island volume as a function of X-ray beam illumination time. The dotted line indicates the average island volume.

CONCLUSIONS

By combining synchrotron radiation and scanning tunneling microscopy, we were able to track the structural stability of a monolayer-high Ni island during continuous hard X-ray illumination for more than half a day. The result shows that high-flux X-ray illumination onto a nanoscale Ni island does not cause beam-induced damage. Although the sample was kept at room temperature, the change of the island volume was negligible.

In the future, beam-damage studies of biological, organic and energy related samples are potential candidates. Furthermore, the combination of SX-STM and advanced imaging techniques, e.g., non-contact atomic force microscopy (NC-AFM) using a q-plus sensor, could allow us to study beam-induced damage on an individual chemical bond in a single molecule [19].

Our study demonstrates that local beam-induced changes can be studied using the SX-STM. The direct access to high-resolution *in situ* information of beam/matter interactions is valuable for many synchrotron applications.

ACKNOWLEDGMENTS

This work was funded by the Office of Science Early Career Research Program through the Division of Scientific User Facilities, Office of Basic Energy Sciences, U.S. Department of Energy, through Grant SC70705. Work at the Advanced Photon Source, the Center for Nanoscale Materials, and the Electron Microscopy Center was supported by the U.S. Department of Energy, Office of Science, Office of Basic Energy Sciences, under Contract DE-AC02-06CH11357. Authors acknowledge the excellent supports from the X-ray microscopy group at CNM.

REFERENCES

1. R. Sanishvili, D. W. Yoder, S. B. Pothineni, G. Rosenbaum, S. Xu, S. Vogt, S. Stepanov, O. A. Makarov, S. Corcoran, R. Benn, V. Nagarajan, J. L. Smith and R. F. Fischetti, *Proceedings of the National Academy of Sciences*, **108**, 15, 6127–6132 (2011).
2. N. Shimizu, K. Hirata, K. Hasegawa, G. Ueno and M. Yamamoto, *J. Synchrotron Rad.*, **14**, 4–10 (2007).
3. P. Sliz, S. C. Harrison and G. Rosenbaum, *Structure*, **11**, 13-19 (2003).
4. T. Beetz and C. Jacobsen, *J. Synchrotron Rad.*, **10**, 280–283 (2003).
5. J. M. Ramallo-López, L. J. Giovanetti, F. C. Vicentin and F. G. Requejo, *J. Physics: Conference Series*, **430**, 1, 012034 (2013).
6. M. Holt, R. Harder, R. Winarski and V. Rose, *Annu. Rev. Mater. Res*, **43**, 183-211 (2013).
7. A. Saito, T. Tanaka, Y. Takagi, H. Hosokawa, H. Notsu, G. Ohzeki, Y. Tanaka, Y. Kohmura, M. Akai-Kasaya, T. Ishikawa, Y. Kuwahara, S. Kikuta and M. Aono, *J. Nanosci. Nanotechnol.*, **11**, 2873-2881 (2011).
8. A. Saito, J. Maruyama, K. Manabe, K. Kitamoto, K. Takahashi, K. Takami, M. Yabashi, Y. Tanaka, D. Miwa, M. Ishii, Y. Takagi, M. Akai-Kasaya, S. Shin, T. Ishikawa, Y. Kuwahara and M. Aono, *J. Synchrotron Rad.*, **13**, 216–220 (2006).
9. M. L. Cummings, T. Y. Chien, C. Preissner, V. Madhavan, D. Diesing, M. Bode, J. W. Freeland and V. Rose, *Ultramicroscopy*, **112**, 22–31 (2012).
10. Y. Hasegawa, T. Okuda, T. Eguchi, T. Matsushima, A. Harasawa, K. Akiyama and T. Kinoshita, *Hyomen Kagaku*, **26**, 12, 752–756 (2005).
11. C.-Y. Chiu, Y.-L. Chan, Y. J. Hsu and D. H. Wei, *Appl. Phys. Lett.*, **92**, 103101 (2008).
12. N. Shirato, M. L. Cummings, H. R. Kersell, Y. Li, B. Stripe, D. Rosenmann, S. W. Hla and V. Rose, *Nano Letters*, **14**, 6499-6504 (2014).
13. R. P. Winarski, M. V. Holt, V. Rose, P. Fuesz, D. Carbaugh, C. Benson, D. Shu, D. Kline, G. B. Stephenson, I. McNulty and J. Maser, *J. Synchrotron Rad.*, **19**, 6, 1056–1060 (2012).

14. V. Rose, J. W. Freeland, K. E. Gray and S. K. Streiffer, *Appl. Phys. Lett.*, **92**, 193510 (2008).
15. V. Rose, K. Wang, T. Chien, J. Hiller, D. Rosenmann, J. W. Freeland, C. Preissner and S.-W. Hla, *Adv. Funct. Mater.*, **23**, 20, 2646– 2652 (2013).
16. K. Akiyama, T. Eguchi, T. An, Y. Hasegawa, T. Okuda, A. Harasawa and T. Kinoshita, *Rev. Sci. Instrum.*, **76**, 083711 (2005).
17. V. Rose, T.Y. Chien, J. Hiller, D. Rosenmann and R.P. Winarski, *Appl. Phys. Lett.*, **99**, 173102 (2011).
18. K. Wang, D. Rosenmann, M. Holt, R. Winarski, S.-W. Hla and V. Rose, *Rev. Sci. Instrum.*, **84**, 063704 (2013).
19. L. Gross, *Nature Chem.*, **3**, 273–278 (2011).

Mater. Res. Soc. Symp. Proc. Vol. 1754 © 2015 Materials Research Society
DOI: 10.1557/opl.2015.637

Non-equilibrium processes in martensitic phase transformations by X-ray photon correlation spectroscopy

Michael Widera[1] and Uwe Klemradt[1],

[1]2nd Institute of Physics and JARA-FIT, RWTH Aachen University, D-52056 Aachen, Germany.

ABSTRACT

Through undulator sources at 3rd generation synchrotrons, highly coherent X-rays with sufficient flux are nowadays routinely available, which allow carrying over photon correlation spectroscopy (PCS) from visible light to the X-ray regime. X-ray photon correlation spectroscopy (XPCS) is based on the auto-correlation of X-ray speckle patterns during the temporal evolution of a material and provides access both to equilibrium and non-equilibrium properties of materials at the Angstrom scale. Owing to technical limitations (detector readout), XPCS has typically been used for the detection of slow dynamics on the scale of seconds. The variety of scattering geometries employed in conventional X-ray analysis can be combined with XPCS. In this work, we report on bulk diffraction (XRD) used to study the prototypical shape memory alloy $Ni_{63}Al_{37}$ undergoing a structural, diffusionless (martensitic) transformation. Two-time correlation functions reveal non-equilibrium dynamics superimposed with microstructural avalanches.

INTRODUCTION

The shape memory effect is based on a diffusionless, structural (martensitic) phase transition. Although shape memory alloys are key functional materials with considerable use in technical applications, the underlying transformation mechanism is still little understood. Being of first order, the martensitic transition (MT) proceeds by nucleation and growth. However, typically the transition is only weakly of first order, e.g. with a small latent heat and accompanied by a hysteresis width on the order of about 10 K. Owing to the reduced symmetry of the low temperature phase, typically several variants (domains) of the martensitic phase are nucleated on cooling. Although these possess the same structure, the variants are nucleated with different orientations (unless prevented by some biasing field). This leads to the buildup of twin-related variants and self-accommodation in order to minimize strain. Since the variants are related to each other by orientation relations, which can be considered compatibility relations of the self-accommodation process, the MT necessarily involves the temperature-dependent up-folding of a surface relief [1, 2]. In contrast to steel, the MT in shape memory alloys appears to be close to a second order phase transition. Precursor effects that herald the new phase well above the actual transition temperature are frequently observed, for example pronounced phonon softening [3-5] in neutron scattering, anomalous elastic constants in ultrasound experiments [6] and tweed patterns observed in transmission electron microscopy [1]. By definition, a prototypical MT proceeds without diffusion [7]. This explains why largely athermal transformations are observed, where the amount of material transformed depends solely on the degree of undercooling, and the conversion of the high temperature phase progresses with nearly the speed of sound, even at temperatures below 100 K. Of course, diffusion is unavoidable at finite temperatures, but is considered not to be a key ingredient of MT. However, there are effects in MT that have been attributed to diffusion superimposed on an essentially diffusionless transformation, in particular ageing effects on long time scales (minutes to hours) [8]. The latter were attributed to short-range diffusion after a change of local symmetry resulting from a MT ("symmetry conforming short-range order", SC-SRO) [9].

Using 3rd generation synchrotron radiation sources, it has become possible to access slow dynamics on the microscopic scale with coherent X-rays. The use of coherent photons had led to novel investigation techniques such as X-ray Photon Correlation Spectroscopy (XPCS), which tracks down time-dependent phenomena in soft and solid condensed matter systems. Using coherent X-ray beams, the individual arrangement of scatterers in real crystals can be shown through a grainy diffraction pattern, also called "speckle" pattern. If the individual arrangement of scatterers changes over time, also the speckle pattern changes and time-dependent intensity fluctuations are observable [10]. The resulting time-dependent evolution of a speckle pattern for equilibrium dynamics can be analyzed using the one-time correlation function (CF) [11]

$$g^{(2)}(\vec{Q},\tau) = \frac{\left\langle I(\vec{Q},t)\cdot I(\vec{Q},t+\tau)\right\rangle_T}{\left\langle I(\vec{Q},t)\right\rangle_T \cdot \left\langle I(\vec{Q},t+\tau)\right\rangle_T}, \tag{1}$$

where $\langle \ldots \rangle_T$ denotes an average over time. The zero-point in time is not significant, since only the time difference $\tau = t_2 - t_1$ enters Eq. (1). Typically, one-time CFs show little change for short time lags τ, but drop drastically in the long run. Experimentally determined CF are frequently parameterized as stretched exponentials, e.g. Kohlrausch-Williams-Watts (KWW) functions [10]

$$g^{(2)} = 1 + A \cdot \exp(-2[\tau/\tau_0]^{\beta}). \tag{2}$$

The stretching exponent β can be different from one, with the numerical value being amenable to physical interpretation: a decay faster than exponential ($\beta > 1$) is associated with solid-like, collective dynamics, a slower decay ($\beta < 1$) with liquid-like, diffusional dynamics [12].

In the case of non-equilibrium systems, the evolving dynamics cannot be meaningfully tracked by the one-time CF. Instead, a two-time CF is more appropriate [13]:

$$C(t_1,t_2) = \frac{\langle I(t_1)\cdot I(t_2)\rangle - \langle I(t_1)\rangle\langle I(t_2)\rangle}{\left(\langle I^2(t_1)\rangle - \langle I(t_1)\rangle^2\right)^{1/2}\left(\langle I^2(t_2)\rangle - \langle I(t_2)\rangle^2\right)^{1/2}}, \tag{3}$$

where $\langle \cdots \rangle$ denotes an average over pixels from a region of interest (ROI), making $C(t_1,t_2)$ also a function of the corresponding wave vectors $\vec{Q}$. Note that in contrast to Eq. (1), in Eq. (3) the zero-point in time now has acquired physical meaning. The average time after start of the experiment, $\bar{t} = \frac{1}{2}(t_1 + t_2) =: t_{age}$, is a convenient measure of the age of the evolving system. This coordinate corresponds in $C(t_1,t_2)$ diagrams to the diagonal from the lower left to the upper right corner. A cut along the time-difference coordinate $\tau = t_2 - t_1$ is perpendicular to that diagonal and provides a characteristic correlation time of the system at t_{age} [13], in contrast to the correlation time averaged over all system ages, provided by Eq. (1).

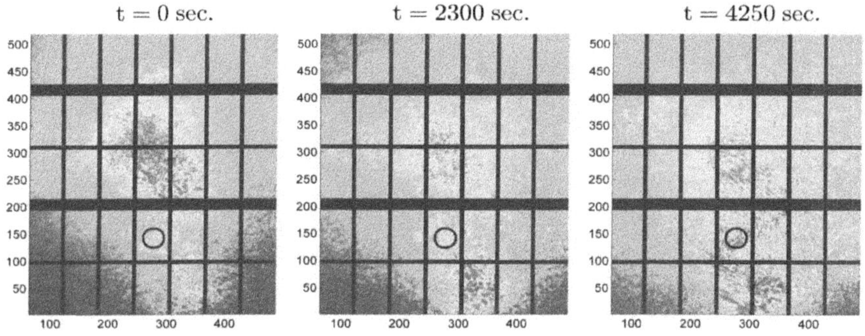

Figure 1. Speckle pattern produced with a partly coherent X-ray beam at the (001) reflection in Bragg geometry for a $Ni_{63}Al_{37}$ crystal at 0 s, 2300 s and 4250 s (time series taken under isothermal conditions at T = 278.5 K). The ROI used to calculate the two-time correlation function depicted in Fig. 2 is indicated schematically as a circle. It corresponds to 79 pixels with a radius of approximately $q_r = 2 \cdot 10^{-3}$ Å^{-1}.

EXPERIMENTAL DETAILS

For the investigation of slow time-dependent phenomena, a $Ni_{63}Al_{37}$ crystal was investigated using XPCS in diffraction geometry. The single crystal with a (001) polished surface was studied at the coherence beamline P10 of the PETRA III synchrotron at DESY. The experiment was carried out in Bragg geometry using the (001) reflection at $\Theta_B = 13{,}51°$ for X-rays of 9.3 keV energy. The undulator beam was focused by compound refractive lenses to a spot size of about 5x5 μm^2 (FHWM) at the sample. The diffracted X-rays were detected by a Pilatus 300K detector (487 × 619 pixels, pixel size 172 × 172 μm^2) placed 4975 mm downstream of the sample. Various times series of the speckle distribution centered at the (001) reflection were recorded for selected temperatures a few Kelvin above and at the MT, as shown exemplarily in Fig. 1. The temperature stability was ensured by a dedicated setup limiting temperature fluctuations to ±3 mK over 24 hrs. Data were taken with an exposure time of 1 sec for intensity reasons, compatible with the focus of the experiment on slow dynamics. The detector readout time was 3 msec.

RESULTS

As can be seen from the typical data shown in Fig. 1, the speckle pattern at the (001) Bragg reflection undergoes partially strong changes while other areas remain essentially unchanged. We can therefore rule out trivial relaxation processes of the entire sample (e.g., associated with the sample mount etc.) and relate these changes to partial transformations in the sample. It is well known that MTs into the low temperature phase proceed by avalanches, which emit acoustic emission events following power laws [14]. We confirmed the occurrence of avalanches in the samples investigated here independently by acoustic emission spectroscopy.

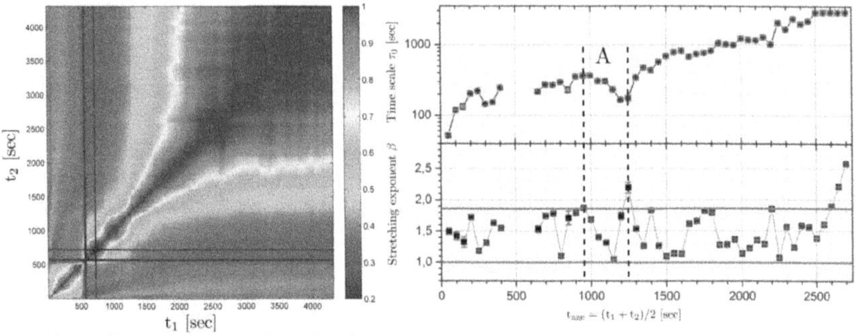

Figure 2. (Left) Two-time CF for $Ni_{63}Al_{37}$ at a temperature of 278.5 K. The contours quantify the degree of correlation between the speckle patterns (The two vertical and horizontal lines are artefacts arising from detector readout error). (Right) Characteristic time scales τ_0 and corresponding KWW exponents β extracted from the two-time CF using non-averaged one-time CF at a given age of the material. The stretching exponent varies repeatedly between 1 and ca. 2, indicating the build-up of internal stress fields that relax temporarily by microstructural avalanches which partially transform the sample.

It should be emphasized that the (001) austenite reflection splits upon the MT due to the lower symmetry of the martensitic phase. Therefore it appears reasonable to relate time-dependent changes of the associated speckle pattern to the phase transformation. More specifically, since the origin of speckle is disorder, a given speckle pattern is closely related to the exact spatial arrangement of the scatterers [11]. Metallic single crystals usually exhibit fairly broad Bragg reflections when measured with incoherent X-rays, hence the corresponding speckle pattern contains information on a variety of related defects. These include (small-angle) grain boundaries separating the mosaic blocks, but also atomic defects, which give rise to Huang scattering around Bragg spots in conventional X-ray scattering [15]. This effect is particularly present in shape memory alloys, for example in $Ni_{63}Al_{37}$ due to the excess nickel [16]. The diffusionless transformation proceeds locally on the order of the speed of sound, so avalanches take extended arrays of unit cells from cubic to tetragonal or orthorhombic symmetry. This changes drastically the exact spatial arrangement of scatterers, which must result in sudden jumps of the related parts of the speckle pattern on the time scale of the experiment.

These features are mirrored by Fig. 2, showing the two-time CF of the ROI from Fig. 1, calculated using Eq. (3). The degree of correlation between the speckle patterns is scale-coded, with higher values representing stronger correlations. The results presented here are essentially independent of the particular choice of the ROI. The local M_s temperature of the spot under investigation was determined to be $M_s = 278.5$ K, since at this temperature the speckle pattern changed dramatically, indicating massive structural rearrangement. To ensure a rather complete record of the non-equilibrium dynamics, a time series extending over more than 4000 seconds had been taken. Two major aspects should be pointed out:
First, the time evolution of the speckle pattern shows occasional jerky movements, mirrored by sharp cuts (breakdowns) of the two-time CF. We attribute these findings to microstructural avalanches, in accordance with the physics of the system and similar to features in previous XPCS measurements of the MT in gold-cadmium [17] and cobalt [18].

Second, as mentioned in the introduction, a system age can be defined via $t_{age} = (t_1+t_2)/2$, which corresponds to the diagonal from the lower left to the upper right corner. For non-equilibrium dynamics which relaxes into a steady or even equilibrium state, also the characteristic time scale τ_0 must evolve over time. The corresponding increase of the correlation time is clearly visible in Fig. 2 (left) as diverging contours. To quantify the evolving dynamics at a given system age, the one-time CF at that particular age was determined using fits of a KWW function (Eq. (2)). The results obtained are shown in Fig. 2 (right), indicating that the stretching exponent β drops repeatedly from values close to 2 to values near 1 (see for example Fig. 1 interval A with $\beta \sim 1.8$ to $\beta \sim 1.1$). We interpret these findings as follows: larger avalanches passing through or near the illuminated volume are comparatively rare events, which are reflected in occasional collapses of the CF. However, owing to the underlying power law distribution, smaller avalanches occur much more often. Far-reaching strain fields still modify atomic positions in the illuminated volume, which do not lead to collapses but modify the CF quantitatively. In addition, slow atomic rearrangements are expected to take place following an avalanche that takes the austenite phase locally into the martensitic phase [9,19]. As detailed in the established SC-SRO model for ageing in shape memory alloys, the symmetry of the configuration of lattice imperfections both in the austenite and the martensitic state should conform to the crystal symmetry under equilibrium conditions. However, after a sudden change of symmetry brought about by a diffusionless transformation (e.g., the avalanches comprising a MT), the previous local configuration is inherited by the unit cells of the martensitic phase, where this configuration gradually changes into the stable one by atomic rearrangement or relaxation [9], or in other words by short-range diffusion. Exactly this behavior is reflected by Fig. 2 (right): repeatedly, the system dynamics in the illuminated volume changes between a stretching exponent $\beta \approx 1$ (interpreted as a signature of diffusional dynamics) and values far above 1 (interpreted as signatures of collective behavior). Hence, the physical picture corroborated here is that of microstructural avalanches building up locally stress in the sample, which is relaxed by further avalanches followed by short-range atomic rearrangements.

CONCLUSIONS

XPCS can provide previously not accessible information for time-dependent phenomena in martensitic transformations. For a $Ni_{63}Al_{37}$ shape memory alloy investigated here, we find at the transition signatures of microstructural avalanches as well as non-equilibrium features on long time scales, in accordance with the macroscopic observation of isothermal ageing. Fits of Kohlrausch-Williams-Watts functions to non-averaged one-time correlation data exhibit solid-like dynamics ($\beta \gg 1$), with β dropping to 1 after stress relaxation by avalanches. This value indicates local atomic rearrangements (short-range diffusion) as suggested by the symmetry-conforming short-range order model.

REFERENCES

[1] Z. Nishiyama, Martensitic Transformation (Acad. Press New York, 1978).
[2] T. Davenport, L. Zhou and J. Trivisonno. Phys. Rev. B **59**, 3421 (1999).
[3] S.M. Shapiro, J.Z. Larese, Y. Noda, S.C. Moss and L.E. Tanner. Phys. Rev. Lett. **57**, 3199 (1986).

[4] L. Manosa, A. Planes, J. Zarestky, T. Lograsso, D.L. Schlagel and C. Stassis. Phys. Rev B **64**, 024305 (2001).
[5] T. Ohba, S. Raymond, S.M. Shapiro and K. Otsuka. Appl. Phys. **37**, 64 (1998).
[6] N. Rusovic and H. Warlimont. Phys. Stat. Sol A **44**, 609 (1977).7
[7] M. Cohen, G.B. Olson and P.C. Clapp. Proc. of the International Conference on Martensitic Transformations ICOMAT-79, Ed. W.S. Owen (MIT, Cambridge, 1979).
[8] K. Nakajima, S. Aoki, K. Otsuka and T.Ohba. Mat. Lett. **21**, 271 (1994).
[9] X. Ren and K. Otsuka. Nature **389**, 579 (1997).
[10] A. Madsen, R.L. Leheny, H. Guo, M. Sprung and O. Czakkel. New J. of Phys. **12**, 055001 (2010).
[11] G. Grübel, A. Madsen and A. Robert. Soft Matter Characterization, chapter 13. Springer Science+Business Media, LCC, New York (2008).
[12] O.G. Shpyrko, E.D. Isaacs, J.M. Logan, Yenjun Feng, G. Aeppli, R. Jaramillo, H.C. Kim, T.F. Rosenbaum, P. Zschack, M. Sprung, S. Narayanan and A.R. Sandy. Nature **447**, 68 (2007).
[13] A. Malik, A.R. Sandy, G.B. Stephenso, S.G.J. Mochrie, I. McNulty and M. Sutton. Phys. Rev. Lett. **81**, 5832 (1998).
[14] E. Vives, J. Ortin, L. Manosa, I. Rafols, R. Perez-Magrane, and A. Planes, Phys. Rev. Lett. **72**, 1694 (1994).
[15] M. A. Krivoglaz, Theory of X-ray and Neutron Scattering by Real Crystals (New York: Plenum Press, 1969).
[16] I.M. Robertson, Phil. Mag. A **64**, 577 (1991).
[17] L. Müller, M. Waldorf, C. Gutt, G. Grübel, A. Madsen, T.R. Finlayson, and U. Klemradt, Phys. Rev. Lett. **107**, 105701 (2011).
[18] C. Sanborn, K.F. Ludwig, M.C. Rogers and M. Sutton. Phys. Rev. Lett. **107**, 015702 (2011).
[19] K. Otsuka and X. Ren. Mat. Sci. Eng A **312**, 207 (2001).

Mater. Res. Soc. Symp. Proc. Vol. 1754 © 2015 Materials Research Society
DOI: 10.1557/opl.2015.760

Application of the Electron Density Correlation Function for Structural Analysis of X-ray Scattering/Diffraction Information from Polymer-based Nano-Composites

Kenan Song [1], Yiying Zhang [1], Navid Tajaddod [1], Marilyn L. Minus [2,*]
[1]Department of Mechanical and Industrial Engineering, Northeastern University, 360 Huntington Avenue, Boston, MA, USA, 02115-5000
[2,*]Department of Mechanical and Industrial Engineering, Northeastern University, 360 Huntington Avenue, Boston, MA, USA, 02115-5000. Correspondence email: m.minus@neu.edu, Phone: 617-373-2608.

ABSTRACT

Modern diffraction and scattering methods of X-ray radiation allow for multi-scale probing of the material morphology for both polymer-based composite films and fibers. These approaches and analyses tools can be used to map the makeup of individual grain structures in various polymer nano-composites in order to examine the effects of the fillers on nano-scale structural changes in the materials. The electron intensity correlation function, derived from Fourier transformations of the X-ray scattering pattern provides a path to analyze acquired data for space resolved domains. Here in this study, polymer-based nano-carbon composite systems are analyzed. The polymers used include polyvinyl alcohol, polyethylene, and polyacrilonitrile as matrix materials. The nano-carbon filler contribution to the grain size evolution is tracked by X-ray scattering/diffraction characterization. These results show that the relevant sizes of crystalline and amorphous domains within the lamellae structures correspond to the dispersion/distribution of the nano-filler in the composite materials. This work mainly illustrates an effective use of the correlation function to provide global morphological analysis in the composite system.

INTRODUCTION

SAXS analysis has been used since the 1950's [1]. SAXS analysis tools developed by Kratky [2], Guinier [3], Hossemann [4], Debye [5], and Porod [6] are now routinely applied to study the microstructure in polymer-based fibers. This analysis is used to obtain long-order structural information (i.e., morphology features at length scales ranging from 10 to 100 nm) for the fibers. SAXS is also commonly used to study the distribution of amorphous and crystalline regions within the lamellae and fibrillar structures in the fibers. Typically small-angle data arises from the scattering contrasts between neighboring domains ranging from 5 to 50 nm in size. D_f and L_f are the diameter and length of the fibrils, respectively. D_L and L_l/L_p are the average single lamella diameter and height. D_l is a unit lamellae diameter, and is typically inclusive of multiple lamella stacks. L_c and L_a are the single lamella crystalline and amorphous height, respectively. D_c and D_a are the diameters for the crystalline and amorphous portions of a single lamella, respectively.

In the SAXS patterns, typically there are two distinct features, a diffused equatorial scattering streak and discrete lobes/reflections along the meridional direction. The equatorial diffuse scattering (EDS) streak from the fiber develops due to elongated cylindrical objects (e.g., voids or fibrils) [7] in the samples. These features may be up to a few hundred nanometers in length and between 1 to 100 nm in diameter. Typically overall scattering due to widely dispersed elongated voids occurs at scattering vector (q_{avg}) less than 0.01 Å^{-1}, while a weaker scattering due to interfibrillar interference occurs at scattering vector more than 0.01 Å^{-1}. q_{avg} is related to the scattering angle (θ) by the relationship provided in Eq. 1, and λ is the X-ray wavelength of 0.15418 nm.

$$q_{avg} = \frac{4\pi \sin\theta}{\lambda} \qquad \text{Eq. (1)}$$

The discrete scattering along the meridional direction (i.e., parallel to the fiber-axis) arises from the presence of lamellae stacks in the fibers, and is referred to as the lamellae meridional peaks (LMP). Both the EDS and LMP data is used to analyze the overall fibrillar structure in the polymer and polymer/nano-filler composite fibers.

CORRELATION FUNCTION THEORY

A one-dimensional correlation (1DCF) function ($K(z)$) is used in order to obtain detailed information regarding structural parameters such as the average lamellar thickness pertaining to the periodic amorphous and crystalline domains [8]. $K(z)$ is derived from the Fourier transformation of the overall SAXS curve. This theoretical treatment for the lamellae stack analysis requires that the $K(z)$ be based on unoriented samples of a partially crystalline polymer, where the lamellae structure is isotropically distributed. For this reason, the multiplication of q_2^2 to $I(q_2)$ should be performed for an oriented system (i.e., anisotropic tapes, wires, and fibers). Eqs. 2 and 3 describe the modified correlation function (i.e., for anisotropic materials) used in this work [9]. From the general principles of diffraction theory it follows that the Fourier transformation of the SAXS data (Eq. 2) describes the distribution of the scattered X-ray intensity in reciprocal space and leads to a measurement of real space features due to the auto-convolution of the electron density variations arising from each diffracting object.

$$K(z) = \int_0^\infty I_1(q_2)\cos(zq_2)dq_2 \,/\int_0^\infty I_1(q_2)dq_2 \qquad \text{Eq. 2}$$

$$I_1(q_2) = \int_0^\infty I_1(q_1,q_2)dq_1 \,/\, 4\pi^2 \qquad \text{Eq. 3}$$

q_1 and q_2 are the scattering vectors along equatorial and meridional directions, and z represents the distance/dimension in real space. A projection operation was first used to obtain the integrated intensity along the meridional direction, $I(q_2)$. In order to obtain scattering intensity profiles solely from the lamellae structures (i.e., meridional lobe), the scattering information within the rectangular region inclusive of the EDS was excluded from this analysis. Practically to obtain the scattering data experimentally, Eq. 2 is rewritten and expressed as Eq. 4. For Eq. 4, the integral is divided into three parts limited by ranges in the scattering vectors q_1 and q_2.

$$I_1(q_2) = \left(\int_0^{q_{1\_initial}} I_1(q_1,q_2)dq_1 + \int_{q_{1\_initial}}^{q_{2\_tinitial}} I_1(q_1,q_2)dq_1 + \int_{q_{2\_initial}}^{\infty} I_1(q_1,q_2)dq_1\right)/4\pi^2 \qquad \text{Eq. 4}$$

The scattering detector is limited to minimum and maximum q_{avg} values, which can be separated into q_1 or $q_{1\_initial}$ and q_2 or $q_{2\_initial}$, respectively. The intensity data for the first integral between 0 and $q_{1\_initial}$ is determined by a linear extrapolation of the corrected scattering data. The intensity for the second integral between $q_{1\_initial}$ and $q_{2\_initial}$ is taken as the corrected intensity calculated from the measured data. The third integral between $q_{2\_initial}$ and ∞ is calculated using Porod's law, where $q_{2\_initial}$ corresponds to the start of the Porod region ($q_{2\_initial}$

is smaller than the maximum limit of q_2). It is important to note that for the fibers in this study a diffuse phase boundary results in enhancement of high-angle scattering leading to a positive deviation for the Porod region [6]. For the present study, extrapolation of the experimental data to higher angles is critical for analysis. Therefore, it is not approximated as an ideal Porod line or one with negative deviation [10].

The values for L_a, L_c, and L_t, can be extracted quantitatively from *K(z)* (Eqs. 5, 6, and 7). Assuming a sigmoidal gradient, with L_t characterizing the transition layer thickness, one obtains Eq. 5 to fit the intensity tails. *B(q)* is the background constant and *K* is termed Porod constant [11]. The *K(z)* and the electron density variations captured by the scattering data are associated. Using the linear correlation function *K(z)*, the lamella stack height L_p is theoretically determined. L_p and L_L (i.e., experimentally determined) values and trends should be similar. The computed L_p values are usually lower as compared to L_L calculated from Bragg's law [7]. This is a common phenomenon for many semi-crystalline polymers and may be due to (i) the presence of a broad distribution in lamella stack heights, and (ii) the existence of the transition region (L_t).

$$\lim_{q\to\infty} I(q) = B(q) + \frac{K}{q^4}\exp(-4\pi^2\sigma^2 q^2) \quad \text{Eq. 5}$$

$$l_c + l_t = \chi_l L_p \quad \text{Eq. 6}$$

$$l_a = (1-\chi_l)L_p \quad \text{Eq. 7}$$

EXPERIMENT

SAXS was performed using a SMAX3000 system equipped with high-brilliance 007HF source with CuK_α radiation (operation voltage 40 kV and current 30 mA, 147 kW), equipped with a 200 nm multi-wire two-dimensional detector (manufactured by Rigaku Americas Corp.). At this distance the effective scattering vector *(q)* range is 0.03 to 0.27 $Å^{-1}$. SAXS patterns were analyzed using the Rigaku GUI software to obtain *q* versus intensity (*I(q)*) curves. All composite fibers discussed were made using solution spinning approaches and characterized by various methods. The PAN/P and PAN/SP films are isotropic, while PE and PVA based fibers are anisotropic.

RESULTS AND DISCUSSION

Polyacrilonitrile/single-wall carbon nanotubes (SWNT) composite films

Intensity (*I*) versus *q* for PAN/P cast and PAN/SP cast films were plotted in Figure 1a. It was observed that no peaks pertaining to polymeric microstructure appeared in these curves. However, correlation function is a useful indicator of regular distance order in material structure. As shown in Figure 1b, there was regularly ordered structure within both composite films. The calculated geometry parameters were also listed in Table 1. It can be seen that more highly purified SWNT induced higher ordered structures.

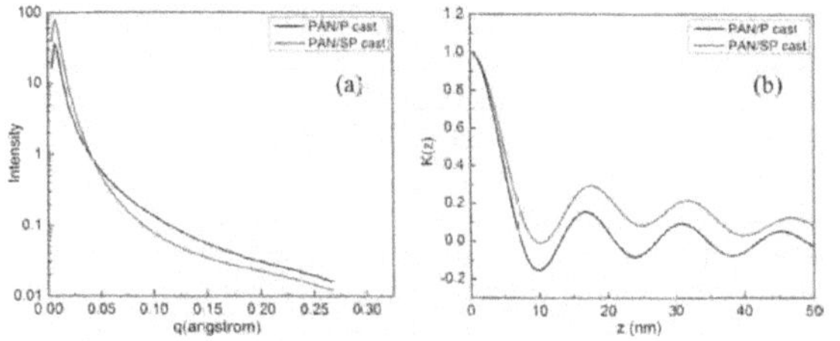

Figure 1. (a) Intensity I *vs.* scattering vector q for PAN/P cast and PAN/SP cast films. (b) Calculated one-dimensional correlation function $K(z)$.

Table 1. Crystalline/amorphous region dimensions and long-spacing order

Samples		L_c (nm)	L_t (nm)	L_a(nm)	L_l (nm)
composites	PAN/P	7.0	1.0	8.5	16.5
	PAN/SP	7.0	1.5	9.0	17.5

Polyethylene/hexagonal boron-nitride (hBN) composite fibers

SAXS could be used to characterize the PE fibers. Due to the shear crystallization approach for making these fibers, they exhibited a shish-kebab structure. A variety of studies have focused on measuring the inter-lamellae long-order spacing for shish-kebabs structures formed using various grade of PE, and measured from 11 to 140 nm depending to material type and processing routes [12, 13]. For this reason, SAXS based correlation function analysis can provide statistical analysis regarding the lamellae structures in the whole bulk material.

DSC may be also used to characterize the crystal structure but is a destructive measurement tool and sensitive to the rate of heating. Therefore, it may not be suitable for routine quantitative analysis. DSC results may also vary due to sensitivity in measurement conditions. For this reason, SAXS was used to alternatively analyze the microstructure of fibers. *I versus q* curves were plotted in Figure 2a for all samples. The 1DCF was used to analyze the microstructure of fibers as well as the lamellae size distribution. This information cannot be obtained based on the experimental I *vs.* q curves (Figure 2a). The 1DCF curves $K(z)$ were plotted in Figure 2b. Based on this analysis, dimensional parameters for crystalline region, amorphous region and transition zone were calculated and listed in Table 2.

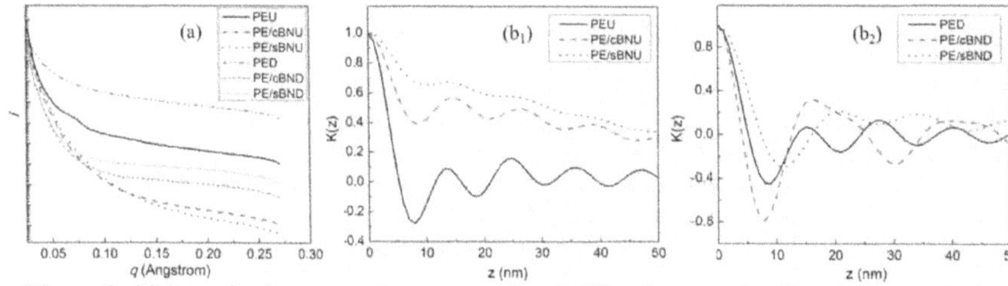

Figure 2. (a) Intensity I *vs.* scattering vector q for all PE and composite fibers before and after drawing treatment. (b_1) and (b_2) Calculated one-dimensional correlation function $K(z)$. Note, there is a variation in lamellae stacks with different thickness in PE/cBND developed during the drawing process indicated by arrows.

Table 2. Long-order spacing calculated using both DSC and SAXS.

Samples		DSC		SAXS			
		L (nm)	L_i (nm)	L_c (nm)	L_t (nm)	L_a (nm)	L_l (nm)
Undrawn	PEU	15.9	13.0	6.0	2.0	5.0	13.0
	PE/cBNU	18.6	15.2	6.0	3.0	6.0	15.0
	PE/sBNU	32.8	26.9	7.0	2.0	4.5	11.0
Drawn	PED	29.0	23.8	6.0	3.0	6.0	15.0
	PE/cBND	31.3	25.6	8.0	1.5	6.5	16.0
				15.0	1.5	6.5	23.0
	PE/sBND	52.1	42.7	9.0	2.0	9.0	20.0

Polyvinyl alcohol/carbon nanochips (CNC) composite fibers

Experimental I *vs.* q scattering profiles for both control PVA and PVA/CNC composites were plotted in Figure 3a. The lamellae stack height (L_L) is estimated from Bragg's law using the q_2 position for the observed meridional peak position in the SAXS pattern (Eq. 1). From this analysis it was found that the L_L increased as a function of fiber drawing and with addition of the CNC. The fully drawn composite fibers (Stage-III, 200 °C) exhibit a L_L increase up to 16.4 nm as compared to the control fiber of 14.8 nm (Figure 3a and Table 3). Similar to the reinforcement of BN in reinforcing PE matrix, the inclusion of CNC was also effective in increasing long-order spacing after heat-treatment and introduced mechanical property increases.

Using $K(z)$, the lamella stack height L_p is theoretically determined. L_p and L_L (i.e., experimentally determined) values and trends are similar (Figure 3b). The computed L_p values showed exactly same trend as compared to L_L calculated from Bragg's law [7]. The $K(z)$ calculated data are provided in Table 3. The computed L_p values were smaller than L_L. This is a common phenomenon for many semi-crystalline polymers and may be due to (i) the presence of a broad distribution in lamella stack heights, which is averaged in the scattering data, and (ii) the existence of the transition region (L_t). The ratios between L_p and L_L were also calculated in Table 3, implying similar values. This also validates the significance of 1DCF in application of obtaining not only long-spacing order but also the sub-lamellar grain size (i.e., geometrical parameters of crystalline, amorphous, and transitional regions).

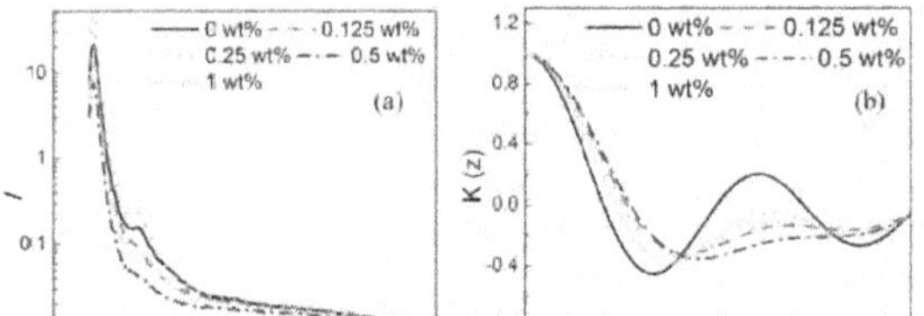

Figure 3. (a) Experimental I *vs.* q scattering profiles at various loadings, and (b) one-dimensional correlation function $K(z)$ associated with a stack of transition zone, crystalline and amorphous layers, obtained for fibers drawn at 200 °C.

Table 3. Experimentally and theoretically determined lamellae parameters based on the one-dimensional correlation function analysis of SAXS data.

Sample (wt%)	L_t *(nm)*	L_a *(nm)*	L_c *(nm)*	L_p *(nm)*	L_L *(nm)*	L_p/L_L
0	1.5	4.6	6.1	12.2	14.8	0.82
0.125	2.0	5.5	6.0	13.5	16.1	0.84
0.25	2.0	5.5	5.8	13.3	15.0	0.88
0.5	2.0	6.0	6.5	14.5	16.4	0.88
1	1.6	5.1	6.3	13.0	15.1	0.86

CONCLUSIONS

The one dimensional correlation function was shown to provide useful tool to analyze grain/lamellae sixe evolution in polyacrilonitrile films, polyethylene fibers and polyvinyl alcohol fibers with variously loaded nano-fillers. These results show that the 1DCF provides information that may not be reflected from experimental *I vs. q* curves. This work illustrates the practical application of the correlation function to provide global morphological analysis toward understanding the polymer structural evolution in the composite system and the relationship to their properties.

ACKNOWLEDGMENTS

Financial support of this work is provided by Air Force Office of Scientific Research (FA9550-11-1-0153).

REFERENCES

1. Klug HP and Alexander. LE. X-ray Diffraction Procedures For Polycrystalline and Amorphous Materials 2, illustrated ed.: New York, Wiley, 1974.
2. Kratky O, Pilz I, and Schmitz PJ. Journal of Colloid and Interface Science 1966;21(1):24-34.
3. Guinier A. X-ray diffraction in crystals, imperfect crystals, and amorphous bodies: Courier Dover Publications, 1994.
4. Hosemann R. Z. Physik 1939;113:751.
5. Debye P and Bueche A. Journal of Applied Physics 1949;20(6):518-525.
6. Porod G. General theory. Small angle X-ray scattering, 1982.
7. Salem DR. Structure Formation in Polymeric Fibers, 1st ed. Cincinnati, OH: Hanser Gardner Pubns, 2000.
8. Saffar A, Ajji A, Carreau PJ, and Kamal MR. Polymer 2014;14(19):3156-3167.
9. Murthy NS, Bednarczyk C, Moore RAF, and Grubb DT. Journal of Polymer Science Part B: Polymer Physics 1996;34(5):821-835.
10. Goderis B, Reynaers H, Koch MHJ, and Mathot VBF. Journal of Polymer Science Part B: Polymer Physics 1999;37(14):1715-1738.
11. Men Y, Rieger J, Lindner P, Enderle H-F, Lilge D, Kristen MO, Mihan S, and Jiang S. The Journal of Physical Chemistry B 2005;109(35):16650-16657.
12. Van Hutten PF and Pennings AJ. Journal of Polymer Science: Polymer Physics Edition 1980;18(5):927-942.
13. Zhou H and Wilkes GL. Polymer 1997;38(23):5735-5747.

AUTHOR INDEX

SUBJECT INDEX

For EU product safety concerns, contact us at Calle de José Abascal, 56–1°,
28003 Madrid, Spain or eugpsr@cambridge.org.

www.ingramcontent.com/pod-product-compliance
Ingram Content Group UK Ltd.
Pitfield, Milton Keynes, MK11 3LW, UK
UKHW020638170926
15229UKWH00001B/1

* 9 7 8 1 6 0 5 1 1 7 3 1 7 *